CLOSING PANDORA'S BOX

CLOSING PANDORA'S BOX

Arms Races, Arms Control, and the
History of the Cold War

PATRICK GLYNN

A New Republic Book
BasicBooks
A Division of HarperCollins*Publishers*

Library of Congress Cataloging-in-Publication Data

Glynn, Patrick.
    Closing Pandora's Box: arms races, arms control, and the history of the Cold War / by Patrick Glynn.
        p. cm.
    "A new republic book."
    Includes bibliographical references and index.
    ISBN 0–465–09809–6: $30.00
    1. Arms control—History. 2. United States—Foreign relations—20th century. 3. United States—Military relations. 4. Cold War. I. Title.
JX1974.G476 1992
327.1'74'09—dc20   91–55464
                                                                              CIP

Designed by Ellen Levine

92 93 94 95 CC/RRD 9 8 7 6 5 4 3 2 1

For Paul Seabury
In Memoriam

CONTENTS

FOREWORD

"Today detachment and objectivity seem to me less important than
to tell a tale of large conceptions, great achievements, and some
failures, the product of enormous will and effort." So wrote
Dean Acheson in the preface to his spellbinding memoir of the early Cold
War, *Present at the Creation*.[1] With odd power, Acheson's phrases capture
something of the drama and the grandeur, the importance and the scope,
of the era that we have just lived through. The Cold War is over. The
twentieth century is really at an end, ten years before its time.[2] And
already the ideas, the passions, the fears, the hopes that were so much a
part of that century and that engulfed all of us who lived through it are
fading from memory.

Today we are embarking on an age seemingly very different from the
age we have just left behind. While nuclear dangers certainly remain, the
threat of global Armageddon no longer appears to hang so heavily over
humanity. The great ideological struggle—the struggle for hearts and
minds, for humanity's future—has been played out. The long war between the dictators and the democracies has been waged and largely won,
and the dictators seem to be in rout.

The Cold War is over. Why, then, a history of the Cold War now? Not
merely to commemorate the past, though it deserves commemoration.
Not merely to celebrate a victory, though a celebration may be in order.
But to learn what the past has to teach us, and to carry that lesson with
us into the uncertain future. That is the purpose of this book.

From the perspective of the liberal democracies, the Cold War in particular, and the twentieth century in general, was a long and very costly tutorial in the realities of power—political power and, above all, military power. It was a tutorial in which the democracies seemed to repeat the same mistakes again and again. Two world wars, Korea and Vietnam, and a host of other struggles—in all of this violence and tragedy, the blunders of democratic statesmen often played an important and sometimes a crucial role. In the end, the democracies triumphed, emerged intact from these trials, graduated from this school of hard knocks. The democracies were victorious, but perhaps without fully understanding how they had prevailed. "Success is a great liar," said Friedrich Nietzsche. The Western victory in the Cold War is already making us complacent and tending to obscure precisely how this war was waged and won. It is important that we examine the nature of this victory while it is still fresh in our minds.

Faults are often the other side of virtues. So it has been with the incomprehension of power in modern democratic life. The democracies became democracies in a sense by diffusing political power, by disguising its operation, by promoting the salutary fiction that power is an unimportant aspect of life. The democratic citizen does not *feel* the power of his or her government very often and is protected from the power of the government by a thousand legal and constitutional guarantees. The very language of democratic governance is euphemistic on the question of power; it disguises power's operation: We have "presidents" who preside rather than kings who rule.[3] Democracies thrive on the myth that power is ineffective; they live, in a sense, by misunderstanding and ignoring power as it operates in more traditional societies. While in aristocracies the few "lord it over" the many, in democracies this relation of superior to inferior—of power—is generally replaced by transactions serving mutual interest, epitomized in the commercial deal.

This disguise and diffusion of power, so essential and salutary to the internal life of a democracy, is a great hindrance in foreign affairs. For the international realm is profoundly unlike the domestic world of a democracy. It is still a Hobbesian realm, a realm anterior to the benign social contract by which democracies live, a world where everyone is potentially at war with everyone else, and where power—including, quintessentially, military power—very much counts. Too often democracies, confronted with the challenge of raw power, have misunderstood the nature of this challenge and attempted to meet it by seeking arrangements of mutual interest, have treated external threats as though they could be solved by internal methods of conflict resolution. Disaster has often been the result.

In the broadest sense, the liberalism of liberal democracies has often proved a liability in foreign affairs. Successful democratic statesmanship—such as that of Dean Acheson or of the preeminent democratic statesman of the twentieth century, Winston Churchill—has always involved somehow marrying or offsetting liberalism with a more traditional foreign policy realism.

This is the story of the arduous path by which liberal societies gradually attained a level of realism in foreign affairs, often only to lose sight of it and then to be forced by events to recover it again. It is the story of three major "wars"—World War I, World War II, and the Cold War; of how these wars originated and how they ended; and of the striking parallels among them.

Since the beginning of the twentieth century, the democratic debate over realism in foreign policy has been, most centrally, a debate about armaments. Beginning in the second half of the nineteenth century, liberal thinking, especially in Britain and America, began increasingly to gravitate to the view that war was a backward, atavistic practice, destined to be abandoned as humanity progressed.[4] The belief grew that preparations for war were wasteful and that the accumulation of armaments could conceivably contribute to fomenting war. As the century turned, advocacy of disarmament began to spread.[5] This new view of war and armaments peculiarly mixed Victorian optimism with pessimism, simultaneously arguing that war was becoming obsolete and that the accumulation of arms somehow posed a danger. In 1899, for example, the Polish financier I. S. Bloch produced a detailed study showing that fearsome modern weaponry had made war too violent and costly to be a rational option for nations. "There will be no war in the future . . . ," affirmed Bloch; "it has become impossible, now that it is clear that war means suicide."[6] Bloch's argument was revived over a decade later by the English journalist Ralph Lane, writing under the pseudonym Norman Angell. His famous book, *The Great Illusion,* preached the obsolescence of major war and became a best-seller on the eve of World War I.[7]

For a civilization that had long believed war to be its way to obsolescence, the Great War of 1914 to 1918 came as a terrible shock. At first the world war was read as a refutation of the new liberal vision of war and peace. But in time an alternative view took hold—on the basis of incomplete and misleading evidence—namely, that armaments themselves had actually brought on the conflict, that the war had been caused by an "arms race." This view in turn inspired the disarmament movement that contributed, disastrously, to the origin of World War II.

At the end of World War II, the notion that the key to controlling war lay in controlling weaponry was given fresh impetus by the arrival of the atomic bomb, a problem that seemed to burst the old bounds of both war and statesmanship.

In short, the debate over foreign policy in the democracies has been most centrally a "Great Debate" over war and armaments. This is the tale of that great debate and of how it helped shape the experience of a violent century.

ACKNOWLEDGMENTS

"This book was several years in the making, and I have many people to thank. In January 1989, Christopher C. DeMuth invited me to join the American Enterprise Institute for Public Policy Research (AEI) in Washington as a resident scholar. Since then, Chris has looked on patiently as my main intellectual energies have gone into a long-term work of history and scholarship, with no visible payoff in the short run. In a city where the time horizon rarely extends more than forty-eight hours in either direction, Chris is rare in emphasizing the role of serious books in shaping the basic framework of public policy discourse. With the help of an unusually committed board of directors and a dedicated staff, he and Executive Vice President David Gerson have created an environment of intellectual excitement, collegiality, and high purpose. All of us at AEI understand ourselves to be extremely fortunate and part of an important enterprise, helping to shape the thinking that will shape our country's future. Those of us in foreign policy studies, under Jeane Kirkpatrick's able leadership, are particularly content.

By the time I joined AEI, I was already well along on this project, thanks in part to Martin Peretz, whom I still remember as the kindest teacher I had during my undergraduate days at Harvard. On a visit to Washington in 1983, I mentioned in passing to my old teacher Marty that I had an idea for a book on the history of arms control; I soon had a contract with New Republic Books. Marty's belief in me at this very early point was critical; it transformed the idea into a potential reality.

This book could not have been produced without the generous support of a number of organizations. I am extremely grateful to the Lynde and Harry Bradley Foundation and the John M. Olin Foundation for major grants in support of my research, as well as to the United States Institute of Peace. (It goes without saying, though I am obligated to say it, that the opinions, findings, and conclusions or recommendations expressed in this book are those of the author and do not necessarily reflect the views of the United States Institute of Peace.) I am also very grateful to Robert Pickus of the World Without War Council and George Weigel, then of the James Madison Foundation, now of the Ethics and Public Policy Center, for their generous roles in administering research grants.

In December 1985, Kenneth Adelman, then director of the U.S. Arms Control and Disarmament Agency, invited me to join ACDA as his special assistant, where I served for a year and a half. Not only did the experience enable me to gain a technical mastery of arms control and defense issues nearly impossible to achieve outside of government, but it also provided an indispensable bird's-eye view of the policy process, of how government really works. The experience was pure pleasure, and the book benefited immeasurably.

In 1987, Owen Harries of *The National Interest* agreed to break precedent at his young magazine and run "The Sarajevo Fallacy" (with minor changes, chapter 1 of this text), the longest article the journal had ever featured, in his fall issue. He then proceeded to cut what this writer believed to be a tightly written 100-plus page manuscript by a third, without losing an ounce of substance. Norman Podhoretz of *Commentary,* whose superb editing I have frequently benefited from over the years, also read and commented encouragingly on some chapter drafts. Charles W. Fairbanks, Jr., offered great encouragement, public and private, at the time "The Sarajevo Fallacy" appeared—especially appreciated both as a personal gesture and as an intellectual vote of confidence, since some of Charles's research into arms races paralleled my own. Carnes Lord read and commented on early chapter drafts. Aaron Wildavsky gave extremely valuable advice on a number of chapters and, most important, had the heart to tell me when drafts I sent to him were simply bad; the book is much the better for it. I am particularly grateful to Midge Decter, who not only offered warmth and encouragement along the way but also, drawing on her firsthand knowledge of publishing, gave valuable counsel on the book project at critical stages.

At several points I received assistance from archivists of the presidential library system. Erwin Mueller at the Truman Library gave me generous attention and even pointed me toward new and largely unexplored material: the vast, unpublished first draft of Harry Truman's memoirs, a treasure trove of information about the early Cold War. David Haight offered valuable guidance through the rich archives of the Eisenhower Library during my two trips to Abilene. David Humphrey at the Johnson Library was similarly helpful, even drawing my attention to newly declassified material shortly after I had left Austin. One bonus of visiting the Johnson Library proved to be Walt Rostow, who occupies an office on the top floor of the library and loves to reminisce and argue about his years in the Kennedy and Johnson administrations. Meeting Walt Rostow made the trip to Austin one of the most enjoyable of the project. At Clemson University, Berniece Holt of the Robert Muldrow Special Collections guided me expertly through the James F. Byrnes papers, which she had personally catalogued. Archivists at the Kennedy Library, the Nixon Presidential Materials Project in Alexandria, Virginia, the Library of Congress, and the United Kingdom Public Records Office were similarly professional and cooperative. Finally, I made extensive use of the fine collection of documents, copied from presidential libraries and other sources, available at the National Security Archive, a nonprofit organization in Washington, D.C.

Back home, AEI's own librarian, Evelyn Caldwell, filled scores of requests for interlibrary loans and for odd bits of information, often on very short notice, and exhibited Job-like patience in the face of my habitual disregard of library due dates.

In the course of this project I was blessed with the help, at different times, of two superb research assistants, Anne Dias, a Georgetown University undergraduate, and Catherine Merrill, a recent graduate of Cornell, both of whom did significant work on a voluntary basis before joining AEI as regular staff. In addition, Michael Rust joined me on short notice midway through the project and worked long hours to help me make a crucial midproject deadline.

Peter Bejger, while editor at New Republic Books, assisted in cutting the manuscript, which in a few weeks' time went from over 1,000 typescript pages to a length of just over half that, while his successor, Peter Edidin, another thorough professional, offered a number of valuable editorial suggestions in the final stages of the editorial process.

Many friends offered personal as well as intellectual support along the way. Walter Lammi was present at the creation of the book and acted as an intellectual sounding board at various points in its formulation, as did our mutual friend Jeff Salmon. Mira Baratta offered endless moral support and, occasionally, valuable criticisms of drafts. Charlie Sorrels read and commented on drafts, bringing to bear his fine eye for detail and his voluminous knowledge of arms control technicalities. E. J. Dionne, an old friend and, more recently, a valued intellectual sparring partner, reminded me continually of my political "roots" and of the range of political views I would have to reach if the book was to have a significant audience. Liz Glynn lived through the long days and the countless weekends, the preoccupations, and—inevitably—the worries and travails of the project, until we parted as good friends in 1990.

Finally, just about the time I began this project, I met Paul Seabury, professor of political science at the University of California, Berkeley. Like many other fortunate younger scholars over the years, I soon found in Paul an invaluable intellectual ally and mentor. During his year in Washington as a fellow at the Institute of Peace, which I suspect was one of the happier of his life, Paul and his wife, Mappie, passed several pleasant spring and summer evenings with Liz and me. At one point Paul and I had collaborated very successfully on a piece about George F. Kennan for *The National Interest,* and Paul's frequently expressed wish was to undertake more such joint ventures. I was eager to do this once my own book was done. I am sad now that it won't be possible. I miss him. This book is dedicated to his memory.

CHAPTER 1

❏

The Sarajevo Fallacy

Our age must learn the lessons of World War II, brought about when the democracies failed to understand the designs of a totalitarian aggressor. . . . But we must remember as well the lesson of World War I, when Europe, despite the existence of a military balance, drifted into a war no one wanted and a catastrophe that no one could have imagined. Military planning drove decisions; bluster and posturing drove diplomacy. Leaders committed the cardinal sin of statecraft: They lost control over events.   —Henry Kissinger, *Years of Upheaval*[1]

For most of the twentieth century, the hope for peace and the fear of war converged on the phenomenon of the arms race. At the root of this hope and fear lay a widely shared conviction that arms races were inherently dangerous and ultimately destabilizing. So firmly established was this belief in Western political discourse that statesmen came to take it for granted.

As a result of this conviction, Western strategy for much of the postwar era remained torn between two fundamentally opposing premises: the notion that military strength deters aggression and the competing belief that the arms race itself could be a cause of war. Throughout the Cold War era, the view that the arms race could lead to catastrophe continually challenged and unsettled the Western faith in nuclear deterrence. Though understanding the need to guarantee peace through military power, Western governments and peoples remained wary of the means at their disposal, haunted by the fear that the very measures they took to secure their safety could be driving them to oblivion.

Hence, in large measure, the intense Western preoccupation with arms control. Much of the urgency with which the United States and other Western governments pursued arms control during the postwar period came from the assumption that arms races could indeed be a cause of war. This conception helped propel arms control to the center of America's national security agenda in the 1960s, setting the stage for the Strategic Arms Limitation Talks (SALT) of the 1970s and subsequent arms limitation efforts.

At issue here was a rarely challenged set of assumptions about international relations that defined a powerful orthodoxy among the Western foreign policy elite: the belief that arms races sprang from an "action-reaction phenomenon"; that the action-reaction spiral was inherently destabilizing and produced mounting tensions; and that finally war, if it came, was likely to arise "accidentally" in this climate of heightened suspicion, as a result of critical "misperceptions" during a crisis.

All these conceptions dated from an era well before SALT and even the nuclear age. They had a specific historical origin: in "revisionist" interpretations of the Sarajevo crisis of July 1914, the crisis that led to the outbreak of World War I. It was the popular understanding of the origins of World War I, not the atomic bomb or the Cold War and the balance of terror, that laid the basic theoretical foundations of modern thinking about arms races and arms control. In this sense, the most important conceptual dividing line in modern reflection on the causes of war is not 1945 but 1919.

The revisionist interpretation of World War I crystallized two fundamentally novel political conceptions: first, that major wars could occur by "accident"; and second, that arms races could cause them. These views were not without precedent. Advocacy of disarmament began to be a factor in British and American politics as early as the mid-nineteenth century, and worries about the "armaments race" had become a staple of British and American liberal thinking even before World War I. As early as 1913, for example, professor and peace activist David Starr Jordan of Stanford University wrote in his book *War and Waste*: "Except as a result of accidental clash in uncontrollable war machinery, international war is already impossible."[2] But it was only after World War I that the arms race/accidental war thesis became codified and popularly accepted, and disarmament and arms control measures began to be thought of by large numbers of people—and governments—as the fundamental method of preserving peace.

The classic statement of the arms race thesis was offered in 1925 by none other than Edward Grey, who had been Britain's foreign secretary at the outbreak of World War I. In asserting a direct causal relation between the war and the arms race, Grey echoed an increasingly widespread view:

> The moral is obvious; it is that great armaments lead inevitably to war. If there are armaments on one side, there must be armaments on other sides. . . . Each measure taken by one nation is noted, and leads to counter-measures by others. . . . Fear begets suspicion and distrust and evil imaginings of all sorts, till . . . every Government regards every precaution of every other Government as evidence of hostile intent. . . .
>
> The enormous growth of armaments in Europe, the sense of insecurity and fear caused by them—it was these that made war inevitable. This, it seems to me, is the truest reading of history and the lesson that the present should be learning from the past, in the interests of future peace, the warning to be handed on to those who come after us.[3]

Conceptions such as these decisively shaped the British (and for that matter the American and French) approach to security problems for the two decades following World War I, producing the disastrous disarmament movement of the interwar decades—that movement which, as the columnist Walter Lippmann said, tragically succeeded in disarming those nations that wished to disarm.[4] These ideas were largely responsible for the debacle of Munich, the culmination of the British policy of appeasement that helped bring on World War II. They survived, in somewhat altered form, into the Cold War, coloring both policy thinking and academic literature about war and peace and the accumulation of military power.[5]

It is worth noting that the revisionist interpretation of Sarajevo also had a critical effect on a pivotal event in postwar American history. In their response to the Cuban missile crisis, President Kennedy and his advisors were decisively influenced by Barbara Tuchman's prize-winning book on the origins of World War I, *The Guns of August*[6]—essentially a popularization of the revisionist thesis. After Soviet missiles were discovered in Cuba, the president told his advisors that he did not wish subsequent generations to read a book titled *The Missiles of October*—that is, that he did not wish to bring about war by accident or "miscalculation."[7] The "arms control" project itself, spurred by the Cuban missile crisis and spearheaded by Kennedy administration defense secretary Robert S.

McNamara, the advisor most influential in shaping the U.S. response to that episode, was conceived, at least in part, as an effort to avoid future nuclear "Sarajevos."

What is ironic is that at the very time when it was beginning to exert a major influence on America's security policy, this historical interpretation of Sarajevo and the origins of World War I was being decisively refuted. In 1961, a year before Tuchman's book captured the imagination of Kennedy's Camelot, the West German historian Fritz Fischer published a painstakingly researched volume that called into radical doubt the whole conventional wisdom about the July 1914 crisis. Using extensive documentary evidence, Fischer showed that Germany in 1914 consciously resolved to risk a "preventive war," and did so knowing that a full-scale Continental war might result. Thus, far from being unforeseen or "accidental," World War I was the product of a deliberate bid by the German leadership for European domination.[8]

Initially, Fischer's book excited enormous controversy. Yet even by the mid-1960s, the work of the Fischer school had revolutionized the historiography of World War I, in West Germany and indeed the West as a whole. Though other historians have since added qualifications and refinements to Fischer's thesis, and some ancillary elements of his case remain in dispute, the main lines of his argument have survived extensive scholarly scrutiny and been confirmed.[9]

Vindication of the Fischer thesis should not have been surprising. The "revisionist" version of the war's origins had arisen during the 1920s and 1930s in response more to contemporary political factors than to any hunger for objective historical scholarship. Eager to free itself of the charge that it was responsible for the war—a charge that legitimated the onerous reparations demanded of the Versailles Treaty—Germany mounted a massive propaganda campaign involving extensive (though selective) publications of state documents. In an effort to discredit the overthrown Russian monarchy, the newly installed Bolshevik regime in Moscow likewise began to release selected archival publications. These documents seemed to shift blame away from Germany—a tendency abetted by appeasement-minded politicians in the West such as David Lloyd George, who for political reasons in the 1930s declared that the great powers had "slithered" into war in 1914.[10] Under these influences, historians, especially in America and Britain, increasingly began to play down German responsibility, shifting blame more and more to impersonal factors such as militarism, nationalism, and the arms race itself.[11]

This view in turn became deeply ingrained in Western thinking about war and peace.

By rights, the findings of the Fischer school should have prompted a radical reevaluation of our entire thinking about the problem of arms races and "accidental" war. Fischer's evidence implicitly challenged a host of orthodox assumptions about international politics. Such a rethinking, however, has been slow to occur. In 1973, the Australian historian Geoffrey Blainey noted in his valuable book *The Causes of War* that Fischer's evidence essentially invalidated the traditional claims either that World War I was "accidental" or that it was caused by the arms race.[12] But remarkably enough, apart from Blainey's critical review of the Sarajevo paradigm, policy discussion for more than two decades failed to absorb, or even to register, the implications of the Fischer thesis. This failure is extraordinary, and important. For as it turns out, the Sarajevo crisis and the period leading up to it teach a lesson quite different from what they have been traditionally thought to teach—a lesson about arms races, disarmament, crisis, and war hardly dissimilar from that taught by Munich itself.

The "Armed Camps"

In one respect the arms race thesis was accurate. Obviously there had been a vast increase in the size of national arsenals before World War I, and in every case—but perhaps most conspicuously in the Anglo-German naval competition—the increases were intensified by an ever more explicit rivalry among the various powers. "The continent," the London *Economist* complained in 1879, "has been converted into a series of giant armed camps, within each of which a whole nation stands in arms."[13]

Figures on defense spending for the various nations indicate the pattern. Between 1870 and 1914, French defense spending roughly doubled, British defense spending nearly tripled, and German defense spending increased tenfold.[14] Reasons for this were several. In part, growing defense expenditures were a natural consequence of Europe's burgeoning industrial and economic might. Governments were spending more on armaments, but they were also spending more on everything else. Indeed, in every nation except Germany, nondefense spending exceeded defense spending in 1914.[15] Technology was also a factor. With rapid technological advances, new "generations" of weaponry began to emerge, and existing weapons quickly became superannuated. This was particularly true in naval construction. Commissioned in 1906, Britain's *Dreadnought,* for example, was so much bigger and faster than any other warship in service that in principle it rendered the whole of the existing British navy—and by implication, the ships of every other power—obsolescent.

Yet the expansion in military and naval forces was also fueled by explicit rivalries, especially the naval competition between Germany and Great Britain. In the years leading up to World War I, the naval programs of the two nations seemed continually to react upon one another. Britain experienced a series of naval "scares" inspired by the apparent surges in the German building program, which led in turn to increases in the British naval estimates. Germany, meanwhile, responded to British technical innovations—notably the commissioning of the *Dreadnought* and subsequent increase in the displacement of ships, thickness of armor, and caliber of guns—with corresponding increases of its own. One of the major foreign policy disputes in prewar Britain concerned the question of how to cope with this escalating arms race.

Advocates of arms control in the nuclear era often suggested that the Anglo-German naval rivalry formed an especially close parallel to the nuclear arms competition between the United States and the Soviet Union. In the words of a 1980s-vintage textbook produced by a Stanford University arms control group:

> The Anglo-German arms race is one of the closest historical analogues to today's U.S.-Soviet arms competition. The weapons involved were major technological systems that had never been tested. They were based on a doctrine very close to today's strategic theories. Their construction was supported by military and industrial interests on each side. And the naval race may have been one of the substantial causes of World War I.[16]

The first point here is valid: There is a close analogy. However, the lessons to be drawn from it are diametrically opposed to what this text suggests and what has usually been taught.

"Moderation Breeds Moderation"

Though the phrase would not be coined by Robert S. McNamara until three-quarters of a century later, the notion of an "action-reaction phenomenon" had already become central to British liberal thinking about armaments by the turn of the century. The "radical" wing of the Liberal party was convinced that the German naval buildup was basically a response to the British program. "The rapid increase in the German Navy is due more to the example set by Britain between 1895 and 1905," argued G. P. Gooch, a young radical writer who later became famous as a historian of World War I, "than to any other cause. . . ." Since, in the words of another radical commentator, the "Germans were merely following the lead of British naval policy," the radical argued that self-restraint and concessions on Britain's part would produce corresponding self-restraint and concessions on the part of Germany. This conviction was summarized by the radicals' slogan, "moderation breeds moderation."[17]

On the German side, meanwhile, signals were mixed. At times, Germany appeared eager to show off its growing naval capability—as when Kaiser William II exhibited virtually the full German fleet in Kiel Bay for his visiting uncle, Edward VII of England, in 1904.[18] On other occasions German officials seemed eager to play it down. In 1907, for example, Admiral Alfred von Tirpitz, the Reich marine secretary and architect of the German naval program, denied before the Reichstag either that the German navy was designed to threaten Britain or that Germany had any intention of challenging British naval hegemony[19]—denials later repeated by the kaiser himself.[20]

As it turns out, however, British efforts at "moderation" failed to bring German moderation in return. The prewar period witnessed a series of British disarmament initiatives, none of which met with success. One of the ironies of August 1914 is that England entered the war under a Liberal government that had come to office in 1905 ambitious for international disarmament.

The first major British attempt to achieve understanding with Germany occurred in the months preceding the Second Hague Conference on disarmament in 1907. (An earlier Hague Conference, in 1899, had failed to yield any disarmament measures.) The radical wing of the Liberal party pressed the cabinet to formulate concrete disarmament proposals. "England as the predominant naval power," argued one radical magazine, "could well afford to take the initiative in such negotiations, and the present government will not fulfill the expectations of its supporters if it fails to do so."[21] Though the government was split between "radical" or pacifist wing and "imperialist" wing of the party, disarmament remained a central plank of the Liberal platform and a key to finding money for the Liberal party's ambitious new programs of social reform.

At the prodding of the Liberal cabinet, the Admiralty agreed to a 25 percent reduction in Britain's 1906–7 naval estimates, including slow-downs in the planned production schedule for large battleships or "dread-noughts," destroyers, and submarines. Dreadnought production was re-duced from four to three, and then, under further pressure from the radicals, to two. The government presented the cuts as an explicit stimu-lus to the disarmament negotiations at the Hague. "We desire to stop this rivalry," the prime minister, Sir Henry Campbell-Bannerman, told the Commons in 1906, "and to set an example in stopping it."[22]

The German reception was less than cordial. In conversations with Edward VII during the English king's visit to Germany in 1906, William II referred to the Hague disarmament talks as "humbug."[23] Convinced by the German response that general disarmament talks would fail, Foreign Secretary Grey proposed some mutual exchanges of information on projected arms increases—in effect, what we now call "confidence-build-ing measures." These, too, were rejected by the Germans. In April 1907 Prince Bernhard von Bülow, the German chancellor, ruled out German participation in disarmament discussions at the Hague. "We confine ourselves," he said, "to allowing those Powers which look forward to some result from that discussion to conduct the discussion alone." The remark was greeted by laughter and cheers in the Reichstag.[24]

It is true that the reductions proposed by the government involved no serious risk to British national security. The Liberal cabinet was forced to claim as much when proposing the gesture. Arthur Balfour, the Conserv-ative leader and an opponent of disarmament, noted the inconsistency of offering to foreign governments as a concession what the government argued at home would have no ill effects. Moreover, the Liberal conces-sions coincided with a significant qualitative improvement in the navy. The technological edge the *Dreadnought* gave Britain was part of what persuaded the Admiralty to consent to the government's scheme of cutting the naval budget.[25]

Nonetheless, there is little question regarding the sincerity of the Liberal cabinet's hopes that this gesture would provide at least the initial impetus to the disarmament process. Unilateral reductions on this scale were, after all, completely unprecedented. As Grey explained to the

French ambassador Paul Cambon: "Great Britain had sometimes been held up to other Parliaments as the nation which was forcing the pace and necessitating expenditure. Now we are anxious to make it clear that we were not forcing the pace, and to get this recognized, in the hope that public opinion abroad would discourage increased [armaments] expenditure by other governments." The foreign secretary told the Commons: "I do not believe that at any time has the conscious public opinion in the various countries of Europe set more strongly in the direction of peace than at the present time, and yet the burden of military and naval expenditure goes on increasing. We are all waiting on each other."[26]

Yet not only did the British initiatives fail to produce results, but the Foreign Office senior clerk, Eyre Crowe, wrote in 1907 that British disarmament efforts were actually stimulating the German buildup: "Our disarmament crusade has been the best advertisement of the German Navy League and every German has now been persuaded that England is exhausted, has reached the end of her tether, and must speedily collapse, if the pressure is kept up."[27] At the end of 1907, Admiral von Tirpitz submitted a supplemental navy bill, providing for a new, previously unscheduled acceleration in the pace of the German buildup.

However, concerned at the effects of their posture on British opinion, the Germans soon thereafter launched a "peace offensive"[28]—a public relations campaign specifically designed to assuage British feeling and prevent a mobilization of English opinion in favor of further arms increases. The kaiser visited England to reassure the British concerning German naval plans. Early the following year, he went so far as to write a lengthy personal letter to the British First Lord of the Admiralty. "It is absolutely nonsensical and untrue," he remonstrated, "that the German Navy Bill is to provide a Navy meant as a 'Challenge to British Naval Supremacy.' The German fleet is built against nobody at all. It is solely built for Germany's needs in relation with that country's rapidly growing trade." The kaiser objected strenuously that the German navy was being used in Britain to stir up public opinion against Germany. Prince Klemens von Metternich, Berlin's ambassador in London, was instructed to reassure the British at every opportunity of the benign character of Germany's intentions.[29]

These protestations of innocence were, to put it mildly, less than sincere. In 1907, it was easy for British liberal opinion to suppose that Germany was merely responding to British naval initiatives; after all, Britain was at that time far ahead, boasting a fleet of forty-seven capital ships plus the *Dreadnought* to Germany's twenty-one.[30] But when Germany accelerated its naval program in 1906 and 1907, it was not, as British disarmament advocates argued, merely responding to British example but actually carrying out a program that had been set down a decade earlier. The reason that British "moderation" failed to inspire reciprocal German self-restraint was essentially that radical opinion had misdiagnosed the motive at the basis of the arms race.

At the basis of the German building effort was an explicit and carefully calculated plan to challenge British naval supremacy, which had been spelled out as early as 1897 in a secret memorandum from Tirpitz to the kaiser: "For Germany the most dangerous naval enemy at the present time is England. It is also the enemy against which we most urgently require a certain measure of naval force as a political power factor. . . . Our fleet must be so constructed that it can unfold its greatest military potential between Heligoland and the Thames."[31] The navy was thus envisioned from the beginning as a "political power factor" to be used against Britain; the whole naval effort posited Britain as the enemy. Germany, Tirpitz said, should concentrate its "efforts on the creation of a battle-fleet against England which alone will give us maritime influence vis-à-vis England." Over the long run, Tirpitz planned nothing less than to create a German fleet that, if necessary, could defeat the Royal Navy at sea. " 'Victorious' is the decisive word," Tirpitz noted in the margins of a secret document. "Hence let us concentrate our resources on this victory."[32]

Analysts in the Reich Navy Office predicted that with a rapid building program executed over twenty years' time, Germany could produce a navy two-thirds the size of Britain's—a ratio that strategists of the day argued was adequate to defeat a naval enemy. The difference in size would be compensated for, Tirpitz argued, by better training, organization, and leadership, and by more modern equipment. This would permit Germany, already Europe's leading land power, to transform itself into at least a practical equal of the world's supreme naval force. The plan, writes the historian V. R. Berghahn, was "with the help of the Navy . . . to overthrow the status quo internationally."[33]

It should be stressed that the German strategy was primarily political. The point was not to launch a surprise attack on Britain; the 2:3 ratio by 1920 that was envisioned—and that was the best that the German economy could sustain given its other commitments—would never have permitted that. The idea instead was to stalemate British naval power—to create a balance such that the Royal Navy, if drawn into a battle, could be defeated by the German force. Having sustained vast losses at the hands of Germany, Tirpitz reasoned, the British navy would then be at the mercy of the French and Russian fleets. With British naval supremacy canceled and Britain unable to risk attack, it would have no choice but to take German demands on the international stage more seriously. Such was the detailed rationale behind Tirpitz's famous "risk theory." With a navy so powerful Germany could, as the admiral put it, "expect 'fair play' from England." "Keep building" went the refrain in the Reich Navy Office, "until they come to us." For all his public protestations to the contrary, William was accustomed to refer to the navy, in the privacy of the German court, as his *"Flotte gegen England,"* his "navy against England."[34]

Liberal efforts to end or slow the arms race thus failed to take into account the political motivation at the basis of the rivalry: the German desire to transform the international status quo. As Crowe noted in a Foreign Office memorandum of 1910: "The building of the German fleet is but one of the symptoms of the disease. It is the political ambitions of the German government and nation which are the source of the mischief."[35]

The fundamental character of Germany's challenge to Britain should be understood. Mutual suspicion of a general sort between sovereign states might have led to continual competition in arms between Germany and Britain resembling the naval competition between Britain and France, or Britain and Russia at the turn of the century. But for the most part Britain, France, and Russia were building their navies to preserve the European balance of power; Germany, by contrast, began arming in order to change it. The hegemonic political ambitions of Germany, directed first toward colonial possessions but later toward the Continent itself, endowed the Anglo-German competition with a special intensity, transforming a generalized rivalry into an all-out arms race. The arms race was merely the outward manifestation of the fundamental incompatibility between the political aims of the two powers. Britain sought, one could say of necessity, to preserve its naval superiority; Germany sought to overthrow it.

Notably, had German ambitions been fully acknowledged, they would not have proved acceptable to even the most pacifistic sectors of British opinion. Most radicals understood well enough that for Britain, an island power, naval supremacy was a life-and-death matter. For one thing, the practical alternative to defending Britain with superior naval strength was a large army, which implied the institution of national conscription;[36] investment in the navy was thus from a certain perspective an antimilitarist measure for the British, reducing the need for a large military influence in British domestic life. But beyond that, the strength of the navy affected Britain's safety—its commerce and even its supply of food—in a way that would never be true in the German case. Winston Churchill angered many Germans but was basically correct when he argued in 1911 that the German navy was to Germany "in the nature of luxury": "Our naval power involves British existence. It is existence to us; it is expansion to them."[37]

The radical agitation for disarmament was inspired not by any acceptance of German ambitions but rather by a denial of their existence—a failure to acknowledge the fundamental political dimension of the problem. Liberal opinion assumed that once the arms rivalry itself was diffused, Germany would be content to coexist on terms compatible with the status quo. This assumption followed naturally from the widespread liberal belief that it was Britain, not Germany, that was "forcing the pace."

German strategy, in turn, depended on keeping German strategic intentions concealed. By comparison with more modern regimes, the government of Wilhemine Germany demonstrated notable ineptitude in this respect. The kaiser, whom Alfred von Kiderlen-Wächter, the German secretary of state, referred to privately as "William the Sudden,"[38] did not count public relations among his strong suits. Nonetheless, German leaders knew that success demanded that the British government not be alerted to the full extent of German plans and, more important, that British public opinion not be aroused to any significant degree by the German threat. "The English," the kaiser affirmed, "must get used to the German fleet. And from time to time we must assure them that the fleet is not built against them."[39] Or as Prince von Bülow, reiterating Tirpitz's "risk theory" asked in 1909, "How can we get through the dangerous zone which we have to traverse until we are so strong at sea that in attacking us England would run a risk all out of proportion to any probable result?" He proposed a consistent foreign policy "without rhodomontade or provocation" designed to lull British statesmen into acceptance of a gradual shift in the status quo.[40]

Yet as regards British recognition of Germany's long-term strategic intentions, the Germans had perhaps less immediately to fear than they sometimes believed. The German leadership thought in terms of the long run; the British in this period were not on the whole accustomed to think in terms of grand strategy, even about the naval question. By the second Navy Law or "Novelle" of 1900, Tirpitz had arranged things so that the Reichstag was voting to approve naval expenditures for projected six-year periods. This political maneuver had the effect of insulating the naval buildup from the vicissitudes of democracy. (The Reichstag was thus not in a position to reciprocate yearly British gestures of "moderation" even had it wished to, which it did not.)[41] Thus the German "procurement cycle," to use a modern term, was established at six years, while the overall navy strategy was designed to unfold over a span of two decades.

The British Admiralty, of course, also planned for the future, but in general the British political system approached naval appropriations empirically, on a year-by-year basis. By the early twentieth century, as the historian E. L. Woodward notes, the "Naval Defense Act of 1899 was almost forgotten" and the British public "remained unfamiliar with any long-range plan of naval construction."[42] The British calibrated yearly expenditures in light of the immediate plans and naval strengths of the other powers. Not surprisingly, the British assumed that the Germans would respond to the environment the way they themselves did: that is, if immediate tensions could be reduced, motives for the German buildup would diminish.

If the British public tended to engage in what we now call "mirror imaging," interpreting German conduct in terms of British psychology, so, in different ways, did the German public and the German leadership. Judging British intentions in light of their own, German officials tended to put the most sinister construction on even the most conciliatory British actions. Thus British disarmament proposals received an entirely cynical reading from Marschall, Germany's delegate at the Hague, who derided the English appeals to "freedom, humanity, civilization" as "catchwords."[43]

From the German viewpoint, professions of goodwill by the British may have been genuine enough, but they were beside the point. They did not alter the fundamental fact of German strategic disadvantage vis-à-vis British naval power. When Philip Dumas, Britain's naval attaché in Berlin, assured Tirpitz in 1906 that British disarmament initiatives were entirely sincere, the latter offered this revealing response:

> Yes, perhaps it is true; but our people do not and will never understand such a scheme. I myself realize the Puritan form of thought such as is possessed by [Prime Minister] Sir Henry Campbell-Bannerman, and that he is perfectly honest and feels [disarmament] is a religious duty; but look at the facts. Here is England, already more than four times as strong as Germany, in alliance with Japan, and probably so with France, and you, the colossus, come and ask Germany, the pigmy, to disarm. From the point of

view of the public it is laughable and Machiavellian, and we shall never agree to anything of the sort. . . . We have decided to possess a fleet, and that fleet I propose to build and keep strictly to my programme.[44]

The clear-headedness and political sophistication of the marine secretary's response are remarkable. Tirpitz himself plainly did not doubt British sincerity. In contrast to the German public, roused to wholly implausible fears of a British "invasion" and inured to the myth of Albion's perfidy by official and unofficial navalist propaganda, Tirpitz and his colleagues in the Reich Navy Office understood the peaceful intentions of the British Liberal cabinet. (Unlike much of the populace, German naval officials had no fear of a British invasion, partly because the British lacked the army to pose such a threat. Bismarck had once remarked that if English troops ever landed on German soil, he would have the police arrest them.) There was a grain of truth in Tirpitz's appeal to the intransigence of German public opinion. But at bottom the marine secretary's intimations of helplessness in the face of it were disingenuous, since the government had at the outset deliberately fostered the popular fear—not to say hatred—of Britain. It was Tirpitz and his long-term strategy of overcoming British naval strength, not public resistance, that ultimately stood in the way of an end to the naval rivalry.

Germany's "Strategic Fear"

Indeed, for all the signs that Germany feared British intentions, German officials came to grasp with remarkable clarity the pacifistic character of the Liberal British government, and insofar as possible they maneuvered to keep the Liberals in and the Conservatives out. In 1907, Tirpitz actually tried to moderate the German buildup slightly so as to avoid arousing British suspicions. As one of his closest advisors in the Reich Naval Office wrote, if the German building tempo increased, the "Liberal cabinet in Britain will be thrown out of office and be replaced by a Conservative one which, even if one hopes for the best, will, by making huge investments in the Navy, completely obliterate all our chances of catching up with Britain's maritime power within a measurable space of time."[45] When the British naval "scare" of 1909 appeared to be getting out of hand, Bülow drew the picture for the kaiser: "A conservative government in England would represent a very real danger for us. . . . We should do all in our power to keep the Liberal party, to which all peace-loving elements in England adhere, at the helm."[46]The whole German strategy depended on nurturing pacifist elements in Britain to get Germany through the buildup period.

To claim that Germany was arming simply from fear of Britain, therefore, would be inaccurate. That Germany feared British power is undeniable; but it is misleading to suggest that Germany was arming out of a simple sense of insecurity. A suggestion of this sort is made by the arms control textbook cited earlier:

> Because Great Britain had an empire and was an island, it had long relied heavily on its navy for defense. In 1889 it authorized construction of seventy ships, including ten battleships, over the next decade. . . .
>
> Germany felt insecure, remembering that in 1807 England had destroyed the Danish fleet at Copenhagen by surprise. Germany moved in 1898, drawing up plans for nineteen new battleships and many lesser ships to be built over six years.[47]

The best that can be said about this piece of conventional wisdom is that it grossly oversimplifies the evidence. It ignores the fact that Britain was sounding out Germany on the possibility of forming an alliance in 1898, the year in which the first German Navy Law was passed. True, a century earlier, the English had preemptively destroyed the Danish fleet in Copenhagen to prevent it from falling into Napoleon's hands and threatening Britain. This incident, wrenched from its context in the Napoleonic wars, became a staple ingredient of German navalist propaganda, and there is little question but that Germans in the early twentieth century came to fear another "Kopenhagen." In 1905, for example, such fears led the kaiser to order a partial mobilization of the German fleet and recall his ambassador from London. Yet it would be ridiculous to explain this fear as the result of a simple defensive sense of "insecurity"; it was a direct consequence of Germany's plan to alter the status quo. As the historian Jonathan Steinberg has put it, "Kopenhagen really stood for a fear of what the British might do if they once found out what the Germans wanted to do."[48] The fear the government felt was a product of what Berghahn has called the "high stakes game" that the Reich was playing; it was the natural consequence of risks deliberately assumed. The "ultimate question," as Tirpitz wrote, was "either to abdicate as a world power or to take risks."[49]

Indeed, rarely was the German government's sense of insecurity focused on British intentions. For all the talk in the Wilhelmstrasse of a "trade war" with Britain, never once did Berlin's ambassadors in London report feeling in favor of such a war.[50] To grasp why Germany's leadership was nonetheless afraid, one must comprehend the structure of German suspicions, which were directed not so much at the aims as at the power of Germany's rivals. The fear that motivated Germany might be characterized as "strategic fear" to distinguish it from defensive or spontaneous fear per se—since it was a consequence primarily of German strategic intentions rather than of the intentions of other states. The German government feared that other powers might have the capacity to frustrate German aims, or threaten German security, if at some point in the future they formed the intention to do so. In the end, the capacity to defeat Germany was, in the eyes of the German leadership, indistinguishable in practice from the intention to do so.

Such strategic fear was in turn a consequence of the Social Darwinist cultural outlook—one might go so far as to call it an "ideology"—that pervaded both the populace and the leadership in Germany at this time. Social Darwinism gained influence with elements of public opinion throughout Europe in the late nineteenth century, but nowhere else did it become so central to national thought and feeling as in Germany. The prevailing German view was that there was to be an eventual struggle for survival among states in which the Reich would either triumph or fall. The possibility of war with Britain was thus on German minds from the turn of the century onward. The tendency was to see Germany as a young state, as it were, "on the make," and to envision Britain, by contrast, as an exhausted and effeminate power in imperial decline. Germany, wrote Tirpitz in 1879, was prompting reactions among other European powers similar to "Society's responses to a social climber." "Old empires are fading away," the kaiser affirmed in 1899, "and new ones are about to be formed."[51] Coexistence with other nations was merely a transitional phase as history progressed toward the final struggle.

Given German paranoia, it was natural enough for Liberal circles in Britain to seek to allay German fears by proposing gestures of conciliation on armaments. Yet efforts to win German trust with unilateral concessions proved to be misdirected because German fears were focused on British power rather than British intentions. Far from diffusing German suspicions, such concessions tended to be ascribed if not to treachery, then to weakness. Following what was perceived in England as one of Sir Edward Grey's more moving appeals for international disarmament before the Commons in 1911, the German naval attaché in London reported in rather typical tones to Berlin: "Grey's surrender is due to the Naval Law alone and the unshakable resolution of the German nation not to allow any diminution of this important instrument [that is, the navy]."[52] The British desire for disarmament was thus equated by German officials with "surrender." The kaiser seconded his emissary's conclusion: "If we had followed the advice of Metternich and Bülow for the last four or five years and ceased to build we should now have had the 'Copenhagen' war upon us. As it is, they respect our firm resolution and surrender to the facts. So we must go on building undisturbed."[53]

Diplomats such as Metternich and Bülow urged moderation in the naval buildup for prudent reasons. But the debate among German officials concerned mainly the buildup's feasibility and risks; the goals and assumptions behind it were quite alien to the issues that occupied liberal Britain. Interestingly, opposition to Tirpitz's plan arose not when Britain offered concessions but rather when British resolve seemed firm enough to raise doubts about the prospect of eventual German success in matching British naval strength, as eventually happened in 1912–13. Then, but only then, pragmatists such as Chancellor Bethmann-Hollweg were able to gain the upper hand in making their case for shifting resources away from the navy. Even so the money was not channeled, as would have been the case in Britain, into "social legislation" but rather into spending for the army—which helps explain why the French remained nervous during the Anglo-German talks. The British Liberal formula of reducing armaments expenditures so as to increase spending for social programs was alien to German ideology and the structure of the German regime.[54]

Thus the action-reaction notion was accurate, if at all, only in the narrow sense that specific actions on the part of the British (for example, the move to dreadnoughts) generally were followed by comparable steps on the part of Germany. True, Britain maintained an edge in naval technology, and Germany was in the position of following its technological lead. But this was an effect rather than a cause of the rivalry. This was not widely understood. As late as 1910 the *Economist* argued, "The German fleet which has struck such panic is largely imaginary, and the supposed danger is entirely due to the fact that the Admiralty invented the Dreadnought and fostered the impression that this type of ship had superseded all others. . . . Nevertheless, spurred on by the contractors, who love these huge jobs in ironmongery, the Admiralty goes on enlarging the size of battleships."[55] Such arguments persisted to the very eve of the war.

Aware in general terms of a new German naval challenge by 1902, by

1906–7 the Admiralty and the Foreign Office were growing increasingly
wary of German intentions and skeptical of the contention that British
attempts at disarmament would curb Germany's ambition. (Notably,
however, perception of a German threat did not figure into the decision
to build the *Dreadnought*.) Winston Churchill, then serving in the cabinet
as home secretary, later summarized the trend of those years:

> No one could run his eyes down the series of figures of British and
> German construction for the first three years of the Liberal administration,
> without feeling in presence of a dangerous, if not malignant design.
>
> In 1905 Britain built 4 ships, and Germany 2.
>
> In 1906 Britain decreased her programme to 3 ships, and Germany
> increased her programme to 3 ships.
>
> In 1907 Britain further decreased her programme to 2 ships, and Ger-
> many further increased her programme to 4 ships.
>
> These figures are monumental.
>
> It was impossible to resist the conclusion, gradually forced on nearly
> every one, that if the British navy lagged behind, the gap would very
> speedily be filled.[56]

Yet the government continued to explore methods of escaping what
Campbell-Bannerman, as prime minister, had termed "the self-defeating
race of armaments."[57]

By the early twentieth century, British politics had begun to exhibit in
full measure that conflict between "hawks" and "doves" that ever since
has shaped disputes about the armaments programs of Western democracies. The dovish, retrenchment-minded Liberals were opposed in general by the more hawkish Tories, while the Liberal party itself was split
fairly evenly between its dovish radical-pacifist and its somewhat more
hawkish "imperialist" wings—a division that dated from the Boer War.
British foreign policy reflected a compromise between these opposing
impulses.

As late as 1908–9, Churchill himself lobbied in concert with Lloyd
George for reductions in the British naval program. They seemed on the
verge of getting their way, moreover, until intelligence reports from
Germany revealed that Tirpitz had secretly laid down two keels ahead of
the officially announced building schedule. The subsequent "panic" fundamentally altered the British outlook on Germany. Until 1909 the British
had viewed France as the most important potential enemy; Britain's
"two-power standard" had been established with the French and Russian
navies in mind. Thereafter, anxiety shifted focus to Germany.

Ironically, the alarming intelligence reports later proved to be over-stated (though not, as some later claimed, manufactured by the government). Nonetheless, the extra four battleships built as a result of the 1909 panic ultimately proved crucial to British security in the opening months of the war, providing nearly the whole of the British margin of superiority in home waters in that class of vessel[58]—a margin that Churchill, head of the Admiralty at the time of the war, later noted did not leave "much . . . for mischance." Churchill praised Reginald McKenna, First Lord of the Admiralty in 1909, for resisting the cuts, noting that while Churchill and Lloyd George were "strictly right" on the facts, "we were absolutely wrong in relation to the deep tides of destiny."[59] The exaggerated intelligence reports thus proved in the long run to serve British security.

Amid the controversy, Grey proposed more confidence-building measures, renewing the request for what we would now term "on-site inspection" of the fleets by the two countries' naval attachés.[60]

What becomes clear is the difficulty that Britain had judging the nature and seriousness of German ambitions. As late as 1909 the cabinet remained split. In a famous memorandum dated January 1, 1907, the Foreign Office's Crowe posed the central question regarding the nature of German intentions: "Either Germany is definitely aiming at a general political hegemony and maritime ascendancy, threatening the independence of her neighbours and ultimately the existence of England; or Germany [is] free from any such clear-cut ambition, and thinking for the present merely of using her legitimate position and influence as one of the leading powers in the council of nations." As the historian Immanuel Geiss has shown, in the absence of a clear answer, Crowe advocated, in effect, a strategy of "containment," acceding to German policy as long as it remained peaceful, opposing it if it became aggressive: "So long as Germany's action does not overstep the line of legitimate protection of existing rights she can always count upon the sympathy and good-will, and even the moral support, of England." He advised strongly against unilateral conciliation or, to use a term favored by the next generation of British statesman, "appeasement": "That is the road paved with graceful British concessions—concessions made without any conviction either of their justice or their being set off by equivalent counterservices. The vain hopes that in this manner Germany can be 'conciliated' and made more friendly must be definitely given up."[61]Pressure to pursue just such a concessionary policy—"moderation breeds moderation"—nonetheless persisted.

Naval talks with Germany continued intermittently up to 1914, with

Grey frequently renewing his proposal for an exchange of technical information, without success. When Theobald von Bethmann-Hollweg came to office as Chancellor in 1909, the Germans opened a new round of negotiations. Bethmann-Hollweg was no believer in arms control; privately he dismissed "arms limitations between two countries who may have to defend their honor and independence against each other" as "chimerical."[62] Nonetheless, unlike Tirpitz, he recognized that the naval race was driving Britain into closer relations with France and Russia, negating the logic of the "risk theory." Tirpitz's original hope of browbeating Britain into an alliance with Germany was beginning to appear bankrupt.

Bethmann-Hollweg attempted to pursue a policy that relied less on the navy per se and more on diplomacy. During negotiations from August through November 1909, the Germans offered a temporary slowdown in naval construction, but the price was high: a British promise of neutrality in any Continental war. This would have ceded to Germany at the negotiating table much of what it was seeking to gain by the naval buildup. The effect, as the British understood, would have been to shatter the Entente with France, leaving Britain isolated opposite a continent under German domination.

Once again, the substantive problem was not so much the arms race as the underlying political cause. Germany had hegemonic ambitions; as long as it had the power, it was inclined to pursue them, whether by military or diplomatic means. The question at issue was whether Britain was willing to accede to German hegemony on the Continent. The British answer was clear enough: "If we sacrifice the other Powers to Germany," Grey wrote in April 1909, "we shall eventually be attacked."[63] Britain was willing to offer a guarantee of nonaggression and a promise of neutrality in the event of an unprovoked attack on Germany—essentially confirmation that the Entente with France was indeed purely defensive; Germany deemed such promises insufficient.

In another round of negotiations in 1912, Britain attempted to end the rivalry by offering Germany a free hand in acquiring colonial possessions. Within Germany Bethmann-Hollweg's position toward Tirpitz had been strengthened by three factors: the spiraling costs of the naval program, aggravated by continuous increases by the British in the displacement of their ships; the demands of the army for an increase in funds; and the elections of 1912, which decisively strengthened the Social Democratic minority in the Reichstag. In 1911, under pressure from the Reich treasury, Tirpitz even began to reformulate his position, arguing that Germany might be able to achieve the "risk fleet" by way of an arms agreement with Britain that ratified the 2:3 ratio, and that in any case if negotiations failed, Germany could go on building with the aim of "enforcing" the desired ratio.[64] Despite Tirpitz's backpedaling, however, Bethmann-Hollweg was still not strong enough to prevent an increase in the Reich's 1912 naval bill. When it became apparent that the new Reich navy law would require yet another matching expansion, the incentive for talks, from the British standpoint, disappeared.[65]

"Moderation," therefore, did not breed "moderation." On the contrary, British disarmament efforts at best had no positive effect on the German resolve to build; and there is considerable evidence to suggest that the persistent British interest in disarmament stoked the fires of the German buildup by persuading for a long time German officials, not least the kaiser himself, that their bid to challenge British power would ultimately succeed. Thus, paradoxically, the effort to achieve disarmament seems to have made an arms race all the more inevitable, while the negotiations themselves had the effect of worsening relations between the two powers by drawing attention to their irreconcilable political differences. When the German naval effort slackened, it was only because of loss of faith in the "risk theory" and financial strains within the Reich— both mainly consequences of the persistence of the British response to the German naval challenge.

In the end, it is probably fair to say that the arms negotiations failed because the underlying cause of the arms race lay beyond the power of diplomats to remedy, since it went to the very nature of German ambitions and of the German regime. In February 1914, responding to yet another campaign for British concessions by the radical wing of his own party, Grey pointed out that the arms race was "not a British matter alone" to control. "Any large increase in the building programme of any great country in Europe," he acknowledged, "has a stimulating effect upon the expenditure in other countries." But he added that "it does not follow that a slackening in the expenditure of one country produces a diminution in the expenditures of others. . . . It does not follow that if the leading horse slackened off, and that slackening was due to exhaustion, the effect would be a slackening on the part of others. It might be a stimulating one." In words that still have resonance, Grey issued a caution: "We must not get into the habit of thinking that if the world does not do what it seems obvious to us it ought to do, it is our fault."[66]

The "Minister for Slaughter"

Those who have argued that war in August 1914 came as a result of action and reaction in arms competition have never satisfactorily explained why Britain, Germany's major competitor in the arms race and the power with the largest per capita arms expenditure in 1914, was the last nation to enter the war, and then did so only reluctantly.[67] The arms race paradigm, at least as it comes down to us today, would seem to suggest that Britain, feeling the same suspicions and driven by the same forces as Germany, would have been equally likely to initiate the conflict. In the event, however, Britain's approach to the Sarajevo crisis was marked throughout by the greatest hesitation and reluctance. The whole British effort was directed at achieving a mediated settlement. "I hate it, I hate it!" the Austrian ambassador reported Grey as saying after the war had broken out; the British foreign secretary, the ambassador wrote to his superiors, "is in despair that his efforts to maintain the peace have gone to ruin."[68]

Indeed, German policy in the Sarajevo crisis—its willingness to escalate the crisis by pressing Vienna to punish Serbia militarily for its alleged involvement in the Sarajevo assassination—was based in part on the belief that Britain would hold back from engagement in a Continental conflict and remain neutral.

The desire for a peaceful resolution to the crisis so manifest in London in 1914 was also apparent, in different degrees and for somewhat different reasons, in Paris and St. Petersburg—a critical fact that recent historiography has increasingly emphasized.[69] For many years, historians assumed that the predisposition to war before 1914 was roughly equal on all sides, particularly among the Continental powers. France, the revisionist argument went, was nursing a grudge over the German appropriation of Alsace-Lorraine in 1871. "For more than forty years," wrote Barbara Tuchman in *The Guns of August,* "the thought of 'Again' was the single most fundamental factor of French policy."[70] At the same time, Russia was long suspected (erroneously) of complicity in the assassination plot. These beliefs supported the impression that the arms race was mere "action and reaction" among more or less equally ambitious and bellicose states.

Recent scholarship has called this whole picture into question. Jean-Jacques Becker's comprehensive study of French political opinion in 1914 shows that nationalism in France was much less of an influence than was long assumed. Far from coming at the culmination of a "nationalist revival," war in July 1914 took most French citizens utterly by surprise.

Active interest in Alsace-Lorraine had for the most part died away. French nationalism itself, Raoul Giradet has written, "even if it remained obstinate in its fidelity to the lost provinces," was "no longer a conquering nationalism, a nationalism of expansion" but "a movement of defense, retreat."[71] Only after the war was underway did France make recovery of Alsace-Lorraine its war aim. While France feared a war and prepared for the possibility of one, President Raymond Poincaré's policy remained fastidiously defensive—a policy of neither provocation nor appeasement, but of strict deterrence.

Essentially the same could be said of Russia. Defeat in the 1904–5 war with Japan had made Russian statesmen cautious, anxious to avoid policies that might lead Russia into another conflict. Among the great powers, Russia was perhaps the least affected by militarism; "turn-of-the-century Russian culture," as the historian D. C. B. Lieven has put it, "was peculiarly inhospitable to military values and virtues."[72] More important, the strength and antigovernment tenor of the left-wing parties meant that war held within it the threat of revolution, as the conflict with Japan had shown, so that even many conservatives counseled against foreign policy risk-taking. Even Tsar Nicholas's own patriotism was balanced by a healthy fear of war,[73] and Sazanov, the foreign minister, talked of maintaining peace so that Russia could pursue "economic reorganization" internally.[74]

Nor were there any illusions in Berlin regarding bellicose intentions on the part of these powers. Only four months before the war broke out, Moltke, chief of the general staff in Germany, wrote his Austrian counterpart, Franz Conrad von Hötzendorf: "All the news which we have from Russia suggests that at present they have no intention of adopting an aggressive attitude." As for France, Moltke continued: "Even less than from Russia should we now expect an aggressive attitude from France. From a military point of view France is at present very unfavorably placed."[75] Of the leaders of these four great powers—Germany, Britain, Russia, and France—German leaders alone were considering and discussing the possibility of a "preventive war"—that is, a war ostensibly designed to prevent the other powers from attacking Germany successfully at some point in the future.

With regard to the arms race itself, the direction of the action-reaction pattern is also clear: Germany was consistently the initiator. The French Chamber of Deputies voted three-year conscription only after Germany passed a massive new army bill in March 1913. The same German bill provoked the tsar to order a large expansion of the Russian army.[76] Nor were French and Russian anxieties unwarranted; unknown to either government, German leaders at the end of 1912 had already begun to lay the groundwork for a preventive war. At a meeting of the kaiser and the leading military officials on December 8, Moltke said: "I believe a war to be unavoidable and: the sooner the better." Bethmann-Hollweg had forwarded the army bill to the kaiser with a note suggesting that the populace must be psychologically prepared for war.[77]

In short, the quantities of arms accumulated before 1914 did not change the underlying characters or policies of the different regimes that amassed them. Underneath the surface of the generalized arms race, there remained a clear distinction between those powers that were wedded to the status quo and were arming defensively, and Germany, which wanted to change the balance of power radically. The fact that France and Russia increased their armies in response to Germany did not mean that their policies had altered in an aggressive direction. Similarly, the outcry of British radicals notwithstanding, the fact that Britain was spending more every year for its navy after 1907 did not mean that it was growing more aggressive; indeed, the opposite was the case.

Historians who have attributed the origins of the war to impersonal forces such as modern nationalism and militarism have neglected to recognize how differently these forces acted upon the different states. George Kennan, for example, cited as critical "the professionalization of the military, the rise of the great military bureaucracies, the growing separation of military and political thought, the abandonment of the concept of limited military operations in pursuit of limited gains."[78] While all of these generalizations clearly hold true of Germany, they do not apply with anything approaching the same force to other powers. As with discussions of nationalism, the tendency in discussing prewar military preparations has been to enforce a false parallelism among the different states.

In fact, only in Germany did the military, in effect, conduct foreign policy (the kaiser himself tending to refer contemptuously to nonmilitary Reich officials, from the chancellor on down, as "civilians"). And only in Germany did mobilization plans constrict political decisions to the point where the distinction between general mobilization and war was cast aside. Russia counted on a minimum of three to six weeks between a general mobilization order and commencement of fighting. Germany, by contrast, planned to attack and mobilize at the same time. The Schlieffen Plan, which formed the basis of German strategy in August 1914, called for an attack through Belgium on France while the Russians were still busy mobilizing, followed by an attack on Russia. This in itself violated existing diplomatic conventions, to say nothing of incipient international law. Yet German planners, and German planners alone, felt no compunction to take such conventions into account.

More recent attempts to attribute the war to a generalized "cult of the offensive" are equally misleading.[79] True, French battle tactics emphasized the offense, or defense by means of counterattack, and from a purely military standpoint this proved a ludicrous and very costly strategy in human terms.[80] But one must keep in mind the elementary distinction between French battle tactics, which may have been "offensive," and France's political posture and foreign policy, which were manifestly defensive. Moreover, while the French general staff may have been unimaginative, it was still under firm government control. "In those states whose regime was democratic and parliamentary," the historian Pierre Renouvin reminds us, "the government, between 1900 and 1914, never stopped supervising the plans of the general staff, perhaps simply because it harbored a secret mistrust of military chiefs . . . on the other hand, in Germany the general staff was freer in its action and freer to yield to the temptation to profit from a superiority in armaments."[81] It may be true, as proponents of the "cult of the offensive" thesis argue, that the strategic ideas and military arrangements of the era created "incentives" for preemption; Germany, however, was alone in yielding to the temptation.[82]

Indeed, most of the lessons that the revisionists applied to all the powers—the predominance of militarism, the blind chauvinism of public opinion, the rigidity of military timetables, the tendency of armaments firms to fuel the arms race—in truth pertained decisively only to Germany.

To a degree that has not generally been appreciated, the forces of "militarism"—if it can be called that—were in fact very much on the defensive in Britain in the years immediately leading up to the war. Germans who had counted on the decadence of French and British culture to undermine the Entente's will in war were surprised at the patriotic fervor that took hold in the supposedly weak democratic regimes once the war was underway. Yet this wartime experience colored the manner in which commentators later interpreted prewar history. "It is true," wrote British socialist J. A. Hobson in 1918,

> that British militarism has come with a rush in war-time and bears the appearance of a merely temporary improvisation. But those who have more closely watched the course of politics in recent years will form a

different judgement. . . . If we look to the trend of British politics and industry in the years before the war, we shall see the same drive towards militarism that we have seen in France and Germany. For the same impelling motives were at work.[83]

Yet these sorts of claims were misleading. The Krupp firm may have played an active role in driving forward the German armaments program, but by 1914 the British government had evolved an elaborate system of bureaucratic checks and balances to keep armament procurement and finance under firm civilian control. The postwar myth that the armaments manufacturers, the so-called merchants of death, had conspired to drive the country into the war for profit had no factual basis.[84]

While it is true in a sense, as the arms control textbook puts it, that naval construction "was supported by military and industrial interests on each side," such a statement ignores the radically different balance between pro- and antimilitarist forces within each of the governments. Tirpitz had the ear of the kaiser and consistently succeeded, until 1912, in circumventing both the "civilian" ministers and the Reichstag. His British counterpart, Admiral Sir John Fisher, reported to a civilian minister, the first lord of the Admiralty. All three first lords before the war—Lord Tweedmouth, Reginald McKenna, and Churchill—successively faced powerful antimilitarist coalitions in both Parliament and the cabinet. In a Liberal government devoted to "Peace, Retrenchment, and Reform," it was no easy task for a British cabinet minister to gain support for new military or naval initiatives. The prevailing views within the cabinet can be gathered from Lloyd George's pet name for Lord Haldane, the war minister, whom he was fond of referring to as "the Minister for Slaughter."[85]

What was true within the governments also held for the societies as a whole. Public opinion in Britain was obviously capable of being aroused by the German threat, as occurred in the naval panic of 1909. Clearly there was a nationalist minority in Britain as in France, some jingoistic newspapers, and a nationalist literature represented most conspicuously by Rudyard Kipling. But in the early twentieth century such influences were on the wane. As the Liberal landslide of 1906 itself suggests, nationalist feeling was more than counterbalanced both within and without the government by pacifist forces. And notably, while both Britain and Germany had industry-financed "Navy Leagues" that pressed for naval expansion, the organizations existed on wholly different scales within the two countries. "In 1901," notes Jonathan Steinberg, "the German Flottenverein had 600,000 members and associates. The Navy League in Britain had 15,000 members and an annual expenditure of under £4,000. The colossal difference in scale of the two organizations underlies the contrast between the role of the Navy in the two societies. In Germany navalism was virtually a mass movement of its own." In fact, the Flottenverein was the largest private organization in Germany.[86]

Far from promoting a dangerous convergence, domestic politics pulled the two coalitions in different directions. In the Entente, public opinion acted as often as not as a brake on policy; in Germany, by contrast, the structure of domestic politics not only permitted but virtually necessitated expansionist or hegemonic policies abroad. Since the time of Bismarck, the leitmotif of German foreign policy had been "export of the social question," the effort, in Friedrich von Holstein's phrase, "to divert the internal struggle to the foreign sphere." "Only a successful foreign policy," wrote Bülow in 1897, "can help to reconcile, pacify, rally, unify." For the ruling elites foreign expansion, success abroad, was a "method of democratic control."[87]

The key to the difference between the two nations lay in the fundamentally contrasting nature of their political regimes. By the close of the nineteenth century, Britain had become, in essence, a liberal democracy. There was a powerful middle class, the economy was largely independent of the state, and British political life was marked by a measure of freedom and tolerance simply unknown in Germany. The aristocracy had ceded control. Not that Britain was unshaken by domestic struggle. In the years leading up to World War I, civil war loomed as a possibility in Ireland and class struggle had risen to fevered crescendo. The violence of suffragettes, the militancy of the trade unions, and the restive mood in the army all threatened domestic tranquillity. Yet, if anything, these developments distracted from rather than promoted the formation of a firm line in foreign policy.

The German situation was quite different. In the latter half of the nineteenth century, Germany underwent an extremely rapid and successful industrial revolution, but economic transformation was unaccompanied by political movement toward genuine democracy. On the contrary, authoritarian forces within German society strove to assure that the emergence of capitalism strengthened their hand. Economic modernization, largely spearheaded by the state, was pursued in the name of state grandeur; key sectors of the economy remained under direct state control. The middle class lacked access to power, while the aristocracy, imbued with a strong militarist tradition, staunchly resisted political change. In-

dustrialization proceeded under an alliance between the agrarian aristocracy and the industrialists, between "blood and iron." It is true that the
parliamentary strength of the Social Democrats grew. But this only increased the impetus for militarist agitation, since nationalism was used by
Germany's authoritarian government to contain the influence of the Left.
The Reichstag, its sole prerogative a veto over government spending,
provided more the trappings than the substance of democratic rule.

In contrast to England, moreover, Germany retained a huge peasant
class, fertile ground for nationalist agitation on the part of the aristocracy.
In this freshly unified country, plagued by conflicts among classes and
ethnic groups, nationalism became the social cement of the regime, while
the success of Weltpolitik constituted the greatest proof that the Reich
itself was a viable political entity.

Together these developments added up to a kind of geological shift in
the European political landscape. Nineteenth-century diplomacy had
been preoccupied with the struggle between revolution and monarchy,
between the threat represented by Napoleonic France and the conservatism represented by the Holy Alliance. Toward the end of the century this
conflict begin to give way to a new opposition, between the emergent
liberal democracies and more authoritarian regimes—by the lights of
liberalism, essentially atavistic states. In actuality, the new authoritarian
states of the twentieth century, as the heirs of Europe's old monarchies,
were to represent a volatile mix of the old and the new—combining
modern economic power and in some measure modern political ideologies (prewar Social Darwinism, postwar Nazism and communism) with
the traditional realpolitik perspective of the old monarchies. The modern
authoritarian regime, lacking the popular legitimacy of the democracies,
would be dependent for its very survival on successes in foreign affairs.
The confrontation between liberal Britain and Wilhemine Germany already exhibited many essential features of the overmastering conflict that
would preoccupy nations for the remainder of the century—the struggle
between democratic and totalitarian states.

"Unintentional" War

In the decade following the war, the question of differences among
political regimes—an issue to which liberal thinking about international
politics was never sensitive—became caught up in the related, though
somewhat distinct, issue of moral responsibility for the war. The growing

reluctance to dwell on the nature of "Prussian militarism" after 1919 was partly due to British and American uneasiness over the Versailles Treaty, branded by John Maynard Keynes a "Carthaginian peace."

Nonetheless, in rejecting, on the grounds of its moralistic overtones, the proposition that "Prussian militarism" was a force endemic to a certain form of government, liberal commentators sacrificed a good deal of practical insight into how the war had begun. One legacy of this oversimplification has been the fallacious notion of "unintentional" or "accidental" war—an idea that gained increasing currency during the early 1960s and became "scientifically" codified in the 1965 research of Ole R. Holsti and Robert C. North. Taking Sarajevo as their model, the two Stanford University researchers exhaustively scrutinized a selection of the state documents of the major powers from June 28 to August 1, 1914, identifying over five thousand discrete "perceptions." By devising various ratios to quantify the psychological relationship between what they termed "units of hostility" and "units of friendship," the researchers thought they had demonstrated a mathematical relationship between mounting anxieties and the escalation of the crisis. The study concluded that feelings of fear and anxiety were decisive in precipitating the war, which they implied had occurred from miscalculation, almost, as it were, inadvertently. In launching the conflict, Holsti and North contended, the kaiser had acted irrationally, which explains why deterrence failed to deter. Indeed, the study went so far as to suggest that the "Kaiser appears to have undergone an almost complete personality change during the critical night of July 29–30." "Perceptions of inferior capability," they wrote, "will fail to deter a nation from going to war," if "perceptions of anxiety, fear, threat, or injury are great enough."[88] However, Fischer's evidence, not yet available in English when Holsti and North wrote, simply invalidated these findings.[89]

First, it was incorrect to assume that the Germans perceived their military capabilities as "inferior." Throughout the July crisis the general staff pressed hardest for war, precisely because the generals believed the odds to be in Germany's favor. As the Bavarian ambassador in Berlin reported to his prime minister on July 31, 1914:

> In military circles here everybody is very confident. Months ago the Chief of Staff, Herr von Moltke, said that from a military point of view the moment was as opportune as it was likely to be in the foreseeable future. The reasons which he gives are:
> 1. The superiority of the German artillery. France and Russia have no howitzers and can therefore not fight troops in covered positions.

2. The superiority of the German infantry gun.
3. The totally inadequate training of the French troops.[90]

Second, the Holsti-North study begged the central question that it posed: It assumed that the cause for the crisis could be discovered in the action and reaction between the powers, that the key to understanding the outbreak of war lay in understanding the immediate emotional states of their national leaders. Ignored was the possibility that the escalation of the crisis to war was the product of conscious intent arrived at analytically. Such indeed was the case. "The events at Sarajevo," as Immanuel Geiss has observed, ". . . turned out to be hardly more than a cue for the Reich to rush into action."[91] As for the kaiser's sudden "personality change," which Holsti and North deduce from marginalia to documents dating from July 29, suffice it to say that there were manifold examples of a peculiarly vehement mode of expression on the part of "William the Sudden" dating from well before the Sarajevo crisis. Moreover, it cannot explain the divergence between the kaiser and Bethmann-Hollweg on July 27, following the Serbian response to the Austrian ultimatum. After reading the Serbians' deferential response to the Austrians, the kaiser wrote that Vienna had scored a "great moral victory" and added that "with it every reason for war drops away."[92] In other words, by all appearances, the kaiser backed away from war at the last minute. Bethmann-Hollweg delayed forwarding William's comments to Vienna, and when he did, he suppressed William's observation that the reasons for war were disappearing.[93] In short, the kaiser's emotional hesitation was overridden by the chancellor on the grounds of the latter's political calculation that Germany had already gone too far in the crisis to back down.

Recent historiography has not dealt kindly with any of the leading assumptions underpinning the conventional model of the Sarajevo crisis: the assumption that "none of the powers wanted war"; the impression that in 1914 Germany genuinely feared imminent aggression from the other powers and that it lacked confidence in its military capabilities; the belief that the Russian general mobilization on July 31 was the event that provoked the subsequent German mobilization and declaration of war.

Far from blundering into the war, German leaders were aware that they were risking general war when they deliberately prodded Austria to take military action against Serbia. The decision to give Austria carte blanche against Serbia was made during July 5–7. By July 12, Count Laszlo Szögyény-Marich, the Austrian ambassador in Berlin, reported that "German circles that mattered" were "one might almost say urging" Austria-

Hungary "to take action which might even mean military action, against Serbia." Four days earlier, after a conversation with Berlin's ambassador, the Austrian foreign minister, Count Leopold Berchtold, told Count Stephen Tisza, the Hungarian prime minister, that "in Germany any deal by us with Serbia would be interpreted as a confession of weakness which must have repercussions on our position in the Triple Alliance and on Germany's future policy." He added that German calculations were based on the assumption "that at present England would not participate in a war which started over a Balkan country, not even if it led to [a] clash with Russia and perhaps also with France."[94]

On July 8 even Bethmann-Hollweg, always more cautious than the generals, had already confided to his personal secretary, Kurt Riczler: "If war comes from the east so that we have to fight for Austria-Hungary and not Austria-Hungary for us we have a chance of winning. If war does not break out, if the Tsar is unwilling or France, alarmed, counsels peace, we have the prospect of splitting the Entente."[95] The chancellor thus explicitly envisioned the possibilities not simply of a localized war involving Austria and Serbia but also of a Continental war involving Germany, Russia, and France. And while Bethmann-Hollweg hoped for British neutrality, he did not totally discount the possibility that Britain would eventually join the conflict. On July 7 he told Reizler: "An action against Serbia . . . can lead to world war."[96]

Given a willingness to risk a major war, the configuration of forces in the crisis was, from the German perspective, ideal: Britain would be called upon to support France and Russia over a question in which Britain had no interest, while Germany would be supporting Austria (as opposed to fickle Austria's being called upon to support Germany) in the likely event that Russia offered military support to Serbia. Popular support in Germany for a European war would be easier to assure if Russia were the enemy. Such were the advantages of a war "from the east." The key to Bethmann's strategy of localization, however, was rapid execution. In late June, European public opinion sympathized with Austria over the death of the archduke. It was essential to his plan that Austria strike while the iron was hot, moving rapidly to exact military punishment from Serbia while still apparently angry, so that Europe would be presented with a fait accompli. Even then, of course, localization of the conflict was by no means guaranteed.[97]

Instead, the Austrian leadership chose to frame a long and careful ultimatum to Serbia. Preparation was held up by technical problems until mid-July. But by that time the French president was scheduled to be in

St. Petersburg, allowing close coordination between France and Russia in responding to the crisis. Publication of the ultimatum was therefore further postponed so that St. Petersburg would not learn of it until after Poincaré had set sail for France. When the Austrian ultimatum finally appeared at 6:00 P.M. on July 23, Europe had for the most part forgotten about the Austrian archduke; by the time of the conciliatory Serbian reply on July 25, it was becoming clear, at least to the foreign offices of the major powers, both that the Austrian action was premeditated and that Berlin must have had a hand in it.

At this point, Bethmann-Hollweg's strategy of limiting the conflict began to look implausible, and attention in Berlin shifted not toward finding a way out of the crisis but rather to delaying German military preparations long enough so that Russia could be made to look the aggressor. This was the crux of German policy in the final days of the crisis—to delay German war preparations until Russia had announced a general mobilization, and then to blame Russia for starting the war that Germany now sought. The purpose was both to persuade Britain to remain neutral, since it was understood that British policy would never back Russian aggression, and, more crucially, to unify the German people. When Germany entered the war, there is no doubt that the populace believed it was being called upon to defend Germany's existence against the Slavic onslaught.

For the Entente nations, the first clear sign that a major crisis was upon them was the Austrian ultimatum to Serbia on July 23. The forty-eight-hour time limit attached to it was not designed to give them a great deal of room to maneuver. Already by late July 25 Eyre Crowe in the British Foreign Office had discerned the crux of the situation: "The point that matters is whether Germany is or is not absolutely determined to have this war now." Yet he added: "There is still the chance that she can be made to hesitate, if she can be induced to apprehend that the war will find England by the side of France and Russia." The "one effective way of bringing this home to the German government without absolutely com-mitting us definitely at this stage," Crowe advised, was to mobilize the fleet at the first sign that others were mobilizing and to inform the French and Russian governments that Britain had decided on this course. This, said Crowe, "may conceivably make Germany realize the seriousness of the danger to which she would be exposed if England took part in the war."[98] Instead, however, Grey temporized, asking Germany to persuade Austria to extend the time limit. The Germans made a show of receptive-ness to this suggestion, but in fact Grey's proposal was deliberately held up in Berlin until after the ultimatum had expired. Russian requests for an extension were similarly deflected. All the while Gottlieb von Jagow, the German secretary of state, repeatedly affirmed (utterly falsely) that Germany had no foreknowledge of the Austrian action.

Russia had from the first resolved to take a firm stand in the crisis. "We will not let ourselves be trampled upon," said Tsar Nicholas.[99] At stake was Russia's whole policy in the Near East—its prestige in the Balkan states by virtue of that its access to the straits (Bosporus and Dardanelles), through which most of its grain was exported. Though Russia opted for a firm stance, two points must be stressed. First, while supporting Serbia, Russia urged a conciliatory response, advising Serbia in the event of an Austrian invasion not to resist but rather to submit the question to other powers for arbitration. According to the Russian chargé d'affaires in Belgrade, moreover, the Serbians in replying to Austria's ultimatum would "meet all demands if they are in the slightest degree compatible with the dignity of an independent state." Grey, when he saw the Serbian reply, called it "the greatest humiliation an independent state has ever been subjected to" and expressed his disappointment to Vienna that Austria "treated the Serbian reply as if it had been a decided refusal to comply with [its] wishes."[100]

Second, even though Russian officials calculated that a firm response might lead to war with Germany, they continued to seek a peaceful solution to the crisis to the very end. The firm line was taken in no small measure because previous experience with Germany—particularly in the annexation crisis of 1909—had persuaded the Russian government that even wholesale appeasement would not necessarily prevent war. Since the turn of the century, all three Entente powers had learned from experience that graceful concessions by no means guaranteed a relenting of Berlin's demands. For example, when the French prime minister Pierre Maurice Rouvier acceded to a German ultimatum demanding the resignation of Théophile Delcassé, the French foreign minister, during the first Moroccan crisis in 1905, the Germans, far from agreeing to a settlement, insisted upon an international conference to negotiate further concessions from France. Russia had suffered similarly brusque treatment by Berlin when it sought mediation from Germany over Austria's annexation of Bosnia and Hercegovina in 1909. The British foreign secretary had learned parallel lessons in the arms negotiations with Germany. It was from such experiences with Germany that the Triple Entente had gradually taken shape. Germany's sense of "encirclement" was largely the product of such aggressiveness on its own part in diplomatic dealings with other powers. "Germany," Berghahn notes, "had 'circled herself out' of the great power concert."[101]

On July 26 Russian Foreign Minister Sazanov attempted to develop an informal mediation proposal with Berlin's ambassador in St. Petersburg, which was rejected by Germany and Austria. Russian requests for mediation, including a request that the question be put before the Court of Arbitration at The Hague, continued to the end, and Russia even attempted to open a new round of talks with Vienna on July 31, after the Russian general mobilization was already in progress.

French policy, meanwhile, was hobbled by the fact that the French leadership was, in John Keiger's phrase, "literally and metaphorically at sea" during most of the crisis.[102] This, of course, was a consequence of the Central Powers' planning. Poincaré and his entourage departed from Russia on the *France* on July 23 before hearing of the Austrian ultimatum, and arrived at Dunkirk on July 29. Maurice Paléologue, the French ambassador in St. Petersburg, gave firm assurances to Sergei Sazanov of French backing in the crisis, and much was made for a long time of Paléologue's encouragements. Nonetheless, historians now tend to agree that he was merely reiterating the mutually understood terms of the Entente between Russia and France, and at all events Sazanov showed no sign of wishing for war.

For a long time it was claimed that the news of the Russian general mobilization, received in Berlin around noon on July 31, provoked German mobilization and, since German plans drew no distinction between mobilization and attack, triggered world war. Thus, it was argued, delay in the Russian general mobilization might have conceivably diffused the crisis. This argument has recently been revived, with some qualifications ostensibly designed to take into account Fischer's evidence, by Steven Van Evera.[103]

Yet the weight of evidence goes utterly against this supposition. The argument was originally made on the invalid assumption that the Russian general mobilization constituted a genuine threat, or at least a provocation, to Germany. On July 28, Austria-Hungary declared war on Serbia, and shelling of Belgrade was begun. Only at this point did Russia order a mobilization—and then a partial one, directed against Austria rather than both Austria and Germany. Notification of the Russian partial mobilization reached Berlin on July 29. On August 1, following the subsequent Russian order for general mobilization and German declaration of war on Russia, a press spokesman for the German Foreign Ministry declared: "Russia alone forces a war on Europe which nobody has wanted except Russia; the full force of responsibility falls on Russia alone."[104]

Yet Berlin's military representative in St. Petersburg had indicated quite clearly on July 30 that Russian preparations were defensive: "I have the impression that they have mobilised because without having aggressive intentions they are afraid of what will happen and that they are now frightened of what they have done." That the German chancellor himself understood the significance, political and military, of the Russian preparation is clear from his remarks at the Prussian ministry of state on the same day. "Although Russia had proclaimed a mobilisation," Bethmann-Hollweg explained, "its mobilisation measures could not be compared with those of the west European [powers]. . . . Russia did not want war, it had been forced by Austria to take this step."[105] When Bethmann-Hollweg fought with the generals to delay the German general mobilization until after the Russian general mobilization was ordered, his aim was simply to make Russia appear the aggressor. On July 27, the chancellor had insisted to the kaiser: "In all events Russia must ruthlessly be put into the wrong."[106] Reflecting agreement with this formula, Moltke telegraphed the Austrian chief of staff on July 30: "Wait for Russian mobilisation; Austria must be preserved, must mobilise immediately against Russia, Germany will mobilise. Italy must be compelled by compensations to fulfil its alliance obligations."[107]

Preliminary military preparations were already underway in Germany, but Bethmann-Hollweg succeeded in persuading the generals to delay the order for German general mobilization until noon on July 31. When news of the Russian mobilization came—as it turns out, only five minutes before the general's deadline, at 11:55 A.M. on the thirty-first—the German reaction was not fear but relief. The following day, as the Foreign Ministry sought publicly to shift blame to Russia, there was rejoicing in government circles in Berlin. Moltke later recalled of August 1: "There was, as I said, an atmosphere of happiness." Admiral Georg von Müller recorded in his diary on the same day: "The mood is brilliant. The government has managed to make us appear the attacked."[108]

Would removal of the pretext provided by the Russian general mobilization have averted war? Van Evera implies as much when he says:

> British leaders were unaware that German mobilization meant war, hence
> that peace required Britain to restrain Russia from mobilizing first. . . . This
> British ignorance reflected German failure to explain clearly to the Entente
> that mobilization did indeed mean war—German leaders had many oppor-

tunities during the July crisis to make this plain, but did not do so. We can only guess why Germany was silent.[109]

Of those who have examined the records of this period, Van Evera is perhaps alone in having to "guess" why the Reich passed up so many "opportunities" to inform the Entente powers of its military secrets during the July crisis. To say merely that mobilization "meant" war for Germany is to obscure the violation of diplomatic convention implicit in the German plan of responding to Russian mobilization with an immediate attack, through neutral Belgium, on France. "Let it never be admitted," Churchill wrote in 1929 of German planning, "that mobilization involves war or justifies the other side in declaring war. Mobilization justifies only counter-mobilization and further parley."[110] Such, moreover, was the understanding among statesmen in 1914.

To hold Britain somehow accountable for failing to advise Russia not to mobilize, by suggesting that peace "required" such an action, is to apply a peculiar standard of conduct to international politics. In effect, it is to blame Britain for lacking knowledge that Germany deliberately withheld from it. By the conventions of diplomacy there was no reason to believe that Germany would respond to Russian mobilization with an immediate attack. In his dispatch to Sir George Buchanan in St. Petersburg on July 25, Grey assumed, not unnaturally, that the crisis would likely get as far as mobilization of Austria and Russia against one another before a solution could be found. The idea was that mediation might then be introduced to solve the dispute.[111]

Grey's error lay in precisely the opposite direction from that implied by Van Evera's theory of a "cult of the offensive." It was not that Britain was insufficiently accommodating to Germany; it was that it was too accommodating. The whole British posture toward Russia was to counsel delay and restraint, predicated on the belief that Austria, under German persuasion, might relent. But by the time the tsar ordered general mobilization, German military preparations were already underway, and Serbia was actually under attack. Britain was in no position to advise Russia's leaders against their better judgment not to take steps that they deemed essential to their country's safety. The power of the German armies and the relative rapidity with which they could be deployed were well known; the Russian mobilization was notoriously sluggish by contrast. In return for a delay, it is likely that Russia would have demanded a signal of unambiguous support from Britain—precisely the kind of support that Grey, cleaving to his preferred role as mediator between the coalitions, did not feel in a position to give.[112] Why take such risks, at any rate, especially when no one outside the German government had reason to suspect that mobilization as such would lead immediately to war?

Germany kept its plans secret from other powers—but for a definite and obvious purpose. Only if one assumes (as Van Evera seems to) that Germany was willing to avert war or wished to cooperate with the Entente powers to diffuse the crisis—and nothing suggests that German leaders had any such intentions—does it make sense to propose that it should have revealed the information. (Even then, who can imagine the German Reich unfolding the details of the Schlieffen plan—which the Reich would not even share with its Austro-Hungarian ally—for all to see? The whole concept verges on the absurd.) Rather than reveal the Schlieffen plan, Germany might as easily have refrained from executing it. Only a kind of stubborn insistence that the key to the crisis lay in the mistaken "perceptions" would lead one to place such stress on exchanges of information alone. At the same time, to blame the secrecy of the Schlieffen plan on the international system or a generalized "cult of the offensive" in which all powers shared is to overlook the obvious fact that only one power—in collaboration with its allies—secretly dispensed with the distinction between war and mobilization and secretly maneuvered toward war while other powers sought peace. Like so much commentary in this vein on Sarajevo, Van Evera's formulation of the problem simply fails to comprehend the political dimensions of the conflict and the seriousness of the German intent.

Such problems aside, however, there is an even more straightforward indication that delay of the Russian general mobilization would have been to no avail: Even before news of it reached Berlin on July 31, Bethmann-Hollweg had drawn up yet another ultimatum demanding cessation of all military preparations on Russia's part. The aim quite obviously was to use the inevitable Russian refusal as a pretext to go to war.[113] Van Evera himself is forced to concede that the effect of the Russian order has been exaggerated: "Germany apparently decided to attack on learning of Russian partial mobilization, before Russian full mobilization was known in Germany. This suggests that the role of inflexible Russian plans in causing the war is overblown."[114] Even here Van Evera clings tenaciously to his "action-reaction" paradigm. The German government had, we must remember, envisioned the likelihood of war from the beginning of the crisis. Preliminary plans for German mobilization had been completed as early as July 18,[115] and on July 27, two days before the Russian partial mobilization, Berlin was poised and waiting. As Admiral von Müller noted on that day: "Tendency of our policy: keep quiet, letting Russia put herself in the wrong, but then not shying away from war."[116] In short, that by July 30 Germany would have gone to war in any event seems virtually assured; most recent analyses have coalesced around this view.

Deterrence "Fails"?

The impulse to find a solution to the crisis in a delay of the Russian general mobilization owes more to the conviction that peace lies down the road of accommodation than to any detailed appreciation of the July crisis. But the question remains: Were there actions within the reach of the Entente powers that might have prevented the outbreak of World War I?

The tendency has been to assume the answer to these questions of necessity lies outside the traditional framework of deterrence. Indeed, the lesson usually drawn from Sarajevo is that in 1914 not only deterrence but the very logic of deterrence "failed." "There is no mystery about the outbreak of the First World War," the historian A. J. P. Taylor once asserted, a bit perversely. "The deterrent failed to deter. This was to be expected sooner or later. A deterrent may work ninety-nine times out of a hundred. On the hundredth occasion it produces catastrophe."[117] Yet this was precisely the "mystery" that kept Sarajevo alive so long in the Western mind: the inexplicable failure of deterrence—an especially troubling lesson, if proven accurate, for the nuclear era. The mysteriousness, however, depended on assumptions about the crisis and German intentions discredited by recent historical investigation. In fact, the framework of deterrence is capable of explaining fairly adequately why the July crisis led to war and of pointing toward actions that might have been taken to avert the catastrophe.

German policy in the Sarajevo crisis was a response not so much to the strength as to the weakness of the Triple Entente. In the wake of the war, there was a tendency among British and American commentators to blame the conflict on the tightness of the opposing coalitions. This was less a conclusion drawn from observation than a restatement of the long-standing liberal conviction that alliances are by nature bellicose arrangements, likely to result in war, a belief that one can trace back through nineteenth-century liberalism to the French enlightenment.[118] The same assumption resurfaces in Van Evera's analysis, which speaks of "the general tendency of alliances toward tightness and offensiveness in an offense-dominated world."[119] But this is simply a misconception. Not only did the Entente, as we have seen, explicitly eschew an "offensive" posture, but also, as Taylor himself has pointed out, "the existing alliances were all precarious."[120] Britain's commitment to France, let alone to Russia, was far from open or obviously assured. A more unambiguous British commitment to France in itself would have done much to undermine German confidence in success. As German planning suggests, the very weakness of the Entente created incentives for a high-risk game, since the possibility that Britain would fail to support her putative friends made the prospects of diplomatic and military victories all the more plausible. The Triple Entente was no NATO. The weakness and elusiveness of its arrangements was especially clear to Russia's Foreign Minister Sergei Sazanov, who lamented to his ambassador in London in February 1914 that "world peace will only be assured the day the Triple Entente, whose existence can no more be proved than the existence of the sea monster, is transformed into a defensive alliance without secret clauses and when this fact is publicly announced in all the newspapers of the world. On that day the danger of German hegemony will finally disappear."[121] Buchanan, the British ambassador in St. Petersburg, endorsed the logic of Sazanov's analysis.[122]

Moreover, we know the hope of British neutrality in a Continental war figured importantly in German calculations. Fear that Britain might fight alongside France was a major factor holding Germany's leaders back in the spring of 1914, even as the generals were urging war. "Our people," Moltke complained to Franz Conrad von Hötzendorf, Austrian chief of staff, in May, referring to his civilian colleagues in the government, "unfortunately still expect a declaration from Britain that it will not join in. This declaration Britain will never make."[123] The only point in the July crisis at which Bethmann-Hollweg actually sought, albeit halfheartedly, to reverse the headlong plunge to war came in the early hours of July 20, after he learned from his ambassador in London that Britain would almost certainly not remain neutral. The chancellor telegraphed Heinrich von Tschirschky, Berlin's ambassador in Vienna, urging that he press "most urgently and impressively" for the "acceptance of mediation" by Vienna. In a second message sent a few minutes later, he warned that Germany, while "ready to fulfil the obligations of our alliance . . . must decline to be drawn wantonly into a world conflagration by Vienna."[124] But the shelling of Belgrade was already underway, and the Austrians, having up to this point been continually pressed and prodded by Germany to go forward, were now unwilling to stop. The news of London's attitude had come too late. Bethmann-

Hollweg's reaction to it suggests that an earlier and firmer signal might well have had effect. The example of the Agadir crisis of 1911, when the clear and early war threat embodied in Lloyd George's bellicose Mansion House speech shocked German authorities and threw cold water on German planning for war, supports that view.[125]

Finally, there is the attitude of William himself, who, on the basis of a selective interpretation of a remark of the English king, had chosen to believe throughout the July crisis that British neutrality was assured. It is significant—and also rather typical—that when the kaiser learned that Britain was in fact to be drawn into the war, he felt that he had been deceived.[126] But far from engaging in fraud, Britain had merely been characteristically indecisive. The point is that its diplomacy failed to translate its military assets into a "political power factor" at a crucial time.

A more open British commitment to the Entente, and especially to France—in effect, the conversion of the Entente into an open defensive alliance—would have enforced a limit on German ambitions; in the absence of such a standing commitment, an early signal of British resolve, such as was advised by Crowe, might have had the same effect. However, the dominant liberal assumptions about foreign affairs prevented Britain from exercising either option. A firm alliance with Russia was politically impossible both because Russia was regarded as an illiberal regime and because alliances themselves were regarded by British liberals as inherently provocative. For the Anglo-American liberal of 1914, there was as yet no such thing as a purely defensive, or NATO-style, alliance. It would require not one but two world wars for liberal thought to absorb the truth that a straightforward alliance or coalition of states committed to maintaining the status quo could be a major force for preserving peace. (To judge from Van Evera's argument, the lesson may still be uncertainly learned.)

During the crisis itself, the idea that a firm and early commitment to the Entente might have forestalled German aggression was not lost on all members of the British government. Yet an attempt to provide such a commitment would have split the cabinet irreparably and brought the government down in the midst of the international crisis.[127] Even had it been possible, the effectiveness of such a commitment would have depended upon the credibility as well as the earliness of the signal. Had the Germans been convinced of British resolve by May, the British position would have proved perhaps more of a deterrent than the gestures that Crowe advised once the crisis was actually underway. Whether the latter action would have deterred the war is still disputed by historians.[128]

In any case, to lay the groundwork for more decisive action at Sarajevo,

Grey would have had to embark much earlier on a long process of public education, instilling in the British populace a clear understanding of the political issues at stake. The British public would need to have been made to see the Entente in a somewhat similar light to that in which Americans through the Cold War saw NATO. Such notions would have gone against radical sentiment in Grey's own party. There was, at any rate, a strong disinclination to engage in such public education, traceable both to anxiety over preserving Liberal party unity and to the distaste of Foreign Office officials for the task of accounting for policy to an uninformed and emotional public. Sarajevo was among the first tests of the ability of modern democracies to conduct foreign policy in a crisis pregnant with the possibility of war. The failure of Britain to respond effectively was in no small part due to a failure to adapt foreign policy to the exigencies of democratic rule, to shape a public mandate for policies essential to Britain's long-range survival and prosperity. This problem is one that the present-day democracies have by no means entirely solved.

To all these circumstances must be added the purely military consideration that, as has usually been true throughout history, everybody, and especially the aggressors, expected a short war—a decisive conflict of several weeks or at most months in duration. The "short-war illusion" was decisive in German military planning.[129] The Germans were by no means alone in failing to understand that the military advantage in modern warfare had shifted decisively from the offensive to the defensive and that consequently a long war of attrition was almost inevitable. But Germany alone sought to exploit the presumed offensive advantage. Whatever their costs on the battlefield, French offensive battle tactics in themselves posed no threat to the peace; German offensive foreign policy did.

Nations do not launch wars because they are afraid, but because they are confident that they will gain more by resorting to force than by refraining from doing so. This was true no less in 1914 than in other cases. It is a fact that Germany was fearful in a sense; fearful not of any immediate attack, but of losing its current advantageous position— "afraid," as Grey later put it, "that she would be afraid." It was by no means clear that in three years' time Germany would be the victor in a Continental war. The generals envisioned a future conflict with Russia as a certainty, and Russia's power was growing. But, as Fischer notes, in Bethmann-Hollweg's discussion of the problem there is no expectation of Russian aggression, merely a suggestion that if a war occurred three years hence Germany would be at a disadvantage.[130]

At all events, to understand the effects of the German fear one must understand how it interacted with the German confidence of victory, which was, after all, the indispensable ingredient of a war-making policy. If Germany were simply fearful, if it were clear that in the "roll of the iron dice" the odds were against it, then even with its predisposition to aggression it doubtless would have refrained from precipitating a war, as it had in 1911. Doubtless, had Germany's leadership been able to foresee the actual outcome of the war, they would have been far less eager to bring it on. But Germany's leaders, and its generals in particular, were confident. What deterrence proposes to offer the potential aggressor is a picture, in effect a discouraging "snapshot" of the future if a power chooses war. The snapshot viewed by the German leadership was manifestly incorrect.

Indeed, World War I revealed a pattern that would pave the road to fighting more than once in the twentieth century: the systematic tendency of democracies to appear weaker and less resolute than they really are in periods leading up to war. This pattern was evident in World War II, in Korea, in the 1982 Argentine invasion of the Falkland Islands, and more recently even in the Gulf War with Iraq. Antimilitarist forces in democracies tend to constrain policy in ways that suggest to more militaristic and authoritarian powers that the democracies lack the wherewithal to resist. Ironically, once democracies perceive themselves under attack, they encounter little trouble in mobilizing public opinion, and nationalism takes on a life of its own. Once galvanized for war, democracies have generally proved to be formidable enemies. This pattern tends to make war more rather than less likely, since it encourages aggression on the part of the ambitious nondemocratic states. Such is the paradox: In the twentieth century, those powers least prone to choose war as a vehicle of policy have also been a fortiori the least prone to take the steps necessary to prevent other powers from choosing it.

As for the notion that "arms races cause wars," it gives a completely distorted picture of the events that culminated in war in 1914. It obscures the source both of the arms race and of the war itself, which lay in German ambitions and conscious decisions made by the German Reich. Eyre Crowe was correct about the Sarajevo crisis almost from the start: The key question was always whether Germany wanted war and was willing to risk it, and whether Entente powers, Britain in particular, could take actions that would render such risks unacceptable. World War I did not result from any "accident"; war came in 1914 for the relatively simple reason that a hegemonic state sought to expand its influence in the world and was persuaded by the apparent momentary weakness and indecision of its opponents to do so by violent means. (In this respect, Sarajevo differs sharply from the Cuban missile crisis, where, by every indication, the Soviet leadership, acutely aware of its inferior capabilities, had no thought of war and sought from the beginning an avenue of retreat.)[131]

Ten years after World War I, Churchill stated, concerning the thorny issue of war responsibility: "Disputes as to responsibility for bringing about conditions which led to various wars are endless. But mankind will be wise in the future to take as the paramount criterion of war guilt the sending of the main armies by any State across its frontier line, and to declare that whoever does this puts himself irretrievably in the wrong."[132] The accurate, and also commonsense, statement of the situation was that Germany had caused the war. For this basic fact, the arms race paradigm substituted the abstraction that "nationalism caused the war" or "the arms race caused the war" or, to use the latest formulation, "the 'cult of the offensive' caused the war." But neither "nationalism" nor "militarism" nor the "cult of the offensive" nor the impulse to improve its fortunes by amassing arms existed in other regimes as in Germany; nor, given the constitution of the democracies, is it likely that such forces could have taken control.

The error of the arms race paradigm lay in generalizing from the German case to the other powers; this derived in turn from a tendency to abstract "militarism" artificially from the particular political setting in which it took hold and became overmastering. The liberal-pacifist paradigm treated "militarism," inaccurately, as a force to which all powers were if not equally subject, then equally susceptible in peacetime—in short, as a kind of communicable disease. Behind this one can sense an almost scientific impulse to identify, isolate, and banish (or at least control) a factor alleged to be at the root of political conflict between states. It amounts to little less than a denial of politics itself, a simple refusal to accept that the phenomenon of the hegemonic or aggressive state is an elemental reality of political life, to be understood on its own terms, irreducible to other factors.

But from the outset the arms race thesis went hand in hand with the idea of rejecting or transcending politics. Those who spoke of preventing war by ending arms races in the 1920s and 1930s also spoke of the dawn of a new international order in which, as Grey put it, "war must be ruled out."[133] The two ideas were closely linked. Those who hesitated to blame Germany emphasized instead that the war was "the child of the European anarchy, of the outworn system of sovereign states."[134] Consonant with the liberal vision of politics, rather than blame the problem on an aggressive or wanton state, the arms race paradigm blamed it on states and governments as such—on the very mechanism, the very nature of politics.

Ironically, at the moment when war broke out in 1914, the event was widely read as a devastating indictment of liberal assumptions about international affairs. In a remarkable gesture, August 8, 1914, *The Nation,* Britain's leading radical journal, printed what amounted to a repudiation of the liberal-pacifist foreign policy vision:

> Who in the future will pay attention to the *Daily News* . . . the *Manchester Guardian* and other journals of the same stamp? These idealists . . . who refuse to look reality in the face and prefer to be deceived and to deceive their followers. . . . Who will heed when the Lord Courtneys and Wedgwoods and the Trevelyans presume to air their baby views on so complicated a subject as foreign politics and our duties toward our friends and allies? I venture to say, after what has happened, no one.[135]

And yet by 1919, the same war that once was regarded as an indictment of the liberal vision of foreign policy was treated as the most compelling argument for its implementation. In the end, the notion that war had been caused by the arms race was less an observation based on events than a complicated reaffirmation of the once-discredited liberal-pacifist vision of international politics.

Yet in setting the framework for efforts to prevent another war, the arms race paradigm pointed the democracies in exactly the wrong direction. It taught that democratic Britain had been too militaristic before the war, when the truth was that it had been not quite firm or vigilant enough. It encouraged at best a certain insouciance about military power, implying that deterrence was an inherently dangerous or simply unnecessary arrangement, something to be transcended or dispensed with—when the real lesson of Sarajevo was that hegemonic states could be prevented from unleashing war only by ensuring that deterrence and defensive alliances remained unambiguously strong. However, from the standpoint of British liberalism, such a conclusion would have amounted to an unpalatable acknowledgment that power politics was—and is—a permanent feature of the human condition.

CHAPTER 2

◻

The Munich Blunder

Much of the revolution in thinking about war now associated in our minds with the invention of the atomic bomb actually took shape in the years during and immediately following World War I. The unprecedented carnage of 1914 to 1918 strengthened the conviction in many hearts that war had ceased to be effective "as an instrument of national policy."[1] In the 1920s and 1930s, it became commonplace to speak of the next war as threatening an end to civilization. The new technology of destruction—machine gun, tank, airplane, poison gas—promised unimaginable horrors should the calamity of world war be repeated. Air power, in particular—described in a manner closely resembling the way in which we now speak of nuclear weapons—was contemplated with growing apprehension. In the next war, it was predicted, bombers would quickly reduce whole cities to rubble; tens of thousands of civilians would perish from aerial gas attacks in a single day. "In war," affirmed British Prime Minister Neville Chamberlain in the late 1930s, echoing the prevailing views of his contemporaries, "there are no winners."[2]

World War I was widely thought to have discredited not merely a particular set of policies but the traditional approach to foreign policy. It was viewed as an indictment not simply of this or that government or foreign office but of the balance of power itself. To prevent another such catastrophe—a cataclysm that promised to be many times worse than the one just concluded—it would be necessary to reconstruct diplomacy on an entirely new foundation. The traditional mechanisms and expedients of statecraft—secret consultations, alliances, military power—must be replaced by alternative arrangements. The principle of deterrence was viewed with particular distrust. The effort to deter war by accumulating military power had, it was widely argued, simply made war more likely. The theorem (fallacious, as we have seen) that an arms race had caused the Great War and that arms limitation arrangements were therefore necessary to prevent a recurrence took hold of the democratic imagination. In place of deterrence based on alliances and armed force, there was to be open diplomacy, "collective security," and above all disarmament.

Modern theories of history have made us skeptical of the influence of theory on history. Yet if we examine carefully the various influences operating in the international system in the postwar period, it is difficult to escape the conclusion that the new internationalist theory of war and diplomacy played a major part, if not indeed the decisive part, in bringing on World War II. From the Treaty of Versailles in 1919 to the Munich Conference in 1938, the effect of the new vision was consistently to obscure the strategic realities that statesmen confronted, disguising genuine dangers and promoting false hopes. The purblindness of democratic leaders in this period is an altogether striking phenomenon. The history of diplomacy is rich in examples of blunder, folly, and miscalculation, of misconceived initiatives and bungled opportunities, but in the 1920s and 1930s, we come upon a series of flagrant and obvious errors that we cannot help but feel a previous generation of statesmen would not have made. Intelligent leaders, shrewd and seasoned politicians with nary a single delusion about the machinations of party politics in their own countries, fell one by one under the spell of the new vision. Where they themselves may have privately deprecated the new internationalist ideals, they were happy to play to that part of the public that had unreservedly embraced them. The rhetoric of peace and disarmament that became the standard fare of the era soon took on a life of its own; when, in response to ominous events in the outside world, democratic leaders sought to reverse the effects of this rhetoric, they found the public resistant. Statesmen and military leaders who sought to urge preparations for war as a means of preventing war were confronted with the widespread belief that armaments were a major cause of war and that war should and could be made obsolete. In the end, their incapacity to conduct affairs on the firm basis of alliance politics and military strength made leaders wish, and eventually anchor policy to the hope, that the new assumptions concerning war and peace were true. In this way many came by a perverse kind of realism to embrace the very illusions that stood in their way.

The Emergence of Wilsonianism

The pervasive influence of the new vision of international politics owed much to the impact of one man. In Woodrow Wilson, liberal-pacifist or "radical" vision of foreign policy found an exponent of unusual eloquence and power. An intellectual imbued with the thinking of the British liberal tradition, as likely, as Lawrence Martin notes, to quote Gladstone, Bagehot, or Mill as an American author to support a point,[3] Wilson attempted to implement the visionary proposals that had occupied the liberal imagination during the previous century.

Nearly all Wilson's major themes—his call for a moderate settlement or a "peace without victory," his League of Nations proposal, his Fourteen Points—were borrowed directly or indirectly from the liberal British intellectuals of his day. Colonel Edward M. House, the president's intimate friend and advisor, consulted frequently with Liberal intellectuals on trips to Britain, and a parade of British radicals called at the White House to confer with the colonel during the war years. Wilson himself imbibed from pages of *The New Republic*—the one journal he was known to read regularly—the writings of such figures as Norman Angell, a leading spokesman for radical opinion in Britain and the author of the best-selling book *The Great Illusion,* which had argued in 1912 that war was becoming obsolete. Angell contributed key suggestions to Wilson's major address of May 27, 1916, in which the American president first set forth his proposal for a League of Nations.[4]

Liberal opinion, as we have seen, had undergone a remarkable reversal in the early days of war. In August 1914 the dominant mood of the British Liberal party shifted overnight from pacifism to jingoism. One reason war became "total" was the ambitious goal that liberal intellectuals helped formulate for it. Within days of the outbreak of hostilities, H. G. Wells had christened the struggle "a war to end wars."[5] But even in the earliest days of the war, a split became apparent in British liberal opinion between the mainstream liberal outlook and more radical Liberals and Labourites. Some in radical circles threw their weight behind the government; *The Nation,* a leading radical journal, recanted its earlier editorial line.[6] But there was also dissent, particularly among socialists. Ramsay MacDonald, the leader of the Parliamentary Labour party, resigned when his party decided to support the government, and along with Philip Snowden he became a vociferous critic of government war policy. (Fifteen years later, as prime minister, he would author a radical disarmament plan for the Geneva Disarmament Conference.) A few days after the start of the war,

MacDonald joined forces with Angell, Arthur Ponsonby, and Charles Trevelyan to establish the Union for Democratic Control. E. D. Morel, another outspoken critic of the government, authored the UDC's peace program the following November, based on four "Cardinal Points" that were to bear a striking resemblance to Wilson's subsequent fourteen.[7]

Whereas mainstream Liberal party members tended to blame Germany for the war, the radical intellectuals, holding firmly to their prewar vision of foreign policy, blamed the outworn international system, what G. Lowes Dickinson would later christen "the international anarchy." In this view Britain shared a responsibility for the war equal with that of Germany. The problem was not German aggression, but the whole apparatus of traditional diplomacy: secret agreements, alliances, the amassing of arms on all sides.[8]

As it took shape in the course of the war, the Wilsonian program for peace proved virtually indistinguishable from the platform of the British Union for Democratic Control. The notion of a moderate peace, what Wilson would later call a "peace without victory," was at the center of the UDC platform.[9] Similarly, the ideas of "open covenants, openly arrived at" to replace "secret diplomacy," of "collective security" to replace "alliances," of "self-determination" and "equality" for all nations, and of "disarmament" itself—all of these central Wilsonian principles could be found in the UDC's manifesto of 1914.[10]

The Versailles Treaty in its final form bore the imprint of this tacit alliance between Wilson and British radicals—an alliance that made it difficult at the end of the war for Lloyd George and Georges Clemenceau to take practical measures on behalf of their own nations that happened to be at variance with the prevailing radical orthodoxy. John Maynard Keynes was speaking for young liberal opinion, for this alliance, when, in his best-selling book *The Economic Consequences of the Peace,* he lashed out at the final treaty in 1919. As Keynes told the tale, Wilson had been too well meaning and too slow-witted to escape the wiles of Clemenceau. France had wished to exact from Germany a "Carthaginian peace," and Wilson and Lloyd George had failed to prevent it. Versailles failed to inaugurate a new order of the ages. The "true voice of the new generation," declared Keynes, had "not yet spoken."[11]

Idealism's Brief Interlude

The perverse effects of the radical formula for peace could be seen almost immediately. Keynes's views notwithstanding, the problem with the Versailles Treaty was not that it constituted in any serious sense a "Carthaginian" or brutally punitive peace but rather that it was virtually a "peace without victory," an armistice rather than a decisive end to the war. The German perception of the injustice of the treaty terms can be explained in no small measure by the fact that the German people had never tasted defeat.[12] In fifty-two months of conflict, no major battle had been fought on German soil; the German army had lost the war before German civilians had experienced directly its horrors.

On October 13, 1918, a week or so after the Germans had signaled to Wilson their willingness to accept an armistice on the basis of the Fourteen Points, Lloyd George in a secret cabinet session asked prophetically whether "the actual defeat of Germany, and giving to the German people a real taste of war, was not more important, from the point of view of the peace of the world, than a surrender at the present time, when the German armies were still on foreign territory." "If peace were made now," said the prime minister, "the Allies would not have occupied a yard of German soil.... In twenty years' time the Germans would say that they had made this mistake and that mistake, and that by better preparation and organization they would be able to bring about victory next time."[13] Yet the growing influence of Wilson's ideas, combined with sheer exhaustion at the duration of the struggle, led the cabinet to bridle at Lloyd George's suggestion. Within a month, the Allies would embrace the armistice.

The Germans, for their part, had resisted peace overtures until their fortunes on the field of battle had suffered decisive reversal. By October 1918 it was clear to the general staff that Germany was headed for disaster. By approaching Wilson rather than the British or the French, and by suing for peace on the basis of the Fourteen Points, the Germans calculated that they could gain better terms than the military situation might warrant. Wilson put forward Fourteen Points as means of transcending policy in the traditional sense of the word; the Germans, in accepting the Wilsonian proposal for an armistice, treated the Fourteen Points as a tool of their own policy, as a means of gaining a more favorable peace than would be dictated out of the barrels of guns.

In the shaping of the peace, meanwhile, democratic public opinion played a curiously problematical role. On the one hand, Wilson's notion of a "peace without victory" and the ideals set forth in his Fourteen Points appeared to have a vast popular following. Wilson had consciously resolved to appeal to European publics over the heads of their leaders, and in no small measure he had succeeded in doing so. "I know that Europe is still governed by the same reactionary forces which controlled this country until a few years ago," he confided privately in July 1918. "But I am satisfied that if necessary I can reach the peoples of Europe over the heads of their Rulers."[14] By the time the armistice was concluded, Wilson's influence was unrivaled in Europe. In France and later in Italy joyous crowds swarmed to greet the American president. Cries of *"Vive le Président!"* and *"Vive l'Amérique!"* went up from the thousands as Wilson's carriage progressed down the Champs Élysées. On the other hand, while Allied publics hungered for peace, they also thirsted for revenge. Lloyd George won a landslide general election in December 1918 on a platform calling for the prosecution of German war criminals and German restitution for the full costs of the war. In France Clemenceau's unsentimentally nationalistic policies had received an overwhelming vote of confidence in the Chamber of Deputies. Nor was the meaning of the welcome offered Wilson by European crowds unambiguous. Wilson's triumphal entry into Paris, as Thomas A. Bailey observed, was "partly the manifestation of a belief that Wilson would carry through his ideals of a lasting and a just peace—which meant, of course, that Germany would be ground down so far into the dust that she could never clench her mailed fist again."[15] The Fourteen Points, in short, had captured the world's imagination, but they could not hold on to it indefinitely. Idealism was bound to give way sooner or later to a politics based on narrower interests, broad hopes for international harmony to desires more concretely rooted in national circumstances. "God has given us the Ten Commandments, and we broke them," said Clemenceau. "Wilson gives us the Fourteen Points. We shall see."[16]

America Abandons Europe

Ironically, the losses suffered by France as a result of the war would prove greater than those suffered by Germany as a consequence of the peace. France was part of the victorious coalition, in a certain sense the main victor of the struggle. The hosting of the peace conference at Paris was intended to symbolize this fact. But France also had paid the heaviest price. The casualties it suffered, while not highest in absolute numbers, were greatest among the Western powers when compared to its population. Britain and Germany had each lost roughly 2 percent of their population on the battlefield, an appalling toll. France had sacrificed nearly twice that proportion. Hardly a family in the northeast of the country was untouched by the grief of war. All the great battles had been fought on French terrain. Acres of farmland lay gouged with trenches and scarred by artillery shells. To make matters worse, evacuating German troops had vandalized the nation's infrastructure, flooding coal mines, tearing down telegraph lines, slaughtering livestock, and burning homes to the ground in a calculated effort to hobble France's capacities for postwar recovery.[17] Nor was the future bright. The German population was 63 million and growing. France, at 39 million, had already shown a declining birth rate before war; now the better part of a generation of young men had been slaughtered on the fields of battle. Twice in the previous half century—1870 and in 1914—Germany had struck across the border; there seemed no permanent guarantee that it would not strike again.

Clemenceau's policy at the Paris Peace Conference was dictated not so much by a desire for revenge—though such a desire was surely present in the French populace—as by a concern for France's future. The reparations from Germany that Keynes made the target of his searing critique were desired by France primarily to finance postwar reconstruction.[18]

What was not clear to Keynes or to historians for many years afterward was how much the reparations problem had followed, at least indirectly, from decisions made by the American administration. In a certain sense, the blame for the apparent severity of the treaty lay ultimately with that power which pressed hardest for leniency: the United States. Originally, French officials had hoped that America would play the central role in financing European recovery, at least by releasing the powers from their war debts, a reasonable hope in light both of France's military contribution to victory and of the U.S. part in financing the war effort itself. More than once the French hinted to the Americans that a coordinated Allied program of recovery—something resembling the Marshall Plan of the late 1940s—would be welcome. Yet by the closing months of the war, American loans to the Allies were rapidly being cut back. Foreign powers were invited to approach Wall Street with their postwar borrowing needs.[19] Free enterprise was as much a part of the Wilsonian liberal vision as disarmament. America might be the savior of Europe, but even under the idealistic Wilson business was business. ("They hired the money, didn't they?" Wilson's successor Calvin Coolidge was later to have said in response to Allied requests for a reprieve on war debts.) It was in no small part America's lack of interest in financing European recovery that forced the French to turn to the galling expedient of German reparations as their chief source of capital for recovery.

In the end, the peace settlement was neither severe nor lenient enough to appear legitimate in German eyes.[20] In addition to paying reparations, Germany was forced to cede territory—Alsace-Lorraine to France, small districts to Denmark and Belgium, upper Silesia to Czechoslovakia, and, most irritating of all, a "corridor" of land west of East Prussia to newly created Poland. Danzig (the Gdansk of our time) became a "free city" under League of Nations administration, and the Rhineland was demilitarized. But the German empire remained intact. This, as A. J. P. Taylor noted, was a momentous fact, pregnant with long-term consequences: The Allied decision—really Woodrow Wilson's decision—to negotiate with the government of the German Reich, to treat the German states as a unified whole, meant of itself that "the German problem" continued unsolved.[21] At the center of Europe lay a coherent, powerful, and always at least potentially hegemonic state; Germany had lost the war, but the back of the German colossus remained unbroken.

Indeed, on the issue of French security, the Wilson administration proved rather less helpful than on the money question. Clemenceau would have preferred to see a dismemberment of the German Reich, a return to the status quo ante of 1870. The Wilsonian armistice already precluded that. Knowing anyway that the American president would revile such a plan, Clemenceau settled instead on the demand for German cession of the Rhineland. The Rhineland was the necessary staging area of any aggression upon French territory; control of the left bank of the Rhine would therefore secure the French indefinitely against German attack. But here again Wilson resisted, and in this he was supported by Lloyd George, who feared that French control of the Rhineland would constitute an irritation to European amity comparable to German possession of Alsace-Lorraine before the war. Lloyd George feared French no less than German hegemony on the Continent. The wartime entente between Britain and its Continental neighbor had by no means entirely allayed their age-old mutual suspicions. At the end of war, anti-French feeling in Britain was running high. Instead of being ceded to France, the Rhineland was made a demilitarized zone. In place of the Rhineland, France received a guarantee of Anglo-American support in the event of

German aggression—a guarantee subsequently repudiated when the Treaty of Versailles was rejected by the U.S. Senate. America, in short, might have given France (and Europe) both economic recovery and security. In the end, it got neither. The French conviction that the peace settlement had not solved its security problem played a critical role in French actions in the early 1920s, including the French decision to occupy the Ruhr in 1920 as a way of enforcing German reparation payments. The Ruhr occupation worked in turn to undermine the process of European reconciliation that Wilson and Lloyd George had hoped to set in motion. The problems of Versailles began to multiply, in short, the moment the treaty was signed. "This is not a peace," said Marshall Ferdinand Foch, the Allied generalissimo, in 1919, "it is an armistice of twenty years."[22]

Historians have said of the Versailles Treaty what G. B. Shaw once said of Christianity: It is not so much that the treaty failed, as that it was never really tried. It would be more correct to say that the treaty was tried selectively, and in large measure which parts were tried was determined by the prevailing outlook of the time. Practically speaking, the centerpiece of the settlement was the Anglo-American guarantee of French security. It was this, looking forward, that could have prevented the recurrence of world war. Victory or defeat in war, as Geoffrey Blainey has observed, is the one certain measure of power in international affairs. At the end of a war, as at no other time in the course of events, it is clear to all which alliances or powers are strong and which weak.[23] The Great War had demonstrated indisputably that the combined strength of the United States, Britain, and France was without equal in the world. Russia had ceased to exist as a great power. Yet however shattered France itself may have been, it was secure with its new allies. Germany demonstrably could never defeat such a combination. It followed that to the degree the wartime alliance or association remained intact, peace would be preserved. But, curiously, the Anglo-American guarantee of French security was regarded by all but the French, not least by Wilson himself, as merely one detail among many in the settlement—indeed, as an unfortunate concession traded for French leniency toward Germany, which itself was believed to be far more crucial to lasting peace. To say that American and British military power were the primary guarantee of French security would be to say that peace was guaranteed by an "alliance," by "power politics"—and this was incompatible with the new order of international affairs that Wilson was promoting and that the treaty was designed to inaugurate.

One of the great ironies of the fight over Senate ratification of the Versailles Treaty is that the leader of the Republican opposition, Henry Cabot Lodge, was a believer both in the Anglo-Franco-American alliance and in the dismemberment of Germany—in short, he had a formula for peace similar to that of Clemenceau.[24] Wilson's most important opponents were not the minority of "Irreconcilables" or isolationists in the Senate but rather mainstream Republicans, a group that Arthur S. Link has called "limited internationalists," who accepted the fact that the United States must play an international role but resisted what they saw as the compromise of American sovereignty and freedom of action implicit in League of Nations membership.[25] The Republicans added reservations to the treaty to protect what they saw as American sovereignty and congressional prerogatives. Wilson, exhausted, ill, and believing falsely that public opinion was on his side, rejected the congressional reservations outright. The consequence of the deadlock was to send the treaty down to defeat.

Yet at the time that Wilson embarked on his crusade for a new international order, there was at least the raw material in Congress for a bipartisan consensus on foreign policy, rooted not in Wilson's vision of a new international order but rather in a more traditional understanding of great-power diplomacy. All this helps to explain the perversity of the final outcome. After all, the real reason that the United States ought to have ratified the Versailles Treaty is that its own security depended on the maintenance of a balance of power in Europe. The real reason to embrace the idea of "collective security" was that without the ability to call upon American military power, the League of Nations would be meaningless as a guarantor of peace. In the end it was American *power* that was necessary to guarantee world stability, not, simply, as Wilson insisted upon arguing, American idealism. Wilson's rhetoric had the effect of obscuring such considerations. It was largely as a result of this that American debate over foreign policy came to be framed during the subsequent decades in terms of the false and mischievous distinction between involvement and isolation.

Far from wishing for any alliance, Wilson argued that American membership was necessary to *prevent* the League from becoming an alliance in the traditional sense of that term.[26] To read Wilson's defense of the operation of Article X of the League charter is to understand why the president's ideas met with a certain measure of skepticism, even when he carried them personally to the American heartland. In the case of aggression by a member state, Wilson explained, League members would absolutely boycott them [the aggressors]. . . . There shall be no communication even between them and the rest of the world. They shall receive no goods; they shall ship no goods. They shall receive no telegraphic messages; they shall send none. They shall receive no mail; no mail will be received from them. . . . It is the most complete boycott ever conceived in a public document, and I want to say to you with confident prediction that there will be no more fighting after that.[27]

Whether the cancellation of its mail would drive an aggressor nation into submission is open to question. Suffice it to say that never before or since have merely economic sanctions operated with anything even remotely approaching the effectiveness of which Wilson dreamed.

In the end, as Thomas Bailey once observed, Wilson's rhetoric of peace proved more effective at rousing the populace to war than at laying a foundation of a lasting postwar settlement. Nonetheless, it was impossible to deny that Wilson had devised a means of reaching the public on foreign policy questions whose efficacy far exceeded anything yet tried. In this sense, Wilsonian rhetoric represented an important solution to the problem of democratic governance, to the task of marshalling public opinion in support of foreign policy. The success of the Wilsonian formula was apparent to everyone, and Wilson's approach would be emulated by democratic statesmen throughout two decades following the war. But the flaw in Wilsonian rhetoric was the failure to fuse idealism with national interest. The effect of Wilson's approach was to promote a dissociation between ideals and interests in discourse on foreign affairs, to open a kind of fissure between the platitudinous surface of international discourse and what Churchill in 1932 called the "iron realities" of international politics. The quandary implicit in Wilson's solution to what we now call the problem of "public diplomacy" would indeed be solved only with the advent of Churchill's own rhetoric—a rhetoric that, however, gained appeal only after the imminence of war made the realities of international power politics impinge unavoidably on the everyday life of ordinary democratic citizens.

The Rush to Disarm

The Wilsonian insistence on the primacy of idealism gave a curious ambiguity and hypocrisy to the whole structure of the Versailles settlement. Nowhere was this clearer than on the issue of disarmament. The fourth of Wilson's Fourteen Points called for "national armaments" to be "reduced to the lowest point consistent with domestic safety." This ambiguous formulation—did "domestic safety" imply security against external aggression or merely against internal unrest?—was not exactly welcome even to the Allies. From the beginning, for example, the British fought against any international conventions that would inhibit their naval power.[28] But disarmament nonetheless came to play an integral role in the Versailles settlement. It was never entirely clear, however, whether disarmament was being undertaken in the old or the new sense of the word. In practice, only Germany was forced to disarm—subjected to disarmament in an older, punitive sense of the term. The provisions of the treaty were quite strict: Germany was limited to an army of 100,000 men; the army was to have no large guns and a fixed number of small ones. The German navy was to consist of no more than six capital ships. Submarines and military aircraft were forbidden.

Though it was ostensibly designed to protect them, the French never much trusted disarmament, arguing—as it turns out, quite accurately—that it could be enforced only so long as it was not needed, and that once disarmament clauses were needed, they could no longer be enforced.[29] But there was an added problem: The treaty portrayed German disarmament merely as the first step toward a universal program of arms limitations. Disarmament in the old sense was to be the prelude to disarmament in the new. The preamble to Part V of the treaty read: *"In order to render possible the initiation of a general limitation of the armaments of all nations,* Germany undertakes strictly to observe the military, naval, and air clauses which follow [emphasis added]."[30] This Allied promise was destined to be used first by Gustav Stresemann, and later more boldly by Adolf Hitler, to provide a pretext for German rearmament. The idea of disarmament, in sum, held within it the seeds of destruction of the security structure.

Nonetheless, of all the elements of Wilsonian vision, it was disarmament whose appeal proved widest and whose influence proved most enduring in the postwar years. Ironically, the United States, having rejected the Versailles Treaty and repudiated involvement in the League of Nations, took the lead in the disarmament effort with its sponsorship of the Washington Naval Conference in 1921. In part the Warren Harding administration was responding to popular agitation. During the lame-duck session of Congress in December 1920, Senator William E. Borah of Idaho, an isolationist Republican and leader of the "Irreconcilables" in the Versailles controversy, sponsored a resolution calling for negotiations on naval reductions with Great Britain and Japan. The Borah resolution launched a popular movement for a naval limitation treaty, endorsed by authorities as diverse as the *New York Times,* William Jennings Bryan, and General John J. Pershing.[31]

The passion for arms limitations that took hold of the United States after the war was the product of two somewhat contradictory tendencies. On the one hand, as we have seen, the Wilsonian vision had given wide currency to liberal views of the armaments question and lent credibility to the notion of "alternative" approaches to national security. Wilson's policies may have been discredited, but his ideals lived on; he had, it appears, forever altered the tenor of democratic discourse on foreign policy. Walter Lippmann years later described the prevailing outlook of the time in mocking tones: "Big warships meant big wars. Smaller warships meant smaller wars. No warships might eventually mean no wars."[32] But disarmament was also congenial with the complacent mood of the times. It is not surprising that Americans, having repudiated that side of the Wilsonian vision which required new involvements abroad, eagerly embraced that side which permitted further withdrawal from foreign military obligations. Americans sought lower taxes and what Warren G. Harding called "normalcy,"[33] while the British rushed to develop new programs of social spending. In 1928, Winston Churchill, as chancellor of the exchequer, made permanent, subject to annual review, the so-called Ten-Year Rule, which specified that defense spending was to be allocated on the assumption that Britain faced no danger for war for ten years.[34]

It was a peculiar marriage of Wilsonian idealism and Republican complacency that guided American disarmament initiatives throughout the 1920s. A succession of Republican presidents—Harding, Calvin Coolidge, Herbert Hoover—out-Wilsoned Wilson in foreign policy, sponsoring a succession of international initiatives in the spirit of the new diplomacy. Yet disarmament, though justified by high idealism, was pursued at least partly because it was the path of least resistance. The ongoing disarmament process served to persuade legislators that, by gutting the military budget they wished to cut anyway, nothing of importance was being sacrificed or risked.

Disarmament at Sea

The Washington Conference of 1921–22 was the first successful international effort to effect large-scale limitations in what might be termed "strategic" arms. But it was also the first of a series of measures that was to have the main effect of paving the way for a second world war. Initiatives such as the Washington Naval Treaty and the Kellogg-Briand Pact, which followed a few years later, in Samuel Eliot Morison's words, "merely served to lull the democracies into a false feeling of security, while giving the militarists everywhere a chance to plot, plan and prepare for a war that would enable them to divide the world."[35] The U.S. handling of the naval disarmament "process" of the 1920s and 1930s illustrates the manner in which modern democracies would permit their faith in disarmament to create conditions conducive to acts of aggression by more ambitious and dangerous powers.

However, if there was a large problem with the Washington Naval Treaty, it was not obvious from the terms of the treaty itself. By almost any standard, and certainly by the standard applied by the age, the treaty was a good arms agreement, far better than most. Signed in February 1922 and based on a surprise radical proposal by the United States,[36] the treaty established a 5:5:3 ratio for battleships and aircraft carriers for the United States, Britain, and Japan. It decreed a ten-year "holiday" or moratorium on the building of such capital ships. And it limited the size of battleships to 35,000 tons. In exchange for Japan's acceptance of inferior tonnage, the United States and Great Britain accepted prohibitions on fortification of their Pacific bases, the United States for possessions west of the Hawaiian islands, Britain for possessions east of Singapore and north of Australia. Under the agreement France and Italy accepted equality of tonnage at slightly more than one-half the level of Japan.[37]

The agreement satisfied a host of diplomatic desiderata: Britain and America agreed to accept naval parity, setting aside a potentially counterproductive rivalry; the Anglo-Japanese alliance, of which Americans were suspicious, was dissolved, to be replaced by a Nine Power Treaty ostensibly guaranteeing the status quo in the Pacific. Japan benefited by the prohibition on fortifications in the Pacific. The United States was relieved of the costly burden of a naval race. And, perhaps best of all, a blow was struck for perpetual peace.

But for all the euphoria that greeted the conclusion of the agreement,[38] there were problems. First, conferees were unable to agree on limitations for cruisers or submarines. Not surprisingly, these loopholes defined the direction of the main naval building effort over the next five years. (A loophole-free arms treaty is no less a contradiction in terms than a loophole-free tax code.) Second, beneath the surface amity there was a residue of bad feeling. In particular, Japan's negotiators had in fact scored a kind of victory for Japan; its position in the Pacific had been materially strengthened; but the 5:5:3 ratio was regarded, especially in Japanese naval circles, as an indignity.[39]

By attempting to solve one set of strategic problems, the treaty merely created another. The prohibitions on base fortification accepted by Britain and the United States actually put them at far more of a strategic disadvantage vis-à-vis Japan than the 5:5:3 ratio might of itself suggest. The Washington treaty was the origin of military problems for the Western powers in the Pacific that would only grow over time. Naval officers in both the United States and Great Britain made some of these problems quite clear, but their warnings went unheeded.[40]

But by far the most fundamental problem lay not in the terms of the treaty itself but rather in the American response to the disarmament "process" that the treaty set in motion. To put the problem simply: Japan made every effort to build to the treaty limits, while the United States made no attempt at all to do so. Beneath the surface of international agreement, different nations responded to the treaty limitations in a manner consonant with the contrasting natures of their political regimes. The Americans, to judge by their actions, tended to regard the treaty as a kind of substitute for a naval force, as an end to the naval competition in the Pacific, while the Japanese saw it more as a set of predictable parameters within which their naval power would continue to expand.

The Growing Threat of Japan

The Congress found in the Washington Naval Treaty a new justification for doing what it had more or less hoped to do anyway—radically cut expenditures for naval power. The British pursued a somewhat less rigorous program of naval retrenchment. The Japanese, meanwhile, built ships. Historians have often said that the Washington Conference was followed by a "race" in cruiser production (where the major treaty loophole lay), but in fact it was an uneven race.

In all, during the five years immediately following the treaty, the United States appropriated funds for construction of a total of 16 new vessels, Britain for 37, and Japan for 116—more than six times the American and four times the British figures.[41] Essentially the same pattern was to persist throughout the life of the naval disarmament process. The power most prone to militarism—Japan—saw in the treaty an opportunity to effect a gradual change in the international status quo, while the Western democracies, and the United States in particular, found in the treaty an excuse to disarm.

The American approach to disarmament was influenced in part by a failure to understand the politics of the agreement. The United States had won agreement from Britain and Japan largely by exerting considerable leverage, by threatening as an alternative an unrestrained naval race that the United States could clearly win. Yet Americans, in characteristic fashion, were inclined to attribute their success at the conference not to the superiority of their power but to the goodness of their intentions. As the threat of an American buildup diminished in credibility, subsequent agreements inevitably became less favorable.[42]

Support for the military in the United States was already weak, but the Washington Conference sapped whatever enthusiasm might have remained for a serious defense effort. Throughout the 1920s, the Japanese navy pursued an aggressive program of technical innovation, perfecting new techniques within the treaty limitations that gradually persuaded naval authorities in Japan that they could defeat even a numerically superior American force. Development of a new torpedo, construction of light cruisers capable of fighting American heavy cruisers, and new tactics of attrition warfare based on use of miniature submarines all worked to shift the naval balance in what the Japanese saw to be their favor.[43] At the same time, Japan built cruisers with power approaching that of battleships (so-called pocket battleships).

A gradual shift began to be evident in the strategic situation in the Pacific. By the London Conference of 1930, Japan was demanding a more favorable ratio than 5:3 in cruisers and was awarded a 7:10 ratio in cruisers and destroyers and parity in submarines.[44] By 1934, the Japanese navy had attained 80 percent of the tonnage of the American navy.[45] In the fall of 1941, Japan had achieved parity with the combined British and American naval forces in the Pacific theater.[46]

By the time of the London Naval Treaty in 1930, the disarmament process was losing what support it had gained among Western naval authorities. During congressional hearings, twenty-two American naval officers testified against ratification of the London treaty, while on the other side of the Atlantic, Winston Churchill argued that the agreement would relegate Britain to the position of "an inferior sea power."[47] Yet political leaders had gotten into the habit of simply ignoring complaints from the military, and the disarmament process continued apace—at least on the Western side.

Within Japan the disarmament process had the additional perverse effect of weakening, rather than strengthening, the parliamentary forces. The arms control negotiations were initially undertaken by the liberal parliamentary governments of the Taisho period. From the start, however, a powerful faction within the navy opposed the treaty. By the time of the London agreement, resistance had turned to open rebellion, and the government came under heavy attack from naval and military authorities for its role in the treaty process. Objectively speaking, Japan's strategic position was in fact improving materially vis-à-vis Western powers; however, anything short of full equality was increasingly regarded by naval officers as an insult. As its strategic position improved, the argument that Japan stood to gain more by going it alone than by remaining within the treaty process grew ever more credible.[48]

The conflict with the Western powers, meanwhile, had strong racial overtones. At the Versailles Conference in 1919, Japan had sought and failed to obtain a declaration of racial equality from the Western nations. In 1924, in a move that could not have been better calculated to sting Japan's prestige, Congress voted to cut off Japanese immigration to the United States. In this way, Congress managed to combine a posture of naval weakness with a policy of gratuitous insults to America's Pacific rival.

Under the combined influence of a dwindling naval capability and an unquestioned faith in disarmament, American policy became ever more passive and lacking in flexibility, while policymakers grew incapable of imagining a response other than disarmament to military problems. "When there were threats to the international equilibrium" during this period, Gerald E. Wheeler has observed, "the reaction in Congress was not for more ships but for another naval conference."[49] As militarist forces gradually assumed control of Japan's government, the United States proved incapable of responding effectively to the change. The Japanese invasion of Manchuria in 1931—a clear violation of the Nine Power Treaty and a major alteration of the status quo in the Pacific—was met with ineffectual verbal protests on the part of the Americans and by a similarly feeble response on the part of the League of Nations. Meanwhile, the Japanese naval buildup continued essentially unabated.

The American "Disarmament Syndrome"

Interestingly, the "disarmament syndrome" that took hold of American policy in the wake of the Washington Treaty prevented the United States from acting in the interests of its own survival even after the disarmament process itself had obviously collapsed. In 1934, the Japanese abrogated the naval treaties. The assumption had always been that in the event the arms control process came to an end, the United States would embark upon a buildup of its own navy. However, between 1935 and 1940 no such buildup occurred.

In part, Western complacency was born of an underestimate of Japanese capabilities, in some measure rooted in racial prejudice.[50] But the most important factor in the paralysis of Western policy was public opinion and politicians' response to it. In the mid-1930s, even the most modest efforts to expand the U.S. navy, ostensibly for the purposes of strengthening the American bargaining position in the arms talks, brought a flood of public protest. Carl Vinson's Senate bill, introduced with Roosevelt's backing in 1934, to build a "treaty navy"—that is, merely to fill out the complement of vessels allowed under the Washington agreement—provoked a public storm. Among the opponents of the bill was one of the president's own delegates to the Geneva conference, Mary E. Woolley, president of Mt. Holyoke College, who argued that passage would undermine disarmament efforts.[51] In the face of poverty and unemployment, critics claimed, it was impossible to justify allocation of government resources to defense.

Though by no means unaffected by the prevailing illusions of the time, Roosevelt, as a former assistant secretary of the navy, was more attuned to strategic problems in the Pacific than his policies might have suggested. It was primarily political instinct, rather than any strong predisposition toward disarmament, that held the president back from openly advocating a stronger U.S. naval posture.

As war approached, the mood in the country became, by all appearances, ever more passive and feckless. Following the sinking of the U.S.S. *Panay* on the Yangtze River by Japanese planes, Congress became absorbed in debate not of sanctions against Japan but of the Ludlow Amendment to the Constitution, which would have required a national referendum before any declaration of war.[52] Following a modest request for two new capital ships, the president was presented with a petition from the National Peace Conference, signed by college presidents, businessmen, and church leaders, protesting the "tremendous increase" in military spending. Even as late as 1938, Congress cut two battleships from a bill requesting three.[53] The slow pace of American naval construction persisted after European war broke out in 1939. In the end, it required nothing less than the Japanese surprise attack on Pearl Harbor to restore the American people to sobriety on questions regarding the maintenance and use of military power.

Germany's Secret Rearmament

Popular memory tends to associate the failure of disarmament policies with the rise of totalitarian governments in the 1930s. Yet the disarmament process had begun to erode the security of the democracies long before either Japan or Germany fell under the control of openly militaristic or totalitarian governments. Just as the technological foundation for the Japanese naval expansion of the 1930s was established under parliamentary governments in the previous decade, so much of the groundwork of Nazi rearmament was laid under the ostensibly democratic Weimar republic, long before Hitler's rise to power.

German violations of the Versailles disarmament provisions began from the moment the treaty was signed. Under General Hans von Seekt, who assumed command of the Reichswehr in 1920, the violations were carefully coordinated by a central command. In Seekt's plan, the tiny allotment of 100,000 troops allowed Germany under the treaty was to serve as the core of a several-million-man army. Bogus military manuals were printed for circulation abroad, while the real manuals reflecting the premises of the new German strategy remained available only to those inside the Reichswehr.[54] Forbidden stocks of weapons and equipment were cached in secret arms depots throughout the country. Clandestine lists were kept of men who could resume active service in the event of hostilities, to flesh out the small standing army. Within the Reichswehr, a skeletal air corps was established, the secret embryo of the air force forbidden to Germany under Versailles. Hunting clubs and other ostensibly private paramilitary organizations provided military training for large numbers of German men. The civil police in Prussia and other German states remained essentially military in function, equipped with armored vehicles, light artillery, and machine guns.[55]

But by far the most flagrant violations of Versailles were those undertaken in secret collaboration with the Soviet Union. Beginning in 1920,

German military authorities concluded a series of secret pacts with the Soviets, offering military advice and war materiel in exchange for military production and training facilities inside Russia. Deep within the Soviet Union the Germans built factories for the production of aircraft and poison gas and established facilities for the training of German troops in poison gas, tank, and air tactics—all weapons forbidden Germany under Versailles.[56]

Within Germany itself, meanwhile, armaments factories owned by the Krupp firm, ostensibly converted under Allied order to civilian manufacturing, remained ready to be retooled for military production.[57] Elsewhere in Europe, companies clandestinely purchased by Krupp and the German government produced war materiel for German consumption. In Amsterdam, an engineering firm secretly financed by the German government kept submarine technology alive by designing and contracting new submarines for the friendly governments of Turkey and Spain.[58] Submarines were built by Krupp-owned holding companies in Barcelona, Bilbao, and Cadiz.[59]

In monitoring German compliance, the allies faced serious problems of what we now would term "verification." The members of the Inter-Allied Military Control Commission (IMCC), charged with overseeing compliance, were continually impeded in their work by uncooperative military and civilian authorities. During the general inspection of 1924, commission members actually came under attack by mobs.[60] For all that, the allies gained a clear enough grasp of the general pattern of German noncompliance. (French and Polish intelligence services even had some knowledge of the Soviet-German military collaboration, which anyway was suspected in some quarters after Germany and the Soviet Union concluded the Treaty of Rappallo in 1922.)[61] But just as the problems posed by the Washington treaty sprang not simply from the treaty terms but also from the U.S. attitude toward the agreement, so the problems verifying and enforcing the Versailles disarmament provisions proved in the end to be not so much technical as political. The problem lay not just in detecting violations but in deciding what to do about them once they were detected.

The British error in handling German disarmament under the Versailles Treaty paralleled the American error in managing disarmament treaties with Japan: Both Western democracies tended to equate an agreement on general principles and an accompanying apparent diminishment of international tensions with an advancement of the cause of peace. In the German case, the problem was complicated by the tactics of a brilliant

German foreign minister, Gustav Stresemann, who understood this point of view well enough to manipulate it to the German advantage.

Stresemann's career was itself emblematic of the pattern of illusion that pervaded the diplomacy of the interwar years. Hailed in his day as an advocate of "world peace" and a champion of "fulfillment" of the Versailles Treaty, Stresemann was revealed after the war by the German archives to be entirely nationalistic in his outlook, aiming with his diplomacy to undermine the treaty structure and lay the groundwork for revision of Germany's eastern borders. As foreign minister he was kept aware of the clandestine Russo-German military collaboration.[62] But to the world at large he showed an entirely different face.

Under the guise of a new "spirit" of European diplomacy, Stresemann perfected techniques that would later be used more boldly and obviously by Hitler. Before World War I, as we have seen, Tirpitz and the kaiser experimented with the "peace offensive" as a means of distracting attention from German plans against Britain. The Soviet Union under Lenin also began to employ disarmament rhetoric as a tool of strategic deception. Stresemann, however, was probably the first statesman to succeed on an important scale in the conscious use of the democracies' hunger for peace as a diplomatic weapon against them.

Stresemann's central achievement was the Treaty of Locarno, concluded in 1926. Locarno was universally regarded as the key to security in Europe during the interwar period, the completion of the unsatisfactory and disrupted work of the Paris Peace Conference. The "spirit of Locarno" was hailed in the mid-1920s as the prelude to an era of lasting peace.[63] The product of ostentatious "conference diplomacy" (what we would call "summit diplomacy" today) involving Stresemann, Aristide Briand of France, and Austen Chamberlain of Britain, Locarno resulted in a British guarantee of French and Belgian borders with Germany. The Rhineland guarantee was also subscribed to by the four other so-called Locarno powers—France, Germany, Italy, and Belgium. For their achievement, Briand and Stresemann shared the Nobel Peace Prize.

Stresemann's tactic was to exploit an essential ambivalence in postwar democratic thinking about strategy and foreign policy, an ambivalence rooted in the tension between the "old" diplomacy and the "new": Which was to be counted more important, a specific set of treaty provisions, or a general improvement in the tone and spirit of international relations? The old diplomacy, while by no means inattentive to such concerns and the tone and mood of international deliberations, would have been heedful of enforcement of treaty provisions, since the assumption was that a potential adversary offered an advantage would be inclined to exploit it. But the new vision of international order, and in particular the new thinking about the causes of wars, pointed toward a new function for diplomacy—what was occasionally spoken of even at this early date as "appeasement."[64] At the foundation of this new approach was the assumption that war was the product chiefly of international tensions, of rising mutual suspicions, resulting especially from alliance polarization and arms races. Under the influence of this assumption, democratic statesmen repeatedly showed a willingness to sacrifice this or that particular advantage to gain broad agreement on larger principles.

The genius of Stresemann was to understand and consciously exploit this feeling. The main technique he employed was to emphasize the "spirit" over the "letter" of international accords[65]—to lay stress on what Roosevelt, in a letter to Ramsay MacDonald on disarmament in 1934, called agreement on the "big principle,"[66] while deprecating treaty details, insofar as they applied to Germany. "I place far less value on the paragraphs of Locarno," he once declared, with not a little irony, "than on the political-psychological consequences of this collaboration."[67]

With the lapse of the Anglo-American guarantee in the early 1920s, German disarmament became the last concrete guarantee of the security of France under Versailles. Anticipating such a contingency, Clemenceau had fought to have inserted in the Versailles Treaty a provision allowing the Allies to prolong their occupation of the Rhineland in the event of German noncompliance with the disarmament provisions.

During 1924, the IMCC undertook a general inspection to determine whether Germany had complied with disarmament. The IMCC report, issued in late December, detailed serious German breaches of the disarmament clauses. No mention was made of the German-Soviet collaboration, which would become common knowledge only two years later. But among the violations cited were the reconstitution of the Reichswehr's general staff, the short-term recruitment and training of volunteers, and retention of military equipment in excess of treaty limits. The commission also cited the Reich's failure to reorganize police along civilian lines, to convert arms works to civilian production, and to regulate export and import of war materiel.[68] In January 1925, Germany was informed that Allied evacuation of the Rhineland would consequently be delayed.

When confronted with accusations of German noncompliance with Versailles, Stresemann did not so much attempt to deny as to disparage the particular charges. "Even if the reproaches levelled against us in the matter of disarmament were true," he told foreign correspondents in

Germany a few days after the IMCC report, "which has been denied by the declarations of the Reichswehrminister in the *Berliner Tageblatt,* what difference would 20 or even 100,000 rifles make in the fact that Germany is actually disarmed?"[69]

What Stresemann offered in the Locarno talks was a *generalized* guarantee of security in exchange for a loosening of the *specific* provisions of Versailles—in particular, the provisions covering disarmament—thus enabling Germany, in his own private description, to "undermine" (*ausholen*) the treaty even while appearing to "fulfill" it.[70]

Stresemann consciously understood the principle that we have already seen operating under the Washington treaty arrangements. He grasped the way in which the democracies would permit agreements themselves to substitute for concrete measures on behalf of their security, while the rhetoric of disarmament took on a life of its own. As he once wrote:

> The ordinary person thinks as follows: Through the Locarno Treaty, peace between France and Germany is secured. Why, then, are there still troops in the Rhineland? Through the Kellogg Pact, the nations have renounced war as a political instrument. Why, then, do the troops remain in the Rhineland? In the League of Nations all powers have equal rights. Why, then, is the territory of one of the members being occupied? When Germany joined the League, Briand said: Away with cannons and machine guns! But why do they remain in the Rhineland? The opponents of the Locarno policy point to these things as weaknesses in Stresemann's policy, and he himself admits that these objects are just and that he has nothing to say in return.[71]

Like the Washington treaty, the "spirit of Locarno" concealed an underlying opposition in interest. In both cases, for those powers wedded to the status quo, agreement on the big principle was desired as an end in itself—a welcome confirmation of the existing state of affairs. For those powers desiring an overthrow of the status quo, on the other hand, agreement on the big principle tended to serve as means to a different end: The appearance of amity led to a relaxation of vigilance on the part of the status quo powers, permitting continued behind-the-scenes efforts to undermine the existing order. (A French quip in circulation a year after the treaty was signed held that there were actually three things involved— "*le Locarno spirit, l'esprit de Locarno, et le Locarnogeist.*")[72]

The most obvious achievement of the Locarno process was the so-called Rhineland guarantee. For this guarantee, Britain and France paid a heavy price. Not only did Stresemann successfully refuse to offer any parallel guarantees concerning Germany's eastern frontiers (German moves against Czechoslovakia and Poland, of course, would later occasion world war), but he also obtained in return for the guarantee a removal of the IMCC inspectors from Germany.

Ironically, a final inspection by the IMCC ordered by the Allies in 1926 preparatory to Germany's admission to the League of Nations resulted in a 500-page report which concluded, as a British representative put it, that "Germany had never disarmed, had never had the intention of disarming, and for seven years had done everything in her power to deceive and 'counter-control' the Commission appointed to control her disarmament."[73] On December 3 and December 6, 1926, the *Manchester Guardian* carried detailed stories on the Soviet-German military collaboration.[74] However, the Locarno "spirit" was at its zenith; not only were the violations ignored, but the IMCC report was suppressed.[75] "Spirit," in short, triumphed over "letter." On December 13, the Allies issued a communiqué stating that of the more than one hundred disarmament questions unresolved, only two remained. To raise a furor over German disarmament violations would be to violate the "spirit" that Locarno had set in motion. The IMCC was withdrawn from Germany, as scheduled, on January 31, 1927. Henceforth, in verifying and enforcing disarmament, the Allies would be entirely at the mercy of German goodwill.

The Kellogg-Briand Pact

Of the triumvirate that negotiated the treaty, Austen Chamberlain, the British foreign secretary, was alone in falling sincerely under the spell of the Locarno "spirit." Briand, the French foreign minister, understood well enough the game that Stresemann was playing.[76] But the isolationist tone of British policy and the pacifistic mood of public opinion seemed to leave the French foreign minister no alternative but to play along. The tactic he chose was to curry public favor in Britain and the United States by excelling Stresemann in pacifistic pronouncements, an approach that earned him the popular title "prophet of peace." But as Stresemann well knew, in carrying Wilsonian rhetoric to an ever higher pitch, Briand was merely digging a deeper grave for the Versailles settlement, and in the long run for the security of France, which depended on it.

Yet in an era when nothing was so feverishly applauded as a peace petition or an initiative to disarm, the temptation was strong for democratic politicians to bask in the new rhetoric of peace, even at the expense of their nations' security. Despotic governments, meanwhile, were learning how to exploit for their own purposes the idealistic mood that engulfed the democracies. In 1928, the United States and France concluded the Kellogg-Briand Pact, to which sixty-two nations, including the aggressors in the subsequent world war, ultimately subscribed, solemnly foreswearing war "as an instrument of national policy." Ironically, this platitudinous treaty—taken seriously enough by United States to be invoked in its condemnation of the Japanese invasion of Manchuria as well as in the Nuremberg trials after the war—originated not in any sudden access of international goodwill but rather in a calculated maneuver by Briand to draw the United States into a kind of bilateral alliance with France. Playing on pacifist sentiment in the United States, he proposed a bilateral agreement to "outlaw war," which he hoped might serve as a prelude to a closer Franco-American collaboration. The pact in its final form was the product of a deft counterstroke by the State Department, designed to turn an unwelcome French bid for a closer bilateral relationship into a bland multilateral affirmation of peace. What began as an all-too-clever effort of the foreign minister of one nation to improve relations with another ended as a grand theatrical event involving all the nations of the world. For his role in helping to craft the treaty, Secretary of State Frank B. Kellogg, like Briand before him, was awarded the Nobel Peace Prize.[77] The public, meanwhile, was left to labor under the impression that aggressive war had been outlawed for all time—an impression that did much to reinforce the faith in disarmament during the subsequent ten years.

Churchill's Warning

The Locarno accords and the Kellogg-Briand Pact ushered in what proved to be an all-too-fleeting era of international amity. By 1929, many of the seeds of world catastrophe had been planted by the diplomatic and military policies of the democracies during the previous ten years. The navies of the Western powers had been allowed to decline to a dangerously weakened state. France had failed to cement any clear security arrangement with its reluctant and complacent former allies, Britain and the United States. The concessions with which the Allies had attempted to purchase German goodwill at Locarno seriously undermined the disarmament provisions, which is to say the last remnant of the security structure, embodied in Versailles. Yet as numerous and fundamental as the errors of democratic statesmen may have been during the 1920s, they had as yet provoked no disasters. Between 1929 and 1933, however, the condition of the world was transformed. Events that supervened in these five years fundamentally altered the configuration of forces in international politics. Three episodes were decisive: in 1929, the Great Crash on Wall Street; in 1931, the Japanese invasion of Manchuria, to which the League of Nations could offer only an impotent response; and in 1933, the accession of Adolf Hitler to the chancellorship of Germany.

To look abroad from the Western democracies in 1933 was, for anyone attuned to the laws and imperatives of strategy, to survey a darkened scene. The most powerful nation in Asia and the most potentially powerful nation in Europe had each fallen under the shadow of authoritarian rule; at home, the once-vital economies of commercial democracies labored under an apparently mortal affliction. But even now the fate of the democracies was by no means sealed. Until this moment, the faith in the Wilsonian experiment of the postwar era, in disarmament, in collective security, in the "new diplomacy," had found in events much apparent justification, however delusory its achievements may have been. No longer would this be so. But the test to come concerned how the leadership of the democracies would act upon this growing revelation—whether democratic statesmen would recognize and respond to the unmasking of the illusions that had guided their foreign policies since Versailles, or whether they would persist down the same course to ruin.

"I cannot recall any time," Winston Churchill told the House of Commons in 1932, "when the gap between the kind of words which statesmen used and what was actually happening in many countries was so great as it is now. The habit of saying smooth things and uttering pious platitudes and sentiments to gain applause, without relation to the underlying facts, is more pronounced now than it has ever been in my experience."[78] By now, as Churchill saw clearly, the Wilsonian drama of "conference diplomacy" was turning into a transparent charade. Disarmament negotiations, then in progress in Geneva, were doing nothing to advance the cause of peace; indeed, they were moving in a direction destined to undermine it. "I am afraid," he said, "that a large part of the object of every country is to throw the blame for an impending failure upon some other country while willing, if possible, to win the Nobel Peace Prize for itself."[79] Yet public opinion, and in particular the advocates of disarmament in Great Britain, appeared blind to the ironies and duplicities so obvious, from Churchill's perspective, in the disarmament process. He stated:

> I have sympathy with, and respect for, the well-meaning, loyal-hearted people who make up the League of Nations Union in this country, but what impresses me most about them is their long-suffering and inexhaustible gullibility. Any scheme of any kind of disarmament put forward by any country, so long as it is surrounded by suitable phraseology, is hailed by them, and the speeches are cheered, and those who speak gain the meed of their applause. Why do they not look down beneath the surface of European affairs to the iron realities which lie beneath?[80]

It was precisely Churchill's continuing attentiveness to strategy, to the "iron realities" of political conflict and war preparations, that would set him apart from the majority of his contemporaries in the subsequent decade.

In 1929, in a generally flattering review of the final volume of Churchill's history of the Great War for *The New Republic,* John Maynard Keynes, that bitter critic of the Versailles settlement, concluded with a disparaging reference to Churchill's "undoubting conviction that frontiers, races, patriotisms, even wars if need be are ultimate verities for mankind, which lends for him a kind of dignity and even nobility to events, which for others are only a nightmare interlude, something to be permanently avoided."[81] If Churchill proved consistently more percipient than many contemporaries concerning events in the 1930s, it was in no small part because he failed to share in the fashionable liberal vision of international affairs—the belief of Keynes and like-minded people that such "ultimate verities" of strategy and military power had been or could be in some sense rendered obsolete.[82]

No one was more eloquent than Churchill in defense of liberal *principles,* in supporting the cause of democracy, in calling attention to the illiberalism of totalitarian regimes in their actions both at home and abroad. But at the same time he enjoyed a kind of immunity to the operational assumptions of the new liberal-pacifist paradigm of international relations—the presumption, in particular, that because of the emergence of new weapons and new diplomatic arrangements, the preservation of peace and the survival of democracy could be guaranteed without serious resort to the traditional tools of statecraft: alliances and military power. It was his detailed alertness to such factors, deprecated by others—his military planner's grasp of the strategic balance and the strategic and political implications of military weakness—that accounted in large measure for the prophetic character of his vision.

In his comprehensive study of the phenomenon of interwar appeasement, Martin Gilbert has usefully distinguished between the "old appeasement" that prevailed during the Locarno period, when Britain sought from a position of strength to reintegrate Germany into the European system, and the "new appeasement" that took hold of British policy during the later 1930s, symbolized by Chamberlain's disastrous concessions to Hitler at Munich in 1938. The old appeasement, accorrding to Gilbert, "was a mood of hope, Victorian in its optimism, Burkean in its belief that societies evolved from bad to good and that progress could only be for the better." The new appeasement "was a mood of fear, Hobbesian in its insistence upon swallowing the bad in order to preserve some remnant of the good, pessimistic in its belief that Nazism was there to stay and, however, horrible it might be, should be accepted as a way of life with which Britain ought to deal."[83] The years from the Geneva Conference in 1932 to Hitler's occupation of the Rhineland in 1936 constituted a period of transition between the two moods. With regard to foreign policy, the dominant hope of the British people appeared to be for disarmament; but even at this time hope for a new international order was laced with a discernible undercurrent of fear.

The Peace Ballot

By the time the Disarmament Conference convened in Geneva in 1932, the conviction was nigh universal in Great Britain that World War I had resulted from an arms race and that disarmament was essential to prevent another major war. To the popular belief that arms races cause wars was added another anxiety—an exaggerated and growing fear of air power. As Harold Macmillan observed many years later, "We thought of air warfare" in the 1930s "rather as people think of nuclear warfare today." Expert opinion, recalled Macmillan, "had indicated that bombing of London and the great cities would lead to casualties on the order of hundreds of thousands or even millions within a few weeks."[84] In 1923, a British strategist predicted that in the wake of bombing "London for several days will be one vast raving Bedlam, the hospitals will be stormed, traffic will cease, the homeless will shriek for help."[85]

Against such horrors, the Air Ministry, influenced by the strategic theories of Air Marshall Sir Hugh Trenchard, maintained that defensive measures were futile. To defend against aircraft with ground-based anti-aircraft weapons was useless; fighter planes were no match for the bomber. Stanley Baldwin, the Conservative party leader and de facto head of the National Government, warned the House of Commons emotionally in 1932 that "the bomber will always get through."[86]

The effect of such predictions was to confirm the already widely held assumption that modern war would be intolerably destructive and unwinnable, and that disarmament was the only sane approach to securing national safety. In a much-publicized debate at the Oxford Union in February 1933, students endorsed by an overwhelming majority the motion "That this House will in no circumstances fight for its King and Country." Fear of air power played no small part in the outcome of this debate.[87]

Influenced by sentiments such as these, peace activists labored assiduously to bring pressure to bear on the British government not to respond to the German threat with an arms buildup of its own. In 1934, even as news was spreading of German rearmament, the League of Nations Union conducted its famous "Peace Ballot," a survey of 11 million Britons. Though the real significance of the vote was ambiguous—a majority of people also paradoxically endorsed "military sanctions" to enforce collective security under the League of Nations—the survey was almost universally read, owing in no small part to its name, as an indicator that public opinion would fail to sustain a major rearmament effort.[88]

The government's own statements encouraged disarmament sentiment. The prime minister of the National Government, Ramsay MacDonald, was, as we have seen, an old socialist, a convinced antimilitarist from prewar days. The foreign secretary, John Simon, was similarly an antimilitarist.[89] According to the Tory leader Stanley Baldwin, no pacifist but a canny reader of the public mood, war was "the most fearful terror and prostitution of man's knowledge that ever was known in the world"; the need to rearm was "a horrible thing to have to say . . . a terrible conclusion."[90]

Both wings of the government, therefore—the socialists out of idealism and the conservatives partly out of idealism and partly out of an imperative of political survival—energetically promoted disarmament.

Hitler and the Geneva Conference

In May 1933, in his famous *Friedensrede,* or "peace speech" to the Reichstag, the new German chancellor, Adolf Hitler, turned the rhetoric of disarmament to uses of his own. Directing his remarks to the Geneva Disarmament Conference then in progress, Hitler invoked all the favorite themes of the proponents of arms limitations. "It is . . . in the interests of all," he avowed, "that present-day problems should be solved in a reasonable and peaceful manner." Indeed, the "application of violence of any kind in Europe could have no favorable effect upon the political and economic position." On the contrary, war would be "unlimited madness" that would result in "the collapse of the present social and political order."[91]

A masterful mixture of blandishments and threats, menace and reassurance, Hitler's rhetoric of the early 1930s was calculated to appeal to those whose ruling passion had become fear of war and whose ruling ideal a new international order based on general disarmament. Germany's intentions were peaceful. The nation "wants nothing for herself which she is not prepared to give others." What Germany desired was simply "equality of rights." On the other hand, the failure to allow Germany equality of rights—which was to say equality of armaments—was itself a threat to peace, or if not to peace precisely, then to "the entire economic structure of the world."

All this could not have been better designed to appeal to the widely held belief that the source of aggression lay in nations' feelings of insecurity and that the relief of insecurity would thereby lead to peace. "Militarism rests on fear," Ramsay MacDonald had written during World War I, "and fear exists because the peoples do not come close enough together."[92] It was in this spirit that MacDonald, addressing the Geneva Conference two months before, proposed a radical plan whereby all European armies would be halved and German armed forces brought up to equality with France. To sense MacDonald's blindness to the strategic realities before him, we need only to juxtapose Churchill's comment on the MacDonald plan in the House of Commons:

> When we read about Germany, when we watch with surprise and distress the tumultuous insurgence of ferocity and war spirit, the pitiless ill-treatment of minorities, the denial of the normal protections of civilized society to large numbers of individuals solely on the ground of race—when we see that occurring in one of the most gifted, learned, scientific and formidable

nations of the world, one cannot help feeling glad that the fierce passions that are raging in Germany have not found, as yet, any other outlet but on Germans.

It was wrong, argued Churchill, to ask France to halve its army and air force while Germany was permitted to double its own.[93]

That Hitler's approach to the disarmament question was patently disingenuous did not deter the advocates of disarmament from exonerating Germany from responsibility for the breakdown in negotiations that it had conspired to destroy. Disarmament advocates generally blamed the Western democracies, Britain and especially France, for the failure of the disarmament process. The unwillingness of the democracies to make sufficient concessions explained German recalcitrance. And in the meantime, the gulf between the British and French widened.

Not only did the failure of the Disarmament Conference provide Hitler with the pretext he needed to justify German rearmament (since French, not German, "militarism" could now be blamed for the resurgence of German military power), but the continuing desire for arms limitations worked to delay the Allied response to the German rearmament during the crucial months of 1934 and 1935.

It is worth remembering that at this point Hitler's military occupation of the Rhineland was less than two years away. From the Rhineland to the Munich Conference it was just another two years, and from Munich to world war in September 1939, a mere twelve months. For some time, historians argued that a show of resolve on the part of the democracies at the time of the Rhineland occupation would have prompted Hitler to retreat. Now, however, the consensus among historians is that an effort to stop Hitler in 1936 could very well have meant war—a limited war, perhaps, a war in which the Western powers would have far more advantages than in September 1939—but war nonetheless.[94] Failure to confront Hitler militarily in 1936 was merely to postpone the inevitable.

Nonetheless, apart from Churchill and his few allies in the Commons and the Foreign Office, and a few pockets of opposition here and there in government, a sense of urgency was nowhere be found. In Britain, the overwhelming concern was still with achieving arms control.

The Turning Point

Even as Britain continued to press France strenuously for concessions in the disarmament discussions with Germany in the early months of 1934, the German government quietly initiated a vast air buildup. The "Rhineland Program," laid down by Hitler and his air minister, Hermann Göring, in January 1934, marked the beginnings of Hitler's Luftwaffe. The plan envisioned the production of 3,715 new military aircraft—an enormous quantity considering that until then secret production had been limited to 30 aircraft per month—by the end of 1935. In July, with the program already underway, the goal was revised upward to 4,021.[95]

Yet for several months after German rearmament had begun on a major scale, the British and French governments deliberately held back on military expansion in deference to the British hope that the disarmament talks might still be salvaged. The British air estimates, released in late February, provided for a budget actually £1 million lower than the 1931 spending level—part of a pattern of unilateral restraint deliberately designed to placate Germany and keep the spirit of arms limitation alive.[96] (The French defense budget, reduced as a gesture of goodwill to Germany in 1932–34, would not increase again until 1936.)[97] As late as April 1934, even as the British air minister, Lord Londonderry, pressed the cabinet to expand the air force, MacDonald resisted: "the Government could not announce a new programme when the question [of disarmament] was still open."[98]

Yet already intelligence estimates were signaling a marked growth in German power. Two days after the 1934 air estimates were published, Sir Robert Vansittart, permanent undersecretary at the Foreign Office, warned of an expansion in the German air force, arguing that Germany "will not be inferior to us in the air for any appreciable time."[99] Responding to such reports, the government announced on March 4 that in the event the arms talks failed, there would be a slight increase—four squadrons—in the Royal Air Force. Even this modest program aroused a storm of indignation in the House of Commons. Clement Attlee, the Labour leader, argued that the increase was unnecessary and would not advance the cause of peace. Another Labour spokesman claimed that "the Government had its hands forced by the wild men like Mr Churchill."[100] Sir Archibald Sinclair of the Liberal party deplored "the folly, danger and wastefulness of this steady accumulation of armaments."[101]

On this occasion, Churchill argued to the House that Britain had "reached a turning point in our affairs." Germany, he said "is arming fast

... and no one is going to stop her."[102] Baldwin responded with a pledge to ensure air parity with other powers, still contingent, however, upon the failure of the disarmament negotiations.[103]

Yet even after the final disarmament talks between France and Germany broke off in April, the British government was slow to act. Responding in July to the charge of a Labour member that he was acting out of "blind and causeless panic," Churchill characterized Britain's situation as "in many ways more dangerous" than 1914.[104]

The "Air Panic"

One might suppose that the collapse of the Geneva conference would have led to a reevaluation of the disarmament process. But this was far from being the case. In 1934 and 1935, majorities in all parties continued to pin their hopes on an arms limitation agreement with Germany, which explains why the sense of urgency expressed by Churchill in 1934 concerning German rearmament aroused only the most limited sympathy. The problem of perception was compounded by the fact that Churchill's earliest warnings of German expansion appeared to be false alarms. Ironically, British attention was focused on the German threat by an "air panic" in 1934–35 that, like the "naval scare" of 1909, proved to be based on incorrect estimates of current German strength. However, Churchill and his allies in the foreign office were right about the general trend: Even as early as 1934, German defense spending had doubled as a percentage of gross national product,[105] and the floor space of the German aircraft industry had vastly expanded.[106]

It should be made clear, however, that Hitler at this time was by no means preparing explicitly for a war with Britain. German ambitions since Versailles had been focused primarily on the east. It was in Czechoslovakia, Poland, and ultimately Russia where, as *Mein Kampf* suggested, Hitler hoped to find *Lebensraum* for Germany's bulging population. Whether Hitler's ambitions would mean war with Britain would depend largely on the British response to his program of Continental expansion. In *Mein Kampf* Hitler had, curiously enough, imagined Britain as a potential ally.[107] Certainly, in this early phase of his campaign—rearmament, recovery of the Saar—he hoped to enlist British support. But one must distinguish between the military and the political functions of the German air force. As a military weapon, the Luftwaffe was designed, at least after 1936,[108] chiefly for close air support of German ground troops. But from 1933 to 1937, Hitler employed his air force primarily as a political weapon against the Western powers, especially the British. To this end, he both exaggerated the strength of the Luftwaffe and portrayed it as a strategic bombing force.

In later years, Stalin was to describe the atomic bomb as a weapon with which to frighten people with weak nerves. Such was the main use to which Hitler put German air power in the mid-1930s. From the unmasking of the German Luftwaffe in 1935 to the Munich Conference in 1938, the Führer continually played upon the fear of air attack to squeeze concessions out of anxious French and British statesmen. In 1935, Hitler manipulated the British fear of air power, and the government's ardent desire for arms agreement,[109] to secure the Anglo-German Naval Treaty, an agreement that ostensibly gave the British an enormous naval advantage over Germany, but that had the effect of legally sanctioning German rearmament.[110] Hitler described the day of the treaty's signature as the "happiest" of his "life."[111]

Churchill was among the few politically influential people in Britain to grasp the political consequences of the British feeling of vulnerability to German air attack. In 1933, he inveighed against the "helplessness and hopelessness . . . spread about"[112] by Baldwin's famous remark about "the bomber" getting through, arguing both that air attack was more likely to be aimed at military targets than at civilian centers and that it could be deterred. "You are not going to get an international agreement," he warned, "which will obviate the necessity of having your own defenses or which will remove the appalling dangers which have been so freely stated,"[113] he said.

Moreover, in 1935, breaking with the prevailing strategic consensus, he urged a crash research program on ground and air *defenses* against air attack. Churchill questioned the view that there was "no defense" against the bomber. "We were told that it was impossible to grapple with submarines, but methods were found which enabled us to strangle the submarine below the water, a problem not necessarily harder than that of clawing down marauding aeroplanes," he said. ". . . I agree that there is nothing which can offer any substitute for an equal or superior force, a readiness to retaliate, but if you could discover some new method the whole of our affairs would be greatly simplified."[114] He even proposed that research could be done on an international basis, with a monetary prize offered by the League of Nations.[115]

Baldwin's decision in 1934 to establish an air defense committee was the result of Churchill's prodding.[116] The work of this committee quickly bore fruit with the invention of radar, which was critical to England's survival of the Battle of Britain six years later.

Chamberlain and the Revisionists

Recent historiography has increasingly stressed the limitations confronting policymakers, especially British policymakers, in the decade leading up to world war. The economic strictures enforced by depression, the intransigence of public opinion, and, most important, the growing discrepancy between British security commitments and British economic and military power all conspired, it is increasingly emphasized, to narrow the options available to decision makers in their efforts to cope with the growing totalitarian threat.[117] The value of this newer historical approach has been to remove some of the element of caricature from our image of "appeasement." Its weakness has been the tendency, among some historians, to obscure the distinction between those who showed good judgment of the political realities of the time and those who simply failed to do so.[118]

Bad political judgment operated to make Britain's options appear considerably more restricted than in reality they were. This was particularly true with regard to assessments of the economic impact of an arms buildup. After 1934, as the German air threat became clear, economic concerns began to replace disarmament sentiment as the major barrier to rearmament. To be sure, circumstances were dire. British unemployment had peaked in 1932 at 3 million. However, Chamberlain, having come to the premiership from the exchequer, viewed everything through an economic prism. While accepting in principle the need to rearm, he fought any measures that would significantly increase the national budget.[119] The modest air rearmament moves undertaken in 1934 were paid for through cuts in the army and navy.[120]

In his opposition to defense increases, Chamberlain was simply following the orthodox economic theory of the day, which put absolute emphasis on the need for balanced budgets and the dangers of deficit spending. To this was added the theory that Britain's economic strength would operate as a deterrent to war. Economic stability, noted Sir Thomas Inskip, minister for supply, as late as 1937, is "the fourth arm of defense." "Nothing," he noted, "operates more strongly to deter a political aggressor from attacking this country than our [economic] stability."[121] In 1934,

Chamberlain killed a Baldwin proposal to float a loan to cover defense expenditures. "If I were to follow Winston [Churchill]'s advice and sacrifice our commerce to the manufacture of arms," Chamberlain wrote to his sister early in 1936, "we should inflict a certain injury on our trade from which it would take generations to recover."[122]

Ironically, Chamberlain ended up rigidly subordinating defense and foreign policy to an economic theory that proved to be questionable in the long run. The economic effect of rearmament was not to impede but rather to enhance recovery in Britain, particularly after 1937.[123] Germany's more rapid recovery can be explained in part by deficit spending for rearmament.[124] ("There is no ceiling on the credit for the financing of rearmament," said Hitler's air minister, Hermann Göring, in 1935.)[125] The stimulative effect of deficit spending had been spelled out clearly enough in Keynes's *General Theory of Employment, Interest and Money,* published in 1936. In 1937, Keynes even wrote a memorandum for the treasury explaining why additional borrowing to finance rearmament would not damage the economy, advice rejected by the government out of hand.[126]

Yet the real error of Chamberlain was not so much to adhere to the wrong set of economic principles as to place economic theory ahead of broader political considerations. The dangers of damage to British trade, bad as they might have been, were hardly greater than the dangers of war or of air attack. Yet in the peacetime environment of a commercial democracy, economic dangers had a kind of immediacy that strategic dangers lacked. Beyond that, faith in the deterrent value of military strength had been undermined by the belief in disarmament and the conventional notion that World War I had come about because of miscalculation owing to the arms race. In Chamberlain's attitudes toward economics, one can see the imprint of the new vision of war and peace.

Chamberlain's misjudgments concerning economics are understandable enough; his misjudgments concerning Hitler are less so. There was no shortage of evidence at the time either of the nature of the Nazi regime or of Hitler's intentions. The persecution of the Jews was no secret; the purport of Nazi ideology was widely known; that Hitler consolidated his power in Germany by the murder of party rivals on the Night of the Long Knives was common knowledge. And yet even so shrewd a politician as Lloyd George would return from Germany singing the praises of this "man of supreme quality."[127] Sir John Simon, the British foreign secretary, described the Führer after meeting him as "rather retiring and bashful and of a certain mystic temperament."[128] In addition, much of the press adopted a pro-German slant, even to the extent of exercising self-censorship. Geoffrey Dawson, editor of the *Times,* wrote to Lord Lothian of the Germans in 1937: "I spend my nights taking out anything which I think will hurt their susceptibilities, and in dropping in little things which are intended to soothe them."[129] Anticommunism played a role in this. Hitler took every opportunity to remind Europe that he was a bulwark against Soviet Russia. (But one of Britain's leading anti-Bolshevists, Churchill, understood nonetheless that Hitler represented something equally as bad.)

There was also a desire to play down ideology. Anthony Adamthwaite describes well the outlook of the age:

> The very bitterness of the war of creeds supplied a rationale for appeasement. British and French leaders tried to bridge the divisions between the democracies and the fascist dictatorships. The means adopted was a so-called realistic, pragmatic diplomacy. "It was necessary to get rid of ideological prejudices and, in the world as it exists today, employ the type of diplomacy which seeks to have as useful relations as possible with every country," declared the French foreign minister, Georges Bonnet, in 1938. Taking sides, it was said, would only divide Europe into armed camps and re-create the international anarchy of 1914. Western statesmen also had their eye on the home front. Avoiding an overt ideological bias was a means of maintaining internal peace.[130]

As G. M. Trevelyan wrote in a letter to the *Times* in August 1937, "Dictatorship and democracy must live side by side in peace, or civilization is doomed."[131]

"If only we could sit down at the table with the Germans," said Chamberlain, "and run through all their complaints and claims with a pencil, this would greatly relieve all tension."[132] Hitler, he thought, was "a man who could be relied upon when he had given his word."[133]

Yet not far beneath the surface of all these feelings was fear. On his return from Munich, Chamberlain would tell his cabinet that he had flown up the river over London. "He had imagined a German bomber flying the same course, he had asked himself what degree of protection they could afford for the thousands of homes which he had seen stretched out below him and he had felt that we were in no position to justify waging a war today."[134]

Hitler, of course, understood this fear of war, and kept alive to the end the hope that conciliation of his desires would lead to a lasting Anglo-German détente. Each threatening action was accompanied by new gestures of reassurance. Even his occupation of the Rhineland came hand in hand with new peace proposals.

Too much has been written of the Munich Conference of September 1938 to necessitate a detailed review of that event here. Suffice it to say that Chamberlain and French prime minister Edouard Daladier's acceptance of the dismemberment of Czechoslovakia proved to be not merely a moral and political error, but also a strategic one. By now a European war was inevitable unless Britain was willing to accept consolidation of a new German empire in Eastern Europe. Hitler had begun naval preparations in 1937 for the coming confrontation with Britain.[135] Owing to the Munich agreement, the Czech army would be lost to the West. At the time of Munich, two thirds of the German army was mobilized against Czechoslovakia. Hitler could bring only ten remaining divisions to bear on France. With the disappearance of Czechoslovakia from the map of Europe, France's fate was sealed. In early September, before the Munich Conference, Churchill confided to a friend: "Owing to the neglect of our defences, and the mishandling of the German problem in the last five years, we seem to be very near the bleak choice between War and Shame. My feeling is that we shall choose Shame, and then have War thrown in a little later on even more adverse terms than the present."[136] Yet Chamberlain, returning from Hitler and Munich with his piece of paper and his promise of "peace for our time," was greeted by jubilant crowds.

Hitler by no means sought protracted, total war. German military plans make it clear that Hitler counted on a succession of quick victories in limited wars to expand Germany's eastern frontiers. Britain was expected to stand aside as Germany gobbled up the Continent. World war came about as a result of Hitler's miscalculation—a miscalculation not unlike that which produced catastrophe in 1914. In both cases, Germany underestimated the strength and, equally important, the will of its potential opponents. In September 1939, Hitler was convinced that Britain and France would repeat with respect to Poland the surrender of Czechoslovakia that had taken place at the Munich Conference a year earlier.

The search for arms limitations and détente on the part of the Western democracies thus played a central role, if not the decisive one, in the precipitation of World War II. Not only did the craving for arms treaties blind democratic leaders to the true nature of the threat that confronted them, but it persuaded the dictators that the democracies lacked the will or the power to resist. The search for disarmament made the democracies appear weaker, both to their own leaders and to their enemies, than they actually were. The illusions concerning strategy and politics forged in the aftermath of the first Great War persisted, in short, to the very eve of the second, and beyond.

⊡

CHAPTER 3

Cold War, Atomic Peace

That Wilsonianism—and disarmament and arms limitation efforts—played an important role in setting the stage for World War II has long been acknowledged by Western commentators and historians (even if it has been forgotten by much of the public). Less widely appreciated even in historical writing of the twentieth century has been the crucial role played by the Wilsonian vision in the genesis of the Cold War. Yet just as liberal-pacifist assumptions blinded Western leaders in the 1930s to the growing threat posed by Nazi Germany, so the Wilsonian perspective continued to blind American officials during World War II to the dangers posed by the emergent power of the Soviet Union.

Curiously enough, Munich—and the disasters that followed from it—did not in any sense settle the Western debate on war and peace. On the contrary, World War II would bring a reenactment, behind the scenes, of essentially the same foreign policy debate that had occupied the British Parliament in the years leading up to 1939. Once again, in the diplomatic councils of the Grand Alliance, Winston Churchill (now the British prime minister) would seek to persuade fellow Western politicians to regard a potential enemy—in this case the Soviet Union—with wariness, and to remain attentive to the details of the military balance of power. Once again, Western leaders would largely ignore him, opting instead for a policy of appeasement anchored in Wilsonian hopes.

By no means could all Soviet gains in the aftermath of World War II be blamed on wartime Western policies: Given Western military weakness at the outset of the war, some significant growth of Soviet power and territory was inevitable. But between 1941 and 1945, under the influence of Wilsonian ideals, the United States made a series of specific policy choices whose effect, perversely, was to strengthen the Soviet position vis-à-vis the West and cede ever greater expanses of European and Asian territory to Soviet control.

At the center of this unfolding tragedy was the enigmatic and mercurial figure of Franklin Roosevelt. A brilliant domestic politician and a powerfully inspiring leader amid both depression and war, Roosevelt nonetheless, like Wilson before him, miscalculated on an almost stupendous scale in attempting to shape a postwar peace. In this miscalculation, Wilsonian hopes and assumptions played a pivotal role. Believing he could see the future more clearly than his British contemporary, and locked within the Wilsonian framework, Roosevelt continually failed to heed the advice of Churchill concerning their third partner in the Grand Alliance, Joseph Stalin.

From early in the Anglo-American defense partnership, Churchill, using all the wiles and persuasive powers at his disposal, sought to persuade his American cousin[1] to share his own suspicions of Stalin, so that when the war ended the two English-speaking democracies might stand together as a united front against potential Soviet aggression or encroachments. From the start, however, Roosevelt rejected Churchill's traditional, balance-of-power approach to foreign affairs. Regarding the British prime minister's views of the Soviet Union (and indeed of international politics generally) as reactionary and anachronistic, cleaving to the hope that Wilson's vision of a united world could be brought to fruition by his own hand, and led by his advisors to believe he could persuade Stalin to share his vision, President Roosevelt made extraordinary efforts to win the trust and goodwill of the Soviet dictator. He did so often not only at the expense of Anglo-American friendship but also at the expense of the sovereignty of many smaller states. Through a series of specific and ill-advised decisions—major territorial and political concessions to Stalin at the Teheran Conference, rejection of Churchill's principle of interposing Western military power in the way of Stalin's inevitable westward advance, refusal to press Stalin on behalf of Poland's government-in-exile in London, refusal to aid the Warsaw uprising in the face of Stalin's objections, failure at Yalta to back British demands for machinery to protect democratic forces in Poland, and, finally, the refusal to permit American armies to march eastward as Soviet armies approached from the west, thereby allowing the Red Army to take Vienna, Prague, and

Berlin—the United States opened the way for a major expansion of Soviet power on the European Continent.[2]

By the time America began to awaken from its Wilsonian reverie—in early 1946, several months after Roosevelt's death—the menacing shadow of Soviet power lay across Central Europe. Millions of unfortunate people who had hoped for liberation from the Nazis now found themselves at the mercy of a new and no less brutal tyranny. For months after the war, as the West stood helplessly by, Soviet power over Central Europe would be consolidated by ruthless methods hardly different from those Hitler had employed to subjugate his Eastern European annexations in the early stages of World War II.

By now, of course, the United States was essentially powerless to reverse Soviet conquests—short of starting another major war. However, three factors would create a climate conducive to a fundamental reevaluation of American foreign policy—first, the pitiless spectacle of Central Europe under Soviet domination; second, bitter American disappointment at Soviet intransigence in face-to-face negotiations and repeated Soviet violations of existing agreements and understandings; and finally—in a sense, the underlying but probably necessary condition of the change—the massive shift in the balance of power occasioned by the appearance of the atomic bomb.

While on the one hand, the arrival of the atomic bomb would temporarily breathe new life into Wilsonianism, reviving hopes for an "end" to "power politics," on the other hand, the bomb would alter the power relations between the Soviet Union and the West in such a way as to permit American officials, when they chose, to assume a far firmer posture toward the Soviet Union than they had in the past. Freed of dependence on the Soviet Union, and assured of its own safety by a monopoly on atomic weapons, the United States would slowly begin to assume its role as the new guarantor of the balance of power, extending the aid and guarantees and drawing the lines that would eventually evolve into the structure of "containment." From the summer of 1945 onward, the fate of freedom would be closely tied, for better or worse, to the fate of the atomic bomb.

Emergence of the Soviet Union

If the greatest penalty for the democracies' descent into military weakness after World War I was to be war with Germany and Japan, then the second greatest penalty was to be military dependence on the Soviet Union. By the late 1930s, as London and Washington gazed with growing anxiety on developments in Berlin, the Soviet Union already loomed in the background as a nation of significant political weight and formidable military power. In a sense, the great, unnoticed development of international politics during the 1930s had been the massive growth of Soviet economic and especially military strength.

Following the Bolshevik takeover of 1917, Russia had essentially disappeared from the ranks of the great powers, its economy shattered, its military eventually reduced to a negligible force. Between 1914 and 1921, the national income of the country suffered a catastrophic drop—declining, according to one estimate, by over 40 percent.[3]

However, beginning with Lenin's New Economic Policy and the Treaty of Rapallo with Germany in the early 1920s, the Bolsheviks embarked on a concerted program to revive the Soviet economy, and began what proved to be a remarkably successful effort to recruit foreign technology and capital—including eventually substantial American technology and capital—to aid development of both the civilian and military sectors.[4] The goal was straightforward—part of Lenin's strategy of "socialism in one country"—to rebuild the country's industrial and military infrastructure while awaiting the moment when, as the Bolsheviks believed, the "correlation of forces" would be more favorable to Communist forces and the world riper for revolutionary change.

Throughout this effort, military production was consistently given highest priority. Even as certain regions of the country labored under famine and Soviet citizens suffered countless privations and shortages of food and consumer goods, contemporary accounts indicate that prime resources were poured into the Red Army, which the Soviets sought to develop as a force superior to its capitalist counterparts.[5]

Figures on defense spending reflected this priority. Estimates later made by Quincy Wright indicate that even by 1929, the Soviet Union was already devoting a significantly larger portion of national income to military spending than any other great power. In that year, the Soviet military budget nearly equaled that of Great Britain (whose national income was 25 percent larger) and significantly exceeded those of France and Imperial Japan. Remarkably enough, by 1937, the largest military budget in the world was to be found not in Hitler's Germany but in Stalin's Soviet Union, which was outspending the Germans in the military area by over 25 percent.[6]

One consequence of this spending was a steady accumulation of military equipment. In 1939, after five years of concerted rearmament, Germany could boast an armored force of just over 3,000 tanks—slightly smaller than that of neighboring France. In 1940, the British expeditionary force in France possessed a mere 400. The Soviet Union, meanwhile, had amassed a force, by one estimate, of over 9,000 tanks.[7] In aircraft the pattern was similar. Germany possessed roughly 1,400 and France roughly 1,300 frontline aircraft at the beginning of the war, while the Soviet Union had amassed 12,000 military aircraft, of which roughly half were frontline.[8] (The world's first all-metal airplane had been constructed in the Soviet Union in the 1920s, at a factory at Fili illegally operated by the German firm Junkers in contravention of the Versailles Treaty.)[9]

Of course, the value of this impressive accumulation of materiel would be fatally undermined by Stalin's strategic errors—first, his failure, despite intelligence warning, to anticipate Hitler's surprise attack in 1941; and second, and perhaps more important, his purge of the Soviet officer corps in late 1930s. In a fit of paranoia, Stalin had more than half the Red Army's senior officers put to death—a circumstance that left Soviet troops bereft of effective commanders when the Germans finally attacked.[10] But in 1938, the consequences of these problems were still in the future.

The impressive growth of Soviet military power helps to explain why Churchill, despite an unwavering anticommunism, welcomed the Soviet Union's call in the crisis-ridden spring of 1939 for a three-power alliance linking France, Britain, and the Soviet Union (Chamberlain rejected the idea).[11]

Such facts also help to explain why the Nazi-Soviet pact several weeks later constituted a major disaster for the West. When the German foreign minister, Joachim von Ribbentrop, traveled to Moscow to conclude the "nonaggression" pact between Germany and the Soviet Union on August 23, an enormous shift occurred in the balance of power. There is little question but that the Molotov-Ribbentrop pact created the final condition necessary for world war. Hitler's armies marched on Poland just one week later.

Captive Nations

Not only did the Nazi-Soviet pact make possible Hitler's aggression, but it also opened the way to a significant westward expansion of the Soviet empire. A secret protocol of the German-Soviet treaty ceded to the Soviet Union a sphere of interest including Latvia, Estonia, Lithuania, Finland, Bessarabia in eastern Romania, and the eastern section of Poland.[12] These were by and large the very states toward which Lenin and his successors had pursued their policy of "peaceful coexistence" during the 1920s and 1930s. The sudden shift in the "correlation of forces" brought an end to both peace and "coexistence" for these unfortunate nations.

In the summer of 1940, Red Army tanks rolled into the Baltic capitals. Almost immediately, thousands of Balts were rounded up and deported en masse to labor camps in the Soviet Union. Countless more died at the hands of Soviet secret police interrogators in their native capitals.[13] In the first year of Soviet occupation, over 32,000 Latvians disappeared— roughly 2 percent of that small country's population.[14]

In Poland, the story was much the same. Between the years 1939 and 1941, whole families of Poles—a total of approximately 1.5 million people—were deported to the Soviet Union, shipped in open cattle cars to the slave camps of the Gulag. Children froze to death, and prisoners, deprived of food and water, resorted to drinking their own urine. At the execution camp of the NKVD (predecessor to the KGB) in the Katyn Forest near Smolensk, in a six-week period between early April and mid-May 1940, over 4,000 Polish officers were trucked in to be shot in the head and dumped twelve bodies deep in a mass grave.[15] When the job was done, the Soviet secret police planted young conifers in the covering dirt to disguise the graves.[16]

Splitting the Atom

If, as it seems reasonable to assume, humanity was doomed from the very inception of modern science eventually to stumble on the secret of the atomic weapon, then the critical question was whether, when the bomb finally appeared, it fell into the hands of a comparatively benign or a comparatively malignant political authority. From this perspective, the situation in the late 1930s was hardly auspicious. It was German scientists, working at the Kaiser Wilhelm Institute in Berlin, who first split the atom, less than a year before the outbreak of World War II.

Indeed, once nuclear fission was discovered in Germany in 1938, it would only be a matter of time before some nation built an atomic bomb—assuming, as then appeared at least possible, that such a device could be made. The fear among the tiny international community of physicists who grasped this fact, understandably enough, was that the nation in question would be Nazi Germany. Imagining the consequences if Hitler had obtained an atomic bomb was not difficult, since a number of the physicists, including Albert Einstein himself, had fled Nazi persecution. The apprehensions of emigré scientists in the United States were compounded when, after invading Czechoslovakia, Hitler cut off uranium sales from that country.[17]

In the summer of 1939, a group of emigré Hungarian physicists led by Leo Szilard convinced the renowned discoverer of relativity to intervene personally. Originally, Einstein's plan was to write to Queen Elizabeth of Belgium, with whom he was acquainted (Belgium controlled a major share of the world's uranium in the Congo). Eventually, however, following the advice of New York businessman Alexander Sachs, Einstein sent his famous letter to President Roosevelt informing the president of the possibility of building an atomic bomb.[18]

It is one of the ironies of the nuclear age that the initial impetus for the American atomic bomb project came not from U.S. military or political officials, who in fact were slow to grasp the urgency of the situation, but rather from foreign-born scientists with distinctly pacifistic views. For Einstein, in particular, it was a curious position in which to find himself, after having so long publicly campaigned against the use of technology for military purposes.[19] Yet not to act was to leave entirely to fate the question of whether the Nazi regime gained a weapon that, in the conditions of the early 1940s, would make world conquest by that nightmare regime considerably more than a farfetched dream. "Here is the last refuge of freedom," Einstein told the American physicist Arthur Compton in 1937 after fleeing Germany and gaining U.S. citizenship. "It is only the United States that can save the world."[20]

Yet, to the dismay of the scientists, the American authorities procrastinated. Only when the British, combining their own research findings with intelligence reports on German nuclear research, urged the Americans forward did Washington finally make the commitment necessary to begin the project.[21]

The bomb, if it was possible, was still five years away. In the meantime, the situation of the West was rapidly deteriorating. In May 1940, Hitler's armies attacked Belgium, Luxembourg, and the Netherlands. By the end of May, the British expeditionary force was being hastily evacuated from Dunkirk. In June, France fell. With the fall of France, Britain was to come under increasing bombardment from German aircraft. Churchill appealed to the United States for military aid. Roosevelt, to his credit, maneuvered behind the scenes—brooking fierce opposition from such supposed foreign policy realists as Republican Senator Arthur H. Vandenberg—to aid Britain.[22]

Still, with public opinion simultaneously running against Hitler and against U.S. involvement in the war, Roosevelt felt he could not draw the nation into the conflict. "I have been so struck by the way you have led public opinion by allowing it to get ahead of you," King George VI commented, in a remark that may have concealed some irony.[23] Meanwhile, as Churchill was to put it in the epigraph to *Their Finest Hour,* the British people "held the fort . . . till those who hitherto had been half blind were half ready."[24]

All this explains why Hitler's invasion of the Soviet Union in June 1941 was to prove so important for the West.

Churchill and Roosevelt

"If Hitler invaded Hell," said Churchill, "I would make at least a favourable reference to the Devil in the House of Commons."[25] John Lewis Gaddis cites a similar remark of Roosevelt's to describe the latter's view of Stalin. "My children," Gaddis quotes the American president as writing to Churchill in 1942 (in a paraphrase of a Balkan proverb), "it is permitted you in time of grave danger to walk with the devil until you have crossed the bridge." However, Gaddis takes this quotation out of context—with quite misleading results. Roosevelt was referring here not to Stalin, but to Admiral Darlan, the vice premier of Vichy France.[26] In fact, Roosevelt was quite suspicious of the French.[27] The Soviets were another matter. Indeed, one searches Roosevelt's correspondence in vain for an expression of suspicion toward the Soviet Union equaling that which the American president routinely expressed for the French. Churchill knew that in doing business with Stalin, he was dealing was the "devil"; there is little evidence that Roosevelt felt any of the same suspicion toward his Soviet comrade-at-arms.

One key to understanding the origins of the Cold War is to recognize the profound differences between Churchill and Roosevelt on the subject of Stalin and the Soviet Union—differences that recent American historians such as Gaddis have acknowledged but downplayed. From the outset, Churchill, while hopeful that long-term relations between the Soviet Union and the West might be improved as a result of the war, understood the essential nature of the Soviet regime and of Stalin. Roosevelt, whatever his other virtues and abilities, never did. To return to Gaddis's metaphor, Churchill was willing to walk with the devil. Roosevelt planned not merely to walk with him, but to earn his intimate trust and to form with him permanent, friendly relations.

How do we explain the two leaders' vastly different assessments of the Soviet reality? Differences in temperament and experience no doubt played a role. But at bottom the profoundly contrasting views of Churchill and Roosevelt reflected the fundamentally different paradigms or frameworks within which they approached foreign affairs—rooted, in turn, in their larger visions of politics.

Churchill's framework was that of traditional power politics. He believed in military power and in alliances. He saw peace as the product not primarily of good feelings among nations but of the balance of power. The world contained a number of relatively peaceful, democratic states along with a number of more authoritarian states that were potential aggressors. Peace required that a preponderance of military power remain in the hands of peaceful nations.

In the relations among great nations, Churchill knew, relative military strength and control of territory always counted, and counted greatly. Churchill was also sensitive to the differences between political regimes— the way in which totalitarianism, whether as manifested under Hitler or under Stalin, stood in natural enmity with democracy. He was not particularly moralistic about the conflict between totalitarianism and democracy; still, he understood how ideology shaped interests.

American policy, meanwhile, was shaped by a combination of Wilsonianism and New Deal "progressivism." Throughout the war, the rhetoric of American diplomacy remained remarkably Wilsonian in tenor. As late as February 1945, Roosevelt was promising that the accords coming out of Yalta would "spell the end of the system of unilateral action, the exclusive alliances, the spheres of influence, the balances of power, and all the other expedients that have been tried for centuries—and have always failed."[28] This was Wilson's language of 1919.

What about Stalin? While Churchill's Britain, in Roosevelt's mind, represented the old order,[29] Stalin's Soviet Union, through its "socialist" ideals, was connected to the new. Wilsonian hopes for a changed world were thus reinforced by the fashionable New Deal view that the Soviet Union, for all its imagined faults and failings, constituted a "progressive" society with elements of real democracy and represented the true wave of the future—a view to which Roosevelt himself subscribed.

Indeed, as Averell Harriman recalled, Roosevelt became a believer in what was later called the "convergence" theory of U.S.-Soviet relations— that the Soviet Union and the United States would gradually become more like one another—the Soviet Union less centralized, the United States more socialistic. Significantly, however, Roosevelt concealed such views from the public.[30]

"For Americans to portray Great Britain as a greater threat to postwar cooperation and peace than the Soviet Union," Warren F. Kimball has written, "may seem absurd." Yet he continues, "American foreign policy from Wilson to Roosevelt had constituted a radical critique of international relations as conducted by the European powers." Kimball goes on:

> *Calls for arms control,* the elimination of trade barriers, and the establishment of governments responsive to the needs and aspirations of their citizens— thus *ending colonialism and 'oppressive' spheres of influence*—were all based on the belief that European leadership had failed. Bolshevism, Nazism, and Fascism were distrusted and feared, but not blamed for the collapse of the interwar order. Most Americans placed responsibility for the world crisis on Great Britain and, to a lesser degree, France. It was British greed and power politics, so the argument went, that prevented the development of effective international cooperation and thus permitted the dictators to run amok."[31]

At bottom, the premises of Roosevelt's diplomacy were precisely the premises of the disarmament and arms control project between the wars. Roosevelt's diplomacy, like disarmament itself, was an effort to transcend "power politics."

Mission to Moscow

Part of Roosevelt's confidence concerning "convergence" and change in the Soviet Union came from Joseph E. Davies, Roosevelt's ambassador to Moscow in the late 1930s and, as a private citizen, a key wartime advisor to the president on the Soviet Union.

A word should be said about Davies, whose pivotal role in American wartime diplomacy—and in the origins of the Cold War—has generally been overlooked by American historians. A Wisconsin "Progressive," lawyer, and New Deal politician who gained wealth by marrying the heiress to the Post cereal fortune in 1935, Davies served as U.S. ambassador to Moscow from 1936 to 1938.[32] Sent by Roosevelt to seek an improvement in relations with the Soviets—Davies replaced the skeptical and well-informed William Bullitt—the New Dealer threw himself into his mission of goodwill with single-minded determination.

Present at the very height of Stalin's Great Terror and the Red Army purge, Davies managed nonetheless to form an overwhelmingly favorable view of Stalin and the Soviet regime during his eighteen months in Moscow. Returning to America after a stint as ambassador to Belgium, he would publish a diary of his Moscow sojourn called *Mission to Moscow*. Eventually made into a hit movie in 1943, *Mission to Moscow* became, in the *New York Times*'s estimate, "the one book above all to read on Russia."[33]

The book presented a remarkably distorted vision of Soviet realities. For example, one 1937 Davies cable to the secretary of state was headlined in the book "STALIN INSISTS UPON THE SECRET BALLOT AND UNIVERSAL SUFFRAGE."[34] Yet of neighboring Estonia, soon to be absorbed bloodily into the Soviet empire, Davies wrote, "The present government is practically a dictatorship."[35]

The Soviet Union as portrayed in Davies's *Mission to Moscow* was changing, reforming. Things had "radically changed since 1935,"[36] he affirmed. Communism was failing, and the Communists under Stalin were turning to capitalistic methods. In the Soviet Union as portrayed by Davies, incentive and profit were reviving, as were social classes. "Human nature," as he put it, was reasserting itself.[37] Communist ideology was giving way to latent Russian national feeling. Above all, there was a strong desire for friendship with the United States.

There is little doubt that the image of a changing Soviet Union was carefully cultivated by Davies's Soviet hosts. The American ambassador was permitted to tour factories (carefully selected and prepared for his visits), where he was able to witness first-hand the phenomenon of reemergent "capitalism" in the Soviet Union; he was shown around museums and palaces where he could see evidence of the deep-rooted appeal of Russian nationalism. As Davies wrote to his close friend Steven Early, Roosevelt's longtime associate and press secretary toward the end of the Moscow sojourn:

Personally, I do not think that the world is in any real danger from communism for many years to come. Communism won't work. It hasn't worked here. This government is not communism. It is a socialism. And this socialism has been modified, and is being compelled to accede more and more to the methods of capitalism and individualism in order to make the machine work. And the crowd in power, the government, has got to make the machine work or lose their jobs.[38]

This was in 1938.

Gifts to "Uncle Joe"

Hitler attacked the Soviet Union on June 22, 1941. A week later, Davies, through Early, had secured a meeting with the president. Davies urged Roosevelt to follow the British example of promising "all-out" aid to the Soviet Union. A Davies memorandum to Harry Hopkins the following week on the "Russian Situation" defended the Soviet Union as having been "driven" to the nonaggression pact with Hitler by Western policies in 1939 and averred that, during the interwar period, the Soviets had actually "led the fight *for the protection of little nations* [emphasis added]."[39] The memo predicted that the Soviet Union would not seek to expand communism in Europe.

In mid-July, Davies secured a blank check from Acting Secretary of State Sumner Welles permitting him unlimited personal contacts with the Soviet embassy in Washington.[40] Armed with this carte blanche, Davies remained in constant touch with both the White House and the Soviet embassy throughout the war, meeting frequently with the president and U.S. high officials to advise them on the Soviet Union even while he was regularly communicating with Soviet high officials through the embassy and directly. The Soviet ambassador was even a regular at Davies's card table. Over time, Davies and his Soviet contacts evolved into an informal "backchannel" through which Roosevelt would conduct confidential negotiations, attempting to maneuver around Churchill and gain Stalin's cooperation in building the "new world."

Davies's extensive Soviet contacts and his special claims to understand the Soviets may help explain Roosevelt's curious remark in a letter to Churchill on March 18, 1942: "I know you will not mind my being brutally frank when I tell you that I think I can personally handle Stalin better than either your Foreign Office or my State Department. Stalin hates the guts of all your top people. He thinks he likes me better, and I hope he will continue to do so."[41] What possible evidence could Roosevelt have had that Stalin "like[d]" him "better"? None, one suspects, apart from Davies's flattering assurances that if only the president could meet face to face with the Soviet leader, Allied problems would be solved and the world put aright.

Roosevelt acted on this self-confident assumption. On April 11, 1942, the president secretly wrote to Stalin, requesting that the two leaders meet in Alaska in the summer. Churchill would not be present. Initially, Stalin, suspicious alike of Roosevelt and Churchill, rejected the president's invitation. However, with time, the Soviets began to recognize to what degree Roosevelt's outlook differed from Churchill's and to what degree it would be possible to drive a wedge between the two Western allies. In this process, Davies was a witting or unwitting agent.

The target of the game was Churchill. The Soviets were extremely suspicious of Churchill, whom they recognized as a formidable political opponent and for whom they blamed the slowdown in convoy deliveries and the Allied decision to postpone the invasion of France—what they liked to call the "second front"—until 1943. The apportionment of blame here was not erroneous. In both cases, Churchill had resisted Soviet desiderata, and in both cases, the key issue had been the loss of Allied lives. Churchill believed the losses from the convoys to be too great to permit continuance at the rate Stalin was demanding. In addition, he and the British staff believed the Allies to be unprepared for a landing in France in 1942; such a landing, while certainly drawing off German troops from Stalin's front, would be a disaster for the West. Interestingly, Roosevelt took Stalin's side in both these arguments—a fact that raises questions about suggestions, mentioned for example in Gaddis's *Strategies of Containment*,[42] that Roosevelt's many concessions to the Soviet Union later in the war may have been part of Machiavellian strategy designed to conserve American lives by allowing Soviets to take the brunt of the war's casualties. Far from wishing the Soviets to take the brunt of Hitler's aggression, as Gaddis suggests, Roosevelt early in the war pleaded with Churchill to send British and American troops onto the Continent to save Russian lives. "I think we should try to put ourselves in his place," Roosevelt wrote to Churchill of Stalin.[43]

Antagonism toward Churchill eventually was to provide the foundation of Soviet-American friendship. To Davies the president would confide his frustrations and resentments at Churchill's "mid-Victorian" and "imperialist" attitudes toward Britain's Asian, Balkan, and Indian interests. In conversation with and memoranda to Roosevelt, meanwhile, Davies would stress Soviet suspicion of Churchill and argue that Britain was played out and would cease to be a force in world politics after the war. As Davies told Roosevelt in April 1943, "friendship between Russia and the United States" was "natural" because neither nation "wanted anything the other had; neither could impose its will upon the other." Not so friendship between Britain and the USSR, which was complicated by British imperial designs. What was needed, Davies affirmed, was someone (that is, Roosevelt) to "allay the old fears and suspicions" of the Soviets and to *"prevent the needs of the British Empire from disrupting [Allied] Unity."*[44]

Yet even as Davies whetted Roosevelt's appetite for a personal conference with Stalin, the Soviets withheld the prize, eventually using it to exact important concessions from Roosevelt prior to the Teheran Conference. In April 1943, Allied relations were suddenly complicated by German discovery of the bodies of the 4,000 Polish officers executed by the NKVD in the Katyn Forest. Poland's government-in-exile in London called for an immediate Red Cross investigation, a demand that Stalin used as a pretext to cut off relations with the London Poles. Churchill initially attempted to moderate the Poles' anger. Yet eventually he persuaded Roosevelt to cooperate in a joint message urging Stalin to reestablish relations with the exile government. When the first message was unavailing, Churchill recommended a second. Instead, Roosevelt acted on his own—sending a special envoy to see Stalin in Moscow: none other than Joseph Davies.[45]

By the time Davies traveled to Moscow, press and intelligence reports tended to confirm Soviet responsibility for the Katyn murders: Davies, interestingly enough, had in his possession a memorandum detailing the evidence.[46] Nonetheless, the purpose of the mission was not to deliver a protest but rather to convey to Stalin a secret request from Roosevelt. The president desired a personal meeting with the Soviet dictator. So eager was Roosevelt to know Stalin's answer that Davies was given a special code to indicate, from Moscow, whether the meeting was to be held in Siberia or Alaska. Before Davies flew back to the States, the Soviets, with great fanfare, painted "Mission to Moscow" in red on the side of his airplane.[47]

Churchill was not informed of any plans for a U.S.-Soviet summit until nearly two months later, when Harriman visited him in late June. When Churchill bitterly protested the idea, citing "the use that enemy propaganda would make of meeting between the heads of Soviet Russia and the United States at this juncture with the British Commonwealth and Empire excluded," Roosevelt lied outright, stating that the meeting had been Stalin's idea.[48]

By now, however, Stalin had decided to play hardball over the Poles and the "second front." In late June, he recalled his ambassadors from London and Washington, thereby raising the prospect that the Soviets might be preparing to negotiate a separate peace with Hitler. Churchill was disturbed enough that on June 29, he reversed himself on the subject of a private meeting between Roosevelt and Stalin, giving Roosevelt the go-ahead to seek one.[49]

Roosevelt quietly took advantage of Churchill's concession, sending Davies to Mexico City in early October to meet privately with the former Soviet ambassador to the United States, now Moscow's ambassador in Mexico, Constantin Oumansky. Davies's mission was to press again for the coveted meeting with Stalin.

After Oumansky aired a long and bitter list of grievances against the Soviet Union's Western allies, especially Churchill, Davies assured him that if a meeting could be arranged between Stalin and Roosevelt, the president and the Soviet leader "would come to a complete and final agreement upon matters which would preserve the vital interests of each country" along lines that Davies himself had previewed to Stalin and Molotov in Moscow.[50]

In short, it is hard to avoid the conclusion that even before the Teheran Conference in 1943, the Soviets had secured broad, in-principle agreement from Roosevelt on their most important demands regarding Eastern Europe. All this was conceded, in effect, as the price for a meeting with Stalin. Ironically, Roosevelt never did get his private summit in quite the form he desired. When he met Stalin for their first tête-à-tête, it was at the three-power Teheran Conference the following month. It appears that the Soviets had more delicacy regarding Churchill's feelings than had Roosevelt himself.

Roosevelt promptly accepted Stalin's invitation to stay during the Teheran Conference in a house in the Soviet embassy compound (the alternatives being the American embassy or the British embassy). Here, insulated not only from his own embassy but from his democratic colleague Churchill, conducting his business under extensive Soviet surveillance,[51] Roosevelt sought to shape the relationship with Stalin that would order the postwar world.

In three private meetings with Stalin, with only his interpreter, Charles E. "Chip" Bohlen, and Stalin's interpreter present, Roosevelt made a series of remarkable statements and concessions. The president professed private agreement with Stalin's wish that the boundary of Poland be moved still farther westward—adding only that for domestic political reasons he could not endorse such a solution publicly. Roosevelt "added jokingly" that "when the Soviet armies reoccupied" the Baltic states (then in German hands), "he did not intend to go to war with the Soviet Union on this point," thus giving up any U.S. leverage in the Baltic countries. And there were matching concessions in Asia: a Soviet protectorate over Mongolia, ceding of China's important ports at Dairen and Port Arthur. In Japan, Stalin obtained the Kurile Islands and the southern half of Sakhalin island.[52]

Perhaps most important, having surrendered on the question of the Polish border, Roosevelt failed to support Churchill's drive to assure a democratic, Western-leaning government for Poland.

Stalin, meanwhile, engaged in some purposeful planting of disinformation, affirming privately to the American president that after its exposure to the West, the Red Army would return home with a new ideological outlook. The Soviet Union after the war, according to Stalin, would chart a middle course between capitalism and communism. The name of the Soviet Union, he volunteered, would be changed back to Russia. (Indeed, shortly afterward, the Soviet ambassador in Washington began to call himself the "Russian ambassador.")[53] This was precisely the impression that Davies had brought home in *Mission to Moscow*. Doubtless it strengthened Roosevelt's faith in "convergence."

Finally, Roosevelt went out of his way to distance himself from Churchill, even poking open fun at the prime minister in Stalin's presence. As he told Labor Secretary Frances Perkins after his return from Teheran, he remarked in a stage whisper to Stalin at the beginning of one conference session that "Winston is cranky this morning; he got up on the wrong side of bed. A vague smile passed over Stalin's eyes." Roosevelt began teasing Churchill "about his Britishness, about John Bull, about his cigars, about his habits. . . . Winston got red and scowled, and the more he did so, the more Stalin smiled. Finally, Stalin broke into a deep, heavy guffaw, and for the first time in three days I saw light. I kept it up until Stalin was laughing with me, and it was then that I called him 'Uncle Joe.' He would have thought me fresh the day before, but that day he laughed and came over and shook my hand. From that time on our relations were personal."[54]

Whether the denigration of his democratic ally was worth the privilege of calling Stalin "Uncle Joe" remains open to question. Churchill and his immediate circle soon recognized that Roosevelt was pursuing a separate course. As Harry Hopkins told Churchill's personal physician, Lord Moran, "Harry tells me that the President is convinced that even if he cannot convert Stalin into a good democrat, he will be able to come to a working agreement with him. After all, he had spent his life managing men, and Stalin at bottom could not be so different from other people." Roosevelt's obvious illusions about Stalin left Churchill in a state of what Moran called "black depression."[55]

Betrayal in Warsaw

Roosevelt's decision to tilt toward Stalin at the expense of Churchill was to have far-reaching strategic consequences. While Roosevelt struggled to maintain a tone of mutual goodwill, Stalin moved to consolidate Soviet power over Poland, ruthlessly eliminating the forces that stood in the way of absolute Soviet control of this historically anti-Russian and anti-Communist nation. The Polish officer corps was dispatched with horrifying efficacy, as we have seen, at Katyn and two other locations.[56] Discovery of the Katyn massacre in turn provided Stalin with a pretext for breaking off relations with the London government-in-exile. The coup de grace was dealt with the betrayal of the Polish underground a year later.

As the Red Army advanced westward toward Warsaw in late July 1944, Moscow established its own provisional government, composed of Polish Communists and fellow travelers and headed by a Pole who had been arrested and deported as a Soviet spy before the war, at Lublin. In Warsaw, meanwhile, the Polish Home Army, loyal to the London government-in-exile, prepared to rise against Nazi captors. Radio Moscow urged the rebellion forward.[57] But when the underground rose against the Nazis on August 1, Stalin halted his armies across the River Vistula from Warsaw and waited.

On August 11, Churchill forwarded to Stalin a note from the desperate rebel commander asking for aid, along with his own request to Stalin for permission to land British planes, so that parachute drops of supplies could be made to the beleaguered rebels in the city. Stalin refused. Claiming falsely that "intensive parachute drops" had already been made to the rebel forces, the Soviet dictator went on to characterize the underground revolt, which Radio Moscow had encouraged, as "a reckless and terrible adventure which is costing the population large sacrifices."[58]

For the first time, by his own account, Roosevelt's ambassador in

Moscow, Averell Harriman, grew suspicious of the Soviet attitude—fearing that Soviet refusal to permit air drops was "based on ruthless political considerations." Meetings with Soviet representatives yielded no results. The American ambassador's instinct to press the Soviets harder was not supported in Washington, which instructed him, somewhat incongruously, that "our chief purpose [in Poland] has already been achieved." Stalin responded to a joint appeal from Roosevelt and Churchill on August 20 by labeling the underground a "handful of power-seeking criminals."[59]

On August 25, Churchill forwarded to Roosevelt a proposal for a second joint message. "I do not consider it advantageous in the long-range general war prospect for me to join with you in the proposed message to U. J. [Uncle Joe]," Roosevelt replied.[60] By now the president was receiving a different kind of advice closer to home. Eleanor Roosevelt had sent her husband a memo on August 21 quoting from a 1919 remark of Churchill's criticizing the Bolsheviks. "It is not surprising if Mr. Stalin is slow to forget!" wrote the First Lady.[61]

More important in Roosevelt's mind perhaps were the negotiations then underway at Dumbarton Oaks on the United Nations. Roosevelt evidently believed pressure over Poland might jeopardize his dream of a United Nations organization.

By October 2, when the Home Army finally surrendered, 100,000 Poles had perished and Warsaw had been reduced to rubble. Only then did Soviet armies liberate the Polish capital.

The Scientist as Idealist

It was in the midst of the August 1944 Allied crisis over the Warsaw uprising that the famous nuclear physicist Niels Bohr paid a private call at the White House. Bohr was the scientist who, on a visit to Princeton in 1938, had first brought to America the fateful news that the atom had been split. When the renowned Danish Nobel Prize–winner finally fled Europe in 1943—after generously helping to operate an underground railway for scientists fleeing Nazi persecution—he was retained by the American government as a consultant to the Los Alamos laboratory.

As perhaps the preeminent nuclear physicist of the age, Bohr was no doubt in a position to provide important assistance on the bomb project. But from the time of his arrival, his own priorities lay elsewhere. "Officially and secretly he came to help the technical enterprise," J. Robert Oppenheimer later wrote, "[but] most secretly of all . . . he came to advance his case and his cause."[62] An idealist and a passionate believer in the possibility of reforming the international system, Bohr was convinced that the American and British governments should inform the Soviet Union at the earliest possible date of the existence of the secret atomic bomb project. Such a gesture, Bohr felt, was necessary to build the trust that would be required to establish effective international "control" of atomic energy at the end of the war. By control Bohr meant complete abolition of nuclear weapons and international cooperation to exploit atomic energy for purely "peaceful" uses. Throughout the spring and summer of 1944, Bohr lobbied Roosevelt and Churchill—sending memoranda and letters and eventually personally visiting each leader—on behalf of his program.

In a sense, the story of nuclear disarmament (as distinct from disarmament and arms control in general) may be said to begin with Niels Bohr. Bohr's ideas eventually formed the core of the earliest American nuclear disarmament proposal—the so-called Baruch Plan of 1946, which called for destroying the U.S. atomic bomb stockpile and establishing complete United Nations control over all aspects of atomic energy. More broadly, the attitudes that Bohr brought to the problem—his powerful idealism, his impatience with ordinary politics, his belief that scientists themselves held better solutions to problems relating to the bomb than political leaders, his faith that a technical solution to these most momentous of political dilemmas could be found—were attitudes that came to characterize a whole generation of scientists who made "control" of atomic weapons their cause. There is one additional point: The story of Bohr's unsuccessful effort of persuasion vis-à-vis Roosevelt and Churchill has come increasingly to be seen as the first in a series of what are perceived by some to have been "lost chances"—squandered opportunities to circumvent and transcend the problem of the nuclear arms race. For Martin Sherwin, Bohr's ideas of cooperation with the Soviet Union define "The Road Not Taken" at the dawn of the nuclear era. Likewise, for Richard Rhodes, the consequences of Roosevelt's and especially Churchill's rejection of Bohr's proposal in 1944 remain "immeasurable."[63]

Was there really a "lost chance" when Bohr tried to persuade Roosevelt and Churchill to share the secret of the bomb with Stalin? That is, would greater openness with Moscow regarding atomic energy on the part of the United States and Britain have forestalled a nuclear arms race or alleviated the Cold War? To answer, one must look closely both at

Bohr's reasoning and the details of the evolving political situation in 1944.

At the heart of Bohr's proposal was the assumption that a gesture of goodwill on the part the United States would be reciprocated by goodwill on the part of the Soviet Union. "An attitude inviting confidence by extending generosity," he wrote (in his peculiarly convoluted English) in April 1944, "might indeed be the only way of furthering a development of the relations between nations."[64]

Even Sherwin is forced to acknowledge that Bohr's vision of the Soviet Union was hopelessly naïve. "He was certain," Sherwin writes, "that among the eminent scientists in Russia, 'one can reckon to find ardent supporters of universal cooperation.' That their influence with the Soviet government on political matters might be nil was a possibility that apparently did not occur to him."[65]

Bohr was evidently basing his views on his own limited contact with Soviet scientists and on the Soviet government's record of courting Western scientists during the interwar period.[66] He apparently assumed from these experiences that scientists could play a key role in opening up Soviet society; what he apparently did not suspect was that the Soviet regime had sponsored such conferences because of its eagerness to gain access to Western technology for its military-industrial base. (It also purchased subscriptions to American technical journals on a large scale for similar reasons.)[67]

And indeed the Soviet government tried to recruit Bohr himself during the war. A renowned Soviet scientist of Bohr's acquaintance, Peter Kapitza, wrote to Bohr after his escape from Denmark inviting him to come to Moscow. When Bohr attempted to have the letter delivered to him in London (where he had traveled from Washington), the Soviet embassy insisted that he retrieve it personally. When he went to the embassy, the counselor pressed Bohr on his attitudes toward Russia and questioned him in some detail about what he knew of scientists' work in America.[68]

Still, the most persuasive element of Bohr's argument for commentators like Sherwin and Rhodes was his seemingly prescient prediction of a postwar arms race. Yet Bohr's prediction hardly required great political acumen—though doubtless for American officials convinced that peace would bring an end to the alliances, spheres of influence, and the balance of power itself, such a forecast might have come as a revelation. Churchill, for one, was certainly aware of the likelihood of such a postwar arms race (which was why he wished to delay Soviet attainment of the Bomb as long as possible, if only for a few years).

What did not follow was that giving the Soviets the Bomb would make such a race any less likely. Given Stalin's overriding priorities in Poland, and the ruthlessness with which he was willing to pursue his aims there and elsewhere in Eastern Europe, it is difficult to imagine how American openness about the Bomb could have changed these objectives, but it would have shortened the duration of the American atomic monopoly. (That Stalin should have known something of the American project from his spies—Klaus Fuchs in particular—seems clear; however, the account in Soviet sources would suggest that atomic research in the Soviet Union, though underway as early as 1942, received top priority only after Potsdam and possibly only after Hiroshima.)[69]

Churchill was acutely aware of these problems. Roosevelt was not, and there are indications that, left to his own devices, the American president might well have divulged the existence of the Manhattan Project to Stalin in 1944 as Bohr suggested.

When Supreme Court Justice Felix Frankfurter originally presented Bohr's ideas to Roosevelt—Bohr had approached Frankfurter, in an exchange that actually breached security regulations—the president and the Supreme Court justice talked enthusiastically for an hour and a half. The president professed to be "worried to death" about the Bomb and the issue of postwar control. Months before actually seeing Bohr, Roosevelt authorized the scientist, through Frankfurter, to act as an unofficial emissary to Churchill on the question of postwar international control (no doubt to Churchill's great vexation). When Bohr himself visited Roosevelt in late August, the president was extraordinarily receptive, giving the scientist a full hour and a half. In light of the later agreement to put Bohr under surveillance, historians have attributed Roosevelt's warm reception of him to the president's temperamental inconsistency,[70] but in fact there is every reason to suppose that, as of August 1944, Roosevelt agreed enthusiastically with Bohr's position.

Churchill, however, was another matter. In contrast to the amiable chat with Roosevelt, Bohr's interview with Churchill the previous May had been brief and unpleasant. Historians again seem eager to provide excuses for the outcome—Bohr's tendency to mumble, Churchill's preoccupation with other issues, all implying that Churchill somehow failed to comprehend the issue.[71] On the contrary, Churchill no doubt understood exactly what Bohr was suggesting and adamantly opposed it. In September, when the prime minister would meet with the president at Hyde Park following the Quebec Conference, he would prevail upon Roosevelt—exactly how we will probably never know—to sign an explicit agreement to the effect that knowledge of the Bomb was not to be shared with other countries without mutual consent and that Bohr himself—who had held unauthorized talks on the subject with Frankfurter and who appeared to be corresponding with a Russian scientist, Peter Kapitza—be restrained in his movements and put under surveillance.[72] (The restraints were never imposed, but Roosevelt never subsequently saw Bohr again.) An agreement between two heads of government to single out an individual citizen for surveillance is an uncommon occurrence in the annals of diplomacy. Evidently, in their quite different ways, Roosevelt and Churchill both took Bohr's ideas and proposals quite seriously, and it was a matter of some contention between them. Even after signing the Quebec agreement, Roosevelt, to Churchill's horror, would casually speak at Yalta of informing Stalin of the Bomb, on the grounds *"that de Gaulle if he heard of [the Bomb] would certainly double-cross us with Russia."*[73] (Such a combination of almost pathological Francophobia and sympathy for the Soviets was typical of FDR.)

Again, the difference between the two men came down to the difference in foreign policy paradigms. Churchill, who focused on the balance of power, recognized that the bomb would eventually provide a critical counterweight to Soviet power. The British were even willing to renounce their postwar commercial interests on atomic energy in order to persuade the rather mean-spirited Americans to continue with the military side of the cooperation—no doubt ultimately with the Soviet threat in view.[74] When Roosevelt heard from his aide Vannevar Bush that the British were primarily concerned about the effect of the atomic bomb on the postwar balance of power, he professed to find the fact "astounding."[75] This is hardly surprising from a president who was anticipating a postwar world from which "the system of unilateral action, the exclusive alliances, the spheres of influence, the balances of power, and all the other expedients that have been tried for centuries" would all but disappear. Indeed, so oblivious were Americans to the military danger or the likely postwar power balance that officials such as Bush and James Bryant Conant were thoroughly absorbed with the postwar commercial implications of the invention, campaigning to exclude British participation on these grounds even as they advised drawing in the Soviet Union.[76]

Finally, the full extent and naïveté of Bohr's faith in "openness" must be understood. As late as June 1948, long after the Cold War was underway and just over a month before the Soviets would launch the first Berlin crisis, Bohr would write a lengthy letter to Secretary of State George Marshall recommending that the United States immediately offer to open *all* its military facilities, including its atomic weapons facilities, to inspectors from other countries on a reciprocal basis. The ostensible purpose of this grand gesture was to end international suspicions and forestall an arms race once and for all. Bohr was once again optimistic. Such a plan, he declared, "would accelerate a change in international relations, more sweeping than can readily be imagined and described."[77] This may have been true, though in a quite different sense from that which Bohr intended. In short, it is easy to see why Churchill, in 1944, responding to the scientist's request for permission to follow up their meeting with a letter, observed bluntly to him that a letter from Niels Bohr was always welcome "but not about politics!"[78]

The Soviet Vise Tightens

"This war is not as in the past," Stalin remarked to the Yugoslavian partisan leader Marshal Tito and his entourage in April. "Whoever occupies a territory also imposes on it his own social system. Everyone imposes his own system as far as his army can reach. It cannot be otherwise."[79] Such were the harsh rules that were to govern the outcome of World War II. Far from creating the "new world" for which Roosevelt hoped, the war at its close left the Soviet Union and the United States competing for territory in an almost traditional sense. Stalin clearly grasped this fact, as did Churchill. Roosevelt, still dreaming his Wilsonian dreams, remained oblivious to such considerations.

Yet, arguably, some of the most consequential and curious American decisions of the war were yet to come. At the end of March 1945, American and British armies stood in striking distance of Berlin and Prague. It was likely that the Soviet army would take Vienna, but the possibility also existed of introducing a large Allied force into Austria as well. Previous Allied planning had presumed that the Americans and British would drive as deep as possible into "the heart of Germany," and before D-Day Berlin had been among explicit American objectives.[80]

Yet on March 30, Churchill received a telegram from the Supreme Allied Commander, General Dwight Eisenhower, stating that Allied forces would halt at the Elbe River and proceed southward, leaving Berlin to be taken by the Soviets. Eisenhower had notified Stalin two days earlier of American intentions, without previously consulting the British. Not surprisingly, Stalin had readily agreed to Eisenhower's plan, even adding that Berlin had "lost its former strategic importance" and the Soviet High Command therefore planned to allot "secondary forces" to the city—a statement, as Churchill later wrote, "not borne out by events."[81]

The strategic consequences of this decision were graver than the Americans understood. By ceding the German capital to Soviet forces, not only was the United States yielding a target of enormous symbolic and political value—a city that, thanks partly to the American abandonment, would be the focal point of Cold War crises and a near occasion of war for the next thirty years—but was also relinquishing hope of gaining leverage over the future of Poland. While historians have generally recognized the importance of Berlin as a strategic target, they have by and large overlooked the effect an occupation of Prussia would have had on the Polish situation, a factor of which Churchill was aware.[82] Had Eisenhower proceeded beyond Berlin, the Anglo-American forces would have come to a halt closer to the Polish border. Not only would the German populace have been spared the horror of the Soviet conquest—during which as Nikolai Tolstoy writes "scarcely a German woman, from grandmothers to four-year-old children, survived unraped east of the Elbe"[83]—but Western requests concerning Poland would have been backed by a nearby military presence.

Two factors lay behind Eisenhower's decision. First, there was Roosevelt's remarkable insouciance concerning the final dispositions of Western and Soviet armies on the Continent—indeed, his apparent desire to *reward* Stalin with the conquest of Berlin.[84] In a private conversation with Stalin at Yalta, the president had actually told the Soviet leader of "bets" FDR had made on board the cruiser coming over as to "whether the Russians would get to Berlin before the Americans would get to Manila"—thereby seeming to encourage Stalin to take the German capital.[85]

The second factor behind the decision was a more general American naïveté about "power politics." General George C. Marshall's response to British urgings that the Western armies take Prague summed up the American attitude. "Personally, and aside from all logistic, tactical, or strategic implications," said Marshall, "I would be loath to hazard American lives for purely political purposes."[86] (Why ever would nations go to war, one is tempted to ask, *except* for "political purposes"?)

The failure of Roosevelt and his generals to attend to the details of the emerging military situation vis-à-vis the Soviet Union was matched by a parallel refusal by the American administration to address the details of the deteriorating political situation in Poland and Eastern Europe generally. At Yalta the president gained Soviet signature to a grandiloquent

"Declaration of Liberated Europe" guaranteeing freedom and self-determination to all liberated peoples. But Roosevelt refused to support British efforts to insist on specific "machinery" to carry it out.[87]

Yet by the closing weeks of Roosevelt's presidency, Soviet violations of the Yalta understandings were becoming ever more egregious and unmistakable. In early March, Molotov made clear that, contrary to Yalta, the Soviets would block a widening of the Polish government, particularly any inclusion of the Polish democratic leader, Stanislaw Mikolajczyk. Meanwhile, within Poland itself, members of the Home Army were being rounded up and either murdered or shipped off to Soviet slave camps. Then on March 27, unbeknownst to the British and the Americans, fifteen Polish leaders, including the commander of the Polish Underground Army and heads of all other major resistance groups, having been offered safe conduct to Soviet headquarters, were promptly taken into custody by the Soviets and shipped off to prison in Moscow. Simultaneously, the Soviets played the UN card against Roosevelt, announcing that Gromyko, the deputy foreign minister, and not Molotov, would be sent to the San Francisco Conference for establishing the United Nations organization, a gesture destined to make Roosevelt even more reluctant to press the Polish case. Indeed, his penultimate cable to Churchill, the day before his death, was yet a further demurral on the Polish issue. "I would minimize the general Soviet problem as much as possible because these problems, in one form or another, seem to arise every day and most of them straighten out." The president then added somewhat contradictorily: "We must be firm, however, and our course thus far is correct."[88]

Harry Truman Takes Over

When Harriman phoned Molotov on the evening of April 12 with the news of President Roosevelt's unexpected death, the Soviet foreign minister rushed to the American embassy. Molotov, according to Harriman, was "deeply moved and disturbed." The next morning, Stalin was in a similar mood. "He greeted me in silence," said Harriman, "and stood holding my hand for about 30 seconds before asking me to sit down."[89] Whatever misconceptions Stalin and Molotov may have entertained regarding the American national character, it is inconceivable that the Soviet leadership had failed to note Roosevelt's unusually accommodating attitude toward the Soviet Union. Harry Hopkins's personal message to Stalin on April 13 that "Russia has lost her greatest friend in America" doubtless rang all too true.[90]

Beginning with the revisionists of the early 1960s, a number of American historians—following, in this, the traditional view of the Soviets themselves—have blamed the Cold War on the shift in policy toward the Soviet Union occasioned by the transfer of power from Franklin Roosevelt to Harry Truman. Revisionists portrayed the changes under Truman as part of a concerted anti-Soviet policy.[91] Postrevisionists, while accepting the existence of such a shift, have argued that it was less clear-cut and consistent than the revisionists portrayed it to be.[92]

However, whether one accepts this shift as the starting point of the Cold War depends on the answer to a more fundamental question: namely, how the "Cold War" itself is defined.[93] Did the Cold War begin when America began resisting Soviet expansion in Europe? Or did the Cold War rather begin when the Soviet Union first began to seek to impose its will on neighboring Central European nations—that is, with the Nazi-Soviet Pact of 1939, the invasion of the Baltic states in 1940, or later with the Teheran Conference in 1943, when Stalin insisted that Roosevelt and Churchill accept such annexations as the price for Soviet support? Only if one accepts the former definition—in essence, equating "Cold War" simply with American resistance to Soviet expansion as opposed to U.S. acquiescence—can responsibility for the Cold War be laid at the feet of Harry Truman.

Still, that there was a change in policy, however halting or uneven, seems clear. In part the difference between the two administrations lay in the simple fact that Truman, in contrast to his airy predecessor, actually listened to his advisors and acted on their advice.[94] Not that the counsel Truman received was in any sense unanimous. A major State Department overview of world affairs prepared for the president on his second day in office, for example, noted that Churchill was "inclined however to press" issues "with the Russians *with what we consider unnecessary rigidness as to detail.*"[95] This was the dominant view.

But by now there were also more skeptical voices to be heard on the subject of the Soviets—most notably that of Harriman, who rushed back from Moscow in order to make certain that the new president was aware of Soviet violations of the Yalta accords. Not even Harriman at this point was counseling a break with Moscow. The Warsaw uprising had marked a turning point in the American ambassador's thinking, but it did not make him anti-Soviet. The firmer line that he recommended was intended to promote better long-term cooperation with the Soviet Union by head-ing off miscalculation in the relationship. Unreciprocated American "goodwill," in Harriman's view, was conveying the wrong message to the Soviets, setting the stage for inevitable problems ahead. While muttering to Truman about the possibility of a "barbarian invasion of Europe," he nonetheless remained "optimistic" about the potential for a Soviet "change of attitude."[96]

Truman's own initial instinct was to be tough and straightforward. Following a conference with Harriman and others, he rebuked Molotov sharply in a meeting at Blair House on April 23. (Following FDR's death, the Soviets had relented and sent Molotov to San Francisco—partly out of anxiety about their relations with Roosevelt's successor.)[97] Truman insisted repeatedly that the Soviet Union was violating the Yalta agreements and should come into compliance with them. "I have never been talked to like that in my life," Molotov said at the end of the interview. "Carry out your agreements," the president snapped back, "and you won't get talked to like that."[98]

This was not the last word, however. Doubting his own foreign policy judgment, and lobbied intensively by, among others, Joseph Davies,[99] Truman subsequently backpedaled and tried a softer stance. (On May 19, during the very period when Davies was struggling to establish his influence with the new president, Moscow announced that the former ambassador had been awarded the Order of Lenin.)[100] In May, following suggestions not just from Davies but from Harriman and State Department advisor Charles E. Bohlen,[101] the president sent Harry Hopkins on a mission of goodwill to Stalin. Davies, meanwhile, was simultaneously dispatched to see Churchill. Toward the Soviet dictator, Hopkins took the most ingratiating approach, not even mentioning the abducted Polish resitance leaders until several days into his visit and then couching U.S. reservations about the episode in the context of its presumed effect on American "public opinion."[102] Davies, meanwhile, argued fiercely with Churchill's critique of Soviet policy and brought back to Truman a report blaming the prime minister's objections to Soviet conduct on wartime fatigue. (Davies also resolved in his diary to report the content of his exchange to Churchill *to the Soviet foreign ministry.*)[103] Churchill, temporarily heartened in April at Truman's original willingness to talk tough to the the Soviets,[104] was again dejected. It appeared as if American policy toward Stalin under the new president was reverting to the Rooseveltian mold.

The Atomic Bomb Alters the Equation

Before his angry exchange with Molotov, Truman had commented that "the Russians needed us more than we needed them."[105] Was this really true? On the one hand, the Soviets would presumably need, or at least want, American economic help for postwar reconstruction, a point emphasized by Harriman.[106] On the other hand, there were two separate reasons why it could be said that the Americans might also "need" the "Russians"—first, Roosevelt's plans for peace and a world organization; and second, the upcoming invasion of Japan. It was indicative of the confusion besetting American policy that Truman made no real effort to distinguish between these objectives in his own mind or to set a separate value on each of them (another sign that in getting "tough" with the Soviets, the president and his chief advisors had no intention of breaking with Moscow). Writing later of his resistance to Churchill's efforts to push Allied lines farther east in late April and early May, Truman said, "I was anxious to get the Russians into the war against Japan as soon as possible, thus saving the lives of countless Americans." Then again: "I was trying to get Churchill in a frame of mind to forget the old power politics and get a United Nations organization to work."[107]

Even if the administration had been inclined to sacrifice its vision of a world at peace under the UN organization—not a likely circumstance—the immediate problem of Soviet help in the Japanese war would remain.

This latter problem would be utterly transformed by the emergence of the atomic bomb. Indeed, the appearance of the Bomb would gradually begin to alter the whole manner in which high American officials viewed the Soviet Union.

The shadow that the atomic bomb would cast on world affairs was already becoming apparent by mid-May. Secretary of War Henry L. Stimson, having heard of the president's plans to meet Stalin in July, was worried that it would not yet have been tested. As he wrote in his diary:

The trouble is that the President has now promised apparently to meet Stalin and Churchill on the first of July and at that time these questions will become burning and it may be necessary to have it out with Russia on her relations to Manchuria and Port Arthur and various other parts of North China, and also the relations of China to us. Over any such tangled wave of problems the S-1 [i.e., atomic bomb] secret would be dominant and yet we will not know until after that time probably, until after that meeting, whether this is a weapon in our hands or not. We think it will be shortly afterwards, but it seems a terrible thing to gamble with such big stakes in diplomacy without having your master card in your hand.[108]

As a result of such considerations, the Potsdam meeting was postponed and the Bomb test hurried.[109]

These decisions have sometimes been taken as the first sign of an American disposition to engage in what Soviet propaganda was later to call "atomic diplomacy"[110]—that is, the use of nuclear weapons for diplomatic leverage. (The Soviet notion of "atomic diplomacy" always embodied a peculiarly one-sided code of international conduct, whereby nations were ostensibly permitted to benefit from the leverage inherent in every form of military power except the one in which the United States enjoyed the decisive advantage—atomic weapons.) There is no evidence that American officials made any threat regarding the atomic bomb either at Potsdam or at the London and Moscow foreign ministers' conferences after the war. Yet not even the idealistic Americans could be entirely oblivious to the impact of the atomic bomb on the balance of power. A popular thesis among recent historians holds that the United States attempted to use the Bomb for diplomatic leverage but that such efforts failed because of the alleged ineffectuality of nuclear weapons for diplomacy.[111] In truth, the situation was almost the reverse: American officials made no visible attempt to use the Bomb, but despite such inaction, the mere presence of the weapon had an enormous impact on the balance of power. (The weaknesses of U.S. policy in the immediate postwar period stemmed not from any lack of weight exerted by the Bomb but rather by the fundamental lack of clarity in American foreign policy. In 1945 and early 1946, American policymakers had not yet decided or even explicitly formulated the question of whether the Soviet Union was to be regarded as basically an ally or an enemy. Until that fundamental issue was settled, the full extent of American power to resist Soviet desiderata could not be known.)

Indeed, when news was received at Potsdam of the Bomb test, there was a visible change in the U.S. delegation. "The President was tremendously prepped up by [the Bomb report] and spoke to me of it again and again when I saw him," Stimson wrote in his diary. "He said it gave him an entirely new feeling of confidence." Harriman observed in the U.S. delegation an "increasingly cheerfulness evidently caused by the news [of the Bomb]." Churchill noted to Stimson that "Truman was evidently much fortified by something that had happened and that he stood up to the Russians in the most emphatic and decisive manner." After being briefed by Stimson on the Alamogordo test, Churchill said "he now understood how this pepping up [of the president] had taken place and that he felt the same way."[112]

Unaccustomed and largely unwilling to base their perceptions of international events on "power politics," American officials nonetheless could hardly remain unaffected by a vast shift in the power equation. The arrival of the atomic bomb brought a radical change in the balance of power within the Grand Alliance, a shift that was apparently felt by American officials at Potsdam, and registered in their sudden sense of exhilaration, even before it was fully understood by them. James Byrnes, for one, believed the mere presence of the Bomb would make the Soviets more tractable in negotiations. He told Davies that "the New Mexico situation had given us great power, and that in the last analysis would control."[113]

With the arrival of the atomic bomb, military dependence on the Soviet Union, with all its attendant complications, moral and political, had basically come to an end. Willy-nilly, the shift in power altered perceptions. Just as dependence had reinforced the American tendency to view Soviet machinations in Europe with comparative indulgence, so the removal of dependence revealed the emerging postwar realities in a clearer and colder light.[114] Now that the atomic bomb had freed the United States from military reliance on the Soviet Union, the gravity of what had, in effect, been conceded to the Soviets in Europe was suddenly beginning to dawn on the Americans. As Byrnes confided to an aide, "somebody made an awful mistake in bringing about a situation where Russia was permitted to come out of a war with the power she will have."[115]

Byrnes's observation was probably influenced partly by the Bomb and partly by Churchill, whose powerful sense of the emerging rivalry between the Soviet Union and the West and whose persuasive personality could not help but influence the thinking of the American delegation at Potsdam. A few weeks later, after Churchill, rejected by the British electorate, had faded from the scene, Byrnes would revert to his customary "Rooseveltian" view of the Soviet Union, confiding to a friend that "Stalin wants peace" and that Byrnes was "fearful for the world if Stalin should die."[116] Though the Bomb altered the power relations between the United States and the Soviet Union, it remained for American officials to grasp where their own interests, and those of the Soviets, lay. Churchill's removal from power would delay by several months the process of reevaluation that was incipient at Potsdam.

The Decision to Use the Bomb

"Now I am become Death, the destroyer of worlds." It was this line of the Bhagavad Gita that occurred to J. Robert Oppenheimer on the other side of the globe as the vast cloud of the first man-made atomic explosion rose above Point Zero at Alamogordo, New Mexico, on July 16, 1945.[117]

In the shorter run, the emergence of the atomic bomb could be blamed on political events. The rapid creation of the atomic weapon was an indirect consequence of the world war. Had there been no war, the emergence of the atomic bomb would doubtless have waited years, perhaps decades. As Churchill had said in the mid-1930s looking back on World War I, "the spur of necessity under war conditions made men's brains act with greater vigor." Had the numerous political errors of the democracies from Versailles and Munich been avoided, a thousand horrors would also have been averted, including the horror of Hiroshima.

One might be tempted to fault the United States and Britain for embarking on the research that led to the creation of the atomic weapon. But they were not alone. As the actions of even the pacifistic Einstein attest, if the Bomb were to prove feasible, it was imperative for the survival of freedom and perhaps of humanity as a whole that the democracies and not the dictators be the first to possess it.

But one could indeed fault the United States for a larger error— permitting the advent of war itself. For this the United States bore a heavy share of the responsibility. In 1919, America possessed the financial wherewithal to succor France and redress German grievances. It possessed the military power, in combination with France and Britain, to police and enforce what might have been an enduring peace. At the time when American power and wealth compared to the rest of the world were at a zenith, the nation lacked the farsightedness, the generosity, and, perhaps most important, the political realism to play the role in which history had cast it, as guarantor and enforcer of the balance of power. Lost in pacifist and isolationist illusions, the nation delivered itself of its military advantages and withdrew, leaving Europe to its own devices. It is ironic that when the most potent weapons possessed by nations were believed to be the great battleships, the United States had voluntarily destroyed them. Yet by relinquishing its military strength at the end of World War I, America helped pave the way for a second war of unsurpassed violence, which unleashed the atomic bomb. The Wilsonian creed believed weapons and "power politics" to be the root of political evil. But far from promoting peace, the unwillingness to conserve and wield military power prudently and resourcefully in peacetime had led to the most prodigal unleashing of that power in time of war.

When war finally came, the choices confronting American leaders were very restricted. One was choosing no longer between good and evil but between degrees of evil. Decisions were being made, moreover, under the most pressured of circumstances. Failure was to be measured in hundreds, thousands, and even tens of thousands of lives.

Such were the circumstances surrounding the decision to use the atomic bomb.[118] At the moment use of the Bomb was being contemplated, Allied servicemen in the Pacific were perishing by the thousands in what ranks with the most savage fighting in history. Every new assault on Japanese-occupied islands meant literally thousands more dead. The United States had begun preparations for an invasion of Japan itself in which it was estimated a half million Americans might perish, along with many millions of Japanese. Projected U.S. casualties for the invasion exceeded the U.S. total for the whole of the war thus far in both theaters. With or without atomic bombs, strategic bombing of Japanese cities would continue. In just two days of conventional bombing over Tokyo in early March, 83,000 people had died, more than would perish at either Hiroshima or Nagasaki as a result of the atomic bomb.[119] Subjugation of a powerful nation whose government and armies are determined to resist, even a nation as exhausted by war as Japan, is no trivial task. Russian participation was believed to be essential to conserve American and British lives, which would have meant a political settlement in wartorn Japan replicating the conflict already emerging in Eastern Europe. This is to say nothing of the sacrifices that would be demanded from the British. It could hardly have seemed possible to ask Britain to send thousands of men to die alongside Americans when a weapon that might have ended the war in a matter of days remained unused in American hands.

A number of the scientists affiliated with the Manhattan Project proposed detonating the Bomb in a remote location to which observers might be invited, to demonstrate to the Japanese what might be in store for them while avoiding military use of the weapon.[120] This suggestion, made by men far removed from the harsh responsibilities of waging war and rejected by those scientists, including J. Robert Oppenheimer, charged with advising the government on the Bomb's use,[121] has gained a certain appearance of plausibility in retrospect. But of course such a measure would have entailed risks of its own. The Bomb would be an "absolute weapon" only once. Its strategic value was closely linked to the element of shock and surprise. Could a demonstration have robbed it of this strategic quality? It is worth recalling that the first postwar public demonstration of the atomic bomb on the Bikini Atoll in 1946 left many observers unimpressed; what they witnessed was merely a large explosion; only three of the ninety-seven target ships assembled for the test sank immediately; even palm trees on the island, to observers' surprise, were left unscathed; for a time indeed, "the Bomb" had lost its mystique.[122] The war party in Japan's government was by all appearances unmoved even by destruction of vast sections of Japan's capital by firebombing. How much less might a mere demonstration in a remote location have provided an incentive to surrender? Add to this the fear that any given Bomb might fail to function and that the American arsenal was limited to two such devices, facts that loomed large for Stimson.[123] Had a demonstration failed, whether physically or politically, the United States would confront again the same decision as to whether the Bomb should be used. With American servicemen continuing to die, with the invasion of Japan imminent or underway, it seems possible that the Bomb would eventually have been employed in any event. But now, with the strategic value of the Bomb vitiated by an unsuccessful demonstration, might it have taken not just two Bombs, but three or four or perhaps half a dozen to accomplish the task—and not just Hiroshima and Nagasaki, but Tokyo itself? American historians sent to Japan after the war by the Strategic Bombing Survey concluded that with or without use of atomic bombs or Russian participation in the war, Japan would have been forced to surrender by November 1 or the latest by December 31.[124] More recent scholarship has in fact suggested that this was too optimistic.[125] That the conclusion remains in dispute even today makes even more clear that such knowledge was manifestly unavailable to decision makers at the time. (Indeed, Herbert Feis has written that in the absence of a second explosion at Nagasaki, Japanese rulers would likely "have delayed, perhaps for some weeks, the response which was preliminary to capitulation.")[126] Now, moreover, in the wake of a demonstration, the use of the Bomb would be a matter of public controversy. It is entirely possible that American prisoners of war might have been moved to Japanese cities (fear of such an eventuality was one factor in leading American officials to refrain from offering a specific warning of attack at Hiroshima and Nagasaki),[127] dividing an American public opinion already absorbed for the first time in the dilemmas of a newborn nuclear age. With casualties mounting and a rancorous public debate underway over use of the Bomb, what then would have been American (and Japanese) fortunes in the war?

To dwell on the consequences that might have flowed from such hypothetical alternatives is to understand why Churchill regarded with impatience the postwar supposition that use of the Bomb might have been avoided:

Up to that moment we had shaped our ideas towards an assault upon the homeland of Japan by terrific air bombing and by the invasion of very large armies. We had contemplated the desperate resistance of the Japanese fighting to the death with Samurai devotion, not only in pitched battles, but in every cave and dug-out. I had in my mind the spectacle of Okinawa island, where many thousands of Japanese, rather than surrender, had drawn up in line and destroyed themselves by hand-grenades after their leaders had solemnly performed the rite of *hara-kiri.* . . . Now all this nightmare picture had vanished. In its place was the vision—fair and bright indeed it seemed—of the end of the whole war in one or two violent shocks. I thought immediately myself of how the Japanese people, whose courage I had always admired, might find in the apparition of this almost supernatural weapon an excuse which would save their honour and release them from their obligation of being killed to the last fighting man. More-over, we should not need the Russians. The end of the Japanese war no longer depended upon the pouring in of their armies for the final and perhaps protracted slaughter. We had no need to ask favors of them. . . . The array of European problems could therefore be faced on their merits and according to the broad principles of the United Nations. We seemed suddenly to have become possessed of a merciful abridgment of the slaughter in the East and a far happier prospect in Europe. I have no doubt that these thoughts were present in the minds of my American friends. At any rate, there never was a moment's discussion as to whether the atomic bomb should be used or not. To avert a vast, indefinite butch-ery, to bring the war to an end, to give peace to the world, to lay healing hands upon its tortured peoples by a manifestation of overwhelming power at the cost of a few explosions, seemed, after all our toils and perils, a miracle of deliverance.[128]

Roosevelt and the Historians

The Bomb ended the war. But by no means did it end the struggle against totalitarianism and authoritarian forces. A new conflict was fast emerging whose seeds had been planted in the war years and in Franklin Roose-velt's ambitious and ill-considered diplomacy toward Stalin. The prevailing effort among recent American historians, even those armed with the latest evidence, has been to defend FDR's diplomacy and attempt to counter, or at least to mitigate, the impression that his approach to Stalin was misguided or naive. Such defenses do not hold up to scrutiny. John Lewis Gaddis, in addition to framing his thesis on Roosevelt's attitude toward Stalin with a quotation misleadingly wrenched from context, quotes Roosevelt's April 6, 1945, letter to Churchill to the effect that "our armies will in a very few days be in a position that will permit us to become 'tougher' than has heretofore appeared advantageous to the war effort."[129] But as Warren Kimball has since revealed, White House logs show the letter was drafted by Admiral William D. Leahy, always more of a hard-liner on the Soviets than FDR, and sent at a moment when Roosevelt, drifting in and out of consciousness six days before his death, was probably too incapacitated to have criticized or even read and absorbed its contents.[130]

Gaddis writes: "Roosevelt's priority, to the end, was to win the war: *quid pro quo* bargaining [with the Soviets] might follow but it would not precede that accomplishment."[131] On the contrary, Roosevelt's dealings with Stalin were shaped as much, if not more, by the president's hopes for the postwar world and his plan of enlisting the Soviets in a Concert of Powers (the United Nations Organization) as by wartime considerations. When Roosevelt refused to cooperate in Churchill's efforts to aid the Warsaw Home Army, it was, as much as anything, to protect the negotiations on the United Nations Organization then in progress at Dumbarton Oaks. As shown again and again by his own words, Roosevelt did not engage in quid pro quo bargaining because he did not believe it was necessary. Stalin was "not an imperialist," FDR said. The Soviets had no "crazy" ideas of "conquest."[132] Such was the great irony of Roosevelt's vision: In the name of a universally free and peaceful world, the United States acceded, time and again, to the imposition of tyranny by the Soviets in particular countries.

Likewise, Robert Dallek, in his 1979 book on FDR's foreign policy, rests his case for Roosevelt's partial realism heavily on the contention that FDR decided against sharing the secret of the Manhattan Project with Stalin.[133] But, as has been shown, Roosevelt was perfectly prepared to divulge the secret to Stalin and would probably have done so had not Churchill strenuously intervened.

Indeed, it would be one thing if Roosevelt had pursued the balanced strategy that Gaddis and Dallek postulate—a strategy in which Western desiderata for the postwar world were carefully weighed against the immediate need for wartime Soviet cooperation. But that description fits Churchill's strategy, not Roosevelt's. Roosevelt's approach was something different—an approach of unilateral gestures of goodwill and gifts, shaped by his dream of a Wilsonian world.[134]

It would, of course, be absurd to say that Roosevelt was practicing arms control. But his diplomacy was based on precisely the same premise as those that have underpinned arms control before and since. Roosevelt followed the formula that democratic leaders had followed at Locarno and to which American leaders would revert during later periods of detente: He focused on maintaining the *spirit* of good relations with Moscow while overlooking incongruous and sometimes intolerable *details* of Soviet behavior; he relinquished the right to exert pressure in *peripheral* areas of conflict such as Poland while attempting to build Soviet cooperation on what Americans viewed as the relationship's *core*. This played neatly into the Soviets' hands.

This is not to detract in any way from Roosevelt's wartime leadership at home. Clearly, Roosevelt's powerful charisma helped preserve vital domestic unity and made the war far less contentious within the United States than, under less inspiring leadership, it might have been. However, whether such unity could be sustained only by promoting Wilsonian illusions and shielding the American public from the "disillusionment"[135] of realities in Eastern Europe is open to question. The Wilsonian vision probably had far more appeal among the liberal-minded intellectuals and newspapermen of the East Coast than among the nation as a whole. It is not self-evident that the American public would have rejected a less Wilsonian and more Churchillian approach.

By the same token, none of this is to underestimate the importance of preserving the alliance with the Soviet Union for the duration of the war, including the war in Asia. But whether Stalin had to be dragged unwillingly into the Asian war, as Roosevelt clearly supposed, remains open to question, especially given the Soviet eagerness to snap up Asian territories after the explosion of the atomic bomb.

The suggestions of some recent American historians, meanwhile, that close cooperation with the Soviet Union was possible at an early stage regarding the atomic bomb—if only Americans had been more open, less secretive, and so forth—constitutes nothing less than a massive failure of historical memory, a misunderstanding of momentous political events, and a lack of recognition of just how far Roosevelt went in every other way to accommodate Stalin's desires. If gestures of goodwill toward the Soviet Union would indeed have brought gestures of goodwill in return, then Roosevelt ought to have converted Stalin, if not to a "good democrat," then at least to a dependable friend of the United States. This he never did.

From Wilsonianism to "Containment"

Even under Truman, American officials were extremely slow to face up to the existence of a fundamental enmity between the Soviet Union and the United States. Soviet brutality in Eastern Europe and Moscow's conspicuous lack of cooperation with Washington on a peace settlement following the war brought mounting frustration and doubt. Yet American officials remained reluctant to complain openly of Soviet behavior, fearing both a breakdown of the wartime alliance and a backlash from an American public believed to be pro-Soviet and wedded to Wilsonian, or Rooseveltian, hopes for peace.[136]

However, a kind of turning point came in February and March 1946 (though even after this point the Truman administration would continue to waver to a surprising degree). First, in February 1946, Stalin's "Election Speech" hinted at the possibility of a future war with the capitalist world and openly revived the hostile anti-Western Soviet rhetoric of the 1930s, raising alarms in the United States.[137] Perhaps even more ominously, in the same month it became apparent that the Soviets, having orchestrated a coup in Iranian Azerbaijan, were refusing to withdraw troops from Iran as promised. Oddly, it would be over this distant country, formerly in the British sphere of interest, that the first important Cold War clash, and U.S. Cold War victory, would come. Truman—surprisingly enough, attuned to the complex problems of the Near East, perhaps from his wide reading of history[138]—took Stalin's adventurism in Iran as a particularly suspicious sign. Sharp U.S. diplomatic warnings—Truman later remembered them as an "ultimatum"—would eventually prompt a Soviet withdrawal.[139]

What was needed, however, was a new paradigm, a framework other than Wilsonianism, both to guide American policymakers and to shape a public mandate for a firmer policy. Two pronouncements in February and March 1946, one classified, the other public, would contribute decisively to the establishment of a new approach. The first was the famous "Long Telegram" of February 22 from George F. Kennan, chargé d'affaires of the U.S. Moscow embassy. A primer of sorts on Soviet history and ideology, Kennan's analysis placed recent Soviet actions in the broader context of the Soviet worldview. It revealed the Soviet Union less as a recalcitrant partner to be cajoled into cooperation than as a force regarding itself as fundamentally hostile to the United States.[140]

The second milestone was Winston Churchill's famous "iron curtain" address in early March. Speaking at Truman's alma mater, Westminster College, in Fulton, Missouri, with the president in the audience, the British conservative leader, deliberately recalling his admonitions of the 1930s, dwelt at length on the dark developments in the Soviet sphere. "From Stettin in the Baltic to Triest in the Adriatic," Churchill declared, "an iron curtain has descended across the Continent."[141] The descripiton of Eastern Europe under Soviet domination presented here—the information blackout, police state rule—was in reality little more than a recap of analyses that the British prime minister had been urgently conveying in private letters to American officials since spring; even the phrase "iron curtain" had been used in an earlier communication to Truman.[142] Yet to the American public, Churchill's depiction of Eastern European realities was news.

Though senior Truman administration officials had privately seen and remarked approvingly on advance copies of Churchill's speech,[143] the president immediately sought to distance himself publicly from the British leader's controversial pronouncement[144]—yet another sign of continuing uncertainty in U.S. policy and of the administration's fear of public "disillusionment." Privately, Truman went so far as to invite Stalin to come to the United States and make a statement of his own.[145]

Nonetheless, Churchill's speech, though unpopular,[146] changed minds. Under the influence of Kennan's "Long Telegram" and Churchill's draft address, American officials were for the first time privately acknowledging that the Soviets probably did not intend to cooperate with the United States in the postwar world.[147] Equally important, following Churchill's speech, public opinion changed. First, the American press, which until now had exercised self-censorship in the interest of preserving cooperation with Moscow, began to report more forthrightly on Soviet misdeeds behind the "iron curtain."[148] Second, opinion polls showed a rising suspicion of Soviet intentions.[149]

Nonetheless, in March 1946, the Truman administration was still far from articulating a clear policy of "containment" and still farther from developing a military doctrine or force posture to support such a policy (the latter would come only in 1950, with the formulation of NSC 68). As late as June 1946, the United States went before the United Nations to offer a utopian disarmament proposal—the so-called Baruch Plan, under which the United States offered to relinquish its atomic arsenal and place all atomic energy activities under UN control. Devised by Manhattan Project scientist Oppenheimer, the plan embodied the vision of Niels Bohr. Far from being a mere propaganda gesture, the Baruch Plan was in a sense a last gasp of the Wilsonian or Rooseveltian vision. The idea of "sharing" atomic energy information with the Soviets had been strongly supported within administration counsels by, among others, the outgoing Secretary of War, Henry L. Stimson, and Undersecretary of State Dean Acheson in the fall of 1945.[150] British Prime Minister Clement Attlee had journeyed to Washington expressly to prod Truman toward moves to internationalize atomic energy.[151] Moreover, Truman, having persuaded himself, probably incorrectly, that American interests and the most vital elements of the "atomic secret" could be protected under such arrangements, favored both an exchange of "general scientific" information with Moscow and some form of plan for "international control."[152] However, by the time U.S. representative Bernard Baruch presented the plan to a UN audience at Hunter College auditorium in New York, skepticism of the idea both in Congress and the Executive Branch had grown.[153] And in any event, as it required an intrusive international presence at uranium mines and atomic energy factilities everywhere, including the USSR, the plan was resisted and ultimately rejected by Moscow (but not before the Soviets hinted a number of times at the possibility of acceptance, in an apparent effort to play on domestic divisions over the proposal in the United States).[154]

Time's epitaph on the Baruch Plan, delivered in the same week as Baruch first presented the American proposal, is worth recalling: "When the U.S. promised to destroy its atomic bombs and turn over atomic secrets . . . ," *Time* wrote, "the U.S. was dealing nobly and sensibly—but it was dealing in superficials. At best, this new issue, the atom, could be 'controlled' as well as the old issues of boundaries, and ideologies, and human rights. How far the world of 1946 was from effective control of the old issues was measured by a half dozen wrecked conferences and a score of uncured sore spots."[155] It was indeed the "old" issues, more than the "new" one, that would continue to govern humanity's fate in what was already being called "the atomic age."

CHAPTER 4

Debating the Absolute Weapon

To the degree that the history of arms control has been written at all, it has generally been told as a series of missed opportunities or "lost chances." Roosevelt's failure to take Bohr's advice and reveal the Bomb's existence to Stalin, Truman's initial hesitancy when faced with Stimson's suggestion to approach the Soviets immediately on "international control," Truman's decision over the objections of Oppenheimer and others to proceed with the H-bomb, the failure of the United States to press harder for a multiple-warhead or "MIRV" ban in the SALT I negotiations in the early 1970s—each of these has been taken as a critical turning point in the arms competition between the United States and the Soviet Union. In each case, as various writers have it, a more enlightened policy on the part of the United States—in particular, a well-timed gesture of unilateral restraint—might well have broken the "action-reaction" cycle and in this way circumvented or at least alleviated the arms race that followed.

The prototypical "missed opportunity"—indeed, perhaps the most widely studied and historically debated weapons decision of the nuclear age—was President Truman's 1950 decision to proceed with the hydrogen bomb. It is this tale of "missed opportunity" that has provided the basic model for many of the others, in part because it was understood very much in these terms at the time. The tale in brief: The General Advisory Committee (GAC), the Atomic Energy Commission (AEC), and a group of scientists including Oppenheimer, recommended in the fall of 1949 that the United States not go forward with the hydrogen, or "super," bomb. After an extended debate within the government, President Truman decided in favor of proceeding with the H-bomb, which was finally tested in 1952. Since then, members of the scientific and arms control community have repeatedly argued that a crucial chance was missed to arrive at a new understanding with the Soviet Union and to gain important control over the arms race at this early stage.

There are two reasons why the H-bomb debate is worth examining today. The first is to evaluate, especially in light of recent evidence, the longstanding contention that an American gesture of restraint at this moment would have had a beneficial effect. The second is to understand the roots of American strategic thinking. For in combination with the surprise Soviet explosion of an atomic bomb in August 1949, the scientists' recommendation not to proceed with the H-bomb provided the catalyst for the first truly comprehensive review within the U.S. government of American military strategy for the nuclear age. In order to better understand the H-bomb decision, we will begin by examining the broader strategic debate.

The Soviets Explode the Bomb

The story of the H-bomb debate begins with the end of the American atomic monopoly. On September 3, 1949, an American WB-29 weather reconnaissance plane on routine patrol over the Pacific detected a radioactive air sample near the Kamchatka peninsula in the Soviet Union. Extensive air sampling and analysis over the next two weeks confirmed the troubling and surprising verdict: The Soviet Union had exploded an atomic bomb.[1]

"This probability has always been taken into account by us," Truman assured Americans as he informed them of the Soviet A-bomb test on September 23. But in reality the United States had no plan with which to cope with such an eventuality. In the absence of something more concrete, Truman recommended redoubled efforts for "international control."[2] Yet the consequences of Soviet attainment of an atomic capability were far graver than Truman implied.

The hard truth was that by 1949, the United States had become crucially dependent on nuclear weapons. "I am certain," Churchill had told a New York audience in March 1949, "that Europe would have been communized and London would have been under bombardment some time ago, but for the deterrent of the atomic bomb in the hands of the United States."[3] Even if he exaggerated the immediate threat of war (and who knows how the world would have looked or how Stalin would have behaved in the absence of the American atomic monopoly?), Churchill by no means overstated the importance of the atomic bomb in the American power position. In 1949, in military terms, the United States really had almost nothing else. U.S. troops had been massively demobilized from Europe. Total U.S. armed forces had declined from a wartime high of more than 12 million to a mere 660,000 men. Ships and other equipment had been massively mothballed. Defense outlays had loped along at $13 or $13.5 billion per year for the previous three years (in 1945 they stood at $85 billion).[4]

Over and above the conventional balance, there was an inherent strategic asymmetry between the United States and the Soviet Union, which made the U.S. atomic monopoly a vital counterweight to Soviet power. The sources of asymmetry were several: geography, which placed literal oceans between the United States and its potential allies in Asia and Europe; political regime and culture, which in the United States encouraged extremely rapid demobilization, more rapid than in the Soviet Union, and made a standing army exceedingly unpopular; and political tradition, which in the case of America included an isolationism offering statesmen little support for intervention or involvement abroad.

The whole of the "containment" policy as it had evolved over the previous two years—the Marshall Plan, military aid to Greece and Turkey, the Truman Doctrine—had, in effect, been orchestrated behind the military shield of the atomic monopoly. The Bomb not only provided the presumption of security that permitted U.S. policy to venture assertively into Europe and the Near East; it also seemed to minimize the cost of such commitments by obviating the need to maintain large forces or to send troops abroad.

Nor had the United States failed to count more directly on its nuclear weapons. When Truman protested the Soviet Union's failure to exit Iran in March 1946, he seems to have had in the back of his own mind the American atomic arsenal, as his later imperfect recollections of the event suggested.[5] Certainly, the Bomb contributed to the self-confidence with which the president felt able to oppose Stalin's designs. More obviously, during the 1948 Berlin blockade, the United States had deliberately sent three squadrons of nuclear-capable B-29 bombers to Britain as a warning to Moscow. The bombers no doubt played a role, alongside the American airlift, in the successful outcome of the crisis.[6]

Soviet attainment of the Bomb thus constituted an important shift in the balance of power, a fact that would become all too apparent in Korea within the course of the next two years.[7] It was the Soviet A-bomb that made it seem necessary for the United States to look harder at the possibility of the H-bomb.

Restraining Technology

Even though nuclear physicists had been aware of nuclear fusion since the 1930s, and even though a group of atomic scientists meeting in Berkeley, California, had concluded as early as 1942 that a hydrogen bomb might be possible,[8] as late as September 1949 President Truman still apparently knew nothing of the possibility of a hydrogen, or "super," bomb. In part this was a product of American insouciance about military strategy; in part it was a legacy of the "domestic control" system for atomic energy that the United States instituted after a long legislative battle in 1946, largely at the atomic scientists' behest. Under the 1946 Atomic Energy Act, nuclear energy matters fell under the jurisdiction not of the military, but of a civilian Atomic Energy Commission answerable directly to the president. The president, in turn, was entirely dependent on the AEC for information about nuclear matters. David E. Lilienthal, the AEC chairman, opposed the hydrogen bomb, as did most of the other AEC commissioners and the scientists in the General Advisory Committee, led by Oppenheimer, on whom the commissioners relied for technical advice. As a result, Truman had heard nothing of the idea even at this late date.

In early October, Lewis L. Strauss, the same AEC commissioner who in 1947 and 1948 had pushed for creation of the air detection program that discovered the Soviet bomb test,[9] met with Sidney Souers, secretary to the National Security Council (NSC). Strauss had originally brought Souers, a former navy colleague, to Washington to work for the AEC. Souers had left the AEC for a job working directly under Truman as NSC secretary. The two former navy men shared a traditional military approach to security questions. Over lunch, Strauss asked Souers whether the president was aware of the super bomb. Souers's 1954 recollection of the meeting is worth reprinting:

Strauss looked upon me as a fellow-security man and asked me whether the President had ever had any information on the super-bomb, and if he had,

had he made a decision with regard to going ahead with it. I said, "Louis [*sic*], as far as I know, he has had none, none from me anyway. Can we build one?" He said, "Yes," and I said, "Then why in the world don't we build it?" He said, "Well, I don't think he [Truman] has been informed because [AEC Chairman David E.] Lilienthal is opposed to it.['] I said, "You should certainly see that it gets to the President so that he can get the facts and make a decision." And he said, "I don't think I can since I'm almost alone in the Commission. All the rest are opposed to it except possibly [Gordon] Dean. The General Advisory Committee of the AEC is almost unanimously opposed." I said, "Well, that doesn't matter. You were appointed by the President. You bring it up letting all your colleagues refute what you are going to recommend, and then the President can do what he thinks is best." He said, "You check with the President, anyway." And he added, "If you'll just tell me to go ahead, I'll accept that from you." So I said, "I'll tell you right now, because I know he would want it done."[10]

Souers asked Truman the next morning whether he was aware of the super. The president responded in the negative. "No," said Truman, "but you tell Strauss to go to it and fast."

Souers's recollection indicates two things. First, Truman favored the H-bomb essentially from the beginning. "It was brought to the President," Souers said, "but he didn't have to be influenced. There was no other decision to make but to go ahead. He listened to all the opposition, but I'm tired of reading all these stories where I got him to do it or that Strauss did. Neither one of us could have kept him from doing it. . . . I am sure he had made up his mind from the very beginning."[11] Souers's remarks square with the tone of the account given in Truman's own memoirs.[12]

Second, Truman was almost deprived of the opportunity to make the decision. "If Strauss had not been the nervous, almost hysterical type and fretting about it," recalled Souers, the topic might not have reached the Oval Office. "It might have reposed there [in the AEC] for a much longer time before coming up," he said.[13] Encouraged by Souers, Strauss submitted a memorandum to his fellow commissioners advocating an "intensive effort" on the super bomb.[14] The Strauss memorandum in turn sparked the report from the General Advisory Committee that was to recommend against the program.

The eight scientists who participated in the GAC report offered some technical arguments against the weapon, but their real objection was always moral. The physicists who, in Oppenheimer's famous phrase, had "known sin"[15] were now being asked, in a sense, to sin again—to sanction development of yet another weapon of mass destruction, this one even more powerful than the first. Ultimately, the H-bomb debate bitterly split the community of atomic scientists between those who rallied to Oppenheimer and the belief that the H-bomb should not be built and those who rallied to Edward Teller, who strongly advocated the weapon and contributed decisively to its design.

In principle, Oppenheimer and many of his fellow scientists were not opposed to military use of atomic weapons. On the contrary, they clung to the hope that smaller fission bombs could be developed and used in a militarily discriminate fashion. During the early 1950s, Oppenheimer would actually be a major force in promoting the development of tactical nuclear weapons, in an effort to direct U.S. strategy away from mass destruction and strategic bombing and toward countermilitary objectives. (This would make him enemies in the Air Force.)[16] In the meantime, however, the H-bomb was viewed as a simple weapon of terror. (Only later would it be realized that H-bombs could be made much lighter than A-bombs and therefore mounted on missiles, eventually giving them, as missiles became more accurate, a primarily military role.)[17] H-bomb opponents were therefore not strictly antinuclear.

That the scientists would object to the weapon on moral grounds was understandable. The problem with the GAC report was that in its analysis moral, technical, and strategic issues were mixed together and confused. The report's emphasis on uncertainties about the H-bomb's feasibility, for example, had its source chiefly in the scientists' moral concerns. More important was the strategic question of what the United States would do in the event the Soviet Union developed such a weapon first. To this crucial question the scientists had no answer.[18] Indeed, Oppenheimer told Strauss that he did not care whether the Soviets obtained the H-bomb first. "I would rather be moral," he said.[19] In an annex to the report, six GAC members, including Oppenheimer, suggested unilateral abandonment of the H-bomb as a means of promoting arms limitation "by example."[20]

The Concept of "Minimum Deterrence"

Side by side with the scientists' theme of restraining technology emerged at this time another major strand of thought about nuclear strategy, the view later known as "minimum deterrence." It, too, could be seen germinating in the weeks of the great H-bomb debate of late 1949 and early 1950. The major spokesman for this perspective proved to be the former head of the policy planning staff and author of the "Long Telegram" and the famous "Mr. X" article in *Foreign Affairs* on "containment,"[21] George F. Kennan.

That Kennan would emerge as a major spokesman for an antinuclear viewpoint at this early stage of the Cold War might seem surprising, given his earlier realism about Soviet power. But Kennan combined the diplomat's professional disdain for military affairs with a strong personal revulsion from war.[22] Significantly, his famous "Long Telegram" did not envision any military steps to contain the Soviet Union. Instead it spoke of maintaining "self-confidence," "morale," and a good moral example in the United States.[23] In 1950, even after the Soviet A-bomb test, Kennan thought the entire job of containment could be done with two crack marine divisions.[24]

Kennan's theory of nuclear weapons, meanwhile, appears to have been heavily influenced by Bernard Brodie, whom Kennan had met at the National War College while the two were serving there together in 1946.[25] Brodie's influential theories are worth examining briefly, for they lay in the background of much of the strategic speculation taking place in the Truman administration, as well as behind later theories of "arms control."

"Thus far the chief purpose of our military establishment has been to win war," wrote Brodie famously in his 1946 volume, *The Absolute Weapon*. "From now on its chief purpose must be to avert them. It can have almost no other useful purpose."[26] This statement encapsulated three somewhat distinct conceptions. First, given the inherent destructiveness of even a single nuclear weapon, air defenses would be largely unavailing and offensive retaliation the only effective counter to attack. Second, the inherent destructiveness of nuclear weapons, and the fear of retaliation, would tend to inhibit rather than stimulate aggression (scientists and others had originally assumed that the invention of the Bomb *increased* the likelihood of war.)[27] Third—the point most unique to Brodie—nuclear weapons would obviate the old strategic calculus of military superiority and inferiority. For purposes of simply deterring war, Brodie contended, superior forces would not necessarily be better. All that mattered was that an enemy's society could be destroyed. This disjunction between winning and preventing war, between the logic of war-fighting and the logic of deterrence, would prove central to the development of arms control theory over a decade later. It would provide the rationale for Robert McNamara's abandonment of the goal of strategic superiority.

Yet this was not as new a way of thinking about war as partisans of Brodie's approach later imagined.[28] The main lines of offensive deterrence theory had been worked out in the 1920s and 1930s by strategists such as Gulio Douhet and Air Marshall Hugh M. Trenchard with respect to conventional bombing.[29] As early as 1940, influenced by such thinking, Brodie had portrayed the "military airplane" as a kind of absolute weapon—an "instrument" of "overwhelming destructiveness" that would make winning war obsolete—on the opening page of his doctoral dissertation at the University of Chicago.[30]

Nor was Brodie alone among his contemporaries in applying the logic of deterrence to the atomic bomb. In 1945, the head of the air force, General H. H. "Hap" Arnold, wrote an essay laying out the essentials of deterrence theory. (Where Arnold did not resemble Brodie was in the latter's insistence that relative strength no longer really counted.)[31]

There was precedent, also, for Brodie's notion that strength had become irrelevant. As he wrote in *The Absolute Weapon*, "If 2,000 bombs in the hands of either party is enough to destroy entirely the economy of the other, the fact that one side has 6,000 and the other 2,000 will be of relatively small significance."[32] Yet as early as 1934, Sir Norman Angell of *Great Illusion* fame had written in a book on the air menace of what he called the "unilateral fallacy"—the traditional belief that "if you are armed you are strong, if you are less armed, you are less strong." In the presence of the bomber, Angell argued, such thinking had become "demonstrable nonsense."[33]

Nor was Brodie as categorical about the irrelevancy of strength as was later imagined. The assertion was heavily qualified: Defenses actually could make a difference, as could the relative efficacy of delivery vehicles.[34] To maintain a minimum force would be "poor strategy," if only because numbers would have a psychological impact.[35] Moreover, somewhat contradictorily, Brodie contended that attacks with the "absolute weapon" might have to be followed up with land invasion and conquest of the enemy.[36]

George F. Kennan and "No First Use"

While Brodie in many ways laid the conceptual foundation for a theory of minimum deterrence, therefore, he did not embrace it. That would be left to Kennan and others. Kennan set forth his views in a lengthy memorandum on international control of atomic energy in January 1950, still the classic statement of the minimum deterrence/"no first use" position and important as an influence on those, such as Paul H. Nitze, who would rethink U.S. strategy in the aftermath of the Soviet A-bomb test.

Kennan carried the antinuclear position to its logical conclusion. Not only should the United States not proceed with the H-bomb, he argued, but it should recast its whole strategy, abandoning its posture of heavy reliance on the atomic bomb in favor of a posture of minimum deterrence and no "first use" of nuclear weapons. It should also sound the Soviets afresh on nuclear disarmament or "international control."

Kennan based his argument, ostensibly, on the Clausewitzian understanding of war as a "continuation of politics by other means." As Kennan put it, "warfare should be a means to an end other than warfare." However, the "weapons of mass destruction . . . cannot really be reconciled with a political purpose directed at shaping, rather than destroying, the lives of the adversary." Nuclear weapons, he wrote, would always lend a certain "top-heaviness" to national planning and strategy.[37]

In addition, distrustful of the masses, Kennan was fearful that the American public, agitated by the nuclear danger and misunderstanding the weapons, might force the hand of officials and call for "decisive" action—that is, preventive nuclear war.

Whether the American public, overcome by "war psychosis,"[38] as Kennan put it, would clamor for nuclear war was to be doubted. But there was a more basic flaw in Kennan's line of reasoning. Suppose that the United States chose minimum deterrence and eschewed the H-bomb? What then would be American's relative position vis-à-vis the Soviet Union? "However a commander may be absorbed in the elaboration of his own thought," Churchill once wrote, "it is necessary sometimes to take the enemy into consideration."

Responding to Kennan's memo, Paul H. Nitze, the new head of Policy Planning, focused on precisely this problem. "It must be assumed," wrote Nitze, "that the U.S.S.R. is proceeding" with an H-bomb program. The "military and political advantages" which the Soviets would gain from getting the H-bomb first made "time of the essence," Nitze believed.[39]

While conceding some merit to Kennan's argument for a "no first use" policy and admitting that the American nuclear advantage would eventually be "neutralized" by growing Soviet nuclear capabilities—a theme that would later appear in the strategy document he authored, NSC 68—Nitze noted that the Soviet Union's preponderance of conventional strength necessitated American reliance on nuclear weapons for the time being.

"The two most difficult points to meet," wrote Nitze, "will be (1) what do we substitute for the present presumed deterrent effect of our atomic bomb policy to Soviet military aggression, and (2) in the event of Soviet military aggression, what do we substitute for our present net atomic strategic advantage."[40] In the end, for Nitze, there was no choice but to go forward with the H-bomb.

Truman clearly saw the decision much the same way. On January 31, he directed the AEC "to proceed to determine the technical feasibility of a thermonuclear weapon." Truman's order has been characterized as a "minimal" decision, which avoided or postponed the most important issues.[41] If this was true at all, it was true only of the decision's form, not its substance. Truman signed a document formulated in a manner that permitted opponents of the decision such as Lilienthal to save face, but the upshot of the decision was clear: The United States would proceed with the H-bomb.[42]

The Dangers of Unilateral Restraint

The classic retrospective statement of the case for unilateral restraint on the H-bomb was set forth by Herbert York, one of the scientists who worked on the H-bomb, in his 1976 book, *The Advisors*. York's book, still the most careful and complete statement of the argument, contended that there would have been little risk for the United States in taking the GAC's advice and forgoing research on the H-bomb, that unilateral U.S. restraint might have opened the way for new initiatives in "arms control" with the Soviet Union, and that in any event Soviet development of the super bomb was stimulated by American development of the super bomb, so that the world would have been better off if the United States had delayed its own program.[43] At the basis of York's case was a view of American "technological exuberance" as the essential driving force behind the nuclear arms race.[44]

Yet even on its face, York's case for unilateral restraint seems curious. First, as York himself acknowledged, Soviet work on the H-bomb was underway *before* the internal U.S. government debate and Truman's decision of January 1950. Indeed, the most recent evidence suggests that the Soviets were probably working on the H-bomb as early as 1947 or 1948[45]; Andrei Sakharov's published autobiographical essay tends to confirm this chronology, since he treats the A-bomb and H-bomb as part of a continuous program (that is, there was no Soviet correlative to the U.S. H-bomb debate).[46] In a careful study of the period, David Holloway concluded that "President Truman's announcement did not provide a major stimulus to Soviet work." More crucial for the Soviets, according to Holloway, was the first American H-bomb test in 1952—and Klaus Fuchs's earlier espionage.[47]

Second, the Soviets tested their first H-bomb within months of the first U.S. "super" test. Moreover, unlike the U.S. "Mike" test of November 1, 1952, which involved a huge, multistory refrigeration device, the Soviet "Joe 4" test of August 1953 involved a deliverable bomb. In other words, the evidence is overwhelming that if Truman had not decided in January 1950 to proceed with the H-bomb, the Soviets would have exploded an H-bomb first.

How can York argue, therefore, that unilateral restraint would not have involved risk? York's argument, as it happens, turns on a technical point. The Soviet "Joe 4" bomb, which involved fusion and was therefore a "hydrogen" bomb, was, he contends, not a true super bomb. It was significantly smaller in yield than "Mike" and subsequent U.S. and Soviet bombs designed on the principle developed by Edward Teller and Stanislaw Ulam. "Mike" was 10 megatons while "Joe 4" was still in the sub-megaton range. (York estimates its size as between 100 and 400 kilotons, although according to Soviet premier Malenkov, it was "many times" more powerful than the Hiroshima and Nagasaki bombs.)[48]

Moreover, he points out that the United States had actually exploded a large fission or A-bomb—the so-called "King" shot—just two weeks after "Mike." York estimates the size of the "King" bomb at 500 megatons. In other words, even by the time the Soviets had devised their first H-bomb, the United States, according to York, had already devised a fission bomb of larger explosive power. (The large fission bomb program had been initiated as a hedge against a Soviet H-bomb.) York's point is this: While the Soviets would have exploded a type of H-bomb in August 1953, the United States would have already perfected an A-bomb of greater size. (The Soviets would not explode a "true" super bomb on the Teller-Ulam design until November 1955.) In addition, the United States would have had a larger arsenal of smaller fission bombs to counteract the new Soviet development. In the wake of "Joe 4," a crash American program on the H-bomb could have been instituted. Because of what York predicts would be greater political unanimity among the scientists, and because of improvements in the computer technology, he argues that the H-bomb program would actually have gone faster, and the United States would still probably have beat the Soviet Union to the super.

Somewhat characteristic of a scientist, York confuses the scientific reality with the political one. Scientifically, Joe 4 may or may not have been a true "super" bomb. Politically, however, it was an H-bomb; and at the time it was actually reported in the *New York Times* as having represented a serious advance, *in both yield and technology,* over the U.S. "Mike" shot. (Evidently the real size of the "Joe 4" explosion was not known even by U.S. experts.) The United States was represented as "catching up" with the Soviet lead.[49] To read York is to gain the impression that the "Joe 4" test was nothing more than an inconspicuous scientific milestone on the Soviet road to a true super bomb. This was emphatically not how it was perceived at the time, either in the United States or in the world at large. It was an H-bomb. Soviet testing of an H-bomb so soon after the United States had tested its own such weapon came as a shock to public opinion. Indeed, there was fear the Soviets had hit on a more sophisticated design.[50]

So wild was speculation that President Dwight Eisenhower was forced to issue an order banning public comment on the test from administration officials, unless comments were approved by the AEC. In a press conference on October 8, the president was forced to admit that the Societ Union had developed "a weapon or a forerunner of a weapon" far more powerful than conventional A-bombs.[51] Nor was Oppenheimer particularly helpful in this regard. When British scientists questioned extravagant claims by a Soviet scientist that the Soviet Union had several types of A-bombs and H-bombs, Oppenheimer urged heeding of the Soviet claim.[52]

Given how nervously the United States reacted to the Soviet explosion of an H-bomb *after* Americans had tested one of their own, how much more frightened would the American public have proved if the "Joe 4" explosion had come—as it was bound to come, if Truman had decided differently in 1950—in the absence of an American program to produce such a weapon? The public would have known that the president had decided against producing the H-bomb in 1950. It would now learn that the Soviets had produced an H-bomb of their own in 1953. The fact that the "King" shot might have been larger than the Soviet "Joe 4" shot—if we assume York's estimates are correct—would hardly have been reassuring if it was believed that the Soviets possessed, as Eisenhower said, "a weapon or a forerunner of a weapon" of far greater magnitude.

In short, York entirely overlooks the political repercussions that would have followed from the "Joe 4" explosion in the absence of an American H-bomb program. As we shall see later in our story, in the two other cases where the Soviet Union was able to steal a march on the United States in the nuclear competition—the launching of Sputnik in 1957 and the breaking of the nuclear testing moratorium in 1961—the apparent Soviet lead in military technology, however temporary or illusory, went hand in hand with heightened Western fears and increased Soviet militancy on the world scene. York—and for that matter Oppenheimer and the other scientists of the GAC—had an example of this principle much closer at hand: namely, Soviet international behavior in the aftermath of the USSR's testing of an atomic bomb in August 1949.

Throughout the late 1940s, the world had seen the rise of a European-wide antinuclear or "peace" movement, dominated by Communist front organizations and largely orchestrated from Moscow.[53] Following the explosion of the Soviet A-bomb in 1949, this movement took on a significantly more belligerent character.[54] Indeed, writing in early February 1950, Nitze noted in Soviet policy "a boldness that is essential new" that foreshadowed "a possible use of force in local areas" and a heightened "chance of war through miscalculation."[55] In a meeting with Nitze, New York businessman Alexander Sachs, conjecturing about the Soviet perception of the effect of their A-bomb explosion on the correlation of forces, prophetically predicted new Communist aggression, possibly in Korea.[56] Contrary to York's supposition, therefore, the diplomatic atmosphere was far from conducive to productive negotiations.

The Birth of NSC 68

At the beginning of 1950, hardly five years after the end of the last world war, the storm clouds of war were gathering again, visible to anyone who chose to peer over the horizon. For Nitze, several developments accounted for the Kremlin's increased boldness: the fall of nationalist China, the Soviet Union's consolidation of power over its European satellites, a brewing economic crisis in the West. But perhaps most troublesome and most decisive of all had been the arrival of the Soviet atomic bomb. Not for the first time in the century, a militarily unprepared and irresolute democracy suddenly found itself face to face with a newly strengthened totalitarian foe.

It was in this circumstance that Nitze and the State Department Policy Planning staff embarked on the strategic review that culminated in what is properly regarded as the master document of U.S. postwar strategy, NSC 68.

Volumes of commentary exist on NSC 68, some of it, unfortunately, quite misleading. John Lewis Gaddis's chapter on the document in his widely read *Strategies of Containment* seems particularly wrong-headed. To begin with, Gaddis comments on the Nitze memorandum cited earlier: "The implications were startling. World order, and with it American security, had come to depend as much on *perceptions* of the balance of power as on what the balance actually was."[57] That a diplomatic historian would be startled by the observation that world order depends on "perceptions" of power is troubling. When has the "balance of power" not been based on "perceptions" rooted in often all-too-elusive realities?

Gaddis's specific commentary on NSC 68—which he harshly labels a "a deeply flawed document"[58]—is marked by several such apparent misconceptions. For example, citing Marshall Shulman's *Stalin's Foreign Policy Reappraised,* Gaddis argues that NSC 68 put too little emphasis on opportunities for productive negotiation in 1950. He cites Shulman to show that even while NSC 68 was being drafted, Stalin was supposedly moving "from the doctrine of 'inevitable conflict' to that of 'peaceful coexistence.' "[59] Not only does this observation demonstrate a misunderstanding of the Soviet doctrine of "peaceful coexistence" (which was never understood by the Soviets as incompatible with, but rather as part of, the doctrine of "inevitable conflict"),[60] but it misstates Shulman's argument. Shulman's characterization of the Soviet "peace offensive" of the period is exactly the opposite of Gaddis's: In Shulman's portrayal, Stalin used the theme of "peace" and "peaceful coexistence" not to conciliate the West, but as a weapon of foreign policy, as a tool of, and cover for, hostile action against Western interests. In fact, Shulman presents some evidence to suggest that the 1950 Stockholm Appeal, or the worldwide "ban the Bomb" petition orchestrated by Moscow in that year, may have been deliberately ginned up by the Soviets in preparation for aggression in Korea.[61]

Also, Gaddis's argument that NSC 68 "vastly" increased "the number and variety of interests deemed relevant to national security" seems to be based on a confusion. The expanded definition of interests was not a result of focusing on "perceptions" or taking a suspicious view of the Soviet Union; rather, it was the natural consequence of acknowledging America's role as a great power, as the new guarantor of the balance of power. Given the position of the United States as the only nation capable of counterbalancing the Soviet Union in the international system, a far more robust U.S. military posture was essential.

NSC 68 recommended two main measures: first, improvement of

relative atomic capabilities, including development of the hydrogen bomb, in order to preserve as much as possible of the original U.S. nuclear advantage; second, a major buildup of conventional forces in order to compensate for the ever-declining value of the nuclear advantage and to enable the United States to meet Soviet and Soviet-sponsored aggression with a less-than-nuclear response.

It was this last recommendation that really constituted the heart of NSC 68. It would also define what emerged as the Democratic party's distinctive position in the strategic debate, as it evolved in subsequent decades: an emphasis on a buildup of conventional strength so as to *avoid* the need to resort to nuclear arms.

Behind NSC 68 was an old truth of strategy: that an excess of capabilities would be necessary to underwrite a restrained use of force. The proposed conventional buildup was not a "militarization" of foreign policy, as Kennan believed, but an effort to deter war and to contain violence on a limited, non-nuclear scale if it were to occur. Implicit in NSC 68 was the doctrine of "limited war" that would govern the Truman administration's handling of Korea and that, in a somewhat altered form, would receive a second major test in Vietnam.

At the time NSC 68 was completed, Nitze and the Policy Planning Staff were extremely pessimistic that its recommendations would gain adoption.[62] What they were calling for was nothing less than a major reorientation of national priorities—what later would be deplored as the birth of the "national security state"—but what in the end amounted to little more than an attempt to compete on reasonably even terms with Soviet foreign policy. To have embarked on a major arms buildup before the Korean war might have been to avoid that war; however, this had not been done. By the time NSC 68 was completed, it was probably already too late. At 4:00 A.M. on June 25, 1950, South Korean peasants were awakened, not for the first time, by the thunder of mortar and artillery fire. This time, however, the explosions signaled more than a border skirmish. The first major war of the nuclear age had begun.

CHAPTER 5

□

Staying Out of Vietnam—The Logic of "Massive Retaliation"

Between the problem of deterring a war and the problem of ending one, there is a close analogy. In war, one seeks the enemy's defeat. In deterrence, one seeks to persuade the enemy, in effect, that he is defeated before he has begun. Deterrence may be expensive; but ending a war is vastly more so. That is because in war a nation is forced to begin *proving* over time what, with deterrence, it merely *asserts* in a moment— namely, that the enemy cannot win. It must prove, moreover, the very thing that its adversary has come to doubt—that it has the will and power to avoid defeat. Time is at the heart of the problem. The longer a war goes on, the longer a war is likely to go on. The sooner one can persuade the enemy that defeat is inevitable, the sooner a war is likely to end. If one proves this early enough, war need not begin in the first place.[1] In the end, the key to deterrence in its purest form is much the same as the key to victory itself: the ability to bring decisive force to bear upon the conflict at the decisive moment in time.

The use of the atomic bomb at the end of World War II showed these relationships with unusual clarity. Before the war, it probably would have been sufficient for preserving peace to maintain the American and British fleets at their post–World War I strength in the Pacific. Owing largely to naval arms control, this was not done. Once war was underway, peace could be restored only by the most extensive expenditure of blood and treasure. To marshal forces decisive enough to end the war required literally years of building and fighting, and hundreds of thousands of lives. Even then the result remained in doubt. As late as the summer of 1945, it appeared that Japan's defeat would have to be "proved" inch by inch, much as Germany's had been—through destruction of its fleet, invasion of its territory, decimation of its army, subjugation of its populace, and the final obliteration of its regime.

The atomic bomb relieved the United States of this awesome undertaking, in essence by restoring deterrence. Curiously, the use of the atomic bomb was itself partly deception and bluff. At the time of the Hiroshima and Nagasaki explosions, the United States had only two atomic bombs in its possession. The use of these two bombs in relatively quick succession was designed to convey the impression that the United States had many more.[2]

The Bomb physically achieved a concentration of force in space and time far surpassing what any other human effort could have replicated. The strategy of using the second bomb so soon reinforced this sense of concentration. Finally, the impact of the two atomic explosions on August 6 and 9 was reinforced on August 10 by some of the heaviest conventional bombing of the war and by Truman's threat that, in the absence of surrender, the Japanese "may expect a rain of ruin from the air, the like of which has never been seen on this earth."[3]

This emphasis on concentration and simultaneity was deliberate, and vital. Hardened by four years of fighting, American decision makers were instinctively following the first law of strategy, namely, that forces should be concentrated at the decisive moment to achieve a decisive result. Instinctively, they acted on the principle, in Clausewitz's words, that "all forces intended and available for a strategic purpose should be applied *simultaneously*; their employment will be the more effective the more everything can be concentrated in a single action at a single moment."[4]

It was this concentration of power that helped produce the deterrent effect, the sudden conviction in Japanese minds that Japan was indeed utterly overwhelmed and that defeat—not to say extermination—was certain and around the corner. The effect was deliberate. As Stimson later said, "I felt that to extract a genuine surrender from the Emperor and his military advisers, they must be administered a tremendous shock which would carry convincing proof of our power to destroy the Empire."[5]

Yet in the final analysis, so "easy" was it to end World War II in August 1945 that it was tempting to forget, not many years afterward, just how difficult the ending of a war could be—especially without the luxury of the "absolute weapon" to accomplish the task. This lesson the United States would learn, the hard way and imperfectly, in Korea.

The experience of Korea, in turn, would help to shape the modern theory of nuclear arms control. In the mid-1950s a series of books and articles would appear on the subject of "limited war." Behind these studies would lie the memory of Korea as, above all, a war in which nuclear weapons had, gratefully, not been used. The theory of limited war would grow up side by side with the theory of nuclear arms control. The two bodies of analysis would in effect be conceptual siblings, children of the same broad assumptions about war, peace, and modern weaponry, drawing on each other's strength and reinforcing each other's influence. They would come of age in the 1960s, when together they would begin to define a new policy consensus. But their deepest roots lay in the early 1950s, in the strategic debate before, during, and immediately following the Korean war.

"Limited War" in Korea

It is an indication of the pitfalls inherent in "limited war" that both limited wars fought by the United States in the Cold War period—Korea and Vietnam—were marked by changes in administration and in party. In each case, the party in power when the war began could not maintain public support for the war's duration. This very fact has contributed to the poor public understanding of where these two wars went wrong. Partly because responsibility for their conduct was divided between parties, the analysis of their outcome has been clouded by partisan recriminations.

In the case of the Korean war, the Truman administration (by its customary method of trial and error) eventually settled upon a model of war limitation. But, owing to a variety of circumstances, it was unable to carry this model through to the war's conclusion. This was a critical fact. The Democrats had not ended the war, and consequently they did not think much later about how it had ended. The Korean example, as the Democrats came to understand it, was really a model for a war without an ending. It overlooked the crucial dimension of time. In war there is a natural trade-off between time and intensity of violence. As was evident at Hiroshima and Nagasaki, great intensity of violence can shorten war. But the converse is also true: Limitations on violence tend, almost inevitably, to prolong it. The model of war limitation that emerged among Democratic strategic analysts in the mid-1950s, in the wake of Korea, had much to say about how to limit war but little to say about how to end it.[6] In the long run, this would prove to be a serious drawback.

The paradigm of "limited war" was by no means born whole at the beginning of the Korean conflict. Rather it evolved somewhat chaotically out of the war experience, and particularly out of two major wartime controversies: General Douglas MacArthur's famous dispute with Truman in April 1951 about whether to push beyond the 38th parallel, and the controversy over whether the United States would be willing to employ the atomic bomb.

There is no need here to review the Truman-MacArthur dispute in full detail. Suffice it to say that as fortunes change in war, so, often, do the objectives of the belligerents. When the North Koreans first attacked, the aggression was believed in the West to be the opening wedge in a new world war that would eventually engulf Europe. By early September, the United Nations forces had been pushed back nearly to the sea at Pusan. MacArthur's daring counteroffensive, including the amphibious landing at Inchon, turned these fortunes around. By the end of the month, the UN forces had attained the 38th parallel, and the Chinese and Soviets still had not intervened. Yet having won this much, MacArthur believed, not unnaturally, he could win more. Persuaded to share his confidence, the Truman administration, despite the misgiving of some officials, approved an advance into the north.

MacArthur overreached. As he approached Manchuria, the Chinese did what some had predicted and poured in over the border. Once again the UN forces were driven back; the Chinese and North Koreans took Seoul. Faced with massive Chinese intervention, mired in an emerging stalemate, MacArthur sought, beginning in December of 1950, to persuade Truman and the joint chiefs of staff (JCS) to carry the war beyond Korea and directly to China with blockade and bombardment.

Wishing for obvious reasons to avoid a world conflagration and emphatically lacking the support of America's European allies (especially the British) for a widened war, the Truman administration ordered MacArthur to hold at his present line. When MacArthur wrote a letter criticizing the administration's strategy that was read on the floor of the House of Representatives, he was relieved of his command. Amid the bitterly partisan climate of 1951, the deposed general came home to a hero's welcome. In an address to a joint session of Congress, he pronounced his famous dictum: "In war there is no substitute for victory." Lengthy hearings were held on his dismissal. But in the end, MacArthur's position was rejected—not merely by Democratic officials of the administration, but by many Republicans and by the joint chiefs of staff.[7]

Clearly, it was wise of the Truman administration to reject MacArthur's overly ambitious proposal for a widened war against China. Such a war potentially would have been a world war, whose costs would have been incalculable and for which there would have been no sustained public or allied support. This is not to say that MacArthur's case was without merit. John Lewis Gaddis writes, "What weakened MacArthur's argument was the fact that he was proposing to end the war by escalating it, a cure that seemed to many worse than the disease."[8] But Gaddis overlooks the fact that escalation is the *normal* means of ending war, presuming one is not prepared to accept defeat. Without escalation it is difficult to make war stop. For two years, MacArthur's argument that there was no substitute for victory would remain essentially unanswered, as the Korean war hopelessly dragged on.

In the background of the MacArthur dispute lay a second controversy, over whether to use the atomic bomb. British opposition to a wider war had been established unambiguously the previous November, shortly after the Chinese intervention. The stimulus was a presidential statement concerning possible use of atomic weapons. The Chinese intervention came as a shock to the West. Americans worried about the possibility of World War III.[9] There was even greater panic in Europe. At a press conference on November 30, Truman stated that the United States would "take whatever steps are necessary to meet the military situation, just as we always have." A reporter asked, "Will that include the atomic bomb?" From the standpoint of traditional military strategy, of keeping one's enemy guessing, Truman's answer was the natural and probably correct one: "That includes every weapon that we have." But reporters being reporters, the president was pressed again: even the atomic bomb? "There has always been active consideration of its use," the president said.[10]

The reaction in London was one of anger and anxiety. In part, the British nervousness could be blamed on Labour antinuclearism. But the British protest also was a measure of the Western European sense of vulnerability, for which there was a real basis. In an atomic war, Europeans felt that they, and not Americans, would be the Soviet Union's first target—a not unjustifiable fear considering that the Soviet Union did not yet have aircraft capable of reaching the United States on two-way missions. It was these predispositions and genuine fears that brought Clement Attlee hurriedly to Washington in 1952.

In reality, Attlee had little reason to worry. Key officials in the Truman administration had been indisposed to use the Bomb in Korea from the start.[11] The whole administration approach to such contingencies as

Korea had been set forth quite clearly in NSC 68, which emphasized the desirability of avoiding nuclear weapons use, of meeting Communist aggression with conventional forces.

However, the effect of the Attlee meeting was to bring the issue of nuclear weapons use to a head in such a way that could only weaken the UN war effort. As a result of Attlee's trip to Washington, Moscow and Beijing were clearly alerted to the Truman administration's self-imposed nuclear taboo. In this sense, the Attlee episode removed an important element of American leverage from the conflict and weakened the UN position. It was the Truman administration's misfortune that an important Soviet spy in the British government, David MacLean, was privy to the president's discussions with the prime minister.[12] But even in the absence of MacLean's reports of Truman's definitive assurances to Attlee, Communist leaders might well have sensed, from the circumstance of the meeting and from the tone of the final communiqué,[13] the existence of a real hesitancy regarding atomic weapons on the Western side.[14]

It was ironic that relations with European allies played such a large role in complicating the Korean war, for the most important beneficiaries of Korea were in a sense these same allies. The crucial consequence of the Truman administration's response to Korea was to solidify the line of containment not only in Asia, but in Europe. The war rallied and coalesced the North American Treaty Organization (NATO) alliance (created in 1949 amid the Berlin blockade) in a way that probably no peacetime military or political effort could. The willingness of the United States to come so wholeheartedly to the aid of such a distant and small Asian nation, a country that had even been placed outside the U.S. defense perimeter by the secretary of state only months before the war, lent mountains of credibility to the American promise to defend Western Europe against Soviet subversion and aggression.[15] The war itself, meanwhile, made real the threat of aggression that had only been a mental figment of defense planners like Nitze a few months before. Korea enabled Nitze and Secretary of State Dean Acheson to do what they had wished to do from the beginning but in the absence of war probably could never have been done: to persuade both the allies and Congress to embark on the major buildup of conventional forces envisioned in NSC 68. It was amid the Korean war that Acheson won the "Great Debate" on Capitol Hill, gaining congressional approval, over the howls of the few remaining isolationists, for American troop deployments in Europe.[16]

The Korean war, and the American response to Korea, thus ended the military and political ambiguity that had haunted the postwar world since

August 1945—an ambiguity that left the Soviet Union unnaturally strong and the United States unnaturally weak. The ambiguity had ended, that is, everywhere but in Korea itself.

The Making of a Quagmire

Having dismissed MacArthur and rejected the possibility of a widened war, the administration was now left with the knotty problem of ending the "limited" war it had chosen. This would not prove easy; indeed, the Truman administration would leave office before the job was done. The war had thus far lasted ten months. It was still *two years* away from conclusion. Ironically, nearly two-thirds of the American fatalities suffered in the war—20,000 lives—would be suffered after the decision had been made to "limit" the conflict.[17]

At the time of MacArthur's dismissal, the United States was clearly prepared for compromise. MacArthur had solidified the UN position in the field. In May, UN forces under General Matthew B. Ridgeway were able to capitalize on their position and repulse a North Korean offensive. From the American standpoint, it was an ideal time to begin talking. In congressional hearings on the MacArthur dismissal in early June, Acheson indicated an American willingness to settle at the 38th parallel.[18] Meanwhile, Kennan was secretly dispatched to the Soviet UN representative, Yacov Malik, to broach a deal for a settlement.[19] On June 23, in a UN radio broadcast, Malik offered a public call for a cease-fire. Two days later, Truman responded favorably. Cease-fire talks began in Kaesong on July 10.

But much as defeat of the original Korean offensive had whetted the American appetite for a clearer military victory, so the American desire for a settlement now whetted Chinese and Korean ambitions for victories of their own. The Western desire for compromise was interpreted— correctly—as a flagging of resolve. For the next two years, the Communist forces would use the negotiations to extract as much of a victory in a military and political sense as could be gotten from the war, confident that time was on their side.[20]

By 1952, Korea had become a quagmire, with no end in sight. Indeed, to end the war it would ultimately prove necessary to lift the self-imposed limitations that had defined it as a limited war. In order to create incentives for the Communist forces to settle, the questions of escalating the conflict into China and of using the atomic bomb would have to be reopened. This would require, and would be accomplished by, a new administration.

Democrats, Republicans, and Strategy

It seems to be the fate of two-party democracies that each major party is condemned to possess only part of the truth. In overcoming isolationist opposition from Republicans and vastly expanding both American conventional forces and the U.S. force deployment abroad, the Truman administration and Democratic party had made a critical breakthrough: It had solidified the balance of power. Indeed, it had stabilized the globe. Months and even years after the Truman administration left office, its Republican successors would live comfortably off the capital of this original achievement. Nor, despite the isolationist rhetoric of Republicans during the early 1950s, would the new administration find it advisable or convenient to bring the forward-stationed troops back home.

But, as odd as it seems today, the Republicans in the early 1950s viewed the Truman foreign policy as a succession of defeats. Eastern Europe had been communized, in defiance of Roosevelt's promises of democracy and self-determination. "Yalta" had become a dirty word. China had fallen to Mao. Senator Joseph McCarthy's charges about Communists in the State Department, the Soviet atomic bomb, and above all the war in Korea had all contributed to an air of weakness and stalemate. Today Truman is probably rightly remembered for his effectiveness in foreign policy; in February 1952, his job approval rating stood at 25 percent.[21]

While all the other foreign policy setbacks might have been weathered, the persistence of an unpopular war could not be explained away. The Truman administration was locked in a seemingly inescapable stalemate, over which hung MacArthur's unanswered rebuke: that there was no substitute for victory. Clearly, if there *was* some substitute for victory, the Truman administration had not yet found it.

Of course, the very willingness of the Democrats to engage in such an onerous buildup of conventional forces had been predicated not simply on the Democratic tolerance for large government expenditures but also on a certain distaste for the atomic bomb. NSC 68 was, at a certain level, an expression of moral responsibility, a call for the nation to invest sufficiently in conventional military capability so as not to have to invoke or use weapons of mass destruction to solve its foreign policy problems. This was both a laudable and sensible position, but it betrayed a certain moral hesitancy, a certain irresolution, that a more ruthless enemy might well exploit. In this sense, the Truman administration was handicapped by its own reasonableness and moderation.

Republican criticisms of the Truman administration were exceptionally narrow and mean-spirited, and seem so even today. John Foster Dulles's famous critique of "containment" in *Life* began with complaints about government spending. "The Administration's 'security policies,' " wrote Dulles, "would this year cost us, in money, about 60 billion. . . . Such gigantic expenditures unbalance our budget and . . . discourage incentive [and] . . . cheapen the dollar."[22] All this in the midst of a *war*.

Much has been written about the intemperate Republican rhetoric of the 1952 presidential campaign—the wild talk from Dulles about "roll-back" and "liberation," his immoderate charges that Democrats would "barter away freedom to appease the Russian rulers," the complaints in the Republican platform about "the negative, futile and immoral policy of 'containment' which abandons countless human beings to despotism and godless terrorism."[23] And in the end, when the Hungarian populace in 1956 erred in taking American words about "liberation" seriously, the rhetoric would be exposed as the unfortunate hypocrisy it was. Yet at the same time, Dulles's bluster gave the new administration a certain flexibility and psychological advantage vis-à-vis its Communist opponents that the Truman administration, with its track record of moderation verging on hesitancy, could never have enjoyed. And there is every reason to believe, from his lack of punch as a campaigner, that Dwight D. Eisenhower's opponent Adlai E. Stevenson would have been even more handicapped by an appearance of moderation than the Truman administration itself had been.[24]

Eisenhower's "New Look"

The country was in one sense fortunate that it did not get a Republican administration in the purest form. Eisenhower, unlike Robert A. Taft and many other Republicans, valued what was then called, in a sense quite different from Wilson's original meaning, "collective security"—that is, the structure of alliances and forward troop deployments that the Truman administration had created. Nonetheless, Ike shared Republican attitudes toward fiscal policy. This would lead him almost immediately to search for alternatives to the Truman administration's comparatively expensive policy of forward deployments and contribute in turn to a strategic rehabilitation of the atomic bomb.

Even before Eisenhower won election and began the lengthy strategic review that culminated in the so-called New Look and massive retaliation strategy, the Republicans had already staked out a clearly pro-nuclear position in the strategic debate. Where the Democrats emphasized the need for forward-deployed ground troops, the Republicans, still isolationists at heart, rejected such expensive and "entangling" commitments. It was isolationism in part that led them to argue for greater reliance on air power and (it inevitably followed) the atomic bomb. Behind this outlook lay the familiar Whig preferences for smaller government expenditures and a smaller standing army—as well as the nineteenth-century liberal disdain for alliances.[25] But there was also an element of classic strategy in this viewpoint: the notion that the best strategy was not to react passively but rather to seize the initiative, capitalize on one's own strengths, and exploit the enemy's weaknesses. As Taft wrote in his 1951 book *A Foreign Policy for Americans,* "The first principle of military strategy is not to fight on the enemy's chosen battleground, where he has the greatest strength." Taft, anticipating Dulles's arguments, rejected NATO-style alliances and instead called for a global coalition of the Anglo-Saxon democracies—the United States, Canada, Britain, and Australia—based on superior air force.[26]

Dulles did not follow Taft in rejecting NATO, but he similarly decried the disadvantages of a perimeter defense. "Containment" was too passive, he argued; the United States could not possibly defend a 20,000-mile perimeter; rather, the best defense would be a good offense. "*There is one solution and only one,*" Dulles wrote. "*That is for the free world to develop the will and organize the means to retaliate instantly against open aggression by Red armies, so that, if it occurred anywhere, we could and would strike back where it hurts, by means of our choosing.*" For Dulles, nuclear weapons were, in Churchill's phrase, the "supreme deterrents." The goal should be to rely on them, to create, as Dulles wrote, "a community punishing force known to be ready and resolute to retaliate, in the event of armed aggression, with *weapons* of its choosing against *targets* of its choosing at *times* of its choosing."[27]

From all this it might appear that a new emphasis on nuclear weapons during the Eisenhower administration was foreordained. Yet after taking office, Eisenhower initially resisted the idea, on grounds that it would not conform with the needs of the "collective security," the core of his basically Atlanticist security vision.[28] Instead of massive retaliation, Eisenhower's ideas initially ran more to what today we would call "burden-sharing"—encouraging allies to shoulder a greater portion of the burden of common defense.[29]

But where Eisenhower agreed emphatically with Dulles and the Taft Republicans was in recognizing an "economic" threat to U.S. national security. The new Republican team believed the Soviets intended to wear the United States down economically by tying down its forces around the globe in limited, proxy wars like Korea. George Humphrey, the treasury secretary, summarized the administration's thinking this way: "As he [Humphrey] saw it, the present Administration was engaged in a dual effort to restore a more normal American economy and at the same time to put the nation in a posture of prolonged preparedness, the idea being that this would frustrate Stalin's design of destroying the power of the United States without war through the sapping of its economic health."[30] Or as Eisenhower himself said, "A bankrupt America is more the Soviet goal than an America conquered on the field of battle."[31]

It was partly this economic perspective, combined with Eisenhower's campaign pledge to decrease taxes, that ultimately drove the strategic review toward a nuclear emphasis. Essentially by process of elimination, by exploring and ultimately rejecting other cost-cutting alternatives—major cuts in Mutual Security Assistance, major withdrawals of American troops abroad—the Eisenhower administration finally settled essentially on what Dulles had proposed from the outset: a policy of increased reliance on nuclear weapons and air power, combined with modest cuts in ground and naval forces.[32] Significantly, however, the option of large-scale troop withdrawals had been rejected: The nuclear emphasis had been restored to American strategy, but in the meantime the Truman administration's containment structure remained in place. In this sense, the strategy produced by the Eisenhower administration, known almost interchangeably as the "New Look" or "massive retaliation," was stronger even than that which the Truman administration had sought. Not only was the United States by 1954 a first-class conventional military power, but the nuclear advantage, lost in 1949, had largely been regained.

Nuclear Arms and the Korean War

That the Eisenhower administration was able to end the Korean war a short six months after taking office was owing in no small part to its ability to reinvoke the nuclear threat and raise afresh the prospect of a widened war. In a sense, this change of policy was implicit in its approach to foreign affairs from the beginning. Throughout the 1952 campaign, the Republican party had associated itself with the policy of ending the stalemate and lifting the emerging nuclear taboo, of pursuing a generally more offensive strategy in both Korea and the Cold War. The keynote address at the Republican National Convention in Chicago had been delivered by Douglas MacArthur.[33] While Eisenhower was careful not to endorse MacArthur's views,[34] the public and the world at large had every reason to assume that the new administration planned to undertake more decisive action in Korea than the previous one. Ike's status as a military man reinforced public confidence that decisive steps would be taken.

In its own thinking, meanwhile, the Eisenhower administration seemed to assume essentially from the beginning that achieving peace in Korea would require an intensification of the war. And from the start, the administration searched for a way to use nuclear weapons to achieve a decisive result. Dulles and Eisenhower differed somewhat on the question of an acceptable final outcome,[35] Dulles being far more eager to drive beyond the 38th parallel to the "waist" of Korea in the process of securing a victory.[36] But they agreed on the desirability of using nuclear weapons. At an early NSC discussion of the Korean problem in February, the president suggested that the United States "should consider the use of tactical weapons on the Kaesong area." "In any case . . . ," said the president, "we could not go on the way we were indefinitely." When General Bradley, the chairman of the JCS, expressed reservations about nuclear weapons use, Dulles deplored "the inhibitions on the use of the A-bomb, and Soviet success to date in setting atomic weapons apart from all other weapons as being in a special category." According to Dulles, "we should try to break down this false distinction."

Eisenhower basically agreed with Dulles's view. Nonetheless, on the basis of Bradley's advice, he backed off. If the allies objected to the use of atomic weapons, said the president, "we might well ask them to supply three or more divisions needed to drive the Communists back, in lieu of use of atomic weapons." Still, Eisenhower agreed that the subject of "military plans and weapons of attack" should not yet be raised in Allied consultations.[37]

Dulles raised his idea of an expanded war with Anthony Eden, the British foreign minister, during the latter's visit to Washington in the first week of March. Perhaps somewhat surprisingly, Eden expressed no objection in principle to Dulles's idea and merely stressed the British desire to be kept informed.[38]

Meanwhile, the administration took the initial steps toward escalating the war. In February, bombing of North Korea was intensified. In early March, General James van Fleet, recently retired as commander of the Eighth Army, publicly urged "limited" use of nuclear weapons.[39] Then on March 17, the United States tested a 15-kiloton prototype of a tactical nuclear weapon in Nevada. On March 18, the picture of the blast cloud was spread across the front page of the *New York Times*.[40] Three days later, retired Admiral William H. P. Blandy was reported as having urged nuclear weapons use in Korea.[41] Behind the scenes, the JCS issued a top-secret report calling for "reevaluating the policy which now restricts the use of atomic weapons in the Far East."[42]

Early March also brought what would prove an extremely fortunate development for the new administration. On March 5, Stalin died. Stalin's death would plunge the Soviet leadership into a protracted crisis. To preserve its power position, as well as to assuage its own lack of self-confidence, the new leadership would embark almost immediately on a policy of reconciliation abroad and at home. Signals of new desire for détente with the West were fast in coming. On March 15, Georgi Malenkov, the new premier, stated that there was no issue between the Soviet Union and the United States "that cannot be decided by peaceful means, on the basis of mutual understanding."[43]

On March 28, perhaps not coincidentally, came the first important breakthrough in truce talks in six months—a letter from North Korean president Kim Il Sung suggesting acceptance of a previous UN proposal for an exchange of sick and wounded prisoners. Two days later, in a radio broadcast, Chinese premier Chou En-lai softened the Communist position on the key outstanding issue of the talks—the Communist demand for forced repatriation of prisoners. Similar conciliatory statements came from Molotov on April 1.[44]

On March 31, Eisenhower took up the subject of Korea again with the NSC. Perhaps because of the hopes raised by the new Communist proposal, the discussion reflected a clearer sense of the pros and cons of the situation, both with regard to expanding the war and with regard to using nuclear weapons. If the United States chose to pursue "a sound tactical victory" in Korea, said the president, the Communists would respond and the United States "would be forced ultimately into a situation very close to general mobilization." Bradley agreed. Again Eisenhower thought nuclear weapons might be the answer. The president acknowledged that "there were not many good tactical targets." But, he said, it would "worth the cost" if "through use of atomic weapons, we could (1) achieve a substantial victory over the Communist forces and (2) get to a line at the waist of Korea." Notably, he saw nuclear weapons in part as an *alternative* to full-scale conventional escalation. At any rate, despite the hopeful signs in the talks, the outlook was not yet clear. The possibility clearly remained, as Eisenhower's special assistant Robert Cutler noted, that the Communists could, as in the past, drag "out their proposals for perhaps a period of three months" with no armistice in prospect. There was common ground in the administration on the potential benefits of employing nuclear weapons. The "President and Secretary Dulles were in complete agreement," the minutes showed, "that somehow or other the tabu which surrounds the use of atomic weapons would have to be destroyed."[45]

Eager to avoid reentry into stalemated talks, Eisenhower resolved to avoid a broader negotiation until Communist good faith could be tested by a prisoner exchange. Meanwhile, planning continued for a widened war. The NSC Planning Board developed six options of increasing intensity, labeled from "A" to "F," with "A" being maintenance of the status quo and "F" a full-scale effort, including bombing attacks on China, to unify Korea.[46]

When the full delegations of the two sides met in Panmunjom for the first time in many months on April 6, there were signs that the trade of sick and wounded prisoners would go smoothly. Settlement had therefore become a real possibility.

Three crucial problems, however, remained. The first was to decide on final U.S. war aims. Did it make sense now merely to accept the existing armistice arrangement, which the present administration had criticized? Or should the United States seek more?

The second problem was America's South Korean ally. As it became apparent that the United States would settle for an armistice and partition of the country, South Korean president Syngmann Rhee, still desiring a unified Korea, would become increasingly intractable.

The third problem, perhaps the key to them all, was to prevent the armistice talks from dragging on until the U.S. position deteriorated again and the war continued: to prevent a recurrence of stalemate.

On the first issue, Dulles and Eisenhower were divided. The secretary of state continued to press his favorite notion of a drive to the waist of Korea. In the end he was overruled by the president.[47]

The handling of Rhee proved more delicate. It demanded a letter from Eisenhower and extremely careful attention on the part of General Mark Clark throughout the truce talks. Rhee threatened to continue fighting and, later, in a bold move designed to derail peace talks, would release North Korean prisoners unilaterally.[48]

But the basic problem of actually ending the war remained. The success of "Little Switch," the exchange of sick and wounded, had raised great hopes during April (even if it did expose conditions in Communist prison camps as utterly appalling). Unfortunately, when negotiations reconvened on April 26, the hopes were shattered. The North Korean representative, Nam Il, proposed an impossibly unreasonable formula for prisoner exchange. It demanded placement of prisoners in a neutral country for six months. During this time, representatives of their governments would be free to attempt to convince them to return. After six months, a political conference would be convened to decide on the ultimate fate of the prisoners. Not only did such an arrangement leave prisoners in limbo, but there was obviously no guarantee that the international conference in question would ever be convened. The smell of stalemate was again in the air.[49]

At this point the administration's willingness, in principle, to escalate the conflict paid off. At an NSC meeting on April 28, George Humphrey recommended that Eisenhower begin a rapid force buildup in Korea to show resolve to wage a widened war. Eisenhower was not yet ready to embark on a real buildup, but wondered whether a deception could be orchestrated. Dulles, reverting to characteristic gamesmanship, codified Humphrey's logic. It "was certainly clear to him," said the secretary of state, "that we were much more likely to get a suitable armistice out of the Communists in Korea if they did not calculate that we were desperately eager to obtain one."[50] This was the kind of thinking generally missing from the Truman administration's approach to strategic matters.

At an NSC meeting in early May, Bradley made clear that an ersatz buildup of the kind the president had proposed was not really possible.[51] At a meeting the following week, General John E. Hull argued for the impracticability of tactical use of nuclear weapons. The weapon tested for the purpose (the Nevada shot) had produced an effect "as of an earthquake" and might not do the job against the entrenched Communist forces.[52]

Eisenhower had pushed the idea of deception or tactical use of nuclear weapons in large part as an alternative to major escalation of the war. Throughout this time Eisenhower remained acutely conscious of the costs of a widened war, especially in relations with U.S. allies. At an NSC meeting on May 13, Acting Secretary of State Walter Bedell Smith urged contemplation of alternative "F"—an all-out war to unify Korea. Eisenhower's response showed a candid understanding of the limits on U.S. policy imposed by the attitudes of the allies:

> The President replied that the simple truth of the matter was that many people in the European countries believe that global war is much worse to contemplate than surrender to Communist imperialism. To many of them there was simply nothing worse than global war, for the reason that it would amount to the obliteration of European civilization. We desperately need, continued the President, to maintain these outposts of our national defense, and we do not wish our allies to desert us.[53]

Nonetheless, in late May, the president proved to be willing in principle to broach the risk. In order to escape the danger of further stalemate, the administration decided to put forward a final offer in the truce talks. In the event of Communist rejection of the plan, the UN commander was instructed to break off the talks and widen the war. On May 20, Eisenhower conditionally approved a JCS plan for major intensification of the war, including large-scale offensive operations and air-atomic attacks on China. The plan, which would require roughly three months to mount, would, conditional upon reexamination, go into effect after the break-off of the truce talks.

It is important to recognize that Eisenhower made this conditional decision with open eyes. The plan ran the risk of Soviet entry in the war, not necessarily confined to China or Korea. Eisenhower's "one great anxiety," he said, was "the possibility of attacks by the Soviet Air Force on the almost defenseless population centers of Japan." That, said the president, "was always in the back of his mind." In addition, Eisenhower fully recognized the bad reaction that such a widened war, involving nuclear attacks, would be likely to arouse among U.S. allies. He resolved nonetheless to attempt to prepare allied opinion for nuclear weapons use. "If the ground were prepared and the seeds planted in a quiet and informal way," said the president, "there was much better chance of acceptance than if we suddenly confronted the allied governments with a full-fledged plan to end the war in Korea by military decision."[54]

The key to securing peace in the next few weeks would be to convey to the enemy U.S. resolve seriously to widen the war. A broad effort was made, through word and deed, to convey the seriousness of the U.S. intent to Pyongyang, Beijing, and Moscow. U.S. allies were informed of the decision to present the final offer.[55] In addition, as Eisenhower later wrote in his memoirs, direct and indirect signals were sent to the Communist world.[56] Clark was explicitly instructed to present the new U.S. offer as a final offer at the truce talks. Dulles, on a visit to India, told Prime Minister Jawaharlal Nehru of U.S. plans to widen the war in the event of no settlement, and assumed his remarks would be relayed to the Chinese.[57] Bohlen in Moscow called on Molotov and informed him of U.S. intentions to widen the war in the event of a new stalemate in the negotiations.[58]

Two points should be made here. The United States was careful to craft its position so as not to have it appear as an "ultimatum"; the final offer did include a concession—in particular an agreement to turn over Korean as well as Chinese prisoners to the Repatriation Commission composed of neutral nations, and to permit the disposition of prisoners by majority rather than unanimous vote. Essentially the message was this: The United States truly preferred a settlement but insisted upon an immediate end to the conflict and was entirely willing to escalate the war massively in the event a settlement was refused. It offered an incentive to settle in the form of a "sweetener"; but the bottom line was the threat of a widened war.

The U.S. position was reinforced by some of the heaviest ground fighting of the war, in particular the terribly costly battle for Pork Chop Hill; by scores of Central Intelligence Agency (CIA)–organized raids across the Formosa straits in the Chinese mainland; and—perhaps deliberately—by the testing of the first operable atomic artillery shell on May 25. At the Bermuda Conference in December 1953, Dulles also recalled that in May the United States "had already sent the means to the theater for delivering atomic weapons. This became known to the Chinese through their good intelligence sources and in fact we were not unwilling that they should find out."[59] Finally, in a radio address to the nation on defense policy just days before the truce offer, Eisenhower spoke of the virtue of "modern weapons" in increasing the destructive capabilities of air power. Today, said the president, "three aircraft with modern weapons can practically duplicate the destructive power of all the 2,700 planes we unleashed in the great break-out attack from the Normandy beachhead."[60] The remarks were not calculated to reassure the Chinese.

Following the May offer, progress in the peace talks was rapid, and the truce was signed on July 26. The Korean war was over.

The Debate over Eisenhower's Nuclear Threat

In recent years a "neorevisionist" school of Cold War historians has attempted to discount Eisenhower's testimony—and Dulles's similar statement only months after the war's end—that willingness to use nuclear weapons played a crucial role in ending the Korean war. Controversy has focused on two issues: (1) whether explicit nuclear threats were made, as the president and his secretary of state indicated, and (2) whether American threats were the crucial factor in ending the war or whether it was rather the death of Stalin.[61]

To some degree, this controversy has been marked by tunnel vision. Following McGeorge Bundy's 1984 assertion that a nuclear threat had probably not been perceived by the Chinese, scholars embarked on a more careful search of the diplomatic record. As it happens, the search has turned up a fair amount of evidence to support the view that Beijing received some nuclear signal.

But might it not simply have been the death of Stalin—combined with the sheer cost of the war—that fundamentally changed Chinese policy in Korea? That is Bundy's contention. In 1984, he wrote categorically, "The decisive shift in the position of the Communists, a shift away from insistence on the forced repatriation of prisoners, occurred before any of these [nuclear] signals was given, shortly after the death of Stalin in March."[62] Significantly, by 1988, he had softened his position. A more complete review of the evidence led him to argue merely that it "seems probable" that "the *most important* Chinese decisions came before the *most important* American signals."[63] So there were signals of the possibility of nuclear weapons use even before the Communist concessions of late March.

But the search for specific nuclear "signals" misses the larger point. The decision of the Soviet leadership to pursue détente after the death of Stalin did not occur in a vacuum. It occurred in a climate in which the military balance had shifted against the Soviet Union. By 1953, the United States really was the superpower that it had rapidly ceased to be following the end of World War II. More important, détente arose in a climate shaped by the Eisenhower administration's promise to lift self-restraint and move to the offensive in the struggle with Communist forces. "Instant retaliation," "rollback," "liberation"—all posed new threats that the shaky new leadership under Malenkov was understandably eager to defuse. Dulles, notes Adam Ulam, "long a *bête noire* of Soviet publicists," was "by the same token treated by them with a respect not accorded to his Democratic predecessors."[64] In short, the imperative for détente arose precisely from the potential aggressiveness of the new administration, precisely from its new attitude toward escalating conflict and using nuclear weapons.

In an effort to play down the nuclear element of the threat, Barry Blechman and Robert Powell note that "Dulles, like Eisenhower, perceived atomic weapons as simply one of several elements of the strategic arsenal."[65] But that is precisely the point. In contrast to the Truman administration, which accepted a major distinction between the two kinds of weapons, the Eisenhower administration sought both operationally and diplomatically to encourage the idea that, as Eisenhower put it during a discussion of Korea, "we have got to consider the atomic bomb as simply another weapon in our arsenal."[66]

Moreover, Bundy's argument notwithstanding, the fact that Moscow had decided to pursue a more conciliatory line in late March did not of itself guarantee a quick end to the war. On the contrary, Nam Il's new positions on prisoner exchange on April 26 made it clear that the Communist side was still willing to delay the endgame, to play for whatever advantage it could derive. As late as mid-May, the Communists had rejected the UN position on prisoner exchange. Side by side with the negotiations, meanwhile, was an intensified psychological warfare campaign, involving loudspeaker broadcasts over no man's land to erode the morale of American troops.[67] The basic Communist strategy remained the same: one of psychological attrition, of erosion of the enemy's will. How long would the Communist side have been willing to permit talks to drag on before it settled—weeks, months, half a year? The point was that the Eisenhower administration's own time was limited. The "honeymoon" phase of the administration would last only so long. In the late spring and summer of 1953, major expansion of the war was still an option. With public support eroding, in time this option would be gone. As Richard Betts has noted in a careful study of the Bundy argument, the chronology of the closing negotiations supports the idea that the late May threats had an important effect.[68]

There is a final point. If one accepts the (entirely reasonable) proposition that Stalin's death made it easier for the new Soviet leadership to end the war, a new question arises: namely, what would the United States have had to do to end the war if Stalin had lived? In such a case, mere threats might not have been sufficient. Under such circumstances, it seems altogether possible that the planned major escalation of the war, involving use of nuclear weapons, might actually have been carried out. In short, with or without the passing of Stalin, the basic form of the problem of ending the war remains the same.

"Massive Retaliation" and Indochina

Having ended one "limited" war, the administration was understandably eager to avoid getting into others. Indeed, to avoid such limited conflicts gradually became a major theme of its policy, for the peculiar mix of economic and strategic reasons we have described. To avoid such wars meant to deter them, to deter them meant, in a sense, to end them before they began—to apply *in advance* the same deterrent principle that the administration believed it had successfully applied to end the war in Korea. That, in the simplest terms, was what Dulles was trying to do in his famous "massive retaliation" speech of January 12, 1954. Dulles's speech was an effort, as it were, to institutionalize the deterrent principle responsible for the Korean war settlement. Moreover, his speech was timed, as Michael Guhin notes, to influence upcoming Berlin negotiations on that second limited war of the early 1950s—Indochina (Vietnam).[69]

The basic themes of Dulles's January 12 address were no different from those of the "Policy of Boldness" article in *Life*. It was essential to achieve security "without exhausting ourselves," said the secretary of state, without risking "practical bankruptcy." "This can be done," he continued, "by placing more reliance on deterrent power and less dependence on local defensive power." "Local" defenses, said Dulles, were not unimportant; but they must be "reinforced by the further deterrent of massive retaliatory power." The secretary declared: "The way to deter aggression is for the free community to be willing and able to respond vigorously at places and with means of its own choosing."[70] "In Korea," Dulles noted, the administration "effected a major transformation" through a threat of escalation. The enemy "was faced with the possibility that the fighting might, to his own great peril, soon spread beyond the limits and methods which he had selected."[71] The speech included a warning on Indochina:

"I have said in relation to Indochina that, if there were open Red Chinese army aggression there, that would have 'grave consequences which might not be confined to Indochina.' "[72]

Perhaps no speech by an American secretary of state has ever been so controversial as this. Whole schools of thought arose in the 1950s in reaction *against* the Dulles speech. To some degree, nuclear arms control theory itself was a product of the reaction against "massive retaliation."

The major objection to this policy was that it seemed to threaten world war every time there was even low-level Communist aggression. As Acheson tersely put it, "If it is said, as it sometimes has been, that we cannot afford another war like Korea, the answer is that such a war is the only kind that we or anyone else can afford. Only a madman would attempt to avoid it by plunging into the unspeakable disaster of a world war."[73] There was merit to Acheson's point. But Acheson presumably did not realize how close Eisenhower had been compelled to come to threatening world war in order to bring an end even to "limited war" in Korea. William W. Kaufmann, another Dulles critic and a leading Democratic strategic writer, noted, "Korea was a tragic and painful experience; with its 137,000 casualties, it scattered suffering and grief throughout the country. But even so, a hundred Koreas would still be cheaper than an American-Soviet exchange of atomic and hydrogen blows."[74]

But would a limited war really be in any sense "cheap"? In a sense the answer would come only years later, in Vietnam. But ironically, it was in Vietnam—or as it was known at the time, French Indochina—that the massive retaliation doctrine faced its first real test.

Interestingly, Indochina was widely portrayed by Dulles's critics as a failure for the massive retaliation doctrine—a verdict that has been accepted, rather uncritically, by later commentators.[75] In fact, this judgment probably rests on a too-narrow reading of what Dulles was attempting to achieve. On the surface, the outcome in Indochina might well have seemed a failure. The United States was unable to use nuclear weapons to avoid a military defeat for the French (though there is a report that Dulles in passing offered French foreign minister Georges Bidault "two A-bombs" to rectify the situation at Dien Bien Phu—whether facetiously or not we will never know).[76] Nonetheless, when one looks at the Indochina negotiations as a whole, it is evident that the United States was able to derive significant diplomatic leverage from the uncertain threat that its superior strategic air forces might be brought into play.

Indeed, viewed from a distance of decades, the 1954 solution in Indochina seems considerably better than the West had any right to expect. Going into the Geneva Conference of 1954, the Western bargaining position could hardly have been weaker. The French, having suffered humiliation at General Vo Nguyen Giap's hands at the battle of Dien Bien Phu, were losing heart in the imperial struggle and eager for a negotiated solution. The British, partly out of national jealousy (having lost India, Churchill was not about to help France keep Indochina), partly out of mercurial temperament (the aging Churchill, once a great warmaker, harbored dreams of ending his career as a great peacemaker),[77] and partly out of fear of atomic warfare (Dulles described the British as "almost pathological in their fear of the H-bomb")[78] adamantly resisted any U.S. plans to intervene in the struggle.

At the same time, Eisenhower, while generous with aid to the French, refused to commit American troops, except on roughly the Korean model. He would intervene only in the context of an allied plan for "united action," in concert with the British, French, and Asian forces. Eisenhower had three concerns. First, he was worried about the loss of moral stature that would follow from lone U.S. support of an old "imperial" power in its struggle against a colony. Second, the president was reluctant to put American prestige on the line in a struggle that might not be winnable and could easily escalate. Finally—a major theme of massive retaliation and the New Look—he was extremely reluctant to brook the economic, political, and human costs of committing U.S. ground troops to another Korea.[79] He did not want another "limited war." Dulles and JCS Chairman Admiral Arthur W. Radford were more ready to intervene, and air strikes in support of the French were seriously contemplated, but Eisenhower remained reluctant to put U.S. prestige on the line.[80]

Despite all this, in 1954 the Chinese agreed, in effect, to restrain Viet Minh leader Ho Chi Minh from undertaking what he was clearly in a military position to accomplish: forcible unification of Indochina under Communist rule.[81] Instead, China consented to accept "half a loaf"[82]—a partition of the country into North and South Vietnam. To be sure, this solution held within it the seeds of future conflict. Yet for a time, at least, the Scylla and Charybdis of full communization of Vietnam and large-scale American troop involvement were avoided. (Under different policies, in later years, we would have both.)

How was the 1954 settlement achieved? Part of the key actually lay in the massive retaliation speech—combined with a series of deterrent threats orchestrated by Dulles during the spring Geneva talks to keep alive in Soviet and Chinese minds the thought that the United States might ultimately intervene in the struggle. Recent historians have increasingly come to admire Eisenhower for his unwillingness to become involved in Indochina, contrasting his policies favorably with those of the Kennedy and Johnson administrations toward Vietnam.[83] At the same time, the massive retaliation strategy is still basically decried as part of the "bad" side of the Eisenhower administration's policies. What historians have tended to overlook is that these two policies—massive retaliation and staying out of Vietnam—were intimately connected. The former was precisely the means of achieving the latter. Precisely by reestablishing the connection between the core of American strategic power—air power and nuclear weapons—and the peripheral conflicts of diplomacy and military policy, the Eisenhower administration was able to benefit from the overall American power position and achieve more decisive results. In effect, the massive retaliation threat prevented the communization of Indochina in 1954.

Dulles's contemporary critics vastly underestimated the impact of his massive retaliation speech in the Communist world. The conventional wisdom of the time was that Dulles's speech had disturbed the allies more than Moscow or Beijing. In the words of the London *Economist,* "The result has been frighten America's allies more than to impress the Communists."[84] Only later in the decade was the impact of the massive retaliation pronouncement on Communist calculations fully documented. By then it had become clear to the American analyst who studied the Soviet reaction most closely that Dulles's speech had in fact caused substantial anxiety in Moscow as well as Beijing.[85]

While the contrast between Dulles's hard-line massive retaliation address and Eisenhower's softer "Atoms for Peace" speech a few weeks later figured in the internal struggle between Malenkov and Nikita Khrushchev, the basic theme of Soviet analysis of massive retaliation was that "the United States would refuse to settle local conflicts, in order to use them as a springboard to larger conflicts."[86] The analysis was applied, as Dulles presumably hoped it would be, specifically to Indochina, where the Soviets doubted the Americans were sincerely seeking a settlement. Ironically, at a time when foreign and domestic pressures were mounting in Washington against intervention,[87] and when the Eisenhower administration was treating intervention only as a reluctant last resort, Moscow began to assume that the United States was actually prepared to impede a diplomatic settlement in Indochina in order to gain the opportunity to intervene.

Dulles did his best, against all odds, to keep such an impression alive. In September, following the Korean armistice, he had warned that Chinese intervention in Indochina would lead to an American involvement that carried the war into China itself. In the massive retaliation speech, he reiterated his September warning. In part because of angry allied and domestic reaction to the massive retaliation address, he was forced to backtrack. On March 19, he stated categorically that the massive retaliation policy had "no application" to Indochina. But he had never implied use of nuclear weapons against the Viet Minh forces; he had only implied use against China in a widened war.[88] That possibility had still not been foreclosed.

On March 29, in his Overseas Press Club speech, Dulles formally spelled out U.S. policy on Indochina. The heart of that policy was the statement that imposition of Communist rule on Southeast Asia as a whole would constitute "a grave threat to the free community." "The United States feels," said the secretary, "that possibility should not be passively accepted, but should be met by united action."[89] The "united action" formula answered to Eisenhower's desire not to go it alone; but it also introduced a certain ambiguity into American policy. Everything now appeared to depend on the consent and resolve of U.S. allies.

Throughout the spring—as the Geneva Conference began its work— the United States performed a precarious balancing act, attempting, first, to assuage the British, who had no desire to intervene on the French behalf, were (probably rightly) skeptical of U.S. military plans, and feared global war; second, to buck up the French, who were demoralized in the struggle and hoping for unilateral rescue from the United States, which the president proved reluctant to supply; and finally, amid all this, to keep alive in Soviet and Chinese minds the prospects of American intervention in the event Indochina as a whole fell to Communist rule. In April, the U.S. aircraft carriers *Essex* and *Boxer* were dispatched to the South China Sea for maneuvers, a provocation duly and angrily noted in the Chinese press.[90] As weeks passed, Dulles issued a series of implicit warnings, usually couched in the diplomatic formula of "united action"; at the same time, he left the Geneva Conference never to return (Undersecretary of State Bedell Smith stayed behind), helping to convey the impression that the United States was not particularly eager for a settlement. The whole U.S. effort was nearly derailed by a British defection. Anthony Eden bitterly disagreed with Dulles's approach, believing a more conciliatory line in the conference would be more productive and help pave the way to a broader détente with the Communist world. The split between Britain and the United States, aggravated by intense personal acrimony between Eden and Dulles, approached crisis dimensions. But in June, when Eden and Churchill went to Washington to mend fences, Dulles and Eisenhower managed to get a private agreement on terms for a partition and at the same time a joint communiqué that seemed to indicate, despite previous tergiversations, that London would support intervention in the event the Geneva Conference failed to reach the right sort of agreement.[91] The following month, the Chinese met the French deadline and agreed to a partition. Despite his disagreements with Dulles, Eden later recognized the value of the nuclear threat. "This was the first international meeting at which I was sharply conscious of the deterrent power of the hydrogen bomb," he later wrote.[92]

We should be clear that there were limits to the utility of this deterrent threat. Dulles's massive retaliation pronouncement, as his critics rightly pointed out, did nothing to deter the Chinese from providing Ho Chi Minh with the wherewithal to defeat the French at Dien Bien Phu. (Dulles himself gave the Chinese no reason to believe that the defeat at Dien Bien Phu would necessarily spark American intervention.) As with Korea, hard-headed military analysis showed the many problems and risks of full-scale military escalation. Nonetheless, events in the spring of 1954 indicate clearly enough that the continuing, implicit possibility of large-scale American intervention helped shape the final settlement in a manner beneficial to the West. Caution in Moscow, born in large part of the massive retaliation threat, played a key role in encouraging Beijing in turn to restrain its Viet Minh ally and settle for partition. As always, there were other factors at play in the Chinese decision to accept the Geneva settlement—in particular, Beijing gained an appearance of international legitimacy from acting as guarantor of a diplomatic settlement; but this minor victory would hardly seem to have compared with the triumph for Chinese foreign policy of expelling the "imperialist" West entirely from Southeast Asia, were that possible. At any rate, the failure of the Chinese to permit the Viet Minh to complete a conquest that would have been in relatively easy military reach in 1954 would be difficult to explain in the absence of a restraining influence. Diplomatic histories of the era attribute Soviet and Chinese willingness to compromise in substantial part to worries about potential American involvement.[93] In short, a restraining influence was provided by American power and, ultimately, American strategic superiority.

Nor in this case either was the Eisenhower administration simply bluffing; military action was seriously contemplated and planned for, including conventional bombing on behalf of the French, the possibility of sending one division of marines, and contingency plans for using atomic weapons to counter direct Chinese intervention[94]; but given the actual attitude of the British toward intervention and Eisenhower's insistence on allied cooperation as a precondition for any U.S. involvement, American power in this instance may indeed have been something of a "paper tiger."

Much as Dulles tried to codify the Korean achievement in the massive retaliation speech, so he tried to codify principles behind the Indochina victory—as well as the administration's success in a 1954 confrontation with China over the islands of Quemoy and Matsu—in an interview with James Shepley in *Life* in 1956. Dulles, Shepley wrote, "believed that he had isolated one of the major underlying causes of war: in a word, miscalculation." War, Dulles told Shepley, generally originated from "miscalculation" by an aggressor who underestimated his victim's capabilities or will to resist. "All the great wars of modern history," Dulles was convinced, "were started by national leaders who thought they could get away with it."[95] To prevent war, therefore, one must demonstrate resolve and be able to outbluff one's opponent. "You have to take chances for peace just as you must take chances in war," he told Shepley. "The ability to get to the verge without getting into the war is the necessary art. If you try to run away from it, if you are scared to go to the brink, you are lost."[96] Thus was born the term "brinksmanship."

What is interesting is the degree to which later testimony from the Communist world indicated that Dulles's tactic had succeeded. Years after Geneva, Chou En-lai commented to James Reston that the Chinese "were very badly taken during the first Geneva Conference."[97] To this we may add Khrushchev's own remarkable tribute to Dulles. "Dulles," Khrushchev wrote, "was a worthy and interesting adversary *who forced us either to lay down our arms or marshall some good reasons to continue the struggle.*" According to Khrushchev, "It always kept us on our toes to match wits with him."[98] Also in *Pravda* in 1961, Khrushchev recalled: "There was a time when American Secretary of State Dulles brandished thermonuclear bombs and followed a 'positions of strength' policy with regard to the socialist countries. . . . That was barefaced atomic blackmail, *but it had to be reckoned with at the time* because we did not possess significant means of retaliation, and, if we did, they were not as many and not of the same power as those of our opponents."[99] In short, Khrushchev openly admitted the effectiveness of the massive retaliation threat—even though, as he later pointed out, Dulles "proved more than once that he really didn't want war."[100]

"Brinksmanship" versus "Limited War"

The reaction in the Communist world to "massive retaliation" was one of admiring and worried accommodation. The reaction in the West was another matter. "Brinksmanship," like "massive retaliation," became a term of derision in the late 1950s. Throughout the decade, the emerging generation of "defense intellectuals"—soon to take the reins of power—heaped scorn upon the supposedly crude and unsophisticated methods of the secretary of state. Among the best and brightest minds of the strategic community, the sense was almost unanimous that Dulles simply failed to understand the realities of the modern world. In a world with nuclear weapons on both sides, the intellectuals pointed out, threats of massive retaliation were both inappropriate and dangerous. The world had changed. As Bernard Brodie wrote, "The ultimate argument in diplomacy has usually been the threat of force, but now the penalties for the use of total force have become too horrible." Instead, declared Brodie, "we must be ready to fight limited wars with limited objectives." Korea was to become the model for a "limited war."[101]

Brodie's disciple William W. Kaufmann, who was to emerge in the early 1960s as a McNamara aide in the Pentagon, was among several theorists to elaborate a theory of "limited warfare" in the mid- to late 1950s in opposition to the strategy of "massive retaliation." In a pair of elegantly written essays in 1956, Kaufmann heaped subtle scorn upon the simplistic notions of the benighted Dulles. The massive retaliation bluff, Kaufmann contended, was both incredible and dangerous. "An examination of our recent diplomatic record, and indeed of the course of American foreign policy during the past fifteen or twenty years, suggests that it is quite out of character for us to retaliate massively against anyone except in the face of provocations as extreme as Pearl Harbor."[102] Communist leaders knew this, Kaufmann insisted. What was more, such threats might actually get the United States into a nuclear war. U.S. policy had to be more reasonable, less provocative, more appropriate to the realities of a nuclear age.

Kaufmann devised a systematic strategy for limited war in which nuclear weapons would be held in abeyance on both sides while fighting was conducted in the limited fashion analogous to eighteenth-century set-piece battles. The key was proportionality, balance, and signaling one's willing self-restraint to the enemy. Especially in the nuclear age, Kaufmann contended, "American policy" should "exhibit a high degree of reasonableness" as a way of lessening the chances of a nuclear war.

Instead of being, as Dulles envisioned it, the first line of defense, nuclear capability should be, Kaufmann argued, only "a last resort." The challenge was "to find deterrents that forecast costs sufficient to discourage the enemy, but not provocative to make him turn, out of fear and desperation, to contingencies of the last resort." Restraint in war would thus breed restraint. "We must, in a word," wrote Kaufmann, "try to fit the punishment to the crime."[103]

To the degree that that was possible, Brodie, Kaufmann, and like-thinking limited war theorists sought to remove nuclear weapons from the power equation. They did not advocate "minimum deterrence." But they championed a strategy where nuclear weapons would not actively be considered part of the preparation for war. On the basis of the Korean experience, the limited war theorists were confident that war could be insulated from strategic capability and conflict could largely be deterred by conventional weapons alone. As Kaufmann wrote, "If we show a willingness and ability to intervene with great conventional power in the peripheral areas, after the manner of Korea, we will have a reasonable chance of forestalling enemy military action there."[104] If war came, the response could be proportionate, graduated, designed so that the punishment would fit the crime. Nuclear weapons would remain in the shadows; to a great degree the nuclear taboo would be restored. How would wars end? One would depend upon the "cost-consciousness" of the enemy. As Kaufmann wrote: "The basic assumption for this kind of conflict—and it is one that appears to correspond accurately with reality under existing conditions—is the assumption of a calculating individual with a multiplicity of values, aware of cast and risk as well as of advantage, and capable of drawing significant inferences from symbolic acts."[105] Such was the new, more sophisticated vision of the Communist enemy.

The concept of limited war would develop side by side with the theory of nuclear "arms control" proper: Both, in effect, would be efforts to remove nuclear weapons from an active role in warfare, to arrive at a stable nuclear "balance" or stalemate, which could provide a stable context for diplomatic and military conflict to continue on a more limited and restrained scale.

Much as the concept of arms limitation itself grew from a misunderstanding of the origins of World War I, so the ideas of limited war and nuclear arms control proper owed something to a basic misunderstanding of the end of the war in Korea. Dismissing the massive retaliation statement as so much blather by an unenlightened man, Dulles's critics failed to heed the factual part of his message: namely, that nuclear weapons, and the renewed willingness of the United States to make use of them, had been a major factor in discouraging Communist aggression and stabilizing the world situation in 1953. The failure to learn this lesson would prove costly. For the Eisenhower administration, a declining stomach for the rigors of massive retaliation and brinksmanship would set the stage for the beginning of a fresh deterioration in global stability and the opening of a new era of crises. As for the evolving theory of limited warfare, its moment of truth was awaiting. The sophisticated new theories of conflict devised in the 1950s would not receive their real test until a decade later—in the jungles of Vietnam.

From the Geneva Summit to *Sputnik*

For all the controversy surrounding it, the policy of massive retaliation therefore brought a certain stability to the world scene. But this stability would prove to be short-lived. Confrontation would soon give way to détente, which would pave the way in turn for another period of confrontation.

Indeed, throughout the postwar era, relations between the United States and the Soviet Union would tend to follow this cyclical pattern—confrontation yielding to relaxation, relaxation yielding in turn to confrontation again. Two tendencies conspired to produce this repetitive cycle. On the Soviet side, a key factor was the tactical oscillation in Soviet foreign policy between open aggression and Leninist "peaceful coexistence."[106] When the balance of power shifted against them, the Soviets, more or less following prescriptions laid down by Lenin in the early 1920s,[107] usually responded by becoming outwardly less aggressive and more accommodating toward the West. However, as the balance began to shift back in their favor, they resumed open confrontation. On the American side, meanwhile, the cyclical alternation was reinforced by a certain tendency to mismanage success. Washington repeatedly achieved a favorable balance of power vis-à-vis Moscow—opening the way to international stability and détente—only to squander its advantage, dissipating its power and paving the way to new crises. A central role was played in this pattern by arms control.

So it was in the mid-1950s. Having achieved an initial stabilization of the world scene through an assertive nuclear deterrence doctrine, Eisenhower, partly adapting to public worries about nuclear weapons (inspired by hydrogen bomb tests as well as by Dulles's massive retaliation rheto-ric),[108] partly expressing his own idealism, became increasingly preoc-cupied with the hope of achieving an arms limitation agreement.[109] The Soviets, for their part, worked actively to soften and diffuse the solid front of Western resistance that their own earlier aggressiveness had provoked. In 1955, partly hoping to stall the rearmament of West Germany, partly seeking a general relaxation of tensions, Moscow surprised the world by voluntarily withdrawing its troops from Austria. The Austrian State Treaty paved the way in turn for the first post-war "summit meeting," bringing Eisenhower and British and French leaders together with Niko-lai Bulganin and Khrushchev in Geneva. (The metaphor of a meeting "at the summit of nations" was coined by Churchill in a May 1953 speech alluding to Edmund Hillary's attempt on Mount Everest, then in progress.)[110]

The 1955 Geneva summit was a short-term public relations success for the United States. Eisenhower's surprise "Open Skies" proposal—a call for mutual opening of air space to reconnaissance flights so as to build "confidence" for arms limitation agreements—gave the United States the propaganda initiative.[111] Arms limitation talks were subsequently intensi-fied. (It was in this era that one saw the first rare casual uses of the phrase arms control, in response to a new emphasis on "limited" or "partial" measures of disarmament.)[112]

But the shift in Eisenhower's focus from arms to arms control did not necessarily serve the goal of stability or Western security in the long run. Amid the new contacts between U.S. and Soviet leaderships and the general relaxation of tensions, the massive retaliation threat rapidly lost its mystique and much of its deterrent value. Eisenhower himself meanwhile became more and more preoccupied with arms control and less and less receptive to efforts designed to press the U.S. arms effort forward. (Min-utes of NSC meetings and other discussions show Eisenhower repeatedly exhorting his advisors to greater effort on arms control and repeatedly complaining about the cost of both the ballistic missile and the earth satellite programs—attitudes with fateful consequences.)[113]

Soon the administration that had cowed or bluffed the Communist world into relative quiescence found itself on the defensive and subject to Communist bluffs. On November 5, 1956, at the height of the Suez crisis, Khrushchev engaged in a first act of open nuclear blackmail, implicitly threatening Britain and France with missile attack (raising the prospect of a "third world war") if intervention against Egypt con-tinued.[114] Almost simultaneously, the Soviets were moving to crush with tanks the anti-Soviet revolt in Hungary. Then on October 4, 1957, the Soviet Union launched the first man-made satellite into space: *Sputnik*.

The shock to American sensibilities caused by *Sputnik* could hardly be overestimated. To the surprise of Americans and the world, the Soviets had bested the United States in the most conspicuous aspect of the technological race. At the same time, the ability of the Soviet Union to put a 184-pound object into orbit lent frightening credibility to an earlier Soviet claim that the USSR had successfully tested an intercontinental ballistic missile (ICBM).[115] The American nuclear guarantee, long perceived as the basis of Western security, was called into question, and America itself appeared vulnerable as never before.

Sputnik dealt a tremendous blow to American scientific and military self-confidence. Public fear and anxiety about U.S. vulnerability to nuclear attack quickly spread. Across the world, the Soviet achievement called into question the whole balance of power: The period of presumed American military preeminence, born in the wake of the Korean war and sustained under the doctrine of massive retaliation, now appeared to be at an end.

The "Missile Gap"

The launching of *Sputnik* marked the beginning of a new phase of the Cold War—of a sustained and coordinated Soviet campaign of strategic deception and nuclear intimidation, aimed at bringing about a significant change in the international status quo.[116] During this era Khrushchev brazenly emphasized Soviet nuclear capabilities against NATO; whole countries would be "put out of commission" or "wiped from the face of the earth."[117] It would be a period of the most severe crises, focused particularly on Berlin, stretching over five years, and ending only at the apparent brink of war in a clash over Soviet missiles in Cuba.

Following *Sputnik,* United States Information Agency (USIA) polling abroad would begin to register a growing European perception that the Soviets had gained military ascendancy over the United States.[118] A similar perception would come to dominate in the United States. In reality, the specter of Soviet strategic superiority remained an illusion throughout these years. Soviet missile capabilities would never equal Soviet claims; as late as 1961, the Soviet Union would have deployed no more than *four* operational ICBMs, while by 1962, the United States would have fielded a formidable missile force of its own.[119] Yet owing largely to the effectiveness of Soviet disinformation, and in no small part to the ineffectiveness of Eisenhower's response to the *Sputnik* challenge,[120] Moscow would convince much of the world of what soon came to be known as the "missile gap." By resisting widespread citizen calls for a redoubled U.S. defense effort, biographer Steven E. Ambrose has written that Eisenhower "saved his country untold billions of dollars and no one knows how many war scares."[121] Dollars may have been saved; war scares, however, were another matter. The atmosphere of apparent unchallenged Soviet military preponderance would in fact bring some of the worst war scares of the Cold War: Berlin in 1958 and 1961, Cuba in 1962. So profound was the loss of national self-confidence in the presence of the "missile gap" that by the end of the 1950s, it would even be commonly questioned whether the United States could compete with the Soviets *economically* over the long term.[122] Not for the first or last time in the Cold War, the military balance would stand in the popular mind as the visible symbol of the relative viability of the two competing systems.

Buoyed by their apparent missile superiority, the Soviets also became more assertive on the disarmament front. In March 1958, after concluding a major series of nuclear tests, the Soviets declared a unilateral moratorium on nuclear testing.[123] Having overtaken Eisenhower in the missile race, Khrushchev now sought to outflank the United States in disarmament. Behind in the missile competition (of which nuclear testing was an important component), but placed on the propaganda defensive by the sudden Soviet gesture,[124] the United States was compelled by the following August to reciprocate and embark on a moratorium of its own.

Ironically, the commencement of talks on a nuclear test ban in October 1958 was followed four weeks later by Soviet initiation of the Berlin crisis—showing the lack of intrinsic connection between ostensible progress in arms control and global stability. Indeed, the intensification of arms control activity after 1955 had gone hand in hand, for whatever reason, with a noticeable decline in world stability and a perceptible increase in Soviet aggressiveness.

Within the testing talks, meanwhile, the Soviets consistently resisted meaningful measures of verification. ("Inspectors criss-crossing around the Soviet Union . . . would have discovered that we were in a relatively weak position," Khrushchev later wrote.)[125] Initially, the United States insisted upon strict measures of inspection.[126] But over time the U.S. position eroded—a process hastened by arms control–minded scientists brought into the government in a consultative role by Eisenhower, ostensibly to assist in rebuilding America's technological and military strength.[127] Scientists on the President's Science Advisory Committee offered far rosier estimates of the verifiability as well as the military impact of a test ban than were accepted by military and Atomic Energy Commission authorities (or even some outside scientists such as Edward Teller).[128] At the same time, the scientists competed increasingly openly with military officials for influence with the president on defense matters. (In August 1960, George Kistiakowski, presidential science advisor, actually excluded the defense secretary and the chairman of the joint chiefs from a presidential briefing on limited war, on the grounds, in Kistiakowski's words, that the briefing concerned "weapons technology rather than strategy and tactics.")[129]

By 1960, spurred partly by the scientists and partly by his own idealistic hopes, Eisenhower was prepared to accept a comprehensive test ban treaty with what many defense-minded observers—and even, at one point, the *New York Times*—regarded as insufficient verification (that is, a ban on tests over 4.75 on the Richter scale with a limited and as yet undetermined number of visits to inspect "suspicious" seismic events, combined with an uninspected "moratorium" on tests under 4.75).[130] Perhaps only Khrushchev's opportunism, and the mishap of the Soviets shooting down an American U-2 spy plane, prevented a treaty. Khrushchev chose to unveil the U-2 shootdown at the May 1960 Paris summit in a manner designed to embarrass Eisenhower, disrupting the meeting, and souring relations for the balance of Eisenhower's term.[131]

Eisenhower had viewed disarmament or arms control as a means of charting a way out of the Cold War conflict.[132] The Soviets, by contrast, following Lenin's well-known advice,[133] had tended to treat arms control as just another weapon in the political struggle. To be sure, aided by the appeal of disarmament, and underwritten by the shock of *Sputnik,* the Soviet blackmail and propaganda offensive of the late 1950s was only partially successful. Certainly, Khrushchev did not succeed in dislodging the West from Berlin; on the other hand, the United States remained on the military and propaganda defensive for the remainder of the decade.

In truth, there was only one final source of "stability" in U.S.-Soviet relations, and that was the relative military power and self-confidence of the United States. Until that power had been rebuilt and American strategic preeminence reestablished, there was little chance of productive agreements of any kind. In this sense, the most important contribution to global stability was taking place not in the test ban negotiations or the summit talks, but offstage, in the steady and increasingly rapid buildup of the modern American missile force. The fruits of this buildup lay in the future. Not until 1960 would the first Atlas missiles come into the American inventory. The first Polaris submarine, carrying 16 missiles, would leave on patrol in November 1960. A power shift was in the making, as the American missile force grew; but growth was gradual, and to establish American strategic preeminence unambiguously in the world's eyes would require more crisis and confrontation. After the recovery of American strength, an atmospheric test ban treaty would actually become possible. Until that moment arrived, arms control was not so much a part of the solution as part of the problem.

CHAPTER 6

□

The Cuban Cauldron

Perhaps even more than most new administrations, John F. Kennedy and his advisors came to office in 1961 supremely confident that they understood the world better than their predecessors and would be capable of doing a decisively superior job of running the country's affairs. Eisenhower, so it was assumed, had presided over a do-nothing, ineffectual presidency. The American economy, once robust, was in recession;[1] perhaps more important, in the coming administration's eyes, American culture was marked by a tired conformism and a vague sense of malaise (although the razor-slim margin of Kennedy's popular-vote victory suggests that some of these dissatisfactions were more prevalent among academics and intellectuals than among the general public). Abroad, the power and prestige of the United States—undercut by the perceived "missile gap" with the Soviet Union—seemed in retreat. Clearly, it was time, in the words of Kennedy's famous campaign slogan, to "get this country moving again."

The long slumber of the Eisenhower years (so it was regarded by Kennedy's advisors) had of course provided Democratic intellectuals with ample time to reflect, ample opportunities to outthink and second-guess the administration, to spin new theories and conceive new designs. Despite a surface conformism, the 1950s had actually been a period of rather intense intellectual ferment, particularly in the universities, where the modern social sciences were just coming of age. At institutions of higher learning such as Harvard and MIT and "think tanks" such as RAND, a new vision of politics was taking shape. Armed with seemingly powerful new methodologies such as econometrics and game theory, American political scientists and experts were reopening and reanswering a host of age-old political and strategic questions, reinventing politics almost from the bottom up. The Kennedy-Johnson years would be full of illustrations of attempts to implement this bold new analytic approach to political matters.

But perhaps in no realm was the revolution of thought more conspicuous or consequential than in the field of nuclear policy and national defense. The 1950s had seen a flurry of writing and debate about nuclear weapons and national strategy. Two major themes had come to dominate Democratic reflection on these issues: "limited war" and "second-strike deterrence." Of the two, limited war was the elder and more established conception. We have already seen its origins in NSC 68.

The second important theme of Democratic strategic thought was that of second-strike nuclear deterrence. The theory of second-strike deterrence had grown up at the RAND Corporation during the 1950s under the influence of such figures as Brodie, Kaufmann, Albert Wohlstetter, Herman Kahn, and later Thomas Schelling.[2] Brodie had set forth most of the key elements of the conception in his essays in *The Absolute Weapon* in 1946, but the 1950s had witnessed a major intellectual effort leading to the formalization of the idea into something of a rigorous theoretical paradigm. Wohlstetter's studies of Strategic Air Command (SAC) base vulnerability[3] played a central role in this, as did the application of game theory to the deterrence problem. In essence, second-strike deterrence theory reduced the problem of nuclear strategy to the technical problem of maintaining an invulnerable retaliatory force of sufficient size to inflict unacceptable damage on an enemy even after absorbing his first strike. The theory differed from ordinary strategic or military thinking in two key respects. First, under this theory, military strength per se became less of an issue than the degree of vulnerability. A very strong strategic force that was vulnerable to preemption would provide far less security than a somewhat weaker force that was *invulnerable* to preemption. As Wohlstetter set forth in a 1959 *Foreign Affairs* article called "The Delicate Balance of Terror," the key to deterrence lay not in the overall size of the force but in the size of the force that could survive an enemy first strike.[4] Second, deterrence theory as elaborated at RAND taught that a preemptive or first-strike strategy was inherently provocative and dangerous— especially if both sides pursued it. Given the inherent horror of global nuclear war, the RAND theorists reasoned, the only likely reason for unleashing such a conflict would be the conviction that it was already inevitable. However, if both sides possessed forces that were catastrophically exposed to preemption, each in a crisis would have a powerful incentive to strike the other first. Nuclear war was therefore most likely to come by "accident," owing to mutual incentives for preemption, much the way World War I was—incorrectly—believed to have begun.[5] To prevent such incentives from arising, it was necessary that one side, and preferably both sides, make a significant portion of its forces invulnerable to the enemy's first strike. In this way, the benefit of striking first would be overwhelmingly outweighed by the cost. The Kennedy team signaled its new outlook by speaking of U.S. "strategic *retaliatory* forces."

One important corollary of second-strike deterrence theory was the theory of "arms control." The stress on invulnerable second-strike forces had led to a further thought: Could negotiations be used to help bring about such "stabilizing" forces on both sides? Schelling, an economist who had studied the general problem of international negotiation from the standpoint of game theory, was a pioneer of this approach.[6] As he and other adherents saw it, arms control was a fundamentally new way of thinking about disarmament. Arms control negotiations would be used not necessarily to *reduce* forces—indeed, in some cases reductions could be dangerous—but rather to help achieve "stable" configurations of forces (that is, secure second-strike capabilities) on both sides. The motivation for such negotiations, the arms controllers reasoned, would be the two sides' mutual interest in avoiding the catastrophe of nuclear war.

Between arms control theory and limited war theory, meanwhile, there was a close kinship. Indeed, as defined by Schelling and his coauthor Morton Halperin in the authoritative book on the subject, the conception of arms control explicitly included limited war. As Schelling and Halperin understood them, both were forms of implicit *cooperation* between enemies with the common goal of averting total war—the ultimate disaster in the nuclear age. What justified hopes for arms control was, in the authors' words, the "recognition" that the "military relation" with "potential enemies" was "not one of pure conflict and opposition," but involved "strong elements of mutual interest." These mutual interests consisted "in the avoidance of a war that neither side wants, in minimizing the costs and risks of the arms competition, and in curtailing the scope and violence of war in the event it occurs."[7]

Such cooperation required an all-encompassing change in the approach to war—and not merely nuclear war itself, but conventional war involving nuclear-armed belligerents. Arms control, as envisioned by Schelling and Halperin, would include "all the forms of military cooperation between potential enemies in the interest of reducing the likelihood of war, its scope and violence if it occurs, and the political and economic costs of being prepared for it."[8] Arms control included not only efforts to limit conventional war but methods of limiting nuclear war. Schelling envisioned the use of "bargaining pauses" between limited uses of nuclear weapons in order to signal a desire to bargain. "Cooperation" would thus extend even into thermonuclear conflict.

By bringing together the concepts of limited war and second-strike deterrence, arms control theory in effect synthesized and systematized the Democratic strategic vision. It also legitimated disarmament negotiations to an unprecedented degree. Notably, teachers of international affairs in universities during the 1950s had not taken disarmament particularly seriously. A leading book on the subject in the early 1960s emphasized the so-called gamesmanship—propaganda and diplomatic maneuvering—involved in disarmament negotiations.[9] It was part and parcel of the Kennedy group's intellectual optimism and idealism their faith in the sheer power of theory—that they believed they had discovered something fundamentally new that could be implemented smoothly in the real world, that they had found a way to make disarmament work.

As the 1950s drew to a close, the new doctrine of arms control won numerous converts in the Democratic camp. Paul Nitze, the author of NSC 68 and probably the major Democratic spokesman for the virtues of strategic nuclear superiority, became something of an adherent, announcing his tentative conversion in a speculative speech at a conference in Asilomar, California, in 1960.[10] Likewise, having largely dismissed the prospect for disarmament in his *Nuclear Weapons and Foreign Policy* in 1957,[11] Henry Kissinger became an attendee of Schelling's arms control seminar in Cambridge and wrote a favorable article on arms control for *Foreign Affairs* in 1962.[12] Indeed, nearly all the first-rank defense and foreign policy officials and consultants of the Kennedy administration had been exposed to arms control theory by the time they joined the administration, either through RAND in Santa Monica or Schelling's seminar in Cambridge. (RAND analysts and Cambridge academics were plentiful both in Robert S. McNamara's Pentagon and the Kennedy White House.) As one Kennedy-Johnson official later remarked, "Everybody was into arms control in those days."[13]

The common element behind this Democratic vision, whether in the earlier version of limited war or the newfangled theory of arms control, was a profound concern with nuclear weapons—a conviction that in the nuclear era, war and military realities had fundamentally altered or must be altered. The prevailing Democratic attitude toward nuclear weapons and toward the relation of those weapons to diplomacy and military conflict was essentially the opposite of that which Dulles had put forward in his massive retaliation address. Insofar as was possible, the Democrats sought to segregate nuclear weapons from diplomacy and even conventional military conflict; they accepted, nay embraced, the inevitability of nuclear stalemate. They sought to establish a firmly stable nuclear "balance" as a context in which lesser conflict could be conducted in a restrained and essentially *cooperative* manner between the two sides.

Yet in reshaping the image of war and negotiation, the Democrats arrived at what in many respects amounted to an unstrategic or astrategic understanding of war and strategy. The limited war/arms control paradigm claimed to preserve the Clausewitzian principle of subordinating means to ends—the concept of war as a continuation of policy. But the new theory completely dispensed with the equally vital Clausewitzian principle of victory as a product of the maximum *concentration* of forces in space and time. That, if anything, was a principle more central to classical strategy even than the notion of relating ends to means. Certainly, the advent of nuclear weapons made the concept of maximum concentration force and therefore of victory itself deeply problematical. Nonetheless, it could be argued that an account of war that excluded the category of victory, as the Schelling-Halperin model essentially did, was no longer truly a description of war proper but of some other kind of conflict. To exclude the concept of victory was not only to beg the question of what should be the purpose of war but ultimately, perhaps, to open the way to defeat. And while it might well be agreed that enemies did in some narrow senses "cooperate" during a war, surely the element of cooperation was overwhelmingly subordinated to the element of conflict. Indeed, what difference was there between war and peace if not that during war conflict was in the ascendancy? Part of the appeal of these theories lay in their novel, counterintuitive character. But that would prove to be precisely their drawback in practice.

From the start, the Democrats showed little hesitancy in recasting national security policy and implementing their new ideas. In the course of the next two decades, this new theory of war and conflict would manifest itself in two major policy initiatives. The two initiatives would develop in tandem and reinforce each other. They would be undertaken by many of the same people. They would produce, in certain respects, somewhat analogous results. One initiative was the origin of strategic arms control and the other was the war in Vietnam. The roots of both could be found in arms control theory—and in a new and misplaced confidence in this theory growing out of the Kennedy administration's interpretation of its experience in the Cuban missile crisis.

Theories and Reality

The main outlines of the Democratic strategic vision were already visible in a memorandum prepared for the president by McGeorge Bundy, the new national security advisor, just days after the new administration took office. The memo cited a "most urgent need" for a comprehensive "review of basic [national security] policy." Bundy pointed, in particular, to policies of the previous administration which, as he wrote, "in the view of *nearly all your civilian advisers* place a debatable emphasis (1) on strategic as against *limited-war* forces, (2) on 'strike-first,' or 'counter-force' strategic planning, as against a 'deterrent' or *'second-strike'* posture, and (3) on decisions-in-advance, as against decisions in the light of all the circumstances."[14] Here was precisely the Democratic formula for strategy that had evolved in the 1950s: limited war, second-strike deterrence, and multiple "options."

To this must be added the president's own special interest in counterinsurgency and guerilla warfare. Kennedy was deeply impressed by Khrushchev's January 6, 1961, address on wars of "national liberation,"[15] which he believed encapsulated Khrushchev's new strategy for the Cold War.[16] Guerilla war and counterinsurgency, Kennedy believed, would be the new front line of the East-West struggle. The young president was eager to meet this challenge. The area of most immediate concern was Laos, where, as Eisenhower had warned Kennedy upon leaving office, Communist guerilla activity was on the rise.[17] In February, Kennedy told the joint chiefs that he wished "to have the maximum number of men trained for counter-guerrilla operations put into the areas of immediate concern" in Southeast Asia and mentioned particularly operations in "Vietminh territory."[18] He also pressed the chiefs for an expansion of "special forces"[19] (Green Berets—as they were later known—and the like) within the services.

When one adds Kennedy's faith in counterinsurgency to the notions of limited war and stable second-strike deterrence, the recipe begins to look familiar. It would certainly be an exaggeration to say that the Vietnam war with all its problems and errors was already implicit in the

Kennedy administration's strategic vision of 1961. Yet between the failed policies of the Johnson years and the ambitious new strategic theories with which the Kennedy administration arrived in office, there was a clear connection.

Signs of certain weaknesses in the new administration's approach to defense and foreign policy, moreover, began to appear early on. Today Kennedy is chiefly remembered in foreign policy for his successful resolution of the Cuban missile crisis and his triumphal speech in West Berlin. Those were significant accomplishments. However, the tale of the first twenty months of the Kennedy administration was quite a different story. Having entered office convinced of their superior clarity and competence, officials of the new administration soon found themselves stumbling uncertainly from crisis to crisis.

First came the abortive Bay of Pigs invasion in April, where Kennedy armed Cuban expatriates and sent them against Castro while at the same time ruling out large-scale American military support—even canceling a second air strike designed to aid the rebels by incapacitating Castro's air force. (The air strike was canceled on grounds that it might compromise the moral position of the United States in the eyes of the UN.)[20] Treated by Kennedy's hagiographers as an anomaly, and sometimes even blamed (unfairly) on Eisenhower,[21] the Bay of Pigs invasion in certain important respects foreshadowed Vietnam. Like Johnson a half decade later, Kennedy rejected a series of more realistic and escalatory military options, settling instead for a limited operation wholly inadequate to the military task at hand.[22] Such a gravitation to the middle course and half-measures in military affairs would be a hallmark of the Kennedy-Johnson approach.

Following the Bay of Pigs fiasco, Kennedy attempted to recoup international prestige by meeting with Khrushchev in Vienna. This meeting proved to be another disaster. Psychologically ill-prepared for the combative approach of the Soviet leader, and encouraged by soft-line advisors to try to reassure Khrushchev so as to avoid accidental war and "miscalculation," the young president was bested again and again by Khrushchev in face-to-face ideological combat. To Khrushchev's endless criticisms of U.S. policy, Kennedy offered the most minimal rejoinders, even confessing his own "misjudgment" with regard to Cuba and the lack of wisdom in U.S. policy regarding the Pacific.[23] By the end of the meeting, according to one former Soviet official, Khrushchev had concluded that Kennedy was "a mere 'boy' who would be vulnerable to pressure."[24]

Bested in a face-to-face encounter, the president returned from Vienna, in *Time*'s later words, "moody, withdrawn,"[25] expecting a resumption of the crisis in Berlin and brooding about the dangers of nuclear war. The expected Soviet moves in Berlin soon came. Here again American hesitancy was to play a role in the escalation of conflict, as Kennedy's advisors, harboring their all-too-characteristic nuclear anxieties, urged a conciliatory response to Moscow's ever-growing provocations. The spirit of the administration's approach to Berlin was brilliantly captured by Jean Edward Smith, who interviewed many Kennedy administration officials for his superb 1963 study, *The Defense of Berlin*:

> The . . . dominant school within the Administration, nominally headed by [Secretary of State Dean] Rusk, included Adlai Stevenson, "Chip" Bohlen, Senators Fulbright and Mansfield, most of the political appointees in the State Department at the level of Assistant Secretary and above, and Ted Sorensen, Walt Rostow and Arthur Schlesinger, Jr., on the President's personal staff. . . . [These] advocates of the "soft-line" urgently sought to improve diplomatic relations with the Soviet Union and felt that this could be achieved through "meaningful" negotiations. Indeed, to these advisers the absolute horror of nuclear war made any other course unthinkable. Thus, since there was no "rational" alternative to negotiations, the mere fact that discussions were going on was considered a virtue; as having an intrinsic value of its own regardless of the subject discussed. It was this sacramental view of negotiations that characterized the Rusk-Stevenson-Bohlen school within the Administration.[26]

In short, the Kennedy advisors by and large failed to understand the political dimension of political conflict. The Berlin crisis began with a harsh aide-memoire handed by Khrushchev to Kennedy at Vienna. When this initial probe failed to provoke a resolute U.S. response, the Soviets successively escalated the crisis, finally closing the border between the two halves of the city in blatant violation of the four-power treaty. When the Kennedy administration remained essentially supine even in the face of the climactic construction of the Berlin Wall, West German morale sunk to a historic low.[27] Kennedy had "talked like Churchill and acted like Chamberlain," wrote James Reston of the *New York Times*.[28]

Kennedy's "Conventional Pause"

The strategic vision of the Kennedy administration took as a given the inevitability of nuclear stalemate; it stressed the primacy of technical "stability" over raw "strength." Yet ironically the whole preoccupation of superpower diplomacy during this period was not with any technical notion of "stability" but rather with the simpler political matter of who was strong and who was weak. The five-year period from the launching of *Sputnik* in October 1957 to the resolution of the Cuban missile crisis in October 1962 could be thought of as a kind of open "debate" between the superpowers over which side had the nuclear advantage. Which side was strategically superior, the Soviet Union or the United States? This was the crucial question on which other world events turned. After *Sputnik*, Khrushchev repeatedly claimed missile superiority, even though the Soviet Union failed to field the forces to back up these claims. Still, it would take the United States several years, in effect, to "prove" to the world that the Soviet boasts were empty. International crises normally occur when the power balance is uncertain. The crisis-ridden years from 1957 to 1962 were no exception.

Of course the Kennedy administration's position was somewhat complicated by domestic political factors. Having campaigned on the existence of an alleged "missile gap," the administration was embarrassed to learn upon arriving in power that no missile gap existed. On the contrary, to the degree that there was a missile gap, it was in the opposite direction: By 1961, the United States had clear missile superiority over the Soviet Union.[29] Yet this was a matter about which it was hard to be entirely frank. Secretary of Defense Robert S. McNamara touched off a controversy when he essentially denied the existence of the missile gap in a background briefing of reporters on February 6.[30] Subsequently, McNamara was less forthright. "There appeared . . . no signs of a Soviet crash effort to build intercontinental missiles," he somewhat cryptically told the Senate Armed Services Committee, "though the overall Russian military preparations continued at a rapid pace."[31] The perverse effect of such carefully hedged statements was to prolong the illusion of Soviet strategic superiority, actually contributing to the strength of Moscow's power position in Berlin and elsewhere.

The problem was compounded by the Democrats' purportedly sophisticated new strategic theories. Had the administration aimed at the simple goal of restoring the political appearance of American nuclear preponderance, it might have been able to establish early on in world opinion that the United States was deploying the superior force. But this was not how the administration conceived the problem. Rather, the task as Kennedy's advisors saw it was to undo the supposedly terrible errors of "massive retaliation," first by overcoming potential *vulnerabilities* in U.S. strategic forces and moving away from a first-strike posture; and, second, by reducing reliance on nuclear weapons through a conventional buildup. Kennedy's campaign rhetoric notwithstanding, the administration saw itself less as restoring American strength than as putting a sophisticated new theory into practice. Item two on McNamara's list of "96 Trombones"—the ninety-six tasks drawn up by the ambitious defense secretary in his bid to reorganize the Pentagon—read as follows: "Prepare and examine a 'doctrine' which, if accepted, would permit controlled response and negotiating pauses in the event of thermonuclear attack."[32] This was Schelling's "bargaining theory" come to life. (The alarmed response of the chairman of the joint chiefs of staff to this particular "trombone" is worth noting. "My personal judgment," wrote General Lyman L. Lemnitzer, "is that we do not now have adequate defenses, nor are our nuclear retaliatory forces sufficiently invulnerable, to permit us to risk withholding a substantial part of our effort, once a major thermonuclear attack has been initiated." Such a policy, he wrote, assumed "a degree of tacit 'cooperation' " with the Soviets "which does not now appear to exist."[33] Professors such as Schelling thought of war as "cooperation." The military knew better.)

Not that the stress on correcting vulnerability was entirely misplaced. McNamara's acceleration of the Polaris and Minuteman programs was a useful step.[34] The only problem was that insufficient attention was being paid to the political issue of relative strength. The measures reducing U.S. vulnerability were politically important precisely because they increased the strength of the U.S. position vis-à-vis the Soviet Union. However, focusing on narrow technical issues, the administration neglected this critical political dimension.

The attempt to reduce reliance on nuclear weapons through an increased emphasis on conventional forces in Europe had similarly perverse results. In late February 1961, the *Washington Star* reported that Secretary of State Dean Rusk had sent to the Pentagon new strategic guidelines calling for sharp curtailment on nuclear weapons use, even in the event of a massive Soviet conventional attack in Europe.[35] The report was subsequently denied,[36] but it indicated the general direction of administration thinking. A major memo on Berlin prepared for Kennedy by Dean Acheson in April bore the imprint of the same limited-war approach. While recommending a firm U.S. stance and counseling against Berlin negotiations, Acheson nonetheless called for large increases in U.S. conventional capability near Berlin, on the grounds that the city's defense could not be credibly based on a threat of nuclear weapons use.[37]

Far from strengthening the U.S. position in the Berlin crisis, however, the emphasis on conventional weapons was almost universally read in Europe as a weakening of Washington's *nuclear* resolve. A November 1961 article in the *Wall Street Journal* reported widespread European dissatisfaction with this doctrine of the "conventional pause." "What do you do," a West German foreign office official was reported as saying, "let the Russians take half of West Germany before you use your full power to stop them?" Interestingly, the West German official cited as analogies the American failures with the North Koreans and, prophetically, the North Vietnamese. "It is obvious," the anonymous German official said, "that the theory is based on the idea: if a shooting war starts, don't try to win the war, pull back, and try to open negotiations as fast as you can." This was precisely the approach the Johnson administration would come to take in Vietnam.[38]

Nowhere were the perverse effects of limited war thinking more apparent than in their dispiriting effect on the morale of West German Chancellor Konrad Adenauer. In November 1961, with the Berlin crisis still in full swing, Adenauer met with Acheson and later with Kennedy in Washington. The chancellor was unremittingly glum. "Either it was a bad morning for him," Acheson wrote of Adenauer after meeting with him, "or he has failed somewhat since last spring. He was either evasive or not making very much sense." Adenauer began with a "gloomy" description of Soviet conventional capabilities: twenty divisions in East Germany, nine East German divisions, and seventy other Russian divisions "near by." "Nothing," said the chancellor, "could be done against" the Soviets "with conventional power." When Acheson questioned the credibility of the Western threat to defend Berlin with nuclear weapons, Adenauer answered, not without a certain shrewdness, that "while we must not use these weapons, we must not tell Khrushchev that we would not do so." Nor was Adenauer impressed with Acheson's theories of limited war. When Acheson "explained" to Adenauer "the Acheson theory of the non-nuclear buildup in Europe," the chancellor responded that the idea was "hopeless" since "no one, except the Germans would do anything."[39] The stress on avoiding nuclear weapons, in short, was failing to have its intended reassuring effect on the Europeans.

Nuclear Testing Resumes

Another factor contributing to the illusion of relative American weakness had its source in the arms control negotiations. Eisenhower had established a pattern of pursuing arms control talks with the Soviet Union even amid an atmosphere of growing crisis and confrontation—permitting Moscow, as had been done in Korea, to talk and fight at the same time. This pattern continued under Kennedy. During the 1960 campaign, Kennedy had written to Eisenhower indicating that, if elected, he would continue to abide by the moratorium on nuclear testing. After assuming office, Kennedy signaled to Khrushchev a serious desire to pursue a test ban.[40]

Throughout the spring of 1961, the Kennedy administration had wrestled behind the scenes with the question of whether to resume nuclear testing. Interestingly, the administration simply did not know whether the Soviet Union was violating the moratorium with secret underground tests. "It is impossible to prove or disprove," Stefan Possony of Air Force Intelligence wrote to White House aide Rostow in May, "whether or not the Soviets have been conducting nuclear tests and other tests designed to enhance their nuclear weapons programs. There are numerous indications which arouse strong suspicions." In effect, wrote Possony, given the uncertainty over Soviet testing, the United States was observing a "unilateral" moratorium.[41] Moreover, as government scientists understood, the moratorium was not without military consequence. Later it would be learned that the testing moratorium resulted in the introduction of a "dud" Polaris warhead into the U.S. arsenal.[42] Politically, however, the fact remained that it was all but impossible for the United States to end the moratorium unilaterally—a political fact of life that Kennedy had little trouble recognizing.

The Soviets, meanwhile, had other plans. On August 13, the Berlin crisis reached a crescendo as the East Germans began to string barbed wire across the middle of Berlin: the beginning of the Berlin Wall. Just over two weeks later, on August 31, the Soviets stunned the world by announcing a resumption of nuclear testing. What followed was the largest test series undertaken by any nation to date, including, on October 30, the explosion of a record 58-megaton weapon.[43] Clearly, the Soviet Union was once again attempting to project an image of military strength; the tests were an act of intimidation. Moreover, they were an act of betrayal. Khrushchev had personally promised Kennedy at Vienna that the Soviet Union would not resume testing so long as the United States observed the moratorium.[44]

The Kennedy administration sought, not too effectively, to combat the impression of superior Soviet strength. A statement from Kennedy following the 58-megaton blast noted that in "terms of total military strength, the United States would not trade places with any nation on earth" and had taken steps "to maintain our lead."[45] Yet these protestations did little to dispel the aura of strength projected by the Soviet Union. Using arms control, the Soviets had succeeded in putting the United States on the defensive.

McNamara's "No Cities" Speech

Yet even though the Soviets had temporarily succeeded in preserving an illusion of strategic preponderance (or at least parity) through their dramatic violation of the nuclear testing moratorium in the autumn of 1961, behind the scenes the U.S. strategic arsenal continued to grow. In the end, the sheer number of new American weapons being deployed—especially when set beside the lagging Soviet missile program—could not help but alter perceptions. At the same time, satellite reconnaissance was permitting the United States to achieve a more accurate picture of Soviet missile capability.[46] Beginning in September 1961, press reports began to explode the missile gap myth. On September 25, the columnist Joseph Alsop—long a missile gap aficionado—noted that instead of the 200 ICBMs that Moscow was previously thought to possess, the Soviet Union was now believed by U.S. intelligence to have "well under 50."[47] (The actual number was closer to 4—as against a total of over 400 ICBMs and submarine-launched ballistic missiles [SLBMs] for the United States.)[48]

As U.S. strategic forces grew, so, perhaps inevitably, did American self-confidence. Addressing the American Bar Foundation in Chicago, for example, McNamara spoke categorically of "our superior nuclear power."[49]"Not even the most boastful Russian rocket rattler," said the defense secretary, "asserts that the Soviet Union has the nuclear power to destroy the United States."[50] Here, if not before, was a de facto denial of the missile gap.

Whether many Americans, much less Europeans, caught the new tone of confidence in administration pronouncements or understood its significance may be doubted. But the press reports of intelligence estimates and the flat statements about U.S. nuclear superiority by McNamara were doubtless read with interest and some dismay in Moscow.

The same was probably true of McNamara's famous "no cities" speech in Ann Arbor in June. In what can only be described as one of the more peculiar and technical commencement addresses ever delivered, the secretary of defense unveiled for the 1962 graduates of the University of Michigan a new U.S. nuclear strategy based, as we now know, on various technical concepts developed by Schelling and analysts at RAND. The strategy envisioned using nuclear weapons to strike Soviet military targets rather than cities (hence the "no cities" shorthand).[51] The idea was that, in the event of nuclear war, the United States would withhold strikes against Soviet cities in the hopes that this policy might encourage the Soviets do the same regarding American cities.[52] As McNamara told the fresh-faced Michigan graduates:

> The US has come to the conclusion that to the extent feasible basic military strategy in a possible general nuclear war should be approached in much the same way that more conventional military operations have been regarded in the past. That is to say, principal military objectives, in the event of a nuclear war stemming from a major attack on the Alliance, should be the destruction of the enemy's military forces, not of his civilian population.
>
> The very strength and nature of the Alliance forces makes it possible for us to retain, even in the face of a massive surprise attack, sufficient reserve striking power to destroy an enemy society if driven to it. In other words we are giving a possible opponent the strongest possible incentive to refrain from striking our own cities.[53]

One suspects that the intended audience here was not so much the students and faculty of the University of Michigan as the Kremlin. The speech was essentially a declassified version of a talk McNamara had given the NATO allies at a meeting in Athens the previous May (to a less-than-glowing reception).

McNamara's plan was to clue the Soviets in to the new American strategy in the hopes of establishing a kind of "cooperative" regime for fighting a general nuclear war (as bizarre as this notion may seem). In essence the speech embodied Schelling's "bargaining pauses" idea. But the general impression conveyed by the speech, in contrast to some administration pronouncements of the previous year, was one of military self-confidence.[54]

In short, by mid-1962, despite the image of strength briefly conveyed by its surprise nuclear tests the previous autumn, Moscow's power position was eroding. The illusion of strategic preponderance on which Khrushchev had based his whole policy of brinkmanship during the past five years was—thanks simply to the shifting realities of the balance of power—in danger of dissolving before the world's eyes. It seems to have been in this atmosphere that the Soviet leader hit upon the daring and risky expedient of deploying missiles in Cuba.

The Cuban Missile Crisis

The final chapter in the long-running "debate" over strategic superiority that began with *Sputnik* came with the Cuban missile crisis of October 1962. On October 16 President Kennedy was informed of a frightening new development: Soviet nuclear missile emplacements had been discovered in Cuba. Thus began what would prove to be perhaps the tensest thirteen days of the Cold War, a period during which the American people came to believe that nuclear war might well be imminent. On October 22, the president delivered a televised address to the nation, revealing the discovery of the Soviet missiles, announcing the imposition of a naval blockade or "quarantine" around Cuba, and warning the Soviet Union that "it shall be the policy of this nation to regard any nuclear missile launched from Cuba against any nation in the Western Hemisphere as an attack by the Soviet Union on the United States, requiring a full retaliatory response upon the Soviet Union."[55] The Strategic Air Command was placed on full alert, bombers dispersed, and a portion of the force kept constantly in the air. Tensions mounted. On October 26, a U.S. U-2 plane was shot down over Cuba and the pilot killed. Finally, after a flurry of communications between Washington and Moscow on October 26 and 27, and with massive preparations for U.S. invasion of the island underway, Khrushchev agreed to remove "offensive weapons" from Cuba in exchange for a public pledge that the United States would not invade Cuba—and secret assurances that U.S. intermediate-range Jupiter missiles would soon be removed from Turkey.[56]

It is important to recognize that while both the U.S. and Soviet governments were aware that America had massive nuclear superiority at the time of the Cuban missile crisis, this fact was not generally recognized outside of government circles. Probably the most important consequence of the crisis was to settle the debate over nuclear superiority—to reveal and confirm American strategic superiority in everybody's eyes. The fact that Khrushchev was forced to withdraw his missiles from Cuba so quickly after deploying them suggested that the disturbing Soviet nuclear threat that had worried everybody in Europe and elsewhere during the previous five years had been a paper tiger all along. As a result, the basis of Khrushchev's power position in world affairs was disastrously undermined. (The effect was dramatically reflected in polling conducted in Western Europe by the United States Information Agency. After the Cuban missile crisis, a majority of European respondents for the first time since 1958 identified the United States as the superior military power.)[57] Not coincidentally, the relentless and frightening Soviet pressure on Berlin, which had defined the reality of the Cold War since 1958, suddenly died down.

The Cuban missile crisis was thus a significant victory for the United States, even if in a sense it was a qualified one. While the prospect of a U.S. invasion of Cuba was certainly unlikely, the U.S. noninvasion pledge had the effect of solidifying Castro's position in Cuba, a problem with repercussions for many years elsewhere in the Western hemisphere. Nonetheless, the unfavorable impact of the crisis on Khrushchev's overall power position was profound. It was as though the Soviets had actually lost a war.[58]

But perhaps most important for our story, Kennedy administration officials portrayed the crisis as a proof of the validity of their own "limited, controlled" approach to superpower conflict—their own theories of second-strike deterrence and limited war. As Walt Rostow observed in a memo to other top Kennedy officials just weeks after the episode, the crisis had been "a first—and brilliantly improvised—exercise" under the administration's "doctrine" of "limited, controlled US-USSR conflict."[59] McNamara aide William Kaufmann, in his quasi-official text *The McNamara Strategy*, sounded the same theme, portraying the crisis as a successful example of "the graduated application of military power" and the "controlled and deliberate application of force."[60] McNamara publicly called the crisis "a perfect illustration of the application of *this* [that is, mutual deterrence/limited war] strategy and *this* force structure."[61] The crisis was thus an important turning point in the thinking of the administration, apparently proving the validity of the strategic theories that it brought into office and would later apply to strategic arms control and the war in Vietnam.

Was this a correct reading of the crisis? Had success in the missile crisis come primarily from "limited, controlled" application of force (that is, limited war)? Also, had the massive U.S. advantage in nuclear weapons—as many Kennedy administration officials now came to insist—really been all but irrelevant to the crisis outcome (that is, mutual deterrence)? There is good reason to doubt both conclusions.

In the first place, in light of now-declassified records of crisis deliberations, the Kennedy administration's various paeans to its own performance in the crisis appear hyperbolic and self-serving. "The performance of the U.S. government during that critical period," McNamara wrote in an introduction to Robert Kennedy's crisis memoir, *Thirteen Days*, "was more effective than at any other time during my seven years' service as Secretary of Defense."[62] Dean Acheson, who saw the Kennedy administration's early crisis deliberations firsthand, had a different impression. After reading Robert Kennedy's self-congratulatory account of the administration's performance, the former secretary of state wrote an article for *Esquire* pointing out numerous flaws in the administration's deliberations and dismissing Kennedy's success in the crisis as an "homage to plain dumb luck."[63]

Declassified records show why Acheson might have arrived at such a harsh judgment. First, there was Robert McNamara's curious and uncomprehending assessment of significance of the Cuban missiles at the outset of the crisis. Incredibly enough, the defense secretary came into the first day of crisis deliberations maintaining that Soviet nuclear missiles in Cuba *made no difference in the strategic balance*; the Cuban missiles simply did not matter.

What basis could the defense secretary have had for such a peculiar judgment? Certainly there were no quantitative grounds for such a conclusion. An analysis produced at the time by Raymond Garthoff at the State Department, and recently declassified, showed how vastly the Cuban deployments increased U.S. strategic vulnerability. In October 1962 the Soviet Union possessed no more that seventy-five ICBMs. According to Garthoff, the Cuban missiles would have increased the portion of U.S. strategic force vulnerable to a Soviet first strike by 30 percent; once the Cuban missiles were fully deployed and operational, Garthoff noted, *only 15 percent of the U.S. strategic force would survive a Soviet first strike*. Roughly 40 percent of SAC bases fell within the range of Cuban-based medium-range ballistic missiles (MRBMs), and 100 percent fell within the range of Cuban-based intermediate-range ballistic missiles (IRBMs), Garthoff reported. In short, the memo noted, the missiles in Cuba represented "a serious dilution of the U.S. retaliatory capability."[64] McNamara's own civilian Pentagon analysts came to identical conclusions.[65]

Yet during the first meeting of what came to be known as the Executive Committee of the National Security Council, or "ExComm," on October 16, Bundy asked the defense secretary how the Cuban missiles would affect the strategic balance. According to the transcript of the tape-recorded discussion, McNamara answered: "not at all." In the defense secretary's opinion, the missiles were not "a military problem." "I'll be quite frank," he told Kennedy. "I don't think there *is* a military problem." Not surprisingly, this judgment completely contradicted that of the joint chiefs of staff as well as Paul Nitze.[66]

Nor did McNamara even seem to appreciate the *political* significance of the Soviet deployment. He did not see the crisis in international political terms. On the contrary, for McNamara, the crisis was, as he assured Kennedy, purely "a *domestic,* political problem" (emphasis added). In other words, Kennedy had made certain public warnings about missiles in Cuba; now that the Soviets had ignored his warnings, he would have to act tough toward Moscow to appease his domestic critics on the American Right.[67] (Acheson was shocked on October 17 to find McNamara maintaining this view, though he did not mention McNamara by name.)[68]

Yet, curiously, the transcript of the October 16 meeting shows that no one was more worried than McNamara about the Cuban missiles, which he then claimed did not matter. In outlining military options on October 16, the secretary of defense insisted that the discussion take as its premise or "foundation" the proposition that U.S. air strikes, if undertaken, would be scheduled "prior to the time that these missiles become operational"— even though McNamara did not know when that time would be. "Because," he said, "if they [the missiles] become operational before the air strike, I do not believe we can state we can knock them out before they can be launched; and if they're launched there is almost certain to be, uh, chaos in part of the east coast or the area, uh, in a radius of six hundred to a thousand miles from Cuba."[69] In short, no one was more worried than McNamara about the prospect of the Cuban missiles being used.

Yet McNamara's unstated premise seemed to be that the Soviets would fire nuclear missiles from Cuba at the United States in immediate response to conventional air strikes on the missile sites—in effect, that in response to conventional attacks on Cuba, the Soviet Union would immediately resort to general nuclear war. He seemed to hold this assumption even though administration analysts suspected that nuclear warheads, if they were present at all in Cuba, would have been stored separately from the missiles, under Soviet control. (There was some question at the time whether the nuclear warheads had even been delivered to the island.)[70] McNamara's premise was especially odd given the administration's whole stress up to this time on the existence of a putative nuclear "firebreak"— that is, the possibility of erecting barriers between "limited" conventional war and nuclear weapons use. In effect, McNamara had been trying for the past twelve months to persuade annoyed and skeptical NATO officials that a vast conventional war could be fought on European soil with the Soviet Union without involving nuclear weapons. Having unnerved the Europeans with talk of a conventional "pause," the secretary of defense was now maintaining with equal certainty that conventional air strikes against Cuba would lead instantaneously and automatically to nuclear strikes upon the United States.

This is not to say that the nuclear danger was nil. McNamara may well have been right about the possibility of conventional air strikes stimulating a nuclear response from Cuba, but if he was right, his conclusion called into question the administration's whole approach to strategy in Europe. Was there or was there not a nuclear threshold or "firebreak"? McNamara's thinking was unclear.

McNamara's fear of nuclear weapons led him to oppose air strikes against the island and propose a naval blockade. (In this he was supported by Bobby Kennedy, who emotionally likened such strikes to Pearl Harbor—that is, an unjustified surprise attack, an analogy from which Acheson passionately dissented.)[71]

Administration officials later credited this decision with playing a key role in achieving a peaceful resolution of the crisis. But ironically, the decision to blockade the island created the very problem that McNamara had made it his "foundation" principle to avoid: It permitted Soviet technicians to begin making the missiles operational. Once this happened, as Acheson later wrote, Cuba became "a combination of porcupine and cobra"—in other words, capable of striking either defensively or offensively at the United States with nuclear missiles.[72] The blockade, later portrayed as a cleverly chosen "limited" option, was in reality, as Acheson later pointed out, not necessarily safer; in certain respects, it increased the danger, by alerting the Soviets to the U.S. discovery of the missiles and giving them time to get the missiles operational. At any rate, the choice of the blockade, as Acheson saw it, was simply a form of procrastination: It "merely postponed confrontation."[73] And it left unsolved the central problem of how the crisis would be brought to an end.

The Meaning of the Crisis

Given McNamara's astonishing claim on the first day of the crisis that the deployment of Soviet missiles in Cuba had no effect whatever on the strategic balance, it is not difficult to see why the defense secretary might have argued later that U.S. nuclear superiority was all but irrelevant to the crisis outcome. If changes in the strategic balance on the scale of the Cuban missiles did not matter, it is hard to see what would. Yet not just McNamara but a number of Kennedy administration officials came to subscribe to this view: In the aftermath of the crisis, Kennedy administration officials stressed the relative unimportance of nuclear weapons, attributing the American success instead to local superiority in conventional forces—in the form of the naval blockade of Cuba. "Nuclear force was not irrelevant," claimed McNamara, "but it was in the background. Non-nuclear forces were our sword, our nuclear forces were our shield."[74] In recent years, the same claim has been put forward in even more categorical form. In October 1982, McNamara, Bundy, and four other like-minded former Kennedy administration officials wrote jointly in *Time*: "The Cuban missile crisis illustrates not the *significance* but the *insignificance* of nuclear superiority in the face of survivable thermonuclear retaliatory forces. It also shows the crucial role of rapidly available conventional strength."[75] Bundy himself has gone so far as to argue that the result of the crisis "would have been the same with strategic parity as it was with American [nuclear] superiority."[76]

But close examination of the crisis events fails to support such a conclusion. One reason that these claims about the irrelevancy of nuclear weapons seem so odd at first glance is that strategic superiority would appear to be precisely what the 1962 missile crisis was all about. By Khrushchev's own later admission, he put the missiles in Cuba in 1962 at least partly to remedy the Soviet Union's strategic inferiority[77] (this was almost certainly his main motive). Kennedy, meanwhile, deliberately invoked the threat of U.S. nuclear forces—not only in his October 22 speech to the nation, but in a highly visible alert of U.S. strategic forces—to get Khrushchev to take the missiles out. Moreover, U.S. strategic superiority at the time was little short of overwhelming—a four-to-one (438 to 75) advantage in ICBMs, a significantly quantitative and qualitative advantage in SLBMs, and a nearly eight-to-one (1,300 to 155) advantage in strategic bombers.[78] One would expect such a margin of advantage to have some impact on the behavior of actors, and, indeed, there is ample evidence to suggest that it did.

First, take the question of the Soviets. It seems clear that U.S. strategic superiority had an inhibiting effect on the Kremlin's actions. As Richard K. Betts, among others, has pointed out, if conventional forces had been the only factor governing the outcome of the crisis, Khrushchev could have easily responded to the U.S. naval quarantine around Cuba by moving against Berlin, where the Soviets had a comparable conventional advantage. He did not. In addition, while the United States went on full nuclear alert, the Soviets never reciprocated, suggesting that the nuclear threat in this crisis was one-sided.[79] And there is Khrushchev's own testimony. In reporting to the Supreme Soviet two months after the crisis, the Soviet leader himself not only drew attention to the U.S. nuclear alert during the crisis but added: "If [imperialism] is a 'paper tiger' now, those who say this know that this 'paper tiger' has atomic teeth. It can put them to work; and it cannot be regarded frivolously."[80] It seems clear that American nuclear capabilities played a prominent role in Khrushchev's calculations.

What about on the American side? While McGeorge Bundy has written that American officials derived "no comfort" from the strategic balance,[81] Betts draws our attention to a revealing letter to McNamara from General Maxwell Taylor, who, like Nitze and others, thought the strategic balance counted very much. "*We have the strategic advantage in our general war capabilities,*" Taylor wrote. ". . . This is no time to run scared."[82]

What, then, is the basis for the Kennedy group's contention that nuclear superiority did not matter? In actuality, the conclusion has its roots not so much in an analysis of the crisis as in mutual deterrence theory. McGeorge Bundy, whose book *Danger and Survival* offers the most complete explication of the Kennedy administration officials' case, lays out the argument in some detail. Implicitly following mutual deterrence theory, Bundy contended that what caused Khrushchev to avoid war in the Cuban as well as Berlin crises of the early 1960s was not any calculation of an American strategic advantage, but the *mutual* danger that nuclear war itself posed for either side. What actually deterred war was not American nuclear "superiority," but a general and shared nuclear "danger."[83]

That is one way of putting the situation, but it misses the point. The point is that in *neither* the Cuban nor the Berlin crises did Khrushchev have any intention whatsoever of going to war.[84] (Kennedy's worries about war by accident or "miscalculation," fed by his recent reading of Barbara Tuchman's *Guns of August,* were in this sense not quite on target. The Cuban crisis differed fundamentally from the Sarajevo crisis of July

1914, since Germany, unlike the Soviet Union in 1962, believed it enjoyed a military advantage and was perfectly willing to go to war.) Rather, Soviet leverage in these crises depended on creating the *illusion* that they might be willing to risk war—an illusion to which the young intellectuals in the Kennedy administration, of whom Bundy was one, proved particularly susceptible at the time.

Since Khrushchev was not interested in war, what was at issue was not so much deterrence itself as each side's subjective and imperfect calculation of the other side's willingness to take risks—in particular, to take political steps or conventional military action that might eventually escalate to nuclear war. Here is where nuclear superiority began to matter. The point is that apart from its direct effect on deterrence, the nuclear balance was bound to affect each side's estimate of the other side's willingness to take military action *even below the nuclear threshold* at any given moment in time, knowing that this might easily escalate to a wider war.

This proved particularly critical on October 26 and October 27—the crucial turning point of the crisis. On October 26, Kennedy received a long, emotional letter from Khrushchev (Dean Acheson later called it "almost maudlin"[85]). The letter stressed the dangers of nuclear war and offered what appeared to be a sliver of light, hinting at the possibility of trading withdrawal of the missiles in exchange for a U.S. promise not to invade Cuba.[86]

This possibility had been raised more explicitly in a curious episode earlier the same day. A senior KGB official in Washington, Alexander Fomin, proposed precisely this formula for a settlement to an intermediary, ABC reporter John Scali, who in turn took the message to the administration. The administration was heartened by the prospect of a way out, and Scali was told to indicate to Fomin that such a solution might be possible.[87]

Then on Saturday came a reversal. Radio Moscow began to broadcast a second Khrushchev letter, this one apparently composed by committee, with harder terms. The new letter demanded removal of Jupiter missiles from Turkey in exchange for withdrawal of Soviet missiles from Cuba. On the same day, the administration received news that U-2 pilot Rudolph Anderson had been shot down and killed over Cuba. The shootdown of Anderson—undertaken, as we now know, by Cuban authorities without specific Soviet authorization[88]—would greatly heighten domestic pressure for decisive action on Kennedy's part.[89]

After long and tense deliberation, the president sent his brother Robert to Soviet ambassador Anatoly Dobrynin with both a secret concession and a kind of ultimatum. The president would be removing the obsoles-cent missiles from Turkey anyway (plans had begun months before), but did not want this to be a part of a public deal. Also, the president's brother was instructed to emphasize, time was short. The Soviets were given until the next day to respond.[90]

As U.S. forces massed for an air attack and invasion, Robert Kennedy's message was fortunately reinforced by an angry Scali, who "denounced" his KGB interlocutor Fomin as" 'a stinking double-cross' " and added: "If you think the United States is bluffing . . . you are part of the most colossal misjudgment of American intentions in history. We are abso-lutely determined to get those missiles out of there. An invasion of Cuba is only a matter of hours away."[91]

Bundy believes that the angry Scali-Fomin exchange—which was en-tirely on Scali's own initiative, without instructions from the president—had a big effect on Khrushchev,[92] and one is inclined to agree, since the public Soviet message on withdrawal of the missiles came the next day. Khrushchev obviously settled because he did not wish to risk the onset of military action by the United States. Scali's encounter with Fomin no doubt helped make this risk seem more real. However, because Khrush-chev had offered the basic terms of the trade on Friday, Bundy argues that these warnings "affected the speed of Khrushchev's response more than its substance."[93]

In politics, as in drama, timing is often everything. Bundy's compla-cency about the importance of the strategic balance goes hand in hand with an effort to discount the importance of the Soviet response to the pivotal American warnings on October 27. This rests in turn on two highly questionable suppositions: (1) that time was on the American side and (2) that a *public* trade of the Jupiter missiles in Turkey for the Cuban missiles—Kennedy's probable fall-back position in the event his Saturday proposal was refused—would not have been a bad outcome.

That time was on the American side hardly seems self-evident. "Each week," Bundy argues, "would have endangered the position of Khrush-chev and his supporters much more than it endangered us."[94] But one must ask: Which sort of government is more likely, over time, to come under domestic pressure to waver from its original purpose or to suffer more when its public loses a sense of urgency about a crisis—a democ-racy or a totalitarian regime? The notion that, in the short run, time was on the side of the democracies in wars or crises, one might argue, would perish in the jungles of Vietnam.

Second and more fundamental, however, was the issue of the Jupiters.

Even though he advised Kennedy otherwise at the time, Bundy has since argued that "a formidable set of arguments" could have been marshaled "in support of [Kennedy's] acceptance of a public trade."[95] Here is where the Kennedy group's argument turns circular. Though Bundy and his colleagues now argue to the contrary, the political difference between a public trade of the Jupiter missiles and the secret deal Kennedy actually got was absolutely fundamental. It was the difference between victory and defeat.

The major outcome of the crisis was the perception that Khrushchev had been forced to back down. He had. The very fact that Khrushchev was compelled to keep the American Jupiter concession secret indicated that the administration had the upper hand. He could use the concession on the Jupiters to save face with his Soviet leadership colleagues, but not with the world at large. That was a fact of critical importance, for it destroyed the illusion of Soviet nuclear predominance that had formed the whole basis of his power position in world affairs.

The problem with the public trade of the Jupiters was the one Bundy saw at the time—in his words then, "it would be clear that we were trying to sell our allies for own interests." Rather characteristically, Bundy told the president the European view would be "irrational" and "crazy" but was nonetheless "a terribly powerful fact."[96] It was not irrational and crazy; the Europeans would have been right—since to permit the perception of a sellout of an ally under Soviet pressure was to sell it out in reality. The effect, in short, would have been roughly the opposite of the secret arrangement. Khrushchev would have been perceived not as losing face but as gaining a significant concession—witness how large the issue of Intermediate-Range Nuclear Forces (INF) missiles has loomed in Western European consciousness in the 1980s—through his daring gambit of putting missiles in the Americans' own backyard.

To argue that a public trade would essentially be the same as the secret trade is essentially to argue that losing in the crisis would have been the same as winning. If one believes that, as Bundy seems to do, then one is not likely to place much importance on the effect the nuclear balance might have had on Khrushchev's calculations or resolve or on *the nature or timing* of his October 27–28 decision. If the political outcome was irrelevant, then whatever marginal effect U.S. strategic superiority may have had on Khrushchev's assessment of the willingness of the Americans to initiate military operations against Cuba makes no difference.

That is to say, to the degree that attention shifts away from the political consequences of particular crises and confrontations, to the mere question of whether nuclear war was or was not avoided, the importance of strategic superiority naturally diminishes. This seems to be the key to the Kennedy officials' approach. When Bundy writes, "I think the result of the confrontation in 1962 would have been the same with strategic parity as it was with American superiority,"[97] it is important to ask what he means by "the same." If by "the same" he means with or without a public trade of the Jupiter missiles, as he apparently does, one might even agree with him. But it is a circular argument, a tautology: If you don't care about political outcomes, you don't have to worry about the details of your power position (of which nuclear superiority would obviously be a major part). However, it should be added the distinction between "winning" and "preserving peace" is a false one. Bundy's implicit denials notwithstanding, an adverse political consequence for the United States over Cuba would have deeply hurt future prospects for peace. If Khrushchev had been perceived as winning the Cuban missile crisis, or even as fighting the Americans to a draw, Soviet pressure on Berlin would doubtless have continued, and new, perhaps more dangerous crises would likely have followed. These crises in turn would have raised anew the specter of possible war.

Indeed, Bundy's account inadvertently shows how close the Kennedy team came to bungling the whole affair, even as they held all the cards. History may owe something of a debt to John Scali, who did what some more official emissary of the president should have been explicitly instructed to do when the Jupiter concession was delivered: tell the Soviets in no uncertain terms this was the last offer.

The Limits of "Limited Means"

In a sense, the choice of limited means in the Cuban crisis—the selection of the blockade or quarantine instead of an early air strike—while it avoided an immediate confrontation, was similar to the choice of limited means in the Korean war: It left entirely unsolved the problem of how to end the crisis, of how to bring the confrontation to a conclusion. Retrospective accounts of the Cuban missile crisis by Kennedy administration officials resembled Democratic accounts of limited war in Korea: They obscured the crucial problem of how wars or crises end.[98] As it happens, there was little truly new in the means by which the Kennedy administration achieved success in the Cuban missile crisis. On the contrary, Kennedy ended the Cuban missile crisis in much the same way that Eisenhower ended the Korean war: with significant, though not debilitating, U.S. concessions, combined with *a virtual ultimatum to escalate the conflict vastly* if quick termination was not achieved.

One reason perhaps that Kennedy loyalists overlooked the crucial role of the threat of escalation in ending the crisis was a belief that Kennedy himself might not have followed through on it. Bundy, for example, contends that if Khrushchev had failed to accept the private concession on the Jupiter missiles, Kennedy would have offered the missiles as a public concession. There is a great deal of evidence to support this view. From the declassified transcript of the administration's October 27 deliberations, it is clear that President Kennedy was strongly inclined to yield to Khrushchev's demand to remove missiles from Turkey. Only repeated argument from various advisors—Nitze, Bundy (who referred to agitated cables warning of the difficulties of a trade from the U.S. ambassador in Ankara, Ray Hare), NATO commander General Lauris Norstad, who wrote emphatically from Brussels, and others—eventually deterred the president from making a public trade. At bottom, it is clear from the transcript Kennedy was deathly afraid of taking military action. As he said on the twenty-seventh:

> I'm just thinking about what—what we're going to have to do in a day or so, which is (censored) sorties and (censored) days, and possibly an invasion, all because we wouldn't take missiles out of Turkey, and we all know how quickly everybody's courage goes when the blood starts to flow, and that's what's going to happen in NATO, when they—we start these things, and they grab Berlin, and everybody's going to say, "Well, that was a pretty good proposition." Let's not kid ourselves that we've got—that's the difficulty. Today it sounds great to reject, but it's not going to, after we do something.[99]

That any military action would have involved grave dangers goes without saying, but at the outset of a war a nation's populace tends not to recriminate against the leadership but rally to it—remember the mood in European countries in 1914. Besides, the case against a trade of the Turkish missiles would hardly have been as difficult to justify as Kennedy believed. The relevant analogy was one that Kennedy, from his undergraduate study of British policy before World War II, should have understood well: Munich. For the United States to have taken missiles away from an ally in response to Soviet extortion would clearly have betrayed the very principle on which NATO was founded; it would have been an act of appeasement that gave the lie to the American nuclear guarantee to Western Europe on which the NATO alliance was centrally based. Indeed, a public U.S. concession on the Jupiter missiles would have transformed the crisis from a victory into a defeat. Once again Kennedy, who liked to talk publicly like Churchill, was talking more like Chamberlain behind the scenes.

The Legacy of the Crisis

For the United States in the twentieth century, avoiding defeat has often proved less of a problem than coping with victory. In this respect, the Cuban missile crisis was no exception. Success in the missile crisis—albeit somewhat inadvertent—put the Kennedy administration in a position analogous to that in which the Eisenhower administration found itself in early 1955. Once again the balance of power had shifted decisively in favor of the United States, and once again, predictably, stability was returning to the world scene. Once again Moscow, in its characteristically rough and ungracious manner, would extend the olive branch, and once again Washington would grasp the branch with characteristic fervor. Once again the attention of the two capitals would turn to arms negotiations. And once again the American administration would grow dangerously careless about the realities of power, with deleterious results.

The Cuban missile crisis marked a pinnacle of American power, and seemed to open a new era of peace. In 1965, Schelling would declare the Cold War to be "dead."[100] But beneath the surface, between 1963 and 1968, the balance of power began shifting against the United States. In November 1963, President Kennedy would fall victim to assassination. By 1968, Lyndon Johnson would bequeath to his successor a nation mired in an interminable war, wracked by internal dissent and violence, its economy bloated with inflation, its relative military power waning, the longstanding bipartisan consensus in Congress in favor of a strong defense disintegrating, if not already destroyed. By 1968, America would be a nation in inner turmoil—economic, spiritual, cultural—and under Richard Nixon the misery would only deepen. Arms control and arms control theory would play a central role in this drama of decline.

Indeed, it would not be too much to say that the Cuban missile crisis inaugurated the era of arms control. This was true in two senses. First, and more superficially, the U.S. victory in the crisis, and the favorable international environment it produced, made possible the first actual arms agreements of the nuclear age—the "hot line" agreement and the Limited Test Ban Treaty, both in 1963. Second, and more fundamentally, the missile crisis inspired Secretary of Defense McNamara to begin a radical revision of U.S. nuclear strategy, designed to remove U.S. policy even farther from the traditional logic of military power and bring it even closer into line with the vision embodied in arms control theory. The experience of the Cuban missile crisis provided the catalyst for what is now understood as the McNamara legacy in defense: the development of the doctrine of "mutual assured destruction" (MAD), the decision to forgo a defense of the United States against Soviet ballistic missiles and, by 1968, the plans to open negotiations with Moscow on strategic arms control.

"Mutual Assured Destruction"

By early 1963, the fundamental revision of U.S. nuclear strategy that would eventuate in "mutual assured destruction" was already underway. A hint of the new direction in McNamara's thinking emerged just weeks after the Cuban missile crisis in an interview with Steward Alsop accompanying a major story on the McNamara "no cities" or "controlled response" strategy in the *Saturday Evening Post*. Asked by Alsop whether the Soviets would eventually achieve a full retaliatory capability against the United States, McNamara not only answered in the affirmative but stated that this would be a positive development. "A nuclear exchange confined to military targets seems more possible, not less, when *both* sides have a sure second-strike capability," McNamara affirmed. "*Then you might have a more stable balance of terror*. This may seem a rather subtle point, but from where I'm sitting it seems a point worth thinking about."[101]

Here was an innovation: an American secretary of defense arguing in favor of strengthening the Soviet strategic arsenal. What lay behind McNamara's unorthodox assertion? Journalist Henry Trewhitt, in a biography of McNamara written in the early 1970s, assumed that McNamara meant that "the Soviets, secure in the knowledge they could retaliate after an American attack, would not be tempted into the folly of a pre-emptive first strike."[102] But there may have been a deeper and more troublesome motive for wishing to strengthen the Soviet Union's strategic capabilities vis-à-vis the United States—namely a desire to reduce *America's* military options in the future so as to decrease the threat of nuclear war from *either* side. This desire may have been rooted in McNamara's personal experience of the Cuban missile crisis only weeks before. After all, in the missile crisis the threat of a Soviet preemptive attack had never been an issue. The president had been informed by the Central Intelligence Agency (CIA) that the Soviets never went on nuclear alert, that their ICBMs had not even been armed with nuclear warheads, and that the warheads may have been stored as far as fifty miles from the missiles.[103] On the contrary, the only real threat of military action came from the *American* side, in the sense that it was the United States, not the Soviet Union, that would have to attack if the Soviets refused to withdraw the missiles.

In an interview many years later, Schelling speculated that what worried McNamara above all during the crisis was that joint chiefs would force his hand, pressuring him, and the president, to initiate military operations.[104]

Had McNamara really believed that the Cuban missiles made no difference in the strategic balance, or was he just saying this to deter the president from taking military action against them? Did he really believe in the wake of the crisis that American strategic superiority made no difference, or was he just saying this to discourage Congress from adding further to U.S. strategic forces? It remains difficult to say. In the end, there was something of hubris in McNamara—a willingness to manipulate and to withhold the truth from his audience in the service of what he regarded as a higher moral end. He lied outright to Congress on the issue of whether Kennedy had secretly traded Jupiter missiles in Turkey for removal of the Cuban missiles, assuring the House Armed Services Committee that there was "absolutely no connection" between the "forced removal" of Soviet missiles in Cuba and the removal of the missiles "in Turkey or Italy."[105] On more than one occasion other administration aides found him manipulating facts in the interest of engineering a particular policy result.[106]

A final point should be made. Among former associates of McNamara there is today wide agreement[107] on a fact that was treated as a closely held secret in the 1960s—namely, that the defense secretary was unusually anxious about the prospect of nuclear war, viscerally antinuclear. At a lunch where his aide Daniel Ellsberg was present, McNamara passionately opposed use of tactical nuclear weapons. "They're the same thing, there's no difference," he said, "once you use them, you use everything else. You can't keep them limited. You'll destroy Europe, everything."

After the luncheon Ellsberg received a call from Adam Yarmolinsky, another McNamara aide who had been present at the meeting. "You must not speak of this lunch to anyone. It is of the highest importance. Not to anyone. It must not get around." As David Halberstam wrote, McNamara had to keep his "almost emotional abhorrence of the weapons" a secret from the joint chiefs and Congress, or "he felt he would be finished as Secretary of Defense."[108]

The imperative moving McNamara during the Cuban missile crisis was that of preventing the onset of hostilities. But interestingly, this meant primarily restraining not the Soviet Union but the United States. The threat of military action really came more from the American side. In a certain sense, therefore, from McNamara's perspective, the problem in the Cuban missile crisis was not that the Soviets were too strong but that they had been too weak.

Was McNamara now prepared to take the extraordinary step of "correcting" the balance of power actually *abetting* the growth of the Soviet arsenal so that in a future crisis there would be no ambiguity, no pressure from the hawks or the military for an American military response? Was he now prepared to ensure that not just the Soviets but that the United States would be deterred by an unambiguous nuclear stalemate? Was he now ready to design policies with the deliberate aim of strengthening the Soviet strategic position—at least the Soviet "second strike" force—in regard to the United States? There are a number of circumstances that point strongly to this supposition.

The first was an extraordinary episode involving the deliberate divulgence of highly classified information by Pentagon General Counsel John T. McNaughton a few weeks after the missile crisis. The incident passed without public notice in 1962 and was revealed in full only many years later in *Newsweek*.[109] McNaughton, who had come into the administration through his close friendship with Harvard colleague Thomas Schelling, was a devotee of arms control theory. In December 1962, at the explicit instruction of Kennedy and McNamara, McNaughton journeyed to an International Arms Control Symposium at Ann Arbor, Michigan, where he proceeded to deliver a speech describing in some detail the technical means by which the United States maintained tight control over the launching or detonation of nuclear weapons even during a nuclear alert— the so-called permissive action links (PALs) designed to prevent unauthorized launch. "It is, of course, hoped—and I wish to emphasize this—that the Soviet Union will see the logic behind these policies and take comparable steps," McNaughton said. U.S. diplomats in Washington and Moscow drew the Soviets' attention to McNaughton's speech, as did some American scientists meeting with their Soviet counterparts.[110]

On the surface, the McNaughton "ploy" was designed to encourage the Soviets to take measures to prevent an accidental or unauthorized launch. But the inevitable—and odd as it may seem, possibly intended— effect was to aid the Soviets technically in developing an arsenal that could be put on instant, full-scale alert like that employed by the United States during the missile crisis, and therefore made war, in a certain sense, more likely. The McNaughton episode, *Newsweek* noted, was "quite probably unparalleled in the history of nations." "In an age," the magazine noted, "when the physical survival of an entire people may well depend upon the strength of its nuclear arsenal, it seems almost inconceivable that a great power would deliberately give away some of its nuclear expertise to its most formidable adversary. Yet . . . during the Administration of John F. Kennedy, the United States did just that."[111] What is clear from the *Newsweek* story is that Kennedy and McNamara plainly understood they were acting in a way that would strengthen the Soviet Union vis-à-vis the United States. One reason McNaughton was chosen for the covert mission was the awareness that such a gesture, if discovered and understood by the Congress, would arouse furious opposition.

The McNaughton gesture suggested the spirit of McNamara's new approach. It was an approach that, as arms control theory had suggested, assumed the possibility of an unusually high degree of communication and "cooperation" between adversaries. McNamara's aim, it would seem, was to nurture the Soviets along—encourage them to develop their own second-strike or, in his famous phrase, "assured destruction" capability. The McNaughton speech began a deliberate process of "educating" the Soviets on the virtues of mutual deterrence.

Two sets of documents from the Kennedy-Johnson years reflect the evolution of McNamara's strategy toward this goal. "Annual Posture Statements" outlining the U.S. strategic conception were published and delivered every year to the Armed Services Committees of Congress. (McNamara was reportedly elated at the number of posture statements purchased by the Soviet embassy. It was interpreted as proof that the Soviets were absorbing and adopting the American strategic conceptions.)[112] But McNamara also spelled out the strategy in classified form in an annual "Draft Presidential Memorandum." In general, the thinking publicly expressed in the "Posture Statements" lagged a few years behind that in the classified "Draft Presidential Memoranda" (DPM). For example, McNamara first publicly outlined his famous concept of "assured destruction" in the 1965 posture statement for fiscal year (FY) 1966.[113] But "assured destruction" originally entered the U.S. strategic lexicon the year after the Cuban missile crisis, in McNamara's December 1963 DPM outlining strategic force posture for FY 1965–1969.[114]

The purpose of the concept of "assured destruction" was twofold. First, it was designed to provide a justification for limiting or capping U.S. strategic forces. McNamara had been unhappy when the services began using the "no cities" doctrine as a justification for buying new weapons.[115] Second, and perhaps more fundamentally, assured destruction served to orient U.S. strategy away from a military or war-fighting approach toward a deterrence-only stalemate.

One key consequence of embracing assured destruction was the rejection of antiballistic missile defenses. This in turn could be traced back to arms control theory. Among the most paradoxical corollaries of the paradoxical doctrine of arms control was that an attempt to defend one's population from missile attack was potentially "destabilizing." The reasoning was as follows: ABM defenses were unlikely to be extremely effective against an attacker's full-scale first strike. However, if an aggressor struck preemptively at an opponent's missile force, destroying a large portion of the opponent's missiles on the ground, then the aggressor could use his ABM defenses to handle the opponent's "ragged" retaliatory strike. In other words, according to the theory, defenses would tend primarily to vitiate the effectiveness of *retaliatory* rather than first-strike forces. In this way, they would create incentives to preemption.

A second indication of McNamara's embrace of stalemate was a policy called in the 1963 DPM "Forcing the Soviets to Harden"—that is, acquiring counterforce weapons so as to encourage the Soviets to harden their ICBM silos. Under McNamara, it became U.S. policy to encourage the Soviets to harden their silos against U.S. attack, ostensibly to encourage mutual stablity.

Third, beginning in 1965, the navy was instructed not to ask for equipment, men, or funds for the purpose of developing antisubmarine warfare capabilities against Soviet ballistic missile submarines[116]—apparently another unilateral gesture designed to assure the Soviets of a second-strike capability against the United States, under the policy of assured destruction.

Like the McNaughton ploy, in other words, assured destruction involved a deliberate decision to permit, and even encourage, an increase in U.S. vulnerability to a Soviet second strike, in the supposed interest of assuring mutual stability.

Determined to restrain the growth of U.S. strategic forces, McNamara took somewhat different lines inside and outside administration counsels. In his classified memorandum to Johnson, for example, the defense secretary assumed a rapid expansion of the Soviet arsenal, thereby justifying his claim that it would be futile to expand U.S. forces. At the same time, addressing the public and the Congress, he sought to reassure that the Soviets were not seeking to match the United States. "There is no indication," the defense secretary announced categorically in April 1965, "that the Soviets are seeking to develop a strategic nuclear force as large as ours."[117]

In general, the shift in strategy outlined in the 1963 DPM took place without major public notice. This was partly because of the complexity and highly classified nature of the issues involved. But it was also partly because of a deliberate guardedness and public ambiguity on the part of McNamara and his chief aides. There was in the arms control brotherhood an element of esotericism and secretiveness. To announce publicly and conspicuously that the United States had now foresworn the goal of strategic superiority and was committed in principle to aid in strengthening the Soviet nuclear arsenal would have been to arouse a public outcry. It was in the nature of the arms control enterprise that the natural passion of the citizen—and in particular, the citizen's instinct for self-defense—was an enemy of the process. McNamara was no more candid than he had to be.

For the military services, for the Congress, and probably for the American people, the most important fact about the American strategic arsenal in the wake of the Cuban missile crisis was its evident superiority over that of any possible adversary.[118] However, it is fair to say that McNamara did not place much value on the superior U.S. strategic position. Indeed, plans were already taking shape to surrender this advantage in favor of a deliberately engineered stalemate.

The new attitude toward defense was linked directly to the Cuban missile crisis, as indicated by a new reference to the problem of the "arms race" in McNamara's 1963 "Annual Posture Statement." "As the events of last October have so forcefully demonstrated," the statement noted, "the expanding arsenals of nuclear weapons on both sides of the Iron Curtain have created an extremely dangerous situation. . . . More armaments, *whether offensive or defensive*, cannot solve this dilemma."[119]

The Limited Test Ban Negotiations

Somewhat characteristically, the Kennedy administration managed to find a reflection of its own change of heart regarding nuclear weapons in the attitude of the Kremlin. Both at the time and afterward, Kennedy administration officials set great store by the change in Soviet behavior following the missile crisis and attributed the shift to a supposed transformation in the Kremlin's view of nuclear arms. Khrushchev, wrote Theodore Sorensen later, "had looked down the barrel of nuclear war and decided that that course was suicidal."[120] But Khrushchev had never really intended to go to nuclear war in the first place; he had simply been bluffing and had gotten caught.

In reality, the Soviets responded to defeat in the Cuban missile crisis in much the same way that they had responded to previous unfavorable shifts in the correlation of forces since 1917—by abandoning the tactics of open bullying and confrontation and moving gradually to a posture of "peaceful coexistence" and détente. "They will . . . try every door in the house," Churchill once told James Forrestal, "enter all rooms which are not locked, and when they come to one that is barred, if they are unsuccessful in breaking through it, they will withdraw and invite you to dine genially that same evening."[121] The negotiations in November and December on removal of missiles and bombers from Cuba were tense—owing perhaps more to Havana's intransigence than to Moscow's—but the invitation to dine soon came. On December 19, Khrushchev devoted the last of a series of letters to Kennedy on Cuba entirely to the test ban negotiations, calling for the "speediest solution which would be mutually acceptable to both sides" and renewing an offer on inspection.[122] Khrushchev's offer did not lead immediately to a treaty, but there is reason to suppose that his letter signaled at least the possibility of a new Soviet receptivity to some kind of an agreement. The offer on inspection—to permit three inspection stations on Soviet soil and allow "2–3 inspections a year" in "seismic regions"[123]—may have been rooted in a misunderstanding. In the letter, Khrushchev claimed to be following a suggestion of U.S. testing negotiator Arthur Dean. However, Dean claimed that he had told Soviet testing negotiator Vasily Kuznetsov that the United States would require a minimum of eight to ten inspections. The Khrushchev formula had evidently come instead from presidential science advisor Jerome Wiesner, who in an October 1962 conversation in Washington with Soviet scientist Yevgeni K. Federov had suggested that Khrushchev offer Kennedy a proposal for three or four inspections a year, with the notion that the United States would make a counteroffer of seven or eight.[124] (It is interesting to see the manner in which U.S. officials strongly committed to arms control, such as Wiesner, would, acting apparently on their own initiative, provide informal guidance to Soviet negotiators in hopes of accelerating the process back home.) Khrushchev, misunderstanding the context of the Wiesner suggestion of two to three inspections, was consequently surprised and disappointed when Kennedy rejected it. Of course such a treaty would have been impossible to police, so in proposing it, Khrushchev was proposing something that the Soviets could have violated.

Nonetheless, the fact that an agreement came within closer reach after the Cuban missile crisis and was eventually achieved suggested an important lesson about arms control, a lesson that was generally not perceived at the time—namely, that it was power relations that determined the success or failure of arms control negotiations rather than the reverse. Throughout the late 1950s under Eisenhower, American negotiators had struggled vainly to arrive at various technical formulations and compromises that might be acceptable to Moscow. Again and again, Moscow had given attainment of an agreement low priority, using the arms negotiations instead to score short-term propaganda victories against the United States. Only now, when confrontational avenues had been closed off, was the Kremlin suddenly apparently receptive to doing business. Since the time of Eisenhower, the United States had striven to stabilize the international environment by engaging in arms control negotiations, to no avail. Ironically, only after the international environment was stabilized—not through negotiations or agreements but through a reassertion of American *power*—did a fruitful agreement with Moscow become possible. This pattern would occur more than once in the Cold War.

Even so, in the end it was not Khrushchev, but Kennedy—heavily prodded by British Prime Minister Harold Macmillan—who provided the main impetus to the final treaty. This, too, conforms to the general pattern of the history of arms control since 1945. In most cases, the Americans were taking the initiative vis-à-vis Moscow, and as often as not they were being pressured to do so by London or other allies. It had been the same with the Baruch Plan.

Despite remarks to this effect by various associates, minutes of meetings do not suggest an overwhelming personal enthusiasm on Kennedy's part for a test ban treaty. To the degree that the president was interested in such an agreement, his interest appears to have been based, somewhat illogically, on the hope that a treaty would halt the Chinese in their development of the bomb.[125] Yet in reality, there was no plan to bring the Chinese into the negotiations and no reason whatever to assume they would follow Moscow's and Washington's example in banning tests.[126]

There was much opposition to the possibility of a total test ban, particularly focusing on the verification problems. News of the exchange of letters between Khrushchev and Kennedy was not well received among Republicans or on Capitol Hill. Until the late 1960s, Congress was basically a force for skepticism regarding disarmament. When news of the December exchange of letters between Khrushchev and Kennedy hit the newspapers in January, the liberal Republican governor of New York, Nelson Rockefeller, lambasted the administration's "bilateral and secret" talks. The House Republican Conference Committee criticized the administration and published a statement from Edward Teller warning against a plan for a small number of "black boxes" and on-site inspections.[127] In a major speech in late February, Senator Thomas Dodd criticized the administration for endangering national security with its concessions on inspection.[128] On March 6, Kennedy finally responded to critics, noting in a press conference that the United States would not agree to a treaty in the absence of "every assurance" of detecting underground tests.[129]

But the administration's hesitant stance toward arms control did not discourage Macmillan, who went into action in March 1963. While Kennedy worried about the Chinese, the British prime minister was apparently anxious about the Germans. "My theory is that unless we can satisfy them by a *general* Test Ban Treaty," Macmillan wrote in his diary, ". . . the Germans are bound to become a nuclear power sooner or later."[130] On March 16, after it became clear that the Geneva talks had stalled,[131] Macmillan sent a lengthy letter to Kennedy pressing for a new initiative. The letter urged a more conciliatory U.S. stance on inspection, arguing that scientific progress would gradually decrease the need for it. Besides, affirmed Macmillan, the Soviets would be "at great risk if they cheat after the signing the treaty."[132] One of Macmillan's suggestions for regaining the initiative was that he, Kennedy, and Khrushchev meet at a summit—which would have been convenient for Macmillan electorally.

Macmillan's pressure evidently had effect. In his March 21 news conference, the president defended the test ban, insisting it was necessary to halt nuclear proliferation. "I see the possibility in the 1970s of the president of the United States having to face a world in which fifteen or twenty or twenty-five nations may have these weapons. I regard that as the greatest possible danger."[133] On March 28, Kennedy sent a basically positive reply to Macmillan. Suspecting the British prime minister's political motives and worried about the reaction of other allies to a three-power summit, Kennedy insisted on postponing any summit meeting with Khrushchev until technical issues were settled. The president instead proposed a joint letter to the Soviet leader and forwarded a draft. While drafts and revisions shuttled back and forth between Washington and London in April, Kennedy asked editor Norman Cousins to use the occasion of an interview with Khrushchev on April 12 to convey a message on the test ban.[134]

Throughout this period, the Soviets continued to use the disarmament talks as a platform for propaganda, attempting both to widen the agenda to include extraneous issues and to shift blame to the United States for lack of progress. All of this suggests—notwithstanding Khrushchev's remarks to Cousins—some discomfort on Khrushchev's side with the actual prospect of a comprehensive ban on nuclear tests. To the end, the Soviets seemed somewhat reluctant to accept a treaty, and a *comprehensive* ban, of course, was never achieved: The final product of the negotiations was a treaty that permitted continued underground tests. However, whatever misgivings Khrushchev may have had about an agreement, there was some desire for détente. It expressed itself most clearly on April 5 when Soviet representative Semyon Tsarapkin, in what Seaborg has described as an "otherwise quite harsh"[135] speech, announced that the Soviet Union was prepared to conclude an agreement establishing a White House–Kremlin "hot line." The hot-line proposal had been in the works since 1962. Interest in the measure rose after the Cuban crisis, where the administration found that it faced four-hour delays—coding, decoding, translation—in sending messages back and forth between capitals.[136]

Partly overshadowed by the hopes for what was perceived as a major step toward disarmament (a ban on nuclear tests), the creation of the hot line—the agreement was concluded on June 5—was the first real arms control agreement of the nuclear age and, in truth, one of the most useful ones. The teletype link made possible an instantaneous communication between the two leaderships—certainly a sensible expedient in an age of worldwide instantaneous communication in which a nuclear holocaust, technically speaking, might be no more than thirty minutes away. It was, in a sense, American political creativity and American "peace" diplomacy at its best.

Khrushchev's initial responses to the April 24 joint initiative from Kennedy and Macmillan were harsh and continued to be harsh in public even as the tone of private communications improved. Khrushchev may well have been looking over his shoulder at the Chinese, who continued to impugn Moscow for insufficient Communist zeal. On May 27, thirty-four senators, led by Dodd and Hubert H. Humphrey, approved a resolution urging the United States to offer a treaty banning tests in the atmosphere and under water, but not underground.[137] The apparent effect of the vote was to tie Kennedy's hands on pursuing a comprehensive ban. But paradoxically, the Senate vote may have made a treaty more feasible, for it pointed to a natural compromise that Khrushchev would doubtless have found somewhat easier to accept than a well-policed comprehensive ban: a limited test-ban treaty that permitted underground testing to continue. On June 8, Khrushchev finally agreed to Kennedy and Macmillan's request for high-level talks in Moscow on tests.[138]

The month of June would bring two of Kennedy's most famous speeches, each pointing in essentially opposite directions. The first, at American University on June 10, marked a major effort to persuade the Soviets to sign a test ban treaty and begin a détente. Kennedy called upon Americans to "re-examine" their attitude toward the Soviet Union and the cold war. "No government or social system is so evil," the president said, "that its people must be considered as lacking in virtue." He emphasized the horrors of nuclear war and decried the arms race. "We are both caught up in a vicious and dangerous cycle with suspicion on one side breeding suspicion on the other, and new weapons begetting counter-weapons," said the president. Both sides, affirmed Kennedy, "have a mutually deep interest in a just and genuine peace and in halting the arms race." The president announced that he was sending Averell Harriman to Moscow for high-level talks on a test ban. He also pledged that the United States would refrain from atmospheric testing as long as other powers did so.[139]

Between the American University address in June and the opening of the Moscow negotiations in July came Kennedy's European trip and a very different kind of speech at the Berlin Wall. The significance of the European trip was more than aesthetic. The reception accorded Kennedy in Western Europe not only marked a high point in the president's personal popularity but a zenith for American power. Not since Woodrow Wilson's triumphal arrival in Paris in 1919 had an American president been so unreservedly embraced by European publics. It was as if the United States had won another major war.

"There are some who say in Europe and elsewhere that we can work with the Communists," Kennedy told the Berlin crowd. "*Lass sie nach*

Berlin kommen! (Let them come to Berlin!)"[140] In part, the choice of such a tone reflected the Kennedy administration's always keen instincts for public relations; two years earlier the administration had turned a deaf ear to pleas of Berliners for resolute action; however, when it came to presidential speech-making and photo opportunities, the administration knew very well what crowds in West Berlin wanted to hear. But the fact that the president now felt free to offer such a provocative utterance within sight of the Berlin Wall was itself a dramatic indication of the preponderance of American power. (Ronald Reagan would make a similar speech at the Brandenburg Gate in 1987.)[141] Such a visit and such a speech by an American president would have been unthinkable in 1961 or before October 1962. One could add that after America had won perhaps the single most important victory thus far of the Cold War and its position was completely unthreatened, it was somewhat easier for the young president to strike a profile in courage.

Seaborg, in his history of the test ban talks, worried retrospectively that Kennedy's tough rhetoric might have derailed the upcoming testing negotiations. This is a very characteristic judgment among members of the arms control community. But one suspects that almost the opposite was the case. The reception accorded to Kennedy in Europe, and the obvious political and military self-confidence of the United States, made détente from the Kremlin's point of view all the more desirable. Why leave Kennedy to bask alone in the new post–missile crisis mood of euphoria? Why not share a place in the limelight? On July 2—during a visit to Berlin—Khrushchev announced the Soviet Union's "readiness to conclude an agreement on the cessation of nuclear tests in the atmosphere, in outer space and under water."[142]

Averell Harriman's twelve days of negotiations in Moscow beginning on July 12, though generally smooth, were not entirely without snags and glitches. The two most significant concerned the Soviet desire for an East-West Nonaggression Pact and the U.S. desire for a withdrawal clause in the treaty. As it happens, the Kennedy administration had enough sense to resist the Soviet Union's effort to draw the United States and Britain into a nonaggression treaty—an agreement that could have strained the broader alliance (since it impinged on vital interests of allies not represented at the table in Moscow) and lulled Western public opinion into assuming that more of the East-West struggle had been resolved than really had been.[143]

The second disagreement concerned the U.S. demand for a withdrawal clause, where the administration's main concern was possible testing by

China. Harriman told Gromyko flatly that without the withdrawal clause there could be no treaty and abruptly left a negotiating session. Harriman's brinkmanship, though provoking a protest from British representative David Ormsby-Gore, nonetheless led to an acceptable compromise formulation.[144]

Debating the Limited Test Ban Treaty

The Kennedy administration showed its characteristic domestic political finesse in handling ratification. Glenn Seaborg later wrote that "Kennedy threw himself into the ratification process with every resource available to him."[145] Numerous private communications with legislators, careful presidential coordination of testimony, a weighing in with his own prestige—such was Kennedy's approach to the delicate process of Senate approval. Theodore Sorensen attributed this to Kennedy's dedication to the test ban,[146] but obviously a measure of self-interest was involved. For the Senate to have rejected the Limited Test Ban Treaty would have been a blow from which Kennedy's presidency would have had difficulty recovering. It was not the first or the last time that the ratification process gave a politician a powerful vested interest in an agreement.

McNamara's testimony was a characteristic performance. So technically charged was the defense secretary's testimony that the *New York Times* even included a "glossary" of terms used by McNamara to defend the treaty. With his usual show of self-confidence, McNamara endorsed the treaty "unequivocally," even claiming that it would maintain rather than diminish U.S. nuclear superiority.[147] (When it was politically convenient to endorse the goal of nuclear superiority, as in aiding the ratification of an arms control treaty, McNamara did not hesitate to do so.)

However, the critical testimony was that of the joint chiefs. It was essential for Kennedy to win their support to gain the two-thirds of the Senate required for approval of ratification. It was this testimony that the senators watched most closely.

The chiefs were not particularly enthusiastic about the Limited Test Ban Treaty. They understood what McNamara would not publicly admit and indeed publicly obfuscated—namely, that from a strictly military perspective, the treaty was essentially disadvantageous to the United States. (It would be particularly harmful to the research necessary to develop an anti-ballistic missile [ABM] system. Because of their violation of the earlier moratorium, the Soviets had much more experience with atmospheric tests.)[148] Kennedy must have understood the chiefs' view of the treaty, because when he met with them on July 23, he encouraged them to consider "political" as well as purely "military" issues in evaluating the agreement.[149] Of course the most important "political" consideration was created by the president's own decision: It would have been extremely difficult, not to say disastrous, for the JCS and for the nation, for the joint chiefs to oppose the treaty after it had been signed. In his testimony, Air Force Chief of Staff Curtis LeMay indicated that the last-minute push to achieve the treaty had actually taken the chiefs by surprise. "I think we were all caught a little bit by surprise at the seriousness of the Administration trying to get a treaty signed," LeMay told the Senate Foreign Relations Committee.[150] As the price for their support, the chiefs insisted on four "safeguards," which Maxwell Taylor spelled out in his testimony during the Senate hearings: conduct of an aggressive underground testing program, maintenance of weapons lab facilities sufficient to attract top talent, maintenance of capabilities to resume atmospheric tests in the event of a Soviet resumption of such tests, and improvement in the ability to detect Soviet violations and assess Soviet nuclear capabilities. Speaking for the joint chiefs, Taylor concluded on the unenthusiastic note that "while there are military disadvantages to the treaty, they are not so serious as to render it unacceptable."[151]

Perhaps the most important military disadvantage, at least as it appeared in retrospect, was the adverse impact of the atmospheric test ban on the development of missile defenses or ABM. Testifying to Congress just six months before the treaty was signed, McNamara had opposed early ABM deployment on grounds that further testing would be necessary (testing would have included nuclear testing, since 1960s-vintage ABMs employed nuclear warheads). Yet now McNamara contradictorily insisted that the ban on atmospheric tests would not adversely affect development of ABMs, even though there had been no atmospheric tests in the interim.[152] What Congress did not realize, and what McNamara was not eager to convey, was that the defense secretary had already effectively decided to forgo ABMs.

Notwithstanding the military disadvantages—the effect on ABMs and the freezing into place of a (less important) Soviet advantage in high-yield weapons—the Limited Test Ban Treaty was on balance a beneficial and important achievement. Above all, in banning atmospheric testing by the two superpowers, the treaty greatly curtailed what could only have been a growing environmental hazard from nuclear testing. In doing so, somewhat ironically, the treaty also probably strengthened public support for nuclear deterrence. In forcing tests underground, the agreement removed a critical provocation for public opinion and a rallying point for antinuclear protests.

The benefits expected by proponents of arms control, however, were generally not realized. The agreement did not "slow" the arms race; indeed, it may have contributed to something of an acceleration, as both sides moved to implement aggressive underground testing programs. Nor did the agreement constitute a "first step" toward accelerated disarmament agreements (the next major arms agreement was the somewhat unspectacular Outer Space Treaty in 1967). The treaty was not so much the source as the *product* of a new stability in U.S.-Soviet relations—a stability born of the American victory in the Cuban missile crisis and of the apparent American superiority in nuclear arms. That stability, however, would prove to be short-lived.

The Limited Test Ban Treaty was approved by the Senate 80 to 19 on September 24. Less than two months later, on November 22, President Kennedy was assassinated.

CHAPTER 7

◻

Limited Arms, Limited War

Historians have debated endlessly how events would have gone—and in particular how the Vietnam war would have gone—if the assassin's bullet had missed, and Kennedy, rather than Lyndon Johnson, had remained president until 1964 or even 1968. On the one hand, there was a surprising degree of continuity between the thinking at the beginning of the Kennedy administration and the policies of the later Johnson years. On the other hand, it is hard not to feel that following Kennedy's departure events were destined to go awry.

The Kennedy administration without John Kennedy somewhat resembled the Eisenhower administration after the death of Dulles: In each case, with the disappearance of a key figure, something of the administration's original ballast and equipoise was lost. Deprived of Dulles's tough-minded advice in the last two years of his second term, Eisenhower surrendered unreservedly to his "peace" impulses, with generally mischievous results. In a similar fashion, deprived of Kennedy's tempering political influence, the Kennedy advisors surrendered wholesale to their ivory-tower vision and their ingenious but flawed theories of deterrence and limited war.

In losing Kennedy the Democrats lost a great deal. First there were the ineffable grace and charm of the man—qualities that actually translated into serious political assets. Even allowing for public-relations manipulations ("We are going to sell Jack like soap flakes," Joseph Kennedy had said when his son first ran for Congress), Kennedy won extraordinary adulation from columnists and reporters and unstinting loyalty from subordinates. There were clearly personal qualities in the man that attracted admiration. Consequently, unlike so many presidents before and since, he had both the news media and the chief officials of his administration generally on his side. The same could not be said, of course, for Lyndon Johnson, whose personality and public presence were of a kind to win him little love

Johnson, though by no means unintelligent, would never command the loyalty or the intellectual respect that the original Kennedy team accorded their young leader. Consequently, Johnson would have less control. Generally speaking, Kennedy's departure would leave the Kennedy advisors free to follow their own vision without restraint. The vision would take them into disaster in Vietnam.

The Soviet Buildup

Between 1964 and 1968, the remarkably favorable power position that the United States had achieved as a result of victory in the Cuban missile crisis would largely evaporate. Many explanations might be offered for this defeat, but for the most part it appears to have been self-inflicted. To a remarkable degree, the decline in the American power position could be attributed to conceptual errors, to policy mistakes rooted in adherence to flawed theories. In particular, in the latter half of the 1960s, the Johnson administration became guilty of a colossal misreading of the nature and intentions of America's two major enemies, the Soviet Union and North Vietnam. At the root of this misreading lay a familiar culprit: theories associated with the new doctrine of arms control.

The first error was in a sense factual: Guided by the new theoretical paradigm, Johnson administration military and intelligence officials severely underestimated the Soviet missile buildup. A huge shift in the power balance was to take place beginning in the mid-1960s essentially without Washington registering the change. Indeed, owing in no small measure to errors traceable to Johnson administration forecasting and planning, the Soviets would effect a major shift in the military balance between 1965 and 1980. Far from opting out of the arms race as McNamara had predicted, the Soviets accelerated their buildup. Between 1962 and 1972, the Soviet Union deployed five new ICBMs, a new SLBM, and four new types of ballistic missile submarine.[1] By 1971–1972, the Soviets would possess 1,510 ICBMs—roughly 500 more than the United

States.[2] (The buildup *after* the signing of SALT in 1972 would be even more rapid.)

Far from accepting a mutual stalemate on the McNamara model, moreover, the Soviets would pursue a first-strike capability against the American ICBM force. By 1969, it would become apparent that the Soviet SS-9 was being designed to destroy U.S. Minuteman missiles in their silos.[3] The successor to the SS-9, the SS-18, would give the Soviets by the early 1980s the capacity to destroy 90 percent of the U.S. ICBM force in its silos. By the mid-1970s, it was clear that the CIA had seriously underestimated the growth of Soviet military power and the Soviet military budget for the past decade and a half.[4]

How did U.S. intelligence fail to predict the Soviet buildup? Several factors contributed, but the most important was McNamara's strategic vision, which he increasingly assumed the Soviets had come to share. McNamara and his "Whiz Kids," assuming Moscow's calculations mirrored their own, saw the Soviets as seeking no more than an "assured destruction" capability.[5] Trained as economists, they assumed Soviet economic problems would impede Soviet military spending. According to McNamara in April 1965, the Soviets had "decided" that they had "lost the quantitative race, and they are not seeking to engage in that contest."[6]

In all this there was a striking absence of thought about Soviet history, culture, or strategy. The portion of Soviet gross national product devoted to military spending had always varied. But the principle of strengthening the military even at the severe expense of civilian economy was, as we know, deeply imbued in the Bolshevik tradition from the 1920s onward.[7] Moreover, it would not have required a deep knowledge of Russian culture to grasp why concepts such as "mutual assured destruction" might not have had a particular appeal for the power-oriented Soviet elite. In addition, there was a body of Soviet strategic writings—including Marshall Sokolovskii's famous tome, by then translated into English—that suggested the Soviets would approach questions relating to nuclear war in a fashion quite different from that of the United States.[8] Finally, there was the Soviet obsession with power. Once the Soviets lost power, as they had in the Cuban missile crisis, it was imperative that they work to regain it. The whole weight of the Soviet Union in the international system depended on its capacity to intimidate. None of this could be predicted by the McNamara analysts' one-dimensional "rational actor" models.

The Vietnam Quagmire

The mistake of underestimating the seriousness and persistence of Moscow's challenge was repeated with respect to Hanoi. Just as the Kennedy-Johnson team wrongly assumed that the Soviets could be drawn into a static relationship of mutual assured destruction in the strategic arms competition, so many Johnson administration officials came to persuade themselves that the North Vietnamese and their surrogates in the South might be drawn into a "cooperative" game of limited war in Southeast Asia.

"The trouble with our policy in Vietnam," Assistant Secretary of Defense Paul Warnke was to remark upon leaving office at the height of the Vietnam turmoil in 1969, "has been that we guessed wrong with respect to what the North Vietnamese reaction would be. We anticipated that they would respond like reasonable people."[9] Interestingly, Warnke, like so many other Johnson administration defense and foreign policy officials, played a central role not only in formulating the administration's Vietnam policy but also in shaping the U.S. approach to strategic arms control. A committed arms controller, he would later go on to negotiate SALT II under Jimmy Carter. Warnke's confession of failure with respect to Vietnam, therefore, offers an interesting perspective on the origins of the SALT talks. Could it have been that the same mistake was made in both efforts?

Certainly, it would be an exaggeration to claim that arms control theory—or more generally, the "limited war/deterrence" paradigm—was solely responsible for America's defeat in Vietnam. But neither is it quite fair to argue that the Vietnam defeat was simply inherent in the American bureaucratic "system" or in the nature of the "containment" policy as practiced by both Republican and Democratic administrations. Such an explanation overlooks the genuinely peculiar assumptions and military methods that governed the Johnson administration's decision making regarding Vietnam from the very start—methods and assumptions rooted in the strategic theories that the Kennedy advisors had brought with them into office.[10]

One may begin by contrasting the Johnson administration's handling of the 1964 Vietnam crisis with the Eisenhower administration's approach to Indochina almost exactly ten years earlier. In 1964, Johnson, like his predecessor, faced a deteriorating situation in Vietnam (a direct consequence of the December 1963 decision by the Ninth Plenum of the North Vietnamese Communist Party to escalate the level of armed violence in the South).[11] In a sense, of course, the 1964 crisis was more serious for Washington, since American prestige was now directly engaged in Vietnam.

Yet the contrast between the Johnson and the Eisenhower/Dulles approaches could hardly have been more vivid. First, Dulles's instinct with regard to Indochina was, characteristically, to keep the enemy guessing. Repeatedly, the secretary of state implied that a Communist takeover of the country would bring large-scale U.S. involvement and even, possibly, atomic weapons use against the Soviet Union and China. Second—a related though somewhat distinct point—through the massive retaliation strategy the Eisenhower administration made clear that no easy line could be drawn between local war in Indochina and general war with China and the Soviet Union—thereby cementing the link between the (inherently weak) U.S. position in the area and the (inherently strong) U.S. strategic capabilities. Third, despite the apparent nonchalance with which the administration threatened military action, Eisenhower behind the scenes remained fully cognizant of the vast costs and risks entailed in actually embarking on new military operations. *Eisenhower listened to the military.* In weighing options in both Korea and Indochina (Vietnam), the president was attentive to the recommendations of joint chiefs and faced up squarely to the fact that favorable military results could not be purchased on the cheap. At the same time, he was a shrewd enough geopolitician not to advertise his reluctance regarding the use of military instruments to the American public or to the other side.

Not so with Johnson. In sharp contrast to Eisenhower and Dulles, Johnson and his advisors continually assured Moscow, Beijing, and Hanoi—and the American public—that the United States wished no wider war with the Soviet Union or China, and indeed would not even threaten the viability of North Vietnam. Far from keeping his adversaries guessing, Johnson—taking his bearings partly from the emphasis on clear communication in Democratic limited war theory—sought to keep the enemy reassured. For example, Johnson's first use of the hot line, amid U.S. bombing in retaliation for the Tonkin Gulf incident in August 1964, was to convey a personal message to Khrushchev that the United States did not seek to expand the war.[12] Repeatedly, Johnson assured the American people and the world: "We seek no wider war."[13] Meanwhile, during the 1964 presidential election, the famous "atomic bomb" TV commercial run by the Johnson campaign—showing a little girl holding a daisy followed by a shot of a mushroom cloud—implied that while Republican candidate Barry Goldwater might use nuclear weapons over Vietnam,

President Johnson clearly would not, another sign that the nuclear option had been excluded, a position reinforced by campaign speeches.[14]

Second, rejecting the massive retaliation principle out of hand, Johnson sought to separate Vietnam from other issues in the superpower relationship. Not only did Johnson avoid threatening the Soviets; he actively pursued other negotiations—especially arms control negotiations—even as Soviet surface-to-air (SAM) missiles destroyed American pilots and Soviet-made weapons were employed by the North Vietnamese and Viet Cong against American ground troops. Johnson's diplomacy created a "delinkage" between Vietnam and strategic capabilities. The United States deliberately did not seek to benefit from its strategic strength and did not use other diplomatic levers to win concessions from Moscow on the war.

Finally, again in clear contrast to Eisenhower, Johnson insulated himself from the advice of the U.S. military. Again and again, at the behest of his civilian defense advisors, Johnson simply ignored the military's counsel to the effect that only major and sudden escalation of the conflict would produce effective results. The degree to which the American military was excluded from top-level Vietnam war decision making was remarkable. During the first two years of the Rolling Thunder bombing campaign, bombing targets were actually chosen at weekly Tuesday luncheons by Johnson and key civilian advisors with *no military representative present*.[15]

Indeed, one key structural difference between the two administrations consisted of the layer of civilian Whiz Kids—the latter steeped in arms control theory—between the president and the military. This new layer of experts fundamentally altered the balance of power within the bureaucracy, preventing the military from exerting what would have been its normal influence. Not only did the civilian "experts" freely substitute their own advice for that of the military on the most detailed matters; they provided Johnson with a ready-made theory to justify the severely self-restrained and "limited" American approach to the conflict.

The Pentagon Papers, the classified history of the war commissioned by McNamara in 1967, make abundantly clear that limited war theory pervaded the administration's thinking and strategizing about the war from 1965 onward—as regards both the bombing campaign and the deployment of U.S. troops.[16]

Straightforward recommendations by the military for large-scale action were pared down in favor of gradual, "controlled" use of force designed to elicit a "cooperative" response from the enemy. McGeorge Bundy's pivotal memo of February 1965, recommending a policy of "graduated and continuing reprisal," which soon evolved into the first major bombing campaign, captured the flavor of the approach: "This reprisal policy *should begin at a low level. Its level of force and pressure should be increased only gradually*—and as indicated above it should be *decreased if VC terror visibly decreases. The object would not be to 'win'* an air war against Hanoi, but rather to influence the course of the struggle in the South."[17] Rationality, proportionality, an ever-scrupulous subordination of means to end, and, above all, the signaling of a clear and open desire to limit conflict and avoid nuclear weapons use—such were the guiding principles of limited war theorists such as Kaufmann and Schelling, and such were the guiding principles of the Johnson administration's approach to Vietnam.

While the joint chiefs argued, from traditional military logic, in favor of a policy of sudden escalation—they called for a bombing campaign hitting ninety-four targets[18]—civilian officials in the State Department Office of the Secretary of Defense cleaved (with no small measure of intellectual arrogance) to their limited war model. The Rolling Thunder bombing campaign, finally initiated in March, was not only designed to build gradually, but even included "bargaining pauses" intended to signal the limited nature of U.S. aims and open the way to a negotiated solution. The aim, to recall Kaufmann's 1956 formulation, was to "find deterrents that forecast costs sufficient to discourage the enemy, but not provocative enough to make him turn, out of fear and desperation, to contingencies of the last resort."[19] In outlining the purposes of the bombing campaign in a June 1965 memorandum, McNamara emphasized the need to "minimize the loss of North Vietnamese face" and "avoid undue risks and costs."[20]

Such a policy approach could not help but undercut military effectiveness. "Unless they secured the president's approval through the Joint Chiefs," Mark Clodfelter has written, "air commanders could not attack targets with a 30-mile radius from the center of Hanoi, a 10-mile radius from the center of Haiphong, and within 30 miles of China. In December 1966, Johnson established 'prohibited areas' around Hanoi and Haiphong. These were zones where no attacks or overflights were permitted."[21]

There were other factors that pushed the administration toward the limited war approach, including the shift in the strategic balance. In contrast to the situation in the 1950s, the Soviet Union now had 200 ICBMs capable of striking at the United States.[22]

Further, Johnson had his own memory of Korea, and of the Chinese intervention.[23] As he asked joint chiefs chairman General Earle Wheeler in 1966 when the latter recommended mining Haiphong harbor, "Do you think this will involve the Chinese Communists and the Soviets?" When Wheeler answered, "No sir," Johnson replied, "Are you more sure than MacArthur was?"[24]

Finally, Johnson feared that a full-fledged war would disrupt his domestic "Great Society" program.[25] Fearful that a right-wing reaction in favor of the war would overwhelm his domestic policies, Johnson downplayed the escalation in Vietnam and sought to keep the public emotionally unengaged.

Yet the very hope that the war could be waged in such a limited fashion—that an adequate solution could be achieved without any risk of confrontation with Moscow, without mobilizing public support, without quick and major escalation, and without raising taxes—owed much to the faulty Democratic memory of Korea and to limited war theory. The existence of a model of limited war, with all its fallacies, clouded the real choice facing the president, which was in truth one between humiliating withdrawal and major escalation entailing large risks. The theory permitted Johnson to believe—or half-believe—that the self-restrained manner in which he was waging war might work.

As a result of this self-restrained behavior and of presidential statements, Clodfelter notes, "North Vietnamese leaders knew that Johnson had no intention of unleashing unrestricted air power against their country."[26] Indeed, the effect was to reassure the North Vietnamese about the limited nature of the threat posed by the United States while at the same time provoking them. As a RAND study concluded, "In terms of its morale effects, the U.S. [bombing] campaign may have presented the [North Vietnamese] regime with a near-ideal mix of intended restraint and accidental gore."[27]

There were those who saw the fallacies of this approach at the time. CIA director John McCone argued it was necessary to "hit" North Vietnam "harder and more frequently and inflict greater damage": "Instead of avoiding the MIGs we must go in and take them out. A bridge here and there will not do the job. We must strike their airfields, their petroleum resources, power stations, and their military compounds. This, in my opinion, must be done promptly and with minimum restraint."[28]

As McCone understood, apart from the physical effect of the bombing, there was the issue of psychological impact. A more thorough and sudden bombing effort—combined with a measure of deliberate ambiguity about American intentions—would have given the North Vietnamese something to worry about. As it was, the North Vietnamese were reassured, understanding the conflict fundamentally as a contest of wills. As General Vo Nguyen Giap said many years afterward: "Our intention was to break the will of the American Government to continue the war. . . . In war there are the two factors—human beings and weapons. Ultimately, though, human beings are the decisive factor."[29]

To a large degree, the administration was misled by its success in the Cuban missile crisis—or its misunderstanding of that success. David Halberstam writes that the example of the missile crisis, with its "slow, judicious" use of force, was "vivid" in McNamara's mind as he planned the Rolling Thunder bombing campaign in March 1965.[30]

Underlying it all was a remarkable lack of basic strategic insight, an almost astonishing incomprehension of the logic of employing military force. William Westmoreland, the Vietnam army commander whose war memoir (like that of his naval counterpart, Admiral U. S. Grant Sharp) bitterly repudiated the civilian decision makers, recalled a particular episode involving the arms controller John T. McNaughton, a key Pentagon Vietnam strategist:

> Some of McNaughton's views, in particular, were incredible. On a visit to Saigon at a time when my air commander, Joe Moore, and I were trying to get authority to bomb SAM-2 (a Soviet-made missile) sites under construction in North Vietnam, McNaughton ridiculed the need. "You don't think the North Vietnamese are going to use them!" he scoffed to General Moore. "Putting them in is just a political ploy by the Russians to appease Hanoi."
>
> It was all a matter of signals, said the clever civilian theorists in Washington. We won't bomb SAM sites, which signals the North Vietnamese not to use them.[31]

In short, the war was being waged from Washington by neophytes without significant military experience and only academic theories to guide them. "Had it not been so serious," wrote Westmoreland, "it would have been amusing."[32]

Neglecting Diplomatic Linkage

During 1966, an average of over a hundred Americans died each week in Vietnam. By the end of the year, the number of American troops in the country had risen to 450,000.[33] Bombing sorties against the Communists were being flown at the rate of 4,000 per month. For the fiscal year ending June 1967, McNamara had projected a budget for Vietnam of $7 to $11 billion. Vietnam would cost $21 billion for that fiscal year, and costs would steadily increase thereafter.[34] By almost any measure—notwithstanding the president's efforts to downplay the importance of the commitment—the country was involved in a major war.

The Soviets, too, were devoting resources to Vietnam. Douglas Pike has estimated that by late 1966, Soviet defense expenditures had increased by from 5 to 15 percent because of Moscow's assistance to the North Vietnamese. Between 1960 and 1975, Hanoi had probably received about $5 billion in military assistance from the Soviets, as well as significant economic aid.[35] By comparison with the American commitment, of course, this was a small outlay. But it was vital to Hanoi's war effort. Without advanced Soviet weapons—and in particular advanced Soviet SAM missiles—North Vietnam would have been defenseless against American bombers. War with the United States on such a scale became militarily and politically possible for the North Vietnamese only with Moscow's support.

Given the deadly importance of the war as measured by both its economic cost and the toll in American lives, and given the indispensability of Soviet aid to the Vietnamese, why was not a greater diplomatic effort made to get Moscow out of the business of funding North Vietnamese aggression against the South? When Johnson speechwriter Jack Valenti, a Houston advertising man uninitiated into the arcane strategic theories of the Johnson defense advisors, asked this naive question in 1966, he was given a curious answer. In a memo of March 29, 1966, NSC staffer Robert Komer pointed out that diplomatic approaches had indeed been made to the Soviets by both Averell Harriman and Dean Rusk. They had been unavailing. Komer attributed Soviet intransigence to competition with Beijing and to Moscow's supposedly "tenuous" leverage with the North Vietnamese.[36]

Yet whatever the limits of Moscow's influence with the North Vietnamese, the fact remained that without Moscow's aid Hanoi would have been helpless. At a time when American soldiers were dying by the hundreds, and pilots falling from the sky to the terrible fate of imprisonment in Vietnamese Communist prison camps, would it not have made sense for the Johnson administration to make Moscow's support of North Vietnamese aggression not merely one subject but the central subject of superpower diplomacy? Would it not have been wise to put other issues on hold until Moscow showed some give on Vietnam?

The administration apparently never considered such an option. Walt Rostow's explanation for this, offered in an interview many years later, was instructive. "We had other interests," said LBJ's national security advisor, "—nonproliferation."[37]

In short, the administration was deterred from pressing what should have been its most important priority partly by its abiding interest in arms control. Indeed, all through the war period, Johnson sought to continue a policy of diplomacy-as-usual with the Soviets—much as he attempted to continue an economy-as-usual (no tax hike) and a poverty-program-as-usual despite the war.[38] In the administration's negotiations with Moscow, Vietnam was kept on the back burner. The focus instead was on arms issues.

The degree to which the administration gave short shrift to Vietnam in its diplomacy with the Soviets seems almost astonishing in retrospect. In the summer of 1966, for example, Secretary of State Rusk decided he would like to make progress with Moscow on the Outer Space Treaty. "I believe Sect. Rusk would like to see if we can get Gromyko over here a week before the U.N. General Assembly to try to nail down the Outer Space Treaty and, if possible, the Non-Proliferation Treaty," Rostow wrote to Johnson in August 1966.[39] One may ask: With American sons dying in the jungles of Vietnam, why was the American secretary of state worrying about the distant possibility of future weapons in outer space? To compound the incongruity, Rusk actually opposed a joint chiefs' recommendation at the time for increased bombing in Vietnam, fearing that such an escalation might spoil the atmosphere for the talks with Gromyko.[40] In effect, the Outer Space Treaty was being given priority over the lives of American soldiers.

Little wonder, then, that the United States got nowhere with Moscow, or for that matter with Hanoi, in its search for a diplomatic settlement of the war. In effect, a total dissociation arose between what the administration considered to be the core issues of superpower diplomacy—mainly arms control issues—and the supposedly "peripheral" question of Vietnam. Yet in a democracy, no war that is costing a hundred lives a week can take any position but center stage in national life. And indeed, Vietnam was to be, from the American perspective, the central event of two decades. It would transform not only American foreign policy but American culture. The prolongation of the war would rend American society and bring a fundamental revolution in politics and morals.

This is not to say that the administration's concern with nuclear non-proliferation was entirely misplaced. Certainly the nonproliferation effort appeared to bear fruit over the long run. By the 1990s, there were far fewer nations possessing nuclear weapons than had once been predicted. To what degree the Nonproliferation Treaty itself was instrumental in achieving this result is a matter for debate. One must recall that the Soviets had an independent interest in preventing the spread of nuclear weapons to other countries, apart from any signature on a treaty. The fact remains: At a time when thousands of American soldiers were dying in a distant conflict, the administration spent what leverage it had with the Soviets to gain Outer Space and Nonproliferation treaties rather than holding good relations with Moscow hostage to a settlement of Vietnam. The Johnson administration's approach contrasts sharply with that of the Reagan administration, which was later to reestablish linkage by making Soviet involvement in so-called regional conflicts one of the pillars of superpower diplomacy.

Debating ABM

Even as the Johnson administration pursued its curious strategy of self-imposed stalemate in Southeast Asia, it took further deliberate steps to institutionalize stalemate in the arms competition with the Soviet Union. The long-running dispute on whether to deploy a U.S. ABM came to a head on December 6, 1966, when Johnson met with McNamara, the joint chiefs of staff, and key civilian advisors at the State Building in Austin, Texas, for a final airing of the issues. The meeting pitted McNamara, arguing against a major ABM deployment, against joint chiefs of staff chairman General Wheeler and the rest of the chiefs, arguing in favor of deployment. Minutes of the meeting, declassified in 1990, make for particularly interesting reading, for they show not only an extremely sharp difference between the defense secretary and the military chiefs but a more effective case for ABM on the chiefs' part than historical accounts of the episode have reflected.[41]

The debate in 1967 turned neither on the issue of technical "stability" nor on the question of feasibility. Evidently neither Johnson nor the chiefs would have been impressed by the stability argument of the arms controllers, and, as Morton Halperin has suggested, after 1963, the basic feasibility of ABM at least at some level was no longer in doubt.[42] Rather, the debate turned on McNamara's contention that the Soviets would react to the U.S. ABM by expanding offensive weapons, eventually negating the value of an ABM and in the meantime causing both sides to spend enormous amounts of money. According to McNamara, the Soviets "would be forced to react to a U.S. ABM deployment by increasing its offensive nuclear forces with the result that: a. The risk of a Soviet nuclear attack on the U.S. would not be further decreased. b. The damage to the U.S. from a Soviet nuclear attack, in the event deterrence failed, would not be reduced in any meaningful sense." Rather than deploying an antimissile defense, the key to nuclear strategy was to maintain the U.S. "assured destruction" capability, according to McNamara.[43]

At the Austin meeting, General Earle Wheeler took direct issue with McNamara's analysis. First, Wheeler pointed to steady growth in both defensive and offensive Soviet forces. Were the Soviets seeking parity, or did they ultimately desire strategic superiority? Wheeler could not say. Clearly, the JCS chairman did not share McNamara's assumption that the Soviets desired no more than parity or an "assured destruction" capability against the United States.

Second, Wheeler took direct issue with McNamara's central contention that the Soviets would "be forced" to react to a U.S. ABM deployment by expanding their offensive forces and could do so relatively cheaply, thereby negating the U.S. ABM advantage. It was impossible to predict, said Wheeler, how the Soviets would react. Perhaps more important, the JCS chairman stressed a point that McNamara's analysis had apparently overlooked—namely, that a Soviet reaction would not be cost-free. "The costs" of responding to a U.S. ABM, said Wheeler, "would constitute an important diversion of resources." For example, if the Soviets moved to multiple warheads in order to counter a U.S. ABM, the move "would reduce the kilotonnage of their nuclear payloads." Wheeler argued that a U.S. ABM would add to deterrence by posing "grave uncertainties" for Soviet planners preparing an attack upon the United States. Deterrence "was not only technology," Wheeler said, "it was a state of mind. Our having an ABM system would increase our deterrence capability no matter what [the Soviets] did."

On the other hand, failure to deploy the ABM, the general said, would be to "increase the possibilities of war by accident." In addition, he noted, it might suggest a lack of resolve—"that the U.S. was not willing to pay to maintain its present nuclear superiority." The general also raised the issue of lives saved in the event of nuclear war. Thirty to fifty million lives might be saved by the Nike-X, ABM, Wheeler noted.

But the crux of the JCS case turned on the need to maintain a favorable balance of power. The joint chiefs recommended deployment of Nike-X "to maintain the kind of favorable power environment which helped us during the Cuba [*sic*] missile crisis."

McNamara responded that the Soviets had been "wrong" in emphasizing defensive systems and were wasting their money; that they would inevitably respond to any U.S. defense by restoring their own "assured destruction" capability; and that the result would be a huge expenditure that would leave both sides "no better off than we are at present."

However, to placate the chiefs and lessen the political impact on Johnson, McNamara recommended a limited ABM deployment aimed at protecting U.S. missiles and insuring against a possible future Communist Chinese ICBM, protecting against accidental launch, and protecting against "a small blackmail Soviet attack." Nonetheless, it was clear that the chiefs would not be satisfied with the limited option.

Nor was Johnson yet completely persuaded by McNamara. In a presidential order to Rostow following the Austin meeting, the president solicited responses from the government's leading foreign policy and Soviet experts on the question of the probable Soviet reaction to a U.S. ABM deployment. Interestingly, the two experts with extensive knowledge of the Soviet Union—Llewelyn Thompson and Foy Kohler—did not share McNamara's assessment of the probable Soviet response, even though they were sympathetic to his general position on ABM and arms control. Both specialists predicted that the Soviets would *not* respond to a U.S. ABM simply with increased offensive forces but would also expand their *defenses*—in line with their traditional priorities. Such efforts to compete with the U.S. ABM, Kohler stressed, would impose heavy, almost impossible costs on the Soviets. "With vast investment requirements in the civilian economy, with $300 billion GNP against our $630 billion and military and space programs running about 80% of our investment, the Soviet leadership would be up against an almost insoluble problem," Kohler wrote.[44]

Consequences of Forgoing ABM

As it turns out, the ABM decision was indeed a critical turning point, but not because it opened the way to controlling the arms race. On the contrary, it created an incentive for the Soviets to race harder. For rather than redirect the arms competition down a path in which the United States would have in all likelihood quickly achieved a decisive qualitative lead—high-technology defensive systems—the Johnson administration chose to close off or at least partially block the defensive path and confine the main arms competition to offensive ballistic missiles—a field in which the Soviets already had gained substantial experience, in which Soviet expertise was constantly improving, and where eventually parity or even loss of parity by the United States was a virtual inevitability. The Nike-Zeus/Nike-X ABM system might not have been able to handle the "sophisticated threat" that McNamara chose to predict for the late 1960s and early 1970s. But it is not clear that Soviet technologies for penetration aids would have been able to match those projected for the United States even in that period. And the early U.S. ABM would have been followed by successor systems, of ever-increasing technological sophistication and effectiveness. There is no reason to suppose that, once defensive technologies became a national priority, the United States would not apply to the ABM program much of the same energy and ingenuity that American scientists had brought to the "missile gap" or the space program, in which the United States had quickly surpassed the Soviet Union. (Even assuming some ideological opposition to ABM in the scientific community—primarily among middle-age "nuclear scientists"—the generous funding for ABM would have placed an abundance of talent at the government's disposal.) In addition, given the inevitable resource trade-offs facing both the United States and the Soviet Union, a sizable U.S. defensive program would also probably have had the additional benefit of reducing the number of *offensive* nuclear weapons acquired by both sides. It was simply inconceivable that both nations could mount sizable ABM systems and at the same time acquire upward of 9,000 strategic offensive weapons—the totals achieved by the mid-1980s after a competition largely confined, thanks to the ABM Treaty, to offensive weapons. The Soviets, who were devoting a full quarter of their GNP to military spending by the late 1980s,[45] would hardly have been in a position to do more. So a world with U.S. defenses would probably have been a world with *fewer* offensive nuclear weapons—to say nothing of the protection ABM would have provided against limited nuclear strikes of whatever kind and even, in some measure, against a full-scale nuclear attack. The decision to forgo ABM simplified the problem the Soviets faced in devising an attack on the United States.

At the root of McNamara's approach to the arms competition was a principle that could be traced back to the thinking of British liberals before World War I—"moderation breeds moderation," or goodwill breeds goodwill. Since the arms race originated in an "action-reaction phenomenon," as McNamara supposed, the key to moderating the arms competition would be unilateral restraint on the American side.

McNamara's Anti-ABM Speech

Unilateral restraint failed to work even in the short run. In his State of the Union message on January 10, 1967, President Johnson announced that he would seek to negotiate a moratorium with the Soviet Union on ABM deployment as a way of curbing the arms race. Administration officials explained that a decision had been reached to forgo a U.S. ABM deployment.[46] The Soviet response was characteristically ambiguous and uncooperative.[47] Even McNamara's emphatic luncheon speech at the June 1967 Glassboro summit outlining the dangers of defenses and supposed advantages of mutual vulnerability failed to arouse visible Soviet interest.[48]

Finally, in frustration, and perhaps with the intention of goading the Soviets to the negotiating table,[49] Johnson announced in mid-September that the United States would deploy a limited ABM directed against China.

If Johnson's initial announcement of ABM deployment failed to galvanize Moscow into action, the lag in the Soviet response may have been owing to the curious speech McNamara gave to United Press International editors in San Francisco on September 18, 1967, ostensibly to justify the ABM decision. The speech, drafted by Halperin[50] and delivered just two months before McNamara's resignation, was the most open and naked statement of McNamara's commitment to the ideology of arms control. Far from supporting the ABM deployment, the speech offered an extensive argument against ABM. McNamara explained the concept of "assured destruction." He characterized the U.S. buildup since 1961 as a mistaken overreaction to Soviet moves, and argued that the arms race of the 1960s had grown out of a series of mutual misinterpretations by each side of the other's intentions. He went on to define the action-reaction phenomenon:

> What is essential to understand here is that the Soviet Union and the United States mutually influence one another's strategic plans.
>
> Whatever be their intentions, whatever be our intentions, actions—or even realistically potential actions—on either side relating to the buildup of nuclear forces, be they either offensive or defensive weapons, necessarily trigger reactions on the other side. It is precisely this action-reaction phenomenon that fuels an arms race.

Having spent most of the speech presenting the argument against an ABM and decrying what he called the "mad momentum" of the arms race, McNamara concluded by endorsing the anti-Chinese ABM deployment.[51]

Given the profound lack of enthusiasm in McNamara's endorsement of ABM, the Soviets might well have had reason to doubt that the United States was serious about deployment and indeed still failed to move on negotiations.

In January 1968, Johnson requested $1.2 billion from Congress for ABM—now re-named Sentinel—with an additional $269 million for research.[52] However, thanks in no small part to McNamara's speech—and the galvanizing effect it had on the opposition forces to ABM in what was already becoming known as the "arms control community"—ABM had become controversial. In June, a motion to postpone deployment came to a Senate vote.[53] The motion was defeated, and initial funds were approved for Sentinel.[54]

One week later, Moscow agreed to begin strategic arms talks. The announcement came as part of the signing of the Nonproliferation Treaty.

In short, only when it become evident that the United States was about to proceed with an ABM did arms talks designed at limiting or curtailing ABM systems became attractive to the Soviets. Did the willingness to enter such talks reflect the adoption by Moscow of a new strategic vision, a new strategic paradigm, an incipient form of "mutual assured destruction"? Or did Moscow's interest in the talks rather reflect a Soviet assessment that the United States was now in a position, if it chose, to win the race in defensive technologies? The latter answer seems far more likely. At all events, the pattern seen in 1967 and 1968 would frequently be repeated. U.S. gestures of unilateral restraint would prove unavailing with the Soviets, while American decisions to go forward with various weapons programs would spur the Soviets into arms negotiations.

Senator Jackson's Warning

The combination of Johnson's unilateral gesture of early 1967 and McNamara's September 1967 speech on the action-reaction phenomenon fundamentally transformed the defense debate. It established as a respectable and commonly held political position that the key to arms control progress lay in unilaterally cutting U.S. defense programs, in the expectation that such gestures would aid negotiations and that the Soviet Union would eventually reciprocate American self-restraint. The appeal of this principle could hardly be overestimated. It fundamentally transformed congressional opinion and fundamentally undermined the congressional consensus in favor of a strong defense. Not only did the strong congressional support for ABM rapidly dissipate, but from 1968 onward, strategic program after strategic program would run into congressional objections on the grounds that the program in question would spur a Soviet reaction and should be forgone in favor of arms control. No longer could an administration count, *as every previous administration since Truman had been able to count*, on strong congressional support for *at least* the level of defense spending that it recommended. The transformation took place against the background of the rising unpopularity of the Vietnam war. But without Johnson's and McNamara's unilateral gesture on ABM, it is not clear that attitudes toward strategic weaponry as such would have taken this course.

Nonetheless, in 1967 and 1968 the decision to forgo a full-scale ABM was basically popular politically. And well it might be: Strategic arms control, as yet untried, held out great promise. The end of the arms race seemed a goal worth attaining.

Yet not everyone accepted McNamara's new strategic vision. The most comprehensive critique of McNamara's San Francisco speech was offered in a speech at the Hoover Institution at Stanford University two weeks later by Senator Henry M. "Scoop" Jackson, Democrat of Washington, who would become, amid the turmoil of the Vietnam and détente years, the leading congressional advocate for a strong defense and the most sophisticated and effective critic of the arms controllers' vision.

In contrast to McNamara's approach, rooted in abstract theory and classical-liberal assumptions about international affairs, Jackson's vision was anchored in traditional power politics. "Top Defense officials are telling us," said Jackson,

> that "nuclear superiority has only limited relevance today" and that "today, in the nuclear age, nuclear superiority is of limited significance." What do statements like that mean? . . . Have top Defense officials accepted the hypothesis that nuclear superiority constitutes a provocation to the other side to build up its strength? Is nuclear parity now our goal? . . . The questions involve what would be a radical change in American policy. I believe it would be a catastrophe.

According to Jackson, the key to restraining the Soviets lay not in parity but in maintaining a favorable balance of power: Where "objective conditions" made possible expansion of their influence, the Soviets sought to expand it; where "objective conditions" prevented such expansion, he argued, they were restrained. Western power and self-confidence were the key. "As I look back upon our experience," Jackson said, "I find a strong correlation between Soviet prudence and restraint and the firmness and prudence of the West."

"As I see things," said Jackson in an echo of Churchill, "international peace and security depend not on a *parity of power* but on a *preponderance of power* in the peace-keepers over the peace-upsetters." He concluded on the prophetic note that given a willingness to maintain military superiority, the "superior industrial and agricultural power of the West" might prove to be "a trump card" in the long run.[55]

It is interesting to compare the McNamara and Jackson speeches as exercises in prophecy. Who would be proved more correct in the long run—McNamara, who predicted that U.S. self-restraint on ABM was the key to breaking the action-reaction phenomenon and slowing the arms race, leading to a leveling off in offensive arsenals, or Jackson, who predicted that the Soviets would continue seeking to expand their military power and influence insofar as they could, and be restrained only when "objective conditions" and Western power placed barriers in their way? Which analysis was to prove sounder—McNamara's, which dealt with the strategic arms competition as a quasi-economic problem in abstraction from Soviet global strategy and events such as Vietnam, or Jackson's, which embedded its consideration of Soviet military behavior in Soviet history and the context of the larger political competition?

Jackson's outlook represented a complete and coherent alternative to the McNamara vision. But for the moment this traditional view, reaching back to Churchill and beyond that to the roots of Western statesmanship, was in eclipse, overshadowed by the hopes and newfangled theoretical conceptions of arms control.

CHAPTER 8

◻

The Age of Arms Control

Probably the most significant and longest-term consequence of the Johnson-McNamara strategy was the transformation it inspired in the consciousness of the nation's political elites. By 1969, the fundamental consensus that had sustained American foreign policy for twenty years of Cold War had effectively been shattered. Throughout the late 1960s and early 1970s, American attitudes toward foreign policy—toward the Soviet Union and toward the use of American military power—began to revert to a state resembling that prevalent in the months before Winston Churchill's Iron Curtain speech in 1946, or even in some respects resembling that prevalent in the 1930s. A new utopianism could be observed among intellectuals and among the young; elite dialogue about foreign affairs began to be marked by a distinct lack of realism about the nature and uses of military power.

It would be hard to overestimate the political significance of this change. The new attitude toward power and force greatly narrowed the options available to any new administration for coping with the myriad foreign policy problems now crowding in upon the United States. In particular, it circumscribed and at times simply cancelled the president's ability to use force or pressure to counter various challenges posed by the Communist bloc. The prolongation of the Vietnam war, the numerical inequities in the SALT I agreements in 1972, the myriad defeats for Western interests in Asia, Africa, Latin America, and the Middle East in the mid- to late 1970s—all could be attributed in some measure to this new elite attitude and the limits it imposed on American foreign policy.

At the center of the problem, of course, was the war in Vietnam. The attempt by Johnson and McNamara to wage a war (in the words of one historian) "without arousing the public ire" had left open the possibility that public ire would be aroused *against* the struggle. The unemotional, intellectualized approach to war pursued by McNamara and his associates had left open an emotional vacuum that was eventually filled by the anger of protest. Deprived of the passions and sense of righteousness that nations normally bring to war, many Americans came to regard the terrible violence—shown nightly on living-room television screens—as simply repugnant and unjust.

At the same time, the Vietnam experience intensified, rather than tempered, the antimilitarist tendencies in Establishment thinking about strategy and foreign policy. In the face of military failure in Vietnam, Establishment figures began to devise theories suggesting that military power was declining in importance in the world and prescribing a reduction in American military power as a cure for the nation's ailments. "Men of independent mind recognize that after twenty years of aggressive military competition with the Soviets our security is not greater and almost certainly less than when the competition began," wrote John Kenneth Galbraith in a tract titled *How to Control the Military.* " . . . Obviously no one who regards himself as a liberal can any longer be a communicant of the military power."[1] McNamara himself contributed significantly to these tendencies of thought. In 1966, even as hundreds of thousands of Americans remained trapped in a war he had conceived and designed, the secretary of defense journeyed to Montreal to confess to the American society of newspaper editors that the United States had overemphasized the military component in its dealings with the Third World and should now give greater stress to economic development. In the emerging modern world, "development," not military power, according to the defense secretary, would be the "essence of security." (Some consolation this must have been to Americans still dying by the hundreds in the jungles of Vietnam.) The speech was later reprinted as the title chapter in McNamara's book *Essence of Security,* published in 1968.[2] The notion that the "essence of security" somehow no longer lay in military power became increasingly fashionable as the 1960s wore on. In 1969, McGeorge Bundy, another former Kennedy advisor, joined the growing chorus with a *Foreign Affairs* article titled "To Cap the Volcano," arguing that the nuclear arms competition had remained in pointless stalemate for some decades and was safely destined to remain so, and then contending (somewhat contradictorily) that arms control agreements were necessary to forestall an arms race "totally unprecedented in size and *danger*" (emphasis added).[3] (How the strategic balance could at once be safely in permanent stalemate and subject to destabilization by a dangerous arms race Bundy never explained.) There were many other such articles and pronouncements about the supposed inutility of both conventional and nuclear military force. In effect, even as the United States continued to struggle with a major war, a kind of taboo was emerging in Establishment thinking against both the use and accumulation of military power.

Finally, as if to compound the difficulties that would confront the new administration, McNamara before leaving office had seriously curtailed the U.S. strategic buildup. For the next decade, no new American strategic missile launchers, strategic bombers, or ballistic missile submarines were scheduled to be constructed. Only qualitative improvements and quantitative MIRVing (multiple independently targetable reentry vehicle—equipping existing missiles with multiple warheads) continued. To be sure, MIRVing would add significantly to the American stock of deliverable warheads. But in other key indices of strategic power—for example, launcher numbers and throw weight—the United States was already beginning to fall behind. In the late 1960s and early 1970s, even as U.S. ICBM construction was slowed and then halted, the Soviets continued to construct ICBMs at the rate of approximately 200 per year.[4] By 1971, the Soviets had actually surpassed the U.S. in the number of ICBMs.[5] By the time SALT I was signed in 1972, the Soviets had secured a symbolic advantage of 800 strategic missiles (ICBMs and SLBMs) over the United States.[6]

A shattered Cold War consensus, a seemingly interminable and badly waged war, an ongoing, unfavorable shift in the strategic balance, and an Establishment in virtual rebellion against both the war and the accumulation of military power—such were the circumstances that Richard Nixon confronted when he assumed the presidency in January 1969.

"Madman" Nixon

It was both unfortunate and ironic that the man who emerged to collect the shattered legacy of the Kennedy-Johnson years in 1969 was the same unhappy Republican candidate whom John F. Kennedy had defeated for the presidency eight years before. Richard Nixon's strong sense of personal enmity with the Kennedy circle and East Coast Establishment and his resentful and unappealing personality were destined only to intensify the nation's political and cultural woes. Less than any other postwar president, with the possible exception of his immediate predecessor, was Nixon capable of communicating persuasively with the nation's political elites. At the same time, his uncharismatic and bitter personality made it all too easy for the Establishmentarians who supported Kennedy to transform Nixon into a scapegoat, abdicating responsibility for the many problems they had created and had now left for him to solve.[7]

One need only compare Nixon's initial handling of Vietnam with Eisenhower's initial handling of Korea to understand how far the country had strayed from elementary strategic awareness and basic common sense. Like Eisenhower in 1953, Nixon came to office in 1969 promising a rapid end to an unpopular war. In sharp contrast to Eisenhower, Nixon proved unwilling and perhaps unable to keep his promise.

To end the war in Vietnam, it would be necessary to *escalate* it—or at least to threaten the enemy credibly with major escalation. That was the elementary strategic truth—so clearly grasped by Eisenhower and Dulles in regard to Korea in 1953—that now seemed to elude nearly everyone who thought about the problem of Vietnam. (Interestingly, none of the recent academic works on the period appears to acknowledge this critical problem.)[8] In the end, only by making the enemy fear an actual U.S. victory—and taste something of the full brunt of American power— would Washington be in a position to gain a diplomatic solution on reasonably acceptable terms. (In the event, a peace settlement—and not a terribly adequate one—was achieved in 1973 only after the heaviest bombing of the war.) As long as the war remained "limited," the North Vietnamese would (and did) assume that time was on their side.

Nixon had some intimation of these relationships. Remembering the essential outlines of Eisenhower's approach in Korea, he hoped in some sense to repeat it. To his aide H. R. Haldeman, he talked of employing what he described as his "Madman Theory": "I call it the Madman Theory, Bob. I want the North Vietnamese to believe I've reached the point where I might do *anything* to stop the war. We'll just slip the word to them that, 'for God's sake, you know Nixon is obsessed with Communism. We can't restrain him when he's angry—and he has his hand on the nuclear button'—and Ho Chi Minh himself will be in Paris in two days begging for peace."[9] But Nixon evidently had no sense of the scale on which such a strategy needed to be executed—or of the need for serious operational planning and action, such as had been undertaken by Eisenhower, in contrast to a mere verbal bluff.

Equally if not more important, Nixon had failed to prepare the public in any sense for the possibility of such an escalation. In 1952 and 1953, Dulles's campaign themes of "liberation," "rollback," and "instant retaliation" gave the Communist world every reason to suppose that the new Republican administration would behave with less restraint in the Korean war than the preceding Democratic one, laying the basis at least for a strong bluff. Nixon's campaign established no such impression. At one point in the campaign a wire service reporter wrote, inaccurately, that Nixon claimed to have a "secret plan" to end the Vietnam war.[10] The inaccurate story inadvertently captured the truth of the situation: Having promised to end the war, Nixon, anxious not to alienate voters, managed to get through the election without explaining how he would accomplish this aim.

The critical question concerned the bombing of North Vietnam. In announcing his intention in March 1968 not to seek reelection, President Johnson had curtailed bombing of the North as a gesture to facilitate peace talks. Then on the eve of the election, in a last-ditch effort to gain a peace and rescue the election for Vice President Hubert Humphrey, Johnson had halted bombing of the North entirely. The hoped-for peace had of course not been gained. Would Nixon be willing to resume bombing of the North when he entered office in January 1969? That, from the North Vietnamese perspective, must have been the acid-test of the new administration's resolve.

The answer proved to be no. The joint chiefs of staff favored such bombing. Moreover, opinion polls suggested, as Nixon realized and later openly acknowledged,[11] that the American public would initially support such a course. Uncertain he could sustain support, Nixon was in the final analysis simply unwilling to sacrifice the "honeymoon" period of his presidency to such a cause.[12]

As the records of his many conversations with Haldeman amply show, Nixon's fondest ambition was to preside over a presidency as outwardly glamorous and glorious as that of his predecessor John Kennedy.[13] One suspects that one reason Nixon eschewed rapid escalation of the Vietnam war in 1969 was that such a policy did not fit in with such a ambition. As Nixon himself later wrote, escalation of the war in 1969 "would have got my administration off to the worst possible start."[14]

On February 22, the day before Nixon was to leave for the Continent—perhaps to repeat Kennedy's glorious trip to Europe in 1963—Hanoi launched a major offensive throughout Vietnam. In response, Nixon ordered secret bombing of North Vietnamese sanctuaries across the border in Cambodia.

Doubtless the North Vietnamese offensive in early 1969 was designed to test the new administration. While the secret bombing of Cambodia was of some military value, it amounted, in the end, to a half-measure not unlike those pursued by the previous administration. It showed North Vietnam that even in the face of a major offensive in which the United States was suffering 400 casualties a week,[15] the Nixon administration lacked the gumption to bomb its homeland or its capital. In May, the administration would aggravate the situation further by beginning withdrawal of American troops—a policy that merely strengthened the public desire for disengagement from the war and condemned the United States to a steadily weakening military and diplomatic position, undermining its hand in negotiations.[16]

By his own later report, Nixon intended the withdrawal as a gesture of goodwill toward the North Vietnamese. Yet how was the Communist side supposed to believe that Nixon was a "madman" if he was at the same time ready to make such a major gesture of goodwill to show his diplomatic "seriousness"?[17]

Despite all this, Nixon persisted in his notion that he could bluff Hanoi and Moscow into accommodation with his Madman Theory. In his own mind, Nixon set a November 1 "ultimatum" after which he planned some vague intensification of the war. In late September, at Nixon's behest, national security advisor Henry Kissinger told Soviet ambassador Anatoly Dobrynin that "as far as Vietnam is concerned, the train has just left the station and is now headed down the track."[18] The administration leaked to columnists Rowland Evans and Robert Novak that Nixon was considering blockading Haiphong Harbor and invading the North. However, on October 15, the Vietnam "moratorium" orchestrated on campuses across the country showed widespread nonviolent opposition to the war and undercut completely Nixon's vague thoughts of escalation. Public opinion had turned; the media portrayed the Nixon presidency as deeply in trouble.[19] With some justification, Nixon later blamed the peace movement for lengthening the war by undercutting his capacity to threaten escalation. Yet whether Nixon intended to follow through on his "ultimatum" is not at all clear, and in reality, November 1 was already too late. (Eisenhower, by comparison, had delivered his essential "ultimatum" on Korea within four months of taking office.)

Nixon had not only failed to end the war; he had virtually destroyed the American bargaining position in the peace talks. The credibility not just of the Madman Theory but of the whole American posture in regard to North Vietnam had been undermined.

Sticks and Carrots

In an environment where the American president was so restricted in his use of coercive "sticks" vis-à-vis the Communist world, it was probably only natural that he would search for "carrots" on the basis of which to conduct foreign policy. In a sense, the essence of the Nixon foreign policy, whether it went by the name of "linkage" or "détente," was the increasing emphasis on carrots rather than sticks in dealing with the Communists—in particular, the attempt to transform the U.S. nuclear arsenal from a big stick into a big carrot. At his first news conference, Nixon proposed that arms talks with the Soviet Union should be conducted "in a way and at a time that will promote, if possible, progress on outstanding political problems" such as "the Mideast" and Vietnam.[20] Briefing reporters on February 6, Kissinger used the novel term "linkage" to describe the relationship.[21]

In the end, the Nixon policy would fail, for two main reasons. First, the administration quickly lost domestic political control over the carrots on which its policy was based; it lost its capacity to withhold or give positive rewards to the Soviets to promote good behavior. In the emotion-charged policymaking environment of the late 1960s and early 1970s, the carrots ultimately proved no easier to manage than the sticks. The Left, in effect, took away the carrot of arms control, while the Right ultimately took away the carrot of trade. Domestic pressure for arms control and against defense programs would lead the administration to concede more to the Soviets in arms control talks than it wished or ought to have done. Having conceded too much in those talks, the administration would then face domestic rebellion on the Right, which subsequently blocked its effort to use trade and credit concessions as a bargaining chip.

Second, and more fundamentally, however, even if Nixon had been more successful in marshaling his "carrots," the Soviets showed no particular inclination to respond constructively to his positive incentives. In the final analysis, the Soviets never really responded positively to carrots; they responded dependably only to sticks. On the two key issues where Nixon hoped "linkage" would enlist Soviet help—Vietnam and the Middle East—the president would ultimately be forced to revert to coercion in order to achieve his basic aims. In the case of Vietnam, Nixon was finally compelled to engage in heavy bombing of the North and mining of Haiphong Harbor in order to gain a face-saving settlement from Hanoi. As to the Middle East, the Nixon administration was ironically led to the expedient of a major nuclear alert—the first such alert since the Cuban missile crisis—to deter Soviet intervention in 1973, only a year after the U.S.-Soviet summit and the signing of SALT I.

Mismanaging Linkage

To base a strategy on carrots required, at a minimum, not only a willingness to proffer carrots but an ability to withhold them until one got what one wanted from the other side. Pressured by liberals and worried about Vietnam, Nixon proved, if anything, too accommodating toward Moscow in the early stages of his administration. Indeed, so eager was he for a better relationship with the Soviets—hoping, in particular, for their help on the problem of Vietnam—that he went so far as to cooperate with a Soviet intelligence operative on the content of his inaugural address. During the transition, a KGB operative named Boris Sedov, nominally a Soviet diplomat at the UN, established contact with Kissinger and pressed him to include a call for détente in Nixon's inaugural. According to the combined accounts of Nixon and Kissinger, it appears to have been Sedov's request that led Nixon to speak in his inaugural of moving from an "era of confrontation" to an "era of negotiations" and to fill the address with peace rhetoric.[22] The Sedov initiative helped Moscow choreograph the front-page news on the day following Nixon's inauguration. On one side of the page was Nixon's inaugural calling for an era of negotiation and peace; on the other side was a statement from Moscow indicating readiness to begin missile talks.[23] In a sense, the Soviets were already undermining linkage by creating independent pressure (in the form of Western public hope) for arms control negotiations and agreements. Nixon's position was also weakened by, in effect, his open overtures to Moscow for help on Vietnam.[24]

On February 14, meanwhile, Kissinger began the first of a series of unprecedented secret "backchannel" meetings with the Soviet ambassador. Kissinger described them as "a series of intimate exchanges" where "the most sensitive business in US-Soviet relations came to be handled."[25] The hope, in particular, was that such meetings would begin to establish a linkage that would lead to Soviet help on Vietnam. But one suspects that the meetings had the contrary effect of demonstrating firsthand to Dobrynin just how frustrated and without recourse on Vietnam the administration was. "On about ten occasions in 1969 in my monthly meeting with Dobrynin I tried to enlist Soviet cooperation to help end the war in

Vietnam," Kissinger later wrote in his memoirs. "Dobrynin was always evasive."[26]

The Push for Unilateralism

Of course, Nixon did not really have the option of withholding carrots—particularly the carrot of arms control. With the pronouncements on "mad momentum" and the "action-reaction phenomenon," Robert McNamara had helped set in motion a kind of political juggernaut. As a result, the East Coast Establishment, the Establishment press, liberals in Congress, atomic scientists, and McNamara aides and arms control advocates in the Executive Branch bureaucracy became in the late 1960s a powerful collective "lobby"[27] pressing for a new arms agreement, with passionate intensity. Of course the idea of strategic arms control was intrinsically very appealing: The promise of an "end" to the arms race, the extravagant (and completely unwarranted) hopes for saving money, the notion of at least partially closing the Pandora's box opened by nuclear weapons—all this was almost irresistible, especially given the mood and problems of the time. Not far in the background lay the Vietnam trauma. A peculiar psychology appeared to be at work. The search for an arms control agreement with the Soviet Union amid an interminable and costly war where the Soviets were extensively supporting America's enemy represented a kind of misdirected and sublimated quest for the ever-elusive "peace" that America could not seem to achieve on the battlefield.

Within the Executive Branch, arms control–minded officials campaigned against linkage, pushing for the start of talks despite lack of progress on Vietnam, with support from a critical media,[28] while in Congress, the proposed ABM came under heavy attack. Much of the popular debate over ABM centered on the question of its feasibility, with a host of scientists—most of them longtime members of the arms control community—testifying on the supposed technical weaknesses of the system.[29] "You can't hit a bullet with a bullet" went the anti-ABM slogan. However, it is unlikely that scientists would have offered such a passionate critique of the technical aspects of the program had it not been for the arms control implications: Arms control theory taught that defenses could be "destabilizing." That the proposed ABM system could shoot down *some* missiles was never in doubt. Besides, even if the first-generation Safeguard was ineffective, more effective successors were bound to follow. What the scientists really feared was not an ineffective defensive system, but precisely an effective one.

Nixon's effort to appease ABM critics by offering a scaled-down version (once called "Sentinel," now renamed "Safeguard"), aimed at defending weapons cites rather than cities, was unavailing,[30] as was his attempt, in an Air Force Academy speech, to brand the attacks on ABM as "unilateral disarmament."[31] Unmoved by the technical aspects of the debate, Nixon understood instinctively that ABM would be an essential "bargaining chip" in arms talks with Moscow.[32] It was symptomatic of the breakdown in the defense consensus that ABM proved to be the major legislative battle of Nixon's first year.

In the end, it was Senator Jackson who rescued Nixon from what might easily have been a devastating defeat. Describing the contest as "war,"[33] Jackson floor-managed the Senate vote for the administration. The final vote was a 50-to-50 tie, with Vice President Agnew casting an unnecessary fifty-first vote to seal the defeat of the amendment to end ABM. Safeguard had survived—barely.

As the ABM vote suggested, American weapons were now coming to be regarded as the chief threat to peace, on the grounds they would spur an escalating and dangerous response from the Soviets. This view would remain strong if not dominant in Congress for decades to come.

The "Horse Trade" in SALT

Nixon's initial political priority in the arms talks was to gain help on Vietnam—a priority that gradually dissipated as linkage dissolved. To the degree that the United States had a military priority going into the SALT talks, meanwhile, it was to gain limitations on Soviet *offensive* missiles: first, on the overall Soviet offensive buildup and, second, and more particularly, on those "heavy" Soviet ICBMs—in particular, the SS-9—thought by some to be potentially capable of destroying the U.S. ICBMs in a preemptive first strike.

There were several reasons why limiting offensive weapons was, or ought to have been, a high priority for American negotiators. First, the basic promise of arms talks, as held out by McNamara, had been that limits on defenses or ABM would lead to a slowing or end of the offensive buildup on both sides, by breaking the supposed action-reaction cycle. Second, the major American advantage going into the talks was clearly understood to be in defensive technologies, while the Soviets' major advantage was in the quantity, pace, and lethality of their offensive buildup. Third, a major function of Safeguard and successive U.S. ABM systems, presuming they were built, would be to protect U.S. ICBM fields from heavy missiles such as the SS-9. Thus if the United States gave up Safeguard, it made sense to obtain in return some kind of negotiated ban or limit on Soviet "heavies." Finally, the notion of limiting offensive first-strike weapons went to the heart of the original purpose of arms control: to limit those systems capable of first-strike missions while strengthening the survivability of those weapons suited for a retaliatory role.

In sum, the basic original American conception of SALT—the "horse trade" supposed to be at the heart of the bargain—was to exchange limits on defenses, in which America was understood to have potential advantage, for limits on offensive weapons, in which the Soviets were understood to be gaining important advantages. It is crucial to understanding the SALT process to grasp that this conception was never realized.

One reason was that the arms control–minded bureaucracy had ceased to think in commonsense, "horse trade" terms. Imbued with the psychology of "moderation breeds moderation" and with the new doctrine of arms control, the large "SALT lobby"[34] in the government concentrated less on bargaining to the U.S. advantage than on transcending the usual psychology of competition.

At the heart of the SALT project lay what proved to be a massive intellectual error. McNamara and the arms controllers had viewed arms talks as the key to obtaining a relationship of mutual restraint; but the Soviets interpreted the eagerness of the United States to participate in arms talks *as a confirmation of the value of their military buildup.*

The basic Soviet view of the arms control and détente process of the early 1970s—expressed from time to time in the Soviet press of the day—was later summarized authoritatively by none other than the Soviet foreign minister of the era, Andrei Gromyko, in his memoirs:

> The improvement in Soviet-US relations in the early 1970s came about primarily through an active Soviet foreign policy, *but also through the steady growth of Soviet influence in international affairs, as Soviet military strength achieved parity with that of the USA. In consequence American foreign policy began to adopt a more realistic posture*: the understanding gained ground in Washington that permanent tension in Soviet-US relations was not in their own interests, and that the only reliable basis for relations with the USSR was peaceful

coexistence and a mutual recognition of the security interests of both states.[35]

Détente was interpreted, in short, as vindication of the Soviet military buildup, the Soviet policy of strength.

In other words, the paradoxical effect of the arms control process was to confirm the Soviets in the belief that their growing military power was improving their leverage vis-à-vis Washington, thereby encouraging them to pursue the buildup further. In the end, arms control probably caused the Soviets to *increase* defense spending and strengthened the hand of the Soviet military in competing for that society's scarce resources. (Soviet defense spending steadily increased during the period 1969 to 1980, notwithstanding a significant decline of U.S. effort in much of this period. By the late 1980s, it accounted for as much as 25 percent of GNP.)[36] With the American president eager to shake hands with the Soviet leader and ready to offer a host of economic carrots in the effort of attaining an arms agreement, the military buildup appeared to be the one aspect of Soviet policy that was paying off.

SALT did not mark any particular watershed in Soviet strategic think-ing. Rather, the Soviets welcomed American proposals to limit ABM for the simple reason that they feared the American ABM, could not dupli-cate it, and wished to take advantage of the fact that the United States was now offering to limit ABM or give it up in negotiations. And they sought to give up as little as possible in return.[37]

All this helps to explain subsequent Soviet behavior—why, despite the sharp limits on ABM, the Soviets continued after SALT I to pour enor-mous resources into active and passive *defenses*, why the Soviets resisted *offensive* weapons limitations during SALT I, and indeed why during and following SALT I Soviet efforts in the area of offensive weapons actually *increased*.

Despite their traditional emphasis on the importance of defensive systems, Soviet military officials evidently came to appreciate that defen-sive weapons per se would be only of limited use, particularly as both sides came to rely more on ballistic missiles. Much of the defensive mission in nuclear war, at least at the present level of technology, would actually have to be accomplished preemptively, with offensive weapons. The best defense in the nuclear age would be a good offense. By this the Soviets did not mean "second-strike" retaliation after the model of McNamara's Whiz Kids. On the contrary, they meant striking first. One could argue that this was the natural military view of the issue—the view any military leadership was likely to take in the absence of interference from civilian theorists like McNamara's Whiz Kids.[38]

The Soviets based their nuclear strategy heavily on preemption, and they were not about to give up such a capability. This fact again defined another constant in the SALT talks. At every turn, the Soviets resisted the most strenuous American efforts to limit their key preemptive weapons or heavy missiles. On this question, they simply would not budge. In other words, the preemptive mission was preserved.

This leads to a startling conclusion: Rather than lead the Soviets toward mutually stabilizing force configurations, the ABM Treaty actually drove them not only toward an intensified arms buildup but also toward an ever more offensive and preemptive strategy. In the absence of strict limits on ABM, and in the presence of a U.S. ABM, the Soviets would have been compelled to allocate significant effort—technology, manpower, even nuclear materials—to their own defensive system, if only to keep up an appearance of equality with the United States. Instead, these energies went into offensive weapons and into meeting what turned out to be an achievable goal: namely, rendering the heart of the U.S. strategic arsenal—the most accurate and prompt U.S. weapons, land-based ICBMs—vulnerable to a preemptive strike and all but obsolete.

All this helps explain the ultimate outcome of SALT I: First, strict limits were agreed to on ABM, but with continued Soviet interest in defense as evidenced by (a) heavy investment in air defenses; (b) continued work on shelters; (c) extensive ABM activities, including activities that were certain and probable violations of the treaty. Second, the Soviets resisted meaningful offensive limitations—leading to the gradual vulnerability of U.S. Minuteman missiles. And finally, despite a treaty ostensibly designed to break the action-reaction phenomenon, there was a continued and massive buildup of offensive weapons on the Soviet side, leading to a gradual shift in the balance of power against the United States.

Could all these problems have been avoided if only the United States had sought a ban on multiple warheads or MIRV as well as ABM? That has been the contention of many in the arms control community since 1969. It was even once endorsed by Henry Kissinger, who in 1974 (when it was completely cost-free to do so) expressed regret for not pursuing a MIRV ban more seriously in SALT I.[39] Yet the fact was that the Nixon administration actually did propose a MIRV ban in the arms talks, albeit linked to a (technically justifiable) demand for on-site inspection. (Most provisions of SALT were shaped so that they could be verified by satellite;

multiple warheads could not be monitored by this means.) Everything depended on the Soviets. Had the Soviets accepted the MIRV ban in principle even while resisting the proposal for on-site inspection, the Nixon administration would have been hard-pressed not to yield. In the event, however, the Soviets expressed no interest whatsoever in banning MIRV,[40] and indeed resisted limits on offensive weapons generally. In retrospect, it seems clear that, far from being subject to persuasion on a MIRV ban, Soviet negotiators were probably under instructions to avoid offensive limits *so as to preserve the preemptive option*, essential to defense of the Motherland now that the Soviet Union was abandoning a full-scale effort at ABM.

The Decline of American Power

By 1970, the Nixon administration, and the nation, was in deepening trouble. The need to escalate the Vietnam war in order to end it had finally come home to roost. In the spring of that year, faced with growing North Vietnamese pressure on the South and Communist pressure on the newly formed pro-Western Cambodian government of Lon Nol, Nixon had ordered an attack by combined U.S. and Army of the Republic of Vietnam (ARVN) troops on Communist sanctuaries in Cambodia. The response at home to the Cambodian incursion was a storm of campus protests. At Kent State in Ohio, National Guardsmen mobilized to deal with the disorder fired on student protesters, killing four. A sense of growing civil unrest and collapsing public order became part of the political background.

On Capitol Hill, the administration's defense program was under heavy assault.[41] In April, the Senate voted 72 to 6 urging Nixon to propose an immediate suspension of further deployment of offensive and defensive strategic weapons to the Soviet Union.[42] In another epic legislative battle, the Safeguard ABM squeezed by the Senate in a 52-to-47 vote.[43]

In the fall of 1970, in an apparent attempt to get American agreement on ABM limits without sacrificing offensive weapons, the Soviets proposed that an agreement be concluded on ABM alone, leaving offensive limits to a future negotiation—a proposal immediately welcomed by the Establishment and the arms control community.[44]

In the White House, meanwhile, Kissinger was becoming increasingly despondent about the future of the West—a state of mind that was ultimately to affect the final outcome in SALT. Elmo R. Zumwalt, chief of naval operations, later described a conversation he had with Kissinger en route to the Army-Navy game in November 1970:

> K. feels that U.S. has passed its historic high point like so many earlier civilizations. He believes U.S. is on downhill and cannot be roused by political challenge. *He states that his job is to persuade the Russians to give us the best deal we can get, recognizing that the historical forces favor them.* . . . I took him on strongly on this, saying that I couldn't accept that the decision to grant the Soviets superior capability in either strategic or conventional fields should be made without putting the issue to the people. K. said, *"You don't get reelected to the Presidency on a platform that admits you got behind. You talk instead about the great partnership for peace achieved in your term."*[45]

The Nixon Summit Obsession

Although the strong Soviet desire for limits on the American ABM program placed a powerful bargaining chip in the hands of the U.S. administration, the White House failed to exploit it to its full potential, partly because of Nixon's extraneous preoccupation with a summit. Nixon's motivations in office, such as his obsession with summitry, were not exactly of the purest sort, or confined, as he sometimes liked to pretend, to a disinterested dedication to the national interest. Other postwar presidents had desired to meet directly with the Soviet leader, but Nixon was probably the first to view the summit meeting in a purely cynical spirit—explicitly, if not primarily, as a tool for boosting his personal popularity. While Kissinger's memoirs indicate that Nixon remained largely aloof from the major technical details of SALT,[46] the Nixon papers show the president nonetheless found time to compose a four-page single-spaced memo to his national security advisor in 1972 describing how the summit must be orchestrated, from a public relations standpoint, so that Secretary of State Rogers and chief SALT negotiator Gerard Smith would not rob Nixon of the political credit for reaching the agreement.[47] At the same time, Nixon worried privately to Haldeman that credit might also be stolen by Kissinger himself.[48]

The decision to press for a summit under such circumstances had a debilitating effect on American foreign policy, as Kissinger understood at the time. The major consequence was to strengthen further Moscow's bargaining position vis-à-vis the United States. Kissinger opposed

Nixon's decision to press for a summit but nonetheless carried the president's orders out.[49] According to Kissinger, Nixon even expressed to his national security advisor a willingness to accept an ABM-only agreement in exchange for a meeting.[50]

Only excessive Soviet demands, in Kissinger's summary, for "a de facto alliance against China, a European Security Conference, and a SALT agreement on their terms—all as an *entrance* price into the summit"[51]— prevented the summit from coming to pass in 1970. However, Nixon had tipped his hand: His overweening desire for a summit was now revealed and could be used against him in the future. Indeed, Nixon's craving for a summit placed in Moscow's hands a bargaining chip probably as potent as the Safeguard ABM was in the hands of the United States. It was one of several reasons why, despite deft moves regarding China and a success-ful manipulation of the Soviets' desire for an agreement over Berlin, the United States still ended up with a SALT I bargain rather too obviously favoring the Kremlin.

Weaving Webs

If linkage as Nixon had originally conceived it was languishing by 1970, then it expired in early 1971 when Nixon approved Kissinger's plan to press Dobrynin privately in "the Channel" (the secret Kissinger-Dobry-nin conversations) for a compromise on SALT. In the first confident days of the administration, the president had envisioned using SALT and summitry in a cool and calculating fashion to wheedle concessions from the Soviets on Vietnam. By late 1970, however, the Nixon administration was increasingly coming to view SALT as a means of simply buying time—getting the best deal it could on strategic weapons amid a cata-strophically declining bargaining position.

Kissinger's account in his memoirs of the negotiations leading up to the May 1971 "breakthrough" on SALT—in which the Soviets ostensibly agreed to link defensive and offensive weapons limitations—gives heavy emphasis to the eroding support for defense on Capitol Hill, partly, one suspects, to explain what he must have recognized in retrospect, if not at the time, to be an unfavorable deal from the American point of view.[52] Under the one-sided "breakthrough" of May 1971, the United States essentially gave up its major bargaining chip—ABM—in exchange for only the most nominal, porous, and temporary limits on Soviet offensive weapons.

In embarking on the "backchannel" SALT negotiations with Dobrynin, Kissinger sought to benefit from a new kind of linkage, this time between arms control talks and the negotiations on Berlin. Since 1969, the West German Social Democratic government of Chancellor Willy Brandt had been pursuing its own policy of détente and normalization with the Soviet Union. In a sense, Brandt's *Ostpolitik* was itself a powerful symptom of the shifting power balance. Rooted in German memory of the 1961 Berlin crisis, in Brandt's anger at Kennedy's supine response to the erection of the Berlin Wall, and in a generally diminishing West German faith in the reliability of American security guarantees, Brandt's *Ostpolitik* reflected calculations that West German interests would best be served by pursuing a more even orientation between the two blocs. In 1971, the West Germans had signed a treaty with the Soviet Union affirming existing Central European borders—that is, effectively acknowledging the independence and legitimacy of the East German Communist government. However, approval of the treaty by the West German parliament hinged on achieving a new agreement regarding access to and freedom for Berlin; a Berlin agreement in turn required the cooperation of Washington.[53] Kissinger proposed to Nixon the "linking [of] the Berlin negotiations to progress in SALT; SALT, in turn, we would make depend on Soviet willingness to freeze its offensive build-up."[54]

This new linkage was typical of the "web"-weaving in which Kissinger engaged throughout the early 1970s. The Berlin negotiations were supposed to help with SALT; SALT in turn would help with the defense budget and make possible Nixon's cherished summit; trade concessions would help sweeten the path to SALT; eventually the opening to China would make the Soviets more desirous of a summit; all of this, it was hoped, might make it easier for Washington to obtain a decent, face-saving settlement in Vietnam. The difficulty with these webs was that it was sometimes difficult to identify the definitive thread. What was Kissinger's major priority: to obtain a sound SALT agreement, to slow the decline in the defense budget by means of a largely cosmetic agreement, or to arrange a summit meeting for Nixon? What was finally more important, the substantive content of the SALT agreements or the aura of achievement they gave to the Nixon foreign policy, permitting the president more maneuverability on Vietnam? Depending on which passage one chooses in the Kissinger memoirs, one can find support for any of these explanations. As time went on, the administration seemed to lose sight of its own priorities, permitting them to shift and all the while adding more and more to the pile of "bargaining chips" ultimately proffered to the Soviets in exchange for the SALT agreements and the summit. Under siege from domestic critics and lacking a clear sense of hierarchy in its own strategy,[55] the administration tended to lose sight of how much it was giving up. In exchange for SALT I, not only did the United States ultimately agree to severe limits on ABM, in which it had a technological advantage; it also agreed to adopt a more forthcoming attitude on the Berlin negotiations; it offered major trade concessions, including a huge subsidized grain sale; it muted human rights concerns;[56] and finally, it made numerous concessions to the Soviets on offensive weapons themselves.

One suspects that a major reason for Kissinger's resort to total secrecy in his talks with Dobyrnin—neither Smith nor Rogers was informed of the backchannel SALT negotiation until it was over—was an implicit awareness that achievement of an agreement would demand concessions that could not easily be made through the more "open" or formal channels.[57] Whether or not Kissinger intended such a procedure from the beginning, his negotiations in SALT repeatedly exhibited a pattern of conceding too much and then deftly explaining away the concession to the public, the bureaucracy, and the press.[58]

Ostensibly, the May 1971 communiqué produced by the secret talks committed the Soviets to simultaneous negotiations on defensive and offensive weapons. But both the language of the communiqué and the details specified in secret letters exchanged between Nixon and Brezhnev were heavily weighted in the Soviet favor.[59] Originally, the American side had sought a single agreement on defense and offense, with equal offensive ceilings, and limits on the most threatening Soviet weapons, "heavy" missiles. Kissinger, by contrast, agreed to a separate, merely temporary or interim agreement on offensive weapons, without equal ceilings, and with no special provision for the priority American concern, Soviet heavy missiles. In addition, instead of being structured as a mutual ceiling, the agreement was to take the form of a "freeze" on new deployments. Eventually, when SALT I was signed, this would mean ceding the Soviets a significant numerical advantage in offensive missiles.

In addition, Kissinger reassured Dobryinin that offensive modernization would be permitted under the agreement, that its duration would be no more than eighteen months to two years, and that the Soviets would receive promised future compensation for "forward-based systems"—in response to Soviet insistence that U.S. nuclear weapons in Europe be included in negotiations. Finally, and perhaps most remarkably, Kissinger had not required that SLBMs be included in the interim freeze. Given the rapidity of the Soviet SLBM buildup, this provision virtually guaranteed a significant and open-ended Soviet numerical advantage.[60] Nixon hailed the joint statement, hyperbolically, as potentially "the beginning of a new era in which all nations will devote more of their energies and their resources not to the weapons of war but to the works of peace."[61]

In the meantime, in line with Kissinger's new policy of proffering carrots, the United States gave approval to Ford Motor Company's long-pending request for the construction of a major truck plant on the Kama River in the Soviet Union.[62] Nine years later, vehicles from what Kissinger called this "civilian truck plant" would carry the invading Soviet army into Afghanistan.[63]

The China Card

Two months after the result of the secret backchannel SALT negotiations was revealed, Kissinger set off on another secretly prepared mission—this time to Beijing. Nixon had actually envisioned the possibility of an opening to China from the earliest days of his administration. Aware of the competition between Moscow and Beijing for "leadership" of the Communist world, Nixon sensed that he could play one off the other to his own benefit.[64] A reflection of his excellent feel for political tactics, and a rare instance where his tactical skill approached genuine strategic vision, Nixon's opening to China was the major foreign policy achievement of his administration.

To open such a rift between Moscow and Beijing was eventually to give the administration more maneuvering room with respect to Vietnam—though it offered no immediate solution. But unfortunately the main uses to which Kissinger put the great bargaining leverage resulting from the "China card" were (1) repairing the too-generous concessions made in his May 1971 "breakthrough" on SALT, and to which the joint chiefs were now objecting,[65] and (2) obtaining a Moscow summit for Nixon.

By February 1972, the Soviets had accepted the principle of a freeze on ICBMs and had agreed to incorporate the freeze into a formal agreement. They had agreed to a prohibition on converting "light" ICBMs to "heavy" ICBMs (though they had resisted defining "light" and "heavy"). Some progress had been made on a joint draft text on the interim offensive agreement. With regard to ABM, the Soviets had accepted in principle a prohibition on ABM defense of territory and agreed to ban deployment of futuristic ABM components unless the treaty was amended. Negotiations continued on provisions governing ABM radars.[66]

Yet significantly, despite the appearance of progress, the Soviets had still revealed almost nothing to the U.S. delegation concerning the actual size of their forces. It is one of the striking facts of the SALT I talks that virtually the entire negotiation was conducted on the basis of American-supplied estimates of Soviet forces, drawn from U.S. intelligence sources.[67] Indeed, so intense was the Soviet preoccupation with secrecy, and so severe the compartmentalization of information on the Soviet side, that the chief military representative on the Soviet delegation, General Nikolai Ogarkov, actually complained to the American delegates that they were revealing too much about the size and specification of Soviet forces to Soviet civilian delegates![68]

Nixon and the Establishment

The intensity of the animosity between Nixon and the Establishment seems a little incongruous in retrospect when one considers that the main features of the Nixon foreign policy as it unfolded in 1971 and 1972—strategic arms control, the opening to China, détente with the Soviet Union—were precisely the objectives that the Establishment was seeking at the time. In the end, there was surprisingly little difference between Nixon and the Establishment at the level of *grand strategy*. Whatever one may say about Nixon's grasp of foreign affairs, there was nothing original or unique in his overarching strategic conception. The notion that the world was passing from an "era of confrontation" to an "era of negotiation," that foreign policy must become less ideological, that it was in some sense time to integrate the Soviet Union and Communist China more fully into the international system, to engage in greater trade with the Communists, to moderate the military competition—this was the conventional wisdom of the age. At the level of *objectives,* Nixon pursued a foreign policy almost indistinguishable from that set forth in McNamara's *Essence of Security.* (The later rehabilitation of Nixon's reputation in foreign policy may have come partly from the Establishment's belated realization that Nixon had actually been pursuing its essential aims all along.)

Where Nixon differed sharply from the Establishment, however, was on *tactics*, and in particular on his residual recognition that power, coercion, and force continued to count in foreign affairs. The Establishment had articulated a new vision of both strategy and tactics based on the deemphasis of military power and the exercise of unilateral restraint. Nixon believed this outlook to be naive. "It's only us non-intellectuals," Nixon told his Cabinet during their first meeting on Vietnam, "who understand what the game is all about" regarding the "need" for "military strength."[69]

Yet rather than attempt to attack the naïveté of the prevailing view publicly and build a working consensus for a tougher policy—the few attempts having proved completely unavailing—Nixon held his realism and cynicism in reserve, as a kind of secret weapon, a hole card with which to trump his critics. In effect, Nixon sought to bring about by secret manipulations and by virtue of his "toughness" the same results his opponents would have sought to achieve by softer means.[70] As he told Haldeman, somewhat proudly, on April 17, with regard to China, he had "already accomp[lished] what no one else c[ou]ld do."[71]

The result was a somewhat peculiar foreign policy, conservative at the tactical level, even as it was liberal at the strategic level, inwardly cynical in its assumptions, yet outwardly dedicated the same goal of "peace" that dominated the mood of the era.

Maneuvering to the Moscow Summit

This interplay of hard and soft could be seen operating in the months between Nixon's visit to Beijing in February and the planned Moscow summit, eventually held in May. Once again, after attempting to conduct policy on the basis of carrots, Nixon was forced to revert to the stick.

Even as relations between Washington and Moscow ostensibly improved and arms negotiations progressed in early 1972, Soviet military aid to North Vietnam was on the increase. At the end of March, tens of thousands of North Vietnamese soldiers streamed across the demilitarized zone—the first cross-border invasion of the war. Linkage had originally been designed to help with Vietnam; now Nixon found himself with the incongruous circumstance of an ostensibly improving relationship with Moscow and a simultaneously escalating Vietnam war.

The North Vietnamese spring offensive of 1972 provided a kind of foretaste of the manner in which Moscow would conduct business throughout détente. One might normally have expected improved relations with another capital to mean *lessened* aid by that capital to one's enemies. But there was nothing normal about the way Moscow conducted its business.

Nixon faced a dilemma: Should he respond to the massive and unprecedented North Vietnamese offensive and risk losing the precious summit, or should he go ahead with the summit and risk losing the war? Throughout the month of April, Nixon brooded, deeply torn.[72]

It turns out that there was a solution to the dilemma, of which Nixon was not yet aware. One had to learn to play the same double game as the Soviets, to continue to improve one's relations with Moscow even while applying violent pressure to its ally. In other words, one could bomb North Vietnam and still have the summit. In a sense, Nixon's gradual discovery of this solution marked the real beginning of the détente era—and a certain end to innocence for American foreign policy. But the solution, such as it was, was still a month away.

The Soviets, for their part, were happy to string the Americans along. Dobrynin invited Kissinger to Moscow for secret summit preparations and hinted that secret talks planned for the end of April between Kissinger and Le Duc Tho would find the North Vietnamese in a forthcoming mood. (Such misleading Soviet hints had been staples of the war since the Johnson years.)

The purpose of this gambit was evidently twofold. First, the Soviets genuinely desired the summit: not just to match Beijing, but also for the commercial benefits—especially a planned and desperately needed grain sale—now being held out by the carrot-conscious Nixon administration.[73] At the same time, the Soviets were happy to do what they could on behalf of their allies to blunt the American response to the North Vietnamese offensive.

The Nixon administration was not completely paralyzed. American air power was readied for a counteroffensive against the North. On April 4, the State Department issued a statement about Soviet arms shipments to North Vietnam, and Kissinger raised the subject with Dobrynin. On the other hand, decisive action was essentially delayed for a month as Kissinger shuttled back and forth between Washington, Moscow, and Paris. Summit preparations continued.[74]

The situation was complicated by an important tactical split between Nixon and Kissinger. Nixon wanted Kissinger to use the opportunity of the Moscow meeting to come down hard on Vietnam, essentially demanding a let-up on the aggression there as a precondition for a summit. Yet contravening Nixon's orders, Kissinger in Moscow dealt summarily with Vietnam, instead concentrating on SALT. On returning, he presented a carrot of his own to Nixon to justify his departure from instructions: "If the summit meeting takes place," he wrote to Nixon, "you will be able to sign the most important arms control agreement ever concluded."[75]

By early May, back from Moscow and a Paris meeting with North Vietnamese negotiator Le Duc Tho, Kissinger was convinced Nixon would have to cancel the summit and commence bombing of Hanoi. Still torn, Nixon sent Kissinger and Haldeman to consult with Treasury Secretary John Connally, the man whom Nixon regarded (no doubt rightly) as the most politically astute member of the administration. It was Connally who hit on the solution: bomb Hanoi, mine Haiphong harbor, and leave the onus on the Soviets to cancel the summit.

Much to the administration's surprise, despite the bombing and the mining, the summit was on as planned. "We've done a lot for those Vietnamese," a Soviet diplomat told the *Washington Post*'s Stanley Karnow, "but we're not going to let them spoil our relations with the United States."[76]

Signing the SALT Accords

Perhaps because of the Kremlin's eagerness for the summit, and the trade and grain deals expected to follow from it, Kissinger was able to make significant progress on SALT during his secret presummit April meeting in Moscow.

The final form of the deal was taking shape. Brezhnev had agreed to an ABM Treaty permitting two ABM sites with 100 interceptors each— one to defend national capitals and one to defend ICBM silos (an approach floated by U.S. negotiators in Helsinki at Washington's authorization in late April). The Soviets accepted a prohibition on construction of new fixed soft ICBM launchers. And they agreed to a five-year duration for the Interim Agreement on Offensive Arms. Finally, Brezhnev had accepted a freeze on SLBMs, but on curious terms. Under the Kissinger-Brezhnev agreement, the United States *and its allies* would be permitted 50 submarines with 800 launching tubes—the United States would be allowed 41 subs with 656 launchers—while the Soviets would be permitted 62 modern submarines with 950 launchers.[77] The agreement, in short, gave the Soviets an advantage of 21 submarines and nearly 300 launchers.

For some time there was some mystery about where the numbers 62 and 950 for the Soviets had come from. Had Kissinger proposed them, or had they come from the Soviets?[78] Chief negotiator Gerard C. Smith's 1979 memoirs threw interesting light on this question. According to Smith, "Some SALT officials later noted a curious coincidence that a then current U.S. intelligence paper containing low, medium, and high estimates of the Soviet strategic submarine program projected *at the high end of this range* a Soviet fleet in 1977 of 62 submarines with about 950 launchers."[79] In other words, faced on the one hand with the necessity of including SLBMs in SALT so as to placate the joint chiefs and faced on the other hand with stiff Soviet resistance to SLBM limits, Kissinger evidently hit on an obvious, if devious, solution: to propose a "limit" to the Kremlin that actually matched or exceeded the expected Soviet building program.

Not unlike previous meetings with the Soviet leadership, the 1972 Moscow summit was marked by the use of sleep deprivation, huge quantities of food and alcohol, and unpredictable late-night meetings as tools of psychological warfare. "You should understand," Kissinger at one point cabled Smith, who remained with the U.S. and Soviet SALT delegations in Helsinki, "that we are operating in a situation where we never know from hour to hour with whom we are meeting or what the topic will be."[80] On one occasion, Brezhnev whisked Nixon away from the Secret Service for a harrowing high-speed drive in his private car to his *dacha*, followed by a gut-wrenching trip on a hydrofoil down the Moscow River.[81] It is not clear whether Brezhnev's intention was to soften Nixon up, or whether this was just the Soviet leader's idea of a good time. The Secret Service was completely panicked. On another occasion, Kissinger sat through multiple toasts at a lavish banquet only to be informed after midnight that Gromyko was awaiting him back at the Kremlin to discuss SLBM limits. As Nixon and Kissinger found, life in the inner sanctums of what Ronald Reagan was later to call, in vivid phrase, the "evil empire" was a strange affair indeed.

In the end, Nixon and Kissinger predictably conceded more than they should. On the SLBM issue, the provisions were mind-numbingly complex, but the essence of the U.S. concession was to permit the Soviets to exempt an older class of submarines from the protocol's replacement provisions—over and above permitting Moscow both higher SLBM and higher "replacement" ceilings.[82] Also the Soviets were assured repeatedly that the United States would not build submarines up to the limits allowed under the Interim Agreement.[83] (There was a later controversy over the alleged secrecy of these assurances. However, Congress was aware that the United States had no plans to build submarines during the five-year Interim Agreement.)[84] In his memoirs, Kissinger states that he gave the SLBM issue highest priority. That is probably because, amid all the confusing complexities of SALT, the anxious attentions of the military, bureaucracy, and the Congress had now converged on the SLBM issue.[85]

Far more important from a substantive standpoint was the still not widely understood issue of "heavy" missiles, to which Kissinger devoted considerably less attention. The failure to obtain meaningful limits on Soviet "heavy" missiles would doom the U.S. ICBM force to vulnerability within just over a decade.

Along with the ABM Treaty and the Interim Agreement on Offensive Arms, eight other agreements were signed in Moscow, including those for cooperation on the environment, health, and space as well as on "basic principles" committing each side, rather quixotically, to eschew "efforts to obtain unilateral advantage at the expense of the other." And of course there were in prospect important agreements on trade, including grain.

Misleading Congress

The Nixon administration's presentation of the SALT agreements to the Congress and the public was less than a model of candor. Perhaps the most scandalous misinformation provided to Congress concerned the heavy missile issue. It is plain now from Smith's memoirs that both Kissinger and the SALT delegates had every reason to be aware they had not solved the heavy missile problem, with all its implications for the eventual vulnerability of U.S. ICBMs; yet Smith and Kissinger clearly did their best to persuade Congress and the press that a firm limit had been achieved.

"We have put them [the Soviets] on clear notice," Smith told a House committee, "that any missile having a volume significantly larger than their SS-11, we will consider a heavy ICBM, and if they deployed weapons, missiles, having a volume significantly larger than the SS-11, we would consider that as incompatible with the Interim Agreement."[86] Members of Congress were given the clear impression that the Soviets would be restrained by the U.S. unilateral statements—precisely the opposite of what Smith now tells us he believed at the time.[87] Indeed, Smith later denigrated claims that the SS-19 successor to the SS-11 was a treaty violation as a "disillusion" based on "ungrounded U.S. expectations"[88] (to which Smith, as he neglects to point out, contributed). There were other such misleading public statements at the time from both Smith and Kissinger.[89]

Meanwhile, a host of academic and think tank experts testifying before the Senate Foreign Relations committee endorsed the conclusion that SALT signified a fundamental shift in Soviet military doctrine. "In a remarkable doctrinal shift, the Soviet Union, in the context of SALT, adopted the view that ABMs are, in fact destabilizing and should be limited to very low levels," testified Jerome H. Kahan of the Brookings Institution, who would later serve in the Carter administration.[90] Paul Warnke, who would later negotiate SALT II, not only predicted that SALT I would protect the Minuteman force but also recommended *additional unilateral restraint* in the U.S. defense effort.[91]

There were, in a sense, two sets of expectations, or at least predictions, for SALT and détente. The more optimistic predictions, from the arms control community, concerned the expected impact of SALT on the arms race. The agreements were said to signify a major change in Soviet doctrine. Now that defenses were limited, the arms controllers believed, the way was open to break the action-reaction phenomenon and gain serious limitations in offensive weapons. Nixon and Kissinger were far less optimistic about arms control,[92] but they professed to see SALT as part of a broader process—the weaving of a "web" of interests that would draw the Soviet Union more fully into the international community. The carrots of arms control and trade would be used to give the Soviets a stake in the international status quo and help moderate their behavior. To the degree that a positive rationale was put forward for détente, it was this effort to "normalize" the Soviet Union.

Neither set of predictions was borne out. Arms control did not cause the Soviet Union to slacken its arms buildup, and détente did not cause it to behave with greater international restraint.

The Soviet Buildup Accelerates

Arms control agreements have sometimes been accused of stimulating the arms race, of providing a pretext for an intensified defense buildup. SALT I may indeed have had a stimulating effect on the arms buildup, but it operated only or mainly on the Soviet side.

While Secretary of Defense Melvin Laird made his support for SALT contingent upon congressional support of a package of "Assurances" developed by the JCS, similar to the "Safeguards" developed for the Limited Test Ban Treaty in 1963, these measures involved an additional expenditure of only $168 million—a figure more than offset by the $711 million cut in ABM funding.[93] *The fact remains that U.S. defense spending, including spending for stratetgic programs, declined steadily until 1977, when it increased only slightly.*[94] Indeed, in 1972, after SALT was signed, Congress slashed 7.2 percent from the administration's fiscal 1973 defense request, the second largest such cut of the Vietnam era.[95]

On the Soviet side, meanwhile, the story was quite different. Within months of the conclusion of SALT, the Soviets began a series of missile flight tests that would eventually lead to a complete overhaul and modernization of their land-based arsenal, a massive growth in the number of their warheads, a huge boost in payload or throwweight, and a significant increase in the vulnerability of the U.S. land-based missile force. Four new ICBMs—the SS-16, 17, 18, and 19—were unveiled, along with advanced MIRV technology and a new "pop-up" or "cold launch" technique. The new systems had been in the design stage during the SALT negotiations; indeed, it seems clear in retrospect that the Soviet negotiating position in SALT I had been shaped to protect them.[96] There were parallel improvements in SLBMs and SSBNs (ballastic missile submarines). Moreover, the Soviets began deploying a new bomber, designated "Backfire."

In effect, the Soviets in the wake of SALT were replicating the kind of dramatic forward leap in missile technology and deployments that the United States had initiated in the late 1950s in response to the *Sputnik* threat. But whereas the American missile buildup of the late 1950s and early 1960s had come in response to an apparent *increase* in the threat from the Soviet Union, the new Soviet program came in response to an apparent *lessening* of the threat from the United States. Far from leading to mutual restraint, therefore, the SALT agreements had opened the way to the greatest single surge of the Soviet buildup.

What was perhaps most noteworthy was the absence of a clear American political response to all this new activity. In many respects, the threat posed by the new generation of Soviet missiles tested immediately after SALT I was substantively greater than the threat posed by *Sputnik* (though *Sputnik* was obviously more dramatic). Yet as Charles Sorrels of the Congressional Budget Office noted in 1976, the U.S. response was considerably less robust than in the earlier period.[97] Indeed, the major concern appeared to focus on the potential effect of the new Soviet missiles on the arms control process.[98] It is hard to accept the now-standard conclusion that SALT I did not produce a "lulling effect" on American thinking about defense,[99] given not only the steady decline in the American defense budget but also the absence of an American response to the post-treaty surge in the Soviet buildup.

Détente and Regional Crisis

There were parallel developments in the political sphere. Here, too, the expectation for détente was disappointed.

The first real test for the new political relationship came in the Middle East. Indeed, it was essentially forced upon the Soviets by their most important client state in the region, Egypt. That the Soviets in some sense *intended* to exercise restraint in various political conflicts around the globe following the Moscow summit was vividly shown by Egypt's decision to expel 15,000 to 20,000 Soviet advisors in July 1972. Egypt's shrewd leader, Anwar el-Sadat, saw plainly that the Soviets were far more interested for the moment in cultivating the new relationship with the Americans than in promoting the aims of Soviet Third World allies.[100]

The eventual reorientation of Egypt's foreign policy toward the West would rank, with the opening to China, as a second great achievement, or at least by-product, of the Nixon-Kissinger foreign policy. Like the China opening, it would stand as something of a tribute to Kissinger's talent for deviousness and double games. But it would also eventually be overshadowed by larger American defeats in Southeast Asia, Africa, and elsewhere as détente increasingly blocked forceful American responses to Soviet encroachments.

For the moment, however, despite some preliminary secret contacts with the Americans, Sadat's aim in expelling Soviet advisors was not to cultivate the West but to get the attention of Moscow. The tactic worked. By October, Sadat was putting out fresh feelers to the Soviets.[101] To win back their position in the Middle East, the Soviets accelerated arms shipments to both Egypt and Syria and began to offer public rhetorical support for a possible war with Israel.[102]

This is not to say that the Soviets actively encouraged hostilities; on the contrary, they privately discouraged them.[103] Still, they were torn: If they failed to support Egyptian designs, they risked the loss of their position in the region and the waste of a decade-long investment in military aid and sales there.

In the end, the Soviets were handicapped less by their conscious intentions than by their very nature and fundamental ideology as a world power. When the Soviets entered a region such as the Middle East, what they brought, primarily, were arms and a "progressive" rhetoric challenging the "imperialist"-dominated status quo. They were by nature a revolutionary power; that was their defining character. In this sense, their thrust was essentially negative. One might say that by their very nature the Soviets were doomed to cause trouble. It also points to the inherent illogic of détente, of basing world order on a cooperative relationship between one power (the United States) fundamentally dedicated to preserving the stability of the international status quo and another power (the Soviet Union) fundamentally dedicated to its overthrow.

All this may help to explain Brezhnev's peculiarly clumsy and bullying attempts to come to grips with the Middle East question at the second Nixon-Brezhnev summit in San Clemente in June 1973. On the final day of the summit, held in Nixon's private California residence, Kissinger was informed around 10 P.M. that Brezhnev wanted to discuss the Middle East. At 10:45 P.M., a groggy Nixon was ushered into a study where the Soviet leader propounded his views on a new Middle East solution. The Soviet formula was characteristically one-sided: It would involve Soviet-American cosponsorship of a peace settlement that involved a complete Israeli withdrawal from territories occupied in the 1967 war.[104]

One suspects that the nature of Brezhnev's recitation had as much to do with the inherent limits of the Soviet position and worldview as with any specific ill intentions on his part. The desire to avoid a war was doubtless sincere. But the fact remained that the Soviets in effect were calling on the Americans to demand vast concessions from an ally (Israel) so as to rescue Moscow from the necessity (the very word suggests the incongruity of the situation) of having to support its own ally in an aggressive war.

Logically speaking, the obvious solution to the problem would have been for Moscow to restrain its Arab allies. But if the Soviets, as the major supplier of arms to the region, opted to play such a role, they would be in the unwelcome position of a drug dealer who suddenly decided to offer his clientele drug counseling instead of drugs.

While the Soviets' role in the Yom Kippur War of 1973 was perhaps not as completely sinister as supposed by many at the time, they did not fail to stir trouble, with accelerated arms shipments and inflammatory radio broadcasts to the region. And when Israel broke the cease-fire, they seriously escalated the crisis, calling upon the United States to intervene jointly, and threatened, failing that, to intervene unilaterally with their own troops (airborne units were put on alert for this apparent purpose). Only when Kissinger ordered a worldwide Defcon 3 alert of U.S. forces did the Soviets abandon this last plan.[105] Ironically, for a full decade, from 1962 to 1972, the superpowers had managed without such a direct collision. Now in the era of "détente" collisions were to become ever more frequent.

The administration could not help but be sobered by the experience. William Quandt, who served on the NSC staff under Kissinger, writes that the "assumption . . . that U.S.-Soviet détente would serve to minimize the danger of regional conflicts" was "undermined" by the October war. "Superpower confrontation was still a possibility in the era of détente and negotiations, and it was this, above all, that preoccupied the senior decision makers. The events of October 24–25 confirmed their worst fears."[106] Publicly, however, beseiged by the Watergate scandal and unwilling to concede the flaws of détente, administration officials stressed how helpful détente had been in solving the crisis.

The Jackson Factor

In a sense, it was ironic that the Nixon-Kissinger policy went by the name of "linkage," since the main effect of this policy was not so much to create new linkages as to dissolve old ones. By breaking the so-called action-reaction pattern, SALT I actually undermined the traditional and healthy linkage between Soviet arms deployments and an American response to them; the main difference in the arms race now was that when the Soviets deployed new weapons, the United States failed to react. Likewise, détente, by capitalizing on the "peace" illusion, destroyed the traditional linkage between American foreign policy and American public opinion. American foreign policy—which admittedly since Woodrow Wilson had always had something of a crusading character—now no longer had this character or particularly reflected American values. Rather, it reflected the Machiavellian calculations of Kissinger and Nixon. But this was not a particularly favorable development for American power. The United States in the 1970s was coming to resemble a human being subject to a neurological disorder or the influence of a narcotic: All the normally powerful reflexes of the American body politic were ceasing to operate, were shutting down. The effect was to leave the Soviets freer to exert their power in various regions of the globe. On a host of different levels, America was no longer behaving in the world like America or like the global power it was. Not for the first time in the twentieth century, a democracy under the influence of the peace illusion was beginning to act in a fashion that communicated to its adversaries far greater weakness and irresolution than actually afflicted it.

In a sense, what was needed in 1973 was a new "Iron Curtain" speech similar to that which Churchill had delivered in March 1946, and which had awakened the American populace from its Wilsonian reverie. What was needed was a dose of realism, the utterance of a statesman capable of jolting the public mind back to reality. What was needed was an open debate over national purpose, over peace and war, over the use of power—precisely the debate that Nixon had pusillanimously evaded from the 1968 campaign onward and that Kissinger presumed the American populace to be too unsophisticated to understand. What was needed, in a sense, was genuine statesmanship, and its two great attributes: clarity of vision and eloquence. But fortune, which had supplied great statesmen at nearly every other critical juncture in American history—the founding, the Civil War, the shaping of the Cold War—saw fit to leave the nation to its own devices during the era of Vietnam.

The closest thing to a Churchillian figure to be found on the American scene in the 1970s was a man whose unspectacular public persona has since condemned him to a certain obscurity: Senator Henry Jackson of Washington. Jackson was marked by one of the two major attributes of great statesmanship. He had genuine clarity about the strategic logic governing American foreign policy. What he lacked, however, was eloquence and public appeal. Famous for his lack of charisma, for his uninspiring television image, Jackson was incapable of arousing the kind of passion Churchill used so effectively to mobilize public opinion and change minds. But working behind the scenes, in the Congress, Jackson fashioned a series of laws and resolutions whose long-term and indirect effect was fundamentally to transform public awareness and help restore the linkages lost in the confusions of Vietnam, arms control, and détente. Through exhaustive congressional hearings and key pieces of legislation, Jackson helped to effect a gradual change in public consciousness almost as profound as the sudden change produced by Churchill's Iron Curtain speech in 1946. It was a kind of legislative statesmanship rare in the history of democracies.

Jackson's first important contribution to a critique of détente was to point out the simple inequities in the SALT I agreement. He did this not only through extensive questioning of administration witnesses during special Senate Armed Service Committee hearings, but by introducing an amendment to the Senate resolution approving the SALT I Interim Agreement. The Jackson amendment called upon the Executive Branch in the future not to "limit the United States to levels of intercontinental strategic forces inferior to the limits provided for the Soviet Union."[107] Unobjectionable enough on the surface, the amendment drew attention to the fact that Kissinger and Nixon had indeed accepted unequal offensive aggregates under SALT I; moreover, it established a concrete criterion against which the results of future negotiations could be measured.

But the most important piece of legislation for the fate of détente was an amendment Jackson originally introduced to the trade bill in 1972, later known as the Jackson-Vanik amendment. The amendment linked the granting of Most Favored Nation (MFN) trade status for the Soviet Union or any other country to the allowance of free emigration. More perhaps than any other utterance or piece of legislation in the decade, the Jackson-Vanik amendment would transform the American foreign policy debate. Indeed, eventually the amendment would play an important role in the collapse of communism and the end of the Cold War.

By the time of the Moscow summit, the United States had already taken major steps toward liberalizing trade and commercial relations with the Soviets. The Kama River truck plant had been approved. A grain deal had been completed at the summit, which resulted in a surprise Soviet purchase of over $1 billion in agricultural products from American firms during 1972, many of them on credit. Indeed, the effect of what became known as the "great grain robbery" was to drive up grain prices in the United States. Nixon's hope at the time of the summit was to dangle the carrot of trade to get further help from the Soviets on political issues, especially Vietnam.[108] However, while withholding approval of joint ventures to exploit Siberian natural gas, the administration was prepared to grant the Soviets Most Favored Nation status *even before the Vietnam war was settled.*[109] And indeed, by October, Commerce Secretary Peter G. Peterson had concluded both a comprehensive trade agreement and an agreement settling Soviet lend-lease debt from the war, opening the way to the granting of Most Favored Nation status to the Soviet Union, presuming Congress approved.

In August, however, possibly in an effort to curry favor with Arab regimes following its setbacks in the Middle East, the Soviet Union had inexplicably begun to impose an exit tax on Jewish emigrants leaving the country. Jewish emigration had increased steadily as détente had developed; now the shift in Soviet policy began to arouse ire on Capitol Hill. It was in light of the new Jewish emigration problem that Jackson hit upon the idea of linking MFN to a demand for full freedom of emigration.[110]

Although Jackson was genuinely concerned about human rights, his amendment also reflected broader geopolitical considerations. In particular, he was concerned that the bushels of carrots being delivered to the Soviets by Nixon and Kissinger were not yielding proportionate results. The bottom-line question remained: What precisely was the United States getting in return for all the concessions being offered to the Soviets under the détente process? The United States had ceded its advantage in ABM. It had accepted an Interim Agreement on Offensive Arms that gave the Soviets a politically significant advantage of 800 offensive missiles, and potentially militarily significant advantages in ICBM throwweight. It had made a billion dollars' worth of grain available to the Soviet Union, inflating the price of domestic grain, and subsidizing the sales at taxpayer expense. Plans were afoot to widen trade relations and extend MFN status to the Soviet Union, a concession that would have the effect of powerfully strengthening the Soviet economy. Increased trade would mean increased Soviet access to Western advanced technologies, many of them with clear military applications.

In return, the Soviets had moderated their rhetoric somewhat and sent Politburo member Nikolai Podgorny to North Vietnam. To end the war in Vietnam, it would still prove necessary to undertake major escalation (both to move Hanoi and to reassure—falsely, as it proved—Saigon). To prevent a major Soviet encroachment in the Middle East, it would eventually prove necessary to go on nuclear alert. And the Soviet missile buildup continued apace through 1972 and 1973. What precisely was being purchased from the Soviets in the way of reciprocal restraint?

The Jackson-Vanik amendment, from Jackson's point of view, replaced vague, difficult-to-pin-down linkages with a clear and concrete quid pro quo: trade in exchange for free emigration.

The importance of this amendment in reshaping U.S.-Soviet relations and the Cold War debate over the next decade and a half could hardly be overstated. The amendment created a fundamental new linkage—between human rights and trade with the Soviet Union—that in some sense would help replace the traditional linkage between the Soviet threat and American vigilance, which arms control had now gravely impaired. Even if, under the influence of arms control, the American elite was no longer capable of recognizing Soviet weapons as a threat to Western security and indeed had come to regard American weaponry as the chief menace, the public was still capable of understanding human rights abuses. The Jackson-Vanik amendment reminded Americans, amid the photo opportunities of summitry and the endless signing ceremonies of détente, that the essential nature of the Soviet domestic political system had not altered. The amendment invoked a natural and longstanding linkage in foreign policy: that is, the link between democratic freedoms and peace. Moreover, at root of the amendment was an important truth: Until the Soviet regime had essentially been converted into a democracy, it would continue to pose a threat, owing to the very logic of totalitarian rule.

Doubtless grasping the potentially far-reaching importance of this new approach, Andrei Sakharov, the father of the Soviet H-bomb and now a prominent Soviet dissident, took the grave personal risk in October 1972 of sending a letter to the American Congress endorsing the Jackson-Vanik amendment.[111] The Sakharov letter had the effect of turning a great deal of liberal opinion in favor of the amendment and against an expansion of East-West trade. By the end of the month, seventy-two senators had signed on as cosponsors of the Jackson amendment.[112]

In a certain sense, Jackson had accomplished what Nixon, Kissinger, or any other American political leader had not been able to do: He had put back together, on a provisional basis, the Humpty Dumpty of the old Cold War coalition; he had reestablished, in effect, the bipartisan alliance of liberals and conservatives that had originally formed the foundation of American power in the Cold War. True, the new coalition was comprised of senators holding very divergent views on issues relating specifically to national defense. Nonetheless, Jackson had recovered common ground for Democrats and Republicans in attitudes toward the Soviet Union. That common ground was the issue of human rights. The creation of this new alliance based on human rights would be extremely important to the reconstruction of the Democratic party.

Kissinger was quite bitter over the Jackson amendment. He later blamed it, along with Watergate, for the breakdown of détente. The debate over it, in his words "blighted US-Soviet relations ever after."[113] Kissinger's objections to the amendment were twofold. First, its passage resulted in the short term in a precipitous decline in Jewish emigration. Second, and far more crucial from Kissinger's point of view, it robbed the Nixon administration of a crucial carrot in dealing with the Soviet Union.

Did the loss of control over MFN status undermine détente? It seems unlikely that congressional haggling over MFN was a factor in Soviet behavior toward the Middle East in 1973. In 1973, Brezhnev still had reason to accept Nixon's assurances that eventually he could bring Congress into line. And by the time the Jackson-Vanik amendment had passed, the Soviets had already given ample indication that they were not prepared to respond constructively to a strategy based heavily on the proffering of carrots.

The American Disease

Kissinger's second explanation for the failure of détente lies in Watergate. That the weakening of the Nixon presidency during Watergate made détente and the Soviets more difficult to manage than they might otherwise have been seems clear enough. Significantly, however, Soviet perception of a shift in the correlation of forces antedated Nixon's Watergate troubles. As early as June 1972, following the Moscow summit and before the Watergate burglary, Georgi A. Arbatov of the Soviet Institute of the U.S.A. assured a Soviet television audience that Nixon had signed the SALT treaties because "new . . . conditions" had forced the choice upon him. SALT reflected, in the *New York Times* paraphrase of Arbatov's analysis, "the increased might of the Soviet Union, American setbacks in Vietnam and such American domestic problems as unemployment, currency difficulties, inflation and race."[114] Détente in and of itself was perceived as a sign of a weakened American power position.

But Watergate could not help but accelerate the decline of American power. The fact that Nixon faced the resignation of his vice president amid the October 1973 Middle East war, for example, could easily have had something to do with the bold course the Soviets chose to follow in that crisis.

Moreover, Soviet bargaining in arms control became even more one-sided. As Nitze told the House Armed Services Committee in July 1974 after resigning from the U.S. SALT delegation, "Soviet officials have indicated . . . that what they call the 'correlation of forces' . . . is moving in their favor and that, even though we may today believe that their proposals are one-sided and inequitable, eventually realism will bring us to accept at least the substance of them."[115] Indeed, chief Soviet delegate Vladmir S. Semenov expressed just such a sentiment to Nitze in the talks.[116]

Kissinger later described the Nixon administration's policy as one of "seeking to dominate the peace issue."[117] Yet there was a question of whether the administration was dominating the peace issue or being dominated by it. Earlier Western statesmen who had attempted to cloak vague and poorly formulated *Realpolitik* objectives in peace sentiment— such as France's Aristide Briand—had ultimately found themselves impossibly encumbered by their rhetorical garments. Having begun as manipulators, they ended as the manipulated. So it was with Nixon and Kissinger and the Soviet Union. Originally, Kissinger had conceived SALT as a concrete test of Soviet intentions. "SALT," he wrote in the first volume of his memoirs, "gave us the opportunity to determine whether détente was a tactic or a new turn in Soviet policy."[118] But by 1974, that original test—having been essentially failed by the Soviets— had been shunted aside, to be replaced by an entirely new one. "Our test," Kissinger wrote in his second volume, "was whether we were, on balance, better off with an accord than without."[119] But of course it was hard to see how such a test could be failed. Given America's steadily declining strategic position, one could always make the case that the country would be worse off if trends were allowed to proceed on their natural course.

By 1974, the Nixon administration's—and the country's—relationship to arms control had come to resemble an addiction. The agreements, like an opiate, treated the symptoms rather than the causes of international instability, giving the illusion rather than the reality of a cure. The fundamental source of the disease lay in declining American power. Arms negotiations and agreements not only failed to alleviate this underlying condition but aggravated the problem both by exposing American weakness to the Kremlin and by further undermining domestic support for American military power. Each summit or agreement brought a temporary illusion of relief—a temporary and illusory "high." Yet after each "high," the patient found himself in a more weakened and drug-dependent state. By 1974, it was seemingly impossible to break out of the vicious cycle. Arms control was failing, but the only cure that anyone could prescribe seemed to be more arms control.

As in recovery from any other addiction, the patient often must grow worse before he or she grows better; so it was with Washington's addiction to arms control. Following Nixon's resignation on August 9, 1974, Kissinger traveled with Gerald Ford, the new president, to Vladivostok in 1974 for a "get acquainted" summit with Brezhnev. To nearly everyone's surprise, Ford emerged from the meeting with a major "agreed framework" for a SALT II treaty. A new ten-year agreement on strategic arms, the administration predicted, was now only months away. Once again, there was the familiar overselling. Vladivostok, said Kissinger, would "mean that a cap has been put on the arms race for a period of ten years."[120]

The reality was otherwise. Superficially, the Vladivostok framework met the test of the Jackson amendment by specifying equal aggregates for both sides. But it did so by setting ceilings so high as to (1) impose no meaningful constraint on the planned Soviet buildup and (2) offer nothing to relieve the growing problem of U.S. ICBM vulnerability. The two sides were to be limited to 2,400 strategic missiles and bombers. But modernization and MIRVing would continue. Moreover, the American effort to reduce Soviet "heavy missiles" was finally shelved, in exchange for an ostensible Soviet agreement to drop the complaints about American "forward-based systems." (Characteristically, the Soviets raised the forward-based systems issue again in subsequent negotiations anyway.)[121]

Interestingly, Vladivostok brought disillusionment even in the arms control community. The leaderships of both the Arms Control Association and the Federation of the American Scientists actually split over the agreement, with many arms controllers arguing that the high MIRV subceilings would encourage a continuation of the arms race and lead to increased strategic instability.[122]

Moreover, no detailed communiqué was produced, and there remained numerous ambiguities and unresolved issues in the accord. Among the most troublesome would prove to be the question of a major new American system—cruise missiles—on which the negotiating record was ambiguous, and a new Soviet bomber—the Backfire—with potentially strategic range, which the Vladivostok framework failed to include.

Hopes that Vladivostok would lead quickly to a SALT II treaty soon faded, as Soviet ardor for an agreement rapidly cooled. The reasons for declining Soviet interest were probably twofold. First, Vladivostok, which the Soviet press praised in the most glowing terms,[123] already had placed effective limits on the American building program, at least precluding any major surges or surprises. Second, American international prestige was rapidly declining. Appalled at the savaging that the Federal Bureau of Investigation and the Central Intelligence Agency were taking at the hands of congressional committees, Dobrynin told Kissinger in January 1975, "Any government that can't protect its intelligence and security agencies is not to be taken seriously."[124] The congressional attack on the intelligence committees was followed by the decision to pull the plug on Vietnam. On March 13, 1975, as Communist forces advanced into the northern provinces of South Vietnam, the House Foreign Affairs Committee rejected a Ford administration plea for military aid to the South. Further pleas to the Congress were unavailing. In the humiliating last days of April, as helicopters lifted Americans and South Vietnamese from the roof of the American embassy in Saigon, North Vietnamese forces closed in on the capital. By April 30, Saigon had fallen.

The American defeat in Southeast Asia appeared to embolden Communist forces, both in Southeast Asia and elsewhere. In the same month as North Vietnamese forces closed in on Saigon, the Khmer Rouge came to power in Cambodia and the Pathet Lao in Laos. Echoes of these developments were to be heard as far away as southern Africa.

Following a military coup in Portugal in 1974, in which Communist-leaning elements were involved, the Soviets stepped up aid to MPLA (Popular Movement for the Liberation of Angola), the Communist-sponsored resistance force in the Portuguese colony of Angola. In 1975, after the defeat of South Vietnam, Soviet involvement became more overt: Large numbers of Cuban troops began pouring into Angola to aid the Communist forces. In December, both the Senate and the House voted to prohibit U.S. aid to Angola. By February 1976, a new Communist government had established itself in the oil-rich former Portuguese colony.[125] As Kissinger told Congress, the Angolan adventure established a fundamentally new precedent: "Angola represents the first time that the Soviets have moved militarily at long distance to impose a regime of their choice. It is the first time that the United States has failed to respond. . . . An ominous precedent is set. . . . If the pattern is not broken now, we will face harder choices and harder costs in the future."[126] Yet not only did Congress preclude an American response, but Kissinger traveled to Moscow in January 1976 to attempt to continue work on SALT II. While criticizing Soviet activity in Angola, Kissinger defended the decision to travel to Moscow: We "have never considered the limitation of strategic arms as a favor we grant the Soviet Union," said the secretary of state.[127]

The debate over "linkage" had come full circle. Having originally hoped to use arms control as leverage to get Soviet concessions on such issues as Vietnam, Kissinger now cautioned against abandoning SALT at any price. In effect, Moscow had begun to use the American craving for SALT as a tool to paralyze the U.S. response to regional Soviet aggression, or perhaps America was merely paralyzing itself.

"The general crisis of capitalism continues to deepen," Brezhnev wrote in 1976. "Events of the past few years are convincing confirmation of this."[128] By the mid-1970s, the Soviets saw their victories in the Third World and their improving military position vis-à-vis the United States as concrete evidence of the inherent superiority of the socialist over the capitalist system. "Socialism is the most dynamic and influential force in the world arena," wrote Gromyko in 1975. "On three continents, from the Republic of Cuba to the Democratic Republic of Vietnam, the new society of the peoples of Socialist states thrives and is being successfully constructed. The inexhaustible resources of these countries, imposing in their economic achievements, *the power of their offensive might* is placed at the service of peace and only peace."[129] At least from Moscow's perspective, it appeared that the great historical contest was being won by the Communist side.

The decade of the 1970s would be a time of terrible violence and awful defeats for the West as Communist power insinuated itself into every corner of the globe and nation after nation fell to Soviet or Soviet-sponsored forces—South Vietnam in 1975, Angola in 1975–76, Ethiopia in 1977, Cambodia in 1978, and Afghanistan in 1979. The death toll from these conquests would be measured in the millions.

CHAPTER 9

The New Morality

You know as well as we do that, when these matters are discussed by practical people, the standard of justice depends on the equality of power to compel and that in fact the strong do what they have the power to do and the weak accept what they have to accept.
—Thucydides, *History of the Peloponnesian War*

Thus conscience does make cowards of us all.   —Shakespeare, *Hamlet*

I s it too obvious to point out that few experiences so shatter the confidence of a nation as defeat in war? Nothing might seem more commonplace, yet for Americans the commonest truths of nationhood have often been the most elusive. Americans did not view war, and particularly the Vietnam war, as a part of them; it was something imposed from the outside, a temporary aberration. Much of the trauma of Vietnam could be traced to the unwillingness of the government even to admit that the country was at war—despite the fact that at the conflict's height half a million troops were committed and up to 400 per week were perishing in battle. By the time the helicopters rose off the roof of the American embassy in besieged Saigon in 1975, with fleeing South Vietnamese reaching desperately for the skids, most of the nation had dissociated itself from the spectacle. It was someone else's problem, perhaps the government's problem. The country was in it but not of it, in the way that a victim in a serious car crash might report an out-of-body experience.

This is not to say that the trauma of defeat had not racked the nation.

It would be reenacted with vividness in cinema and fiction for a decade to come. Films such as *The Deerhunter* and *Apocalypse Now*, books such as James Webb's *Fields of Fire*, Michael Herr's *Dispatches*, and Gustav Hasford's *The Short-Timers* reenacted the trauma. The literature of Vietnam bore a certain distant relationship in atmosphere and tone to the kind of poetry that came home from the front in World War I—verse such as that of Wilfred Owen, Robert Graves, and Siegfried Sassoon. Indeed, there was a certain passing resemblance between the cultural impact of Vietnam and that of the Great War. There was, first of all, the same widespread cultural repudiation of war and its violence. But more than that, there was a similar revulsion from the public, the official, the political, the same impulsive turning inward toward the erotic and appetitive side of life. In the 1920s, this tendency had expressed itself in poems such as T. S. Eliot's "The Wasteland," novels such as Joyce's *Ulysses*, painting such as that of Picasso and Braque. The fragmentary idiom of modern art and writing, though in evidence before the war, implied a certain delegitimation of public reality and an elevation of the private sphere, a tendency strengthened by the war experience. While American mass culture of the mid-1970s had nothing quite so elegant to offer, there was a clear elevation of the private—even expressed in something so trivial as the conceit of the "me generation." There was the same shrinking from the political order that would conduct war. There was the same cynical distrust of official purposes. In sum, there was a rejection of politics.

Jimmy Carter's candidacy could be understood on one level as an expression of this phenomenon. Other presidential candidates had run against the opposing party, but Carter ran against Washington. His was an antipolitical message. His deepest theme, so appealing in the wake of Vietnam and Watergate, was that politics, even international politics, should be conducted by the standards of private life. As he wrote in *Why Not the Best?* "A nation's domestic and foreign policy actions should be derived from the same standards of ethics, honesty and morality which are characteristic of the individual citizens of the nation. The people of this country are inherently unselfish, open, honest, decent, competent, and compassionate. Our government should be the same, in all its actions and attitudes."[1] Carter's faith in his fellow man was touching; but whether a foreign policy based on compassion was capable of coping with the reality of Soviet totalitarianism and Soviet international ambition remained to be seen.

Nearly all the strengths and weaknesses of the Carter presidency, nearly all the successes, nearly all the characteristic failures came from Carter's moralism. It caused him to give enormous emphasis to arms control; at the same time, it led him to pursue arms control in such a way that exposed the flaws of the process more readily than Kissinger would have ever permitted. It caused him to make human rights a central issue of his foreign policy, but at the same time, it led him to use human rights to undermine the strategic position of the West. Again and again, it led him to embrace political opposites, on the grounds that moral not political standards should be the basis for political choice.

The Old Morality versus the New

One major problem that Carter faced in substituting moral for political judgments was that the Democratic party harbored not one but two conflicting moralities, divided along political lines. One might be called the "old morality," the other the "new morality." The old morality was essentially the party's traditional anti-Communist faith, dominant among Democrats since Truman. It had as its central value the preservation of freedom. It saw American power, even in the wake of Vietnam, as an essentially constructive force. And it believed firmly in the rightness of the use of force in defense of freedom. The old morality found its adherents in the so-called Jackson wing of the party—dominated intellectually by such figures as Ben Wattenberg, Jeane Kirkpatrick, and Senator Jackson himself.

The new morality, by contrast, was the party's post-Vietnam faith. It had as its central value the post-Vietnam preoccupation with peace. It saw American power as a basically disruptive and sometimes pernicious force in the world. It believed the key to moral action in the international sphere lay in the deemphasis of the military instrument. The new morality prevailed in the so-called McGovern wing of the party, represented within the administration by such figures as Paul Warnke, Charles William Maynes, and Cyrus Vance.

Each of these "moralities" derived from a fundamentally different orientation toward politics. The old moralists harked back to John F. Kennedy's exaltation of the public sphere. They emphasized political modes of action; they retained a belief in the irreducibility of power politics as an international reality and kept a faith in the public and the official purposes of the nation. The new moralists, by contrast, saw the Churchillian side of the Kennedy rhetoric as having been discredited by

Vietnam. They were often less comfortable with the political and official as such; their deepest wish was to transcend power politics and to reduce international politics insofar as was possible to standards of private ethics. In this sense, Jimmy Carter himself was at heart more a new moralist than an old one. (Indeed, Woodrow Wilson, the political grandfather of the new morality, was Jimmy Carter's idol.)[2]

The old moralists pressed human rights as their most politically appealing foreign policy issue, while the new moralists gave priority to arms control. But in reality, each faction had its distinct position on these two master issues of the Carter foreign policy.

The old moralists meant by human rights chiefly freedom and the struggle against the West's traditional enemy, Communist totalitarianism. Human rights was a repackaging of anticommunism amid détente. The new moralists, by contrast, saw human rights in more apolitical, anti-Western terms. The main targets of the new moralists' human rights concerns were authoritarian governments allied with the United States (beginning with the Thieu regime in South Vietnam). The inclusion of a strong statement on human rights in the 1976 Democratic platform was viewed as a victory for the old moralists, for the Jackson wing. But to achieve this inclusion, the Jackson adherents had to accept language that made human rights evenhanded vis-à-vis right and left-wing dictatorships.[3]

Similarly with arms control. The new moralists, whose issue arms control was, saw it chiefly as a means of establishing cooperative relations with the Soviet Union, of transcending what they regarded as an outmoded power-politics competition. By contrast, the old moralists, to the degree that they accepted arms control at all, saw it chiefly as a means of achieving concrete *reductions* in weapons that would reduce the strategic military threat that the Soviet Union might pose to the United States. In the end, Carter would give high priority to arms control, but out of a combination of ambition for greater disarmament and deference to the moral appeal of the old moralists, he would briefly attempt serious arms reductions.

The Carter foreign policy, as it emerged from the convention and the campaign, proved a contradictory amalgam of these two conflicting views. On the one hand, Carter would in effect tilt toward the right wing of the party by giving tremendous emphasis to the theme of human rights. On the other hand, his implementation of human rights would emphasize criticism of allied regimes. On the one hand, no priority of his administration exceeded arms control. On the other hand, even as he pursued arms control, he tried, temporarily at least, to implement the conservatives' ideas of "deep reductions."

Whiz Kid Warnke

Yet to suggest that Carter's policy was somehow evenly balanced between "old" and "new" moralities would be misleading. In both his own preferences and his choice of personnel, Carter clearly favored the new morality over the old.

There was no clearer expression of this new morality—of the Democratic party's post-Vietnam security vision—than that offered in the mid-1970s by the man whom Carter was to appoint as chief negotiator in arms talks with the Soviet Union, Paul C. Warnke.

An exceptionally cogent and articulate Washington attorney, Warnke was among the last crop of Whiz Kids to pass through McNamara's Pentagon in the late 1960s. Warnke had worked side by side with Morton Halperin on the original preparations for the SALT talks. A dedicated arms controller like Halperin, he had favored not just limits, but a total ban on ABM.[4] When McNamara resigned to be replaced as secretary of defense by the Establishmentarian Clark Clifford, Warnke became, in effect, Clifford's *éminence grise*, gradually converting the elder man to opposition to the Vietnam war.[5] (Johnson later complained that Clifford had been misled by "McNamara trainees.")[6]

Warnke's sensibility was an almost uncanny reincarnation of the liberal-pacifist outlook of nineteenth- and twentieth-century British radicals. His views also represented a kind of logical culmination of the McNamara doctrine. Most other foreign policy officials of the Carter administration shared this view to some degree, but Warnke was its leading proponent and its perfect incarnation. Like nineteenth-century liberals, Warnke saw the impulse to arm and to fear an enemy as an expression of an unappealing national chauvinism. (One reason some Americans seemed to be alarmed about the shifting military balance in the mid-1970s, he told an interviewer in 1976, was that "Americans" were by nature "chauvinistic.")[7] Like the British liberals of old, he believed that authoritarian states armed in imitation of the democracies. And like the proponents of the liberal-pacifist vision, believed that moderation in arming against an opponent would lead to moderation in return.

Warnke's 1975 article for *Foreign Policy*, "Apes on a Treadmill,"[8] still stands as perhaps the most complete and synoptic expression of the arms control ideology that came to dominate American security thinking in the 1970s. Written in the wake of the Vietnam defeat, and strongly imprinted by the "Vietnam syndrome," Warnke's article called for a comprehensive "re-evaluation of the role of the American military in today's world"—in effect, a major retrenchment of the U.S. defense effort. "Too often in the past 20 years," he wrote, "we have behaved as if our ability to influence world events required military force." On the contrary, Warnke argued, "contemporary experience should indicate that most of the world wants none of our military intervention." Indeed, the "last decade and a half has done much to teach us that the injection of American firepower into a local conflict is rarely compatible with our foreign policy interests."

Warnke described what he called "two major fallacies" that drove defense expenditures to what he termed "their present giddy heights" (though in reality by 1975 U.S. defense expenditures were declining). The first was "the fiction" that "protection of our interests" implied a "global military mission" requiring capabilities for "a congeries of contingencies throughout the world." The second was that "failure by the United States to maintain a cosmetic military 'superiority' " would "cause us political disadvantage." Warnke in short wanted to see both a global withdrawal of American power and an even less robust effort of countering the Soviet Union.

Warnke's thesis was that Soviet participation in the arms race came largely from reaction to, or—in a striking parallel to early twentieth-century British liberal thinking—from *imitation* of the United States. "As its only living superpower model, our words and our actions are admirably calculated to inspire the Soviet Union to spend its substance on military manpower and weaponry," Warnke wrote. "There is every reason to feel that we have persuaded the Soviets on this score and that they too will not negotiate from a position of military inferiority." The notion that the Soviets might be arming out of their own hegemonic ambition, irrespective of U.S. actions, had come to be seen by Warnke and his allies as hopelessly old-fashioned and naive.

Warnke's response to this problem was the same as that of early twentieth-century British liberals: unilateral restraint, or what British radicals liked to call "moderation" breeding "moderation." The Soviet Union, Warnke said, "has only one superpower model to follow." It was "far more apt to emulate than to capitulate." Therefore, the United States should set a "sound example" for the Soviet Union through unilateral self-restraint. To end what he called "this irrational arms competition,"

Warnke advocated the announcement of a unilateral moratorium on virtually every U.S. strategic program then underway.

Warnke's article was all the more remarkable for coming in the wake of a tightly reasoned pair of essays by Albert Wohlstetter, also in *Foreign Policy*, demonstrating, in effect, that the notion of an arms "race" between the U.S. and the Soviet Union was fallacious.[9] (The Soviet effort was steadily expanding, Wohlstetter showed in some detail, even as the American effort was slowing down; for some years the United States intelligence community had been consistently *underestimating* the Soviet effort.) Wohlstetter's articles were among the earliest examples of a growing literature questioning the validity of the major assumptions undergirding the arms control process. (Nitze was another important contributor to this debate.)[10] Notable in Warnke's depiction of the arms race was a failure to come to grips in any detail—beyond asserting a disagreement—with Wohlstetter's technical criticisms of the arms controllers' model.[11] Warnke wrote with the confidence that came from representing a still-dominant consensus, at least among foreign policy intellectuals.

That Carter chose such a man to head the negotiating team confronting the Soviets confirmed the president's own strong affinity for the liberal-pacifist vision. But the appointment proved to be a political blunder, in two respects. First, Warnke's views were hardly conducive to a strong bargaining position in regard to Moscow: It was as if a labor union had chosen as its bargaining agent a man with strong management sympathies who believed on principle that workers' wages were generally too high. Second, and more important to Carter in the short run, the appointment was bound to alienate the conservative wing of his own party. Senator Jackson used Warnke's confirmation hearings to expose the new nominee's antimilitarist views in some detail and to lay down markers for a possible SALT II confirmation fight. At one point Jackson reviewed Warnke's record on key defense issues:

SENATOR JACKSON. . . . I would like you to tell the committee whether I have accurately summarized your prior recommendations on these U.S. programs.

You recommended:
(1) Against the B-1.
(2) Against the Trident submarine and the Trident II missile.
(3) Against the submarine-launched cruise missile.
(4) Against the AWACS programs.
(5) Against the development of a mobile ICBM, by the United States.

(6) Against MIRV deployment.

(7) Against improvements to the U.S. ICBM force, including improved guidance and warhead design.

(8) Against the development of the XM-1 tank and for reductions in the procurement of the M-60 tank.

(9) For the reduction of U.S. tactical nuclear weapons in Europe from 7,000 to 1,000. I believe you just said a moment ago that you did not recommend a reduction in nuclear weapons in Europe.

(10) For the withdrawal of some 30,000 troops from NATO without waiting for the conclusion of an MBFR [Mutual and Balanced Force Reduction] agreement.

(11) For holding the army at 13 rather than 16 divisions, after improved efficiency made creation of three new divisions possible within existing manpower ceilings.

(12) For a $14 billion cut in the defense budget in the fiscal year 1974 submission and a $11 billion cut in fiscal year 1975.

(13) For reduction in fiscal year 1975 dollars of 3 percent per year in the defense budget, with the result that, applied to the fiscal year 1978 budget, the total reduction would amount to some $26 billion from the Carter recommendation to Congress.

MR. WARNKE. Yes, sir, Senator, that is absolutely correct.[12]

That such a man would be representing the United States in arms negotiations with the Soviet Union did not give the Senate comfort. Jackson's questioning had its intended effect. While the Democrat-controlled Senate, deferring to the new president, approved Warnke as director of the Arms Control and Disarmament Agency by a 70-to-29 vote, the vote confirming him as chief SALT negotiator was only 58 to 40, six votes shy of the two-thirds that would be needed to ratify a SALT treaty.[13] The split between those who believed in and those who had become skeptical of arms control was growing.

Senator Jackson Sets the Tone

Despite Carter's neo-Wilsonianism and his overwhelming commitment to what we have called the new morality, Senator Jackson had a surprising degree of influence on the new administration's foreign policy agenda in its initial months. Once again, Carter's moralism and populism were key factors: Moralism made Carter susceptible to the moral arguments that Jackson had been framing—almost irrespective of their political consequences—while populism made the new president more prepared than another chief executive might have been to try fundamentally new approaches. Curiously, the two distinctive early themes of the Carter foreign policy—human rights and "real arms control"—could both be traced back, the former indirectly, the latter quite directly, to Jackson.

Though the language on human rights in the 1976 Democratic platform reflected a compromise between left and right, between the McGovern and Jackson Democrats, the *Washington Post*'s Stephen Rosenfeld viewed the inclusion of such language in the platform as a clear victory for the Jackson forces.[14] Jackson had seized the human rights issue in 1973 and 1974 as a means both of restoring realism about the nature of the Soviet Union and of linking progress in détente to concrete improvements in Soviet behavior. It was ironic that Jackson, an indifferent campaigner who as a candidate fell by the wayside early in the 1976 presidential primaries, was able to identify perhaps the most potent and popularly appealing foreign policy issues of the presidential campaign. Drawn to the human rights theme by his own moralism, Carter discovered that he could use the issue to good effect against President Gerald Ford. In particular, Ford's refusal, on Kissinger's advice, to host exiled Soviet dissident Aleksandr Solzhenitsyn at the White House in 1975 proved to be a vulnerability that Carter could exploit.[15] Within the administration, national security advisor Zbigniew Brzezinski encouraged Carter to pursue the human rights theme—at least in its anti-Soviet dimension—believing that the theme put America on the right side of the struggle for history, for the future, and would necessarily goad and pressure the Soviets.[16]

Jackson also played an even more direct role in Carter's resort to the theme of arms "reductions." Jackson had staked out a position favoring actual arms reductions under arms control as early as 1974.[17] Like the human rights theme, the arms reduction theme was in part an effort to find a new moral anchor amid détente, a new test for Soviet conduct. If arms control was indeed going to deliver on its promise of reducing the strategic threat, Jackson seemed to be arguing, then the logical outcome should be a reduction in weapons. The willingness of the Soviets to accept weapons reductions would be a measure of their commitment to genuine arms control.

The human rights and deep reductions themes operated—and perhaps were intended by Jackson to operate—as a kind of reality test for détente.

If the United States was going to pursue a genuinely closer relationship with the Soviet Union, such as had been envisioned, for example, by Roosevelt at the end of World War II, then it made sense that the two governments somehow have closer views on key matters of principle. The issue of human rights, in this sense, would define a natural limit to cooperation—much as it had been found to do at the end of World War II. Similarly, if major arms control treaties were going to be pursued, it made sense that the military threat be somehow concretely reduced. If the arms control process was to be continued, at some point real reductions in the Soviet capacity to damage the United States should be arrived at. These were the kinds of common-sense "linkages" that Jackson sought to encourage as an antidote to the anesthetic effects of the Nixon-Kissinger détente.

In a sense, the Jackson issues were tailor-made for the Democratic sensibility, appealing to the strong moral concerns of the party. They also proved to be especially appealing to Carter. But they would have political consequences that the president did not anticipate.

Moscow Is Annoyed

Already by March 1977, a bare three months into the administration, the new Carter program was causing great consternation both in Moscow and at home.

First, the human rights theme had taken on a momentum of its own. Having campaigned on the issue and included a ringing call for respect for human rights in his inaugural, Carter was not unnaturally pressed on the issue by the media. In late January, the State Department issued statements condemning human rights abuses in Czechoslovakia and Rhodesia. Then on January 27, in response to a reporter's question the previous day, the State Department issued a brief statement concerning Moscow's warnings to dissident Soviet physicist Andrei Sakharov. Initially, both Carter and his secretary of state, Cyrus Vance, attempted to distance themselves from that statement, claiming they had not cleared it. But on January 28, the administration's hand was forced. Carter received a personal letter from Sakharov smuggled out of the Soviet Union; in the first days of February, Soviet authorities arrested Aleksandr Ginzburg, a prominent dissident. Having campaigned against Ford for refusing to receive Solzhenitsyn at the White House, Carter had little choice but to respond. Vance expressed administration concerns about the arrest to

Dobrynin, and a public statement condemning the Ginzburg arrest was issued by the State Department. Carter responded to Sahkarov's letter. Dobrynin called at the State Department to protest.[18]

The Soviets were exercised by this—so much so that by March, it appeared as if Carter's human rights policy might endanger SALT. In effect, the Soviets sought to establish their own form of linkage between progress in arms control and American silence on the topic of human rights. On March 13, *Pravda* warned that Carter's outspokenness on human rights might undermine SALT,[19] a position echoed by Soviet commentator Georgi Arbatov in a BBC interview three days later.[20] However, the leadership itself was more cautious. On March 21, Brezhnev delivered a speech criticizing the Carter human rights stance as an interference in internal Soviet affairs, but added that the Soviets remained interested in the SALT negotiations.[21]

At the same time that Carter was making points about human rights, he was conceiving a more ambitious agenda for the arms control negotiations. Here again Jackson was an important influence. In two breakfast meetings, Jackson shared with Carter his misgivings about the high level of weaponry embodied in the Vladivostok accords. He also submitted to the president a powerfully argued memo drafted by his aide Richard N. Perle, outlining the case for going beyond Vladivostok and attempting real reductions in nuclear weapons.[22]

The Jackson-Perle memorandum carried an implicit warning—especially in conjunction with the narrow Warnke confirmation vote—namely, that a SALT II treaty based simply on Vladivostok would not have Jackson's support. But it also reinforced an existing preference among Carter and several of his advisors—including Zbigniew Brzezinski, deputy national security advisor David Aaron, and defense secretary Harold Brown—for a bolder approach to the Soviets involving actual reductions in nuclear weapons.

There were several reasons why various members of the Carter team found the idea of arms reductions appealing. Brzezinski, the most attuned to power politics of the Carter advisors, tended toward the conservative view of SALT as a means of limiting the Soviet military threat to the United States. Brzezinksi had advocated lower SALT ceilings in a memo to Carter as early as February 1976.[23] Brown, as a technically oriented arms controller and former member of the SALT I delegation, understood that the Vladivostok formula would not really contribute to technical stability. A believer in arms control, he was hoping to make it work. His particular concerns included limiting warhead fractionization (the number of MIRVed warheads per missile) and Soviet heavy missiles (SS-18s), which increasingly threatened the survivability of U.S. Minuteman ICBMs.[24] The "deep cuts" idea probably appealed to Carter himself on at least three levels. First, it fit in with his moralism and populism to press for "real" disarmament as opposed to (by now) traditional arms control. Second, given Jackson's position and the mounting criticism of SALT on the outside, a treaty incorporating such cuts would be far easier to ratify.[25] Third, a more ambitious approach to SALT would differentiate his policy from that pursued by Ford and Kissinger. Like many new administrations, the Carter administration wanted to distinguish itself from and show that it could surpass its predecessor. The attempt to negotiate actual arms "reductions" seemed a natural way to do that.[26] Fourth, he apparently believed (mistakenly) that the call for deep reductions would signal goodwill to the Soviets.[27]

The Carter deep cuts proposal of March 1977 foreshadowed the Reagan strategic arms reduction (START) proposal. It called for a lowering of the overall Vladivostok ceiling from 2,400 strategic launchers to between 1,800 and 2,000. It lowered the ceiling on MIRVed missiles from 1,320 to between 1,200 and 1,100, and introduced a new ceiling on MIRVed land-based missiles of 550—the number of U.S. MIRVed ICBMs or Minuteman IIIs. Finally, and perhaps most significantly, it called for cutting Soviet "heavy missiles" in half, from approximately 300 to 150.[28] To this was added a fallback position: If the Soviets did not wish to accept deep cuts, the United States would be willing to conclude a more limited accord based on Vladivostok, from which the two key disputed systems—the Soviet Backfire bomber and cruise missiles—would be excluded. Vance was to be sent to Moscow to negotiate the proposals.

In a characteristic departure from accepted diplomatic practice, Carter unveiled the basic proposal at a news conference on March 24.[29] Here again we see Carter's bull-in-a-china shop attitude toward purely political categories and conventions. A populist and a self-styled Wilsonian, he eschewed "secret diplomacy."

Moscow Gets Angry

For the Soviets, the combination of public human rights protests and public calls for deep arms reductions were less than welcome. Accustomed by now to Kissinger's dependable discretion and Nixon's penchant for secrecy, and to having the propaganda field largely to themselves, the Soviets were now suddenly faced with an administration apparently seeking to seize the rhetorical high ground and imposing new demands. This is to say nothing of the obnoxiousness of the idea of reductions themselves.

It is one of the minor mysteries of the Carter era that Carter's softer-line advisers did not anticipate[30] the vehemence of the Soviet reaction to the March 1977 deep reduction proposal. Ironically, this failure to anticipate may have rested on a basic misunderstanding of Kissinger's diplomacy. One suspects that Vance and Warnke simply had no idea just how one-sided the arms control process had become under Kissinger, or how loath Kissinger had become to impose serious demands on his Soviet interlocutors. Inadvertently, Carter's new proposals violated what had become the cardinal principle of Kissinger's arms negotiations—namely, to set mutual limits so high that the Soviets could not possibly object to them.

When Vance arrived in Moscow, the Soviets dismissed the new American proposals out of hand. Neither the deep cuts idea nor the modified Vladivostok formula was acceptable.[31] So exercised were the Soviets that Gromyko took the unprecedented step of calling a press conference in Moscow to denounce the Carter proposals as seeking unilateral advantage, while complaining that the administration's public style and emphasis on human rights "poisons the atmosphere."[32]

The March 1977 flap was the closest thing to a major crisis in U.S.-Soviet affairs since the October 1973 war (Soviet and Cuban intervention in Angola might conceivably have led to a crisis in 1975, except that the atmosphere of détente encouraged American complacence). So abrupt was the change in mood that one anonymous congressional staffer invoked the memory of the Cuban missile crisis.[33] The moment actually bore a closer resemblance to the end of the Reykjavik summit nine years later, when the two sides similarly split openly over radical arms proposals.

The March 1977 episode was another experience similar to Vladivostok. It showed how arms control was not destined to deliver actual stability or real changes in the power balance. It widened the rift between those, such as Nitze, who were willing to accept arms control so long as it accomplished something concrete, and those, such as Warnke and Vance, who saw the process as something to be pursued essentially for its own sake. The original Schelling-Halperin views of arms control as a method of substantially altering stability was gradually being overshadowed by a faith in the negotiating process. "Negotiability" was becoming an end in itself.

Soothing the Soviets

In most other administrations, the major pressure for progress in arms control had come from the outside, but in the Carter administration, the most important pressure came from within. From April onward, Vance and especially Warnke pressed Carter for concessions that would make the U.S. position more acceptable to the Soviet Union. Brzezinski noted in his journal after an April 25 meeting in which he and Defense Secretary Harold Brown successfully held off Warnke and Vance demands for a further softening of the U.S. position that "there is a tendency on our side to want an agreement so badly that we begin changing our proposals until the point is reached that the Russians are prepared to consider it."[34]

The Vance-Warnke program extended beyond limitation of arms to the supply of a vast range of technological and economic concessions to the Soviet Union. In the spring of 1977, Vance sent Carter a memo proposing a significant broadening of détente to include, among other things, granting to the Soviets remote access to the Cyber 76 computer for use in weather observation, increased Soviet involvement in global and North-South questions, development of new bilateral scientific agreements, opening of a banking office in New York (giving them access to the U.S. banking system), expansion of visa privileges for Soviet citizens (giving them vast intelligence benefits), and, in Brzezinski's paraphrase, "greater consideration of the effect on the Soviets of our forthcoming announcements regarding weapons procurement or deployment."[35]

Why so many concessions to Moscow on both arms and economics? The assumption of Warnke and Vance seemed to be that U.S. concessions in arms control and other areas held the key to a general improvement with relations with the Soviet Union. Paradoxically, however, they proved willing to turn a blind eye to Soviet misconduct on numerous specifics in the service of this general improvement in relations. In the end, the approach resembled Roosevelt's handling of Stalin—an attempt to preserve central agreement with Moscow at the sacrifice of numerous specific Western interests. Indeed, détente and arms control under Carter could be said to have combined the worst aspects of Roosevelt's approach to Stalin with the British radicals' approach to the kaiser.

Vance described his preferred policy in his memoirs as a "more balanced approach toward the Soviet Union." The vagueness of the phrase was somewhat characteristic; one of his key contentions was that the rationale for détente was, in essence, ineffable or incommunicable. "This more balanced approach toward the Soviet Union, merely labeled 'détente' or relaxation of tensions, was not easy to define or to defend to the American public," he later wrote. One reason may have been that the rationale for the policy was not terribly clear. The one clear thing was that arms control was its "centerpiece":

> The SALT process was the centerpiece of the Nixon-Kissinger-Rogers strategy of "détente" to engage the Soviet Union in a cooperative effort to avoid military confrontation, and to establish an international framework within which the U.S.-Soviet political competition could be contained. There were other elements of the strategy: increased U.S.-Soviet and East-West trade; greater Soviet access to U.S. technology and capital; and mutual agreement on some general principles of international conduct, a kind of "rules of engagement" to reduce the risks of direct U.S.-Soviet confrontation in the increasingly volatile Third World regions.[36]

The detached reference to "the increasingly volatile Third World regions" suggested the nature of the view. Why, one might ask, was the Third World becoming more "volatile"? One major answer, of course, was that the Soviets were vastly increasing transfers of arms and advisors to Third World countries.

It was characteristic of the confusions in Establishment and liberal thinking in the second half of the 1970s that at the very time when Soviet arms shipments and adventurism in the Third World were increasing unprecedentedly, the conventional wisdom held that North-South issues were replacing East-West conflict in determining the fate of Third World countries. Soviet adventurism in Third World regions was genuinely on the rise. "The USSR had been involved militarily in local conflicts before, of course," wrote Bruce D. Porter in the most comprehensive and careful study of Soviet involvement in the Third World, "but the magnitude, scope, and apparent success of its efforts in the 1970s were perhaps without precedent." "The 1970s," Porter noted, "witnessed three massive Soviet airlifts and sealifts to client regimes at war, the deployment in combat of over 40,000 Soviet-armed Cuban troops in Africa, and the outright invasion and occupation of a Third World country by the USSR—all phenomena unheard of during the Cold War."[37] Cuban troops in Africa were an entirely new phenomenon, but Vance saw the United States as primarily responsible for turning Angola into an East-West conflict,[38] while Carter's UN ambassador Andrew Young claimed to see Cuban troops in Africa as the source of "a certain stability and order."[39] Even as the United States pressed for arms control, Soviet arms were pouring arms into the Third World. Between 1973 and 1977, Soviet arms exports to the Third World totaled $16.5 billion, according to one government estimate.[40] By comparison, Soviet military aid to North Vietnam between 1960 and 1975—without which the North Vietnamese could never have won the war—totaled perhaps $5 billion.[41]

One important dissenter from the conventional wisdom was Brzezinski, who was concerned both about Soviet involvement in the Third World and the unremitting intensity of the Soviet strategic buildup. By late fall 1977, U.S. allies and moderate states in the Middle East, including Iran, Saudi Arabia, Egypt, and the Sudan, were expressing increasing concern at Soviet involvement in the Ethiopian-Somali border dispute on behalf of Ethiopia's left-wing Mengistu government. Sudan's president wrote to Carter of what the Sudan perceived as a "sinister grand strategy" on the part of the Soviets in Africa and complained of American passivity.[42] By mid-January, Cuba had inserted several thousand military personnel into Ethiopia in an apparent attempt to repeat the earlier Communist success of Angola. "Soviet leaders may be acting merely in response to an apparent opportunity," Brzezinski wrote to Carter in January 1978, "or the Soviet action may be part of a wider strategic design. In either case, the Soviets probably calculate, as previously in Angola, they can later adopt a more conciliatory attitude and that the U.S. will simply again adjust to the consolidation of Soviet presence in yet another African country."[43]

Brzezinski obtained permission from Carter to begin briefing the press on Soviet activities in Africa. At Brzezinski's urging, Andrew Young gave a UN speech decrying Soviet-Cuban involvement in the continent. In private counsels, Brzezinski urged the dispatch of an aircraft carrier to the region to signal U.S. attention to the conflict.[44] Still, Vance and the State Department, in this instance supported by Harold Brown, strongly resisted any effort to take action. "In Washington," Vance later wrote, "we in the State Department saw the Horn as a textbook case of Soviet exploitation of a local conflict. In the long run, however, we believed the Ethiopians would oust the Soviets from their country as had happened in Egypt and the Sudan. Meanwhile we should continue to work with our European allies and the African nations to bring about a negotiated solution of the broader regional issues. We believed that in the long run Ethiopian-Soviet relations undoubtedly would sour and Ethiopia would again turn to the West."[45] One wonders what Vance meant by "the long run." In the event, the rule of Ethiopia's Mengistu outlasted that of Communist leaders in Eastern Europe.

It appeared to be a central tenet of Vance and the State Department that no Soviet local encroachment was to be resisted, particularly if this resistance might endanger SALT. In a press conference on March 1, Brzezinski suggested that Soviet global adventurism might eventually endanger SALT by creating a public and congressional climate hostile to the treaty's ratification—not only a reasonable political prediction, but a gentle way of warning the Soviets to exercise restraint. "We are not imposing any linkage," said Brzezinski, recalling the Kissinger term, "but linkages may be imposed by unwarranted exploitation of local conflict for larger international purposes."[46] Vance was bitterly angry at Brzezinski's suggestion. On the same day, he categorically told the Senate Foreign Relations Committee, "There is no link between the SALT negotiations and the situation in Ethiopia."[47] At a meeting the following day, the two advisors openly clashed, with Vance complaining bitterly of Brzezinski's mention of linkage. "We will end up losing SALT," said the secretary of state, "and that will be the worst thing that could happen. If we do not get a SALT treaty in the President's first four years, that will be a blemish on his record forever."[48]

Strategic Deterioration Under Carter

Conservatives of the period attacked SALT chiefly on the basis that it was eroding the military balance. But in fact there were two interrelated problems, one military, the other political. The military problem was real enough. Beginning in 1968, the year after McNamara's action-reaction speech, U.S. military spending began a long and steady decline, while Soviet military spending during the same period continued to increase. Essentially, a lessening of effort on the U.S. side did not result in the predicted reciprocal restraint from the Soviets. On the contrary, the greatest surge in the Soviet strategic buildup came *after* the signing of SALT I, when as part of a massive modernization effort, the Soviets deployed four new ICBMs, three new SLBMs, five new ballistic-missile submarines, and a new medium-range bomber. During the same period, it should be noted, the United Stated added significantly to its stock of deliverable warheads through MIRVing but deployed no major new systems.

The complacency about military power extended to the maintenance of general purpose forces. Throughout the Carter era, readiness, sustainability, morale, and training continued to deteriorate. In 1980, Senator Sam Nunn, a ranking Democratic member of the Armed Services Committee, enumerated the multiple problems that had developed within the U.S. military structure:

- First, we have lost strategic nuclear superiority, and during the next five to seven years our strategic position will be something less than essential equivalence. . . .
- Second, the Soviets have achieved an advantage in long-range theater nuclear forces in Europe. . . .
- Third, NATO has a questionable capacity to sustain a conventional defense of Europe because of continuing severe shortages in available stocks of ammunition and war reserve equipment, a lack of sufficient strategic sealift and airlift resources, and the absence of a reliable manpower mobilization base. . . .
- Fourth, because of the shortages in strategic lift, the U.S. capability to rapidly deploy sizable forces to the Indian Ocean, the Middle East, or elsewhere is questionable at best. . . .
- Fifth, the chronic shortages in funding for training, operations, maintenance that have plagued all the services during the past decade have reduced the readiness of much of our force structure. . . .
- Sixth, our dwindling navy today is spread too thin.[49]

But even more serious than the military problem was the pattern of American political behavior under arms control. Notwithstanding the endless, remorselessly technical disputes on the prospective military balance under SALT, the real difficulty with SALT did not lie in the technical details of the military balance, though they were important enough. The real problem lay in the perverse politics of the arms control process itself. If the United States was failing to respond to various Soviet encroachments around the world, it was not because Washington was being deterred in any sense by superior or growing Soviet strategic strength, however formidable this strength had become. *Rather*, as Vance's remark to Brzezinski suggests, *the United States was being deterred from resisting Soviet regional aggression chiefly by the arms control process itself. Arms control, in effect, and the moral or even quasi-religious imperative of preserving the arms control process at all costs, was causing the United States to behave as if it was weaker than it really was.*

In a sense, the overriding U.S. preoccupation with arms control in the second half of the 1970s led to the classic miscalculation that at earlier points in the century had led to major war: A democracy, under the influence of liberal-pacifist ideals, was behaving in a fashion that suggested to its authoritarian adversary that it was weaker than it really was. On the

Western side, the miscalculation consisted of excessive timidity, while on the Soviet side, the miscalculation led to imperial overstretch. Throughout the later 1970s, the Soviet Union was beginning to pour an enormous portion of its resources into a combination of the military buildup and fomenting Third World aggression and revolution. Eventually, these investments would take their toll on the Soviet domestic economy. When the United States shifted outlooks and began to behave in a fashion consonant with its real power in the world, the Soviets would quickly find how fragile was the imperial structure that all its resources had built.

Carter and the Neutron Bomb

The problem was intensified by Carter's own millenarian and quasi-pacifist views toward weaponry. Having served in Admiral Hyman Rickover's nuclear navy, and having studied nuclear engineering in the process of qualifying for that duty, Carter knew more about the operation of nuclear weapons than most presidents and approached nuclear matters with a self-confidence[50] not seen since Eisenhower. At the same time, in clear contrast to Eisenhower, Carter's Christian convictions, reinforced by the "new morality" of Wilsonianism, gave his opposition to nuclear weapons a passionate and almost visceral quality. In his diary, Carter described the decision toward the end of his presidency to approve the MX missile, a precondition for gaining Senate approval for SALT II, as "nauseating."[51] He believed in the doctrine of minimal deterrence—namely, that one submarine's worth of nuclear weapons was enough to deter a direct Soviet nuclear attack on the United States (it probably was; but whether such a minimal force would deter conventional aggression or nuclear blackmail in all its many forms was to be doubted). When he spoke in his inaugural of the possibility of eliminating nuclear weapons entirely from the earth, he was speaking from the heart.[52]

It should not be surprising that in the two major weapons decisions Carter faced in his first two years—regarding the B-1 bomber and the enhanced radiation weapon (ERW), or neutron bomb—Carter decided against the weapons system. The decision to forgo the B-1 bomber was defensible on purely technical grounds. The decision rested heavily on two calculations: first, that the United States would depend heavily for the air-breathing leg of its deterrent on cruise missiles, which could still successfully penetrate the Soviet Union when launched from B-52s; and, second, that the still top secret Advanced Technology (or "Stealth")

Bomber (later known as the B-2) would prove a better successor to the B-52 in the long run.[53] One could dispute these contentions, but they were not without merit.[54] Still, coming on the heels of so many other cuts in defense, the effect of the B-1 cancellation politically was to reinforce the impression that the United States no longer took military power seriously. (Shortly after the Carter B-1 decision, Senator John Tower of the Senate Armed Services Committee was in Moscow. He asked Alexandr Shchukin, Nitze's old counterpart from SALT I days, what the Soviets were prepared to do to reciprocate Carter's cancellation of the B-1. "Sir," responded Shchukin, "I am neither a pacifist nor a philanthropist.")[55] Ironically, the Soviets portrayed the cancellation of the B-1 as *increasing* the threat to them, since it implied increased U.S. reliance on cruise missiles.[56]

The decision on the neutron bomb was another matter, more serious in political as well as military terms. Of all the weapons contemplated in the 1970s, the neutron bomb might have done the most materially to alter the strategic balance in the West's favor. Killing by radiation rather than by blast, the weapon was capable of devastating use against the personnel in large tank formations. As a smaller explosive, the weapon would cause far less collateral damage to the European countryside. As a particularly frightening weapon particularly effective against tanks massed for attack, it would have gone a long way toward counterbalancing NATO's acute numerical disadvantage in armor and rendering deeply problematic any scenario for Soviet aggression against Western Europe. Possibly for the first time since the 1950s, it would have rendered NATO's nuclear strategy credible, transforming it into a genuine tactical doctrine rather than a mere suicide pact or bluff.

The neutron bomb had a political importance that went beyond its tactical applications. SALT I had contributed to anxiety in Europe over the firmness of the U.S. nuclear guarantee. Since the 1940s, Europeans had linked their security to the counterbalance that the American nuclear arsenal provided to massive Soviet conventional strength. If the "massive retaliation" doctrine had intensified this state of nuclear dependency, then McNamara's "flexible response" doctrine had not ended it. SALT I, however, raised decisive doubts about the logic of this arrangement. If, as the SALT agreement seemed to indicate, the superpowers now possessed essentially equal nuclear deterrents, if indeed the agreement allowed the Soviets an advantage of 800 missiles, then how could American nuclear strength be said to counterbalance Soviet conventional superiority in Europe?[57]

The problem was compounded by the intensity of the Soviet building program following SALT I. Along with introducing four new strategic missiles beginning in 1973, the Soviets began in 1977 to deploy a major new intermediate-range missile in Europe and Asia, the SS-20. With three warheads and far greater accuracy and range than the existing SS-4 and SS-5 intermediate-range missiles, the SS-20 threatened fundamentally to alter the existing nuclear balance in the European and Asian theaters.

Carter and Brzezinski were slow to acknowledge the significance of the SS-20. While Carter stated in his first press conference that he would like to see the Soviets "cease deployment" of the SS-20,[58] he was unsympathetic to West German Chancellor Helmut Schmidt's insistence during 1977 that the SS-20 demanded a specific Western response.[59] In October, Schmidt, a former defense minister and a competent nuclear strategist, delivered a lecture at the International Institute of Strategic Studies in London calling attention to the problem of the SS-20 (which he did not name), in an attempt to force the Carter administration's hand.[60] Noting that SALT had established ostensible parity between the superpowers at the strategic level, Schmidt warned that greater attention had to be devoted to real and potential disparities at the tactical nuclear and conventional levels. In line with the prevailing politics of the day, Schmidt recommended intensified arms control in these areas; but the implication was that in the absence of successful arms control, a buildup might be necessary. However, as late as 1979, Defense Secretary Harold Brown's Annual Report discounted the significance of the SS-20 as a new threat.[61]

Perhaps the most natural Western counter to the SS-20 would have been the neutron bomb. But instead of attempting to see the neutron bomb in 1977 as, in effect, an appropriate response to the SS-20 and resolutely assuming leadership of the alliance in advocating deployment of the weapon, Carter vacillated, concerned that the weapon might spoil his coveted reputation as peacemaker.

Problems with the neutron bomb began in July 1977, when the existence of the previously secret weapon was revealed in a *Washington Post* story.[62] Carter publicly expressed support for the weapon, but from the outset was privately irresolute about it. In an August meeting, he told Brzezinski, Vance, and Brown that "he did not wish the world to think of him as an ogre" in deploying such a weapon. Rather than lobby European governments to support the system, he sent a Defense Department team to present "both sides" of the neutron bomb issue and "solicit views of the allies."[63]

U.S. vacillation bred allied irresolution. In the face of evident American indecisiveness, European governments that had previously supported the neutron bomb program began to balk.[64] In the meantime, the Soviets launched an effective propaganda campaign against the bomb, branding it a "capitalist" weapon that destroyed human beings but left property intact.[65] In October, protesters were arrested for disrupting Sunday services at Carter's Baptist church.[66]

Essentially, Carter treated the issue as a hot potato, wishing Schmidt to take responsiblity for supporting deployment of the weapon, while Schmidt, in turn, in an effort to protect himself from the left wing of his own party, wanted some other European government to accept deployment of the weapon as well. Brzezinski developed a formula linking an offer to forgo the neutron bomb to Soviet willingness to forgo the SS-20, and involving arms negotiations. The formula was sent in a Carter letter to Schmidt. But then Carter changed his mind and decided not to deploy the weapon anyway. "I don't think that I have ever seen the President quite as troubled and pained by any decision item," Brzezinski recorded in his diary. "At one point he said: 'I wish I had never heard of this weapon.'" Carter told his advisors that "he did not wish to go through with it." He had, he said, "a queasy feeling about the whole thing." A decision to deploy the weapon meant "that his Administration would be stamped forever as the Administration which introduced bombs that kill people but leave buildings intact." He wished "to find a graceful way out."[67]

There was, of course, no graceful way out. The decision not to deploy the weapon shook the Alliance, reinforcing European doubts about America's ability both to lead and to offer an umbrella of security. It left the Soviets to deploy the SS-20 entirely unopposed. It was one thing to leave the Soviets unopposed in the Horn of Africa; it was quite another to permit them to change the balance of power in Europe. In a very short time, arms control and the impulses behind it had gone from inhibiting the United States in peripheral areas to deterring the United States from a robust response to threats to the very core of the Western security system. It was a measure of waning confidence in Western strength that for the first time since the Marshall Plan years, a European government— Italy—came close in late 1977 and early 1978 to adopting a Communist government.[68] The neutron bomb controversy was to be the first episode in a protracted battle for influence in Europe, in essence a battle for the heart and soul of Germany. It was a battle the West would eventually win, but only after Carter's successor adopted attitudes and tactics diametrically opposed to those for which Carter became famous.

The neutron bomb decision was a deeply personal one; but for this it was no less irresponsible. Jimmy Carter acted on the basis of his conscience. But one might argue that Jimmy Carter had the kind of conscience that, while sometimes desirable in a citizen, a nation can ill afford in a president. "The Sermon on the Mount is the last word in Christian ethics," wrote Churchill. "Everyone respects the Quakers. Still, it is not on these terms that Ministers assume their responsibilities of guiding states."[69]

Ironically, Carter's decisions on the B-1 and the neutron bomb did not even serve his long-term aim of gaining an arms accord. In both instances, he passed up the chance to use the weapons as bargaining chips in negotiations. More important, the cancellations undermined public and congressional confidence in his judgments on defense, detracting from public faith in SALT.[70]

Back to the China Card

Watching the United States lose ground in Europe, powerless to reverse the trend in the strategic balance, Brzezinski turned to the expedient that Kissinger had used: strengthening the relationship with China. Like the Nixon policy, the Carter China policy was driven largely by weakness. Unfortunately, under Carter the strengthening of ties with China involved the sort of betrayal of an ally for which the Carter administration became noted: On January 1, 1979, the United States established full diplomatic relations with the People's Republic of China and simultaneously severed long-standing relations with the Republic of China (Taiwan).[71] One might argue that geopolitical calculations dictated such an approach. Yet had the United States done a better job of keeping its own strategic house in order, improvement of relations with the People's Republic could have been pursued at a more measured pace, without the dishonorable sacrifice of a longstanding alliance.

No one was more sensitive to shifts in the power balance than the leadership in Beijing, and it is interesting in this regard that Deng Xiaoping, seeing the United States chiefly as a valuable counterweight to Soviet power, complained of the SALT process. "To be candid with you," the Chinese leader told Brzezinski during the latter's visit to Beijing, "whenever you are about to conclude an agreement with the Soviet Union, it is the product of concessions on the U.S. side to please the Soviet Union."[72]

Indeed, such was the pattern in the SALT II negotiations. Step by step,

Washington came closer to an agreement largely by yielding on key points. First, on the crucial issue of heavy missiles, Washington's position slid from a limit of 150 to 190. When Gromyko rejected the 190 figure in May 1977, the United States raised the number to 250. The key "breakthrough" in the negotiations came in a meeting between Gromyko and the Carter team in Washington in Septmber 1977, when the United States gave up entirely on the effort to limit "heavy" missiles below the existing Soviet level (of around 300).[73] The administration's rationale was that the SS-19 (which had come through a loophole of SALT I) posed equally as serious a danger as the SS-18 and that the problem would best be gotten at through an overall limit on MIRVed ICBMs. But the basic problem was that the Soviets would not agree to limit their precious heavies.[74]

On the issue of cruise missiles, the pattern was similar. After Vladivostok, the status of cruise missiles had remained in dispute. The United States had struggled for inclusion of the Backfire bomber in SALT II, while a high Soviet priority was limiting the range and number of U.S. cruise missiles. The final SALT II treaty and protocol included limits on cruise missiles and cruise missile ranges[75] but did not cover the Backfire bomber, which was handled in a side letter in which the Soviets pledged not to build more than 30 Backfires a year (a pledge they later apparently violated[76]).

The SALT II negotiating team even failed to secure unambiguous acknowledgment from their Soviet counterparts that the major new U.S. strategic program planned to counter Minuteman vulnerability—the multiple-aim-point (MAPs) deployment of the MX missile, which would have placed 200 MX missiles in a massive sheltering system in the Southwest[77]—was permitted under the treaty.[78]

Much was conceded and more would have been had it not been, first, for Brzezinski and Brown, and second, for significant intervention by Congress. It was Senator Charles Mathias who persuaded the Soviet chief delegate, Vladimir S. Semenov, that the Senate would not approve the treaty *unless the Soviets actually provided data on the size of their forces* (which they had not done for the most part under SALT I). Even after Mathias's warning, Semenov attempted to *trade* revelation of basic data on Soviet forces for U.S. agreements to limits cruise missiles.[79] To the degree that the U.S. delegation resisted Soviet efforts to limit cruise missile range, it was owing in part to intense pressure from Jackson.[80] To the degree that options such as the Ground Launched Cruise Missile were protected on behalf of U.S. allies, it was the result of pressure from Jackson and Senator Sam Nunn.[81]

Warnke was not particularly solicitous about protecting cruise missiles. He despised the MX.[82] When it became apparent that the Soviets were resisting meaningful limits on telemetry encryption, Vance recommended that the United States yield on the position so as not to jeopardize a treaty. Only the most strenuous lobbying by Brown and CIA director Stansfield Turner prevented a U.S. cave-in.[83]

The Bureaucracy versus Brzezinski

While Vance and Warnke resisted any position in SALT that might threaten to delay or undermine conclusion of the agreement, lesser officials both resisted and occasionally acted deliberately to undercut Brzezinski's efforts to communicate greater overall firmness to Moscow. On March 17, 1980, Carter was prevailed upon to deliver a speech at Wake Forest University in North Carolina in which he noted that the pursuit of arms control would be balanced with an effort to proceed with U.S. defense programs. Marshal Shulman, Vance's leading advisor on Soviet affairs in the State Department, told the Soviet embassy without White House knowledge "that the President's speech should be viewed primarily as designed for domestic consumption and therefore should not be interpreted as indicating declined U.S. interest in SALT or accommodation."[84] When Brzezinski proposed Carter visit Poland to pursue a policy of differentiation, Shulman opposed the visit as overly provocative.[85] (Later Carter's visit, and the connection it established, would be instrumental in helping the administration take action that helped deter Moscow from making a Hungary-style crackdown on Solidarity.)[86] When Carter decided against deployment of the neutron bomb, the State Department recommended that Moscow be informed of the decision before U.S. allies were.[87] State had even gotten to the point of recommending against the prosecution of Soviet spies.[88]

Vance and Warnke, meanwhile, proved tireless in devising more new concessions to sweeten relations with Moscow. In 1978, they submitted a memo to Carter recommending commencement of negotiations with Moscow on an immediate cutoff of production of fissionable materials. (Brzezinski forwarded the memo to James Schlesinger at the Energy Department, who wrote a scathing response.)[89] Willing to supply endless carrots, they eschewed the stick. The Soviets put two well-known dissidents, Anatoly (later Natan) Sharansky and Aleksandr Ginzburg, on trial.

In response, Vance bitterly opposed a proposal by Brzezinski, supported by Brown largely on national security grounds, to curtail technology transfer to the Soviet Union as a sanction. Only when Carter's domestic advisors intervened, stressing the urgent need for the president to show a strong response for domestic political reasons, did Carter override Vance's objections. As a result, Carter denied an export license on a Sperry Univac computer for use in the 1980 Olympics, reestablished export controls on oil production technology, put oil production technology on the commodity control list, and deferred decisions on export licenses for Dresser Corporation for a drill-bit factory and an electron beam welder.[90] Unfortunately, the Dresser drill-bit factory sale was later approved.[91] Partly in the service of the prevailing belief that trade would soften the Soviets, the United States had pursued an extremely permissive approach to the sale of technology under both Ford and Carter, including militarily significant technologies. In 1977, the chairman of a Defense Science Board Task Force on Export of U.S. technology told a Senate committee that "the transfer of militarily significant technology has been of major proportions."[92]

Institutional Momentum for Arms Control

Carter's policies were succeeding neither with the Soviets nor with domestic constituencies; simultaneously the administration was attacked for proceeding too slowly with arms control and for being too soft on the Soviets. In early June 1978, the *Washington Post* published a false story suggesting that the administration was "freezing" SALT.[93] Had arms control partisans within the administration deliberately planted the story to put pressure on Carter for further concessions in the arms talks? (The final years of the Carter administration saw proxy battles in the press as Brzezinski confided in Richard Burt of the *New York Times* and Brzezinski's opponents at State used their own press sources in turn.) At the same time, public and congressional support for SALT was declining. Senator Byrd told a news conference on June 10 that the Senate would not consider a SALT II treaty in 1978 even if Carter were to sign one because of growing concern with Soviet adventurism in Africa and elsewhere.[94] At the end of June, a *New York Times*/CBS News poll showed 48 percent of Americans favoring a break-off of arms talks until the Soviet Union withdrew from Africa.[95]

Carter's effort to reconcile these opposing positions in a speech at the Naval Academy in early June was notably unsuccessful. "The Soviet Union can choose either confrontation or cooperation," said Carter. "The United States is adequately prepared to meet either choice."[96] Hardly ringing rhetoric, the Carter utterance was viewed as a transparent attempt to straddle the political fence.[97]

Brzezinski had sought to resolve the contradictions in the Carter policy by advocating what he called a "comprehensive and genuinely reciprocal" détente. In essence, Brzezinski's formulation was linkage by another name. His notion, accurate enough, was that the Soviets were seeking to pursue a "selective" détente involving Western arms control and trade concessions while they busily advanced their interests in the Third World.[98] Yet Brzezinski faced two major problems. The first was Carter himself. Prompted by Brzezinski and his political advisor Hamilton Jordan to mention Soviet activities in Africa and human rights, Carter nonetheless closed a meeting with Gromyko by expressing his eagerness for a summit and SALT accord.[99] The second was the dominance of what writer Carl Gershman later called the "new foreign policy Establishment"[100] in the State Department. Brzezinski may have been keyed to pursue a tough policy, but the whole government bureaucracy was poised to offer new concessions. So sensitive were Vance and other State Department officials to any effort to make demands on the Soviets that the relatively anodyne terms "comprehensive" and "reciprocal" were systematically excised from references to détente in drafts that Brzezinski would submit to State for clearance.[101]

The third problem was the arms control process itself. While doubts about the effectiveness of the administration's conciliatory approach to the Soviets were growing, these doubts had not yet crystallized. The arms control process maintained enormous institutional momentum. It was the one positive achievement that the conciliators could point to as justifying the host of concessions that had been yielded to Moscow.

SALT Under Attack

Yet by the time Carter departed for his long-awaited meeting with Brezhnev in Vienna in June 1979, the SALT process was under open attack.[102] "To enter a treaty which favors the Soviets as this one does on the grounds that we will be in a worse position without it," said Senator Jackson on the eve of Carter's departure, referring to the now-standard justification for signing SALT, "is appeasement in its purest form."[103] The summit was noteworthy for Carteresque departures from protocol—the president's ostentatious jog around Moscow and his embrace of the bearlike Brezhnev in the traditional Slavic kiss. Yet arms control no longer had the recuperative effect on presidential popularity that Nixon had so often counted upon. Carter returned to a divided and dissatisfied nation. The next six months would bring an unwelcome harvest as the seeds of hesitancy in foreign policy sewn over the previous years began to bear conspicuous fruit. Carter would face four interlocking crises: (1) an energy crisis spurred by a boycott by the Organization of Petroleum Exporting States (OPEC); (2) the fall of the shah of Iran and the subsequent takeover of the American embassy by Iranian radicals; (3) a devastating Senate controversy over SALT II; and (4) the Soviet invasion of Afghanistan.

After inviting a parade of prominent citizens to Camp David to discuss the state of the nation, Carter delivered a speech on July 15 claiming there was a "crisis of confidence" in the country.[104] Carter's perception of a declining mood was certainly accurate; but the national doldrums had to do as much as anything with the new morality of national self-abnegation that Carter and his advisors had been attempting to impose upon the nation. As a cure to the problem, Carter seemed to be recommending more of the same. At any rate, the speech did little to reassure the public about his own leadership.

While souring the mood at home, Carter continued to show the same mixture of hesitancy, moralism, and bad strategic judgment abroad. The Carter administration's handling of the shah of Iran exhibited in miniature all the principles and habits that had guided the Carter foreign policy in other realms: (1) a Hamlet-like hesitancy and indecision; (2) a misplaced moralism by which human rights concerns became a club to be employed against U.S. allies; (3) a total discounting of U.S. strategic interests in the region; and (4) a State Department tendency to undercut U.S. policy. At a time when the shah was under severe pressure, looking for reassurance to Washington, and needing to impose a temporary repression to restore order in his troubled country, prepatory to instituting democratic reforms, Vance and fellow State Department official Warren Christopher consistently opposed the idea of a military government to restore order, while the U.S. ambassador on the scene undermined the shah's already shaky self-confidence.[105] All the Carter administration's scruples about human rights did nothing to serve the cause of human rights in the long run; the shah's imperfect authoritarian regime was replaced by a far more fanatically repressive and violent one. In security terms, the fall of the pro-Western shah, the linchpin of stability in the Persian Gulf and the main counterweight to the aggressive Saddam Hussein of Iraq, would reverberate for decades: in the Iranian hostage crisis, in the emboldened attitude of the Soviets toward the region leading to the invasion of Afghanistan, in the protracted Iran-Iraq war, and finally in Saddam Hussein's invasion of Kuwait in 1990.

As the shah's situation deteriorated, meanwhile, the SALT II treaty came under close and highly public scrutiny in the Senate. Jurisdiction over the treaty lay primarily with the Senate Foreign Relations Committee, but as with SALT I, the most important hearings on the agreement proved to be those dominated by Jackson in the Senate Armed Services Committee. In certain respects, the televised SALT II hearings constituted the most dramatic public spectacle since Watergate.

The SALT II hearings of 1979 had roughly the same relation to the election of 1980 that the Lincoln-Douglas debates of 1858 had to the election of 1860. They were both a preview and a clarification of the questions that would determine the country's strategic, if not moral, fate. The SALT II debate was the debate of the decade, if not of the half-century. It pitted one against another two fundamentally opposing views of foreign policy and national security: one that emphasized the inutility of military force, the importance of unilateral restraint, and the primacy of negotiations; and another that emphasized the enduring relevancy of force, the continuing problem of Soviet expansionism, and the primacy of the balance of power.

The very fact that such a debate took place could not help but alter perceptions. Until the time of the SALT II hearings, the ordinary citizen's exposure to the arcana of arms control was generally filtered through large media organizations overwhelmingly sympathetic to the arms control cause—the *New York Times*, the *Washington Post*, and the major television networks. The hearings provided the first chance for the critics to present a detailed case against the treaties to the widest possible audience.

The debate was intensified by a chance event: the discovery on August 14 of a Soviet combat brigade in Cuba. Briefed on the discovery by the administration, Senator Frank Church of Ohio, running for reelection and attempting to compensate for his dovish image, revealed the news at a press conference.[106] The episode was arguably blown out of proportion. But the row over the Cuban brigade was a symptom rather than a cause of the problem. It crystallized much broader suspicions about the Soviet Union.

SALT partisans later tended to blame the treaty's failure to gain ratification on a combination of the Cuban brigade discovery and the Soviet invasion of Afghanistan (an event itself largely traceable to the low estimate Moscow had formed of the Carter administration's resolve). Yet in retrospect, it seems likely that the treaty was in trouble anyway. The founding fathers' requirement for two-thirds Senate approval of a treaty imposed a stringent test. (Carter, never any stickler for political tradition, would have preferred to dispense with this particular constitutional inconvenience; thought was given to submitting the SALT II treaty as an Executive Agreement requiring simply majority approval of both houses.[107] Indeed, Carter states in his memoirs that the Soviet Union, with its more "consistent" policies, was better at conducting arms control negotiations than the United States.[108]) It implied an overwhelming consensus.

By 1979, that consensus had been lost. The leading witness against the treaty, Paul Nitze, in a sense symbolized the consensus that no longer existed for arms control. A close associate of Dean Acheson and a major formulator of the nation's basic national security strategy for the Cold War in 1950, Nitze was for many years the chief Democratic spokesman on nuclear strategy and a chief proponent of the doctrine of nuclear superiority. In the late 1950s, he had become a thoughtful convert to arms control. To the degree that arms control retained respectability among serious strategists, Nitze represented their outlook. His defection was a loss from which the arms control process was not likely to recover.

Nitze's testimony against SALT II, overwhelming in its detail and relentless in its technical mastery of the issues, was nothing less than devastating. The United States had initiated SALT II negotiations with three objectives, Nitze pointed out, and four constraints. The objectives included (1) a treaty of indefinite duration; (2) essential equivalence; and (3) an improvement in "crisis stability." The constraints included (1) verifiability; (2) regard for allies' interests; (3) the need for a continued strategic modernization program that was both economic and politically feasible; and (4) the requirement that the agreement be negotiable with the Soviets and ratifiable by the Senate. According to Nitze, the three objectives and three of the four constraints had been sacrificed to meet part of the fourth one: negotiability, or acceptability of the treaty to the Soviet Union. "At the same time," noted Nitze, "the U.S. side has been inhibited in publicizing Soviet recalcitrance in the negotiations because of the other aspect of the fourth constraint—that the agreements be ratifiable by the Congress." The story of the negotiations had been a story of U.S. concessions: "Each negotiating 'breakthrough' since the Moscow conference has involved a further retreat from our original objectives."

One by one, Nitze's written testimony ticked off the technical issues: the fact that SALT II would permit the Soviets a vast advantage in counterforce capability threatening preemptive destruction of 90 percent of the Minuteman force; the fact that the Minuteman III production line had been shut down while the Soviets would be permitted to continue deployment of their four new ICBMs; the fact that the limit on "new types" of ICBM would not prevent continued modernization of the Soviet missile force; the fact that cruise missiles and cruise missile carriers were constrained while the air defenses designed to counter them would run free; the fact that SALT II would do nothing to constrain the medium-range SS-20. "The SALT II proponents assert that the agreements are adequately verifiable," Nitze told the senators. "Strict adherence to many of the provisions of the agreements cannot be confidently verified. But the agreements so one-sidedly favor the Soviet Union that verifiability is not the major issue." "It is quite evident," he said, "that strategic parity is slipping away from us and that the Soviets can be expected to achieve meaningful strategic superiority, probably by 1982 and most certainly by 1985, unless we take most urgent steps to reverse current trends."

But the key problem with the agreement was political. "The present situation is the result of an American tendency toward self-delusion," he wrote. "Throughout the 1960s and 1970s American intelligence analysts consistently underestimated Soviet military growth. The SALT process, regrettably, has contributed to this tendency by creating the illusion that a fundamentally new era in the strategic competition had arrived." Instead, as Nitze told the senators, the correlation of forces was shifting against the United States. The Soviets could not be expected to bargain more reasonably in SALT until this trend had shifted. "Soviet officials took the view that the correlation of forces has been moving and would continue to move in their favor. They deduced from this the proposition that even though we might, at a given time, believe their proposals to be one-sided and inequitable, realism would eventually bring us to accept at least the substance of them."[109]

Nitze's criticisms of the treaty were seconded by General Edward Rowny, the Pentagon's representative to the talks, who had asked to be relieved of his duties because of disagreement with the treaty.[110] To have, in effect, the chief Democratic spokesman on defense topics and the JCS representative both opposing the treaty publicly, and a host of other well-known Democrats supporting them, was devastating.

The central reality was that ten years after the beginning of strategic arms talks and seven years after the conclusion of SALT I, the Soviet strategic arsenal was expanding at an unslackened or even increased pace—despite severe cutbacks in the comparable American building effort. "We have found that when we build weapons, they build," Harold Brown acknowledged to members of the Senate Foreign Relations Committee: "When we stop, they nevertheless continue to build."[111]

One consequence of the effort to ratify SALT II was an unusual degree of attention, for the Carter administration, to weapons systems. Brzezinski and Brown had managed to win Carter's approval for the MAPS MX. Nunn and Byrd wrested from the president a commitment to increase defense spending by more than 3 percent.[112] On December 12, after the Senate Foreign Relations Committee split 9 to 6 on approving the treaty, Carter upped the ante and promised a five-year 4.5 percent annual increase.[113] At the same time, Carter administration aides moved to allay NATO concerns, convening NATO to approve a Western counterdeployment of intermediate-range nuclear missiles in Europe to counter the Soviet SS-20. Reflecting the preoccupations of the time, the deployments were to be preceded by four years of arms control negotiations to determine whether agreed limits could be found on intermediate-range systems.

From a historical perspective, it is remarkable to note to what degree the decisions taken by the Carter administration at the end of the 1970s were essentially designed to undo decisions taken by Robert McNamara during the previous decade. The increase in military spending was needed to begin to make up for the slowdown in American strategic programs begun under McNamara. MX in MAPS was needed to overcome Minuteman vulnerability. Deployment of intermediate-range missiles in Europe was needed because the U.S. unilateral withdrawal of such missiles from Europe following the Cuban missile crisis had not led to any slackening of the Soviet effort in that theater.

The Carter administration was willing to undertake all these steps; none was quite enough to counteract the impression of weakness. On December 20, the Senate Armed Services Committee voted 10 to 0 with 7 abstentions that SALT II as it stood was "not in the national security interests of the United States."[114] The treaty appeared to be in deep trouble. However, the entire issue was mooted days later, when Soviet tanks poured into Afghanistan.

□ □ □

If nothing else had done so, the Afghanistan invasion called into question the whole approach the Carter administration had adopted toward the Soviet Union. The first cross-border aggression by the Soviet Union since World War II symbolized the shift in the correlation of forces.

For Brzezinski, the event was a kind of vindication. "Had we conveyed our determination sooner," he later wrote, "perhaps the Soviets would have desisted [in the Horn of Africa], and we might have avoided the later chain of events which ended with the Soviet invasion of Afghanistan and the suspension of SALT."[115]

Carter, meanwhile, discredited his own position by admitting, with the kind of politically inappropriate candor for which he was famous, that Afghanistan had utterly transformed his view of the Soviets[116]—which suggested that these views had in fact been more naive than many might have suspected. The administration began to take a series of steps—bars on wheat sales and an eventual boycott of the 1980 Olympics—in response to Soviet aggression. The steps, interestingly, brought Carter's popularity to its highest level since the election.[117] But the damage was done. Carter spent the final year of his presidency enduring the consequences of his imprudent policies toward Iran and the Soviet Union and of his otherworldly contempt for the balance of power, reaping what he had sown.

CHAPTER 10

Tough Cop, Good Cop

T he most harrowing periods of the Cold War had always been those in which the apparent balance of power had shifted in favor of the Soviet Union. In 1949, the Soviet explosion of an atomic bomb had prepared the way for actual "hot" war in Korea. In 1957, the launching of the *Sputnik* satellite had inaugurated five years of crisis, culminating in the Cuban missile showdown. In 1979, the Soviet invasion of Afghanistan marked the beginning of yet a third period of protracted confrontation.

To many observers, tensions following the Afghanistan invasion seemed as high as at any time in the Cold War. "We are all being carried along at this very moment," George F. Kennan wrote in alarmed tones in the year after the Soviet invasion, "towards a new military conflict, a conflict which could not conceivably end, for any of the parties, in anything less than disaster." "Not for thirty years," he wrote, "has the political tension reached so high and dangerous a point as it has today. Not in all this time has there been so high a degree of misunderstanding, of suspicion, of bewilderment, and of sheer military fear."[1]

The causes of the turn-of-the-decade crisis were complex, and its roots could be traced to many sources. Yet to a remarkable degree, the impasse at which the United States and the Soviet Union had together arrived could be traced to the practice of arms control. For over a decade, the Western conception of arms control, reinforced by the closely related attitudes of the "Vietnam syndrome," had led the United States systematically both to underequip its military forces and to understate its role in world affairs—even as the Soviet Union was enticed, again and again, to overplay its hand. With the American advocates of arms control (within and outside of government) continually advocating unilateral military cutbacks, advising restraint in the face of a growing Soviet arms buildup, and counseling benign neglect vis-à-vis expanding Soviet encroachments in the Third World, it was little wonder that the Kremlin developed a misguidedly scornful attitude toward American power. Like some Gulliver bound by a thousand Lilliputian strings, the United States was behaving, as the 1970s wore on, more and more like Richard Nixon's famous "helpless giant."

Yet if the West appeared to be losing out in the struggle with communism, particularly in the Third World, the Soviets did not always see their own victories as unalloyed. In a sense, the end result of the eastward shift in the balance of power was to heighten anxieties on both sides, by adding to unpredictability and instability everywhere. Initially, the shift in the correlation of forces had been greeted with pleasure in the Kremlin. In the mid-1970s, the height of the Kissinger era—the classic age of the arms control—high-level Soviet commentators pointed to Soviet victories in the Third World and growing socialist military "might" vis-à-vis the West as historical evidence of the intrinsic superiority of the socialist system over its capitalist counterpart.[2] But by the later 1970s, especially with Carter's shifting to and fro, the original optimism was giving way to new hints of pessimism and uncertainty.[3] Somehow failing to consider that they might have been provoking an adverse American reaction with their adventurism in the Horn of Africa, the new missiles they were rapidly deploying in Europe, and their outright invasion of Afghanistan, the Soviets tended to regard Carter's behavior in the closing year of his presidency as inexplicably anti-Soviet.

The Americans, for their part, might have been understating their power vis-à-vis the Soviets, but they were not entirely prepared to give up on the Cold War. Jimmy Carter's hectoring of the Kremlin on human rights was one symptom of a residual political, economic, and moral strength on the American side of which the Soviets would have done well to take note. They did not. As the decade came to a close, the troubled but still overconfident Soviets overreached—sending their armies across their borders into Afghanistan—only to be shocked by the vehemence of the American reaction. It was a classic case of a dictatorship's miscalculation based on a democracy's false appearance of weakness, an error repeated in the twentieth century again and again.

The American administration taking power in 1981 had the unenviable task of righting the power balance after a decade of military and political decline. Carter had belatedly started the process with a change in nuclear targeting doctrine, a proposal for a mobile-based multiple-warhead missile (the MX), and (when the bidding was done) a projected 5 percent real increase in the defense budget. But the strength of the incumbent president's commitment to this prospective military buildup was far from clear. In the final phases of the presidential campaign of 1980, Carter found it convenient, probably for both personal and political reasons, to position himself well to the left of his Republican opponent, identifying himself as the "peace" candidate and painting his Republican adversary Ronald Reagan (with some success) as a bellicose Republican in the Barry Goldwater mold. "Inflation, unemployment, the cities are all very important issues," Carter declared in his televised debate with Reagan in late October 1980, "but they pale into insignificance in the life and duties of a President when compared with the control of nuclear weapons."[4] Having withdrawn SALT II from the Senate in response to the Afghanistan invasion, Carter pledged to resubmit the treaty to the Senate following the election.[5] As the campaign came to a close, it appeared likely that Jimmy Carter's priority in his second term, as in his first, was once again going to be arms control.

Whether Carter would have ultimately implemented the promised military buildup following a 1980 victory was far from clear. But, in any event, the defeat of Reagan would have been read as a vote for the peace candidate, and Carter would have returned to a policy *mixing* hard and soft in some new combination. Given the overriding emphasis on arms control, the policy of Carter's second term would necessarily have been a *policy of ambiguity*, sometimes hard, sometimes soft, in this sense not fundamentally different from the policy of his first term.

The most important change introduced by Ronald Reagan (much as was true of John F. Kennedy in the Cuban missile crisis of 1962) was to bring the era of ambiguity to an end. With Reagan one had all the advantages of clarity—and all of the disadvantages, at least in the short-term. Reagan did not steer a middle course. On the contrary, he and his followers considered it imperative to turn the country completely around. Deliberately eschewing Nixon's approach of attempting to work within the Establishment consensus on foreign policy, they sought instead to transform the consensus fundamentally. The impact of this effort was enormous. Foreign policy controversy during the Reagan administration was as great as during any administration in the postwar era. Tensions with the Soviets were extraordinarily high—the highest they had been since the Eisenhower and Kennedy era crises over Berlin and Cuba. But when the day was over, the power relationship between the United States and the Soviet Union was finally clear. By late 1980s the superior power position of the United States was no longer in doubt, at least in the assessment of the Kremlin. The experience, to be sure, had proved a bit harrowing, but the payoff was to be greater than anyone had hoped. For one unforeseen by-product of this final shift in the correlation of forces was the collapse of communism and an end to the Cold War itself.

Reagan's Game Plan

Reagan's conduct of foreign policy, especially in his first term, was marked by something of the same instinctive feel for power, bluff, and gamesmanship that had characterized the policy of John Foster Dulles. Indeed, the Reagan foreign policy was the most Dulles-like of any post-war president's since Eisenhower's. In part, this was a matter of party pedigree. Recalling Dulles's themes of "rollback" and "liberation" in the 1952 campaign, the Republican platform of 1980 explicitly called for pursuing what it called (in somewhat more cautious phraseology) "positive nonmilitary means" to "roll back" the "growth of communism."[6] For the conservative wing of the Republican party, these were old, not to say hallowed, political themes. But in part the new stress on gamesmanship also came from Reagan himself. Genial, relaxed, often simplistic in his spontaneous public utterances, Reagan had a better intuitive grasp of power politics—whether in the foreign or the domestic sphere—than his opponents generally gave him credit for.[7]

The distinctive advantage of Dulles's approach had been that it kept the Soviets off-guard by genuinely frightening them; the disadvantage was that it tended to scare Western publics and the allies half to death as well. Reagan's policy would have the same double-edged effect. Reagan's policies seriously frightened the Soviets with, one could argue, eventually quite salutary results. But in the meantime, they caused a tremendous furor in both Western Europe and the United States. Indeed, the huge controversy that engulfed the Reagan administration in foreign policy could be seen, at least in part, as paralleling, on a somewhat larger scale, the earlier postwar controversy over the "massive retaliation" doctrine.

By his own account, Reagan deliberately set out to send harsh new signals to the Soviets—probably for much the same reason that Eisenhower had permitted Dulles to use "massive retaliation" and other notoriously vivid utterances to create a deterrent effect on the Soviet Union. When, in his first press conference, the new president stated bluntly that "détente" had "so far" been "a one-way street" and went on to describe the Soviets' explicit goal as "the promotion of world revolution and a one-world Socialist or Communist state," adding that they "reserve[d] unto themselves the right to commit any crime, to lie, to cheat"[8] in order to achieve it, the statement was not, as it was widely viewed at the time, merely accidental. By Reagan's own account, it was part of a deliberate strategy that he actually labeled in his memoirs (perhaps without excessive precision) the "foundation" of his "foreign policy." Such utterances—repeated again and again—were meant, Reagan wrote, to send a "powerful message" to the Soviets "that we weren't going to stand by anymore while they armed and financed terrorists and subverted democratic governments" and "that there were some new fellows in Washington who had a realistic view of what they were up to and weren't going to let them keep it up."[9]

The policy was not confined to Reagan. "Every official of the State Department, in every exchange with a Soviet official," wrote Reagan's first secretary of state, Alexander M. Haig, "emphasized American determination that the U.S.S.R. and its clients—especially Fidel Castro and Qaddafi—must moderate their interventionist behavior, and that Poland must be spared."[10]

The change in tone was designed to create a deterrent effect across the spectrum of U.S.-Soviet conflict. But the issue of greatest urgency in the first weeks and months of the new administration proved to be Poland, where Soviet and Warsaw Pact forces seemed poised to intervene, and where Reagan and his advisors were particularly anxious to deter Soviet action.[11]

More than has been realized, it was the Polish situation that tended to shape the administration's initial handling of arms control in the opening months of its tenure. Like Nixon, Reagan found himself upon entering office without significant sticks to wield against Soviet policy. Like Nixon, he sought to gain leverage using carrots, though Reagan in the end proved better at managing them than had his Republican predecessor. As Alexander Haig, Reagan's first secretary of state, later wrote: "Certainly there could be no summit while the shadows of Budapest and Prague fell across Poland. Every bit of leverage and influence we possessed must be mustered in an effort to influence Soviet calculations and modify Soviet actions."[12]

In his first press conference, Reagan committed himself categorically to "linkage." The decision to begin new arms talks with the Soviets would be contingent upon improvements in Soviet behavior in other areas. "I believe in linkage," he said.[13]

Privately, he wrote to Brezhnev in the spring that "the Soviets could forget any new nuclear arms agreements or better trade relations with us and expect the harshest possible economic sanctions from the United States" if they invaded Poland.[14]In early April, Secretary of Defense Caspar Weinberger persuaded NATO defense ministers in Bonn to endorse a statement explicitly linking the prospect of European arms talks to Soviet restraint on Poland.[15] Given the eagerness of NATO ministers to undertake the arms talks[16] and the palpable lack of sympathy among the European Left for the Polish plight,[17] this was a substantial achievement. But such employment of linkage was regarded with both suspicion and impatience in certain quarters in Western Europe and among the arms control community at home. In his contemporary history of the negotiations, published in 1984, Strobe Talbott, a *Time* correspondent with views closely reflecting those of the arms control community, offered an extremely unsympathetic portrayal of Weinberger's performance in Bonn. To delay arms control negotiations for an "issue of the hour" such as Poland, Talbott implied, was to mistake real priorities.[18]

Reagan's warnings on Poland went farther than most Americans realized. At the time of the imposition of martial law in December 1981, Reagan implicitly raised the war threat, warning Brezhnev over the "hot line" that direct Soviet intervention "could unleash a process which neither you nor we could fully control."[19]

The Euromissile Crisis

Nearly every new administration overestimates its ability to wipe the slate clean and make a fresh start of things, and the Reagan administration was far from an exception to this rule. Temperamentally, Reagan and his advisors were perfectly willing to subordinate the quest for arms control to larger geopolitical concerns such as Poland and to wait until doomsday, if necessary, for a new arms agreement. (Some, but not all, Reagan advisors were, as it were, theologically opposed to arms control; with a few exceptions, most regarded it as, at best, problematic and secondary.) Not everyone else was so patient. Even as the administration concentrated its energies on the crisis in Poland—and on communism in Central America, and the arms buildup, and a host of pressing domestic economic concerns—a new crisis was brewing at the core of the Western security system, in NATO, based on a major arms control decision inherited from the Carter administration.

The so-called Euromissile crisis from 1981 to 1983—when NATO struggled to deploy new American intermediate-range missiles in Western Europe in response to the Soviet SS-20—proved, more than Poland, more than Central America, to be the central foreign policy crisis of the Reagan administration. Indeed, in importance, function, and intensity, the Euromissile episode resembled the two Berlin crises and the Cuban crisis in the period 1957 to 1962. Like the earlier experiences, the Euromissile confrontation involved a major struggle of wills. As with the Cuban crisis, the experience turned on the deployment of intermediate-range missiles (the Cuban crisis involved Soviet insertion of missiles in Cuba, while the Euromissile crisis involved American insertion of missiles in Europe in response to earlier Soviet deployments there; the Euromissile episode was a kind of Cuban crisis in slow motion and reverse). As with the Berlin crisis, a central question in the Euromissile episode concerned the fate and ultimate orientation of West Germany in regard to the West and the East. Finally, as in the earlier episode, the eventual Western victory brought a major shift in the balance of power and a major subsidence in the power struggle.

The Soviet SS-20 missile was a classic illustration of how arms control had worked, or clearly failed to work, through the previous decade. SALT I had limited "strategic" missiles, defining such missiles as having a range of 5,500 kilometers or more. In 1977, the Soviets began to deploy the SS-20, a modern, triple-warhead mobile missile with a range approaching 5,000 kilometers—just below the SALT I limits.[20] The SS-20 was, in effect, the "pocket battleship" of the SALT process. Like the pre–World War II Japanese and German cruisers of that name, it eluded the limits of arms control but packed the same wallop as weapons controlled by agreement—at least within its range, which happened to include all of Europe, Asia, and a good chunk of Africa and the Mideast.[21]

A by-product of arms control, the problem of the SS-20 was also aggravated by arms control. For most of the postwar era, Soviet advantages in conventional weapons in Europe had been seen to be offset by an American advantage in nuclear weapons: Western Europeans liked to speak of an American nuclear "umbrella." SALT I, by establishing official "parity" between the superpowers in 1972, had the unintended consequence of spelling an end to any special U.S. nuclear advantage, and thus seemed to suggest, willy-nilly, that the nuclear umbrella had become porous. In a climate of nuclear "parity," the huge numerical advantages possessed by the Soviets in conventional arms again seemed to loom large. To this, then, the Soviets added the SS-20, which created, or seemed to create, yet a new disparity at the "theater-nuclear" level. Having gained parity at the strategic level, in other words, the Soviets now seemed to enjoy superiority in both conventional and theater-nuclear weapons. (The equivalent U.S. missiles in Western Europe had of course been removed in 1963 as a secret part of the Cuban missile crisis deal.) In short, the balance of forces was shifting against NATO, with all the potentially mischievous political consequences that such a shift implied.

All of this was adumbrated by West German Chancellor Helmut Schmidt in his famous Alastair Buchan lecture in London in 1977.[22] Written in Aesopian terms and couched as a new call for arms control, Schmidt's lecture did not even mention the SS-20 by name. But clearly that was the problem on the West German chancellor's mind. It was Schmidt, a defense expert by background, who worried most about the political consequences of the shifting balance and who pressed the generally complacent Carter administration for some kind of concrete response to the SS-20.[23] But just as the problem of the SS-20 had been produced by arms control, so, in the view of NATO leaders of the 1970s, the response to the SS-20 had to be couched in terms of arms control.[24]

In 1979, after much agonizing, not least in Jimmy Carter's Washington, NATO finally agreed to approve a counterdeployment of new U.S. intermediate-range missiles to offset the SS-20. At NATO's behest, the U.S. would deploy 108 Pershing II ballistic missiles and 464 Ground Launched Cruise Missiles in various European countries including West Germany (which alone would receive the Pershing IIs). But these missiles would not be ready for deployment until 1983, and in the meantime, NATO committed itself to pursue a second "track" of arms control negotiations with the Soviet Union.

The baroque twists and turns of the Euromissile story suggest the unholy complexities into which arms control had led the Western security effort. One could no longer simply counter Soviet weapons by building weapons of one's own. Everything had to be couched in terms of the arms control process.

The so-called dual-track decision, straddling the Carter and Reagan eras, was in a sense a relic of Kissinger's world of the 1970s, when Western political leaders, swamped by the powerful utopian currents of public opinion, struggled to manipulate peace themes subtly in the service of the national interest. Kissinger and Schmidt had both approached this task in a similar way and with somewhat similar political styles; both were practitioners of *Realpolitik* who positioned themselves as figures of the center; both sought to build and balance coalitions through subtle maneuvers at a time of leftward-leaning public opinion. Moreover, one sensed that, at a certain level, both Kissinger and Schmidt relished these complexities. The Reagan advisors, with notable exceptions such as Haig and Lawrence Eagleburger, both formerly of Kissinger's staff, had almost no patience at all with them. In February, in a meeting with British Prime Minister Margaret Thatcher, Reagan had committed himself to the dual-track decision.[25] But for a time, the Reagan administration seemed to behave almost as if the "dual-track" decisions did not exist, preoccupying itself instead with what it saw as more pressing and serious concerns in Poland.

Leftist opposition to NATO's Euromissile decision had emerged as early as 1980, before Reagan's election.[26] But by early 1981, Schmidt was under increasingly heavy fire from the West German Left—with an assist from the Soviet Union. The Soviets, for their part, were absolutely committed to preventing the deployment of new American missiles in Europe. Having succeeded a few years earlier in turning back Jimmy Carter's decision to deploy the neutron bomb, partly by arousing public protest against it, they had some confidence in their ability to achieve this goal.

Indeed, the boldness, not to say insolence, of Soviet efforts to dictate whether or not NATO could deploy new missiles was a symptom of the Soviets' assessment of the manner in which the correlation of forces had shifted against the West. In March, Bonn openly complained about Soviet efforts to influence West German public opinion through, for example, interviews Soviet officials had given to West German television.[27] By spring, a protest movement against the missiles was gaining momentum. Some 15,000 demonstrators marched in Bonn against the NATO missile deployments in early April.[28] Schmidt, meanwhile, was coming under increasing attack within his own party. It seems likely that Schmidt was going to have these problems anyway, but the Reagan administration's delays on getting dual-track talks underway with Moscow could not have made his position easier.

Reagan finally wrote to Brezhnev in early May formally requesting talks. Yet far from lessening the pressures against the alliance, the move toward talks only increased them. Valentin Falin, a Soviet spokesman, immediately charged that the U.S. missiles were designed to alter the balance of power in Europe.[29] Tass twice dismissed the call for arms talks as a "maneuver" designed to make the American deployments possible.[30] On May 17, under increasing pressure from the Left in his own party, Schmidt threatened to resign as chancellor if the NATO dual-track decision was not sustained.[31]

The arms control track had originally been designed to lessen the negative public impact of the deployments. But as the talks became more imminent, the apparent effect was to draw ever greater attention to the missiles and fuel antinuclear protest. In late September, Haig, meeting with Gromyko in New York, worked out the details for intermediate-range missile talks to begin on November 30. (On the day before the agreement was announced, Gromyko went before the UN General Assembly to accuse the United States of starting an arms race to counter a nonexistent Soviet threat.)[32] Less than three weeks later, some 250,000 people marched in Bonn against the planned NATO deployment. Similar massive demonstrations followed over the next three weeks in London, Paris, Brussels, and Milan. Not even in the late 1950s, during the *Sputnik* era, had there been demonstrations of this size. The Euromissile crisis was on.

Matters were not helped on October 17 when Reagan, in a question-and-answer session with news editors in Washington, noted that "you could have an exchange of tactical weapons against troops in the field without it bringing either one of the major powers to pushing the button"[33]; nor when the supposedly subtle Atlanticist Haig two weeks later inexplicably disburdened himself to a congressional committee of NATO contingency plans for a nuclear "demonstration" shot in the event of a Soviet conventional attack.[34] Later, the administration's so-called loose talk was sometimes blamed for having spawned the European antinuclear movement. But in fact Reagan's remark, which was little more than a spectacularly ill-timed restatement of NATO's longstanding flexible response doctrine, followed, rather than preceded, the first major demonstration in Bonn; and Haig's remark followed most of the rest. Still, the remarks fit nicely with the favored Soviet propaganda theme that the purpose of the U.S. missiles was to "Europeanize" a nuclear war, or fight a nuclear war confined to Europe, and contributed to Reagan's growing reputation in Europe as an irresponsible nuclear cowboy.[35]

Under the dual-track plan, arms control was supposed to make the NATO deployment easier. In the end, somewhat predictably, it had the opposite effect. Had NATO decided, bravely, merely to deploy new weapons in response to the SS-20 and then waited until the weapons were built in 1983 to deploy them, there would have been two major moments of controversy: at the time of the decision and at the time of the deployment. Those two moments, especially the second, might have been difficult, but between them it would have been hard to sustain popular interest in the problem. As it was, the arms control process kept the problem of the Euromissiles alive and in the headlines week after week and month after month. Endless NATO meetings and communiqués, endless negotiating sessions and press conferences, endless expectations followed by endless disappointments—the process was tailor-made to intensify and draw out the crisis. That NATO finally succeeded in deploying the American missiles in 1983 was something of a miracle under the circumstances.

The "Zero Option"

The problem remained of developing the American position for the talks. In November 1981, Reagan surprised observers by publicly proposing a so-called zero option for the Euromissile talks: The United States would agree to forgo its Euromissile deployment entirely if the Soviet Union would agree to destroy its intermediate-range missiles (SS-20s, SS-4s, and SS-5s) in Europe and Asia. The proposal was initially quite well received in Western Europe, where leftist parties and even governments had for some time discussed a *Null Lösung*, or "zero solution."[36] Reagan's proposal neatly co-opted the position of the Western European Left and in the process momentarily diffused tensions.

Indeed, whether from the standpoint of propaganda, superpower gamesmanship, or concrete military consequences, the so-called zero option was actually one the better crafted American arms proposals of the nuclear era. Nonetheless, throughout the years 1981 to 1984, the alleged nonnegotiability of the zero option became a rallying cry of Reagan's adversaries in the arms control debate.[37]

Seen at the time largely as a simple ploy to avoid an arms agreement, the zero option was in reality the solution to a complex conundrum involving many elements—military, diplomatic, political. The brainchild of Richard Perle, Senator Jackson's former chief aide for defense and now Weinberger's *éminence grise* at the Pentagon for arms control, the proposal reflected, as it were, Jacksonian habits of thinking. The chief problems with the Kissingerian stress on negotiability had always been two: It paid insufficient attention to the concrete military consequences of an agreement; moreover, it ceded the diplomatic and propaganda initiative to the Soviets. Perle had begun by focusing on the concrete military issues, asking Pentagon specialists to determine precisely how many Soviet SS-20 missiles would be needed to accomplish the SS-20's mission. When Pentagon analysts responded that with as few as fifty SS-20s (with three warheads each), the Soviets could execute a disabling preemptive strike on the relevant NATO command centers, air fields, weapons depots, and so on, it was clear that NATO had a problem. What Perle, by his own later account, feared above all was a deal that traded zero American missiles for a sharp reduction in Soviet SS-20s—a deal that might look superficially beneficial but would leave the new Soviet preemptive capability intact. (The SS-4s and SS-5s had never been accurate enough to perform such a preemptive mission.)

Second, there was the issue of public relations. The State Department was favoring an ostensibly more "negotiable" option that would have reduced missiles on both sides to the lowest level the Soviets would accept. (Whether in reality this was any more "negotiable" is not so clear: It seemed likely that the Soviets would refuse any American proposal involving actual deployment of the U.S. missiles for as long as it appeared that deployment might be prevented.) In contrast to the State Department plan, the zero option gave the European Left at least a theoretical stake in the negotiation and shielded the American proposal from attacks on the basis that it was insufficiently radical or visionary.

Third, there was the issue of verifiability. The verification problem presented by an INF Treaty was orders of magnitude greater than that attempted in SALT, where the main unit of account had been missile silos, or fixed, concrete holes in the ground. Mobile missiles were another story. Even with a combination of stringent inspection and "national technical means" of verification (satellites), it was essentially impossible to verify a *limit* on such systems. Not even a total *ban* of mobile missiles was terribly verifiable by SALT standards, but it was somewhat more manageable.

Fourth, there were less tangible political elements that weighed in Perle's calculations—Reagan's own desire for nuclear arms reductions and the president's natural interest, as a politician, for a clear, politically saleable proposal. In choosing the zero option over the State Department's comparatively colorless alternative, Reagan showed typically good political instincts—but this is not to deny that his passive management style necessitated unseemly maneuvering to make certain that the right piece of paper arrived in front of him at precisely the right time. The memo drafted by Perle outlining the case for the zero option was cabled from Weinberger's plane (en route to Europe) directly to the White House, where counselor Edwin Meese II, a conservative ally of Weinberger, was poised to hand the paper off to Reagan at the right moment. (The Reagan administration was filled with such tales of paper maneuvering.) To sweeten the proposal further, moreover, Weinberger had added to Perle's memo outlining the rationale for the zero option one sentence: that the proposal would win Reagan the Nobel Prize.[38]

The "Nuclear Freeze" Movement

The zero option did not win Reagan the Nobel Prize, but it did temporarily defuse the rising peace movement in Western Europe. But no sooner had Reagan momentarily distracted Western European protesters with his proposal for the zero option than he faced a new wave of protest back home.

Culturally as well as politically, the great "nuclear freeze" controversy that engulfed the United States in the early 1980s—as reflected in numerous books, articles, TV movies, public debates, large protest gatherings, and so forth—was essentially a reprise of the debate over the Vietnam war. The issues were parallel, the configuration of political forces similar, and the cast of characters in many cases the same. The backbone of the protest was formed by the old Vietnam generation, grown somewhat balder and grayer with years. (The prevalence of physicians' and attorneys' groups in the new movement—Physicians for Social Responsibility, Lawyers Against Nuclear War, and the like—could be explained by the fact that many college protesters of the 1960s had now grown up to be doctors and lawyers.) These were people who in the course of the Vietnam era had come to regard protest as the highest expression of citizenship and who would probably have acknowledged finding in protest activities something positive to fill the spiritual void in modern life. There was, moreover, the same alliance of convenience between the Establishment and the Far Left, as prominent Establishment figures—now conspicuously including Robert S. McNamara—lent their prestigious approval to the rising protest. There was, in the background, a similar clash between a Republican president and an Establishment contemptuous of an administration that it did not regard as one of its own.

But there was a difference. By the early 1980s, the Establishment no longer enjoyed an intellectual monopoly on foreign policy discourse, and the Left, if not yet on the defensive, was under intellectual challenge. During the 1970s, as the Establishment foreign policy vision had become more and more narrowly "liberal-pacifist" in orientation, a growing number of liberal Democratic intellectuals had defected to the conservative camp. By the 1980s, "neoconservatism" had become a potent intellectual force in both domestic and foreign policy, as reflected in such journals as *Commentary, The Public Interest,* and, increasingly, even that traditional flagship of American liberalism, *The New Republic.* The origins of this movement were complex, and the subject would merit a book in itself. But the upshot was that Reagan, like John Kennedy, came to office with the support of an intellectual community—albeit a small one. Unlike the Vietnam debate, the nuclear freeze debate definitely had two sides, and both sides had "ideas."

Launched by two left-wing activists, Terry Provance and Randall Forsberg, the nuclear freeze movement had already achieved something a local following, especially in the Northeast, by the time of the 1980 campaign, in response to Carter's shifts toward a tougher defense policy.[39] But it was in the fall, winter, and spring of 1981–82, after Reagan took office, that the antinuclear movement gradually became a national phenomenon. By early 1982, the freeze effort encompassed as many as 1,400 separate organizations nationwide.[40] The publication of Jonathan Schell's "Fate of the Earth" series (later published in book form) in *The New Yorker* in February of 1982 was a pivotal event.[41] A passionate description of the horrors of nuclear war and a wide-ranging political meditation with philosophical pretensions, Schell's series purported to show the way toward an alternative to the balance of terror that had dominated life since the early 1950s. Like Norman Angell's *The Great Illusion* many decades earlier, Schell's antinuclear tract seemed to catch the crest of a new wave of pacifist feeling.

Why did Schell's antinuclear vision resonate so? One could discern both broad cultural and narrow political trends at work. At the cultural level, Schell's vision was in part a continuation of the revulsion against politics that followed from the Vietnam experience—yet another cultural manifestation of the demythologization and disillusionment, the loss of faith in received values, so characteristic of the 1960s generation. Arguing that no merely political value was worth a nuclear holocaust, worth the destruction of humanity, Schell contended that world political leaders had the responsibility to fashion some new global system in which conflicting political values could exist amicably side by side. At the heart of Schell's vision was a devaluation of the political, a tendency to treat such fundamental differences as that between freedom and totalitarianism as a kind of epiphenomenon or afterthought. It reflected the mental habits of a generation whose political thinking had formed amid the moral mire of the Vietnam war and who had been schooled in the nation's better universities to believe that all human values were ultimately "relative." For such a generation, Schell's message was particularly congenial.

But the rise of antinuclear sentiment was also a specific consequence of the Reagan policies, on three levels. First, the mere need to launch a nuclear buildup in response to the Soviet buildup was bound to arouse some protest. The freeze idea, after all, emerged during the Carter administration. Second, Reagan's efforts to conjure up a kind of "massive retaliatory" deterrent—the "tough talk" and "loose talk" so prevalent in the first two years—was bound to cause a backlash at home, as Dulles's similar statements had in an earlier era. But, finally, in turning his back on the arms control paradigm and mutual assured destruction, Reagan aroused the collective ire of the arms control community and the foreign policy Establishment, who by providing collateral intellectual support to the freeze movement lent it respectability and strength.

Schell's book, for example, was prominently reviewed by Jerome Wiesner, president emeritus of MIT and an ardent advocate of the arms control cause since serving on Eisenhower's science advisory council. When Robert Scheer of the *Los Angeles Times* published a book misleadingly cobbling together out-of-context quotations from Reagan officials to suggest that the administration was planning to fight and win a nuclear war, he was able to gather warm jacket endorsements from the likes of Wiesner, Herbert York, Spurgeon M. Keeny, Jr., and former Carter administration secretary of state Cyrus Vance.[42]

McNamara's role was especially interesting. In the spring of 1982, with Western Europe still in the grip of antinuclear hysteria and the completion of the "dual-track" deployment far from certain, McNamara and three prominent Establishment colleagues—McGeorge Bundy, George F. Kennan, and former SALT I negotiator Gerard Smith—published a major article in *Foreign Affairs* calling for abandonment of NATO's nuclear-based "flexible response" strategy and adoption of a new doctrine specifying "no first use" of nuclear weapons.[43] With NATO in the midst of the worst crisis in its history, its survival dependent on a successful deployment of new nuclear weapons amid a massive wave of antinuclear protest, it would have been hard to imagine a more inopportune moment for leading American figures to initiate major controversy on the overall validity of NATO's nuclear strategy. Indeed, Atlanticist West Germans reacted with notable anxiety to the suggestion.[44] But McNamara, notwithstanding his eagerness in an earlier era to exclude the public from debate on Vietnam, was now evidently interested in stirring public controversy, however harmful to NATO, on an issue where he happened to be on what he regarded as the right side.[45]

What McNamara and his Establishment colleagues somewhat characteristically failed to grasp was that the West was in the midst of a critical power struggle, a struggle of wills, with the Soviet Union. Nothing would contribute more to peace than American success in this power struggle, and nothing would contribute more to instability than failure. Whether NATO's strategy was in some technical sense sound or not was far less important in 1982 than that NATO not be seen to change its strategy under pressure from the antinuclearists and the Soviet Union. But McNamara and company were doing all they could to undermine NATO's strategy and the existing administration's approach. In effect, having started a war that destroyed two presidencies, McNamara was now busily engaged in the de facto attempt to destroy a third.

The "no first use"/nuclear freeze battle posed a critical challenge to Reagan. Had he lost this domestic battle, his foreign policy credibility would have been shattered, the mandate of 1980 turned back, and the process of restoring the balance of power dealt a huge blow. Nothing would have been more likely to prolong the age of ambiguity and with it the Cold War.

The contest was narrow. In March 1982, Senators Edward M. Kennedy of Massachusetts and Mark O. Hatfield of Oregon announced that 17 senators and 122 House members had agreed to sponsor a resolution calling for a nuclear freeze. Not for the first time, an administration was rescued by Senator Jackson, who with Senator John Warner of Virginia gained a total of 58 Senate co-sponsors for an alternative resolution in late March calling for a freeze at equal and sharply *reduced* levels of weapons. Jackson's maneuver meant that no freeze could pass the Congress in 1982, and a freeze motion was ultimately defeated in a narrow House vote of 204 to 202 on August 5, 1982.[46]

In May, Reagan belatedly put forward his proposals for strategic arms control in a commencement address at his alma mater, Eureka College in Illinois. The most remarkable thing about Reagan's proposals for, in effect, SALT III—now called the Strategic Arms Reduction Talks, or START—was how little controversy they aroused. Whether because the

State Department had won a number of the internal battles leading up to the proposal[47] (State had better relations with the media), or because of the intrinsic design of the proposal, or because of the delays, there was far less criticism than one had a right to expect. Perhaps by delaying so long, Reagan had begun to wear his opponents down. *Time* commented that the proposal was so long in coming that it was greeted with "relief."[48] Both *The Economist* and the *New York Times* editorialized favorably on the proposal, which called for cuts of far more radical strategic significance than even the "zero option."[49]

The proposal, embodying Reagan's 1980 campaign theme of "reductions," envisioned a one-third cut in ballistic missile warheads on both sides, only half of which would be permitted on land-based missiles. If accepted, the cuts would have involved a major restructuring of the Soviet arsenal—Haig again condemned the proposal in his memoir as "unnegotiable."[50] But the restructuring would have been, theoretically at least, in the direction of greater stability. The idea was to force the Soviets to take bilaterally the kinds of steps that the United States had already taken unilaterally over many years—that is, deemphasize relatively destabilizing ICBMs and emphasize more stabilizing submarine-based missiles. But in reality, whether the START treaty would actually stabilize the balance was far from clear. At the time, many in the government understood that the lower numbers called for in the American proposal could lead to greater instability.[51] But even the hawks understood they would be saved from the worst consequences of "deep cuts" by the Soviets' dependable refusal to accept them.[52]

The Racetrack and the Bishops

How long could a democracy live under the corrosive reality of complete vulnerability to nuclear missile attack and sustain the will for deterrence's upkeep?[53] As the year 1982 wound to a close, the answer to this question seemed increasingly uncertain. Despite Reagan's provisional victory over the nuclear freeze, support for nuclear deterrence seemed to be eroding rapidly, on both a strategic and a moral plane. The two most visible signs of the crisis were Congress's refusal to approve the MX missile and the Catholic bishops' draft "pastoral letter" on nuclear war.

The rejection of the MX missile was in large part the result of the Reagan administration's serious mishandling of the issue. But it was also partly a consequence of the political and moral liabilities inherent in an offense-only nuclear strategy.

In development since the time of SALT I,[54] the MX missile constituted the centerpiece of the U.S. strategic modernization program, the main American answer to the relentless Soviet missile buildup of the previous decade. In 1986, MX was to be the first new ICBM deployed by the United States in over ten years.[55] It was a large "medium" ICBM—between a "light" and a "heavy"—more on the order of the larger missiles the Soviets had been deploying. It was also designed to have 10 extremely accurate warheads capable of destroying hard targets. In other words, it was a "counterforce" weapon.

The MX was criticized by some arms controllers as a first-strike weapon, and as a counterforce weapon, it certainly had some first-strike potential. But that was not its real role. Over the years, the number of hardened targets in the Soviet Union had vastly increased, including not just missile silos, but shelters for the leadership, command and control centers, and other military installations.[56] If the Soviet Union were ever to launch a first strike against the United States—presumably, a preemptive strike against ICBM silos, airfields, ports, and other military installations—it would still have a huge number of active hard targets, including silos containing as-yet unfired missiles, worth striking. A nation's first priority in the wake of such a horrible eventuality would be to destroy these hardened targets—using a weapon such as the MX—in the hope of ending or curtailing the Soviets' ability to continue to wage nuclear war. (There might also be a distant hope that after such devastating mutual exchanges aimed primarily at military installations, the two sides might have an incentive to cease further hostilities before wholesale targeting of urban centers commenced.) In other words, the MX was a "damage-limiting" weapon, a weapon designed to destroy the Soviet Union's war-making capability and to strengthen deterrence by providing the president with a credible intermediate step between surrender and total counter-city retaliation.

One could avert one's eyes from these horrible scenarios, but that was to quit the game of deterrence itself. Indeed, the question of the hour seemed to be whether the nation—and certainly the nation's political class—was ready to opt out of the game of deterrence, much as it had previously opted psychologically out of the Vietnam war.

With the MX missile, the Carter administration had also attempted to solve another pressing strategic problem—the vulnerability of American ICBMs. After playing down ICBM vulnerability for two years, the Carter administration in 1979 had concocted an elaborate basing scheme for the MX, designed at once to shield it from preemptive destruction and to meet the requirements of verifiability under SALT. The so-called race-track basing scheme envisioned 200 MXs moving in special trucks in an elaborate "shell game" among 4,600 separate shelters connected by an underground network of tunnels covering some 40,000 square miles in Nevada and Utah, at an estimated cost of $30 to 40 billion.[57] Requiring approximately 20 percent of the combined area of the two states, as well as vast quantities of scarce water for the actual construction,[58] the "race-track" scheme was never popular, lacking a real constituency either among arms controllers or hawks. Resistance from Utah and Nevada legislators was so strong that by the spring of 1980, the Carter administration itself had backed off the original racetrack, outlining a scaled-down "linear" approach.[59]

In a sense, the MX racetrack was a physical correlative of the NATO dual-track decision—an exceedingly complex scheme born of the effort to reconcile the mutually conflicting imperatives of arms control and defense. But like the dual-track, it was also the basis for a critical political consensus—in this case in the Congress, where Democratic and Republican legislators on the Armed Services Committees had been induced to support the scheme. Just as Thatcher had persuaded Reagan, despite Weinberger's misgivings, not to jettison the dual-track decision in 1981,[60] so it would have been nice if someone had persuaded President Reagan not to jettison racetrack. Unfortunately, there was no domestic Thatcher to do the job. On the contrary, on the advice of Reagan's chief defense advisor in the campaign, William R. Van Cleave (who, along with many right-leaning defense experts, had doubts about the enormous costs and Rube Goldberg complexity of the scheme), as well as the urging of his close friend Nevada Senator Paul Laxalt (whose constituents were up in arms), Reagan openly attacked the racetrack during the 1980 campaign. After his appointment as secretary of defense in 1981, Weinberger, too, began to express public skepticism about the scheme, proposing alternatives such as basing the MX on airplanes or on surface ships (such suggestions showed Weinberger's fundamental ignorance of the defense debate at this stage: the whole point of the MX as an upgrade to the *land-based* missile force, and not the sea or air legs of the triad). By May, doubtless thanks in no small part to Reagan's and Weinberger's public opposition, the Mormon church declared itself against the racetrack, and Utah and Nevada senators had gone on record as firmly against it.[61] Racetrack at this point was probably dead. In October, Reagan finally shelved the racetrack scheme publicly and announced plans provisionally to base 36 MXs in "superhardened" silos, pending a study on permanent basing for the missile.[62]

Shorn of its special basing mode, the MX, never popular, became a kind of arms controller's nightmare—a vulnerable first-strike weapon, technically the most destabilizing combination of all. Congressional support for the missile rapidly dissipated. On March 23, 1982, the Senate Armed Services Committee voted to deny funding for the interim basing plan for MX until the administration developed a permanent basing scheme.[63] When the Reagan administration returned to Congress with a so-called dense pack plan, Congress put the missile completely on hold. Technically, dense pack might have had some merit. But by now the administration had lost all credibility on the issue. At the suggestion of Senators Sam Nunn of Georgia and William Cohen of Maine, the president was to appoint a special bipartisan commission to sort the issue out. The Scowcroft Commission would recommend procurement of 100 MX missiles; but Congress would in the end approve just over 50.[64]

However costly or imperfect racetrack might have been, it would have provided some measure of protection for MX. True, the Soviets could overwhelm the system by targeting all 4,600 shelters; but such an attack, whether using one or two warheads per shelter, could never be construed as "limited." In short, there was every reason to believe that racetrack would strengthen deterrence against preemption. Equally important, Reagan's support of racetrack would have made deployment of 200 MX missiles with 2,000 accurate warheads politically viable. (There is every reason to suppose that a combination of Reagan's strong support with that of key Democratic senators could have overawed local opposition in the Southwest.)

While Reagan and Weinberger showed bad judgment in their handling of racetrack, the congressional reaction also indicated the fragility of the defense consensus. Reagan's congressional opponents were by no means free of blame. As Richard Perle pointed out in a *Washington Post* op-ed, the same liberal critics who for years had "dismissed the idea of a Soviet attack on our land-based force as an obsessive delusion of worst-case defense planners" were now regaling Congress "with the several ways in which MX might be destroyed, earth-penetrating warheads, attacks timed to within millionths of a second, 'pindown' attacks, and the like." "That liberal lawmakers should now arrive at the conviction that the Soviets will go out of their way to destroy our land-based deterrent," wrote Perle, "is too richly ironic to pass without comment."[65]

MX, in a sense, defined the cul-de-sac into which McNamara's strategy of assured destruction had led the nation. Under McNamara, the country had gone to an offense-only strategy on the premise that the Soviets would concentrate merely on development of a reciprocal "second-strike capability." Instead, the Soviets had relentlessly moved toward first-strike weapons. Now the United States was faced with an unpleasant choice: Should it respond to the Soviet effort with a counterforce weapon of its own, or should it permit the Soviets a monopoly in such first-strike systems and continue to base its deterrent on what remained of an increasingly vulnerable retaliatory capability? Some were content to remain with the latter. Deterrence in an offense-only world was fast losing its moral and political appeal.

Deterrence was dealt an even more serious blow with the issuance in October of the Catholic bishops' draft "pastoral letter" on nuclear war. Actually only the latest in a long series of left-leaning pronouncements on foreign policy produced by the bishops' liberal staff,[66] the pastoral letter nonetheless caught the administration and the country by surprise. An institution (misleadingly) perceived as a bastion of conservatism appeared to be raising fundamental questions about the administration's nuclear strategy. The letter called for a "no first use" posture on nuclear weapons in Europe and questioned whether deterrence based on massive nuclear retaliation could ever be moral.[67] The letter created potentially terrible problems of conscience for Catholics in the administration and the armed services. It pointed to a fundamental breakdown in the moral consensus on which deterrence had been based. The troubles with the MX and the action of the Catholic bishops would help precipitate two of the most famous and, as it turns out, important steps of the Reagan foreign policy in March 1983: the "evil empire" speech about the Soviet Union and the Strategic Defense Initiative.

"Star Wars" and the "Evil Empire"

Reagan was no consensus politician. The bad news about this was his neglect, almost to the point of irresponsibility, of carefully built consensuses like that behind the MX or (in the early months of 1981) the dual-track decision. The good news was his comparative immunity to the fashionable assumptions of the day and his serious commitment to redefining his era's moral and political agenda. At a time when nuclear armageddon was the talk of the West and virtually any other politician—certainly, for example, Richard Nixon—would have sought to curry favor with the electorate by advertising his dedication to arms control, Reagan instead strove to reframe the defense argument in terms that would be more advantageous to the West in the long term. Perhaps only a president with an extraordinary media presence and speech-making skill, not to mention a following of conservative ideologues prepared to pen vivid speeches, could have ventured this; at any rate, the importance of Reagan's rhetorical and psychological contributions to the foreign policy debate of the day could not be overestimated. In the end, they probably made up for poor decisions, such as that on the MX. Indeed, they probably played a major role in winning the Cold War.

In June 1982, at the height of the Euromissile crisis, Reagan, in the course of a European trip, addressed the British Parliament. Almost any other president could have been depended on to devote the speech, defensively, to alliance policy and arms control. Reagan, instead, went on the offensive. Celebrating the virtues of liberal democracy, he all but predicted the collapse of communism. In retrospect, his comments are remarkably prophetic:

> In an ironic sense Karl Marx was right. We are witnessing today a great revolutionary crisis, a crisis where the demands of the economic order are conflicting directly with those of the political order. But the crisis is happening not in the free, non-Marxist West, but in the home of Marxist-Leninism, the Soviet Union. It is the Soviet Union that runs against the tide of history by denying human freedom and human dignity to its citizens. It also is in deep economic difficulty.[68]

Seven years before the collapse of communism and the fall of the Berlin Wall, when the weakness of the Soviet system was far from self-evident, Reagan predicted that Marxism-Leninism was destined for "the ash-heap of history." Outlining the Soviet Union's severe economic problems, Reagan expressed "optimism" about the long-term triumph of democracy. He cited both Solidarity in Poland and a recent election in El Salvador (where American aid was helping to fend off a Marxist-Leninist insurgency) as signs of a worldwide trend toward democracy, and exhorted his audience to a symbolic "crusade" on its behalf.[69]

In post-Vietnam America, moral and military self-doubt had gone hand in hand; national guilt made military effort seem unjustified; military failure in turn reinforced moral self-doubt. Reagan, in effect, sought to reverse both trends, simultaneously rebuilding American military strength and speaking in a manner designed to restore Western moral confidence.

But the major break with the dominant consensus of the previous decades would come in two major speeches in March 1983. March was indeed a fateful month of the Cold War. Early in the month, West Germans went to the polls and returned a conservative government, in the face of massive Soviet pressure, a victory for Reagan and the "zero option." In the same month, Ronald Reagan called the Soviet Union an "evil empire" and proposed the Strategic Defense Initiative (SDI). In one fell swoop, Reagan left behind both the value-neutrality of the McNamara model and "mutual assured destruction." A new era was about to dawn.

It is not often remembered that the reference to the evil empire actually came in a speech to a religious group—the annual convention of the National Association of Evangelicals, in Orlando, Florida. The speech also had a practical political purpose: In the wake of the Catholic bishops' letter, Reagan was trying to head off a politically disastrous pro–nuclear freeze vote in a core religious constituency.[70] The language he chose was appropriate to a religious audience; nonetheless, it shattered a kind of taboo. Characterizing Soviet totalitarianism as "the focus of evil in the modern world," Reagan enjoined the evangelicals not to remain neutral between the West and what he called "the aggressive impulses of an evil empire."[71]

No sooner had the Establishment—and the Soviets—absorbed the shock of that remark than Reagan appeared again, this time on national television, with a major proposal essentially overturning the security consensus of the previous fifteen years. In a surprise conclusion to a nationally televised address on defense, Reagan called for a major new program of research into defenses against ballistic missiles, with the ultimate aim of rendering Soviet missiles, as he put it, "impotent and obsolete."[72] The proposal for what eventually became known as the Strategic Defense Initiative (and was quickly branded by Democrats as "Star Wars") was to dominate the defense and arms control debate for the remainder of the decade.

The strategic defense speech should not have been as surprising as it seemed. In 1980, the Republican platform had included language specifi-cally condemning "MAD" and calling for "vigorous research and devel-opment of an effective anti-ballistic missile system."[73] And in early 1981, Weinberger had expressed doubts about the ABM Treaty.[74] But Reagan had deliberately prepared the strategic defense speech in secret with only a few advisors and special consultations with the joint chiefs of staff. It was the fruition of an idea of his that had been percolating in his mind since a visit to NORAD (North American Aerospace Defense Command) in 1979—when it was brought home to the former California governor that even in the event of a limited ballistic missile launch against the United States, the country had no defense whatever. Weinberger and Shultz had no part in preparing the SDI speech (White House officials probably rightly feared leaks from the State or Defense departments would kill the initiative), and even the JCS were surprised by the dramatic unveiling of the initiative on March 23.[75] Yet as the support of the chiefs suggested, there were sound policy reasons for wishing to strengthen emphasis on defense—many experts had come to recognize that offensive deterrence had become a kind of dead end. However, even many who favored greater emphasis on strategic defense regretted the dramatic and symbolic fashion in which Reagan unveiled the subject.

Yet rarely have speeches had such impact on world events. Reagan's speeches of March 1983, in effect, redefined the superpower agenda. Mikhail Gorbachev's dramatically new approach to Soviet foreign policy beginning in 1985 could be seen, not entirely unfairly, as an attempt, first, to kill the Strategic Defense Initiative and, second, to prove to the world that the Soviet Union was not in fact an evil empire.[76]

The Roots of *Perestroika*

As long ago as 1946, George Orwell had identified qualities in totalitarian regimes that made it difficult for them to keep a firm grasp on objective reality; it was these qualities that seemingly came most into play as the Soviet Union attempted to cope with the phenomenon of Ronald Reagan.

"The organised lying practised by totalitarian states," Orwell wrote in his essay "The Prevention of Literature,"

> is not, as is sometimes claimed, a temporary expedient of the same nature as military deception. It is something integral to totalitarianism. . . . Totalitarianism demands, in fact, the continuous alteration of the past, and in the long run probably demands a disbelief in the very existence of objective truth. . . . A totalitarian society which succeeded in perpetuating itself would probably set up a schizophrenic system of thought, in which the laws of common sense held good in everyday life and in certain exact sciences, but could be disregarded by the politician, the historian, and the sociologist.[77]

By the 1980s, Westerners had probably come to underestimate how simply delusory the Soviet worldview had become after seventy years of totalitarian rule. American conservatives, on the one hand, tended to assume that the Soviets, in repeatedly lying about themselves and others, were privately keeping careful track of the truth. On the other hand, forces on the Western Left routinely did their best to find what truth they could in Soviet lies. To put the situation slightly differently, conservatives assumed the Soviets must be fully aware that they were the evil empire, while at least part of the Western Left tended to act as if the United States were the real evil empire.

Certainly, few American conservatives, least of all Reagan himself, probably imagined that the turn toward a tougher rhetorical and military policy would be equated by some in the Soviet power structure with the first steps toward a preemptive nuclear war. Yet there is evidence that such a delusion took hold of the Soviet intelligence bureaucracy in the early 1980s. In January 1984, Columbia professor Seweryn Bialer returned from Moscow reporting "feelings verging on rage" and a "mood of dark defiance" among the Soviet political elite, which, he argued, had been "pushed into a corner." Bialer wrote, "the Soviets are waiting for an opportunity to reassert their international status and teach Reagan a lesson. Meanwhile, they are waiting for the outcome of this year's presidential election." Bialer saw "great danger," the possibilities of "a new Cold War," and "an expensive and dangerous new round in the arms race."[78] At the time, one might have been inclined to dismiss such reports as so much bluster and disinformation from Soviet officials, but in retrospect, Bialer's reports probably conveyed accurately the feelings of the Soviets with whom he spoke.

According to Oleg Gordievsky, a former KGB head of station in London who defected in the early 1980s, Reagan's tough rhetoric, combined with the massive U.S. military buildup, persuaded some people very high in the Soviet power structure that the United States might actually be planning a nuclear war. In 1981, Yuri Andropov, the head of the KGB, apparently argued in a speech that the United States was actively preparing for nuclear war. Beginning in 1981, the KGB and the GRU (military intelligence) embarked on a worldwide intelligence operation designed to unearth the (nonexistent) Western plans for a nuclear strike on the Soviet Union. The operation, code-named RYAN (for Raketno Yadernoye Napadenie, or "Nuclear Missile Attack") persisted, according to Gordievsky and his British co-author, into 1984.[79] Gordievsky further recalled that on November 8 or 9, 1983—ironically, just over a week before the

ABC-TV movie *The Day After* vividly depicted the consequences of a nuclear holocaust—a flash notification was sent out to KGB stations reporting a (nonexistent) worldwide American military alert. While the alert was explicitly linked to the bombing of U.S. Marines in Beirut, there was some hint from Moscow Center that the alert could be the first stage of the feared "RYAN."[80]

Is this to say that Reagan's tough posture brought a heightened chance of nuclear war in the early 1980s? Ironically, to argue that it did so would be to invalidate any claim as to the efficacy of "mutual assured destruction." If nuclear war had indeed been a serious possibility, then this would imply that deterrence based on the prospect of overwhelming retaliation was a great deal weaker than the advocates of MAD (or for that matter almost anyone else) claimed it to be. If under the circumstances, the Soviets were willing to contemplate and seriously prepare for a "preventive" war, it would mean that the nuclear balance had indeed dangerously shifted in the Soviet favor, and that therefore the claims of the most extreme conservative alarmists about the state of the nuclear balance were ultimately correct. In reality, however, there was almost certainly negligible chance of actual war. There was, after all, a long distance, and many, many steps, between the kinds of paranoiac fears apparently exhibited by the KGB in its operation RYAN, on the one hand, and the planning that would be necessary for a Soviet preemptive strike, on the other. Even a rather neurotic and delusory individual will not frequently act on his delusions in a way that grossly endangers his very existence. But this is not to deny that tensions were excruciatingly high—as high as they had been at any time since the Cuban missile crisis.

The psychological mechanism behind such delusions is not hard to fathom. In a sense, the Soviet delusion of American plans for a nuclear strike came from a perverse form of "mirror-imaging" (hard-minded officials of the Soviet military-intelligence bureaucracy could very well imagine themselves, from a certain perspective, planning a "preventive" nuclear war against an adversary). Also, inhibited from admitting that it was their own conduct—the arms buildup, the deployment of new missiles in Europe, Third World adventurism, and the invasion of Afghanistan—that had, in a sense, created the phenomenon of Reaganism (at least in a foreign policy sense), the Soviets could only ascribe Western actions to the most diabolical of intentions.[81]

Reagan brought the Soviets to a new pitch of agitation, which fostered in turn new heights of delusiveness. But the troubles of the early 1980s also brought self-doubt. Faced with Reagan, the Soviets could sustain little of the complacency they exhibited in the mid-1970s, when détente with the West and Communist victories in the Third World had led them falsely to imagine that socialism was surpassing capitalism as a world force. Whatever the Soviets might say about Reagan in the early 1980s— and in his climactic September 1983 statement Andropov said some very harsh things[82]—it was hard for the Soviets, in any event, to argue that their plans and their system were succeeding. The end of complacency, in a sense, was the beginning of reflection. Whatever else he had or had not done, Reagan had shattered the Soviet illusion of success.

One response to the difficulties with Reagan was the KGB's paranoiac search for NATO's secret plans for nuclear war. A second response was a more honest search for the source of the Soviet Union's growing troubles, internal and external. Significantly, it was in 1982, at the height of Reagan's Cold War "crusade" against communism, that Andropov protégé Mikhail Gorbachev, by his own later account, set forth with his new Politburo colleague Nikolai Ryzhkov on the investigation that eventually bore fruit in *glasnost* and *perestroika*. According to Paul Nitze, in 1987, Gorbachev related to Secretary of State George Shultz that in 1982 he and Rhyzkov "exchanged views on the serious internal problems facing the Soviet state—the political structure of the party, the backwardness of the economy, the excess allocation of resources to defense, and more."[83] Gorbachev and Rhyzkov then appointed some 100 teams of leading intellectuals and analysts to survey the problems and prescribe solutions. It seems to have been these teams that, by 1985, produced the 110 research papers that Gorbachev later described as having been prepared for a large conference of leading Communist intellectuals scheduled for March of that year. Gorbachev, by his own account, was to serve as rapporteur for this comprehensive conference on reform. But in that month Chernenko died, and Gorbachev assumed an even more weighty role of General Secretary of the Communist party.[84]

The roots of *perestroika*, therefore, lay in the depths of Reagan's new Cold War. That the Soviets would have eventually arrived at some realization of their failings—certainly by the end of the millennium, if not before, seems more than possible. The question was when. As long as the West exhibited self-doubt, a flagging economy, a weakening military position, while at the same time trading with and subsidizing the Soviets economically, the moment of truth was likely to be delayed. Insight, when it came, depended on three things: loss of military initiative, American economic recovery, and an absence of American aid. That they would have arrived at this moment in the mid-1980s without the unambiguous challenge posed by Ronald Reagan seems in doubt.

Victory in Europe

At the same time, behind the scenes Reagan was quietly laying the groundwork for a better relationship with the Soviet Union. As early as 1981, Reagan had penned a handwritten note to Brezhnev—deliberately sent alongside a tougher, more formal communication when Reagan lifted the U.S. grain embargo against Moscow. An attempt, by Reagan's own later account, to reach the Soviet leader on a more "human" level, the note reminded Brezhnev of the two men's first meeting when Reagan was California governor. While refuting Soviet charges of U.S. "imperialism," the informal note also raised the possibility of a "meaningful and constructive dialogue which will assist us in fulfilling our joint obligation to find lasting peace." An as-yet isolated (and from the Soviet perspective, probably incongruous) communication among harsh signals, the note, according to Reagan's later account, received an "icy reply" from Moscow.[85] Nonetheless, it gave evidence of Reagan's early interest in developing a second "track" alongside confrontation and showed the instinctive "tough cop/good cop" logic in Reagan's approach. (Haig later related that Reagan had penned an even earlier "handcrafted" note to the Soviet leader, raising hopes of a nonnuclear world; Haig, "astonished" at the softness of sentiment expressed by the hard-line Reagan, vetoed sending the earlier letter.)[86] Similarly, in 1983, around the time of the evil empire and SDI addresses, Reagan told Shultz of a desire for a presidential trip to Moscow. The president actually met secretly with Soviet ambassador Anatoly Dobrynin to begin laying the foundation for such a visit.[87] Reagan's notion had always been that rebuilt American strength would create (in the old Acheson phrase) "situations of strength" for productive negotiation. He was now apparently ready to begin laying groundwork for such talks. It was here that Reagan parted ways with his most conservative followers, who by and large feared that negotiations could only lead to damaging U.S. concessions. Reagan's confidence in the strength of the U.S. bargaining position and his belief in the possibility of actually changing the Soviet system were vindicated over the fears of his more pessimistic conservative adherents.

In 1983, nonetheless, the possibility of a significant lessening of tensions, let alone an end to the Cold War, appeared remote. On the contrary, in every dimension the superpower crisis seemed to deepen. In August, as if to confirm Reagan's description of them as an evil empire, the Soviets shot down a civilian airliner that had strayed into their air space—Korean Air Lines Flight 007. The Soviets bitterly defended their action, charging the United States with sending the airliner on a spy flight—a charge repeated by sympathetic parties in the West. They were, as usual, lying. As later Soviet press revelations showed, the Soviets themselves discovered the nature of the flight when they recovered the plane's "black box" from the sea. They concealed the discovery and even planted a false "pinger" to draw American searchers away from the real black box.[88]

KAL 007 put the Soviets on the extreme defensive. In September, Andropov issued one of the most blistering denunciations of the Cold War, accusing Reagan and the United States of developing an "outrageous militant psychosis."[89]

Indeed, as if to confirm the Soviets' worst fears, in October, the United States actually invaded the small island of Grenada and, much to the joy of the local populace, deposed a new Marxist-Leninist government there. The first such American intervention in the Western Hemisphere since Lyndon Johnson sent troops to the Dominican Republic in 1965, this too seemed to turn back the Cold War clock. In the United States, the successful intervention won popular support.

The Euromissile crisis, meanwhile, moved toward its climax with the Soviets threatening to walk out of the missile talks if American missiles were deployed in Germany. Barely a week before the Euromissiles were due to arrive, ABC-TV's movie *The Day After* not so subtly predicted that the American missile deployment would lead to a nuclear war, whose effects on the town of Lawrence, Kansas, were depicted in gruesome detail. After the program, the secretary of state spoke in what were intended to be reassuring tones. A panel of experts including Henry Kissinger and death camp survivor Elie Wiesel was convened by ABC to discuss the movie. (Kissinger, to his credit, was alone in dismissing the production as the purest emotionalism.)

Despite the anxiety, and the fanfare, however, the West Germans held solid. On November 22, the West German Parliament approved deployment of the Euromissiles. The following day, the missiles were flown to West Germany, and the Soviets walked out of the arms talks. Though it was not immediately clear, the Euromissile crisis had been brought to a successful conclusion.

1984

Ever since the publication of George Orwell's famous novel, the century had anticipated the year 1984 with a measure of trepidation. Orwell's fictional 1984, of course, marked the final victory of the totalitarians. The real 1984, interestingly enough, brought the first real signs of spring after the long winter of the Cold War. Not that anyone recognized the blossoming for what it was, or saw ahead to the century's spectacular climax in the collapse of communism. But looking back today, one can discern some early signs that the long freeze was ending.

The clearest such sign was the mood of the summer Olympics in Los Angeles that year. In May, the Kremlin announced that the Soviets would be boycotting the Los Angeles games in retaliation for the 1980 U.S. boycott of the Moscow games. (Like the walkout from the arms talks, the gesture was self-defeating.) At first it might have seemed that the absence of the East Bloc would take the wind and joy out of the 1984 summer Olympics.

On the contrary, the absence (with the exception of Romania with its dazzling young gymnasts) of the East Bloc countries, with their burdensome quasi-moral mission of struggle against the West and their Olympic judges committed to skewing scores in the Communist favor, gave the Los Angeles games a lightness of tone and aura of playfulness unique among the Olympic games in the Cold War era. In Los Angeles that summer, the world caught a foreshadowing glimpse of the post–Cold War world, a world in which communism was no longer a factor, a world dominated by the Western democracies and above all by the crazy-quilt pop culture of the United States. For the first time since Vietnam, America was in a patriotic mood. "America's Moment," said the cover of *Time* that August.[90] And when the games were over, another *Time* cover summed up a new national spirit: "I ♥ U.S."[91]

In such a climate, the sackcloth-and-ashes campaign of former Carter vice president Walter Mondale in the fall of 1984 probably never had a chance. Not that the Establishment did not wish to drive Reagan from the White House. Throughout 1984, an Establishment critique of the Republican administration's foreign policy was taking shape, focusing on its supposed mishandling of arms control. The Establishment's point man in the attack was Strobe Talbott, *Time* editor, translator of the Khrushchev memoirs, and Council of Foreign Relations expert on foreign policy.

Talbott's attack unfolded in two books published in that year. The shorter of the two, *The Russians and Reagan*, attacked Reagan's anti-Communist crusade, even printing the British Parliament and evil empire speeches in an appendix as examples of Reagan's misdirected approach, while the lengthier and more sensational *Deadly Gambits*, published on the eve of the 1984 election, criticized Reagan's policies in arms control.

In retrospect, the Talbott books tend to show how mechanistic and shortsighted the Establishment vision of foreign policy had become. Policies that improved the immediate atmosphere in U.S.-Soviet relations were rated by Talbott as beneficial, while policies, such as Reagan's, that increased tensions even in the short run were thought to be misguided and if not dangerous. It is sobering to recall that it was on the basis of this wonderfully sophisticated and complicated formula that the Reagan foreign policy was widely dismissed by the East Coast elites as misguided and simplistic.

Of nothing did Talbott appear more certain than that Reagan's hopes of changing the Communist system were misplaced. "Some members of the Administration," he wrote, "persisted in *an unprecedented assertion that the United States had the ability to effect crucial changes at the very core, and at the very top, of the Soviet system.* The Reagan administration believed, for a long time, *that it could influence the composition and orientation of the post-Brezhnev leadership.*"[92] This was not only wrongheaded, Talbott implied, but possibly dangerous, contributing to the deterioration of "the tone and substance of Soviet-American relations" to "the worst" level "in more than two decades."[93]

Deadly Gambits caused far more of a splash. A detailed, behind-the-scenes history of arms control policy based on extensive background interviews with the participants, the book received wide notice and was used by Mondale in one of the presidential debates. It told essentially two tales: first, the story of an unauthorized and unsuccessful effort by Paul Nitze to reach a compromise in the Euromissile negotiations, the then-famous "walk in the woods" episode; and second, what became known as the "battle of the two Richards," the struggle between Richard Burt and Richard Perle—or between State and Defense, the Kissingerites and the Reaganites within the administration—over U.S. policy in the arms negotiations.

Talbott's premise was that the failure of the Reagan administration to achieve an arms agreement by the end of its first term constituted a major foreign policy blunder. Talbott was particularly critical of the administration's neglect of the value of "negotiability"—that is, crafting proposals that the Soviets might accept. Those who paid homage to the value of negotiability were cast as heroes in the book, while those who resisted negotiability were cast as villains. Perle, particularly, was portrayed as a kind of diabolic figure, the "Prince of Darkness."[94]

Much was made of the Nitze's "walk in the woods" episode at the time. A play was even written about it.[95] (In the play, in a kind of characteristic demonstration of post–Vietnam era American self-doubt and self-hatred, the characters were reversed, with the American delegate cast as a younger man—Sam Waterston—and the Soviet delegate as a sage elder statesman—played by the appealing Robert Prosky[96]—whereas, in reality, Nitze, the elder statesman, liked his younger Soviet counterpart Yulii Kvitsinski but remembered him as a liar.[97]) Believing he had an obligation to negotiate in good faith, assuming certain prerogatives as an elder statesman, and possessing the temperament of what Perle called "an inveterate problem-solver,"[98] Nitze attempted on his own to devise a compromise formula for the Euromissile negotiations. The compromise, worked out in a chat with Kvitsinski during a walk in the woods, would have traded elimination of the U.S. Pershing II ballistic missiles for limits on the SS-20s. From the American point of view, the problem with the compromise was its political inequality: It would have left the Soviets in possession of ballistic-missile warheads capable of reaching Western European targets in a matter of minutes, while NATO would have been restricted to slower-flying cruise missiles. Talbott derided Reagan for rejecting the compromise on the basis of a supposedly simplistic distinction between "slow-flyers" and "fast-flyers."[99] But once again Reagan's political instincts were probably right: The compromise would have been given the *appearance* of an American concession (also, it raised complex political questions since the Pershing IIs, the only weapons to be eliminated under the compromise, were also the only missiles scheduled to be deployed in West Germany). Indeed, one could easily have imagined Nitze, out of government, criticizing the same compromise he fashioned while within. But the more fundamental problem, which Talbott could not fail to acknowledge, was the absence of any sign of Soviet interest in the compromise. There was no reason to suppose that the Soviets were prepared to accept any deal allowing U.S. missiles in Western Europe so long as a chance remained that the U.S. deployment could be entirely turned back. At any rate, Reagan's response to Nitze's compromise, quoted by Talbott, still resonates: "Well, Paul . . . you just tell the Soviets that you're working for one tough son-of-a-bitch."[100]

Reagan was able to defuse campaign criticism of his arms control position by the simple expedient of scheduling a meeting with the Soviet foreign minister—the first of his presidency—and giving a conciliatory speech about arms control at the United Nations. By now, having been put through the wringer of Reagan's new Cold War, worrying about SDI, and believing in all likelihood they would have to cope with Reagan for another four years, the Soviets were more than eager for a meeting, as it were, with the "good cop." In the meantime, the strong U.S. economic recovery, combined with Mondale's ill-advised pledge to raise taxes once elected, was enough to send the Democrats down to defeat. Reagan won by the largest electoral vote margin in history.

Gorbachev Winds Down the Cold War

Given the cyclical pattern of postwar history, it was predictable enough that Reagan's confrontational first term would be succeeded by a less confrontational second term, a period of détente. What was not at all predictable was that this new détente would resolve itself into the collapse of communism and the end of the Cold War itself. How do we begin to explain this complex turn of events?

Outwardly, what the new Soviet leader Mikhail Gorbachev undertook beginning in March 1985 was not fundamentally new, especially at the beginning. The pattern of internal renewal and external accommodation following a period of protracted outward confrontation and internal repression had been repeated before in Soviet history—at the end of the Civil War under Lenin, following Stalin's death under Malenkov and later Bulganin and Khrushchev, and after the Cuban missile crisis again under Khrushchev. In many respects, the Soviet Union at the time of Konstantin Chernenko's death found itself in circumstances parallel to those after Stalin's death. Isolated politically, diplomatically, and economically, the Soviets had everything to gain from a softening of relations with the external world. Stagnant, corrupt, and ossified within, meanwhile, the system was sorely in need of fresh air.

Yet if history had played itself out according to script, Gorbachev's thaw would have been succeeded by a new freeze. Either Gorbachev himself would have turned, like Khrushchev, toward confrontation, or, like Malenkov, he might have been deposed, to be succeeded by a harder-line leadership. Following the pattern under Eisenhower and later under Johnson and Nixon, meanwhile, the West would have frittered away its position of strength. How was all this avoided?

Certainly there were no indications at the beginning under Gorbachev that the Soviets had any plans of giving up on the Cold War. Fighting in Afghanistan was intensified under him.[101] Arms shipments to Nicaragua actually increased.[102] KGB espionage and "active measures" operations were, if anything, on the upswing.[103] The Soviet military buildup continued at its rapid pace, particularly in the area of strategic nuclear weapons.[104]

Yet one can point, in particular, to four key factors that conspired to make the new détente quite different from the old.

First, influenced by the bad experiences of the past and by a strong suspicion of détente, the Reagan administration—especially Reagan's most conservative advisors—made it extremely difficult for the Soviets, far more difficult than at any time in the past, to achieve accommodation with the United States. The Americans did not shun détente, but they made its price extremely high. By the end of 1988, Gorbachev had handed over an enormous number of concessions. However, he had still not achieved his twin overriding goals of ending the Strategic Defense Initiative and opening large-scale trade with the West. As late as 1989, the Soviet Union had still not gained the Most Favored Nation status that Scoop Jackson had denied them in the 1970s. Between them, Reagan and his advisors played, whether always deliberately or not, another effective variant of the "tough cop/good cop" game, extending the "carrot" without ever quite giving it away. They accomplished in practice what Nixon and Kissinger had set out in theory but never managed to execute.

Second, partly owing to the general shift in the balance of power, partly owing to their special fear of SDI, the Soviets after 1985 were never at the point where they could afford to reverse course and revert to confrontation. This was true both in a narrow military and a broader economic sense. From the narrower military standpoint, Gorbachev—or a hard-line replacement—lacked a *Sputnik,* a military-technological breakthrough that would permit the Soviets to repeat Khrushchev's performance and turn the tables on the United States. On the contrary, with each passing year, the American advantage in high technology weaponry appeared to be increasing.[105] Meanwhile, the Soviet Union was falling desperately behind in the world economy, especially in the high-technology industries that were coming to dominate the world's "second industrial revolution." Particularly after the Reagan administration effort to strengthen Western export controls in the early 1980s, the Soviets needed good relations with the United States in order to get large-scale access to technology and capital in Europe and Asia.

Third, faced with insurmountable internal difficulties, the Soviets, apparently, were losing heart for the struggle. Few in the West understood the depth of the Soviet economic crisis in the mid-1980s, though Reagan later claimed to have sensed it from the intelligence briefings he received.[106] The Soviets must have sensed that a return to external confrontation and internal totalitarianism simply could not solve their problems. There was also perhaps a simple human unwillingness on the part of Gorbachev's generation to return to the rigors of Stalinism. As had been true in a far less fundamental sense for the United States in the 1970s, the sense of strategic and moral failure tended to go hand in hand. Knowing that they were losing the superpower economic and arms race made the charge of evil empire sting all the more deeply.

Fourth, there was Gorbachev himself. Two qualities, in particular, proved important—first, his radicalism,[107] and, second, his tactical skill. A hugely ambitious man envisioning himself as a kind of second Lenin,[108] Gorbachev was willing to tinker with the existing Soviet system to an unprecedented degree. Rearranging the nuts and bolts of the structure, he eventually undermined its stability. At the same time, despite actions that undercut Soviet power, he was able repeatedly to outmaneuver his domestic opponents and remain in office. Frequently, Gorbachev would use the credit he had built in foreign relations—in particular, the relationship with Reagan—to strengthen his position at home. But this was, in a sense, shortsighted, for to win the good relationship with Reagan, Gorbachev made concessions that undermined the long-term power position, and ultimately the very existence, of the Soviet empire, a consequence that by all appearances he did not anticipate.

The Strategic Defense Initiative

The military buildup was important; the American economic recovery was important; the change in rhetoric and tone, especially the reference to the "evil empire," was important; the restrictions on trade were important; the use of American military power in 1983 to remove a Communist government from tiny Grenada was probably not unimportant; the successful deployment of INF missiles in Europe was certainly very important; but nothing weighed more heavily in Soviet geopolitical calculations after 1983 than Reagan's proposal for what eventually became known as the Strategic Defense Initiative.

It was SDI, first, that provided the incentive for the Soviets to resume arms talks. In March 1984, Reagan appointed Air Force Lieutenant General James Abrahamson to head the new SDI program. The ginning up of the SDI program was partly a deliberate move on the part of Reagan's new national security advisor, Robert McFarlane, to restart the arms negotiations.[109] In May, Abrahamson outlined the new program for Congress.[110] The following month, on the same day that army ABM units reported the first successful interception of a ballistic missile warhead in space, Soviet leader Konstantin Chernenko proposed talks on banning antisatellite and space weapons.[111] The United States counterproposed across-the-board talks on arms control. In September, amid the presidential campaign, Gromyko met with Reagan. Then in December, after Reagan's election victory, Mikhail Gorbachev, until then a comparatively unknown member of the Politburo, was given the task of delivering the good news that the Soviets were willing to resume arms talks. The news came in a speech to the British Parliament during Gorbachev's first-ever trip to Great Britain.[112]

Gorbachev's foreign policy focus from the first was on eliminating or curtailing SDI. In meeting with Thatcher (the famous meeting in which the Iron Lady said she could "do business" with him),[113] he concentrated on persuading her against SDI.[114] At his first meeting with Reagan in Geneva, Gorbachev was again centrally occupied with getting Reagan to give up SDI.[115] And the elimination of SDI would be Gorbachev's main objective in what proved to be one of the most peculiar and remarkable summits of the postwar era, the Reykjavik summit of October 1986.

Why were the Soviets so concerned about SDI? With American scientists writing and testifying at great length about the program's supposed infeasibility,[116] one might have thought the Soviets would be happy to watch the United States throw its money down a technological rat hole. But the Soviets did not view the problem in quite this way.

For fifteen years the Soviets had built a vast military-industrial complex, much of which was aimed at one task: creating better and better ballistic missiles. It was a task that the Soviets had mastered well, so well that they had essentially surpassed the Americans in the narrow offensive missile race as McNamara had defined it. Now the rules of the game suddenly threatened to alter. If, of a sudden, the arms race were to shift to defensive technologies stationed in space, the Soviets would essentially have to begin anew. As the West German Sovietologist Christian Schmidt-Häuer wrote in 1986: "For the first time the Soviet Union fears that, although it has so far been able to equal all American innovations in Western technology more quickly than expected, it will be unable to make the leap from simple offensive systems to as yet unknown and cost-intensive defensive systems. All objections to Star Wars can be reduced to one basic formula: Moscow does not wish to have its future overall strategy dictated by the Americans."[117]

Doubtless there were members of the Soviet military-industrial bureaucracy who remembered well the massive American missile surge after *Sputnik,* which it had taken the Soviets essentially a decade and a half to match. What is more, this time around, the Soviets simply did not have the technologies. To be sure, the Soviets had greater operational experience with ABM through their Moscow system and greater capability for putting payloads in space. And in basic research in certain of the most advanced potential SDI technologies, such as particle beams, they were actually ahead.[118] But in microelectronics and computers, the crucial heart of any ABM system, they were hopelessly and irretrievably behind. Moreover, even as they faced new Western restrictions on technology transfer, their own technological infrastructure—the mechanism for translating basic research into mass production items—was hopeless.[119]

To a degree that not even Reagan understood, the SDI proposal spoke to the core of the Soviet inferiority complex. Miraculously, overnight, the SDI speech by itself had shifted the balance of power in a fundamental way, translating vastly superior American technology once again into a political power factor.[120]

The Reagan Style

For much of Reagan's second term, Gorbachev was perceived as winning the propaganda battle—despite the fact that in specific instance after specific instance, Reagan tended to come out on top. The first such test came at the Geneva summit of 1985. At the time, it was expected that the vigorous young Soviet leader would upstage his elderly American counterpart; in the event, the opposite occurred. Reagan's political and public relations victory at Geneva foreshadowed the relationship between the two men as a whole.

The Geneva summit proved to be a U.S. victory on three levels. First, the Reagan administration successfully broke the Nixon-Carter pattern requiring that a summit include the singing of a major arms agreement—thereby showing that some improvement could be achieved in U.S.-Soviet relations without American arms concessions.

Second, at the level of media imagery, Reagan, somewhat to the surprise of the American media, actually outshone his Soviet counterpart. Walking out, coatless, in the wintry Geneva air to greet his bundled Soviet guest—circling an arm behind Gorbachev's back—the American president flawlessly played the one-up role of host, turning the age and vitality issue on its head.

Finally, less obvious at the time but still quite crucial was the broadening of the emphasis in the summit agenda to include issues other than arms control. This accomplishment was largely owing to conscious effort by Reagan's conservative advisors. At a preparatory meeting in Moscow for the resumption of arms talks in 1985, Richard Perle encouraged Secretary of State Shultz to raise the issue of human rights with the Soviets. Donald Fortier, an NSC staffer who later died of cancer, crafted a "regional initiative" designed to highlight the Soviet role in Third World struggles—Afghanistan, Nicaragua, Ethiopia, Angola, and Cambodia—which Reagan put forward in a speech to the UN General Assembly in September 1985. Kenneth Adelman, the arms control director, had helped to persuade Reagan *not* to include a new arms initiative in his UN address, keeping the focus on regional conflict. Shultz became very proficient at unpleasant conversations with the Soviet leader or foreign minister in which the United States simply stated its view that this or that Soviet action in human rights or regional disputes was unacceptable. Eventually the State Department under Shultz's direction developed a formal four-part agenda for U.S.-Soviet relations that was to include, besides arms control, regional issues, human rights, and other elements of bilateral relations.[121] Moreover, Reagan's correspondence with Gorbachev routinely incorporated discussion of regional conflicts.[122]

Perhaps Reagan's finest hour in Geneva consisted in the discussion of regional disputes, where, in his genial way, Reagan accused Gorbachev to his face of sponsoring "genocide" in Afghanistan. (Reagan had, not surprisingly, been particularly appalled by photographs of Afghan children maimed by Soviet mines deliberately disguised as toys and dropped from helicopters.)[123] Reagan's ability to blend hard and soft, to continue his anti-Communist "crusade" even as he attempted to reach Gorbachev at the personal level, expressing genuine cordiality and good nature, probably had much to do with the productive direction in which U.S.-Soviet relations eventually went. (Significantly, Reagan fell down in Geneva on human rights, where he took his old friend Richard Nixon's advice to emphasize "quiet diplomacy.")[124]

Nothing would more clearly foreshadow the end of the Cold War than the gradual shift of the superpower dialogue away from arms control toward "regional" conflicts and human rights.

Soviet Noncompliance

Yet arms control continued to dominate the public and the media's view of superpower relations, almost to the exclusion of any other issue. Nothing showed this more clearly than the overwhelmingly emotional reaction to Reagan's decision in the spring of 1986 to jettison SALT II.

Reagan, of course, had campaigned against SALT II. Most of his key arms advisors in his second term—Nitze, Perle, Adelman, Rowny—had made names for themselves in the 1970s opposing it. Almost inexplicably, however, upon assuming office in 1981, Reagan had been led to approve a statement declaring that the United States would not act to undercut SALT II so long as the Soviets did the same. The influence here came from Haig—always willing, in Kissingerian fashion, to pay lip service to arms control in deference to U.S. allies—and Admiral Bobby Inman, deputy CIA director, who sat in on the meeting in place of the far more conservative William Casey. Haig and Inman had argued (not without some basis) that nothing in U.S. plans envisioned going beyond SALT II. They added that in the meantime the treaty might marginally restrain the Soviets.[125]

The latter point did not prove to be true—first, because as numerous members of Reagan's own administration had once argued, the SALT II limits were too high to provide meaningful restraints, and, second, because the Soviets would end up violating the treaty anyway.

Since 1984, under congressional mandate, the Reagan administration had been issuing both classified and unclassified reports on Soviet violations of various arms agreements. The Reagan reports reflected two changes—not only a new willingness by an American administration to publicize Soviet violations (previous administrations had swept ambiguous situations under the rug),[126] but also an increase in the actual seriousness of Soviet contravention of the agreements. As it happens, the Soviets violated virtually every arms agreement of the nuclear era in some way (even the Limited Test Ban, under which they continued carelessly and illegally to vent radioactive gases from their underground nuclear tests).[127] But the new violations of the ABM Treaty and SALT II in the 1980s were particularly serious.

Nothing showed the one-sided agenda of the American arms control community more clearly than its tendency to whitewash Soviet violations of arms agreements. When the Reagan administration cited Soviet violations, anger was inevitably directed not at the Soviet Union for violating the agreements, but at the Reagan administration for daring to bring the subject up. Not only was doubt expressed about the veracity of the administration's findings—despite careful sifting of evidence and extensive interagency debate before the publication of charges—but it was argued that merely to raise the subject of Soviet violations was to put future agreements in jeopardy.[128] Within the government, arms control partisans fought bitterly to prevent publication of the violations; when violations were publicized, arms controllers outside the government lambasted the administration for doing so. (When, in October, of 1989 Soviet foreign minister Eduard Shevardnadze finally admitted that the Soviets' large phased-array radar in Krasnoyarsk as an "open violation"[129] of the ABM Treaty, there was, or should have been, egg on many American faces, since for five years the arms control community and its allies in the Executive Branch and the Congress had played down the significance of the Krasnoyarsk installation.) The Krasnoyarsk radar violation of the ABM Treaty was particularly blatant. The several-football-field-size radar grossly contravened the careful provisions on early warning radars that Nitze had helped craft in the treaty so as to provide a trip-wire, or early warning, of Soviet intention to break out. Indeed, taken in conjunction with a host of other questionable ABM activities, Krasnoyarsk suggested, as the presidential report on noncompliance noted, that the Soviets "may be preparing" an ABM defense of their territory.[130] (One suspects that if Reagan had not proposed SDI, the Soviets would have pursued illicit ABM activities even more energetically; as it was, the threat of SDI provided an incentive for Soviet self-restraint.)

The violations of SALT II were equally important. In particular, instead of limiting their modernization to the permitted one "new type" of ICBM, the Soviets tested and would eventually deploy two. They had also encrypted missile telemetry to the point of impeding verification. And they were careless enough also to violate the overall numerical limit in the treaty.[131] At the time SALT II ratification was under debate, arms controllers such as Paul Warnke had heralded the "new type" and "encryption" provisions as breakthroughs;[132] yet when the Soviets violated the same provisions, Warnke and others dismissed the provisions in question as "tangential" to the "core elements" of the treaty.[133] They were, in the words of another arms controller, "militarily insignificant technical violations."[134]

Such was the arms control community's prescription for U.S. security: One was supposed to be willing to accept unequal provisions in arms treaties; then one was supposed to act with even more self-restraint than the treaty provisions required (as Warnke had explicitly recommended to Congress after SALT I); and then when the Soviets violated the agreements, one was supposed to turn a blind eye or at least keep publicly silent.

When in the spring of 1986 Reagan officially ended American compliance with SALT II—given his natural instincts as a politician, somewhat reluctantly—the arms control community in Washington bristled with alarmist predictions, which the media faithfully reproduced. Apocalyptic forecasts that the SALT II decision would, in Warnke's words "open the floodgates for massive Soviet increases"[135] were repeated in the newspaper and on the Senate and House floor. According to Warnke, the Soviets would respond to the American decision by expanding their arsenal by 10,000 ballistic-missile warheads (they did not even yet possess 10,000 deployed strategic warheads). Referring to the administration's SALT decision, Warnke declared, "the nuts have won."[136]

Yet not only did the apocalyptic predictions of the arms control community fail to come true (the Soviets were already building new missiles too rapidly to be able to accelerate the process),[137] but two days after the decision, the Soviets tabled a new and more forthcoming proposal in the strategic arms talks.[138] If anything, the jettisoning of SALT added to American bargaining leverage.

Reagan, Gorbachev, and SDI

Of course, the primary Soviet concern continued to be the Strategic Defense Initiative. From 1985 to 1988, Gorbachev's hope that he could persuade or compel Reagan to give up SDI drove Soviet diplomacy forward. SDI was both stick and carrot: Its prospective deployment frightened the Soviets; its prospective derailment seemed, irrationally perhaps, a potential answer to their many problems.

Yet two major barriers existed to Reagan's abandonment of SDI. First, there were the conservatives inside and outside the administration, who, whether with justification or not, increasingly came to see SDI as the key to future American security. As Adelman writes, SDI "had gone from being a Pentagon research program to a conservative cause."[139] The second, and far more important, barrier was Reagan himself.

Reagan's own understanding of SDI, not widely grasped at the time even within the U.S. government, was quite peculiar. Others, including McFarlane, saw SDI as a kind of technological goad to the Soviets, to be traded eventually for arms control concessions.[140] Not so Reagan. For Reagan, SDI transcended politics and transcended arms. Somehow it became linked in his mind with disarmament and his dream of a nuclear-free world.

In the end, Reagan's view of nuclear arms issues amounted to an odd amalgam of ideas[141]—fortunately ballasted by enough instinctive feel for traditional power politics and sufficiently checked by his conservative advisors within the government not to have led to disaster. The president was, for one thing, perfectly serious about the idea of "sharing" SDI with the Soviets—despite the fact that this would have made available to them some of the most advanced military technologies America could produce.[142] He was also perfectly serious about the idea of eventually eliminating nuclear arms.[143] Eventually, Reagan envisioned building SDI in conjunction with a program of radical disarmament. As both sides disarmed, both sides would build missile defenses. As Reagan liked to say "We all got together in 1925 and banned the use of poison gas. But we all kept our gas masks."[144] No one had really eliminated poison gas, of course, but one got the idea. Ironically, the view in the arms debate closest to Reagan's own was that of Jonathan Schell, who had written a follow-up to his *Fate of the Earth*, called *The Abolition*, outlining just such a scheme of combining radical disarmament with the erection of strategic defenses.[145]

The Reagan idea was formalized in a proposal linking abolition of ballistic missiles to postponement in SDI deployment, which was sent to Gorbachev in late July 1986[146] and put forward in a Reagan speech to the UN General Assembly in September.[147] (There were two surprises here: The zero ballistic missile idea actually originated at the Pentagon, in effect as another "zero option," and was made public long before its coming to light at Reykjavik seemed to surprise everyone.)[148]

How a conservative president like Reagan arrived at the same formula for world peace as a utopian writer like Jonathan Schell remains something a mystery; how the United States managed to go through four summit meetings with such a visionary at the helm without suffering a major strategic or political setback is another. As it happens, disaster came quite close at Reykjavik. But two things might be said. First, in contrast to more conventional thinkers about disarmament, Reagan somehow understood that a kind of enforcement mechanism would be necessary in a nonnuclear world: Distrustful of treaties,[149] he sensed that parchment would never be enough. Some kind of physical "insurance" would be required: hence SDI. Ironically, his insistence on physical insurance—in a form obnoxious to the Soviets—saved him from the consequences of his own visionary hopes for a nonnuclear world. Second, Reagan, an old negotiator, must have grasped instinctively that SDI was the source of his bargaining leverage with Gorbachev. The moment he gave SDI up, Reagan must have sensed, the party would be over. In the meantime, his dream of a nonnuclear world—and, as it were the characteristically American good nature involved in this new version of the 1946 Baruch Plan, when the Truman administration offered to give up the bomb itself—served as a kind of "carrot" drawing Gorbachev in. Given Gorbachev's need of détente for reasons of his own, the Soviet leader was led to make more and more concessions. Almost inadvertently, Reagan and his conservative advisors had begun to play a game of good cop-tough cop—holding out hope of major concessions while failing in the final analysis to produce them.

For Gorbachev, meanwhile, nothing would have served better than a comprehensive arms settlement involving the effective abandonment or crippling limitation of SDI. In one fell swoop, such an agreement would have vindicated his leadership in the eyes of the most hard-line elements in the apparatus, the military, the KGB, as well as in the eyes of the Soviet populace as a whole. With such an agreement, he would have ended the presumed major threat to Soviet military preeminence into the twenty-first century while at the same time bringing symbolic "peace" to his country. And he would almost certainly have opened the doors again to the promise of capital and technology flows from the West that had marked the Nixon-Kissinger détente, and on which the Soviet Union was now desperately counting.

Ironically, this was precisely the agreement that many of Reagan's less conservative advisors wished to see. McFarlane implemented the SDI program with the precise objective of making such a deal. Under the name "grand compromise," it would essentially have repeated the ABM pattern—trading fresh limits on strategic defenses for offensive weapons limits, or rather cuts. Nitze was another advocate of this approach.[150]

Yet there is reason to suppose that the "grand compromise" was exactly what the United States needed to avoid if it was to put relations with the Kremlin on a better footing. Not only would the grand compromise have appeared to vindicate Gorbachev's program of "reforming" the existing Communist system (as opposed to leaving communism and the Soviet imperial structure behind), but it might well have inaugurated another Nixon-Kissinger style détente. (Such a détente was precisely what advisors such as Michael Deaver and the president's wife, Nancy, hoped for.)[151] The outward technological thrust of the American arms effort would have been blunted. The West would have become more forthcoming with economic aid to the Soviet Union and at the same time felt subtly that its security had been diminished. Just possibly the Kremlin power structure would have survived. Whether the grand compromise in 1988 was enough to save the Soviet Union is not at all certain. But clearly that was Gorbachev's intention. And it is worth remembering the most revolutionary Soviet reforms—in particular, elections—came after START failed to materialize in 1988.

It was in the hopes of achieving, or forcing, a grand compromise, that Gorbachev invited Reagan to a summit in Reykjavik.

The Reykjavik Drama

Reykjavik originated in the least auspicious of circumstances. In the fall of 1986, Reagan accepted Gorbachev's sudden and less than cordial invitation, amid a small superpower crisis over the imprisonment of *U.S. News* Moscow correspondent Nick Daniloff, to meet in some European city (Gorbachev suggested London or Reykjavik) ostensibly to prepare for the summit that had previously been promised for Washington. The invitation came not only at an awkward time—the Soviets had arrested Daniloff in unjustifiable retaliation for the FBI capture of a real Soviet spy—but also in a particularly unappealing form. Adelman later described Gorbachev's letter to Reagan including the invitation—since reprinted only in part in Reagan's memoirs[152]—as the harshest of the Reagan-Gorbachev correspondence.[153] Reagan's readiness to snap up the invitation clearly indicated a certain impatience for further contact with Gorbachev.

The Reykjavik summit proved to be one of the more dramatic and peculiar episodes in modern diplomacy. In two days and nights of meetings at Hofdi House in the Icelandic capital, Reagan and Gorbachev, each with a high-level arms control team working into the wee hours of the morning, engaged in some of the most free-wheeling and radical diplomacy of the twentieth century. The two leaders seriously discussed the total elimination of nuclear arms and the total elimination of ballistic missiles over a ten-year time frame; the main features of a START agreement specifying 50 percent cuts in ballistic-missile warheads were hammered out; and a compromise was reached that soon led to an INF or Euromissile Treaty.

In retrospect, the Soviet game plan for the meeting seemed simple enough, indeed almost too simple—though almost no one on the American side had apparently foreseen it.[154] Gorbachev went to Reykjavik with the intention of offering Reagan a series of radical arms proposals that at the last minute he planned to link to severe restrictions on SDI. Gorbachev's target, once again, was the Strategic Defense Initiative. The Soviet leader's aim was to force Reagan to relinquish SDI or risk public opprobrium of standing in the way of radical arms cuts. The plan backfired: Reagan refused the deal on the grounds that it would kill SDI. Gorbachev's attempt to put Reagan on the spot at Reykjavik actually *strengthened* American public support for SDI,[155] while the two leaders' radical discussions of arms control created in Western Europe, for the first time in memory, anxiety that the arms talks were progressing too *quickly*.[156]

Most surprising, however, was American behavior at the meeting. That this avowedly most conservative of postwar presidents would engage in free-wheeling face-to-face talks about total nuclear disarmament with the General Secretary of the Soviet Communist Party was something few would have predicted in 1981. Reagan, moreover, was not alone in feeling exhilaration in these negotiations. Shultz was visibly—indeed for public relations purposes, somewhat too visibly—disappointed when the agreements outlined at Reykjavik failed at the last minute to materialize. And Nitze, that dean of American arms negotiators, remembered the summit as "more fun than I've almost ever had."[157]

In retrospect, the Reykjavik experience suggests that the Baruch Plan—the original 1946 American proposal to eliminate nuclear arms—represented something more integral to the American character than it might have appeared at first glance. After all, the essential reality of the nuclear age had been Soviet *resistance* to meaningful arms control. When at Reykjavik the Soviets showed serious willingness to discuss major arms reductions, the floodgates of American enthusiasm seemed to open.

The more responsible elements of the American foreign policy community back home were perhaps rightly appalled at the U.S. performance at the meeting—though more reflexive arms controllers were quick to blame the failure of the summit on "Star Wars."[158] To go heedlessly into such discussions and agree to such radical arms cuts in the wee hours of the morning—it was a textbook case on how not to conduct superpower diplomacy. In the end, Reykjavik was a close-run thing. If Reagan had actually embraced such radical arms cuts on the spot—as not only the president but his secretary of state and his most venerable arms advisor (Nitze) were apparently prepared to do—the blow to Western self-confidence would have been severe. As it was, Reykjavik left the NATO allies shuddering.[159] Only Reagan's commitment to SDI, and his more conservative advisors' last-minute indication that the deal would cost him this program, prevented a debacle. When asked what quality he prized most in his generals, Napoleon once answered "luck." Reagan was nothing if not a lucky general.

Reagan's "Teflon" (to recall Representative Pat Schroeder's famous metaphor) was in fine working order, and, despite the cries from the arms control community that "Star Wars" had "sunk" the summit, all of this flowed off his back—at least as far as the average American citizen was concerned. Despite everything, Reagan emerged from the Reykjavik summit without undue public relations damage. Once again, in other words, Gorbachev had challenged Reagan, in effect, to a political duel, and, however close it may have been, Reagan once again had somehow come out ahead.

The Key Role of SDI

It remains remarkable in retrospect to what degree superpower diplomacy continued to be driven by Reagan's idea of an antimissile shield. Gorbachev would seemingly have done anything to destroy the program; Reagan seemingly would do anything to keep it. It was remarkable what resources were being marshalled on both sides, what lengths were being gone to, over what remained thus far little more than a presidential fantasy. And yet it was not surprising once one recognized that what SDI symbolized or embodied above all was potential American power, American technological capacity, which the Soviets feared.

The role of SDI lent a peculiar kind of symmetry to the story of strategic nuclear arms control. For if America's willingness to give up strategic defenses made strategic arms control possible beginning with the ABM Treaty in the early 1970s, then Reagan's unwillingness to surrender his missile defense idea made strategic arms control impossible in the late 1980s. And while strategic arms control in the 1970s went hand in hand with a steady deterioration of the country's strategic position, then the absence of a strategic arms agreement at the end of the 1980s coincided—for a number of reasons—with an almost miraculous upturn in the country's strategic fortunes. The conventional wisdom had preached that only by controlling strategic weapons, the core of the two states' arsenals, could one stabilize the superpower relationship; but in fact, essentially the opposite proved to be the case. Precisely at the moment when weapons issues became intractable because of American unwillingness to compromise on a key program (SDI), attention on both sides turned instead to political issues such as human rights and regional conflicts, and genuine progress began to be made toward a resolution of the underlying conflict of the Cold War.

SDI operated in two steps. First, it worked to arouse urgent Soviet interest in an arms agreement; then it prevented this arms agreement—at least a big strategic agreement—from coming to fruition. The effect was eventually to encourage the channeling of political energies in a different, more productive direction.

This is by no means to argue that SDI was the only influence operating on the Soviets. But the negative contribution of SDI—in preventing a return to strategic arms control and the détente pattern of the past—was doubtless important in forcing substantive attention to the underlying political conflicts.

As ever, Gorbachev was the one making the major concessions—though most did not understand this at the time. Three months after the failure of Reykjavik, Gorbachev reversed himself and offered yet another concession, raising the possibility of a separate Euromissile or INF Treaty "de-linked" from a settlement on SDI.[160]

Evidently Gorbachev had concluded that the requirement for political détente—and some kind of partial arms agreement to formalize it—was more urgent than the need to cripple SDI, for the time being. Such surprise gestures were typical of his new flexibility. However, Gorbachev was continually achieving short-term political victories at the expense of the longer-term power position of the Soviet Union, though, again, this was far from apparent at the time. In a sense, Gorbachev was living off the capital of fear built up by his predecessors. The view of him in the West—in Gromyko's famous phrase—as having a "nice smile" but with "iron teeth"[161] was shaped less by his own actions than by the fear aroused by the system he represented.

In the long run, Gorbachev's "de-linking" of INF actually lessened the pressure on the Reagan administration for major arms control, and for concessions on SDI, in two ways. First, it allowed the administration to satisfy the Establishment and public hunger for arms control without giving up SDI or signing a START agreement. Thinking ahead to the 1988 election, Republican strategists doubtless were hoping for some kind of arms agreement to take into the campaign. Politically speaking, the comparatively limited INF agreement satisfied this requirement. However visionary Reagan might have been, he was primarily a politician. With the arms control "requirement," so to speak, essentially filled, the overriding imperative to push hard for START or a comprehensive strategic agreement was no longer present.

Second, INF actually inoculated the political system against START. Especially coming on the heels of the seemingly wild Reykjavik summit, the arms reductions embodied in the INF "zero option" actually aroused a measure of anxiety in Western political elites, both here and in Europe. Support for agreement among informed opinion was far from unanimous. The NATO commander retired and opposed it;[162] respected figures such as Brent Scowcroft and Congressman Les Aspin spoke out against it;[163] even Nixon and Kissinger teamed up to express public reservations.[164] While Reagan was able to win overwhelming Senate support for the treaty, many senators issued public statements suggesting that they would not look as favorably on "deep reductions" in a future strategic arms treaty.[165] Senate examination of the INF Treaty highlighted the far more serious verification problems inherent in START.[166]

Reagan and the Republicans made much of the claim that the INF Treaty was a different kind of arms treaty because it embodied actual "reductions" in weapons.[167] But in reality, INF had many of the liabilities we have seen in other arms agreements of the twentieth century.

First, the agreement was attended by a bad political odor. The endgame of the INF negotiations came during the height of the Iran-Contra scandal. Indeed, 1987, the year of the INF Treaty, was in fact the weakest year of the Reagan presidency. Whether timed deliberately or not, Gorbachev's offer to "de-link" INF on February 28, 1987, had the appearance of a life preserver thrown by the Soviet leader to an American president besieged by a potentially Watergate-style scandal. The offer appeared to be snapped up by the White House in just such a spirit. Whether justifiably or not, Reagan seemed throughout the period to be acting out of weakness.

Second, the INF endgame imposed serious strains on relations between Washington and Bonn—particularly over the issue of seventy-two Pershing Ia missiles owned by the West Germans, which Gorbachev insisted on making part of the agreement.

In reality, the prospect of arms "reductions" was not all that consoling to Western European elites as long as the basic Soviet threat remained. In 1987, the Cold War still seemed to be going strong, even if changes were beginning to be seen in the Soviet Union and the INF Treaty marked a kind of temporary thaw. Quite naturally, the prospect of losing American missiles that everyone had fought so hard to deploy fostered anxiety among defense-minded European elites—notwithstanding that the Soviets were going to be destroying an even greater number of missiles as part of the deal. "At the governmental level in Paris, London, and Bonn," wrote James Markham of the *New York Times*, "there is something approaching dread that the Reagan administration, partly out of domestic necessity, is taking decisions that, willy-nilly, will undermine NATO's deterrence doctrine and lead to a radically diminished American commitment to the defense of Europe."[168]

Moreover, from the perspective of friends and allies in Asia, the Reagan administration came perilously close to concluding a self-evidently bad deal. The tentative INF agreement, as it emerged from the confusions of the Reykjavik summit, envisioned retention of 100 warheads on both sides, though none in Europe. On the Soviet side, this meant 33 SS-20 missiles aimed at Asia. (Under the deal, the United States retained an empty right to deploy Pershing IIs in Alaska—hardly an attractive option.) Not only was this read in the Pacific as an American betrayal of Asian interests,[169] but it posed many of the problems of verification that Perle had sought to evade through the zero option formula.

Eventually the Americans persuaded the Soviets to accept "true zero"[170]—that is, a ban on both intermediate-range missiles and a second tier of slightly shorter-range intermediate-range missiles—one suspects by convincing them that anything short of zero would run into serious trouble in the Senate.[171] But Gorbachev played a tactically strong hand by proposing a third "zero," insisting on inclusion of some West German missiles (Pershing Ias) not originally meant to be part of the deal. Recognizing the White House's urgent desire for the agreement, and pressured by their own coalition partners to sacrifice the missiles, West German conservatives eventually caved in on the Pershing Ias, but not without experiencing bitterness and a strong sense of betrayal.[172] Gorbachev had evidently hoped to create momentum toward "denuclearization" of Europe with his INF gambit, and his pressure succeeded. West German support for NATO's nuclear doctrine was significantly weakened by the episode. It was well that NATO did not have to depend for too many more years on the threat of nuclear "first use" to counter a threat from the Warsaw Pact.[173]

The ascendancy of arms control coincided with the ascendancy of Gorbachev. The Washington summit, during which the INF Treaty was signed, was the one moment in the Gorbachev-Reagan relationship in which the Soviet leader seemed to dominate. Washington was aflutter with "Gorbymania."[174] The Soviet leader did his best to play to the Western media, suddenly stepping from his ZIL limousine on Connecticut Avenue to work the crowd in the manner of a Western politician.

Yet the occasion was not free of Soviet threats. If Reagan failed to give up SDI, Novosti Press Agency head Valentin Falin told Flora Lewis of the *New York Times*:

> We won't copy you any more, making planes to catch up with your planes, missiles to catch up with your missiles. We'll take asymmetrical means with new scientific principles available to us. Genetic engineering could be a hypothetical example. Things can be done for which neither side could find defenses or countermeasures, with very dangerous results.
>
> If you develop something in space, we could develop something on earth. These are not just words. I know what I'm saying.[175]

It was discordant moments such as this that made the Washington summit a still-uncomfortable experience, redolent of the ambiguity of the Nixon-Kissinger years.

Reagan's Final Victory

The conventional wisdom of two decades would have suggested that a strategic arms or START Treaty was essential if relations between the United States and the Soviet Union were to move to a new level. But essentially the opposite proved to be the case. Indeed, while by 1988, the collapse of communism may already have been foreordained by destiny, perhaps the only thing that might have forestalled or delayed this climactic event was the conclusion of a START Treaty and a debilitating compromise on SDI. For only this might have altered the balance of power, which until now had been shifting steadily against the Soviet Union. There is little question but that the START treaty in 1988 would have had a profound psychological effect in the West, and not necessarily a beneficial one. Among Reagan's enemies as well as his friends, the signing of START would have been read almost universally, for better or worse, as marking a return to full-fledged Nixon-style détente, complete with new trade agreements, Most Favored Nation status, expanded scientific exchanges, and so forth. It was precisely such a détente that the Establishment craved and that Reagan's conservative supporters abominated. It proved to be the path not taken.

Two new factors now stood in the way of START: increasing restiveness from Reagan's natural political allies outside the government[176] and increasing reservations expressed within by the joint chiefs of staff.[177] The chiefs were particularly concerned about (1) the uncertainties still hanging over the U.S. ballistic missile modernization program and (2) the status of Sea-Launched Cruise Missiles in the agreement. The U.S. intelligence community was also upset about a lack of resources for monitoring the complex new treaty.[178] Within the government, Nitze and Shultz still attempted to push the treaty forward (even as Weinberger resisted). Outside the government, meanwhile, experts worried that the START cuts would not actually be stabilizing, as advertised, and would pose major problems of verification.[179]

While Reagan may have entertained a vague desire for total nuclear disarmament, he was apparently not eager in the twilight days of his administration to undertake a major battle both with his conservative allies and the joint chiefs. Besides, the Soviets—perhaps ambivalent themselves about the purely military implications of the planned reductions—were proving less than forthcoming in the negotiations.[180] In late February, the president sought publicly to dampen expectations that START would be completed in time for the coming Moscow summit.[181]

As in the case of the INF or Euromissile deal, Gorbachev continued to set politics and symbolism ahead of arms control substance. With or without the START Treaty, he evidently deemed it essential to keep the momentum toward accommodation alive, which meant another summit (though he nearly cancelled the meeting over the continued anti-Communist and human rights themes in Reagan speeches—the president even amid accommodation was keeping elements of the "tough cop" approach alive).[182] Yet a summit had to have content, and in the absence of a START Treaty other issues naturally came to the fore. These proved to be human rights and the Soviet war in Afghanistan.

In the long run, the changes introduced by Gorbachev into Soviet human rights practices during these years had a far more profound effect on Western security than all the arms negotiations of the 1980s, for in the long run these changes undermined the very power and legitimacy of the Soviet totalitarian regime. As this story has emphasized again and again, it was never the weapons themselves, but always the regime that wielded them that posed the real threat. What lay behind Gorbachev's *perestroika*? In part, Gorbachev's policy merely repeated past "thaws," under Lenin, under Khrushchev. In part, it was an effort to appeal to the West, to gain arms and trade concessions. But in part, too, the Gorbachev human rights policy constituted an effort to become a more "normal" country. This was significant, for Gorbachev and his generation had subtly begun to accept the West's—and not Marxism-Leninism's—definition of normalcy.

In the final analysis, though internal factors were obviously crucial, it is hard not to see Gorbachev's *glasnost* as something of a response to Reagan's claim that democracy was the wave of the future, and the president's effective "proving" of this claim through economic recovery and a rebuilding of American military strength. Only against the background of American economic recovery and renewed military power were the flaws and historical weaknesses of the Soviet system fully revealed to the Soviet elite. In effectively losing the military race, the Soviets knew that they had lost the future.

One other reason the Soviets may have permitted so many internal changes was a certain overconfidence in their ability both to manipulate Western opinion and to control matters at home. Certainly by 1987, Gorbachev was outdistancing Reagan in Western opinion polls.[183] In a rather bald statement of Soviet policy goals on the eve of the Washington summit, Georgi Arbatov wrote in the *New York Times* of a new Soviet "secret weapon":

> And here we have a "secret weapon" that will work almost regardless of the American response—we would deprive America of The Enemy. And how would you justify without it the military expenditures that bleed the American economy white, a policy that draws America into dangerous adventures overseas and drives wedges between the United States and its allies, not to mention the loss of American influence on neutral countries? Wouldn't such a policy in the absence of The Enemy put America in the position of an outcast in the international community?[184]

The still-hostile tone of Arbatov's remark clearly partook of the Cold War. The Soviets apparently saw American power as deriving from their own challenge to the West (a theme present in Soviet thinking at least since the days of Malenkov).[185] But Arbatov was, so to speak, overly optimistic about America's dim future in the absence of a Soviet threat, as was Gorbachev, who predicted in his book *Perestroika* that if the superpower competition turned from swords to plowshares, the Soviet Union would win this "final argument."[186] Few predictions have been farther from the mark.

The unwarranted optimism of the Soviet leadership found its counterpart in the unwarranted pessimism of many American conservatives, who thought they understood well enough Gorbachev's foreign policy game plan and who feared it might work. Both misread the balance of power, which was shifting almost irrevocably to the American side.

In April, the United States and the Soviet Union concluded an agreement embodying Soviet withdrawal from Afghanistan. It was not the best agreement. The Soviets withdrew, but years later the war continued to rage, waged by a government armed as a Soviet proxy.

The most important achievement of the Moscow summit itself the following month proved to be simply Reagan's presence there, openly bringing the message of human rights. It was a remarkable contrast to earlier summits, which had preoccupied themselves with signing ceremonies and arms control agreements. Visiting with Soviet dissidents, speaking to students at Moscow state university, Reagan celebrated human rights in much the same terms he had used in the earlier British Parliament speech, speaking of the "information revolution" now dominating the world economy. The "key" to that revolution, Reagan argued, was "freedom—freedom of thought, freedom of information, freedom of communication."[187] It was American freedom that Reagan glimpsed for his audience:

> But freedom doesn't begin or end with elections. Go to any American town, to take just an example, and you'll see dozens of churches, representing many different beliefs—in many places, synagogues and mosques—and you'll see families of every conceivable nationality worshiping together. . . . Go to any courtroom, and there will preside an independent judge, beholden to no government power. . . . Go to any university campus, and there you'll find an open, sometimes heated discussion of the problems of American society. . . . Go into any union hall, where the members know their right to strike is protected by law.[188]

For an American president to utter such words in Moscow beneath a statue of Lenin was, in 1988, a triumph indeed. But it was not a triumph simply of idealism. Reagan had earned the right to be in Moscow at this moment through his arms buildup, by first challenging the Soviets and then beating them, as it were, at their own game. Yet the message was extended with grace, not in a spirit of boasting or accusation (in his eagerness to avoid offense, Reagan blamed Soviet "bureaucracy"[189] for human rights abuses, as if the bureaucracy could somehow be separated from the regime). His clear aim was to encourage, to nurture, the new era opening in Soviet society. "Americans seek always to make friends of old antagonists,"[190] said this president who had been communism's greatest antagonist of the Cold War.

A word should be said about the humanity and good nature inherent in the Reagan approach. To arrive at this point in Moscow, it was not enough to have won, or potentially won, the arms race—though that was clearly essential. It was also important after having won to be willing to extend an open hand—without at the same time undercutting one's position of power. It was necessary not only to practice power politics but to soften power politics with an idealism and goodwill specifically American in nature. Reagan, in combination with his conservative followers, found a way to do this. If Reagan had taken the advice of his most hard-line followers and shunned summitry and rapprochement in any form, the end of the Cold War would probably have been delayed—just as it would have been delayed, even more catastrophically perhaps, if Reagan had taken the not-so-friendly advice of the arms controllers and the Establishment and abandoned his hard-line positions in the early 1980s. In defeat, defiance, Churchill had said; in victory, magnanimity. Such was the Churchillian principle that Reagan, partly by conscious intention, partly by serendipity, observed. There was, in the end, a kind of symbiosis between Reagan's good nature and the hardness of the conservative movement with which he was so closely tied: Together they achieved the most effective fusion of American power and American ideals since Truman.

Yet the path Reagan pursued was not a simple middle course between soft and hard, left and right, arms controller and "hawk." It was an approach, from beginning to end, quite at odds with, indeed almost diametrically opposed to, the liberal-pacifist paradigm, the standard arms control formula. Where the arms control establishment had advocated unilateral restraint as the key to peace, Reagan had pursued a massive military buildup, which indeed continued, at only slightly slower pace, as he visited Moscow. Where the arms control establishment had insisted on shaping negotiating proposals that the Soviets might accept, Reagan put forward proposals considered nonnegotiable. Where the arms control establishment had advised disinvolvement in Third World struggles, Reagan had increased aid to anti-Communist Third World forces from Central America to Afghanistan. Where the arms control establishment had observed a taboo against use of American military force, Reagan had openly employed it. Where the arms control establishment had advocated increased trade with the Soviets, Reagan had severely restricted it. And where the arms control establishment had advocated a muting of Cold War rhetoric, Reagan had branded the Soviet Union an evil empire. In a sense, Reagan's ability to extend effective goodwill had depended on dispelling the arms control paradigm: Only by doing so could he assure that the Soviets would not mistake American goodwill, as they nearly always had in the past, for simple weakness.

It was the man willing to call the Communists an evil empire who was able to bring the message of freedom directly to Moscow. And nothing suggested more clearly the coming triumph of this message than the gradual fading of arms control from the scene.

The ascendancy of the arms control paradigm had coincided with a weakened and self-doubting period in American history, a period of sad domestic turmoil and foreign defeat. The history of arms control showed how easily and how often democracies could be debilitated by certain flawed but appealing ideas. The waning of the arms control idea as the overmastering concept in U.S.-Soviet relations was a symptom of America's—and freedom's—recuperation.

EPILOGUE

❏

The experience of history teaches that when an aggressor sees that he is not being opposed he grows more brazen. Contrariwise when he meets opposition, he calms down. It is this historic experience that must guide us in our actions.

—Nikita Khrushchev, August 7, 1961[1]

The breaching of the Berlin Wall and the spectacular collapse of Communist governments in Eastern Europe in November 1989 brought an end to the Cold War but also raised a question: Had Soviet power simply been an illusion? In a sense, of course, it must have been so, at least for some years. While Gorbachev's policies had clearly undermined Soviet ideology in a way that contributed to rapid disintegration after 1985, "stagnation," to use the Soviet term, had obviously been eating away at the Soviet power structure for some time.

But though in a sense an illusion, at least in recent years, Soviet power had been, paradoxically, no less real. In international affairs, there is no practical distinction between the illusion of power and the reality, as long as the illusion is credited. The history of twentieth-century diplomacy showed this repeatedly—whether in Germany's power under Hitler, which began as an illusion and then became a reality, or in the Soviet Union's power under Khrushchev after *Sputnik,* which began as a partial illusion and was later unmasked as such. International struggle was itself little more than the interplay among ambition, fear, and illusion. War alone—and in the nuclear era, the crisis or showdown[2]—was the arbiter of reality, the unmasker of illusion, the final proof of each nation's true power. But it was an expensive and risky mode of discovery, naturally shunned.

At any rate, it was foolish to awaken from the Cold War and imagine that the Soviet threat of forty-five years had somehow been a simple dream—a creation of hawkish Western "threatmongers."[3] In truth, Soviet power and the illusion of Soviet power had affected Western hawks and doves equally—influencing hawks toward an arms buildup, doves toward measures of arms control and sometimes anxious accommodation. (For example, in 1990, *Time*'s arms control-minded Strobe Talbott, dismissing the Soviet Union, with the benefit of hindsight, as an "ossifying, demoralizing, brutalizing system of institutionalized inefficiency," incapable of posing a serious threat to the West,[4] forgot his warnings only six years earlier that the Soviets were "poised on the starting block" for a technological "race"[5] with the United States in SDI.) One side in the Western debate claimed to fear the Soviet Union, while the other claimed to fear nuclear war or the arms race itself; but both sides were affected by the reality, or perhaps at times the illusion, of Soviet power.

❋ To unmask the illusion of Soviet power, it was necessary to "disprove" it. And to disprove it, it was necessary to rebuild and demonstrate relative American military strength. One saw this pattern not simply under Reagan, but under Kennedy, and before that under Truman and Eisenhower. Indeed, the debate over Reagan's role in the winning of the Cold War becomes less of an issue when placed in the context of earlier Cold War experiences. Previous Soviet "thaws," under Malenkov and Khrushchev from 1953 to 1955 and under Khrushchev again in the mid-1960s, had invariably been preceded by assertive American policies and a shift in the power balance to the Western side. The final "thaw" under Gorbachev was in this respect no different.

At the end of the Cold War, an elemental truth about power should have been clear: It was not enough to call attention to the supposed weaknesses of the playground bully while he continued to terrorize the schoolyard; one had to unmask his weakness by confronting him and forcing him to back down. The failure to understand these elemental realities, so widely and instinctively appreciated by more primitive societies, remained a conspicuous failing of advanced liberal democracies in their conduct of foreign affairs.

The Gulf War

Interestingly, one could see similar phenomena operating in 1989 with Saddam Hussein of Iraq. Just as the collapse of the Berlin Wall brought an end to the story of the Cold War, so the Persian Gulf crisis and war of 1990–1991, precipitated by Iraq's invasion of Kuwait, brought an end to the story of "limited war." If the 1980s controversy over the "nuclear freeze" constituted a "second" Vietnam debate, then the Gulf crisis debate constituted a third.

With some notable exceptions,[6] opinion on the Gulf crisis divided along predictable lines, with key representatives of the arms control Establishment opposing decisive military action and counseling delay. Robert McNamara, for example, warned of "heavy causalities" and recommended an extension of economic sanctions over "12 to 18 months," with the institution of a rotation policy for U.S. troops already massively deployed to the Saudi desert. Reviving his Vietnam era reasoning, McNamara argued that such gradualism would cause Saddam's resolve to collapse before the West's (an unlikely supposition either then or in retrospect, given Saddam's continued willingness to cause mischief even after losing the war).[7]

A conscious attempt to avoid the pitfalls of Vietnam, the Bush administration's war policy, by contrast, marked a return to traditional strategic principles. First, the administration, and especially the president, fully grasped the basic logic of a power struggle with a dictator, even invoking the "Munich" analogy. Second—in contrast to the Establishment approach—the president remained acutely conscious of the factor of *time*, recognizing that a brief "window" existed for decisive action during which Western and Arab morale could be sustained and after which gradual defeat was all but guaranteed. Third, the administration avoided military minimalism or proportionalism, massing forces in the Middle East, as good strategy would dictate, far in excess of the basic level that might be deemed necessary by some abstract calculation. Fourth, while maintaining overall strategic control, it allowed the military proper freedom in executing strategy. Fifth, it avoided gradualism, employing force in a concentrated, massive fashion early in the struggle. Sixth, it played to its own strategic strengths, using air power and precision weapons to maximum advantage before engaging in a land war.[8]

Of course, the Gulf war differed fundamentally from Korea and Vietnam insofar as the administration was able to enlist Soviet support in the crisis (itself something of a diplomatic achievement). But the testimony of McNamara and others strongly suggests that had the Establishment been at the helm, it would have repeated Vietnam-style errors notwithstanding.

The war was doubtless essential: To have left Saddam astride Kuwait and on the border of Saudi Arabia, with a vast army and a well-advanced nuclear weapons program in progress, was not only to leave the world economy hostage to a tyrant but to invite a host of future disasters; including Saddam's imminent development of the atomic bomb. To pursue a policy of simple "containment," as so many Establishment figures urged, would have been to elevate Iraq to the status of a new Soviet Union, feeding the illusion of Saddam's power, while doing nothing to eliminate his nuclear or missile assets. Fortunately, the war, especially well managed, proved far cheaper, in American lives, than anyone could have hoped. To gain victory with no more than 124 killed in action (and 207 lost as a result of accidents) was a remarkable achievement indeed. It showed the efficacy of traditional strategic principles, the value of the Reagan military buildup, the logic of advancing, rather than retarding, Western military technologies, and the virtues of possessing, in Churchill's phrase, a "preponderance of power" over inimical forces. And, like victories in the past, the Gulf war had a revivifying effect on national morale, exorcising the ghosts of Vietnam.

However, the Bush administration did not entirely overcome the paradox of "limited war"—though its model of war limitation fortunately resembled Eisenhower's more than the Kennedy-Johnson alternative. The Bush administration stopped the war before Saddam Hussein had been removed from power. While this early end to the war may have been preferable to further action involving greater American casualties and certainly the complications of an extended occupation of Iraq, it left the original problem incompletely solved. The relevant analogy was Indochina in 1954: The problem had been cut down to size; but containment of a diminished Saddam would require sustained attention in the future; and further strategic errors were possible down the road, especially as overall American military power declined.

Disarmament and Proliferation

"It is the greatest mistake," Churchill had said in 1934, "to mix up disarmament with peace. . . . Europe will be secure when nations no longer feel themselves in great danger, as many of them do now. Then the pressure and the burden of armaments will fall away automatically, as they ought to have done in a long peace; and it might be quite easy to seal a movement of that character by some general agreement."[9]

Had the West finally arrived at this moment? The disappearance of Mikhail Gorbachev's Soviet Union and the rise of Boris Yeltsin's Russia and the Commonwealth of Independent States at the end of 1991 seemed to herald the dawn of a new era. Now, at last, radical reductions in nuclear weapons seemed possible—perhaps urgently desirable, given the instabilities of the former Soviet Union. The notion of minimal deterrence articulated by George F. Kennan in 1950—neither possible nor appropriate during the Cold War—appeared a logical choice in a post–Cold War world where Communist imperialism no longer threatened the survival of freedom, and the main hope of civilized nations would be to keep the nuclear Pandora's box closed. Remarks by Yeltsin at the end of January 1992 suggested the possibility not only of major nuclear disarmament measures but even of cooperation with Russia on global defenses against nuclear missles. Ronald Reagan's once-quixotic dream of a world combining significant nuclear disarmament with a protective umbrella of missile defenses suddenly seemed a real possibility. Indeed, even more ambitious forms of cooperation seemed conceivable.[10]

The crucial change, of course, had been political. As critics of the arms control paradigm had argued throughout the Cold War, arms were never the cause of conflict, but always merely a symptom. The arms race was not the product of a "mutual" misunderstanding, but of the driving ambitions of one side. The change in the Russian outlook demonstrated the truth of this proposition. So long as the Soviet Union, with its inherent hostility to the West, remained, an arms race was inevitable. However, once attitudes within the Soviet Union had fundamentally altered—altered so fundamentally that the Soviet Union could no longer survive—nuclear disarmament on a major scale became not only a possibility, but a certainty.

Hopeful possibilities now abounded, but dangers had by no means entirely disappeared. The end of the Soviet Union did not mean the end of power politics, or of the nuclear danger.

First, there was Russia itself. The emergence of a democratic Russian nationalism in the wake of Communist rule was a development of enormous propitiousness and importance. But whether Yeltsin and his democratic allies in the Russian leadership could survive the rigors of the Russian economic transformation remained unclear, and the possibility of a neo-facist reaction or a military coup in Russia could not be entirely excluded. Under almost any conceivable circumstance, Russia would retain a significant nuclear arsenal. With a hostile government at the helm in that country, nuclear blackmail might again become a factor in world politics. Like Weimar Germany in the 1920s, the former Soviet Union would require massive infusions of Western aid merely to avoid chaos and would harbor instabilities for years to come.

Second, there was China. As the United States embarked on nuclear disarmament, it had to take care not to reduce its arsenal to the point of transforming China—still under totalitarian rule—into a nuclear super-power. China's nuclear capabilities—including an ICBM capability—continued to grow,[11] while its government ruthlessly repressed its populace and nurtured irredentist ambitions toward neighboring Taiwan.

Third, nuclear and other mass-destruction weapons were spreading. It was ironic that at the very moment that the West had succeeded in vanquishing Soviet communism, mass-destruction weapons were passing into the hands of other tyrannical and aggressive states. At the time of the Gulf war, for example, Iraq was possibly within as little as a year of creating a nuclear weapon. The State Department indicated that a North Korean atomic bomb might be as little as two years away.[12] In the Middle East, Iran pursued a nuclear program, while Syria continued to add to its missile force. The breakup of the Soviet Union threatened to aggravate the problem, with elements of the old Soviet military-industrial complex potentially selling nuclear hardware in exchange for Third World cash.

It was important that in focusing on new hopes for nuclear disarmament, the United States not overlook these other dangers. It was important, in particular, that disarmament and defense cutbacks not undercut the ability of the United States to project conventional power or fight a conventional war.

In the wake of the Gulf victory and the Soviet breakup, it was tempting to imagine, as Western democracies had always imagined after similar victories in war and peace, that military power was finally becoming less necessary in the world, indeed almost obsolete. With the collapse of the Soviet threat, Congress seemed in the mood to slash away at American defense programs relentlessly. Several factors contributed: the continued prevalence of "liberal-pacifist" thinking in both the Senate and (especially) the House, resurgent American isolationism, perhaps justifiable dismay at massive deficits, and a general sense that domestic problems were being neglected.

With the totalitarian threat removed, was not the world destined to be a safer place? With democracy expanding on every continent, could not the United States finally afford to let down its guard? Circumstances in 1991, after all, resembled those of the 1920s, when even comparative realists such as Churchill had pressed for military cuts.

But the lessons of the 1920s were perhaps as germane to the post–Cold War era as the lessons of the 1930s had been to the era of the Cold War. The decline of Western militaries and the disappearance of American power from Europe and the Pacific in the 1920s had created a power vacuum for other states to fill. American withdrawal had proved to be a major blunder and an important cause of World War II. Would the pattern be repeated?

In 1991, the world was much smaller than in the 1920s, in a military as well as a cultural and economic sense. A Japanese invasion of Manchuria could be viewed with comparative complacency by Western powers in 1931, as unwise as this complacency may have been; an Iraqi invasion of Kuwait in 1990 manifestly could not. Could the world economy afford to lose Taiwan, with the destabilization of the Pacific Basin that would necessarily follow? Was a war in Korea something from which the United States could easily stand aside? Moreover, technology was bringing military dangers closer and closer to home: A single renegade state with nuclear bombs or long-range missiles could pose a global threat. By the end of the millennium, according to *Russian* estimates, fifteen to twenty states or more would possess ballistic missiles; half of these states would have missiles of 5,000-mile range or more.[13] U.S. estimates were substantially the same.[14] Arms control nonproliferation measures, while worth pursuing and strengthening, might do little ultimately to prevent the efforts of determined authoritarian regimes to obtain the bomb, as shown by the examples of North Korea and Iraq.

The United States had a choice; following the apparent inclination in Congress, it could massively disarm, waiting until dangers landed on the doorstep, tolerating increasing global instability and the inevitable decline in its own influence. Or following more prudent advice, it could continue to extend a more modest but still solid umbrella of stability over the globe. The ability to repeat the Gulf war performance—with the logistical capability, the comfortable superiority of global forces, and the life-saving advantage in technologies such as "Stealth"—was the test. One did not want a mere "balance" between the forces of order and the forces of disorder in the post–Cold War world; one wanted a "preponderance of power" in the hands of the peace-keeping forces. The size and mix of forces specified in the Bush administration budget plan as of 1990 would

probably be sufficient to repeat such a performance in the future. The
Bush budget would reduce defense spending to 3.6 percent of GNP by
1996—the lowest such proportion since before World War II.[15] But
Congress was likely to cut even deeper and rearrange priorities.

One critical issue was that of missile defenses. At a time of heightened
instability in the former Soviet Union and expanding missile proliferation,
one unfortunate legacy of "assured destruction" thinking was that the
United States, despite its ability to perform virtual technological miracles
in the battle theater, remained completely defenseless against attack on
the American homeland with even a single ballistic missile. Not only did
the Gulf war provide vivid televised evidence of the horrors of such
attack and the value of defensive systems (in the dramatic battle between
American Patriot defensive missiles and Iraqi SCUD ballistic missiles),
but the post–Cold War era offered new prospects for cooperation with
the Russians on such defenses. In 1991, Congress began to move in the
direction of deploying at least land-based defenses. But the process was
slow and resistance within the arms control community remained.

The liberal-pacifist prejudice against weaponry ran deep, a seemingly
permanent part of the political landscape in Western democracies. At the
end of the Cold War, moreover, ideological and moral opposition to
weaponry was reinforced by isolationist sentiment from the Right—from
figures arguing either that America did not owe the world protection or
that a significant American defense effort would hobble the United States
in economic competition with powers such as Germany and Japan.

It was true that in employing its own resources and citizen-soldiers to
underwrite global stability, the United States faced something of a "free
rider" problem from allies—though allies had proved willing to contribute large sums, and in some cases troops, to the Gulf war effort. More
cooperation, and new cooperative arrangements, would be needed. But
the alternative was simply to permit anarchy to spread unchallenged. In
the post-Vietnam era it had become almost axiomatic to say that America
could not be the world's "policeman"; but the decade in which America
shrank from that role was one of the more unstable of the century. In a
world still capable of producing Saddam Husseins, some international
police force was manifestly required; and the fact remained that no other
power was equipped, economically, politically, or culturally, to lead the
effort. When the United States chose to stand aside, as in Yugoslavia, the
field was left to more violent forces. The abortive attempts of the European Community to forestall and mediate civil war in disintegrating state
in 1991 showed the incapacity of the European powers, acting alone, to

oppose violent forces. (Only when Germany took decisive action, recognizing Croatia and Slovenia, was there a break in the crisis. And even then, German ability to manage the crisis was hampered by the absence of military leverage.) U.S. leadership—and military protection—remained the *sine qua non* of a stable world.

As for international economic competition, it was far from self-evident that the small portion of U.S. GNP spent on military forces explained, for example, the loss of domestic auto markets to the Japanese. And in any event, the natural leadership role simply required that the United States find some way to put its economic house in order while exerting leadership in foreign policy and defense. In this sense, the degree of challenge posed for the United States by the post–Cold War era might not be very different from the challenges of the Cold War.

In the wake of the Cold War, the United States once again possessed the capacity, acting in concert with the other industrial democracies, to underwrite and preserve global stability, much as it originally had in 1919. With America deeply involved in international efforts to resolve disputes, control the spread of mass-destruction weaponry, and preserve peace, and with Washington maintaining a preponderance of military power to back such efforts, the nightmare of the twentieth century could be safely left behind and the dangers of the new era of weapons proliferation probably averted. The Cold War had provided an intense and often costly lesson in the logic of power politics and in the deterrent value of military strength. But whether by the closing decade of the century that lesson had been learned by the democracies was still far from clear.

NOTES

Foreword

1. Dean Acheson, *Present at the Creation* (New York: W. W. Norton, 1969), n.p.
2. Compare John Lukacs, "The Short Century—It's Over," *New York Times,* February 17, 1991, E13.
3. A point I borrow from Harvard professor Harvey Mansfield.
4. See, for example, Walter E. Houghton, *The Victorian Frame of Mind* (New Haven and London: Yale University Press, 1957), 42–43.
5. I. S. Bloch [Jan Gotlib Bloch], *The Future of War in Its Technical, Economic, and Political Relations,* intr. Sandi E. Cooper (New York and London: Garland Publishing, 1972).
6. See Merze Tate, *The Disarmament Illusion* (New York: Russell and Russel, 1971).
7. Howard Weinroth, "Norman Angell and *The Great Illusion:* An Episode in Pre-1914 Pacifism," *The Historical Journal* 17 (1974): 551–74. Compare Barbara W. Tuchman, *The Guns of August* (New York: Macmillan Publishing Co., Inc., 1962), 10.

Chapter 1

1. Henry Kissinger, *Years of Upheaval* (Boston: Little, Brown, 1982), 237–38.
2. David Starr Jordan, *War and Waste* (Garden City, NY: Doubleday, Page, 1913), 53.
3. Edward Grey, Viscount Grey of Fallodon, *Twenty-five Years, 1892–1916* (London: Hodder and Stoughton, 1925), 1:91–92.

4. Walter Lippmann, *U.S. Foreign Policy: Shield of the Republic* (Boston: Little, Brown, 1943), 55.

5. See, for example, Ole R. Holsti and Robert C. North, "The History of Human Conflict," in Elton B. McNeil, ed., *The Nature of Human Conflict* (Englewood Cliffs, NJ: Prentice-Hall, 1965), 155–71; and Dean G. Pruitt and Richard C. Snyder, eds., *Theory and Research on the Causes of War* (Englewood Cliffs, NJ: Prentice-Hall, 1969). A more recent version of the revisionist argument can be seen in Steven Van Evera, "The Cult of the Offensive and the Origins of the First World War," in *International Security* 9, no. 1 (Summer 1984): 58–108, reprinted in Steven E. Miller, ed., *Military Strategy and the Origins of the First World War* (Princeton, NJ: Princeton University Press, 1985), 58–107.

6. Barbara W. Tuchman, *The Guns of August* (New York: Macmillan, 1962).

7. Robert F. Kennedy, *Thirteen Days* (New York: W. W. Norton, 1969), 62, 127.

8. Fritz Fischer, *Germany's Aims in the First World War* (New York: W. W. Norton, 1967); Fischer, *War of Illusions: German Policies from 1911 to 1914*, trans. Marian Jackson (London: Chatto and Windus, 1975); and Fischer, *World Power or Decline: The Controversy over Germany's War Aims in the First World War* (New York: W. W. Norton, 1974). See also V. R. Berghan, *Germany and the Approach of War in 1914* (New York: St. Martin's Press, 1973) and Immanuel Geiss, ed., *July 1914 the Outbreak of the First World War: Selected Documents* (London: B. T. Batsford, 1967).

9. William R. Keylor, *The Twentieth-Century World: An International History* (New York: Oxford University Press, 1984), 44; Berghahn, *Germany and the Approach of War*, 1–3.

10. David Lloyd George, *War Memoirs 1914–1915* (Boston: Little, Brown, 1933), 49.

11. Examples of revisionist accounts include, inter alia, Harry Elmer Barnes, *The Genesis of the World War: An Introduction to the Problem of War Guilt* (New York: Alfred A. Knopf, 1929), and G. P. Gooch, *Recent Revelations of European Diplomacy*, 4th ed. (London: Longmans, Green, 1940). The rise of the revisionist controversy is chronicled in Immanuel Geiss, "The Outbreak of the First World War and German War Aims," *Journal of Contemporary History* 1, no. 3 (July 1966): 75–92; James Joll, *The Origins of the First World War* (London: Longmans, 1984), 1–5; A. J. P. Taylor, *The Struggle for Mastery in Europe 1848–1918* (Oxford: Oxford University Press, 1971), 569–77; and Dwight E. Lee, ed., *The Outbreak of the First World War: Causes and Responsibilities,* 4th ed. (Lexington, MA: D. C. Heath, 1975).

12. Geoffrey Blainey, *The Causes of War* (New York: Free Press, 1973), 131–47.

13. Quoted in ibid., 135–36.

14. See Quincy Wright, *A Study of War*, 2nd ed. (Chicago: University of Chicago Press, 1965), 1:670–71.

15. Ibid.

16. Coit D. Blacker and Gloria Duffy, eds., *International Arms Control: Issues and Agreements*, 2nd ed. (Stanford, CA: Stanford University Press, 1984), 84.

17. A. J. Anthony Morris, *Radicalism Against War, 1906–1914* (London: Longmans, 1972), 123–24; see also Howard Weinroth, "Left-Wing Opposition to Naval Armaments in Britain before 1914," *Journal of Contemporary History* 17, no. 3 (1974): 109.

18. Arthur J. Marder, *From the Dreadnought to Scapa Flow: The Royal Navy in the Fischer Era, 1904–1919* (London: Oxford University Press, 1961), 108.

19. Morris, *Radicalism Against War*, 122.

20. Berghahn, *Germany and the Approach of War*, 66.

21. Morris, *Radicalism Against War*, 135.

22. Ibid., 108.

23. E. L. Woodward, *Great Britain and the German Navy* (Oxford: Oxford University Press, 1935), 125.

24. See Morris, *Radicalism Against War*, 113–14.

25. Ibid., 106–7; Woodward, *Great Britain and the German Navy*, 4–5 and 103–4.

26. Quoted in Woodward, *Great Britain and the German Navy*, 125, 131.

27. Morris, *Radicalism Against War*, 121.

28. Berghahn, *Germany and the Approach of War*, 66.

29. Ibid., 67.

30. Woodward, *Great Britain and the German Navy*, 450–51.

31. Quoted in Jonathan Steinberg, *Yesterday's Deterrent: Tirpitz and the Birth of the German Battle Fleet* (London: MacDonald, 1965), 209.

32. Berghahn, *Germany and the Approach of War*, 38.

33. Ibid., 40.

34. Ibid., 36; Steinberg, *Yesterday's Deterrent*, 24, 148.

35. Quoted in Marder, *Dreadnought to Scapa Flow*, 105.

36. Woodward, *Great Britain and the German Navy*, 117.

37. Quoted in Winston S. Churchill, *The World Crisis* (New York: Charles Scribner's Sons, 1931), 65.

38. Woodward, *Great Britain and the German Navy*, 275.

39. Ibid., 170.

40. Ibid., 195.

41. Taylor, *Struggle for Mastery*, 447.

42. Woodward, *Great Britain and the German Navy*, 31.

43. Ibid., 136.

44. Quoted in Marder, *Dreadnought to Scapa Flow*, 131–32.

45. Quoted in Berghahn, *Germany and the Approach of War*, 62.

46. Quoted in Marder, *Dreadnought to Scapa Flow*, 172.

47. Blacker and Duffy, *International Arms Control*, 85.

48. Jonathan Steinberg, "The Copenhagen Complex," *Journal of Contemporary History* 1, no. 3 (July 1966): 44.

49. Quoted in Berghahn, *Germany and the Approach of War*, 108.

50. Woodward, *Great Britain and the German Navy*, 46.

51. Quoted in Berghahn, *Germany and the Approach of War*, 35–36.

52. Quoted in Woodward, *Great Britain and the German Navy*, 303.

53. Quoted in ibid., 303–4.

54. See Berghahn, *Germany and the Approach of War*, 117.

55. Quoted in Woodward, *Great Britain and the German Navy*, 503.

56. Churchill, *World Crisis*, 26.

57. Morris, *Radicalism Against War*, 121.

58. Marder, *Dreadnought to Scapa Flow*, 179.

59. Churchill, *World Crisis*, 137, 25.

60. Woodward, *Great Britain and the German Navy*, 212.

61. Geiss, *July 1914*, 31–32.

62. Quoted in Konrad H. Jarausch, *The Enigmatic Chancellor: Bethmann-Hollweg and the Hubris of Imperial Germany* (New Haven, CT: Yale University Press, 1973), 146.

63. Quoted in Taylor, *Struggle for Mastery*, 458.

64. Quoted in Berghahn, *Germany and the Approach of War*, 106.

65. Marder, *Dreadnought to Scapa Flow*, 272–87.

66. Quoted in Woodward, *Great Britain and the German Navy*, 425–26.

67. Blainey, *Causes of War*, 138.

68. Lee, *Outbreak of the First World War*, 32.

69. See, inter alia, Jean-Jacques Becker, *1914: Comment les Français sont entres dans la guerre* (Paris: Presses de la Foundation Nationale des Sciences Politiques, 1977); Raoul Giradet, ed., *Le nationalisme français 1871–1914* (Paris: Armand Colin, 1966); John F. V. Keiger, *France and the Origins of the First World War* (New York: St. Martin's Press, 1983); D. C. B. Lieven, *Russia and the Origins of the First World War* (New York: St. Martin's Press, 1983).

70. Tuchman, *Guns of August*, 29.

71. Giradet, ed., *Le nationalisme français*, 18; Keiger, *France and the First World War*, 75; see also Becker, *1914*.

72. Lieven, *Russia and the First World War*, 21, 17.

73. Ibid., 120–21, 64.

74. Quoted in Fischer, *War of Illusions*, 433.

75. Quoted in ibid., 397.

76. Berghahn, *Germany and the Approach of War*, 171.

77. Quoted in Fischer, *War of Illusions*, 162, 164.

78. George F. Kennan, "World War I; Then II; Then . . . " *New York Times*, November 11, 1984, E21. Also see Paul Seabury and Patrick Glynn, "Kennan: The Historian as Fatalist," *The National Interest* (Winter 1985/86): 97–111.

79. See, especially Van Evera, "The Cult of the Offensive and the Origins of the First World War," in Miller, *Military Strategy and the First World War*, 58–107.

80. See Tuchman, *Guns of August*, 31–35.

81. Lee, *Outbreak of the First World War*, 39.

82. Van Evera, "Cult of the Offensive," in Miller, *Military Strategy*, 72.

83. J. A. Hobson, *Democracy after the War* (New York: Macmillan, n.d.), 61–64.

84. See Clive Trebilcock, "Legends of the British Armaments Industry 1890–1914," *Journal of Contemporary History* 5, no. 4 (1970): 3–19.

85. Morris, *Radicalism Against War*, 81.

86. Steinberg, *Yesterday's Deterrent*, 29n.

87. See Michael R. Gordon, "Domestic Conflict and the Origins of the First World War: The British and the German Cases," *Journal of Modern History* 46 (1974): 212, 217, 201.

88. Holsti and North, "History of Human Conflict," 155–71.

89. For a later and only slightly revised version of the Holsti-North thesis ostensibly taking Fischer's work into acount, see Eugenia V. Nomikos and Robert C. North, *International Crisis: The Outbreak of World War I* (Montreal: McGill-Queen's University Press, 1976), 265.

90. Quoted in Fischer, *War of Illusions*, 402–3.

91. Geiss, "Outbreak of the First World War," 82.

92. Quoted in Geiss, *July 1914*, 222.

93. Ibid., 223.

94. Quoted in Fischer, *War of Illusions*, 481.

95. Quoted in ibid., 479.

96. Quoted in Berghahn, *Germany and the Approach of War*, 191.

97. The account here follows Berghahn over Fischer in taking Bethmann-Hollweg's hopes of localizing the conflict seriously. See also "The Illusion of Limited War" in Jarausch, *The Enigmatic Chancellor*.

98. Quoted in Geiss, *July 1914*, 198.

99. Quoted in Lieven, *Russia and the First World War*, 65.

100. Quoted in Geiss, *July 1914*, 167, 221.

101. Berghahn, *Germany and the Approach of War*, 47.

102. Keiger, *France and the First World War*, 147.

103. Van Evera, "Cult of the Offensive," in Miller, *Military Strategy*, 58–107.

104. Quoted in Fischer, *War of Illusions*, 504.

105. Quoted in ibid., 492.

106. Quoted in Berghahn, *Germany and the Approach of War*, 207.

107. Quoted in Fischer, *War of Illusions*, 499.

108. Quoted in ibid., 504–5.

109. Van Evera, "Cult of the Offensive," in Miller, *Military Strategy*, 99.

110. Winston S. Churchill, *The Aftermath* (New York: Charles Scribner's Sons, 1929).

111. See Luigi Albertini, *The Origins of the War of 1914*, 3 vols. (London: Oxford University Press, 1952–57).

112. Grey, *Twenty-five Years*, 1:330–35.

113. See Lieven, *Russia and the First World War*, 151.

114. Van Evera, "Cult of the Offensive," in Miller, *Military Strategy*, 88.

115. Quoted in Fischer, *War of Illusions,* 487.

116. Ibid., 483.

117. A. J. P. Taylor, *War by the Time-Table: How the First World War Began* (New York: American Heritage Press, 1969).

118. See Felix Gilbert, *To the Farewell Address* (Princeton, NJ: Princeton University Press, 1961), and Tate, *Disarmament Illusion.*

119. Van Evera, "Cult of the Offensive," in Miller, *Military Strategy,* 100.

120. Taylor, *Struggle for Mastery in Europe,* 518.

121. Quoted in Fischer, *War of Illusions,* 433

122. Quoted in ibid.

123. Quoted in ibid., 400.

124. Quoted in Geiss, *July 1914*, 292–93.

125. See Fischer, *War of Illusions*, 82–88.

126. See Geiss, *July 1914*, 288–90.

127. SeeGrey,*Twenty-five Years*, 1:333–39, and Churchill, *World Crisis,* 109.

128. See, for example, Zara S. Steiner, *Britain and the Origins of the First World War* (New York: St. Martin's Press, 1977).

129. See Tuchman, *Guns of August,* 17–27 and 118–19.

130. Fischer, *War of Illusions*, 470.

131. See, for example, Arkady N. Shevchenko, *Breaking with Moscow* (New York: Alfred A. Knopf, 1985).

132. Churchill, *Aftermath*, 467.

133. Grey, *Twenty-five Years*, 2:27.

134. G. P. Gooch, *Recent Revelations of European Diplomacy,* 4th ed. (London: Longmans, 1940).

135. Quoted in Morris, *Radicalism Against War*, 419.

Chapter 2

1. The language is that of the Kellogg-Briand Pact of 1928.

2. Keith Feiling, *The Life of Neville Chamberlain* (London: Macmillan, 1946), 320.

3. Lawrence W. Martin, *Peace Without Victory: Woodrow Wilson and the British Liberals* (Port Washington, NY: Kennikat Press, 1973), 18.

4. Ibid., 13, 103, 110.

5. Ibid., 50.

6. See chapter 1.

7. Martin, *Peace Without Victory*, 57, 62–63.

8. See Martin Gilbert, *The Roots of Appeasement* (New York: New American Library, 1966), 14–15.

9. Martin, *Peace Without Victory*, 62–63.

10. Ibid., 57–58.

11. John Maynard Keynes, *The Economic Consequences of the Peace* (New York: Harcourt, Brace and Howe, 1920), 298.

12. Cf. Sally Marks, *The Illusion of Peace: International Relations in Europe 1918–1933* (New York: St. Martin's Press, 1976), 16.

13. Quoted in Gilbert, *Roots of Appeasement*, 38–39.

14. Quoted in Martin, *Peace Without Victory*, 179.

15. Thomas A. Bailey, *Woodrow Wilson and the Lost Peace* (New York: Macmillan, 1945), 111.

16. Quoted in Arnold A. Offner, *The Origins of the Second World War: American Foreign Policy and World Politics, 1917–1941* (New York: Praeger Publishers, 1975), 25–26.

17. Keylor, *The Twentieth-Century*, 81.

18. See Marc Trachtenberg, *Reparation in World Politics: France and European Economic Diplomacy, 1916–1923* (New York: Columbia University Press, 1980). Cf. Etienne Mantoux, *The Carthaginian Peace, or The Economic Consequences of Mr. Keynes* (London: Oxford University Press, 1946).

19. Walter A. McDougall, *France's Rhineland Diplomacy, 1914–1924* (Princeton, NJ: Princeton University Press, 1978), 72–77; Keylor, *Twentieth-Century World*, 82–84.

20. Marks, *Illusion of Peace*, 15.

21. A. J. P. Taylor, *The Origins of the Second World War*, 2nd ed (New York: Fawcett Premier, 1961), 27–28.

22. Quoted in Anthony Adamthwaite, *The Making of the Second World War* (London: George Allen & Unwin, 1977), 28.

23. Blainey, *The Causes of War*, 118.

24. Arthur S. Link, *Wilson the Diplomatist: A Look at His Major Foreign Policies* (Baltimore, MD: Johns Hopkins Press, 1957), 138.

25. Ibid., 135.

26. Quoted in ibid., 145.

27. Quoted in ibid., 143.

28. Stephen Roskill, *Naval Policy Between the Wars*, vol. 1, *The Period of Anglo-American Antagonism* (New York: Walker, 1968), 83–84.

29. Winston S. Churchill, *The Aftermath* (New York: Charles Scribner's Sons, 1929), 226–28. Cf. Winston S. Churchill, *The Second World War*, vol. 1, *The Gathering Storm* (Boston: Houghton Mifflin, 1948), 16.

30. J. A. S. Grenville, *The Major International Treaties, 1914–1973* (London: Metheun & Co., Ltd., 1974), 68.

31. Harold and Margaret Sprout, *Toward a New Order of Sea Power: American Naval Policy and the World Scene, 1918–1922* (Princeton, NJ: Princeton University

Press, 1940), 112–13; Gerald E. Wheeler, *Prelude to Pearl Harbor: The United States and the Far East, 1921–1931* (Columbia: University of Missouri Press, n.d.), 131–32.

32. Lippmann, *U.S. Foreign Policy,* 54; cf. John Chalmers Vinson, *The Parchment Peace: The United States Senate and the Washington Conference 1921–1922* (Athens: University of Georgia Press, 1955), 45.

33. Quoted in Wheeler, *Prelude to Pearl Harbor,* 106.

34. See Martin Gilbert, *Winston S. Churchill,* vol. 5, *1922–1939 The Prophet of Truth* (Boston: Houghton Mifflin, 1977), 65–91, 290–92.

35. Samuel Eliot Morison, *The Oxford History of the American People* (New York: Oxford University Press, 1965), 922.

36. Yamoto Ichihashi, *The Washington Conference and After* (Stanford, CA: Stanford University Press, 1928), 34–37.

37. Ibid., 365–85.

38. See L. Ethan Ellis, *Republican Foreign Policy, 1921–1933* (New Brunswick, NJ: Rutgers University Press, 1968).

39. Asada Sadao, "The Japanese Navy and the United States," in Dorothy Borg and Sumpei Okomoto, eds., *Pearl Harbor as History: Japanese American Relations, 1931–1941* (New York: Columbia University Press, 1973), 235; cf. Ichihashi, *Washington Conference,* 144.

40. Wheeler, *Prelude to Pearl Harbor,* 57–58 and 135–38.

41. George T. Davis, *A Navy Second to None* (New York: Harcourt, Brace, 1940), 131, 314.

42. Wheeler, *Prelude to Pearl Harbor,* 142.

43. Stephen E. Pelz, *Race to Pearl Harbor: The Failure of the Second London Naval Conference and the Onset of World War II* (Cambridge, MA: Harvard University Press, 1974), 25–40.

44. Ibid., 2.

45. Ibid., 25.

46. Ibid., 221.

47. Ibid., 2–3.

48. Ibid., 27–29.

49. Wheeler, *Prelude to Pearl Harbor,* 123.

50. Roskill, *Period of Anglo-American Antagonism,* 531; Pelz, *Race to Pearl Harbor,* 182.

51. Ibid., 81.

52. Ibid., 201.

53. Ibid., 202.

54. Churchill, *Gathering Storm,* 45–46.

55. F. L. Carsten, *The Reichswehr and Politics 1918 to 1933* (Oxford: Oxford University Press, 1966), 220–32; John W. Wheeler-Bennett, *The Nemesis of Power: The German Army in Politics, 1918–1945* (London: Macmillan, 1954), 92–102.

56. Gustav Hilger and Alfred G. Meyer, *The Incompatible Allies: A Memoir-History of German-Soviet Relations 1918–1941* (New York: Macmillan, 1953), 187–208; Hans W. Gatzke, "Russo-German Military Collaboration during the Weimar Republic," in Hans W. Gatzke, ed., *European Diplomacy between Two Wars, 1919–1939* (Chicago: Quadrangle Books, 1972), 40–65; Carsten, *Reichswehr and Politics*, 232–38; Wheeler-Bennett, *Nemesis of Power*, 128.

57. Wheeler-Bennett, *Nemesis of Power*, 145.

58. Carsten, *Reichswehr and Politics*, 242–43.

59. Wheeler-Bennett, *Nemesis of Power*, 145.

60. Hans W. Gatzke, *Stresemann and the Rearmament of Germany* (Baltimore: Johns Hopkins University Press, 1954), 27.

61. Gatzke, "Russo-German Military Collaboration," 54.

62. See Gatzke, *Stresemann,* and Gatzke, "Russo-German Military Collaboration." Cf. Marks, *Illusion of Peace*, 64–65.

63. Churchill, *Aftermath*, 488, and cf. explanation in Churchill, *Gathering Storm*, 30.

64. Gilbert, *Roots of Appeasement*, 54.

65. Annelise Thimme, "Stresemann and Locarno," in Gatzke, ed., *European Diplomacy,* 73–91.

66. Quoted in Pelz, *Race to Pearl Harbor*, 120.

67. Quoted in Thimme, "Stresemann and Locarno," 81.

68. Gatzke, *Stresemann*, 28–29.

69. Quoted in ibid., 30.

70. Ibid., 4, 12.

71. Quoted in ibid., 85.

72. Anthony P. Adamthwaite, *The Making of the Second World War* (London: George Allen & Unwin, 1977), 33.

73. Quoted in Wheeler-Bennett, *Nemesis of Power*, 185–86.

74. Carsten, *Reichswehr and Politics*, 255.

75. Quoted in Gatzke, *Stresemann*, 71.

76. Marks, *Illusion of Peace*, 64–65.

77. See Robert H. Ferrell, *Peace in Their Time: The Origins of the Kellogg-Briand Pact* (New Haven, CT: Yale University Press, 1952).

78. Winston S. Churchill, *While England Slept: A Survey of World Affairs 1932–39,* (New York: G. Putnam's Sons, 1938), 30.

79. Ibid., 28.

80. Ibid., 24.

81. Quoted in Gilbert, *Churchill*, 318–19.

82. Winston S. Churchill, *The World Crisis* (New York: Charles Scribner's Sons, 1931), 14.

83. Gilbert, *Roots of Appeasement*, 185.

84. Quoted in Uri Bialer, *The Shadow of the Bomber: The Fear of Air Attack and British Politics 1932–1939* (London: Royal Historical Society, 1980), 158.

85. J. C. F. Fuller, *Reformation of War*, quoted in George Quester, *Deterrence Before Hiroshima* (New York: John Wiley & Sons, 1966), 56.

86. Quoted in ibid., 67.

87. Telford Taylor, *Munich: The Price of Peace* (New York: Vintage Books, 1979), 197–98.

88. Churchill, *Gathering Storm*, 169–70; Taylor, *Munich*, 226.

89. Bialer, *Shadow of Bomber*, 18–19.

90. Quoted in F. S. Northedge, *The Troubled Giant* (New York: Frederick A. Praeger, 1966), 385. Cf. Pelz, *Race to Pearl Harbor*, 98–99.

91. Norman H. Baynes, ed., *The Speeches of Adolf Hitler, April 1922–August 1939* (New York: Howard Fertig, 1969), II: 1041–58. Cf. Alan Bullock, *Hitler: A Study in Tyranny*, 2nd ed. rev. (New York: Bantam Books, 1961), 277.

92. Quoted in Gilbert, *Roots of Appeasment*, 106; cf. 128–29.

93. Churchill, *While England Slept*, 48–49.

94. See D. C. Watt, "German Plans for the Reoccupation of the Rhineland: A Note," *Journal of Contemporary History* vol. 1 (October 1966): 193–99. Cf. Adamthwaite, *Making of the Second World War*, 55.

95. Matthew Cooper, *The German Air Force 1933–1945* (London: Jane's, 1981), 36.

96. Bialer, *Shadow of Bomber*, 43; Gilbert, *Churchill*, 505. J. Nere, *The Foreign Policy of France from 1914 to 1945* (London: Routledge & Kegan Paul, 1975), 130.

97. Nere, *Foreign Policy of France,* 130; Adamthwaite, *Making of Second World War,* 38.

98. Quoted in Bialer, *Shadow of Bomber*, 62–63.

99. Gilbert, *Churchill*, 506.

100. Quoted in ibid., 507.

101. Quoted in ibid.

102. Quoted in ibid.

103. Quoted in Churchill, *Gathering Storm*, 113.

104. Quoted in Gilbert, *Churchill*, 552.

105. Berenice A. Carroll, *Design for Total War: Arms and Economics in the Third Reich* (The Hague: Mouton, 1968), 184.

106. Cooper, *German Air Force*, 61.

107. Adolf Hitler, *Mein Kampf*, trans. Ralph Mannheim (London: Hutchinson, 1969), 596–98.

108. See Taylor, *Munich*, 236n.

109. Bialer, *Shadow of the Bomber*, 158.

110. Taylor, *Munich*, 220–24.

111. Quoted in Charles Block, "Great Britain, German Rearmament, and the Naval Agreement of 1935," in Gatzke, *European Diplomacy*, 126.

112. Churchill, *While England Slept*, 38.

113. Ibid., 40.

114. Ibid., 204.

115. Ibid., 206.

116. H. Montgomery Hyde, *British Air Policy Between the Wars* (London: Heinemann, 1976), 322.

117. See especially Taylor, *Origins of World War*; also Maurice Cowling, *The Impact of Hitler: British Politics and British Policy, 1933–1940* (Cambridge: Cambridge University Press, 1975); also D. C. Watt, "Appeasement, the Rise of a Revisionist School?" *Political Quarterly* 36, no. 2 (April–June 1965). Cf. Alan Bullock, "Hitler and the Origins of the Second World War," in Gatzke, ed., *European Diplomacy,* 221–48; and Adamthwaite, *Making of Second World War,* 67–68.

118. Adamthwaite, *Making of Second World War,* 95.

119. Keith Middlemas, *Diplomacy of Illusion: The British Government and Germany, 1937–39* (London: Weidenfeld and Nicolson, 1972), 33.

120. See Pelz, *Race to Pearl Harbor,* 99–122.

121. Donald Cameron Watt, *Too Serious a Business: European Armed Services and the Approach of the Second World War* (Berkeley: University of California Press, 1975), 113–14.

122. Quoted in Feiling, *Life of Chamberlain,* 314.

123. See H. W. Richardson, *Economic Recovery in Britain, 1932–9* (London: Weidenfeld and Nicolson, 1967), 231–35.

124. Ibid., 304–5.

125. Quoted in Cooper, *German Air Force,* 61.

126. Robert Paul Shay, Jr., *British Rearmament in the Thirties: Politics and Profits* (Princeton, NJ: Princeton University Press, 1977), 277–78.

127. Quoted in Taylor, *Munich,* 262.

128. Quoted in ibid., 217n.

129. Quoted in ibid., 143–44.

130. Adamthwaite, *Making of Second World War,* 44.

131. Quoted in Gilbert, *Roots of Appeasement,* 167.

132. Quoted in Adamthwaite, *Making of Second World War,* 62.

133. Quoted in ibid.

134. Quoted in Bialer, *Shadow of Bomber,* 157.

135. Admathwaite, *Making of Second World War,* 67.

136. Quoted in Martin Gilbert, *Winston Churchill: The Wilderness Years* (Boston: Houghton Mifflin, 1982), 277.

Chapter 3

1. Churchill and Roosevelt were eighth cousins once removed. See Frederick W. Marks III, *Wind Over Sand: The Diplomacy of Franklin Roosevelt* (Athens: University of Georgia Press, 1988), 194.

2. See Robert Nisbet, *Roosevelt and Stalin: The Failed Courtship* (Washington: Regnery Gateway, 1988). In sketching the triangular relationship among Roosevelt, Stalin, and Churchill, the author is indebted to Nisbet's analysis. For a second skeptical account of Roosevelt's diplomacy, see Marks, *Wind Over Sand.*

3. Wright, *A Study of War*, 1:670–71; cf. Harriet Fast Scott and William F. Scott, *The Armed Forces of the USSR* (Boulder, CO: Westview Press, 1979), 284.

4. See Anthony C. Sutton, *Western Technology and Soviet Economic Development*, vol. 1, *1917 to 1930* (Stanford, CA: Hoover Institution Press, 1968).

5. D. Fedotoff White, *The Growth of the Red Army* (Princeton, NJ: Princeton University Press, 1944), 285; cf. Scott and Scott, *Armed Forces of the USSR*, 16.

6. Wright, *Study of War*, 1:670–72.

7. Edgar O'Ballance, *The Red Army* (New York: Praeger, 1964), 124. Cf. Janusz Piekalkiewicz, *Tank War, 1939–1945*, trans. Jan van Heurck (Poole, England: Blanford Press, 1986), 329. See also Nicholas Bethell, *The War Hitler Won* (New York: Holt, Rinehart and Winston, 1972), 170; Piekalkiewicz, *Tank War*, 329; Barton Whaley, *Covert German Rearmament, 1919–1939: Deception and Misperception* (Frederick, MD: University Publications of America, 1984), 69–70.

8. Cajus Bekker, *The Luftwaffe War Diaries*, trans. Frank Ziegler (Garden City, NY: Doubleday, 1968), 23; T. Dodson Stamps and Vincent J. Esposito, *A Military History of World War II*, vol. 2, *Operations in the European Theater* (West Point, NY: West Point, 1953), 6, 60; Bethell, *War Hitler Won*, 170; Wright, *Study of War*, 1:670–72; O'Ballance, *Red Army*, 124, 127; Scott and Scott, *Armed Forces of the USSR*, 16, 22; *Conway's All the World's Fighting Ships, 1922–1946* (London: Conway Maritime Press, 1980), 320; Whaley, *Covert German Rearmament*, 70; Scott and Scott, *Armed Forces of the USSR*, 287.

9. Sutton, *Western Technology and Soviet Economic Development*, 1: 260.

10. Nikolai Tolstoy, *Stalin's Secret War* (New York: Holt, Rinehart and Winston, 1981), 143.

11. Winston Churchill, *Gathering Storm*, 362–65.

12. See "Secret Protocols: A Look into the Files," *Vestnik* [magazine of Soviet Foreign Ministry] (March 1990): 62.

13. Tolstoy, *Stalin's Secret War*, 194.

14. Quoted in ibid.

15. Ibid., 102, 177–80.

16. See note 46.

17. Jeremy Bernstein, *Einstein* (New York: Viking Press, 1973), 224.

18. Richard Rhodes, *The Making of the Atomic Bomb* (New York: Simon and Schuster, 1986), 306.

19. Albert Einstein, *Ideas and Opinions*, trans. Sonja Bargmann (New York: Dell, 1954), 103.

20. Quoted in Arthur H. Comptom, *Atomic Quest: A Personal Narrative* (New York: Oxford University Press, 1956), 30.

21. Arnold Kramish, *The Griffin* (Boston: Houghton Mifflin, 1986), 54–55. See also "Appendices to a Report to the President by Special Committee of National Security Council on Atomic Energy Policy with Respect to the United Kingdom and Canada, March 2, 1949," Truman Library, President's Secretary's File (hereafter PSF), Box 200, Subject File—Atomic Energy, Agreed Declaration of US, UK, and Canada; Attlee to Truman, June 7, 1946, Truman Library, PSF, Box 200, Atomic Energy—agreed declaration by U.S., United Kingdom, Canada (Folder 1); Rhodes, *Making of the Atomic Bomb*, 317.

22. Arthur H. Vandenberg, Jr., ed., *The Private Papers of Senator Vandenberg* (Boston: Houghton Mifflin, 1952), 10.

23. Quoted in Marks, *Wind Over Sand*, 206.

24. Winston S. Churchill, *Their Finest Hour* (Boston: Houghton Mifflin, 1949), ix.

25. Winston S. Churchill, *The Grand Alliance* (Boston: Houghton Mifflin,1950), 370–71.

26. Roosevelt to Churchill, November 19, 1942. See John Lewis Gaddis, *Strategies of Containment: A Critical Appraisal of Postwar American National Security Policy* (Oxford: Oxford University Press, 1982), 3, 361n; cf. Francis L. Loewenheim, Harold D. Langley, and Manfred Jonas, eds., *Roosevelt and Churchill: Their Secret Wartime Correspondence* (New York: Saturday Review Press, 1975), 282; and Warren F. Kimball, ed., *Churchill and Roosevelt: The Complete Correspondence* (Princeton, NJ: Princeton University Press, 1984), 2: 22.

27. Marks, *Wind Over Sand*, 211–16.

28. Quoted in Robert Dallek, *Franklin D. Roosevelt and American Foreign Policy, 1932–1945* (New York: Oxford University Press, 1979), 520. Cf. Lynn Etheridge Davis, *The Cold War Begins: Soviet-American Conflict over Eastern Europe* (Princeton, NJ: Princeton University Press, 1974), 141.

29. Nisbet, *Roosevelt and Stalin*, 95.

30. W. Averell Harriman and Elie Abel, *Special Envoy to Churchill and Stalin 1941–1946* (New York: Random House, 1975), 169–70.

31. See Kimball, *Complete Correspondence*, 1:14, emphasis added.

32. Biographical note, Davies Papers, Library of Congress.

33. Joseph E. Davies, *Mission to Moscow*, 2nd rev. ed. (New York: Pocket Books, 1943), frontispiece.

34. Ibid., 120.

35. Ibid., 207.

36. Joseph E. Davies, *Mission to Moscow* (New York: Simon and Schuster, 1941), 423.

37. Ibid., 122–24.

38. Ibid., 318.

39. Ibid., 495.

40. Ibid., 492.
41. Roosevelt to Churchill, March 18, 1942, in Kimball, *Complete Correspondence*, 1: 421.
42. Gaddis, *Strategies of Containment*, 8–9.
43. Roosevelt to Churchill, July 29, 1942, in Kimball, *Complete Correspondence*, 1: 545.
44. Diary, April 12, 1943, Davies Papers, Box 13, Folder "1–12 April, 1943," emphasis added.
45. Dallek, *Franklin D. Roosevelt*, 401–2.
46. "Alleged Soviet Massacre of 10,000 Polish Army Officers," April 17, 1943, Davies Papers, Box 13, Folder "13–19 April 1943."
47. "FDR's Last Instructions on Moscow," Diary, May 5, 1943, Davies Papers, Box 13, Folder "1–10 May 1943." Account of painting of plane also in Box 13.
48. Churchill to Roosevelt, June 25, 1943; Roosevelt to Churchill, June 28, 1943; Churchill to Roosevelt, June 29, 1943—in Kimball, *Complete Correspondence*, 2: 278, 283, 290.
49. Ibid.
50. Diary, October 2, 1943, Davies Papers, Box 14, Folder "1–29 October 1943."
51. Nisbet, *Roosevelt and Stalin*, 45.
52. U.S. Department of State, *Foreign Relations of the United States [FRUS]: The Conferences at Cairo and Tehran 1943* (Washington: GPO, 1961), 482–86; 529–33; 594–96; Nisbet, *Roosevelt and Stalin*, 44–45; Marks, *Wind Over Sand*, 170–71.
53. Jan Ciechanowski, *Defeat in Victory* (Garden City, NY: Doubleday, 1947), 247–48; cf. Marks, *Wind Over Sand*, 170.
54. Quoted in Frances Perkins, *The Roosevelt I Knew* (New York: Harper & Row, 1964), 82–83.
55. Lord Moran (Sir Charles Wilson), *Winston S. Churchill: The Struggle for Survival, 1940–1965* (London: Constable and Co., 1966), 133, 140.
56. Tolstoy, *Stalin's Secret War*, 179–80.
57. Harriman and Abel, *Special Envoy*, 336.
58. Quoted in André Fontaine, *A History of the Cold War: From the October Revolution to the Korean War 1917–1950*, trans. D. D. Page (New York: Pantheon Books, 1968), 208.
59. Harriman and Abel, *Special Envoy*, 340–43.
60. Roosevelt to Churchill, August 26, 1944, in Kimball, *Complete Correspondence*, 3:296.
61. Quoted in Kimball, *Complete Correspondence*, 3:288.
62. Quoted in Martin J. Sherwin, *A World Destroyed: The Atomic Bomb and the Grand Alliance* (New York: Vintage Books, 1977), 92.
63. Ibid., 65, and Rhodes, *Making of the Atomic Bomb*, 538.

64. Memorandum by Niels Bohr, April 2, 1944, Felix Frankfurter Papers, Bohr File, Library of Congress.

65. Sherwin, *A World Destroyed*, 98.

66. Niels Bohr, "Notes Concerning Scientific Co-operation with the U.S.S.R.," Frankfurter Papers, Bohr File, Library of Congress.

67. Sutton, *Western Technology and Soviet Economic Development*, 1:6.

68. Kapitza to Bohr, October 28, 1943, and "Memorandum of Conversation between Dr. Bohr and Soviet Counsellor Zurcheko," Frankfurter Papers, Bohr File, Library of Congress.

69. See David Holloway, "Entering the Nuclear Arms Race: The Soviet Decision to Build the Atomic Bomb, 1939–45," *Social Studies of Science* 11 (1981): 182–84; and David Holloway, *The Soviet Union and the Arms Race* (New Haven, CT: Yale University Press, 1983), 18–20.

70. See, for example, Sherwin, *A World Destroyed*, 109.

71. The argument for this view is found in McGeorge Bundy, *Danger and Survival* (New York: Random House, 1988), 115–17; Rhodes, *Making of the Atomic Bomb*, 530, and Sherwin, *A World Destroyed*, 111, stress, by contrast, the deliberate nature of Churchill's response.

72. The agreement is reprinted in Sherwin, *A World Destroyed*, 284.

73. Ibid., 290–91.

74. Appendices to a Report to the President by Special Committee of National Security Council on Atomic Energy Policy with Respect to the United Kingdom and Canada, March 2, 1949," Truman Library, PSF, Box 200, Subject File—Atomic Energy, Agreed Declaration of US, UK, and Canada.

75. Richard G. Hewlett and Oscar E. Anderson, *A History of the Atomic Energy Commission*, vol. 1, *The New World, 1939/1946*, (University Park: Pennsylvannia State University Press, 1962), 274.

76. Sherwin, *A World Destroyed*, 68–87.

77. Bohr to Marshall, June 10, 1948, Frankfurter Papers, Bohr File, Library of Congress.

78. Quoted in Rhodes, *Making of the Atomic Bomb*, 530.

79. Quoted in Milovan Djilas, *Conversations with Stalin*, trans. Michael B. Petrovich (New York: Harcourt, Brace & World, 1962), 112.

80. Forrest C. Pogue, "The Decision to Halt at the Elbe," in Kent Robert Greensfield, ed., *Command Decisions*, (New York: Harcourt, Brace and Co., 1959), 375–77. Cf. Martin Gilbert, *Winston S. Churchill*, vol. 7, *Road to Victory 1941–1945* (Boston: Houghton Mifflin, 1986), 1169.

81. Winston S. Churchill, *Triumph and Tragedy* (New York: Houghton Mifflin, 1953), 460.

82. Gilbert, *Winston S. Churchill*, 7:1276.

83. Tolstoy, *Stalin's Secret War*, 268.

84. Nisbet, *Roosevelt and Stalin*, 83–90.

85. *FRUS: The Conferences at Malta and Yalta* (Washington: GPO, 1955), 570–71. Cf. Nisbet, *Roosevelt and Stalin*, 83–84.

86. Quoted in Pogue, "Decision to Halt at the Elbe," 384.

87. Davis, *Cold War Begins*, 187.

88. Roosevelt to Churchill, April 11, 1945, in Kimball, *Complete Correspondence*, 3: 630.

89. Memorandum of Conversation, by the Ambassador in the Soviet Union (Harriman)," *Foreign Relations of the United States (FRUS) 1945*, vol. 5, *Europe*, 826.

90. Ibid., 825–26, 829.

91. See, for example, Gar Alperovitz, *Atomic Diplomacy: Hiroshima and Potsdam: The Use of the Atomic Bomb and the American Confrontation with Soviet Power* (New York: Penguin Books, 1985), 68–72.

92. For example, John Lewis Gaddis, *The United States and the Origins of the Cold War, 1941–1947* (New York: Columbia University Press, 1972), 204–6.

93. Cf. Paul Seabury, *The Rise and Decline of the Cold War* (New York: Basic Books, 1967), 3–17.

94. Robert J. Donovan, *Conflict and Crisis: The Presidency of Harry S Truman, 1945–1948* (New York: W.W. Norton, 1977), 20.

95. Quoted in Harry S. Truman, *Memoirs by Harry S. Truman*, vol. 1, *Year of Decisions* (Garden City, NY: Doubleday, 1955), 14, emphasis added.

96. Truman, *Year of Decisions*, 71; Harriman and Abel, *Special Envoy*, 343–46, 447–48.

97. Davies notes of his meeting with Truman, April 30, 1945 (handwritten original and typewritten copy with editing), Davies Papers, Box 16, Folder "30 April 1945."

98. Quoted in Truman, *Year of Decisions,* 81–82.

99. See especially Davies to Truman, April 15, 1945, Davies Papers, Box 16, Folder "13–20 April 1945"; "First Talk with President Truman," April 30, 1945, Davies Papers, Box 16, Folder "30 April 1945"; Davies to Truman, May 13, 1945, Davies Papers, Box 16, Folder "13 May 1945"; and "Sustaining Opinion from Justice Frankfurter," Davies Diary, May 13, 1945, Davies Papers, Box 16, Folder "13 May 1945."

100. Davies Diary, May 19, 1945, and press clipping, "Davies Awarded Reds' Order of Lenin," *Washington Times-Herald*, May 20, 1945, Davies Papers, Box 17, Folder "14–20 May 1945."

101. Charles E. Bohlen, *Witness to History 1929–1969* (New York: W.W. Norton, 1973), 215; see also Harriman and Abel, *Special Envoy*, 459.

102. Much of Hopkins's personal correspondence with Truman about the mission—far more revealing than the official State Department memoranda of conversation reproduced in *Foreign Relations of the United States*—is reproduced in the lengthy, unpublished first draft of Truman's memoirs, held at

the Truman Library (hereafter Truman Draft Memoir). The Truman Draft Memoir provides a far more detailed account of this crucial period in the early Cold War than any published source. See Hopkins to Truman, June 3, 1945, Truman Draft Memoir, Truman Library, Post-Presidential Memoirs, Box 17, 757. Cf. *FRUS: The Conference of Berlin* (Washington: GPO, 1960), 2: 24–62.

103. *FRUS: Conference of Berlin*, 64–78; compare Diary, May 26, 1945 and Diary, May 27, 1945, Davies Papers, Box 17, Folder "24–26 May 1945."

104. Martin Gilbert, *Winston S. Churchill*, vol. 8, *Never Despair 1945–1965* (Boston: Houghton Mifflin, 1988), 7–8; and also Truman, *Year of Decisions*, 247–48.

105. Truman, *Year of Decisions*, 71.

106. Ibid., 70.

107. Truman Draft Memoir, Truman Library, Post-Presidential Memoirs, Box 17, 490–91.

108. Stimson Diary, May 15, 1945, Sterling Library, Yale University (Library of Congress microfilm copy).

109. Sherwin, *A World Destroyed*, 191–92n, 222.

110. On the origins of the phrase in 1945, see Bernhard G. Bechhoefer, *Postwar Negotiations for Arms Control* (Washington: Brookings Institution, 1961), 47.

111. Proponents of this case include Gregg Herken, *The Winning Weapon* (Princeton, NJ: Princeton University Press, 1988), and Robert L. Messer, *The End of an Alliance: James F. Byrnes, Roosevelt, Truman, and the Origins of the Cold War* (Chapel Hill: University of North Carolina Press, 1982).

112. Stimson Diary, July 19 and July 23, 1945. Cf. Messer, *End of an Alliance*, 103.

113. Davies Diary, July 29, 1945, Davies Papers, Box 19, Folder "29 July 1945."

114. Stimson Diary, July 19, 1945.

115. "W. B.'s Book," July 24, James F. Byrnes Papers, Robert Muldrow Cooper Library, Clemson University.

116. Ibid., September 21.

117. Quoted in Rhodes, *Making of the Atomic Bomb*, 676.

118. A useful collection of documents relating to the bomb decision can be found in Barton J. Bernstein, *The Atomic Bomb: The Critical Issues* (Boston: Little, Brown, 1976).

119. United States Strategic Bombing Survey, *Effects of Incendiary Bombing Attacks on Japan: A Report on Eight Cities* (Washington: GPO, 1947), 102.

120. See Alice Kimball Smith, *A Peril and a Hope: The Scientists' Movement in America 1945–47* (Chicago: University of Chicago Press, 1965), 14–72.

121. Hewlett and Anderson, *New World*, 358.

122. Ibid., 580–82; "Operation Crossroads: Explosion over 97 Ships at Bikini," *Time*, Feb. 11, 1946, 23.

123. Henry L. Stimson, "The Decision to Use the Atomic Bomb," *Harper's*, February 1947, 101.

124. Ibid., 19; cf. *The United States Strategic Bombing Survey: The Effects of Atomic Bombs on Hiroshima and Nagasaki* (Washington: GPO, 1946), 22; Herbert Feiss, *The Atomic Bomb and the End of World War II*, (Princeton, NJ: Princeton University Press, 1966), 191.

125. See Margaret Gowing, *Britain and Atomic Energy, 1939–1945* (London: Macmillan, 1964), 376.

126. Feis, *Atomic Bomb*, 199.

127. Hewlett and Anderson, *New World*, 358.

128. Churchill, *Triumph and Tragedy*, 638–39. The impact of the atomic bomb—and the heavy conventional bombing that Japan was undergoing at the same time—was apparent in the emperor's statement to his counselors on August 14: "I appreciate how difficult it will be for the officers and men of the army and navy to surrender their arms to the enemy and see their homeland occupied. . . . In spite of these feelings, so difficult to bear, I can not endure the thought of letting my people suffer any longer. A continuation of the war would bring death to tens, perhaps even hundreds, thousands of persons. The whole nation would be reduced to ashes. How then could I carry on the wishes of my imperial ancestors?" Quoted in Robert J. C. Butow, *Japan's Decision to Surrender*, (Stanford, CA: Stanford University Press, 1954), 207–8.

129. Gaddis, *Strategies of Containment*, 6.

130. See Roosevelt to Churchill, April 6, 1945, and accompanying note in Kimball, *Complete Correspondence*, 3: 617.

131. Ibid., 15.

132. Nisbet, *Roosevelt and Stalin*, 73.

133. Dallek, *Franklin D. Roosevelt*, 534.

134. Cf. Marks, *Wind Over Sand*, 172–73.

135. Dallek, *Franklin D. Roosevelt*, 596.

136. On the latter point, see Bohlen, *Witness to History*, 247.

137. Joseph Stalin, "New Five-Year Plan for Russia," *Vital Speeches*, March 1, 1946, 300; Gaddis, *Origins of the Cold War*, 300.

138. Interview with Dean Acheson by Hillman and Noyes for Truman Memoirs, February 17, 1955, Truman Library, Truman Papers, Post-Presidential, Box 1.

139. A historical controversy has long raged concerning whether (1) Truman, as he later stated on several occasions beginning at a presidential press conference in 1952, issued some form of "ultimatum" to the Soviets and (2) as he apparently told Senator Henry M. Jackson on one occasion (see "Gold Old Days," *Time*, January 28, 1980, 13), he threatened the Soviets with use of atomic weapons. Jackson's secondhand report of Truman's views is hard to assess, given much parallel hearsay around Washington but little cor-

roborating evidence, but inspires skepticism concerning Truman's memory. However, the president's repeated insistence that his warnings to Stalin had been abrupt probably warrants more than the dismissal it initially received. Kuross A. Samii, *Involvement by Invitation* (University Park: Pennsylvania State University Press, 1987), 69–94, builds a strong case for the validity of Truman's recollection, while suggesting that the bluntest U.S. warnings may have come via U.S. ambassador to Moscow William Bedell Smith in conversations with Stalin *after* the initial Soviet decision to withdraw. Samii also provides a thorough review of the controversy. A contrasting account, focusing more narrowly on the issue of the nuclear threat, can be found in Bundy, *Danger and Survival*, 232–33. Clearly, however, the firm U.S. policy stance on Iran, whatever the specifics of its mode of conveyance, had an impact on the Soviet decision to withdraw, a fact granted by the most authoritative Western history of Soviet foreign policy. See Adam Ulam, *Expansion and Coexistence: The History of Soviet Foreign Policy, 1917–67* (New York: 1968), 425.

140. Kennan to Byrnes, February 22, 1946, in *FRUS 1946*, vol. 6, *Eastern Europe; the Soviet Union* (Washington: GPO, 1969), 696–709.

141. Robert Rhodes James, ed., *Winston S. Churchill: His Complete Speeches 1897–1963* (New York: R. R. Bowker, 1974), 7: 7290.

142. Churchill to Truman, May 12, 1945, in *FRUS: The Conference of Berlin 1945* (Washington: GPO, 1960), 1:8–9.

143. Gilbert, *Winston S. Churchill*, 7: 195–96; Secretary of State Byrnes had also visited Churchill while he was drafting the speech in Florida. Byrnes to B. M. Baruch, February 13, 1946, Byrnes Papers, Robert Muldrow Cooper Library, Clemson University. It is probable that Churchill's draft and conversation influenced Byrnes's relatively hard-line Overseas Press Club speech of February 28. Cf. Messer, *End of an Alliance*, 189.

144. Gilbert, *Winston S. Churchill*, 206.

145. Clark Clifford on the Cold War," *United States Institute of Peace Journal* 3 (October 1990): 12.

146. George H. Gallup, *The Gallup Poll: Public Opinion 1935–1971*, vol. 1, *1935–1948* (New York: Random House, 1972), 567.

147. Charles E. Bohlen later remembered Secretary of State Byrnes first taking this view in a meeting during February 1946. See Charles Burton Marshall, "The United States," in Kurt London, ed., *The Soviet Impact on World Politics* (New York: Hawthorn Books, 1974), 221. Cf. Walter Isaacson and Evan Thomas, *The Wise Men* (New York: Simon and Schuster, 1986), 352–76.

148. The self-censorship was explicitly described by *Newsweek* writer Harry F. Kern in a September 3, 1945, story mentioning Soviet depredations in East Germany. The shift in reportage was evident, for example, in "Policy and Police States," *Newsweek*, March 11, 1946, 45–46; "Iron Curtain," *Life*, April

1946, 27–35; and "Behind the Iron Curtain," *New York Times Magazine*, July 28, 1946, 10–11.

149. Gallup, *Gallup Poll 1935–1948*, 524, 565, 567.

150. Henry L. Stimson and McGeorge Bundy, *On Active Service in Peace and War* (New York: Harper and Brothers, 1948), 642–44; Acheson to Truman, September 25, 1945, *FRUS 1945*, vol. 2., *General; the United Nations* (Washington: GPO, 1967), 48–50. See also Walter Millis, ed., *The Forrestal Diaries*, (New York: Viking, 1951), 94–95, and "Cabinet, Atomic Bomb," September 21, 1945, Matthew J. Connelly Papers, Set 1, Truman Library.

151. On Attlee's views, see Attlee to Truman, October 16, 1945, Public Records Office, United Kingdom, PREM 8/116. Records of the meeting can be found in the Truman Library, PSF, Box 200, Subject File—NSC—Atomic —Atomic Energy—Agreed Declaration by U.S., U.K., and Canada (folder 1). An account can also be found in Hewlett and Anderson, *New World*, 462–66.

152. Truman's attitude has been misrepresented as skeptical, owing apparently to inadvertent scholarly error. Gaddis, *United States and Cold War*, 273, misquoted a Davies diary entry from the Davies Papers, attributing apparently skeptical statements about sharing the bomb to Truman; the statements were actually paraphrases of Davies's own remarks to Truman. Truman's leading biographer, Robert J. Donovan, relied on Gaddis's evidence to paint Truman's attitudes as skeptical. See Donovan, *Conflict and Crisis,* 130. Davies, not surprisingly, favored sharing the Bomb with the Russians, and his diary presents Truman as sympathetic to the idea. See Journal, September 18, 1945, Davies Papers, Library of Congress, Box 22, Folder "18–20 October 1945." Typewritten copy, dated "8–22–50," is a fairly accurate transcription of handwritten notes in pencil, possibly original notes of the Truman meeting, headed "Sept. 18, 1945." Notes of cabinet meetings, though sparse, seem to suggest Truman's sympathies (see notes to cabinet meetings of September 21 and October 26, 1945, Matthew J. Connelly Papers, Truman Library). This accords in turn with a Truman remark to Stettinius, presumably correctly recorded by Gaddis, that there was "no precious secret" for the United States to withhold from other nations. Gaddis, *United States and Cold War*, 253.

153. See, for example, "U.S. Safety First, Baruch Promises," *New York Times*, March 28, 1946, 7; "$660,000 Approved for Baruch Board," *New York Times*, June 27, 1946, 4; also Baruch to Truman, March 13, 1946, *FRUS 1946*, vol. 1, *General; the United Nations* 757–58. Cf. Hewlett and Anderson, *The New World*, 590–610.

154. See, for example, "Molotov Agrees to Arms Inspection to Verify Cuts and Ban on Atom Bomb; Accepts Idea of Freedom of Danube," *New York Times*, November 29, 1946, 1. A good discussion of the rationale behind Soviet

resistance to the plan can be found in Adam Ulam, *The Rivals: America and Russia Since World War II* (New York: Viking Press, 1971), 105–7.

155. "Atomic Age, Beyond the Bomb," *Time*, June 24, 1946, 25.

Chapter 4

1. Richard G. Hewlett and Francis Duncan, *Atomic Shield, 1947/1952*, vol. 2, *A History of the Atomic Energy Commission* (University Park: Pennsylvania State University Press, 1969), 362–66; Lewis L. Strauss, *Men and Decisions* (Garden City, NY: Doubleday, 1962), 201–7.

2. Quoted in Strauss, *Men and Decisions*, 205.

3. Speech of 25 March 1949, James, *Churchill: Complete Speeches*, 7:7800. Cf. Gilbert, *Winston S. Churchill*, 8: 464.

4. U.S. Department of Commerce, Bureau of the Census, *Historical Statistics of the United States: Colonial Times to 1970* (Washington: GPO, 1975), 2:1116.

5. See "Gold Old Days," *Time*, January 28, 1980, 13, and cf. chapter 3, note 13.

6. George H. Quester, *Nuclear Diplomacy* (New York: Dunellen, 1970), 49–50.

7. See Paul H. Nitze, "The Development of NSC 68," *International Security* 4, no. 4 (Spring 1980):173–74.

8. Edward Teller with Allen Brown, *The Legacy of Hiroshima* (Garden City, NY: Doubleday, 1962), 35–36.

9. Strauss, *Men and Decisions*, 201–7.

10. Interview of Admiral Sidney W. Souers by William Hillman and David M. Noyes for Truman Memoirs, Kansas City, Missouri, December 16, 1954, Truman Library, Post-Presidential Papers, Box 2. Hereafter, "Souers Interview."

11. Ibid.

12. Harry S. Truman, *Memoirs of Harry S. Truman*, vol. 2, *Years of Trial and Hope* (New York: Da Capo Press, 1986), 308–10.

13. Souers interviews. Cf. Hewlett and Duncan, Atomic Shield, 373–75. Truman, *Years of Trial and Hope,* 308–12.

14. Strauss, *Men and Decisions*, 216–17.

15. J. Robert Oppenheimer, *The Open Mind* (New York: Simon and Schuster, 1955), 88.

16. Robert Gilpin, *American Scientists and Nuclear Weapons Policy* (Princeton, NJ: Princeton University Press, 1962), 111–21.

17. Edmund Beard, *Developing the ICBM: A Study in Bureaucratic Politics* (New York: Columbia University Press, 1976), 154.

18. Herbert F. York, *The Advisors: Oppenheimer, Teller, and the Superbomb* (San Francisco: W. H. Freeman, 1976), 153–59.

19. Souers interview, December 16, 1954.

20. York, *The Advisors*, 157.

21. George Kennan, "The Sources of Soviet Conduct," in Kennan, *American Diplomacy*, (Chicago: University of Chicago Press, 1984), 107–28.

22. Kennan, *Memoirs 1925–1950*, 198. Cf. Paul Seabury and Patrick Glynn, "Kennan: The Historian as Fatalist," *The National Interest*, no. 2 (Winter 1986): 97–111. Helpful light was shed on Kennan's position in this debate by Paul Nitze in a personal interview with the author.

23. Ibid., 128.

24. Nitze, "Development of NSC 68," 171.

25. George F. Kennan, *The Nuclear Delusion* (New York: Pantheon Books, 1983), xiv.

26. Bernard Brodie, ed., *The Absolute Weapon: Atomic Power and World Order* (New York: Harcourt, Brace, 1946), 76.

27. In November 1945, *Time* listed "Twelve Points" summing up expert opinion on the atomic weapons. Point 10 read: "Atomic weapons increase the incentive to aggression by multiplying the advantage of surprise." "Twelve Points," *Time*, November 12, 1945, 28. Cf. Brodie, *Absolute Weapon*, 72–73.

28. See, for example, Leon Wieseltier, "The Great Nuclear Debate," *The New Republic*, January 10 and 17, 1983, 28.

29. Lawrence Freedman, *The Evolution of Nuclear Strategy* (New York: St. Martin's Press, 1983), 3–9.

30. "It requires no great conversance with the principles of strategy to concede at the outset that the invention and development of the military airplane, particularly of the bomber, constitute one of the most arresting *motifs* in the international political drama of our own times. It is apparent that the threat contained in *this instrument of overwhelming destructiveness* merely to the capital equipment of a nation may relegate to a position of relative unimportance a consideration of its potentialities in the tactics of warfare, whether on land or sea. *What it may boot a nation to win a war* if her capital accumulation of a half-century or more is largely wiped out is a question. *Whether it can win a war* while undergoing such punishment to its industrial home is another. And *whether it will not at times bow before so appalling a menace without further regard for the likely eventuation of a military campaign* is still another." (*motifs* italicized in original; other emphasis added). Bernard Brodie, "Major Naval Inventions and Their Consequences on International Politics, 1914–1918," Ph.D. diss., University of Chicago, 1940, 1.

31. H. H. Arnold, "Air Power in the Atomic Age," in Dexter Masters and Katharine Way, ed., *One World or None* (New York: McGraw-Hill, 1946), 26–32.

32. Brodie, *Absolute Weapon*, 46–49.

33. Norman Angell, *The Menace to Our National Defence* (London: Hamish Hamilton, 1934), 19, 98, and passim.

34. Brodie, *Absolute Weapon*, 79.

35. Ibid., 48–49.

36. A contradiction noted in Robert Maynard Hutchins's 1946 review of the book. See Robert M. Hutchins, "Scholarly Opinions on Atomic Energy— and Its Control," *New York Times*, June 9, 1946, 7:6. Cf. Brodie, *Absolute Weapon*, 48–49.

37. *FRUS 1950,* vol. 1, *National Security Affairs; Foreign Economic Policy* (Washington: GPO, 1977), 38. All quotations of the document are from this text, which appears on pages 22–44.

38. Ibid.

39. Ibid., 1:13–17.

40. Ibid.

41. Warner R. Schilling, "The H-Bomb Decision: How to Decide Without Actually Choosing," *Political Science Quarterly* 76, no. 1 (March 1961): 24–46.

42. Hewlett and Anderson, *The New World*, 406–9.

43. York, *The Advisors*. Cf. Bundy, *Danger and Survival*, 214–19 and 668n.

44. Herbert F. York, *Race to Oblivion: A Participant's View of the Arms Race*, quoted in York, *The Advisors*, viii–ix.

45. York, *The Advisors*, 88–89.

46. Andrei D. Sakharov, *Sakharov Speaks*, ed. Harrison E. Salisbury (New York: Alfred A. Knopf, 1974), 29–31.

47. David Holloway, "Research Note: Soviet Thermonuclear Development," *International Security* 4, no. 3 (Winter 1979/80): 192–97.

48. York, *The Advisors*, 90–91.

49. "Soviet Atom Lead Overcome by U.S.," *New York Times*, March 31, 1954, 5.

50. "High Officials Say Nation Is Menaced by Hydrogen Bomb," *New York Times*, October 5, 1953, A1.

51. "Eisenhower Says Soviet Can Attack with Super Bombs," *New York Times*, October 9, 1953, A1.

52. "Soviet Scientist Reports on Bomb," *New York Times*, November 4, 1953, 4; "Oppenheimer Warns U.S.," *The New York Times*, November 5, 1953, 9.

53. Marshall D. Shulman, *Stalin's Foreign Policy Reappraised* (Cambridge, MA: Harvard University Press, 1963), esp. 80–103.

54. Ibid., 104–38.

55. *FRUS 1950*, 1:145.

56. Nitze, "Development of NSC 68," 173–74.

57. Gaddis *Strategies of Containment*, 92.

58. Ibid., 106.

59. Ibid., 106 and 378n.

60. See Franklyn Griffiths, "Origins of Peaceful Coexistence," *Survey*, no. 50 (January 1964):195–201, and cf. Walter C. Clemens, Jr., "Lenin on Disarmament," *Slavic Review* 23 (September 1964):504–25.

61. Shulman, *Stalin's Foreign Policy*, 134.

62. Personal interview with Paul Nitze.

Chapter 5

1. Fred C. Iklé has described deterrence as "ending wars before they start." See Fred Charles Iklé, *Every War Must End* (New York: Columbia University Press, 1971).

2. Henry L. Stimson, "The Decision to Use the Atomic Bomb," *Harper's Magazine* 194, no. 1161 (February 1947):106.

3. Robert J. C. Butow, *Japan's Decision to Surrender* (Stanford, CA: Stanford University Press, 1954), 181; Harry S. Truman, *Year of Decisions* (Garden City, NY: Doubleday, 1955), 422.

4. Carl von Clausewitz, *On War*, ed. and trans. Michael Howard and Peter Paret (Princeton, NJ: Princeton University Press, 1976), 204, 209.

5. Stimson, "The Decision to Use the Atomic Bomb," 101, 106.

6. See, for example, Bernard Brodie, "Unlimited Weapons and Limited War," *The Reporter*, September 18, 1954, 16–21.

7. David Rees, *Korea: The Limited War* (New York: St. Martin's Press, 1964), 180–229; cf. Max Hastings, *The Korean War* (New York: Simon and Schuster, 1987), 192–203.

8. Gaddis, *Strategies of Containment*, 119.

9. Rees, *Korea*, 172.

10. Truman, *Years of Trial and Hope*, 395.

11. Acheson, *Present at the Creation* (New York: Norton, 1969), 472.

12. Richard K. Betts, *Nuclear Blackmail and Nuclear Balance* (Washington: Brookings Institution, 1987), 35–36.

13. Truman, *Years of Trial and Hope*, 413.

14. Rees, *Korea*, 170.

15. Keylor, *Twentieth-Century World*, 289.

16. Acheson, *Present at the Creation*, 488–89.

17. Iklé, *Every War Must End*, 54–55.

18. Hastings, *Korean War*, 230.

19. Clay Blair, *The Forgotten War* (New York: Anchor, 1987), 911.

20. Hastings, *Korean War*, 231; cf. Iklé *Every War Must End*, 89.

21. Robert A. Divine, *Foreign Policy and U.S. Presidential Elections 1952–1960* (New York: New Viewpoints, 1974), 7–8.

22. John Foster Dulles, "A Policy of Boldness," *Life*, May 19, 1952, 146–60.

23. Quoted in Divine, *Foreign Policy and Elections*, 44, 53, 34–35.

24. On Stevenson's lack of effectiveness as campaigner, see ibid., 64–65.

25. Dulles, "A Policy of Boldness," 146.

26. Robert A. Taft, *A Foreign Policy for Americans* (New York: Doubleday, 1951), 78–79.

27. "A Policy of Boldness," 151–52.

28. Memorandum of Discussion at the 132nd Meeting of the National Security

Council, February 18, 1953, Eisenhower Library, Ann Whitman File, NSC Series, Box 4.

29. Ibid.

30. *FRUS 1952–1954*, vol. 2, *National Security Affairs*, 1111.

31. Quoted in Samuel Huntington, *The Common Defense* (New York: Columbia University Press, 1966), 64–66.

32. See especially Memorandum of Discussion at a Special Meeting of the National Securiy Council, March 31, 1953, and Memorandum of Discussion at the 164th Meeting of the National Security Council, October 1, 1953, Eisenhower Library, Ann Whitman File, NSC Series, Box 4. The best accounts of the development of the "New Look" remain Huntington, *Common Defense*, 64–88, and Glenn H. Snyder, "The 'New Look' of 1953," in Warner R. Schilling, Paul Y. Hammond, and Glenn H. Snyder, *Strategy, Politics, and Defense Budgets* (New York: Columbia University Press, 1962), 379–524.

33. Divine, *Foreign Policy and Elections*, 33.

34. Hastings, *Korean War*, 317–18.

35. But not on the issue of employing nuclear weapons. Stephen E. Ambrose, relying on Eisenhower's later recollections in a personal interview, paints the president as opposing nuclear weapons use in Asia "only seven years after Hiroshima." On the contrary, as explained in the chapter text below, NSC transcripts abundantly show that Eisenhower, even more than Dulles, was eager to find some use for nuclear weapons in the war. See Stephen E. Ambrose, *Eisenhower*, vol. 2, *The President* (New York: Simon and Schuster, 1984), 35 and 680n and cf. main chapter text following.

36. *FRUS 1952–1954*, vol. 15, *Korea*, pt. 1, 806, 693–94.

37. Ibid., 769–770.

38. Ibid., 805–6.

39. "Van Fleet Said to Favor 'Limited' Atomic Attacks," *New York Times*, March 9, 1953, 8.

40. "35th U.S. Nuclear Blast Tests Tactical Weapon," *New York Times*, March 18, 1953.

41. " 'Whole Works' Urged to End War in Korea," *New York Times*, March 21, 1953, 2.

42. Quoted in Hastings, *Korean War*, 318.

43. Quoted in Ambrose, *Eisenhower*, 2:91. Cf. Ulam, *Expansion and Coexistence*, 541, and Mikhail Heller and Aleksandr M. Nekrich, *Utopia in Power* (New York: Summit Books, 1982), 514.

44. *FRUS 1952–1954*, 15:818–19; Hastings, *Korean War*, 320.

45. *FRUS 1952–1954*, 15:826–27.

46. Ibid., 835, 839–75.

47. Ibid., 894.

48. Clark, *Danube to Yalu*, 261–81.

49. Ibid., 259–60.

50. *FRUS 1952–1954*, 15:946.

51. Ibid., 976.

52. Ibid., 1014.

53. Memorandum of discussion at the 144th meeting of the National Security Council, May 13, 1953, Eisenhower Library, Ann Whitman File, NSC Series, Box 4.

54. *FRUS 1952–1954,* 15:1066.

55. Ibid., 1052–56.

56. Dwight D. Eisenhower, *White House Years,* vol. 1, *Mandate for Change, 1953–1956* (Garden City, NY: Doubleday, 1963), 181.

57. *FRUS 1952–1954,* 15:1068, 71.

58. Ibid., 1095–96, 1103–11.

59. Eisenhower, *White House Years,* 181.

60. U.S. President, *Public Papers of the President: Dwight D. Eisenhower, 1953* (Washington, D.C.: GPO, 1960), 82.

61. See McGeorge Bundy, "Atomic Diplomacy Reconsidered," *Bulletin of the American Academy of Arts and Sciences* 38, no. 1 (October 1984):29–31, and Barry M. Blechman and Robert Powell, "What in the Name of God Is Strategic Superiority?" *Political Science Quarterly* 97, no. 4 (Winter 1982–83):589–602. In a more detailed analysis in *Danger and Survival,* Bundy significantly qualified his original case. See Bundy, *Danger and Survival,* 239–45. A review of the arguments is presented in Betts, *Nuclear Blackmail and Nuclear Balance,* 37–47.

62. Bundy, "Atomic Diplomacy," 30.

63. Bundy, *Danger and Survival,* 240, emphasis added.

64. Ulam, *Expansion and Coexistence,* 541.

65. Blechman and Powell, "Strategic Superiority," 595.

66. *FRUS 1952–1954*, 15:977.

67. Rees, *Korea,* 408–9.

68. Betts, *Nuclear Blackmail,* 45.

69. Michael Guhin, *Dulles* (New York: Columbia University Press, 1972), 232–33.

70. John Foster Dulles, "The Evolution of Foreign Policy," *Department of State Bulletin,* January 25, 1954, 107–8.

71. Ibid., 108.

72. Ibid.

73. Dean Acheson," 'Instant Retaliation': The Debate Continued," *New York Times Magazine,* March 28, 1954, 77.

74. William W. Kaufmann, ed., *Military Policy and National Security* (Princeton, NJ: Princeton University Press, 1956), 107.

75. See Dean Acheson, "The Parties and Foreign Policy," *Harper's,* November 1955, 32, and Kaufmann, *Military Policy,* 12–25 (see discussion in text below).

For more recent accounts echoing the contemporary view, see John Prados, *The Sky Would Fall: Operation Vulture: The U.S. Bombing Mission in Indochina, 1954* (New York: Dial Press, 1983), 199, and Betts, *Nuclear Blackmail*, 53. Betts's assessment of Indochina in 1954, like his analysis of Korea in 1953, focuses narrowly on the issue of whether a specific nuclear threat was made (none was), but again overlooks the broader diplomatic and political context. In contrast, diplomatic histories of the Indochina crisis and the Geneva conference have tended to stress the importance of Dulles's deterrent threats in overall Chinese and Soviet calculations. See, for example, Robert F. Randle, *Geneva 1954: The Settlement of the Indochinese War* (Princeton, NJ: Princeton University Press, 1969), and Melvin Gurtov, *The First Vietnam Crisis: Chinese Communist Strategy and United States Involvement, 1953–1954* (New York: Columbia University Press, 1967), 116–19. Interestingly, McGeorge Bundy, despite a general stress on the supposed diplomatic inefficacy of nuclear weapons, acknowledges some usefulness of the atomic threat at the Geneva Conference of 1954. See Bundy, *Danger and Survival*, 271–73.

76. For a recent discussion, see Prados, *The Sky Would Fall*, 145–66.
77. Moran, *Churchill*, 423, 543, 563.
78. *FRUS 1952–54*, vol 13; *Indochina*, 1467, 1474, 1433. Cf. Betts, *Nuclear Blackmail*, 52.
79. Ambrose, *Eisenhower*, 2:177–79.
80. Prados, *The Sky Would Fall*, traces internal debate on military intervention. See esp. 165–66.
81. See Philippe Devillers and Jean Lacouture, *End of a War* (New York: Praeger, 1969), 301. Also see Gurtov, *First Vietnam Crisis*, 149.
82. Gurtov, *First Vietnam Crisis*, 152.
83. For the influence of the Vietnam issue on Eisenhower's "rehabilitation" among younger historians, see Richard A. Melanson and David Mayers, eds., *Reevaluating Eisenhower: American Foreign Policy in the 1950s* (Urbana: University of Illinois Press, 1987), 4.
84. "Alliance in Danger," *The Economist*, May 8, 1954, 429–30.
85. H. S. Dinerstein, *War and the Soviet Union* (New York: Praeger, 1959), 108–9; Randle, *Geneva*, 148–49.
86. Dinerstein, *War and the Soviet Union*, 91–129; Randle, *Geneva*, 138–51; Gurtov, *First Vietnam Crisis*, 117.
87. Gurtov, *First Vietnam Crisis*, 145.
88. Randle, *Geneva*, 71.
89. Quoted in Randle, *Geneva*, 60.
90. Gurtov, *First Vietnam Crisis*, 118.
91. Ibid.
92. Anthony Eden, *Full Circle* (Boston: Houghton Mifflin, 1960), 139.
93. See Randle, *Geneva*, 556; Gurtov, *First Vietnam Crisis*, 152–55.
94. Prados, *The Sky Would Fall*, 75—102, 189.

95. James Shepley, "How Dulles Averted War," *Life*, January 16, 1956, 70. Dulles made essentially the same point during an NSC meeting on March 31, 1953, where he cited the danger of "global war" arising from "Soviet miscalculation" of the intentions of the United States: "Beyond this, Secretary Dulles pointed out, we must take clear positions so that war could not result from Soviet miscalculations. There must be no repetition of the fuzzy situation in Korea in the spring of 1950, which constituted an invitation to the Soviets to move against South Korea." Memorandum of Discussion at a Special Meeting of the National Security Council, March 31, 1953, Eisenhower Library, Ann Whitman File, NSC Series, Box 4.

96. Quoted in Shepley, "How Dulles Averted War," 78.

97. Quoted in Prados, *The Sky Would Fall*, 193.

98. Nikita Khrushchev, *Khrushchev Remembers: The Last Testament*, ed. and trans. Strobe Talbott (Boston: Little, Brown, 1974), 363, emphasis added.

99. Quoted in Arnold L. Horelick and Myron Rush, *Strategic Power and Soviet Foreign Policy* (Chicago: University of Chicago Press, 1966), 30.

100. Khrushchev, *Last Testament*, 362.

101. Brodie, "Unlimited Weapons and Limited War," 18–21.

102. Kaufmann, ed., *Military Policy and National Security*, 21.

103. Ibid., 115, 28, 29.

104. Ibid., 29.

105. Ibid., 117.

106. See Franklyn Griffths, "Origins of Peaceful Coexistence," 195–201.

107. The best account of Lenin's strategy of "strategic retreat" remains John W. Wheeler-Bennett, *The Forgotten Peace: Brest-Litovsk March 1918* (New York: William Morrow, 1939).

108. See, for example, "The Road Beyond Elugelab," *Time*, April 12, 1954, 21–22; " 'Let Us All Thank God,' " *Time*, April 12, 1954, 30; cf. Memorandum of Discussion at the 204th Meeting of the National Security Council, June 24, 1954, Eisenhower Library, Ann Whitman File, NSC Series, Box 5.

109. In early discussion of various international proposals for a nuclear testing moratorium (which the administration rejected), Eisenhower had staked out a position far more favorable than his advisors to nuclear disarmament. Memorandum of Discussion at the 199th Meeting of the National Security Council, May 28, 1954, and Memorandum of Disucssion at the 203rd Meeting of the National Security Council, June 23, 1954, Eisenhower Library, Ann Whitman File, NSC Series, Box 5.

110. "If there is not at the summit of the nations the will to win the greatest prize and the greatest honour ever offered to mankind, doom-laden responsibility will fall upon those who now possess the power to decide." James, *Winston S. Churchill: Complete Speeches*, 8: 8485. Churchill's language bore a close relationship to that of a London *Times* special supplement on

Edmund Hillary's Everest expedition six days earlier. See "The Pyramid of Hard-Won Experience," *Times*, May 5, 1953, special supplement.

111. A superb brief account of "Open Skies" by a participant in the policy process, complete with reprints of many primary documents, is to be found in Walt W. Rostow, *Open Skies* (Austin: University of Texas Press, 1982). On the propaganda impact of the initiative, see pp. 57–62.

112. The first public reference to "arms control" discovered by the author is to be found in "It's Official: U.S. Won't Give Up Her Bombs," *The New Republic*, August 29, 1955, 3. Dulles also made reference to "disarmament and arms control" in an NSC meeting in February 1955. See Memorandum of Discussion at the 236th Meeting of the National Security Council, February 10, 1955, Eisenhower Library, Ann Whitman File, NSC Series, Box 6. The term would be later be appropriated by theorist Thomas Schelling. See chapter 6.

113. Eisenhower's urgency regarding disarmament is expressed in minutes of NSC meeting for February 7, 1956; his basic dislike of missiles is clear from minutes of an August 1, 1956, NCS meeting (Eisenhower Library, Ann Whitman File, NSC Series, Box 7). His skepticism about the strategic importance of missiles is reflected in Eisenhower to Montgomery, May 2, 1956, Ann Whitman File, DDE Diary Series, Box 15; Memorandum of Conference with the President, March 15, 1956, Ann Whitman File, DDE Diary Series, Box 13, March 1956, Goodpaster; Conversation with Bernard Baruch, March 28, 1956, Ann Whitman File, DDE Diary Series, Box 12, March 1956 Diary; and Supplementary Notes of Legislative Leadership Meeting, February 14, 1956, Ann Whitman File, DDE Diary Series, Box 13, February 1956 Miscellaneous (3). Finally, his lack of enthusiasm for, and concerns with costs of, the earth satellite can be seen in minutes of the May 3, 1956, NSC meeting, Ann Whitman File, NSC Series, Box 7, as well as in minutes of NSC meetings on January 24, May 10, and July 25, 1957, Ann Whitman File, NSC Series, Boxes 8 and 9. The inadvisability of Eisenhower's attitude is discussed in Rostow, *Open Skies*, 76–77 and 98 ff. However, Soviet attainment of an ICBM before the United States was owing not primarily to neglect under Eisenhower but to program cutbacks in the late 1940s. See Edmund Beard, *Developing the ICBM* (New York: Columbia University Press, 1976), 83–105, 216–19, and cf. James L. George, *The New Nuclear Rules* (New York: St. Martin's Press, 1990), 28.

114. "Russia Warns of Force to End Suez War; Loses U.N. Bid for Joint U.S.-Soviet Action; British-French Commandos Land in Egypt," *New York Times*, November 6, 1956, 1. Cf. Arnold L. Horelick and Myron Rush, *Strategic Power and Soviet Foreign Policy* (Chicago: University of Chicago Press, 1966), 31.

115. James R. Killian, Jr., *Sputnik, Scientists, and Eisenhower* (Cambridge, MA: MIT Press, 1977), 2–4.

116. Chronicled extremely ably in Horelick and Rush, *Strategic Power.*
117. Ibid., 49.
118. Beginning in November 1957, the USIA began to ask European respondents, "All things considered, which country do you think is ahead in total military strength at the present time—the U.S. or the Soviet Union?" Until February 1963—after the Cuban missile crisis—a majority or plurality of respondents in European countries placed the Soviet Union ahead. The results were summarized in a graph in "West European Opinion on the Outcome of the Cuban Missile Crisis," USIA Research and Reference Service Report, R-102–63 (R), July 1963, USIA Library.
119. Fred Kaplan, *The Wizards of Armageddon* (New York: Simon and Schuster, 1983), 286.
120. Eisenhower's resistance to a meaningful military response was apparent from his exchanges with representatives of the Security Resources Panel of the Science Advisory Committee (the Gaither panel) in 1957. Memorandum of Discussion at the 343rd Meeting of the National Security Council, November 7, 1957, Eisenhower Library, Ann Whitman File, NSC Series, Box 9. On the more general question of Eisenhower's attitude to defense in this period, see Rostow, *Open Skies*, 70, 74, 98–102.
121. Ambrose, *Eisenhower*, 2:435.
122. See, for example, Adlai Stevenson, "Putting First Things First: A Democratic View," *Foreign Affairs* 38 (January 1960):192; and Henry C. Wallich, *The Cost of Freedom* (New York: Collier Books, 1962), 14 (originally published 1960). The author is grateful to Charles Sorrels for drawing attention to these sources.
123. Robert A. Divine, *Blowing on the Wind: The Nuclear Test Ban Debate 1954– 1960* (New York: Oxford University Press, 1978), 200.
124. As reflected clearly in Dulles's remarks during an anxious meeting convened on March 24; Memorandum of Conference with the President, March 24, 1958, Ann Whitman File, DDE Diary Series, Box 31.
125. Quoted in Divine, *Blowing on the Wind*, 288.
126. Ibid., 207–8.
127. By July 1960, "Arms Limitation" was second on a list of six major "Topics Suggested" by members of the President's Science Advisory Committee "for Discussion with the President"—after "Science Organization in Government" and *ahead* of "Science, Technology, and the Economy" and "Military R & D." Eisenhower Library, President's Science Advisory Committee Series, Box 3. Cf. Divine, *Blowing on the Wind*, 246–47.
128. For example, in Memorandum of Conference with the President, April 17, 1958, Eisenhower Library, Ann Whitman File, DDE Diary Series, Box 32, Staff Notes April 1958 (2); contrast General Maxwell Taylor's Memo to the Secretary of Defense, 13 March 1958, Eisenhower Library, White House Office, Office of the Special Assistant for National Security Affairs, NSC

Series, Briefing Notes Subseries, Box 2 [Atomic Testing] Killian Report—Technical Feasibility of Cessation of Nuclear Testing [1958]. Cf. Divine, *Blowing on the Wind*, 209, 281, 304–8.

129. George B. Kistiakowski, *A Scientist at the White House*, (Cambridge, MA: Harvard University Press, 1976), 385. See also Divine, *Blowing on the Wind*, 284–86.

130. Divine, *Blowing on the Wind*, 299–310.

131. Ibid., 311–13.

132. Ibid., 301.

133. "You and I have both fought against pacifism as a programme for the revolutionary proletarian party. That much is clear. But who has ever denied the use of pacifists by that party to soften up the enemy, the bourgeoisie?" Lenin to Chicherin, February 16, 1922. V. I. Lenin, *Collected Works* (1960–70), 45:474–75. Lenin actually developed a broad strategy for using disarmament as a political weapon. See Clemens, "Lenin on Disarmament," 504–25; and Griffiths, "Origins of Peaceful Coexistence: A Historical Note," 195–201.

Chapter 6

1. Theodore C. Sorensen, *Kennedy* (New York: Harper & Row, 1965), 217.

2. Thomas Schelling was kind enough to provide me with a number of illuminating comments on the personal and intellectual origins of this theory in a personal interiew.

3. Albert J. Wohlstetter, Fred S. Hoffmann, and Henry S. Rowen, *Selection and Use of Strategic Air Bases*, RAND R-66 (Santa Monica: RAND Corporation, 1954). Also see Kaplan, *Wizards of Armageddon*, 97–102, 171–73.

4. Albert Wohlstetter, "The Delicate Balance of Terror," *Foreign Affairs* 37 (January 1959): 211–34.

5. Thomas C. Schelling and Morton H. Halperin, *Strategy and Arms Control* (New York: Twentieth Century Fund, 1961), 10.

6. Personal interview with Thomas Schelling.

7. Schelling and Halperin, *Strategy and Arms Control*, 1.

8. Ibid., 2.

9. John W. Spanier and Joseph L. Nogee, *The Politics of Disarmament: A Study in Soviet-American Gamesmanship* (New York: F. A. Praeger, 1962). Personal interview with Morton Halperin.

10. Paul H. Nitze, with Ann M. Smith and Steven L. Rearden, *From Hiroshima to Glastnost* (New York: Grove Weidenfeld, 1989), 170–3.

11. Henry A. Kissinger, *Nuclear Weapons and Foreign Policy*, (New York: Harper & Brothers, 1957), 206–21.

12. Henry A. Kissinger, "Arms Control, Inspection, and Surprise Attack," *Foreign Affairs* 38 (July 1960):555–75.

13. Personal interview with Walt Rostow.

14. Bundy to Kennedy, January 30, 1961, Kennedy Library, National Security File, Meetings and Memoranda Series, Box 313, National Security Council Meetings 1961, No. 475, 2/1/61, emphasis added.

15. Arthur M. Schlesinger, *A Thousand Days* (Boston: Houghton Mifflin, 1965), 302–3.

16. Ibid., 303.

17. Memorandum of Conference with the President, January 25, 1961, John F. Kennedy Library, National Security File, Meetings and Memoranda Series (Chester V. Clifton), Box 345, Conference with the President, Joint Chiefs of Staff, 1/61–2/61.

18. Memorandum of Conference with the President, February 23, 1961, and Memorandum for the File, February 24, 1961, Kennedy Library, National Security File, Meetings and Memoranda Series (Chester V. Clifton), Box 345, Conference with the President, Joint Chiefs of Staff, 1/61–2/61.

19. Schlesinger, *A Thousand Days*, 340–42.

20. Ibid., 272–73.

21. Ibid., 238, 294–97; Sorensen, *Kennedy*, 294–309.

22. A problem noted by Raymond Aron at the time. See Hans J. Morgenthau, "The Trouble with Kennedy," *Commentary* 33, no. 1 (January 1962):51–55.

23. Memorandum of Conversation, Vienna Meeting Between the President and Chairman Khrushchev, June 3, 1961, 3:00 P.M. Now-declassified memoranda of conversation from the summit can be found in Kennedy Library, President's Office Files, Country Files, USSR, Vienna Meeting (I)—Memos of Conversations—Final Versions, Box 126.

24. Arkady N. Shevchenko, *Breaking with Moscow* (New York: Alfred A. Knopf, 1985), 110.

25. Quoted in Jean Edward Smith, *The Defense of Berlin* (Baltimore: Johns Hopkins University Press, 1963), 241.

26. Ibid., 293–94.

27. Willy Brandt traced the orgins of his policy of *Ostpolitik* to this moment. See Gordon A. Craig, "A New, New Reich?" *New York Review of Books* 36, no. 21 and 22 (January 18, 1990):30.

28. Quoted in Smith, *Defense of Berlin*, 313.

29. Kaplan, *Wizards of Armageddon*, 289.

30. Henry L. Trewhitt, *McNamara* (New York: Harper & Row, 1971), 20.

31. Quoted in Trewhitt, *McNamara*, 21.

32. Memorandum for the Secretaries of the Military Departments, Director, Defense Research and Engineering, Assistant Secretaries of Defense, Chairman, Joint Chiefs of Staff, Assistants to the Secretary of Defense from

Robert S. McNamara, March 1, 1961, Kennedy Library, President's Office File, Box 77, Defense, 1/61–3/61 (National Security Archive copy).

33. Lemnitzer to McNamara, April 18, 1961, National Security Archive.

34. Statement of Secretary of Defense Robert S. McNamara Before the Senate Committee on Armed Services, Tuesday, April 4, 1961, Kennedy Library, National Security File, Departments & Archives Series, Box 273.

35. "Rusk Hints Sharp Curb on Nuclear Arms Use," *Washington Star*, February 27, 1961.

36. "U.S. Denies Report on Rusk Policies," *New York Times*, February 28, 1961, 5.

37. Acheson to JFK, April 3, 1961, Kennedy Library, President's Office Files, Box 127a, U.K. Security, 3/27/61–4/30/61 (National Security Archive copy). Large sections of the Acheson memorandum remain classified. However, a fuller account of its contents can be found in Kaplan, *Wizards of Armageddon*, 294.

38. Ray Vicker, "Discredited Doctrine," *Wall Street Journal*, November 9, 1961.

39. Memorandum of Conversation with Konrad Adenauer, November 21, 1961, Truman Library, Acheson Papers, Box 85 (National Security Archive copy).

40. Telegram for Ambassador Thompson, Kennedy Library, President's Office File, Box 125a, Folder 7, USSR Security, 1/61–5/61.

41. Possony to Rostow, May 8, 1961, Kennedy Library, National Security File, Box 299, Nuclear Weapons Testing, 2/61–4/61 (National Security Archive copy).

42. Caspar Weinberger, "Congress Must Not Bottle Up Testing; Defects in Weapons, Arms Control Demand Continuation," *Los Angles Times*, May 13, 1987.

43. Glenn T. Seaborg, *Kennedy, Khrushchev, and the Test Ban* (Berkeley: University of California Press, 1983), 114.

44. Memorandum of Conversation, Vienna Meeting Between the President and Chairman Khrushchev, June 4, 1961, Luncheon, Kennedy Library, President's Office Files, Country Files, USSR, Vienna Meeting (I)—Memos of Conversations—Final Versions, Box 126.

45. White House Press Release, November 2, 1961, National Security Archive.

46. Lawrence Freedman, *U.S. Intelligence and the Soviet Strategic Threat* (Princeton, NJ: Princeton University Press, 1986), 77.

47. Horelick and Rush, *Strategic Power*, 83.

48. Kaplan, *Wizards of Armageddon*, 289.

49. Robert S. McNamara, "The Communist Design For World Conquest," *Vital Speeches*, March 1, 1962, 297.

50. Ibid.

51. Robert S. McNamara, "The United States and Western Europe," *Vital Speeches*, August 1, 1962, 628.

52. Ibid.

53. Ibid.

54. Ibid., 626–30.

55. David L. Larson, *The Cuban Crisis of 1962: Selected Documents and Chronology* (Boston: Houghton Mifflin, 1963), 61–62.

56. The classic sources for the Cuban story include Graham T. Allison, *The Essence of Decision* (Boston: Little, Brown, 1971), 141–43, and Robert F. Kennedy, *Thirteen Days* (New York: W. W. Norton, 1969), 94–95. See also James G. Blight and David A. Welch, *On the Brink* (New York: Hill and Wang, 1989).

57. "West European Opinion on the Outcome of the Cuban Missile Crisis," USIA Research and Reference Service Report, R-102–63 (R), July 1963, USIA Library.

58. Raymond Aron, *The Great Debate,* trans. Ernst Pawel (New York: Doubleday, 1963), 207.

59. Rostow to Executive Committee of the National Secruity Council, November 10, 1962, Johnson Library (National Security Archive copy).

60. William W. Kaufmann, *McNamara Strategy* (New York: Harper & Row, 1964), 94.

61. Ibid., 294, emphasis added.

62. Kennedy, *Thirteen Days*, 14.

63. Dean Acheson, "Dean Acheson's Version of Robert Kennedy's Version of the Cuban Missile Affair," *Esquire* 71 (February 1969), 76.

64. Raymond L. Garthoff, "The Meaning of Missiles," *Washington Quarterly* 5, no. 4 (Autumn 1982):78–79.

65. Personal interview with Henry S. Rowen.

66. Cuban Missile Crisis Meetings, October 16, 1962, Kennedy Library, President's Office Files, Presidential Recordings Transcripts. Hereafter referred to as October 16 transcript.

67. Ibid.

68. Acheson, "Dean Acheson's Version," 76.

69. October 16 transcript.

70. Ray S. Cline, "Nuclear War Seemed Remote . . . ," *Washington Post*, February 5, 1989, D7.

71. Kennedy, *Thirteen Days* , 31; see also Acheson, "Dean Acheson's Version," 76.

72. Acheson, "Dean Acheson's Version," 77.

73. Ibid.

74. Quoted in Kaufmann, *McNamara Strategy*, 273.

75. "The Lessons of the Cuban Missile Crisis," *Time*, September 27, 1982, 85, emphasis added.

76. McGeorge Bundy, *Danger and Survival* (New York: Random House, 1988), 450.

77. See Ronald R. Pope, ed., *Soviet Views on the Cuban Missile Crisis* (Washington: University Press of America, 1982), 125.

78. Raymond L. Garthoff, "The Meaning of Missiles," *Washington Quarterly* 5, no. 4 (Autumn 1982):79.

79. Betts, *Nuclear Blackmail*, 127–29.

80. Quoted in Pope, *Soviet Views on the Cuban Missile Crisis*, 105.

81. Bundy, *Danger and Survival*, 448.

82. It is interesting that Taylor became another latter-day convert to the view that nuclear weapons had been unimportant in the crisis. Betts, *Nuclear Blackmail*, 121, emphasis added.

83. Bundy, *Danger and Survival*, 447.

84. A fact that has become especially clear in the Cuban case from the Castro-Khrushchev missile crisis correspondence released by Castro in late 1990. As Khrushchev wrote to Castro on October 30, 1962: "If, giving in to popular sentiment, we had allowed ourselves to be led by certain inflamed portions of the population and if we had refused to conclude a reasonable agreement with the U.S.A., war probably would have broken out, causing millions of deaths, and the survivors would have said that it was the leaders' fault for not having taken the necessary measures to avert this war of annihilation." Khrushchev to Castro, October 30, 1962, in Jean Edern-Hallier, "Castro Embattled: History: Fervent anti-Americanism," *Los Angeles Times*, December 9, 1990, M2.

85. Dean Acheson, "Dean Acheson's Version," 44.

86. Pope, *Soviet Views on the Cuban Missile Crisis*, 47–48.

87. Allison, *Essence of Decision*, 220.

88. Castro to Khrushchev, October 28, 1962, and Khrushchev to Castro, October 30, 1962, in Edern-Hallier, "Castro Embattled," M2.

89. Allison, *Essence of Decision*, 224–25. Cf. Bundy, *Danger and Survival*, 423–24.

90. Bundy, *Danger and Survival*, 406.

91. Quoted in ibid., 439.

92. Ibid.

93. Ibid.

94. Ibid., 426.

95. Ibid., 436.

96. Ibid. See also Cuban Missile Crisis Meetings, October 27, 1962, Kennedy Library, Presidential Recordings, 4–5. Hereafter referred to as "October 27 transcript."

97. Bundy, *Danger and Survival*, 446.

98. Arms control theory included the notion of "war termination," that is, an ending to war that was neither a victory nor a defeat. But this was precisely the problem—the failure to grasp that the logic of war and crisis

implied that it must end in something approaching either a victory or a defeat.

99. October 27 transcript, 27.

100. Quoted in Jerome B. Wiesner, "The Cold War Is Dead, but the Arms Race Rumbles On," *Bulletin of Atomic Scientists*, (June 1967):6.

101. Stewart Alsop, "Our New Strategy: The Alternative To Total War," *Saturday Evening Post*, December 1, 1962, 18.

102. Trewhitt, *McNamara*, 116.

103. Edward Klein and Robert Littell, "Shh! Let's Tell the Russians," *Newsweek*, May 5, 1969, 46–47.

104. Personal interview with Thomas Schelling.

105. U.S. Congress, House of Representatives, Committee on Armed Services, *Hearings on Military Posture and H.R. 2440*, 88th Cong., 1st sess., January 30, 1963, 264.

106. For example, in attempting to make the case in favor of missiles at the expense of bombers in early 1964, McNamara offered figures on relative "dependability" of the two systems that showed a larger percentage of missile weapons than bomber weapons reaching their targets. When the joint chiefs pointed out that bomber weapons were more accurate than missile weapons and hence were more likely to *destroy* the targets they reached, thereby reversing the advantage, McNamara simply ignored their correction and redefined "dependability" to mean the capability of *reaching* a target rather than *destroying* it. He then took his original figures to Congress. See W. Y. Smith (of NSC staff) to McGeorge Bundy, Feburary 6, 1964, LBJ Library, National Security File, Agency File, DoD, 1 1/63, vol.1 (2) (National Security Archive copy). On another occasion, an NSC aide reviewing the draft of a McNamara speech questioned "the desirability of using stacked figures to prove the case of numerical superiority" of Western conventional forces. David Klein to McGeorge Bundy, November 13, 1963, Kennedy Library, National Security File, Departments and Agencies, Box 274, Department of Defense, McNamara Speech, 11/18/63.

107. A conclusion based on personal interviews with Schelling, William W. Kaufmann, Henry Rowen, and Alain Enthoven.

108. David Halberstam, *The Best and the Brightest* (New York: Random House, 1972), 243.

109. Klein and Littell, "Let's Tell the Russians," 46–47. Cf. Kaufmann, *McNamara Strategy*, 138–48.

110. Quoted in Klein and Littell, "Let's Tell the Russians," 47.

111. Ibid. 46.

112. Lawrence Freedman, *The Evolution of Nuclear Strategy* (New York: St. Martin's Press, 1982), 248.

113. Committee on Armed Services, House of Representatives, *Hearings on Miltary Posture and H.R. 4016*, 89th Cong., 1st sess., 1965, 172–74.

114. Draft Memorandum for the President, Recommended FY 1965–FY 1969 Strategic Retaliatory Forces, December 6, 1963, U.S. Department of Defense (made available under Freedom of Information Act).

115. Kaplan, *Wizards of Armageddon*, 316–19.

116. Paul A. Nitze's 1979 testimony on SALT II. See U.S. Congress, Senate, Committee on Armed Services, *Military Implications of the Treaty on the Limitation of Strategic Offensive Arms and Protocol Thereto (SALT II Treaty)*, 99th Cong., 2d sess. (Washington: GPO, 1979), pt. 3, 885.

117. "Is Russia Slowing Down in Arms Race? Interview with Robert S. McNamara," *U.S. News and World Report*, April 12, 1965, 52.

118. See U.S. Congress, House of Representatives, Committee on Armed Services, *Hearings on Military Posture and H.R. 2440*, 88th Cong., 1st sess., (Washington: GPO, 1963), 327.

119. Ibid., 306–7, emphasis added.

120. Sorensen, *Kennedy*, 724.

121. Walter Millis, ed., *The Forrestal Diaries* (New York: Viking Press, 1951), 145.

122. Khrushchev to Kennedy, December 19, 1962, Kennedy Library, National Security File, Box 183, Khrushchev Correspondence, vol. 3-C, 11/28/62–12/30/62.

123. Ibid.

124. Seaborg, *Kennedy and Test Ban*, 178–81.

125. Ibid., 182.

126. Ibid., 181.

127. See "Rockefeller Is Critical," *New York Times*, January 30, 1963, 2; "G.O.P. Makes Issue of Kennedy Stand on Banning Tests," *New York Times*, February 1, 1963, 1.

128. "Dodd Denounces Test Ban Retreat," *New York Times*, February 22, 1963, 1.

129. "Text of President Kennedy's News Conference on Foreign and Domestic Affairs," *New York Times*, March 7, 1963, 4.

130. Quoted in Alistaire Horne, *Harold Macmillan*, vol. 2, *1957–1986* (New York: Viking Press, 1989), 507.

131. "Rusk Is Doubtful on Test Ban Pact, *New York Times*, March 9, 1963, 3.

132. Horne, *Macmillan*, 2:506–7.

133. "Kennedy to Push Test Ban Treaty," *New York Times*, March 22, 1963, 4.

134. Seaborg, *Kennedy and Test Ban*, 208–9, 179–80.

135. Ibid., 207.

136. Ibid., 206.

137. "34 Senators Ask for New Efforts to Limit A-Tests," *New York Times*, May 28, 1963, 1.

138. Harold Jacobson and Eric Stein, *Diplomats, Scientists, and Politicians: The United States and the Nuclear Test Ban Negotiations* (Ann Arbor: University of Michigan Press, 1966), 450.

139. John F. Kennedy, "A Strategy for Peace," *Vital Speeches*, July 1, 1963, 558–61.

140. Quoted in Seaborg, *Kennedy and Test Ban*, 224.

141. "Excerpts from Reagan's Talk at the Berlin Wall," *New York Times*, June 13, 1987, 3.

142. Seaborg, *Kennedy and Test Ban*, 227.

143. Ibid., 243–44.

144. Ibid., 246–47.

145. Ibid., 265.

146. Sorensen, *Kennedy*, 745.

147. "Text of McNamara's Statement Upholding the Limited Nuclear Test Ban Treaty," *New York Times*, August 14, 1963, 14.

148. Benson D. Adams, "McNamara's ABM Policy, 1961–1967," *Orbis* 12 (Spring 1968):200–25.

149. Seaborg, *Kennedy and Test Ban*, 271.

150. Quoted in Adams, "McNamara's ABM Policy," 210.

151. U.S. Congress, Senate, Committee on Foreign Relations, *Nuclear Test Ban Treaty*, 88th Cong., 1st sess. (Washington: GPO, 1963), 274–75.

152. See Adams, "McNamara's ABM Policy," 207.

Chapter 7

1. U.S. Department of Defense, *Soviet Military Power 1989* (Washington: GPO, 1989), 88 (chart).

2. International Institute of Strategic Studies, *The Military Balance 1971–1972* (London: International Institute for Strategic Studies, 1972), 3, 5.

3. John Prados, *The Soviet Estimate* (New York: Dial Press, 1982), 210.

4. David Binder, "New C.I.A. Estimate Finds Soviet Seeks Superiority in Arms," *New York Times*, December 26, 1976, A1; Drew Middleton, "American Security and Expanding Soviet Military Strength," *New York Times*, January 21, 1977, A10.

5. Freedman, *U.S. Intelligence*, 115.

6. Quoted in ibid.

7. See chapter 3.

8. Vasilii Danilovich Sokolovskii, *Military Strategy* (New York: Praeger, 1963).

9. Quoted in Leslie H. Gelb and Richard K. Betts, *The Irony of Vietnam: The System Worked* (Washington: Brookings Institution, 1979), 139.

10. A suggestive treatment of the connection between arms control and limited war strategy in Vietnam is provided in Wendell John Coats, Jr., "The Ideology of Arms Control," *Journal of Contemporary Studies* 5, no. 3 (Summer 1982):5–15, to which the author is indebted.

11. William J. Duiker, *The Communist Road to Power in Vietnam* (Boulder, CO: Westview Press, 1981), 222.

12. Stanley Karnow, *Vietnam: A History* (New York: Viking Press, 1983), 369.

13. Quoted in ibid., 396.

14. Edwin Diamond and Stephen Bates, *The Spot: The Rise of Political Advertising in Television* (Cambridge, MA: MIT Press, 1984), 333, 360; Bundy, *Danger and Survival*, 537.

15. Mark Clodfelter, *The Limits of Air Power: The American Bombing of North Vietnam* (New York: Free Press, 1989), 122.

16. *The Pentagon Papers: The Defense Department's History of United States Decision-Making on Vietnam,* Senator Gravel Edition (Boston: Beacon Press, 1971–72), 5 vols. Also see Stephen Peter Rosen, "Vietnam and the American Theory of Limited War," *International Security* 7, no. 2 (Fall 1982):83–113, to which the author's discussion is indebted.

17. Quoted in Admiral U.S. Grant Sharp, *Strategy for Defeat: Vietnam in Retrospect,* (San Rafael, CA: Presido Press, 1979), 60, emphasis added.

18. Clodfelter, *Limits of Air Power*, 51, 60.

19. Kaufmann, *Military Policy and National Security*, 1956; cf. Kaplan, *Wizards of Armageddon*, 329–36.

20. Quoted in Sharp, *Strategy for Defeat*, 94–95.

21. Clodfelter, *Limits of Air Power*, 119.

22. Institute for Strategic Studies, *The Military Balance 1964–1965* (London: Institute for Strategic Studies, 1965), 3.

23. Quoted in Clodfelter, *Limits of Air Power*, 42.

24. Quoted in ibid., 97.

25. Quoted in Doris Kearns, *Lyndon Johnson and the American Dream* (New York: Harper & Row, 1976), 251–52.

26. Ibid., 138.

27. Quoted in ibid.

28. Quoted in Sharp, *Strategy for Defeat*, 73–74.

29. Quoted in Stanley Karnow, "Giap Remembers," the *New York Times Magazine,* June 24, 1990, 36.

30. Halberstam, *Best and Brightest*, 515. Cf. Peter W. Rodman, "The Missiles of October: Twenty Years Later," *Commentary* (October 1982):39–45.

31. William C. Westmoreland, *A Soldier Reports* (Garden City, NY: Doubleday, 1976), 120.

32. Ibid.

33. George C. Herring, *America's Longest War: The United States in Vietnam, 1950–1975* (New York: Alfred A. Knopf, 1979), 151.

34. Karnow, *Vietnam*, 487.

35. Douglas Pike, *Vietnam and the Soviet Union* (Boulder, CO: Westview Press, 1987), 118–22.

36. Komer to Valenti, March 29, 1966, Lyndon B. Johnson Library and Mu-

seum, National Security File, Memos to the President (Rostow), Box 7, Walt Rostow, vol. 1, April 1–30, 1966.

37. Personal interview with Walt Rostow.

38. Norman Podhoretz, *Why We Were in Vietnam* (New York: Simon and Schuster, 1982), 79–80.

39. Rusk to Johnson, August 8, 1966, LBJ Library, National Security File, Files of Walt W. Rostow, Box 1, Meetings with the President, April–December 1966.

40. Rostow to Johnson, September 22, 1966, LBJ Library, National Security File, Files of Walt W. Rostow, Box 1, Meetings with the President, April–December 1966.

41. See, for example, Morton Halperin, "The Decision to Deploy the ABM," *World Politics* 35, no. 1 (October 1972):79.

42. Ibid., 80.

43. Notes on Meeting with the President in Austin, Texas, December 6, 1966, LBJ Library, National Security File, Memos to the President (Rostow), Box 11, Walt W. Rostow, vol. 16, December 1–13, 1966. All quotations of the discussion are from this source.

44. Kohler to Rostow, December 10, 1966; Thompson to Rostow, December 10, 1966; Rostow to Johnson, December 10, 1966; LBJ Library, National Security File, Memos to the President (Rostow), Box 11, Walt W. Rostow, Volume 16, December 1–13, 1966.

45. "Intelligence Fiasco," *New York Times*, April 27, 1990, A35; "Soviet Experts Say Their Economy is Worse Than U.S. Has Estimated," *New York Times International*, April 24, 1990; Igor Birman, "The Size of Soviet Military Expenditures: A Methodological Aspect," ms., American Enterprise Institute Conference, April 19–22, 1990.

46. "Message Asks Soviet Pact to Halt Race on Missiles," *New York Times*, January 11, 1967, A1.

47. "Excerpts from Transcript of Kosygin News Parley," *New York Times*, February 10, 1967, 13.

48. Halperin, "Decision to Deploy ABM," 87; Lyndon Baines Johnson, *The Vantage Point* (New York: Holt, Rinehart, and Winston, 1971), 484.

49. Halperin, "Decision to Deploy ABM," 87.

50. Personal interview with Morton Halperin.

51. See Robert S. McNamara, "U.S. Nuclear Strategy," *Vital Speeches* 33, no. 24 (October 1, 1967): 742–43.

52. "Defense Figure $3 Billion Higher," *New York Times*, January 30, 1968, A1.

53. "Senate Defeats a Move to Delay Sentinel System," *New York Times*, June 25, 1968, A1.

54. Ibid.

55. Henry M. Jackson, "National Security: Basic Tasks," *Vital Speeches*, November 1, 1967, 34–37, emphasis added.

Chapter 8

1. John Kenneth Galbraith, *How to Control the Military* (Garden City, NY: Doubleday, 1969), 43, 60.
2. Robert S. McNamara, *The Essence of Security: Reflections in Office* (New York: Harper & Row, 1968), 141–58.
3. McGeorge Bundy, "To Cap the Volcano," *Foreign Affairs* 48, no. 1 (October 1969): 1.
4. Figures from Institute for Strategic Studes, *The Military Balance, 1969–1972.*
5. Institute for Strategic Studies, *The Military Balance, 1970–1971* (London: Institute for Strategic Studies, 1971), 1–2, 6.
6. Roger P. Labrie, ed., *The SALT Handbook* (Washington: American Enterprise Institute, 1979), 40.
7. See Raymond Aron, *The Committed Observer*, trans. James and Marie McIntosh (Chicago: Regnery Gateway, 1983), 238.
8. See, for example, Gaddis, *Strategies of Containment*, 313; Karnow, *Vietnam*, 582–589.
9. Quoted in H. R. Haldeman with Joseph DiMona, *The Ends of Power* (New York: Times Books, 1978), 83.
10. Karnow, *Vietnam*, 582.
11. Richard Nixon, *RN: The Memoirs of Richard Nixon* (New York: Simon and Schuster, 1990), 347.
12. See Henry Kissinger, *White House Years* (Boston: Little, Brown, 1979), 239.
13. For example, Haldeman's handwritten notes for April 15, 1971, record the following from Nixon:

> look Kennedy—he was colder, more ruthless etc.
> but look at his PR.
> PR is right if it emphasizes truth
> wrong—*for us*—if it isn't true
> but untrue worked for JFK.

Or again, speaking of Victor Lasky's book on Kennedy:

> read Lasky's book re JFK
> all of him was myth—created by talk

"We have not created [a] mythology," Nixon complained to Haldeman and went on to describe the image he desired:

> courage, boldness, guts
> not true that everything is political

most important fact 1st two years: GUTS
boldness, coolness under fire, stands alone

Haldeman Notes, 4/15/71, Nixon Presidential Materials Project (Alexandria, VA), White House Special Files, H. R. Haldeman, Box 43, H Notes April–June 1971 [April 1, 1971–May 19, 1971], Part I (hereafter referred to as "Haldeman Notes" with box numbers).

14. Nixon, *RN*, 347.
15. Kissinger, *White House Years*, 240.
16. Ibid., 271.
17. Nixon, *RN*, 392.
18. Quoted in Nixon, *RN*, 399; cf. Kissinger, *White House Years*, 304.
19. Nixon, *RN*, 401–2.
20. "Nixon Would Link Political Issues to Missile Talks," *New York Times*, January 28, 1969, 1; "Transcript of the President's News Conference," *New York Times*, January 28, 1969, 12.
21. Kissinger, *White House Years*, 129. Cf. James Reston, "The Kissinger Approach to the Soviets," *New York Times*, January 29, 1969, 40.
22. Kissinger, *White House Years*, 50, 127; Nixon, *RN*, 346–47.
23. "Soviet Tells U.S. That It Is Ready for Missile Talks," *New York Times*, January 21, 1969, 1.
24. See Nixon remarks in early March press conference: U.S. President, *Public Papers of the Presidents of the United States: Richard Nixon: 1969* (Washington: GPO, 1971), 187.
25. Kissinger, *White House Years*, 138.
26. Ibid., 144.
27. See John Newhouse, *Cold Dawn: The Story of SALT* (New York: Holt, Rinehart and Winston, 1973), 150.
28. Kissinger, *White House Years*, 133–37.
29. See, for example, Abram Chayes and Jerome B. Wiesner, eds., *ABM: An Evaluation of the Decision to Deploy an Antiballistic Missile System* (New York: Harper & Row, 1969).
30. Kissinger, *White House Years*, 205–10.
31. "Excerpts from President's Speech at the Air Force Academy," *New York Times*, June 5, 1969, 30.
32. Nixon has since written that this was his major reason for desiring ABM, though he could not reveal so at the time. Nixon, *RN*, 415–16.
33. Nixon, *RN*, 417; cf. Haldeman Notes, 3/19/69, Box 40, H Notes Jan.–June 1969 [Jan.–April 1, 1969], Part 1.
34. Newhouse, *Cold Dawn*, 150.
35. Andrei Gromyko, *Memoirs*, trans. Harold Shukman (New York: Doubleday, 1989), 278, emphasis added.
36. "Intelligence Fiasco," *New York Times*, April 27, 1990, A35; "Soviet Experts

Say Their Economy Is Worse Than U.S. Has Estimated," *New York Times International*, April 24, 1990; Igor Birman, "The Size of Soviet Military Expenditures: A Methodological Aspect," ms., American Enterprise Institute Conference, April 19–22, 1990.

37. As a young defector from the staff of the Soviet Institute of World Economics and Politics told Paul Nitze in 1973, "At the time of SALT One, the unanimous view of the Soviets was that their ABMs were worthless. They had second generation computers and his Institute had Bis II, which was used to run war games. It wasn't very good; certainly not good enough for ABM use. In the preparatory work for SALT One—in which the Institute had participated—the object was to control U.S. Safeguard, which they feared very much. The people at the Institute spent their time on studies analyzing what the Soviets could give in order for the U.S. to give up Safeguard. Grechko [the Soviet Minister of Defense] insisted that it was not necessary to give up anything. The Institute turned out to be wrong—he turned out to be right." Quoted in Elmo R. Zumwalt, Jr., *On Watch* (New York: Quadrangle, 1976), 427.

38. See Thomas W. Wolfe, *The SALT Experience* (Cambridge, MA: Ballinger, 1979), 112.

39. Seymour M. Hersh, *The Price of Power* (New York: Summit Books, 1983), 155.

40. Newhouse, *Cold Dawn*, 173–74; Gerard Smith, *Doubletalk* (New York: University Press of America, 1985), 154–78.

41. "Senate, 70–2, Votes Defense Fund Bill," *New York Times*, December 30, 1970, 12; "Outlay for the Military Is Sliced to Smallest Share in 2 Decades," *New York Times*, February 3, 1971, 22.

42. "Senate, 72–6, Bids President Seek Halt on Missiles," *New York Times*, April 10, 1970, 1. See also "Nixon Panel Asks Moratorium Now in Missiles Race," *New York Times*, April 8, 1970, 1.

43. "Expansion of ABM Backed by Senate by 52-to-47 Vote," *New York Times*, August 13, 1970, 1; Smith, *Doubletalk*, 148–49.

44. "Russia's SALT Offer," *New York Times* January 17, 1971, 14; G. B. Kistiakowski and G. W. Rathjens, "A Chance to Freeze ABM's," *New York Times*, January 27, 1971, 37.

45. Zumwalt, *On Watch*, 319, emphasis added.

46. Kissinger, *White House Years*, 1162.

47. RN to Kissinger, March 11, 1972 *EYES ONLY*, Nixon Presidential Materials Project, White House Special Files, H. R. Haldeman, Box 45, HRH Notes Jan.-Feb.-Mar. 1972 [Feb. 19, 1972 to March 31, 1972], Part 2.

48. Haldeman Notes 4/24/72, Box 45, H notes April-May-June, 1972 [April 1, 1972, to May 15, 1972], Part 1.

49. Ibid.

50. Ibid., 556.

51. Ibid., 557.

52. Kissinger, *White House Years*, 811–13.

53. Ibid., 405–12, 529–34, 794–802; cf. Adam Ulam, *Dangerous Relations: The Soviet Union in World Politics, 1970–1982* (New York: Oxford University Press, 1983), 63–65.

54. Kissinger, *White House Years*, 802.

55. I am indebted for the latter observation to Paul Nitze.

56. In October 1970, for example, Haldeman, responding to a critical letter in the conservative *National Review*, questioned Kissinger on the administration's handling of "Captive Nations Week"—a week when it was customary for the president of the United States to issue a strong proclamation deploring Communist domination in the East Bloc and various Soviet republics. "Clearly," replied Kissinger, "we cannot issue a proclamation that stresses the 'captive nations' of Romania and Yugoslavia—two countries that have received the President. *And we had to keep in mind the possibility of a summit conference at some point.* What we have tried to do in the last two proclamations issued by this Administration is to broaden the original context to stress human freedom, *a more positive goal than the negative condemnation of specific nations.*" Kissinger to Haldeman, October 17, 1970, NPMP, White House Special Files, H. R. Haldeman, Box 66, Haldeman Staff Memos/Kissinger-M-October, 1970 [Folder 1].

57. Smith, *Doubletalk*, 234.

58. Nitze, *Hiroshima to Glasnost*, 309–10, 313, 331–32.

59. Smith, *Doubletalk*, 223. See also Haldeman Notes 5/20/71 (Cabinet), Box 43, H Notes April—June 1971 [April 1, 1971, to May 19, 1971], Part 1.

60. Smith, *Doubletalk*, 226–34; Newhouse, *Cold Dawn*, 218–19.

61. Quoted in Smith, *Doubletalk*, 224.

62. Kissinger, *White House Years*, 840.

63. W. Scott Thompson, ed., *National Security in the 1980's* (San Francisco: Institute for Contemporary Studies, 1980), 193.

64. Haldeman Notes, 6/16/72 (Cabinet), Box 45, H Notes Apr.-May-June 1972 [May 9, 1972-June 30, 1972], Part 2; Haldeman Notes, 4/17/71, Box 43, H Notes April–June 1971 [April 1, 1971 to May 19, 1971], Part 1.

65. Kissinger, *White House Years*, 763–70; Newhouse, *Cold Dawn*, 223.

66. Smith, *Doubletalk*, 349.

67. U.S. Congress, Senate, Committee on Armed Services, *Military Implications of the Treaty on the Limitations of Anti-Ballistic Missile Systems and the Interim Agreement on Limitation of Strategic Offensive Arms*, 92nd Cong., 2d sess., 1973, 167–86. Hereafter referred to as SALT I Senate Armed Services Hearings.

68. Newhouse, *Cold Dawn*, 56.

69. Haldeman Notes, 2/20/69, Box 40, H Notes Jan.–June 1969 [Jan–April 1, 1969], Part 1.

70. This is another way of explaining the discrepancy between the outward

dedication to peace and the secret resort to coercion that Tad Szulc made the subject of his study of the Nixon foreign policy. See Tad Szulc, *The Illusion of Peace* (New York: Viking Press, 1978).

71. Haldeman Notes, 4/17/71, Box 43, H Notes April–June 1971 [April 1, 1971 to May 19, 1971], Part 1.

72. The Haldeman notes from late April 1972 vividly reflect this dilemma. The "real prob[lem]," deputy security advisor Alexander Haig told Nixon, was that a "summit" with the Russians with "blood on their hands won't look good here." Nixon was anxious. "P. obviously feels we're trapped," Haldeman jotted on his yellow pad on April 23, 1972. ". . . concern is deep." Haldeman Notes, Box 45, H Notes Apr.-May-June 1972 [April 1, 1972–May 15, 1972], Part 1.

73. Nixon, *RN*, 587.

74. Kissinger, *White House Years*, 1124–74.

75. Quoted in Nixon, *RN*, 592.

76. Quoted in Karnow, *Vietnam*, 646.

77. *Doubletalk*, 370–71.

78. See Newhouse, *Cold Dawn*, 245.

79. Smith, *Doubletalk*, 372, emphasis added.

80. Quoted in ibid., 417.

81. Ibid., 1224.

82. Ibid., 419–21, 427–29.

83. See Labrie, *SALT Handbook*, 225–35; Smith, *Doubletalk*, 396–429; Wolfe, *The SALT Experience*, 8–13, 87–90.

84. Labrie, *SALT Handbook*, 39. Cf. "U.S. Aides Deny Kissinger Made Secret Arms Deals," *New York Times*, June 24, 1974, A1; "Kissinger Denies Secret Arms Deal," *New York Times*, June 23, 1974, A9.

85. Henry Kissinger, *Years of Upheaval* (Boston: Little, Brown, 1982), 1147–51.

86. U.S. Congress, House of Representatives, Committee on Armed Services, *The Military Implications of the Strategic Arms Limitation Talks Agreement*, 92nd Cong., 2d sess. (1972), 15092. Quoted in Congress of the United States, Congressional Budget Office, *SALT and the U.S. Strategic Forces Budget*, Background Paper No. 8, June 23, 1976; hereafter CBO 1976 Report.

87. Smith, *Doubletalk*, 414.

88. Ibid., 460.

89. For Smith, see SALT I Senate Armed Services Hearings, 100; for Kissinger, see SALT I Senate Armed Services Hearings, 128, and cf. Labrie, *SALT Handbook*, 351.

90. U.S. Congress, Senate, Committee on Foreign Relations, *Strategic Arms Limitations Agreements*, 92nd Cong., 2nd Sess. (Washington, D.C.: GPO, 1972). 202.

91. Ibid., 184–85.

92. Haldeman Notes 6/16/72 (Cabinet), NPMP, White House Special Files, Staff Member and Office Files, H. R. Haldeman, Box 45, H Notes April-May-June 1972 [May 9, 1972–June 30, 1972], Part 2.

93. Sean M. Lynn-Jones, "Lulling and Stimulating Effects of Arms Control," in Albert Carnesale and Richard N. Haass eds., *Superpower Arms Control* (Cambridge, MA: Ballinger, 1987), 251.

94. U.S. Department of Commerce, Bureau of the Census, *Statistical Abstract of the United States 1990* (Washington: GPO, 1990), 330.

95. Lynn-Jones, "Lulling and Stimulating Effects," 247.

96. "A Soviet Success Reported in Test of New Missiles," *New York Times*, August 18, 1973, 1; cf. Congressional Budget Office 1976 Report, 17–19.

97. CBO 1976 Report, 29.

98. "Soviet Missile Test May Chart a New Course for the Arms Talks," *New York Times*, August 18, 1973, 4.

99. See, for example, Lynn-Jones, "Lulling and Stimulating Effects," 223–73.

100. Anwar el-Sadat, *In Search of an Identity* (New York: Harper & Row, 1978), 228–31.

101. Ibid., 237–38.

102. See, for example, William B. Quandt, "Soviet Policy in the October Middle East War—I," *International Affairs* (London) 53 (July 1977):381; Foy D. Kohler, Leon Gouré, Mose L. Harvey, *The Soviet Union and the October 1973 Middle East War: The Implications for Détente* (Miami: University of Miami Center for International Studies, 1974), 36–37; and cf. Karen Dawisha, "Soviet Decision-Making in the Middle East: The 1973 October War and the 1980 Gulf War," *International Affairs* (London) 57 (Winter 1980/81):48, 65.

103. See, for example, Galia Golan, *Yom Kippur and After* (Cambridge: Cambridge University Press, 1977), 44–49.

104. Kissinger, *Years of Upheaval*, 297–300.

105. Ibid., 545–613.

106. Quandt, *Decade of Decisions*, 201.

107. Quoted in Labrie, *SALT Handbook*, 147.

108. Haldeman Notes, 5/22/72, Box 45, H Notes Apr-May-June 1972 [May 9, 1972–June 30, 1972], Part 2.

109. Kissinger, *White House Years*, 134.

110. Paula Stern, *Water's Edge: Domestic Politics and the Making of American Foreign Policy* (Westport, CT: Greenwood Press, 1979), 18.

111. Stern, *Water's Edge*, 86.

112. Ibid., 86; Kissinger, *White House Years*, 1272.

113. Kissinger, *Years of Upheaval*, 249.

114. "Soviet Sees Politics Behind Arms Pact," *New York Times*, June 9, 1972, 4.

115. Wolfe, *SALT Experience*, 95, 327n.

116. Nitze, *Hiroshima to Glasnost*, 337.

117. Kissinger, *Years of Upheaval*, 979.
118. Kissinger, *White House Years*, 1245.
119. Kissinger, *Years of Upheaval*, 985.
120. Wolfe, *SALT Experience*, 179.
121. Ibid., 183–88.
122. Ibid., 180.
123. Ibid., 181–82.
124. Nitze, *Hiroshima to Glasnost*, 344.
125. Constantine Menges, *The Twilight Struggle* (Washington: AEI Press, 1990), 110–11.
126. Quoted in ibid., 111.
127. Labrie, *SALT Handbook*, 355.
128. Quoted in Roger Hamburg, "Soviet Perspectives on Military Intervention," in Ellen P. Stern, ed., *The Limits of Military Intervention* (Beverly Hills, CA: Sage Publications, 1977), 51.
129. Quoted in ibid.

Chapter 9

1. Quoted in Betty Glad, *Jimmy Carter* (New York: W. W. Norton, 1980), 316.
2. Jimmy Carter, *Keeping Faith* (New York: Bantam Books, 1982), 19, 21; Zbigniew Brzezinski, *Power and Principle* (New York: Farrar, Straus, Giroux, 1983), 432.
3. Joshua Muravchik, *The Uncertain Crusade* (Washington: American Enterprise Institute, 1986), 2–3.
4. Personal interview with Morton Halperin.
5. Karnow, *Vietnam*, 553–55.
6. Report by Alexander Haig of a conversation with Johnson at the LBJ Ranch in July 1972. (Haig was sent by Nixon as an emissary to clear up a misunderstanding over credit for SALT.) Haig to Haldeman, July 6, 1972, Nixon Presidential Materials Project, White House Special Files, Staff Member and Office Files, H. R. Haldeman, Box 106, Alexander Haig 1972.
7. "The Real Paul Warnke," *The New Republic*, March 26, 1977, 22. (Excerpts from an interview conducted in 1976.)
8. Paul C. Warnke, "Apes on a Treadmill," *Foreign Policy*, no. 18 (Spring 1975): 12–29.
9. Albert Wohlstetter, "Is There a Strategic Arms Race?" *Foreign Policy* no. 15 (Summer 1974): 3–20; Albert Wohlstetter, "Rivals, But No 'Race,'" *Foreign Policy* no. 16 (Fall 1974): 48–81; Albert Wohlstetter, "How to Confuse Ourselves," *Foreign Policy*, no. 20 (Fall 1975): 170–98. Related articles can be found in the same issues of *Foreign Policy*.
10. Paul H. Nitze, "The Strategic Balance: Between Hope and Skepticism,"

Foreign Policy, no. 17 (Winter 1974–75): 136–56; Paul H. Nitze, "Deterring Our Deterrent," *Foreign Policy,* no. 25 (Winter 1976–77): 195–210; Paul H. Nitze, "Assuring Strategic Stability in an Era of Détente," *Foreign Affairs* 54, no. 2 (January 1976): 207–32.

11. Warnke, "Apes on a Treadmill," 12–13.
12. U.S. Congress, Senate, Committee on Armed Services, *Consideration of Mr. Paul C. Warnke to be Director of the U.S. Arms Control and Disarmament Agency and Ambassador,* 95th Cong., 1st sess. (Washington: GPO, 1977), 17–18.
13. "Senate Confirms Warnke, 58–40; Vote Falls Short of Carter's Hopes," *New York Times,* March 10, 1977, A1.
14. Muravchik, *Uncertain Crusade,* 8.
15. Ibid., 6.
16. Interview with Zbigniew Brzezinski. Cf. Brzezinski, *Power and Principle,* 3, 150.
17. Dorothy Fosdick, ed., *Henry M. Jackson and World Affairs: Selected Speeches 1953–1983* (Seattle: University of Washington Press, 1990), 156.
18. Muravchik, *Uncertain Crusade,* 23–27.
19. "Pravda Cautions U.S. On Rights Criticisms," *New York Times,* March 14, 1977, A1.
20. "Moscow's Expert on U.S. Asserts Rights Issue May Cloud Arms Talks," *New York Times,* March 17, 1977, A2.
21. "Brezhnev Criticizes U.S. Stand on Rights; Warns on Relations," *New York Times,* March 22, 1977, A1.
22. Strobe Talbott, *Endgame* (New York: Harper & Row, 1979), 52–54. Cf. Carter, *Keeping Faith,* 67.
23. Brzezinski, *Power and Principle,* 150; Talbott, *Endgame,* 48.
24. Talbott, *Endgame,* 50–51.
25. Alexander Moens, *Foreign Policy Under Carter* (Boulder, CO: Westview Press, 1990), 68.
26. Ibid., 50–63.
27. Ibid., 73.
28. Ibid., 60.
29. "Carter Says Vance, In Soviet, Will Seek Deep Weapons Cuts," *New York Times,* March 25, 1977, A1.
30. Moens, *Foreign Policy Under Carter,* 79.
31. "Arms Talks Break Off As Soviet Rejects 2 Key Proposals by U.S.; Carter Says He Isn't Discouraged," *New York Times,* March 31, 1977, A1.
32. "Gromyko Charges U.S. Seeks Own Gain in Arms Proposals," *New York Times,* April 1, 1977, A1.
33. "After a Rebuff in Moscow, Detente Is Put to the Test," *New York Times,* April 1, 1977, A1.
34. Quoted in Brzezinski, *Power and Principle,* 167.
35. Ibid., 172.

36. Cyrus Vance, *Hard Choices: Critical Years in America's Foreign Policy* (New York: Simon and Schuster, 1983), 21–22.

37. Bruce D. Porter, *The USSR in Third World Conflicts* (Cambridge: Cambridge University Press, 1984), 1–2.

38. Vance, *Hard Choices*, 24.

39. Quoted in "State Disputes Young's Angola Remark," the *Washington Post*, February 3, 1977, A1.

40. Porter, *USSR in Third World*, 30.

41. Douglas E. Pike, *Vietnam and the Soviet Union* (Boulder, CO: Westview Press, 1987), 118–22; cf. Porter, *USSR in Third World*, 22.

42. Brzezinski, *Power and Principle*, 178–79.

43. Quoted in ibid., 180–81.

44. Ibid., 179–82.

45. Vance, *Hard Choices*, 73–74.

46. Quoted in Brzezinski, *Power and Principle*, 185.

47. Quoted in ibid.

48. Brzezinski's rejoinder was prophetic: "It will be a blemish on his record also if the treaty gets rejected by the Senate." Ibid. 185–86.

49. Sam Nunn, "Defense Budget and Defense Capabilities," in W. Scott Thompson, ed., *National Security in the 1980s* (San Francisco: Institute for Contemporary Studies, 1980), 382–83.

50. A point noted by Zbigniew Brzezinski in an interview with the author.

51. Quoted in Carter, *Keeping Faith*, 241.

52. Thomas Powers, "Choosing a Strategy for World War III," *Atlantic Monthly* (November 1982):84.

53. See Harold Brown, *Thinking About National Security* (Boulder, CO: Westview Press, 1983), 72–74.

54. For a review of the risks and rationale of the Carter decision, see Charles A. Sorrels, *U.S. Cruise Missile Programs* (New York: McGraw-Hill, 1983), 25–35.

55. Personal communication from John Tower.

56. See Talbott, *Endgame*, 105.

57. Cf. Adam B. Ulam, *Dangerous Relations: The Soviet Union and World Politics, 1970–1982* (New York: Oxford University Press, 1983), 38.

58. Quoted in Sorrels, *U.S. Cruise Missile Programs*, 56.

59. Jeffrey Herf, *War by Other Means: Soviet Power, West German Resistance, and the Battle of the Euromissiles* (New York: Free Press, 1991), 54.

60. The text of Schmidt's address can be found in Wolfram F. Hanreider, ed., *Helmut Schmidt: Perspectives on Politics* (Boulder, CO: Westview Press, 1982), 23–37.

61. Sorrels, *U.S. Cruise Missile Programs*, 56–57.

62. Brzezinski, *Power and Principle*, 301.

63. Ibid., 301–2.

64. Ibid., 302.

65. J. A. Emerson Vermaat, "Moscow Fronts and the European Peace Movement," *Problems of Communism* 31 (November–December 1982):47–48. Herf, *War by Other Means*, 61–62.

66. "Protesters Disrupt Carter Services," *New York Times*, October 17, 1977, 12.

67. Brzezinski, *Power and Principle*, 303–4.

68. Ibid., 311–12.

69. Churchill, *Gathering Storm*, 320.

70. Cf. Talbott, *Endgame*, 160.

71. "U.S. and China Mark Resumption of Ties in Peking Ceremony," *New York Times*, January 2, 1979, A1.

72. Quoted in Brzezinski, *Power and Principle*, 215.

73. Talbott, *Endgame*, 86, 100, 101, 103, 124–27.

74. Ibid., 136–37.

75. U.S. Arms Control and Disarmament Agency, *Arms Control and Disarmament Agreements* (Washington: GPO, 1982), 270–71.

76. U.S. Arms Control and Disarmament Agency, *Soviet Noncompliance*, ACDA Publication 120 (Washington: GPO, 1986), 11.

77. See chapter 12.

78. U.S. Congress, Senate, Committee on Armed Services, *Military Implications of the Treaty on the Limitation of Strategic Offensive Arms and Protocol Thereto (SALT II Treaty)*, 96th Cong., 1st sess. (Washington: GPO, 1979), pt. 3, 887. Hereafter referred to as Senate Armed Services SALT II Hearings.

79. Talbott, *Endgame*, 96–97.

80. Ibid., 185.

81. Ibid., 187.

82. Ibid., 57, 105, 168.

83. Brzezinski, *Power and Principle*, 329–30.

84. Ibid., 189.

85. Ibid., 297.

86. Ibid., 300.

87. Ibid., 318.

88. Ibid., 338.

89. Ibid., 316–17.

90. Ibid., 323.

91. Carl Gershman, "Selling Them the Rope," *Commentary* 67, no. 4 (April 1979):43–44.

92. Ibid., 42.

93. "White House Imposing Freeze on Strategic Arms Talks," *Washington Post*, June 2, 1978, A1; cf. Brzezinski, *Power and Principle*, 320.

94. "Senate Leader Sees Delay on Arms Pact," *New York Times*, June 11, 1978, 12.

95. "Carter's 17-Month Rating in Poll Is Below that of 5 Predecessors," *New York Times*, June 30, 1978, A1.

96. Quoted in Brzezinski, *Power and Principle*, 320.

97. "Carter on Soviet: An Ambiguous Message," *New York Times*, June 9, 1978, A3.

98. Brzezinski, *Power and Principle*, 147–50, 188.

99. Ibid., 319.

100. Carl Gershman, "The Rise & Fall of the New Foreign-Policy Establishment," *Commentary* 70, no.1 (July 1980):13–24.

101. Brzezinski, *Power and Principle*, 147.

102. See, for example, Eugene V. Rostow, "The Case Against SALT II," *Commentary* 67, no. 2 (February 1979): 23–32.

103. Quoted in Talbott, *Endgame*, 5.

104. *Weekly Compilation of Presidential Documents*, July 23, 1979, 1235–41.

105. Brzezinski, *Power and Principle*, 344–78.

106. Ibid., 347.

107. Talbott, *Endgame*, 83–84, 215–16.

108. Carter, *Keeping Faith*, 213.

109. All quotations of Nitze testimony from Senate Armed Services SALT II Hearings, pt. 2, 668–769.

110. Ibid.

111. U.S. Congress, Senate, Committee on Foreign Relations, *The SALT II Treaty*, 96th Cong., 1st sess., pt. 1, 111.

112. Brzezinski, *Power and Principle*, 345.

113. "President Calls for 4.5% Increase in Military Budgets for Five Years," *New York Times*, December 13, 1979, A1.

114. "Senate Panel Votes Antitreaty Report," *New York Times*, December 21, 1979, A10.

115. Brzezinski, *Power and Principle*, 186.

116. See "Transcript of President's Interview on Soviet Reply," *New York Times*, January 1, 1980, A4.

117. Austin Ranney, ed., *The American Elections of 1980* (Washington: American Enterprise Institute, 1981), 16.

Chapter 10

1. George F. Kennan, *The Nuclear Delusion* (New York: Pantheon Books, 1983), 143, 146.

2. Roger Hamburg, "Soviet Perspectives on Military Intervention," 51.

3. Cf. Margot Light, *The Soviet Theory of International Relations* (New York: St. Martin's Press, 1988), 63–64.

4. "Transcript of the Presidential Debate between Carter and Reagan," *New York Times*, October 30, 1980, A26.

5. "There's a Greater Uncertainty than the Outlook for SALT," *New York Times*, August 24, 1980, IV, 4E.

6. Quoted in Seyom Brown, *The Faces of Power* (New York: Columbia University Press, 1983), 565.

7. Lou Cannon, *Reagan* (New York: Perigee Books, 1982), 71.

8. *Weekly Compilation of Presidential Documents*, February 2, 1981, 66.

9. Ronald Reagan, *An American Life* (New York: Simon and Schuster, 1990), 267, 269.

10. Alexander M. Haig, Jr., *Caveat* (New York: Macmillan, 1984), 110.

11. Reagan, *An American Life*, 301; Caspar Weinberger, *Fighting for Peace* (New York: Warner Books, 1991), 34–35.

12. Haig, *Caveat*, 105–6.

13. *Weekly Compilation of Presidential Documents*, February 2, 1981, 66.

14. Reagan, *An American Life*, 302.

15. "Text of Statement on Poland," *New York Times*, April 9, 1981, A11.

16. "NATO Defense Aides Issue Joint Warning to Soviet on Poland," *New York Times*, April 9, 1981, A1.

17. See Walter Laqueur, "Pity the Poor Russians?" *Commentary*, February 1981, 33.

18. Strobe Talbott, *Deadly Gambits: The Reagan Administration and the Stalemate in Nuclear Arms Control* (New York: Alfred A. Knopf, 1984), 47.

19. Quoted in Reagan, *An American Life*, 304.

20. See, for example, Talbott, *Deadly Gambits*, 29.

21. Charles A. Sorrels, *U.S. Cruise Missile Programs: Development, Deployment and Implications for Arms Control* (New York: McGraw-Hill, 1983), 57.

22. Hanreider, *Helmut Schmidt*, 23–37.

23. Herf, *War by Other Means*, 54–55.

24. Sorrels, *U.S. Cruise Missile Programs*, 169.

25. Lou Cannon, *President Reagan: The Role of a Lifetime* (New York: Simon and Schuster, 1991), 302.

26. Herf, *War by Other Means*, 118–22.

27. "Bonn Assails Soviet Bid to Sway Public Against New Missiles," *New York Times*, March 18, 1981, A9.

28. "Europeans Demonstrate Against NATO Missiles," *New York Times*, April 5, 1981, 3.

29. "Soviet Warns of 'Reply' to NATO Over Missiles," *New York Times*, May 6, 1981, A14.

30. "Moscow Says U.S. Offer to Discuss Missiles in Europe Is a 'Maneuver,'" *New York Times*, May 7, 1981, A10; "Moscow, Piqued, Assails Haig Speech," *New York Times*, May 11, 1981, A3.

31. Herf, *War by Other Means*, 125–26.

32. Gromyko, at U.N., Says U.S. Fosters a New Arms Race," *New York Times*, September 23, 1981, A1.

33. "President Says U.S. Should Not Waver in Backing Saudis," *New York Times*, October 18, 1981, 1.

34. "Allied Contingency Plan Envisions a Warning Atom Blast, Haig Says," *New York Times*, November 5, 1981, A1.

35. See U.S. Arms Control and Disarmament Agency, *Soviet Propaganda Campaign Against NATO* (Washington: GPO, 1983), 16.

36. West Germany and the Netherlands had urged such a "zero option" on the United States at an October 1981 NATO defense ministers' meeting in Scotland. Sorrels, *U.S. Cruise Missile Programs*, 174, 235n. Also see Herf, *War by Other Means*, 132; Talbott, *Deadly Gambits*, 56.

37. See especially Talbott, *Deadly Gambits*, passim.

38. Interview with Richard Perle.

39. Adam M. Garfinkle, *The Politics of the Nuclear Freeze* (Philadelphia: Foreign Policy Research Institute, 1984), 5–7.

40. Ibid., 80–81.

41. Jonathan Schell, "Reflections: The Fate of the Earth," *New Yorker*, February 1, 1982, 47ff; February 8, 1982, 48ff; February 15, 1982, 45ff. Republished as Jonathan Schell, *The Fate of the Earth* (New York: Alfred A. Knopf, 1982).

42. Robert Scheer, *With Enough Shovels: Reagan, Bush & Nuclear War* (New York: Random House, 1982).

43. McGeorge Bundy, George F. Kennan, Robert S. McNamara, and Gerard Smith, "Nuclear Weapons and the Atlantic Alliance," *Foreign Affairs* 60, no. 4 (Spring 1982): 753–68.

44. Karl Kaiser, Georg Leber, Alois Mertes, and Franz-Josef Schulze, "Nuclear Weapons and the Preservation of Peace," *Foreign Affairs* 60, no. 5 (Summer 1982): 1157–70.

45. See Scheer, *With Enough Shovels*, 220.

46. "House Supports Reagan on Arms, Adopting His Idea of Atom Freeze," *New York Times*, August, 6, 1982, A1.

47. See Talbott, *Deadly Gambits*, 233–73.

48. "Starting the Great Debate," *Time*, May 24, 1982, 28.

49. "Freeze or Thaw," *The Economist*, May 15, 1982, 15–16; "The Conversion of Ronald Reagan," *New York Times*, May 16, 1982, E22.

50. Haig, *Caveat*, 223.

51. See also Thomas C. Schelling, "What Went Wrong with Arms Control?" *Foreign Affairs* 64, no. 2 (Winter 1985/86): 226.

52. Talbott, *Deadly Gambits*, 272–73.

53. See Fred C. Iklé, "Nuclear Strategy: Can There Be a Happy Ending?" *Foreign Affairs* 63, no. 4 (Spring 1985): 810–26.

54. See Thomas B. Cochran, William M. Arkin, and Milton M. Hoenig, *U.S. Nuclear Forces and Capabilities* (Cambridge, MA: Ballinger, 1984), 125.

55. See ibid., 118.

56. U.S. Secretary of Defense, *Annual Defense Department Report FY 1978* (Washington: GPO, 1977), 106–7.

57. Herbert Scoville, Jr., *MX: Prescription for Disaster* (Cambridge, MA: MIT Press, 1981), 56, 22, 170, 161–62.

58. Ibid., 178–80.

59. Ibid, 113.

60. Cannon, *Reagan,* 302.

61. Ibid., 387–93.

62. "Reagan Drops Mobile MX Plan, Urges Basing Missiles in Silos; Proposes Building B-1 Bomber," *New York Times,* October 3, 1981, A1.

63. "Senate Panel Rejects Reagan Interim Plan for MX Missile Base," *New York Times,* March 24, 1982, A21.

64. President's Commission on Strategic Forces, *Report of the President's Commission on Strategic Forces,* April 1983 (Washington: GPO, 1983). Figures on congressional action supplied to author by U.S. Department of Defense, Office of Public Affairs.

65. Richard Perle, "The Wondrous Turnabout of the MX's Enemies," *Washington Post,* December 13, 1982., A15.

66. See Patrick Glynn, "Pulpit Politics," *The New Republic,* March 14, 1983, 11–15.

67. "Proposed Catholic Bishops' Letter Opposes First Use of Nuclear Arms," *New York Times,* October 26, 1982, A1.

68. *Weekly Compilation of Presidential Documents,* June 14, 1982, 766.

69. Ibid., 764–69.

70. "Reagan Denounces Ideology of Soviet as 'Focus of Evil,' " *New York Times,* March 9, 1983, A1.

71. *Weekly Compilation of Presidential Documents,* March 14, 1983, 369.

72. *Weekly Compilation of Presidential Documents,* March 28, 1983, 448.

73. Quoted in Martin Anderson, *Revolution: The Reagan Legacy* (Stanford, CA: The Hoover Institution Press, 1990), 87.

74. "U.S. Might Consider Reviving the ABM's," *New York Times,* January 16, 1981, A11.

75. Anderson, *Revolution,* 80–99; Cannon, *Reagan,* 319–33.

76. This last point owes something to discussions I have had with my American Enterprise Institute colleague Michael Novak.

77. George Orwell, *The Collected Essays, Journalism, and Letters of George Orwell,* ed. Sonia Orwell and Ian Angus, vol. 4, *In Front of Your Nose 1945–1950* (New York: Harcourt Brace Jovanovich, 1968), 63–64.

78. Seweryn Bialer, "A Wounded Russian Bear Is Dangerous," *Washington Post,* January 22, 1984, C1.

79. Christopher Andrew and Oleg Gordievsky, *KGB: The Inside Story* (New York: HarperCollins, 1990), 582–83.

80. Ibid., 600.

81. Cf. Margot Light, *Soviet Theory of International Relations*, 64.

82. See note 89.

83. Paul Nitze, "America: An Honest Broker," *Foreign Affairs* 69, no. 4 (Fall 1990):6.

84. "Gorbachev Address to Science and Culture Figures, January 6, 1981," *Foreign Broadcast Information Service*, FBIS-SOV-89–005, January 9, 1989.

85. Reagan, *An American Life*, 270–73.

86. Cannon, *Reagan*, 301.

87. Don Oberdorfer, "Reagan and the Russians: Revising History's 'First Draft,' " *Washington Post*, September 29, 1991, C5.

88. James Oberg, "Soviets Report: Moscow Lied About KAL 007," *Wall Street Journal*, April 23, 1991, A22.

89. Strobe Talbott, *The Russians and Reagan* (New York: Random House, 1984), 121.

90. *Time*, July 30, 1984.

91. *Time*, September 24, 1984.

92. Talbott, *Russians and Reagan*, 74, emphasis added.

93. Ibid., 3.

94. Talbott, *Deadly Gambits*, 15.

95. Lee Blessing, *A Walk in the Woods* (New York: New American Library, 1988).

96. "Stage: 'A Walk in the Woods,' " *New York Times*, February 29, 1988, C15.

97. Interview with Paul Nitze.

98. Quoted in Talbott, *Deadly Gambits*, 54.

99. Ibid., 132, 143.

100. Quoted in ibid., 144.

101. Zalmay Khalilzad, "How the Good Guys Won in Afghanistan," *Washington Post*, February 12, 1989, C1.

102. In 1985, according to U.S. government figures supplied to the author by the State Department, the Soviets sent $280 million in military aid to Nicaragua. In 1986, Gorbachev's first full year in power, that total rose to $600 million. In 1987, $505 million was sent. "Soviet Arms Shipments to Nicaragua Increased Last Year," *Washington Times*, February 28, 1989, A10.

103. Robert M. Gates, Deputy Director of Central Intelligence, "Developments in the Soviet Union: Implications for U.S. Intelligence," Speech to Air Force Symposium, October 21, 1988.

104. Ibid.

105. In 1985, Ogarkov published a revealing monograph stressing the primacy of new technologies in strategy. See Leon Gouré and Michael J. Deane, "The Soviet Strategic View," *Strategic Review* 13, no. 4 (Fall 1985):97–112.

106. Reagan, *An American Life*, 237. One book that provided a prescient portrait of Soviet internal decline and imperial overstretch was Henry S. Rowen and

Charles Wolf, Jr., eds., *The Future of the Soviet Empire* (New York: Institute for Contemporary Studies/St. Martin's Press, 1987).

107. See Charles H. Fairbanks, Jr., "Gorbachev's Cultural Revolution," *Commentary*, (August 1989): 23–32.

108. See Mikhail Gorbachev, *Perestroika* (New York: Harper & Row, 1987), 25, 45–46.

109. Strobe Talbott, *The Master of the Game: Paul Nitze and the Nuclear Peace* (New York: Alfred A. Knopf, 1988), 200–8.

110. "Plan for Weapons in Space Is Told," *New York Times*, May 10, 1984, A23.

111. "Army Test Missile Is Said to Destroy a Dummy Warhead," *New York Times*, June 12, 1984, A1; "Soviet Urging Talks Insists, Space Arms Can Be Verified," *New York Times*, June 12, 1984, A18.

112. "Gorbachev Vows Soviet Readiness for Big Arms Cut," *New York Times*, December 19, 1984, A1.

113. "A Disarming Russian Steals the Scene on Weapon Talks," *New York Times*, December 23, 1984, E1.

114. "Gorbachev Meets with Laborite Leaders," *New York Times*, December 20, 1984, A8. Cf. Christian Schmidt-Häuer, *Gorbachev: The Path to Power*, trans. Ewald Osers and Chris Romberg, ed. John Man (Topsfield, MA: Salem House, 1986), 8.

115. Schmidt-Häuer, *Gorbachev*, 161–62; Kenneth L. Adelman, *The Great Universal Embrace* (New York: Simon and Schuster, 1989), 136–37.

116. See, for example, "Study Assails Idea of Missile Defense," *New York Times*, March 22, 1984, A11.

117. Schmidt-Häuer, *Gorbachev*, 156.

118. See U.S. Department of Defense, *Soviet Military Power 1984* (Washington: GPO, 1984), 32–37; U.S. Department of Defense and U.S. Department of State, *Soviet Strategic Defense Programs* (Washington: GPO, 1985).

119. David R. Tanks, "The Coming Soviet Crisis: A Western Policy Dilemma," ms., September 1, 1989, Institute for Foreign Policy Analysis; Donald M. Snow, "Soviet Reform and the High-Technology Imperative," *Parameters* 20, no. 1 (March 1990):76–87.

120. This commentary on SDI owes something to Michael Rühle of the Konrad Adenauer Foundation.

121. Adelman, *Great Universal Embrace*, 95, 131–34.

122. Reagan, *An American Life*, 642–74.

123. Adelman, *Great Universal Embrace*, 141.

124. Ibid., 144. See also Larry Speakes, *Speaking Out* (New York: Charles Scribner's Sons, 1988), 125.

125. Adelman, *Great Universal Embrace*, 260.

126. An account of the development of noncompliance policy in the Reagan administration by a key participant can be found in Sven F. Kraemer, "The Krasnoyarsk Saga," *Strategic Review* 18, no. 1 (Winter 1990): 25–38.

127. U.S. General Advisory Committee on Arms Control and Disarmament, "A Quarter Century of Soviet Compliance Practices Under Arms Control Commitments: 1958–1983," Washington, October 1984.

128. See, for example, Strobe Talbott, "Questions about Soviet Cheating," *Time*, December 3, 1984, 19; Gloria Duffy, "Administration Redefines Soviet Violations," *Bulletin of the Atomic Scientists*, 42, no. 2 (February 1986):13–17; Jozef Goldblat, "Charges of Treaty Violations," *Bulletin of Atomic Scientists* 40, no. 5 (May 1984):33–36. "Soviet Arms Pact Breaches: Charges Questioned," *New York Times*, June 6, 1986, A6. In February 1987, Stanford University's Center for International Security and Arms Control published an extensive report questioning and playing down Soviet arms control violations. See "Few Treaty Violations Found," *New York Times*, February 13, 1987, A15.

129. "Moscow Says Afghan Role Was Illegal and Immoral; Admits Breaking Arms Pact," *New York Times*, October 24, 1989, A1.

130. White House, Office of the Press Secretary, "The President's Unclassified Report to the Congress on Soviet Noncompliance with Arms Control Agreements," February 1, 1985.

131. Ibid.

132. Walter Pincus, "Pass the SALT: An Interview with Paul Warnke," *New York Review of Books*, June 14, 1979, 43.

133. "The Folly of Scrapping SALT," *Arms Control Today* (May/June 1986): 4.

134. Jack Mendelsohn, "Proportionate Response: Sense or Nonsense?" *Arms Control Today*, (January/February 1986).11.

135. Ibid. See also Paul C. Warnke, "Arms Policy: By Logic or Ideology?" *Los Angeles Times*, June 22, 1986, V1.

136. "U.S. Is 'No Longer Bound' by SALT II, Weinberger Says," *Washington Post*, May 29, 1986, A1.

137. The false prediction that an end to SALT II would result in a massive acceleration of the Soviet buildup received wide currency. See, for example, David Ignatius, "Without SALT, the Race Is On," *Washington Post*, June 8, 1986, F5. The erroneous assumptions on which such predictions were based were discussed in U.S. Department of State, Bureau of Public Affairs, "Interim Restraint: U.S. and Soviet Force Projections," Special Report No. 151, August 5, 1986.

138. Adelman, *Great Universal Embrace*, 288.

139. Ibid., 70.

140. Cannon, *Reagan*, 326; Talbott, *Master of the Game*, 204.

141. The best and most sympathetic—to the point of indulgence—description of Reagan's views on nuclear weapons is to be found in Anderson, *Revolution*, 72–75.

142. Adelman, *Great Universal Embrace*, 318–19.

143. Ibid., 64–69.

144. Quoted in Reagan, *An American Life*, 548.

145. Adelman, *Great Universal Embrace*, 68. See Jonathan Schell, *The Abolition* (New York: Alfred A. Knopf, 1984).

146. Reagan, *An American Life*, 665.

147. Adelman, *Great Universal Embrace*, 34, 62.

148. Ibid., 28–29.

149. Anderson, *Revolution*, 74.

150. See Talbott, *Master of the Game*, 200 ff.

151. Michael K. Deaver with Mickey Herskowitz, *Behind the Scenes* (New York: William Morrow, 1987), 39, 129.

152. Reagan, *An American Life*, 669–72.

153. Adelman, *Great Universal Embrace*, 25.

154. There are conflicting accounts in the Adelman and Nitze memoirs. Adelman portrays the Soviet game plan as unexpected (Adelman, *Great Universal Embrace*, 36), while Nitze indicates that "[a] few days before the meeting, the State Department received reports that Dobrynin, while on a trip to South Asia, had said that Gorbachev was planning to come to Reykjavik with significant new proposals and then trap us into refusing to meet him halfway." See Nitze, *Hiroshima to Glasnost*, 429.

155. Adelman, *Great Universal Embrace*, 80.

156. Ibid., 83–84.

157. Quoted in Talbott, *Master of the Game*, 18.

158. See, for example, "No Deal: Star Wars Sinks the Summit," *Time*, October 20, 1986, 19.

159. Adelman, *Great Universal Embrace*, 83.

160. "Moscow, in Reversal, Urges Agreement 'Without Delay' to Limit Missiles in Europe," *New York Times*, March 1, 1987, A1.

161. Quoted in "Winds of Kremlin Change," *Time*, July 15, 1985, 38.

162. "What's Wrong with 'Zero,'" *Newsweek*, April 27, 1987, 27.

163. John Deutch, Brent Scowcroft, and R. James Woolsey, "The Danger of the Zero Option," *Washington Post*, March 31, 1987, A21; Brent Scowcroft, "INF: Fewer Is Not Better," *Washington Post*, April 20, 1987, A15; for Les Aspin, see "ABC News This Week with David Brinkley," April 19, 1987 (transcript).

164. Richard M. Nixon and Henry A. Kissinger, "An Arms Agreement—on Two Conditions," *Washington Post*, April 26, 1987, D7.

165. "Senators Using INF Debate to Preview Questions on START," *Christian Science Monitor*, March 28, 1988, 3.

166. "Hill Asks White House Not to Rush into START," *Washington Times*, March 30, 1988, A3; "Verification Is About to Become Even Harder," *New York Times*, April 3, 1988, E3.

167. Kenneth L. Adelman, "Why an INF Agreement Makes Sense," Address,

Brandeis University, April 28, 1987 (U.S. Arms Control and Disarmament Agency text).

168. James Markham, "Bonn and Arms Plans: Kohl in a Bind," *New York Times*, April 18, 1987, A8. Charles Sorrels drew my attention to the quoted passage.

169. Adelman, *Great Universal Embrace*, 237–38.

170. Kenneth L. Adelman, "For True Security, 'True Zero,' Not 'Near Zero'" *New York Times*, July 9, 1987, A27.

171. Talbott, *Master of the Game*, 339.

172. "Bonn Asks More Time on Rocket-Ban Ruling," *New York Times*, May 12, 1987, A11. "Soviet Missile Proposals Put Kohl in Tough Spot," *New York Times*, May 19, 1987, A3; "Kohl Shifts on Short-Range Missile Ban," *New York Times*, May 24, 1987, A10; M. S. Forbes, Jr., "To Get an Impactful Feel for How Upsetting," *Forbes*, August 24, 1987, 25; Josef Joffe, "*Achtung*: Too Much Disarmament Too Fast," *U.S. News and World Report*, December 7, 1987, 43.

173. Josef Joffe, "The Revisionists: Moscow, Bonn, and the European Balance," *National Interest,* no. 17 (Fall 1989):41–54; Robert W. Tucker, "INF: The *NOs* Have It," *National Interest,* no. 10 (Winter 1987/8):115–19.

174. Charles Krauthammer, "The Week Washington Lost Its Head," *New Republic*, January 4 and 11, 1988, 18–19.

175. Quoted in Flora Lewis, "Moscow at a Crossroads," *New York Times*, December 11, 1987, A39.

176. In which the author, having resigned from the Arms Control and Disarmament Agency in September 1987 out of concern with START, played a role. See Patrick Glynn, "Reagan's Rush to Disarm," *Commentary*, March 1988, 19–28.

177. See the account of this period in Talbott, *Master of the Game*, 369–94.

178. Ibid.

179. See Charles Krauthammer, "The End of Arms Control," *New Republic*, August 29, 1988, 29–30; also Glynn, "Reagan's Rush to Disarm," 22–24.

180. "U.S.–Soviet Arms Talks Stumble," *Washington Post*, April 23, 1988, A1.

181. Talbott, *Master of the Game*, 388.

182. "U.S.–Soviet Arms Talks Stumble," *Washington Post*, April 23, 1988, A1.

183. See, for example, "Gorbachev Outpolls Reagan in West Germany," *New York Times*, March 17, 1987, 18.

184. "It Takes Two to Make a Cold War," *New York Times*, December 8, 1987, A38.

185. Dinerstein, *War and the Soviet Union*, 128.

186. Gorbachev, *Perestroika*, 131.

187. *Weekly Compilation of Presidential Documents*, June 6, 1988, 703–4.

188. Ibid., 705.

189. Ibid., 712.

190. Ibid., 707.

Epilogue

1. Quoted in Smith, *The Defense of Berlin* (epigraph).

2. Aron, *The Great Debate*, 207.

3. Strobe Talbott, "Rethinking the Red Menace," *Time*, January 1, 1990, 70.

4. Ibid., 66.

5. Strobe Talbott, "The Case Against Star Wars Weapons," *Time*, May 7, 1984, 81ff. John O'Sullivan of *The National Review* pointed out this contradiction in an address to the Pumpkin Papers Irregulars, Cosmos Club, Washington, DC, October 31, 1990.

6. Including Zbigniew Brzezinski and James Schlesinger, who opposed the war option. See United States Congress, Senate, Committee on Armed Services, *Crisis in the Persian Gulf Region: U.S. Policy Options and Implications*, 101st Cong., 2d sess. (Washington: GPO, 1990).

7. U.S. Congress, Senate, Committee on Foreign Relations, *U.S. Policy in the Persian Gulf*, 101st cong., 2d sess. (Washington: GPO, 1991), pt. 1, 2–7.

8. Behind-the-scenes decision making in the crisis was chronicled in Bob Woodward, *The Commanders* (New York: Simon and Schuster, 1991), 197–376.

9. Quoted in Churchill, *The Gathering Storm*, 102.

10. See Fred Charles Ilké, "Comrades in Arms: The Case for a Russian-American Defense Community," *National Interest*, no. 26 (Winter 1991–92): 22–32.

11. See Chong-Pin Lin, "From Panda to Dragon," *National Interest*, no. 15 (Spring 1989): 49–57.

12. Patrick Glynn, "Bombs Away: The Nuclear Proliferation Boom," *New Republic*, October 28, 1991, 13.

13. Remarks of Major General Viktor L. Samoilov, Department Chief, State Committee on Defense, Russian Federation, from transcript of "Change and Continuity in Soviet Military Policy," Conference sponsored by International Security Council, Madison Hotel, October 7, 1991 (transcript from National Institute for Public Policy).

14. See remarks by Secretary of Defense Dick Cheney to the Inland Press Association, Chicago, Illinois, October 22, 1991.

15. Statement of the Secretary of Defense, Dick Cheney, before the House Budget Committee in Connection with Long-Term Defense Budget Issues, July 31, 1991 (U.S. Department of Defense text).

INDEX